THE JUSTICE IMPERATIVE

An Introduction to Criminal Justice

LEWIS R. KATZ

John C. Hutchins Professor of Law
Director, Center for Criminal Justice
Case Western Reserve University Law School

CJ Criminal Justice Studies
Anderson Publishing Co.

THE JUSTICE IMPERATIVE
An Introduction to Criminal Justice

Library of Congress Catalog Card Number: 79-55209
ISBN: 0-87084-475-X

This book was edited by Candice Piaget and designed by William A. Burden

Cover design by David R. Lang

to JAN,
and to BRETT, ADAM, and TYLER

INTRODUCTORY NOTE

At different levels of awareness, Americans are grappling with the criminal justice system. Lawyers, judges, and legal scholars wrestle with its philosophies and operational complexities. Citizens remain home-bound at night and yearn for a return for a simpler, less violent way of life. The overall feeling is that the system is not working. Out of the musings, out of the fears, and out of the mood of our country comes the message that justice is imperative.

The command is clear but an understanding of the criminal justice system and why it is failing is not. This text addresses the purposes, goals, and actual functions of the system. The material is presented so that the student will develop an understanding of the derivation of each phase of a criminal case, as well as the mechanical operation of each and its attendant strengths and weaknesses. Beginning with the constitutional framework in which the system is enclosed, this text follows the criminalization process from investigation and arrest, through court procedures, to trial and appeal, to punishment of the guilty. The goal behind this undertaking will be satisfied if the reader develops a critical understanding of how our criminal justice system evolved, how it is presently working, and how it could be improved.

Certain persons assisted me in the preparation of this book and I am indebted to them. In 1972, along with Lawrence B. Litwin and Richard Bamberger, I wrote *Justice is the Crime,* published by the Press of Case Western Reserve University. While that book dealt with pretrial delay, some of the material, especially historical, has been incorporated into this text and I am indebted to Messrs. Litwin and Bamberger. I wish to express my appreciation to Rick Anderson, Hal Arenstein, John Lipps, and Bryan McCormick, former law students at Case Western Reserve University, who assisted me in preparing certain materials and researching footnotes. I am also indebted to Candice Piaget, my editor, for her editorial counseling and assistance, and to Bob Haley, publisher's staff attorney, who contributed to the discussion in Chapter Twelve on the death penalty.

Finally, I wish to thank my wife, Jan Katz, who not only provided encouragement but who spent most evenings over the course of many months translating what I had written into a text that could be understood without first going to law school. Where that end has not been achieved, I alone am to blame for failing to heed her suggestions.

CONTENTS

Part I Notions of Justice

1 American Justice *5*
- "Victim Justice" *8*
- "Criminal Justice" *9*
- The Bill of Rights *9*
- Procedural Regularity *11*
- The Warren Court *13*
- The Sixth Amendment *14*
  - Right to a Speedy Trial *14*
  - Right to a Trial by Jury *15*
  - Right to Present a Defense *15*
  - Right to Counsel *16*
- The Fifth Amendment *16*
  - Right Against Double Jeopardy *16*
  - Privilege Against Self-Incrimination *17*
- The Fourth Amendment *17*
  - Right of Privacy *18*
- Due Process in State Courts *18*
- Equal Protection *19*
- The Rule of Law and Discretionary Justice *21*
- Order or Justice? *22*
- Discussion Questions *24*

2 A Failing Ideal *29*
- "Son of Sam" *30*
- State of Ohio v. Ralph Johnson *31*
  - Johnson's Story *31*
  - Root's Story *36*
- Discussion Questions *41*

Part II Preserving Order

3 Policing *47*
- "Hue and Cry" *47*
- The Throes of Police Professionalism *49*
  - The Police "Problem" *50*
- The Officer on the Beat *53*
  - Keeping the Peace and Community Relations *54*
- The Investigative Function and Process *56*
  - The Right of Privacy *58*
  - Stop and Frisk *59*
- Arrest *65*
  - Probable Cause *68*
  - Reasonable Force *69*
- After Arrest . . . *70*

The Decision to Arrest: A Practice in Discretion *73*
Overcriminalization and Police Discretion *76*
"Quality Control" *77*
Arrest/Conviction Rates *77*
Departmental Policies *77*
External Review of Police Decisions and Policies *80*
Discussion Questions *81*

4 Policing the Police *89*
Operation of the Exclusionary Rule *91*
Application of the Rule *92*
To Searches *92*
Incident to a Lawful Arrest *94*
With Consent *94*
Automobiles *95*
Other General Exceptions *95*
To Eavesdropping *95*
To Confessions *96*
To Derivative Evidence *97*
"Because the Constable Has Blundered . . ." *99*
Discussion Questions *103*

Part III Pursuing Fairness

5 The Prosecuting Power *109*
The Prosecutorial Role *109*
Prosecutorial Policies *110*
Prosecutorial Discretion *113*
Case Screening *115*
Criteria and Methodologies *116*
Options *123*
The Charging Decision *126*
The Decision Not to Charge *126*
The Decision to Charge *127*
The Formal Charge *129*
"Unbridled Power" *131*
Discussion Questions *133*

6 Bail or Jail? *139*
The Preliminary Appearance *139*
Misdemeanors *141*
Felonies *142*
Bail *145*
History *146*
The Constitutional Right to Bail *148*
Bail Determination *149*
Money Bail *153*
The Bail Bondsman *154*
The Effect of Pretrial Detention *155*

Bail Reform *157*
Release on Recognizance *158*
Conditional Release *160*
Ten Percent Deposits *161*
Preventive Detention *162*
Discussion Questions *164*
7 Screening the Case *169*
The Preliminary Hearing *170*
History *170*
How It Works *171*
The Grand Jury *177*
History *177*
How It Works *180*
The Defendant as a Grand Jury Witness *183*
Return of an Indictment or Information *187*
Are They Both Necessary? *188*
Discussion Questions *190*
8 Defending the Accused *197*
The Need for Counsel *197*
The Defense Attorney's Role *199*
The Attorney - Client Relationship *201*
The Right to Counsel *201*
A Privilege or a Right *202*
Development of the Constitutional Right *203*
Effective Assistance of Counsel *206*
Waiver of Counsel *210*
The Right to Self-Representation *211*
Defense Services for the Poor *211*
The Public Defender *215*
Discussion Questions *218*
9 Sporting Justice *225*
The Arraignment *225*
Pleas *226*
No Contest *226*
Guilty *227*
Withdrawal of a Guilty Plea *228*
Not Guilty *229*
The Motions Practice *229*
Discovery *231*
...for the defense *232*
...for the prosecution *234*
Time Pressures *235*
Controlling Delay *237*
Right to a Speedy Trial *237*
Federal and State Statutes *239*
Discussion Questions *241*

10 **The Bargained Plea** *245*
Why the Prosecutor Bargains *246*
Why the Defendant Bargains *247*
The Issues *248*
Plea Bargaining *248*
...as an avenue toward repentance *248*
...as an out *248*
...as a means of disguise *249*
...as a delaying tactic *249*
...as a false concession *250*
...as a penalization *250*
...as a handmaiden of discretion *251*
...as a constitutional issue *252*
The Prosecutor's Role *253*
The Defense Attorney's Role *257*
Judicial "Interests" *260*
The Need for Reform *263*
Discussion Questions *266*

11 **The Juvenile Justice System** *273*
Children Subject to Juvenile Court Jurisdiction *275*
Status Offenders *276*
Delinquency *277*
Miscellaneous Jurisdiction *277*
Trying the Juvenile Offender as an Adult *277*
Constitutional Rights of Juveniles in Delinquency Proceedings *279*
Juvenile Court Procedures *281*
Disposition *283*
Discussion Questions *285*

Part IV The Resolution

12 **Trial and Appeal** *291*
Defendant's Initial Trial Rights *291*
Pretrial Publicity *294*
Jury Trial *297*
Jury Selection *298*
Rules of Evidence *300*
Direct/Examination *302*
Cross-Examination *303*
Defendant's Right to Confront His Accusers *304*
Defendant's Privilege Against Self-Incrimination *305*
The Trial Process *306*
Opening Statements *306*
Presentation of the State's Case *307*
Motion for Acquittal *307*
Presentation of the Defense *307*
Rebuttal and Surrebuttal Evidence *307*

Motion for a Directed Verdict or Acquittal *308*
Summations *308*
Charge to the Jury *309*
Jury Deliberation and Verdict *310*
Appeals *312*
Direct Appeals *312*
Defendant's Right to Appeal *314*
Prosecutor's Right to Appeal *315*
Habeas Corpus Appeal of Custody *316*
Discussion Questions *318*

13 Sentencing and Punishment *323*
A Brief Look at the Past *323*
Objectives and Justifications *326*
Retribution *327*
Restraint *328*
Deterrence *328*
Rehabilitation *329*
Sentencing Model *331*
The Indeterminate Sentence *332*
The Presumptive Fixed Sentence *333*
The Determinate Sentence *334*
Mandatory Minimum Sentences *335*
Codification *336*
Sentencing the Accused *337*
Punishment Options *341*
Fines *341*
Community-Based Corrections Programs *342*
Imprisonment *344*
The Death Penalty *347*
...And Now *348*
"Death Wish" *348*
Renewed Debate *349*
The Supreme Court and Capital Punishment *350*
The First Breakthrough *350*
Furman v. Georgia 351
A Divided Court *352*
The Court's Holding *352*
The Court's Analysis *353*
Procedural Requirements *354*
No Mandatory Sentences *354*
Prisoner's Rights *356*
Access to Courts *358*
Disciplinary Hearings *358*
Freedom of Speech *358*
The Right to Organize *359*

The Freedom to Worship and Proselytize *359*
Freedom from Racial Discrimination *360*
The Right to Medical Treatment *360*
The Reentry into Society *360*
Discussion Questions *363*

Glossary *367*
Appendix: Supreme Court Litigation and The Development of Selected Constitutional Rights *373*

Index *438*

THE JUSTICE IMPERATIVE

IN CONGRES

he unanimous Declaration of the thirteen u

When in the Course of human events, it becomes necessary for one people t
ong the powers of the earth, the separate and equal station to which the Laws of Nature and of Nature's God
re the causes which impel them to the separation. —— We hold these truths to be self-e
unalienable Rights, that among these are Life, Liberty and the pursuit of Happiness. — That to secu
the consent of the governed, — That whenever any Form of Government becomes destructive of these ends, it
laying its foundation on such principles and organizing its powers in such form, as to them shall seem
Governments long established should not be changed for light and transient causes; and accordingly all
ie, than to right themselves by abolishing the forms to which they are accustomed. But when a long t
to reduce them under absolute Despotism, it is their right, it is their duty, to throw off such Government
sufferance of these Colonies; and such is now the necessity which constrains them to alter their former Syste
of repeated injuries and usurpations, all having in direct object the establishment of an absolute Tyrann
—— He has refused his Assent to Laws, the most wholesome and necessary for the public good. ——
tance, unless suspended in their operation till his Assent should be obtained; and when so suspended, he
accommodation of large districts of people, unless those people would relinquish the right of Representation
— He has called together legislative bodies at places unusual, uncomfortable, and distant from the deposi
easures. —— He has dissolved Represtative Houses repeatedly, for opposing with manly firmness hi
dissolutions, to cause others to be elected; whereby the Legislative powers, incapable of Annihilation, have r
osed to all the dangers of invasion from without, and convulsions within. —— He has endeavoured t
ation of Foreigners; refusing to pass others to encourage their migrations hither, and raising the conditions o
by refusing his Assent to Laws for establishing Judiciary powers. —— He has made Judges dependen
ies. —— He has erected a multitude of New Offices, and sent hither swarms of Officers to harass our
g Armies without the Consent of our legislatures. —— He has affected to render the Military independent
urisdiction foreign to our constitution, and unacknowledged by our laws; giving his Assent to their Acts
For protecting them, by a mock Trial, from punishment for any Murders which they should commit
world: — For imposing Taxes on us without our Consent: — For depriving us in m
nces: —— For abolishing the free System of English Laws in a neighbouring
ple and fit instrument for introducing the same absolute rul
ns of our Governments: — For suspending ou
here, by declaring us out of his Pro
time transporting

Part I
Notions of Justice

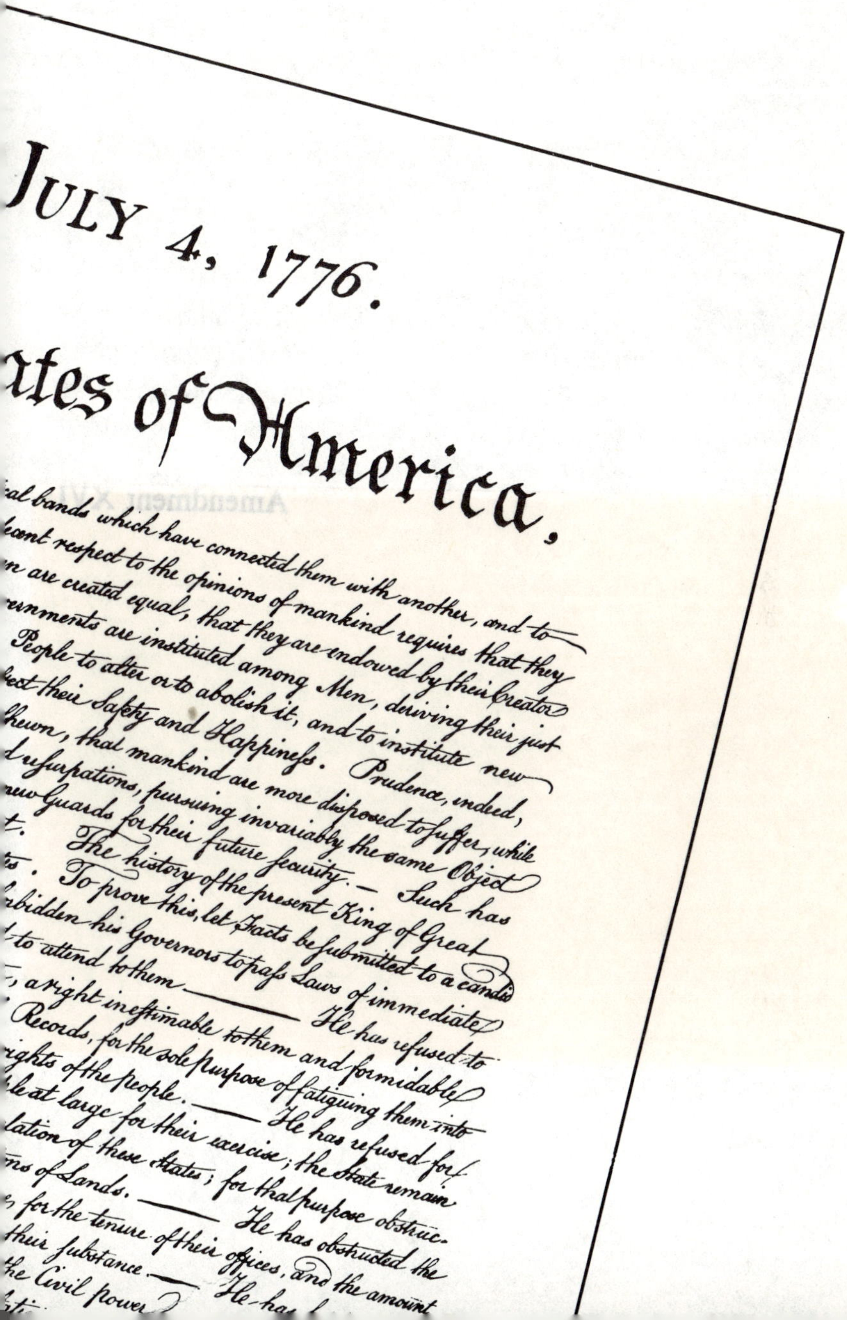

1.

. . . No State shall make or enforce any law which shall abridge the privileges or immunities of citizens of the United States; nor shall any State deprive any person of life, liberty, or property, without due process of law; nor deny to any person within its jurisdiction the equal protection of the laws.

Erratum, page 4:

Amendment XVI should read Amendment XIV

(Use this peel-off label to make correction)

Amendment XIV

American Justice

The proliferation of crime and the inability to control or prevent it are epitomized by the New York City blackout of 1977. In 1965 when a similar catastrophe hit the entire northeastern side of the United States, solidarity and cooperation prevailed as citizens and law enforcement agencies worked together to avoid chaos and to reestablish order. Relatively few crimes occurred, and those that did were contained with ease by responsible police officers.

The blackout of 1977, however, demonstrated that law-abiding citizens can no longer expect their own codes of behavior to be reflected among large masses of people. It also demonstrated that citizens can no longer expect the professional commitment of those appointed to enforce the law.

In 1965 there were 96 arrests as a consequence of the blackout; in 1977 police stopped counting at 3,776[1] arrests. At the same time the "predatory animalism of the marauding poor blacks and Hispanics" occupied the minds of journalists; on the other hand, the societal implications of such massive examples of immorality alerted politicians, social scientists, and academicians alike. While the newspapers emphasized the number of television sets snatched up by the desperate and greedy, others were more carefully observing that "the power blackout is a warning to the 'system' in all senses and at all levels."[2]

The blackout was such a warning. Foremost, the chaotic "free-for-all" indicated that respect for law and order had drastically declined since 1965. One looter remarked, "We made a mistake in '65 [but] we're going to clean-up in '77."[3] The "mistake" this person was referring to was the mistake of observing a moral code during the 1965 blackout. Poverty, it was implied, has no relief in morality. Consequently, "Why not?" was the common rationale most looters offered for their actions.

This attitude was to be expected. From 1965 to 1977 little in the way of social reform had alleviated the conditions of poverty in this country. Instead, despite countless programs and expenditures of vast sums of money, the plight of the impoverished worsened. But poverty was not the only cause of the '77 fiasco. One observer remarked, "it [was] never clear that most of the looters were the neediest."[4] The violence that took place during this blackout was as much a gesture of general disrespect for the law as it was a reaction against poverty. For instance, on Times Square middle-class "partiers," as they called themselves, took part in the destruction "just for the helluva it."

In New York City the criminal justice system failed on two counts. First, the police, the courts, and the jails did not by any means control, adjudicate, or contain the looters according to professional standards. Philip Leshin stated in Newsweek:

> What happened was that a system which is barely able to handle hundreds of cases a week was suddenly asked to handle thousands.[5]

The system was criticized for being totally ineffective in the wake of a crisis. Yet the extremity of the situation helped to mitigate instances of police violence, prolonged pretrial delay, and overcrowded jailhouses.

What could not be explained or, for that matter, justified in the eyes of the public was the failure of the entire police force to react to the disaster. The department had already been ravaged by the city's financial crisis and its numbers had been reduced to 25,000 officers. When the blackout occurred, there were only 8,000 officers on duty. The police commissioner ordered all off-duty police to report immediately, *but more than 11,000 failed to heed or did not hear the order to report.* While city officials were calling the blackout a "night of terror," virtually half of the city's police officers were turning deaf ears to the orders of their superiors and were refusing to uphold their sworn duty.[6] Such a lack of commitment was even more distressing to the national concern than the conduct and attitudes of the looters.

In this decade we have seen immorality and illegality reach the highest elected office in the country. The general lack of moral standards and a brazen disrespect for law *or* order must force this nation to not only look hard at its social policies, but also to question the foundations and efficacy of its criminal justice system.

The Federal Bureau of Investigation publishes annually a "crime clock" that reports the frequency of reported crimes in the United States. In 1970 there were 11 serious crimes reported every minute; by 1975 that number had nearly doubled to 21. A violent crime was reported every 43 seconds in 1970 and by 1975, those reports were coming in every 31 seconds.[7]

The crime clock statistics are shocking; yet what is even more alarming is that these reported crimes may represent only the tip of the iceberg. Federal studies have demonstrated that substantial numbers of crimes are not reported in this country. The reasons cited by citizens for not reporting crimes are that they do not want to become "involved," that they are afraid, or that nothing would be accomplished even if they did react.[8]

The attitude that nothing would be gained if one did report a crime cannot be discounted. Under-staffed and over-worked police departments cannot match the zeal or satisfy the expectations of an outraged citizen who has just experienced a purse snatching or witnessed a violent altercation in the streets. Moreover, even if the police do react immediately, arrest does not necessarily lead to prosecution, conviction, or punishment. For example, recent studies of seven major cities indicated that 60 percent of the defendants charged with felonies were never convicted and that another 80 percent were not incarcerated.[9]

The ever-increasing crime rate is creating public fear. The collective response has been the development of an American psychology with two different tendencies. On one hand, America has abandoned its city streets after dark. Behind doors with multiple locks, many Americans will not go out at night except under very controlled conditions. The tragic irony is that the desolate, abandoned streets increase the likelihood of crime. Those cautious people who will no longer get involved, who won't report a crime they've witnessed or come to the aid of a victim, are in themselves hindering the system's ability to apprehend and convict offenders.

At the same time that this passivity has developed, our citizens have been also acquiring guns at an alarming rate. The once predicted "greening"[10] of America has turned into the "arming" of America. What is equally disconcerting about the growth of private ownership of weapons in this country is the fact that neither the federal nor local governments pay heed to the public opinion polls suggesting that an overwhelming majority of the American people are in favor of restrictions on the sale and possession of handguns.[11] Instead, legislators at all levels of government have been influenced by well-organized and financed gun lobbies. Some gun groups assert a highly aggressive stance, such as the federation of 135 pistol and rifle clubs in New York which in 1977 offered a $200 reward to any victim of a robbery or assault who shot and killed his assailant.[12]

In this atmosphere of fear, rampant crime, and public dissatisfaction with our criminal justice system, the system itself is overwhelmed by a multiplicity of problems. When we know the details of any given case, the inability to arrest, convict, or punish may be understandable and even justifiable. But the frequency of these apparent failures has undermined the respect of citizens and public officials alike for the criminal justice system.

"Victim Justice"

Before 1868, when crime was simple and its control relatively straightforward, "victim justice" prevailed throughout the United States and its territories. "Victim justice" characterizes the frontier justice system that focused on the primary right of the victim to revenge. In developing communities, predominantly rural, crime was not tolerated and altruistic concern for the criminal's fate was virtually non-existent. What was deemed criminal in those communities was largely based upon the views of the large land-owners who also controlled, by virtue of their wealth, the political processes and officials in the area. At this period in American history, lynchings, tar-and-featherings, and other extreme methods of punishment were not repugnant to the American conscience. Self-help was the rule, often executed by undiscerning posses who considered the chase and administration of punishment a sport. In the course of restoring order and satisfying the victim's need for revenge, the law, such as it was, was quick to punish without philosophic musings about the rights of the accused. Because community attitudes were relatively primitive and single-minded, reaction to crime was emotional and the need for resolution immediate.

When communities became more urban and thus complex, crime increased and there was a concomitant increase in blatant miscarriages of justice. Although courts were functioning, they were hardly palaces of justice. While innocent people were often being condemned, criminals were frequently getting away. At the same time, the archaic methods of disposing of convicted persons were starting to grate on the nerves of an increasingly sophisticated society, and the voices of penal reformers were beginning to be heard.[13]

By the late nineteenth century, the American public was ready for a semblance of fairness in the administration of its criminal laws. The vehicle for the introduction of fairness into the states where most crimes are prosecuted became the due process and equal protection clauses of the Fourteenth Amendment.[14] Historians and legal scholars still differ as to whether the Amendment was ever intended to apply to how a state dealt with any of its citizens other than newly freed slaves,[15] but through its promise of due process and equal protection for all citizens, the notion of "criminal justice" was introduced into the administration of our criminal law. Although concern for the rights of victims has never been in question, the law turned from the obvious—revenge for the outrage against the victim—to the very complex—protection of a criminal's rights. Indeed, the shift from "victim justice" to "criminal justice" has been so extreme during the past hundred years that our legal system now suffers from accusations that, by over-emphasizing and "over-protecting" the criminal's rights, the victim's plight and the need to protect law-abiding citizens are often forgotten.

"Criminal Justice"

AMENDMENT XIV (1868)

All persons born or naturalized in the United States, and subject to the jurisdiction thereof, are citizens of the United States and of the State wherein they reside. No State shall make or enforce any law which shall abridge the privileges or immunities of citizens of the United States; nor shall any State deprive any person of life, liberty, or property, without due process of law; nor deny to any person within its jurisdiction the equal protection of the laws.

Prior to the Civil War, the federal Constitution played no role whatsoever in determining how a state treated its citizens in its justice system.[16] Only after the adoption of the Fourteenth Amendment, providing that no state might deprive an individual of due process or equal protection of the law, did a tool exist to monitor how a state dealt with its citizens, and especially how a state went about depriving a citizen of his liberty. Until the second half of the twentieth century, however, the Fourteenth Amendment did not prove, in and of itself, to be an effective tool to guarantee fairness in criminal proceedings throughout the country. It was then that an activist Supreme Court, under the stewardship of Chief Justice Earl Warren, vigorously made use of the Fourteenth Amendment to examine how well the rights of citizens were being protected in the states.

The Warren Court in the 1960s turned to the Bill of Rights for guidance in designing a due process model of fairness for the federal and state courts. Within the Bill of Rights were the substance and spirit of criminal justice as we know it today.

The Bill of Rights

The Bill of Rights was an afterthought to the Constitution. The document that was originally submitted to the colonies for ratification made no mention of the rights that were to be enumerated and appended and later known as the Bill of Rights. Because the national government was to have very limited powers, the drafters of the Constitution did not feel it was necessary to include a statement of rights. Yet the citizens of the various colonies distrusted all forms of government; without a reassurance that their rights would be protected, they were reluctant to ratify the powers of the so-called "limited government." Notwithstanding the good faith of the drafters of the Constitution, then, failing to include a statement of rights seriously jeopardized the likelihood of the document's ratification.[17]

James Madison, eventually the principal proponent and author of the Bill of Rights, discounted the value of such a document. In a letter to Thomas Jefferson, Madison questioned whether "parchment barriers" could have any effect upon "overbearing majorities" when such a document's "control is most needed."[18] Jefferson replied with a timeless exposition of the need for a statement of rights:

> Experience proves (critics say) the inefficacy of a Bill of Rights. True. But though it is not absolutely efficacious under all circumstances, it is of great potency always, and rarely inefficacious. A brace the more will often keep up the building which would have fallen with that brace the less. There is a remarkable difference between the characters of the inconveniences which attend a declaration of rights, and those which attend the want of it. The inconveniences of the declaration are that it may cramp government in its useful exertions. But the evil of this is short-lived, trivial and reparable. The inconveniences of the want of a Declaration are permanent, afflicting and irreparable. They are in constant progression from bad to worse. The executive in our governments is not the sole, it is scarcely the principal object of my jealousy. The tyranny of the legislatures is the most formidable dread at present, and will be for long years.[19]

When the new government began its operation in 1789 under its barely ratified Constitution, half of the former colonies formally requested an addition to the new charter consisting of a formal statement recognizing the inalienability of some individual rights.[20] Madison, whose opposition to a bill of rights had been overcome either by Jefferson's persuasiveness or by the fact that he had nearly been defeated in his bid for a seat in the first House of Representatives when it was rumored that he opposed such a document, introduced a bill during the opening days of the first Congress. This bill, after amendment, became the Bill of Rights.

For nearly a century the provisions of the Bill of Rights were applicable only to protect against intrusions upon those fundamental rights by the national government.[21] The framers of the Constitution and the Bill of Rights were primarily afraid of a centralized, powerful government operating autonomously, and not specifically in the interests of the states. As these individuals represented the controlling interests of their states, it is understandable why they did not fear the operation of their own state governments. Thus, the provision of the Bill of Rights guaranteeing due process in the application of the criminal laws applied only to the relatively few criminal cases that were prosecuted and tried in the federal courts.

Procedural Regularity

The mainstay of the American criminal justice ideal, predating both the Bill of Rights and the Fourteenth Amendment, is *procedural regularity.* Simply put, this means that all government—federal, state, and local—must abide by its own rules when dealing with its citizens. The government may not cut corners and ignore established procedures to achieve a desirable end. Procedural regularity is especially critical in the administration of the criminal laws where a person's liberty is at stake. Thus, no matter how heinous the crime the government must abide by its own rules and proceed according to law when it seeks to convict and punish the offender.

The American reliance upon procedural regularity to insure fairness is hardly surprising since the American system of justice was born out of a revolution against England's abuse of its own procedural rules that resulted in violations of the colonists' rights. Justice Felix Frankfurter, an immigrant at the turn of this century who had risen to the Supreme Court, stated:

> The history of American freedom is, in no small measure, the history of procedure. (1945)[22]

Procedural regularity was a familiar concept to the states, most of which had well-defined procedures set forth in their own constitutions. And the Bill of Rights was recognition of the new nation's commitment to procedural regularity. The Bill of Rights sets forth rights that were regarded as so fundamental that the framers forever barred their abridgement by the new government. The enumerated rights were not haphazardly selected. Derived from the traditional English common law, they were included to insure that American governments respected the rights of their citizens, did not tamper with a citizen's basic freedoms, and observed their own procedural rules and restrictions when attempting to deprive a citizen of his liberty.

The Bill of Rights was designed to assure procedural regularity and enhance the two basic values fundamental to the Anglo-American concept of justice. These two principles which are intrinsic to the American justice ideal are (1) *that a man is innocent until proven guilty, and (2) that each accused will be guaranteed a fair trial.*

The presumption of innocence guarantees that an individual will not be treated as guilty until his guilt has been proven at trial. A person may not be denied liberty, except in extraordinary circumstances, prior to a finding of guilt.[23] And most importantly that guilt may neither be assumed nor extracted from the accused.[24] And finally, it is the government's responsibility when it attempts to deprive an individual of his liberty to bear the burden of assembling its own case, presenting the evidence, and proving the individual's guilt beyond a reasonable doubt.[25]

This nation's concept of a fair trial, which is complex and will be treated throughout this text, demands: that a determination of guilt is based upon the evidence presented at the trial, after the accused has had an opportunity to challenge that evidence and present his own and that a guilty verdict is arrived at by a judge or jury who will consider only that evidence and not extrinsic factors such as the passions of the community or the race of the accused. The fair trial standard strives to protect the integrity of the guilt-determining process by underwriting the reliability of the verdict. Thus, the multiple procedures and rules that grew out of this principle were initially designed to protect the innocent and insure that only the guilty were convicted.

As early as the 1930s it became apparent to the Supreme Court that defendants in many state courts were being deprived of their fundamental rights due to an absence of procedural regularity and that the guilt-determining process was, by no means, always fair, despite state statutory and constitutional provisions similar in content to the Bill of Rights.[26] In order to insure a fair trial by providing procedural regularity, the federal judiciary began to intervene by imposing the national Constitution upon state criminal trials. The due process clause of the Fourteenth Amendment provided the means for that intervention.[27]

The early intervention was hesitant and confined to extreme situations. The first cases that were reversed by the Supreme Court on due process grounds, beginning in 1923, were mob-domination cases in which angry lynch mobs threatened violence if defendants were not found guilty.[28] The trials were devoid of any semblance of fairness as guilty verdicts appeared to be an appeasement of an angry public. As a result of these cases, the Court realized that no state, regardless of public pressure, coercion, or any other reason, should be allowed to violate the fundamental right of any citizen to a fair trial as guaranteed in the due process clause of the Fourteenth Amendment. From these first tentative steps, the following rights were recognized by the Supreme Court as essential to a fair trial and as rights of the accused that should not be sacrificed under any circumstances:

1. The accused must have the right to know what the charges are against him.[29]
2. The accused must have the right to a public trial so that he will not be "railroaded."[30]
3. The accused must have the right to a trial that is free from threats and violence.[31]
4. The accused must have the right to present a defense.[32]
5. Evidence of guilt pertaining to each and every element of an offense must appear in the record.[33]

Thus, even before the activist period of the 1960s, the Supreme Court had begun to define the essentials for a fair trial.

The Warren Court

During the 1960s cases involving violations of these fair trial rights continued to reach the Supreme Court. Now, however, these cases were being heard by a new majority within that Court that was not satisfied with the generalized notion of a fair trial that had been applied to the states through the Fourteenth Amendment. Despite prior rulings by the Supreme Court, the dual promises of due process and equal protection were being disregarded in many state criminal courts. The new majority turned to the Bill of Rights for its definition of due process. In the course of determining which of the rights enumerated in the Bill of Rights were applicable to the states through the due process clause of the Fourteenth Amendment, and consequently which state procedures violated those enumerated rights, the current American notion of "fairness" in criminal justice evolved. Through a process defined as "incorporation," specific rights contained within the Bill of Rights that the majority regarded as essential to achieving a fair trial were made applicable to state criminal proceedings and made binding upon the states through the Fourteenth Amendment. The Warren Court did not confine itself to a concept of fairness limited to the reliability of the guilt-determining process; in short, this Court recognized the necessity to insure the dignity of all those who come in contact with the law.[34]

A due process model, then, was imposed upon the states. Although the model has been subject to redefinition by subsequent Supreme Court majorities or constitutional amendment, it did define the meaning of due process and the minimal level of fairness acceptable in state criminal courts. Through this model, a certain amount of uniformity was imposed upon the criminal justice systems of all the states. While each state remains free to develop its own criminal procedures, those rules and practices may not fall below the announced due process standards.

The due process revolution has not been an easy one. While the ultimate authority for interpreting the Constitution and its effect on the laws and procedures of the national government and each of the states rests with the United States Supreme Court, critics have charged that the Supreme Court assumed too great a supervisory role over the states.[35] Within the Supreme Court itself dissenting justices denounced the incorporation process as an act of imposing provisions from the Bill of Rights that were never intended to be levied upon the states.[36] And finally, some have attributed the near-breakdown of criminal court machinery in many states to the high standards imposed by the Warren Court.[37]

Regardless of these criticisms, it cannot be denied that by defining and interpreting the meaning of due process, the Court was exercising its constitutional authority. And the Fourth, Fifth and Sixth Amendments were the foundations of the Supreme Court's efforts to insure fairness and preserve the dignity of defendants in both federal and state courts. Through the incorporation of all but one provision of those amendments[38] into the due process clause of the Fourteenth Amendment, and to a lesser extent, through its utilization of the equal protection clause as an access to equal justice for the poor, the Warren Court was characterized as "putting flesh and blood" on our ideals.[39] By giving solid meaning to due process by enunciating its minimal requirements, the Warren Court gave our system of justice the potential, for the first time, to become a true system of "criminal justice."

The Sixth Amendment

AMENDMENT VI (1791)

In all criminal prosecutions, the accused shall enjoy the right to a speedy and public trial, by an impartial jury of the State and district wherein the crime shall have been committed, which district shall have previously ascertained by law, and to be informed of the nature and cause of the accusation; to be confronted with the witnesses against him; to have compulsory process for obtaining witnesses in his favor, and to have the Assistance of Counsel for his defense.

The Sixth Amendment, concentrating as it does on trial rights, provides the basic underpinnings for a fair trial. Its ultimate contribution is that it has given constitutional status to our adversary system of justice. Equipped with the rights spelled out in this amendment, the defendant does not stand powerless before the law. A balance is established where the prosecutor is required to prove every element of the accused's guilt and where the accused is afforded the right to a meaningful and effective defense. The incorporation of the Sixth Amendment has given constitutional support to a set of procedures that has developed across the span of almost five hundred years—procedures that define the essence of democratic justice.

Right to a Speedy Trial

Related to the earlier concern with an accused's right to a fair public trial that grew out of the mob-domination cases is the requirement that the trial also be "speedy." This requirement, always applicable to the federal government, was made binding upon the states for three reasons: a speedy trial (1) affords the accused an opportunity to vindicate himself before the criminal charges against him damage his reputation; (2) enhances the reliability of the guilt-determining process; and (3) allows the defendant the opportunity to prepare a meaningful defense before his case grows stale with time.[40]

The Supreme Court recognized the difficulty in establishing absolute time requirements for bringing a defendant to trial. Although many states have established specific times within which an accused must be tried, the Supreme Court has not. Instead, it has adopted criteria for judging whether or not a trial has been unnecessarily and thus unconstitutionally delayed. The factors considered by the Court are: (1) the length of the delay; (2) the reasons for it; (3) the defendant's timely assertion of his rights; and (4) whether the accused suffered prejudice.[41]

Implicit in this right is the belief that unnecessary delay in bringing a person to trial damages the character of the defendant. If a trial is unnecessarily delayed and the accused's freedom is in the meantime denied, the state's case and the defendant's defense, along with his reputation, erodes.

Right to a Trial by Jury

The Sixth Amendment right to a trial by jury was made applicable to the states in 1968. In *Duncan v. Louisiana*[42] the Supreme Court thoroughly examined and analyzed the purposes and policies promoted by the right. Although recognizing that a fair criminal process could be achieved without a jury trial, the Court pointed out the historical significance of trial by jury in the development of freedom in England and in the United States. The Court concluded that the function of a jury trial is to protect against government oppression, whether from a corrupt or overzealous prosecutor, or a compliant, biased, or eccentric judge. The Court's decision to protect the accused's right to a jury trial reflects a fundamental decision about the exercise of power in this society: a refusal to entrust plenary power over an individual's life and liberty to one judge or group of judges.

Right to Present a Defense

The compulsory process[43] and confrontation[44] clauses of the Sixth Amendment provide the guarantees that the accused will have an opportunity to present a defense. Compulsory process requires that the defendant be able to utilize the state's authority and machinery to compel witnesses in his favor to appear. Consequently, subpoenas will be served upon defense witnesses by the official designated to summon witnesses and the court's power will be used to compel the presence of unwilling witnesses. The right of the defendant to prepare a strong defense has been supported to such an extent that valid state evidentiary rules which would normally bar certain evidence must sometimes give way to allow the defense to present that evidence and thus prove the defendant's innocence.[45]

Intertwined with the right to present a defense is the concept of a meaningful opportunity to attack the state's evidence. The opportunity is provided through the Sixth Amendment requirement that the defendant have an occasion to confront his accusers at trial and a chance at significant cross-examination.[46] By challenging the accuracy and veracity of a witness' testimony through vigorous cross-examination, the jury can make a more accurate determination of the witness' credibility and reliability.

Right to Counsel

Since the Court determined earlier that fundamental fairness required that an accused have the right to present a defense, the Sixth Amendment right to counsel provided the principal tool to make that a substantial right. The Court had pointed out much earlier that the lay person would have difficulty in defending against a criminal charge and presenting a defense;[47] it was inevitable, then, that the Court would utilize the Sixth Amendment right to counsel to assert that any defendant, regardless of his ability to pay, was entitled to counsel.

Twenty years before the Warren Court, the Supreme Court had deemed it fundamentally unfair for a defendant charged with an offense carrying the death penalty to have to represent himself.[48] The Warren Court incorporated the right to counsel into the Fourteenth Amendment but limited its extension only to serious offenses,[49] which in most states was interpreted to mean felonies carrying a penalty of more than one year in prison.[50] Ultimately, it was the Burger Court in 1972 that extended the right to counsel to any criminal charge that may result in the imposition of a jail or prison sentence.[51]

The Fifth Amendment

AMENDMENT V (1791)

No person shall be held to answer for a capital, or otherwise infamous crime, unless on a presentment or indictment of a Grand Jury, except in cases arising in the land or naval forces, or in the Militia, when in actual service in time of War or public danger; nor shall any person be subject for the same offense to be twice put in jeopardy of life or limb; nor shall be compelled in any criminal case to be a witness against himself, nor be deprived of life, liberty, or property without due process of law; nor shall private property be taken for public use, without just compensation.

Right Against Double Jeopardy

The doctrine opposed to placing a man twice in jeopardy for the same offense was recognized under English common law as early as the thirteenth century. The Fifth Amendment prohibition against double jeopardy reflects the awareness of those responsible for the Bill of Rights that a legal system which fails to place limits upon the number of opportunities available to government for establishing a defendant's guilt runs a serious risk of abuse.[52]

The double jeopardy clause has been made a part of the Fourteenth Amendment due process requirements because it offends our sense of justice to permit a state to force a defendant to run the trial gauntlet multiple times until that state obtains a result which it considers satisfactory.[53]

Privilege Against Self-Incrimination

The presumption of innocence is an essential ingredient of American due process. Placing the burden of proof upon the state is an example of this principle in operation, but its core is found in the Fifth Amendment prohibition against compelling a defendant to be a witness against himself, which has also been extended to the states through the due process clause of the Fourteenth Amendment.[54]

When a police officer makes an arrest, the rules guarding the presumption of innocence are designed so that the defendant need never say anything from the moment of arrest to the final determination of guilt or innocence. What this means is that the state must develop and prove its own case and not utilize the accused to prove his own guilt. The state must justify the grounds for the arrest and must justify compelling the defendant to stand trial, in addition to proving the defendant's guilt at trial. The defendant does not have to talk his way out of trouble at the police station, and the police are obligated to abide by an accused's decision to invoke his Fifth Amendment right to remain silent. If an accused makes a statement to the police after being taken into custody, the prosecution may not use that statement at trial unless it is first established that the defendant, advised of the right to remain silent, *freely and voluntarily* waived that right.[55] Certainly, the defendant does not have to testify at trial, and the prosecution is not permitted to comment upon the defendant's silence to the jury or attempt to substitute that silence for evidence of guilt.[56] In fact, the defendant need not present a defense and may still be acquitted because the burden of proving guilt rests with the state.[57]

The Fourth Amendment

AMENDMENT IV (1791)

The right of the people to be secure in their persons, houses, papers, and effects, against unreasonable searches and seizures, shall not be violated, and no Warrants shall issue, but upon probable cause, supported by Oath or affirmation, and particularly describing the place to be searched, and the persons or things to be seized.

Right of Privacy

In a free society an individual is entitled to a certain amount of dignity, and that dignity must be respected even when the state is attempting to deprive the individual of his liberty. This principle, together with the notion of fairness, defines due process.

America's comprehension of the full import of due process ripened after World War II; the police state tactics practiced in Europe had alerted Americans to the necessity of guaranteeing the personal dignity of all citizens, even those suspected or accused of crimes. Even in this country, there was a general fear that the police were prone to strong-arm tactics and violence.[58] Consequently, the government as well as the public, wanted to be assured that the police, while enforcing the law, obeyed the law.

One right that is fundamental to a democratic system and essential to protection of individual dignity is the right of all citizens to privacy.[59] The denial of this right was one of the central issues between the American colonists and England. Its principal embodiment in the Constitution is found in the Fourth Amendment, prohibiting "unreasonable searches and seizures" of persons or their property. Shortly after World War II, the Supreme Court ruled that this provision of the Fourth Amendment was binding upon the states through the due process clause of the Fourteenth Amendment because it was essential to a free society.[60]

The constitutional standard governing official intrusions into individual privacy is "reasonableness."[61] The word is not susceptible to easy definition, and the problem is complex when applying the standard to the facts of a particular arrest or search. Essentially, the information that police base their decision to arrest or search is weighed against the nature of the intrusion of a citizen's privacy to evaluate the legitimacy or "reasonableness" of that intrusion. For a relatively minor intrusion, such as an on-the-street stopping and questioning, the police need not have as much information concerning the individual's involvement with a crime as they must have to justify a major intrusion, such as an arrest.[62] Consequently, if police make an unreasonable (illegal) arrest or conduct an unreasonable (illegal) search, the evidence which they secured during the intrusion cannot be used to convict the person so arrested or searched.[63] This is an incredible commitment to individual rights. Even though the evidence is reliable and may prove beyond a reasonable doubt the accused's guilt, it will be suppressed if the accused's right to privacy has been violated.

Due Process in State Courts

Prior to the Warren Court, criminal proceedings in state criminal courts were, in many instances, notoriously unfair. The Court's struggles and debates to determine the breadth of due process protections forced the country to reevaluate and redefine its notion of fairness in the criminal justice process.

The due process model developed by the Court was not designed to insure conformity or to dictate the mechanics of state criminal trials. As stated previously, the model was not intended to impose an ideal. Nevertheless state courts did not welcome the interference of the Supreme Court in what they considered the purely state and local matter of maintaining order and administering their criminal laws. Often state judges sympathized with law enforcement officers who believed that the net effect of the due process revolution was to coddle criminals and handcuff the police.[64] Even after the Warren era ended and the Burger Court started cutting back on the extent of federal constitutional involvement in state criminal procedure, criticism of the due process model did not abate.

Some state supreme courts, however, have not accepted the cutbacks offered by the Burger Court. Through interpretations of provisions in their own state constitutions, which are often identical in wording to the provisions of the Bill of Rights, the highest courts in several states have imposed higher standards of due process upon their own criminal justice systems than the Supreme Court has said the Fourteenth Amendment requires.[65] For instance, while the Supreme Court has decided that the Fourteenth Amendment right to a jury trial does not require that a jury number twelve persons[66] or that a jury verdict in a non-capital case be unanimous,[67] the vast majority of the states continues to require unanimous verdicts by juries of twelve.[68] In an entirely different area, the Supreme Court has ruled that it is reasonable for a police officer to conduct a full body search of every person arrested and taken into custody, no matter how trivial the offense.[69] A handful of state courts has ruled differently under their own state constitutions and limited full-body searches to those offenses where evidence of the crime might be found, thereby eliminating complete searches for traffic arrests.[70]

Before the due process model was imposed on state courts, the freedom of the states to adjudicate defendants on their own terms often led to abuse. While the due process revolution has in no way created a utopian criminal justice system, and has in fact exacerbated other problems within the system, it has helped to make the two-hundred-year-old promise of a fair trial more of a living reality.

Equal Protection

The other essential promise within the Fourteenth Amendment is that all citizens will be afforded "equal protection of the laws." What this pledge means, very simply, is that all citizens will have equal access to the law and the laws will be applied equally to all citizens. In short, the Fourteenth Amendment requires that a state not discriminate between persons who come before the law.

As everyone knows, all citizens of the United States do not enjoy equal advantages. And the law does not have the power to equalize the position of all the defendants who come before the courts. The state's obligation does not and cannot extend so far as to furnish an indigent with all the assistance and services that a defendant with an unlimited purse may choose. Yet few would suggest that differing financial resources will not affect the quality of the defense an accused is able to muster. What the courts are required to do is regard wealth (as well as race, religion, and sex) as an irrelevant factor in administering the law.

By no means, then, is the equal protection guaranteed by the Constitution unlimited: poverty can and does affect an accused's defense. But if a defendant cannot retain counsel or obtain the testimony of an expert witness, the state *is* obligated to assist the accused in obtaining these services. This principle was upheld by the Supreme Court when it ruled that to deny a person who is seeking an appeal the transcript of his criminal trial is to deny him equal protection of the law:

> Such a denial is a misfit in a country dedicated to affording equal justice to all and special privileges to none in the administration of its criminal law. There can be no equal justice where the kind of trial a man gets depends on the amount of money he has.... In criminal trials a state may no more discriminate on account of poverty than on account of religion, race, or color....(1956)[71]

Equal protection exists within the confines of the state's responsibility to insure that an accused's poverty does not bar his access to the legal process, does not bar him from presenting an effective defense, and does not result in injustice. Thus, the poverty of an accused must not interfere with the orderly and fair application of the law: poverty must not cripple an accused's defense to the extent that the due process guarantee of a fair trial is violated.

States are obligated to provide effective legal assistance for all indigents, but effectiveness has proven to be an illusive standard and one that is difficult to enforce. The Supreme Court has consistently recognized that the issue is not one of absolutes but of degrees and that the Fourteenth Amendment "does not require equality or precisely equal advantages."[72] Even though a poor man's defense may be a far cry from the defense a wealthy man is able to secure, this difference is not regarded as a violation of the equal protection guarantee as long as the indigent defendant has "an adequate opportunity to present his claims."[73]

The application of the equal protection principle to criminal procedure has been limited.[74] The equal protection clause, for example, has been the means to successfully attack convictions secured from all white juries where blacks were systematically excluded from jury service.[75] Similarly, the equal protection clause has been the vehicle to insure that women are not systematically excluded from grand and trial juries,[76] and may be used in the future to insure that juries represent an economic cross-section of the community.[77]

The equal protection guarantee has not had as great an impact as due process upon developing notions of fairness and justice in the criminal process. Its greatest impact has been in the civil area where it has helped to transform this society by attacking racial, religious, and sex-based discrimination in education, employment, and housing. While it has played a secondary role to due process in the developing notions of criminal justice, that role has been a complementary one in the fight to insure fairness and justice for all defendants.

The Rule of Law and Discretionary Justice

We often hear that America is a country where the rule of law, not man, prevails. Due process and equal protection are two principles that help to make the concept of the rule of law a living reality. Equally important to fulfilling the promise that the rule of law will prevail in our justice system are limits on the discretion that a public official exercises. We have already seen that due process, through its insistence upon procedural regularity, seeks to limit the exercise of discretion, and that equal protection, through its promise of equal justice, seeks to insure that all people will be treated alike irrespective of race, religion, sex, or position. We must recognize, however, that these propositions are always being tested. The notion that "no man is above the law" is constantly being challenged in every context, and failures to abide by that principle have resulted in a public loss of confidence in the criminal justice system.

In a modern, crowded, and complex society, discretionary decisions cannot be eliminated. Monitoring and controlling discretion at every level of the process is the only way to insure the integrity of the justice process. Reality demands our recognition that the police officer does not arrest every violator whom he detects; nor does the district attorney prosecute everyone arrested; nor is everyone tried and convicted who is guilty; nor everyone convicted punished, or punished the same.[78] There is tremendous discretion at every step of the justice process, and the application of the rule of law to this process depends upon the mechanisms that exist to monitor and control the exercise of discretion.

Individualized justice is as important to our notions of fairness as are the principles of due process and equal protection. Individualized justice depends on a certain amount of flexibility in our justice system. Police, prosecutors, judges, and all criminal justice professionals must exercise some discretion in determining the individual fates of those who come in contact with the law. The problem of discretionary decisions is not to eliminate responsible interpretation of the law in relation to individual cases, but to establish "... the elusive balance between structuring decisions and providing for individualized justice."[79]

Discretionary justice is a reality. For it to compliment the principles of due process and equal protection, it is necessary that controls exist so discretion is not abused in an arbitrary and capricious manner; that individuals are treated fairly; and that individual cases that are substantially alike will not be treated differently without justification.

Order or Justice?

The criminal justice system in this country has two discreet and distinct functions: it must (1) battle crime and, at the same time, (2) protect and preserve individual liberty. Often these two functions are contradictory and in open conflict.

Maintaining order and preserving freedom involves the exercise of immense power by the police, prosecutors, courts, and correctional agencies. Divisions of such power and responsibility naturally tend to cause suspicion among the repositories. For example, consider the tensions that arise between the police and the courts when judges exclude evidence because of the manner in which it was discovered by the police. It would hardly be in the interest of fairness if the courts over-emphasized their relationship with the police, rather than remaining detached and dispassionate when making decisions based on constitutional considerations and the evidence on record. In addition there are interfaces of authority that meet head on. Prosecutors, by the very nature of their responsibility, have authority over the police, and the courts have supervisory power and the final say as to the correctness of police and prosecutorial decisions. The fact that these relationships exist in an era when there is too much crime, too few police officers, prosecutors, judges, and willing witnesses, compounds the problems created by the dual responsibilities of the system and the uneasy sharing of power.

The criminal justice system in this country has been weakened even further because an increased emphasis has been placed in the last twenty years on results—on numbers of cases disposed of—and not on quality, despite the fact that every decision made affects the liberty of individuals and the safety and security of the community. Consequently, our system has been characterized as mass production justice. In simply moving people through the process, the system is failing to achieve either order or justice.[80]

Order without a concern for justice would be a much easier governmental objective than attempting to achieve both order *and* justice. The recorded history of mankind abounds with examples of societies and regimes that have achieved order through rigid systems of law that operate without concern for individual rights. In societies that demand unmitigated order individual rights have been subordinated to governmental interests. In such societies the law is totally dependent for its content and impact upon the decisions of those who are in control of the government. The rule of law, even in an imperfect condition, has no meaning within that context because decisions at every level are within the discretion of the people who exercise control.

Achieving the balance between an ordered society and individual freedom may be an arduous task, one that has required a constant struggle to maintain even in an imperfect condition; but it is the quintessential difference between enforcement of the law in a free society and a repressive society. We cannot afford to decrease our efforts at either building an ordered society or protecting individual rights. The safety and security of our persons, homes, and streets are dependent upon the ability of the criminal justice system to achieve order; at the same time, however, a great proportion of our national ideals has to be invested in the criminal justice system's capacity to insure fairness as it tries to build order. To abandon or diminish either order or fairness would be to surrender to lawlessness and anarchy and to relinquish much of our heritage that sets us apart from most other societies. The effort to realize both democratic goals is essential to the maintenance of the best aspects of this society as we know it.

Discussion Questions

1. What is meant by the term "criminal justice"?

2. What was the Warren Court's contribution to the American system of criminal justice?

3. Why was it deemed necessary to incorporate the Fourth, Fifth, and Sixth Amendments into the Fourteenth Amendment?

4. What does the following statement mean?

"The problem of discretionary decisions is not to eliminate responsible interpretation of the law in relation to individual cases, but to establish 'the elusive balance between structuring decisions and providing for individualized justice.' "

5. Walter Miller states in his article, "Ideology and Criminal Justice Policy" (J. of C.L. and Crim., 64:2, 1973) that America is "experiencing a major transitional phase—a period in which long-established social arrangements . . . are undergoing substantial change." One of the changes he discusses is the switch in national emphasis from criminal justice ideals to the "eye-for-an-eye" mentality of the past. In short, Miller maintains we are now witnessing a return to "victim justice." The reinstatement of the death penalty, the increased respect for harsher sentences, the tendency toward treating many juvenile offenders as adult offenders, and a renewed concern with victims' rights rather than criminals' rights all attest to a deterioration of criminal justice ideals. Is "victim justice" compatible with democratic ideals? Is "criminal justice" possible or even desirable in light of an ever-increasing crime rate?

Notes

1. Number of arrests in 1968, *New York Times,* July 15, 1977, § 1, p. 3; number of arrests in 1977, § 1, p. 1.
2. "The Plunderers," *Newsweek,* July 25, 1977, p. 25.
3. Ibid., p. 26.
4. "Blackout Justice," *Newsweek,* August 1, 1977, p. 67.
5. Ibid.
6. *New York Times,* July 15, 1977, § 1, p. 3.
7. *Uniform Crime Reports, 1970-72, Advisory Committee on Uniform Crime Records,* "Crime Clocks," p. 31, Chart 16 (1970); *Uniform Crime Reports, 1975, Advisory Committee on Uniform Crime Records,* "Crime Clocks," p. 9, Chart 1 (1975).
8. *Crime in Eight American Cities: National Crime Panel Surveys on Atlanta, Baltimore, Cleveland, Dallas, Denver, Newark, Portland, and St. Louis* (U.S. Department of Justice, July 1974), p. 5.

9. Patrick R. Oster, "Revolving Door Justice: Why Criminals Go Free," *U.S. News and World Report,* May 10, 1976, p. 37.
10. Charles A. Reich, *The Greening of America* (New York: Random House, 1970).
11. *Gallup Poll,* "Handgun Laws," October 1975.
12. *New York Times,* April 14, 1977, § 2.
13. Sol Rubin, *The Law of Criminal Correction* (St. Paul, Minn.: West, 1963), p. 40 and p. 41.
14. Fred P. Graham, *The Due Process Revolution: The Warren Court's Impact on Criminal Law* (Rochelle Park, New Jersey: Hayden, 1970), p. 32.
15. Adamson v. California, 332 U.S. 46, at 72-75 (1947), Justice Black, dissenting opinion.
16. Adamson v. California, supra, at 59, Justice Frankfurter, concurring opinion.
17. Nelson B. Lasson, *The History and Development of the Fourth Amendment to the United States Constitution* (New York: Da Capo Press, 1970), p. 96.
18. Bernard Schwartz, *Bill of Rights: A Documentary History* (New York: Chelsea House, 1971), vol. 1, p. 616.
19. Ibid., p. 620.
20. Bernard Schwartz, *Bill of Rights: A Documentary History* (New York: Da Capo Press, 1971), vol. 2, p. 983.
21. Barron v. Mayor of Baltimore, 32 U.S. 243 (1833).
22. Malinski v. New York, 324 U.S. 401, at 414 (1945).
23. Stack v. Boyle, 342 U.S. 1 (1975).
24. Brown v. Mississippi, 297 U.S. 278 (1935).
25. In re Winship, 397 U.S. 358 (1970).
26. Comment, "Cracks in the Foundation of Criminal Justice," 46 *Ill. L. Rev.* 385, (1951-52).
27. Powell v. Alabama, 287 U.S. 45 (1932); Brown v. Mississippi, 297 U.S. 278 (1935); Rochin v. California, 342 U.S. 165 (1952).
28. Moore v. Dempsey, 261 U.S. 86 (1923).
29. Cole v. Arkansas, 333 U.S. 196 (1948).
30. In re Oliver, 330 U.S. 257 (1942).
31. Moore v. Dempsey, supra.
32. Snyder v. Massachusetts, 291 U.S. 97 (1934).
33. Thompson v. Louisville, 362 U.S. 199 (1960); Schware v. Board of Bar Examiners, 353 U.S. 232 (1956).
34. Mapp v. Ohio, 367 U.S. 81 (1961); Malloy v. Hogan, 378 U.S. 1 (1964).
35. Clifford M. Lytle, *The Warren Court and its Critics* (Tucson: The University of Arizona Press, 1968), p. 12.
36. Malloy v. Hogan, supra, dissenting opinion of Justice Harlan, at 14, 15.
37. Lytle, *The Warren Court,* p. 73.
38. Twining v. New Jersey, 211 U.S. 78 (1908).
39. Walter v. Shaefer, 54 *Ky. L.J.* 521 (1966).
40. Klopfer v. North Carolina, 386 U.S. 213 (1967).
41. Barker v. Wingo, 407 U.S. 514 (1972).
42. Duncan v. Louisiana, 391 U.S. 145 (1968).
43. Washington v. Texas, 388 U.S. 14 (1967).
44. Pointer v. Texas, 380 U.S. 400 (1965).
45. Chambers v. Mississippi, 410 U.S. 284 (1973).

46. Bruton v. United States, 391 U.S. 123 (1968).
47. Powell v. Alabama, supra at 69.

"... even the intelligent and educated layman has small and sometimes no skill in the science of law. If charged with a crime, he is incapable, generally, of determining for himself whether the indictment is good or bad. He is unfamiliar with the rules of evidence. Left alone without the aid of counsel he may be put on trial without a proper charge, and convicted upon incompetent evidence, or evidence irrelevant to the issue or otherwise inadmissible."

48. Powell v. Alabama, supra.
49. Gideon v. Wainwright, 372 U.S. 335 (1963).
50. Patterson v. Warden, 372 U.S. 776 (1963), where the Supreme Court reversed a misdemeanor conviction carrying a jail sentence of typical felony length (2 years) because of the denial of counsel.
51. Argersinger v. Hamlin, 407 U.S. 25 (1972).
52. Bartkus v. Illinois, 359 U.S. 121 (1959).
53. Benton v. Maryland, 395 U.S. 784 (1969).
54. Malloy v. Hogan, supra,
55. Miranda v. Arizona, 348 U.S. 436 (1966).
56. Griffin v. California, 380 U.S. 609 (1965).
57. In re Winship, supra.
58. *National Commission on Law Observance and Enforcement: The Wickersham Commission,* "Lawlessness in Law Enforcement," vol. 5 (1931) pp. 4-5.
59. Katz v. United States, 390 U.S. 347 (1967).
60. Mapp v. Ohio, supra.
61. Ker v. California, 374 U.S. 23 (1963).
62. Terry v. Ohio, 392 U.S. 1 (1968).
63. Mapp v. Ohio, supra.
64. Silver, "The Supreme Court, the State Judiciary and State Criminal Procedure: An Example of Uncreative Federalism," 41 *St. John's L. Rev.* 331 (1967); Inbaw, "Public Safety v. Individual Civil Liberties: The Prosecutor's Stand," *Journal of Criminal Law, Criminology, and Police Science* (1962); Lytle, *The Warren Court,* p. 94.
65. Wilkes, "More on the New Federalism in Criminal Procedure," 63 *Ky. L.J.* 873 (1975); Howard, "State Courts and Constitutional Rights in the Day of the Burger Court," 62 *Va. L. Rev.* 873, 891-907 (1976); People v. Jackson, 391 Mich. 323, 217 N.W.2d 22 (1974); People v. Brisendine, 13 Cal.3d 528, 531 P.2d 1099 (1975).
66. Williams v. Florida, 399 U.S. 78 (1970).
67. Apodaca v. Oregon, 406 U.S. 404 (1972); Johnson v. Louisiana, 406 U.S. 356 (1972).
68. 1978 Ky. Rev. Stat. & Rules Serv. § 9.32; 1978 Iowa Rules of Court, Rule 21; N.Y. § 310.40 [Verdict] *Law* (McKinney).
69. Robinson v. United States, 414 U.S. 218 (1973); Gustafson v. Florida, 414 U.S. 260 (1973).
70. 22 *Crim. L. Rep.* 1013, October 26, 1977.
71. Griffin v. Illinois, 351 U.S. 12 (1956), majority opinion of Justice Black, at 19 and at 17.
72. Griffin v. Illinois, supra, concurring opinion of Justice Frankfurter, at 20.
73. Ross v. Moffitt, 417 U.S. 600, at 615 (1974).

74. Brown v. Board of Education, 347 U.S. 483 (1954); Swann v. Charlotte-Mecklenburg Board of Education, 402 U.S. 1 (1971); Keyes v. School District No. 1, Denver, Colorado, 413 U.S. 189 (1973).
75. Strauder v. West Virginia, 100 U.S. 303 (1880).
76. Taylor v. Louisiana, 419 U.S. 522 (1975).
77. Kamisar, LaFave & Israel, *Modern Criminal Procedure,* 4th ed. (St. Paul, Minn.: West, 1974), pp. 1317-1318.
78. Frank M. Miller, *Prosecution: The Decision to Charge a Suspect with a Crime* (Boston: Little, Brown and Company, 1969), p. 173.

    "Sometimes the problem encountered is whether to prosecute when the victim—initially, at least—is insistent but the prosecutor does not desire to charge, either for reasons of evidence sufficiency or he believes that prosecution would not be in the community interest." Ibid., at 179.

    "A desire to conserve the limited resources of the criminal justice system may cause the prosecuting attorney to decide not to charge an offender who would be otherwise prosecuted." Ibid., at 186.
79. Burton Atkins and Mark Pogrebin, *The Invisible Justice System* (Cincinnati: Anderson, 1978), p. 2.
80. Charles H. Whitebread II, *Mass Production Justice and the Constitutional Ideal* (Charlottesville, Virginia: The Michie Company, 1970), p. 1.

2.

The criminal law's reach has been extended in this country far beyond its competence, invading the spheres of private morality and social welfare, proving ineffective, corruptive, and criminogenic.

Norval Morris

A Failing Ideal

Criminal justice is a product of the American democratic conscience. As an ethos, it has informed the character and practices of our criminal courts since before the Warren Era. Yet criminal justice as a controlling principle behind law enforcement and administration has had a short-lived popularity. In fact, today we are now witnessing a pendulum swing from the altruistic stance of criminal justice to what might be regarded at the very least as a less "sentimental" posture. Today, the return of the death sentence, the rejection of rehabilitation as a correctional ideal, and the demand to try certain types of juvenile offenders as adults in criminal courts all point to a relaxation of the national conscience in regard to the defendant's position.

The courts and criminal justice professionals themselves are disillusioned with our present system of justice. Daily, they see their own lack of impact upon crime and criminals. They, perhaps more than anyone else, are aware that the reforms of the past two decades have not improved the quality of justice. They are also watching the public shift its attention more and more to the plight of the victim. Yet the courts know with certainty that this concern for the victim cannot be translated into concrete action within the life of a criminal case because the victim, by necessity, must simply be just another witness. The courts cannot guarantee that justice will be done and, at the same time, they are not geared to service the victim's needs.

Why has our sense of moral obligation toward the defendant diminished? Why is the public telling the criminal justice system to "get tough with criminals"? The answers can be found in the two cases described in this chapter. Both of these cases, one sensational, the other quietly ironic, illustrate that criminal justice is far from perfecting a reasonable and fair compromise between the state, the victim, and the defendant.

"Son of Sam"

Between 1976 and 1977, six young women were killed and seven other persons were wounded in the New York City area. In a "Jack-the-Ripper" style, the murderer would gun down his victims in the night and escape without a clue to his identity. In the summer of 1977, the killer was finally caught. David Berkowitz, a shy postal clerk, was charged with six counts of murder in the first degree.[1]

After remaining in custody for ten months, Berkowitz was finally convicted of the murders. When he was brought in for sentencing, however, the courtroom became a stage for Berkowitz's tantrums and planned hysterics. Consequently, sentencing had to be postponed so Berkowitz could be subjected to more psychiatric tests. The victims' relatives, understandably eager to see "justice done," even in the muted style of life imprisonment instead of through the death sentence, were outraged. Berkowitz, a self-confessed, proud killer, was able to stall the final pronouncement of his fate. Yet as one observer remarked, "In the meantime, what about the families? How much can *they* take?"

"Son of Sam" was a sensational case. Foremost, the case indicated that by protecting a criminal's rights, the court often sacrifices the emotional needs of the victims or their families. Berkowitz's rights were fully protected throughout the criminal justice process. He was given every opportunity to prepare a defense. Finally, regardless of his guilty plea, punishment was delayed because a possibly effective insanity defense might be available to the defendant.

Clearly, a reasonable and fair compromise could not be struck between the interested parties in this case: while the families of the dead girls languished, Berkowitz benefited from the careful hand of criminal justice. And the public, clamoring for the death sentence, was calling justice a "sham."

Although our justice system does not exist, as it could not exist in a civilized society, as an instrument for personal vendettas, the drawn-out, complicated nature of criminal trials like Berkowitz's frustrates not only victims but the public as well. The multiple steps that must be heeded ("the history of American freedom is, in no small measure, a history of procedure")[2] before an obviously guilty person is sentenced are often hindrances rather than aids to realizing justice. This fact has brought renewed respect for the concept "swift and sure" justice or "swift and certain" punishment. But swift and sure justice in practice would necessitate eliminating several procedural steps and rules originally designed to protect the innocent and reveal the guilty. Yet these procedures have been an intrinsic part of our justice system; and the underlying fear felt by even the most adamant of critics is that once certain procedural rules are circumvented to facilitate swift and sure justice, the democratic character of our criminal justice system will fade.

State of Ohio v. Ralph Johnson

The point to be learned by the "Son of Sam" case was that the criminal justice system is obligated to protect the rights of even the most culpable criminals, and by protecting those rights, the system alienates the victims, their families, and the public.

State of Ohio v. Johnson is not as sensational as *People of the State of New York v. Berkowitz.* Yet the implications the *Johnson* case has for criminal justice are even further reaching than the "Son of Sam" trial. Every phase in the *Johnson* case (described in full in the remainder of this chapter) illustrates a major malfunctioning in our justice system.

Johnson's Story

A letter of grievances was sent early in 1971 to an attorney's office from twenty inmates held in Cleveland's Cuyahoga County jail awaiting disposition of their cases.[3] The letter complained that its signers had been in jail from nine to sixteen months—living in barbaric conditions—while they waited for an opportunity to answer the criminal accusations that had been brought against them. Their protest went beyond the conditions of the cells in which they were forced to live. They claimed that imprisonment had really cost them their jobs, the comfort of their homes, and alienation from their families. Their letter ended: "It is little or no consequence to be found innocent after losing everything." Soon after this letter was received, the principal author of the letter, Ralph Johnson, was acquitted and shortly thereafter requested an interview with the attorney to whom the letter had been sent. In this interview, Johnson, a tall, good-looking young black man, spoke softly but intensely about what had happened to him...

According to Johnson, at about 11:30 p.m. on April 12, 1970, he had retired for the night in his second floor bedroom. He had locked the doors and made sure the windows were secured but had left the front porch light on for his roommate who had not yet returned home. Johnson was awakened by a loud voice calling, "Hey, Ralph, hey, Ralph" at about 3:15 a.m. and thought the sounds were coming from the direction of his roommate's first floor bedroom. He groped his way downstairs, and as he turned the light on in his roommate's bedroom, he saw his roommate, Cal Root, dressed in a pair of jockey shorts kneeling down alongside his bed clutching his stomach. Root repeated several times, "I thought it was you, Ralph." Johnson observed a knife wound just above his roommate's navel, and he lowered the victim on his back to the floor and placed two pillows under Root's legs. The two men had no phone in their house, so Johnson ran out of the house to find a telephone. He ran down the residential street until he saw a house with lights on. The people who answered his frantic knocking would not open the door, but they did summon the police.

Police arrived on the scene at 3:54 a.m. and were waved down by Johnson, wearing underwear and a bathrobe, who told them that the victim said that he had surprised an intruder who had broken in and that the intruder stabbed Root and ran out through the front door. The police entered the bedroom and found Root unconscious; they immediately took him to the hospital, with Johnson accompanying them.

At the hospital, Johnson remembered, the police asked him all sorts of questions. "Then a detective asked me to accompany him to the police station. When I got to the police station, the detective just pointed his finger and said, 'I charge you.' "

When told that he was under arrest, Johnson asked the detective why:

> He told me I was the most likely suspect in the case. That's all. He proceeded to fingerprint me and everything. After he fingerprinted me he took me to a little card on the board and told me to read it which was informing me of my rights. The detective then read the card to me. I asked for an attorney because I knew one I could call, but they didn't give me an attorney. There was nothing said. There was a continuation of processing. Everything they were doing was in such a rush that they practically paid no attention to the things that I was saying. And that was it.

Johnson was placed in the municipal jail. The decision to charge Johnson had a momentous effect upon his life. At the time of his arrest the twenty-nine year old unemployed Johnson had just decided to return to his native South and enroll in college. The transplanted southerner had no family to turn to in the Cleveland area and had never been charged with a crime or been in jail before.

The following morning, April 14, Johnson appeared in the municipal court of the suburb where he had been arrested; he was charged with intentional stabbing,[4] an offense carrying a penalty of from one to twenty years. During that initial court appearance, Johnson was informed of the charge and his rights, and a preliminary hearing was scheduled:

> They took me to court the next day. I don't recall whether the judge informed me of my rights. I was wearing handcuffs until the time when the bailiff or whoever it was called my name. There was a gentleman there who was prosecuting and he charged me at that point with stabbing with intent. They went through the process. I wasn't paying too much attention because, to tell the truth, I was afraid and I didn't exactly know what they were doing and what was going on at the time.

Intentional stabbing is not a capital offense, and Johnson was eligible for release on bail. His perceptions of how the municipal court judge set bail are instructive:

> I talked and the judge asked me questions. Then what got me was the detective who arrested me and was in court with me walked around to the judge and whispered something in his ear. After that the detective came around and stood with me and the judge set the bail at $5,000. The judge asked me if I could make the bond. I had some money but it was in check form at home, and nobody could go in the house and get it from what I understood. So therefore, I had to stay in jail, and the judge continued my case.

After the preliminary appearance, Johnson was taken to the county jail where, except for court appearances, he would spend the next ten months. The preliminary hearing to ascertain probable cause was set for April 22, but it was continued to May 4 "with the consent of both parties."[5] One of those parties, Ralph Johnson, did not recall having been asked or agreeing to the continuance. On April 23 the victim of the stabbing, Cal Root, died and Johnson was charged with first-degree murder,[6] a nonbailable offense,[7] and the lesser stabbing charge was dismissed. A preliminary hearing was held May 6 on the murder charge. At its conclusion the municipal court judge found that there was probable cause to believe that the defendant had committed the offense and bound Johnson over to the grand jury:[8]

> When the date rolled around for me to appear, the detectives came and got me and I appeared, but the hearing was rescheduled. I never consented to anything, postponement or otherwise. After this I was informed that the person had died and that they charged me with murder. When I appeared for the preliminary hearing I had this attorney appointed by the court. This gentleman was peculiar. I sat down and talked with him and when he got in court he didn't say or do anything. He just did nothing. I said, My goodness. I wanted to know what was going on, because when we stepped in court I never seen an attorney who was defending a person, supposed to be defending a person, go and become chummy and shake hands and everything with the prosecutor and everybody else. I mean it's all right to remain on friendly terms with them, but I think the way he was going at it they knew more than I knew and he knew something more too. It seems as if I'd been put on rails and I was getting ready to be shipped. The police, a doctor from the hospital, and a coroner were the only witnesses at the hearing. My attorney maybe asked them one or two questions. I'm no attorney but I would have asked more questions in more depth and detail than the ones that he asked. Then from there the judge, after everything, bound me over to the grand jury. This was while I was still learning about the process because I had never been in any trouble before and

> never had to go through anything like that. From there I was taken to the county jail.

An indictment charging Ralph Johnson with the first-degree murder of his roommate was returned by the grand jury on June 12.[9] Six days later Johnson was arraigned[10] on the indictment in the court of general jurisdiction. The court determined that Johnson was indigent and appointed two attorneys to handle his case. A plea of not guilty was entered on his behalf at the arraignment:

> I didn't know about the grand jury indictment until I received it. As far as I know, the only evidence presented was by the prosecutor, and as far as I'm concerned it seems as if a person is being tried at that particular moment while not being there. Anyway, at my arraignment hearing, my name was called off, and the indictment was read. I was asked if I understood the indictment and I said yes, as far as reading it, but as far as anything else concerning the indictment, no. The judge told me that I could give no plea so he entered a plea of not guilty. The judge also said I was entitled to attorneys and an attorney should be present, but at the time I had no attorney, so he said he would appoint me an attorney and that attorney should be in contact with me in the next week or two and these are his words. I believe it was almost three weeks later that I saw an attorney. We had a nice conversation because I told him that I was putting my confidence in him. I knew he was appointed by the courts and indications to me are that a person appointed by the courts to some degree are subject to that court, but I told him that I was putting my confidence in him to a point that I wanted him to defend me. I knew, because the judge told me, that I was entitled to two attorneys since the case was murder. I didn't see the second attorney for some time, but I received a couple of letters from him to let me know that he was working.

Johnson's experience in the county jail was not atypical. The eight-story jail Johnson was taken to was nearly fifty years old. Although the jail was built to accommodate three hundred inmates, its population at the time of Johnson's incarceration was approaching six hundred. Cells designed to house two inmates were being shared by four and cells intended for four persons were housing eight. Inmates denied bunks were lucky if they received a mattress and a blanket—not everyone did. Old plumbing was constantly subject to sabotage by frustrated inmates who caused water and refuse to flood the cell ranges. Johnson was initially placed on the fifth floor, a place he described as "not fit for pigs." It seemed to him that there were twenty or thirty men roaming around the range of cells; many of them had been in jail before and "those people tend to make suffer the ones that they know have never been in jail before, and suffer quite a bit."

Johnson, shortly after being placed on the range, was attacked by a group of prisoners who attempted to initiate him by a process he later heard called "ripping off." Johnson was told that he would have to accommodate the sexual desires of the group that advanced on him. On that first occasion he resisted and had all of his clothes ripped off. As he continued to resist, the group attacked him and he was knocked unconscious. When he came to, he "checked [himself] to know that nothing had happened." When he told the deputies what had happened, he was taken to the dispensary where first aid was administered and then he was returned to the same range. After another attack Johnson was rushed to the hospital suffering from chest and head injuries and received eight stitches. When he was returned, the jailers placed him on another floor.

During the period between Johnson's plea of not guilty at the arraignment on June 18 and the impaneling of the trial jury on February 16, the defense filed several motions, including a motion to suppress the alleged dying declaration of the victim. The last motion was filed on February 10, one day after the pretrial conferences began. While arguing on the motion to suppress, the assistant prosecutor admitted that the state could not prove the premeditation element of first-degree murder. The judge ruled in light of that admission that the charge could not go to trial; whereupon the prosecutor amended the indictment to second-degree murder,[11] which does not require premeditation. The amended indictment meant that Johnson was eligible for bail, but he was not released. On February 16 the jury was impaneled and the trial began:

> Throughout this period I saw my attorney quite often and many times I called he was right down. I was told both attorneys were going to file motions but I never knew exactly what those motions were, because I put my complete confidence in them. I think I learned they were only trying to get me for second-degree murder at the pretrial conferences which ran into the trial. I really didn't know what was happening then because I didn't understand what they were saying as far as the legal terms they were using and all that. Then I remember the trial starting when the jury was sworn in. No one ever told me I could get bail when the charge was changed. I sure didn't think I could get bail then. But I could have gotten somebody to bail me out, if I had been told.

Even while the jury was being impaneled, the assistant prosecutor and Johnson's attorneys continued to plea bargain,[12] just as they had for the previous seven days. After reduction of the charge to second-degree murder, which carried a life sentence with parole available after ten years, the assistant prosecutor offered, and Johnson's attorneys urged him to accept, a plea of guilty to manslaughter,[13] which carried a penalty of one to twenty years with parole available after ten months. Johnson was repeatedly asked by his attorneys to plead guilty. The last time he was asked, the morning the jury was to be impaneled, he came very close to acquiescing:

> I had become so disgusted. Everybody was saying that you don't have a chance, you don't have a chance and this and that and the other. I said maybe I don't have a chance after being in jail almost a year.

Johnson's lawyers informed the judge that their client was ready to change his plea to guilty. Johnson stood before the judge, flanked by his attorneys and a short distance away from the prosecutor:

> The judge had gotten to the point where he said, "Are you pleading guilty to this crime?" All of a sudden it hit me, why should you plead guilty? This was what was running through my mind, now why should you plead guilty to something you didn't do? All of a sudden I said, "No, I don't want to plead guilty. Continue with these proceedings." The judge got up from his bench and stood in the door with his hands on his hips and looked at me. He didn't know what to think.

A jury was quickly selected and the trial lasted three days. At the end of the trial, the jury retired to deliberate its verdict and, after forty-five minutes, returned a verdict finding Ralph Johnson not guilty. After ten and a half months in jail Johnson was a free man.

Root's Story

The police files containing information on Johnson's case cast a different light on the homicide. At the same time, although nothing in the report contradicted anything that Johnson related about his experiences in jail or court, the material raised additional questions about the efficacy and fairness of our criminal justice system.

Johnson had related that on the night Cal Root was mortally wounded he was asleep in his room and was awakened by the sounds of a struggle and calls for help coming from the lower floor of the house. Johnson repeatedly told the police after his acquittal that he went downstairs and found Root in his first floor bedroom alongside his bed clutching his stomach. Johnson insisted that the stabbing had been committed by, as he claimed his roommate had related, an intruder who had broken into the house.

Ralph Johnson's roommate did not die immediately but languished, mortally wounded, for ten days. During that period Root told police officers, doctors and nurses, and his mother and sister what had really happened on the night he was stabbed.

Root told the police that he and Johnson were homosexuals. They had purchased the house in order to establish a permanent relationship but that shortly after, Johnson had lost his job and financial problems had set in. Root continued working and carried the house payments, but financial problems and disagreements arose between the two. On the night he was stabbed Root recounted that he had returned home around three in the morning. After walking his two dogs Root returned to the house and went to his bedroom where he readied himself for bed. Johnson entered the bedroom. He was upset that his roommate had been out and had not left him any money. Their discussion soon developed into an argument. Root told police that he wanted to end the argument so he turned off the bedroom light and started to get into bed. The next thing he knew he felt a searing pain in his stomach and saw Johnson holding what he believed was one of their kitchen knives. Root also told police that Johnson had told him while they were waiting for the police to arrive that he was sorry and begged him to tell the police that he had been stabbed by a burglar.

That version of the incident was told to the police by the victim as he was treated in the emergency room at the hospital. He repeated the essentials later that day upon awakening after surgery and reiterated the same version several times before he died. The police confronted Johnson at the hospital with the victim's version of the stabbing. He indignantly denied that either he or his roommate were homosexuals and insisted that the stabbing had been committed by an unknown intruder. He maintained both positions throughout the investigation and insisted that his version was the truth even after his acquittal.

Although subsequent police investigation during the period that the victim was still alive cast doubt upon Johnson's claims, the police were unable to find enough hard evidence to convince a jury beyond a reasonable doubt that Johnson was guilty. It was not enough that the police could prove that four months before the stabbing Johnson was discharged from his work in the post office, and one of the grounds for that discharge was that "he engaged in homosexual behavior." In addition, several knives were found in the kitchen and in Johnson's bedroom; but because they were all clean with no traces of blood on them, they as well as the fact that Johnson lied about his homosexuality, would be useless as evidence unless Root would be available for trial.

When Root failed to recover normally from the abdominal wounds and his condition began to deteriorate, the police began to see their case disintegrate. As long as the victim remained alive, the case against Ralph Johnson was formidable. The victim promised his cooperation in the prosecution of his assailant and was prepared to testify against Johnson. If the victim were to die, the crime, of course, would be more serious—murder, or at least, manslaughter—but the state might not have any evidence.

Cal Root told at least seven persons about the stabbing and, presumably, all seven would be available to testify at Johnson's trial if subpoenaed by the prosecution. But no matter how many witnesses could relate Root's account, the rules of evidence might prevent the jury from ever receiving that evidence because the witness' testimony would be *hearsay.* Hearsay is information that is offered to prove a fact which is not based upon the personal knowledge of the witness and, instead, is based upon what he has been told by another person.[14] Hearsay is excluded as evidence because the credibility of the person who made the original statement cannot be judged because he is not present in court, under oath and subject to cross examination. To permit Cal Root's account of the stabbing to be presented to the jury by the police or by Root's doctor, nurses, mother, or sister would deny the defense the right to cross examine the credibility of the victim, the only person who actually could accuse Ralph Johnson.

The hearsay rule is riddled with exceptions and one of the oldest and most basic exceptions is that a dying declaration is admissible if it is the statement of a victim in a homicide case relating the events and circumstances preceding the fatal wounding. But a verbal statement of a dying victim, by itself, is not sufficient. Consequently, Root's claim that Ralph Johnson stabbed him, no matter how many times he repeated it to the police and others, would be inadmissible unless it fulfilled the other legal requisites. The law supposes that a person on his deathbed, who knows he is about to die, would not lie about the cause of his dire situation. Therefore, in order for a dying declaration to be admissible, it must be also stipulated, generally in the person's own writing, that he understood that his death was certain and imminent.

Ten days after the stabbing in question, the police were notified that Root was close to death. He had not responded to treatment after surgery and developed a gross infection of the abdomen, a condition which had brought about a kidney shutdown. Detectives hurried to the hospital with a dying declaration form and a stenographer to record his statement.

As soon as the police arrived at the hospital they ran into a roadblock that was to ultimately undo their case. The attending physician confirmed the seriousness of his patient's condition and stated his opinion that the patient was not likely to live. But the doctor had not informed the patient of his condition and was not about to do so, feeling that Root could not psychologically handle this information. The police advised the doctor how crucial it was to obtain Root's statement and his acknowledgment of his impending death if there was to be any prosecution.

We now come to a bizarre factual disagreement that complicates an understanding of what happened throughout the next ten months up to and including the trial. Two strikingly different versions exist of what occurred in the hospital between the police and the doctor and again, most crucially, between the police and Root.

The police report indicates that upon being advised of the hopelessness of prosecuting Johnson without Root's knowing dying declaration, the doctor relented and agreed to a compromise. That compromise according to the police report provided that neither the doctor nor the detectives would tell Root that he was about to die, but that Root would be given the dying declaration form to fill out and sign and then his statement would be taken. The report states that the form contained this critical question:

> "Do you believe you are about to die, and have given up all hope of recovery?"

The police report claims that the doctor instructed the detectives that when Root came to the critical question, he was to be allowed to fill in the answer as he thought without expansion or clarification because of the adverse psychological impact any information might have upon him. Root filled out the form, according to the police version, in his own handwriting and then repeated his account of the stabbing, implicating Johnson.

Nothing in the police report indicates any additional conversation as the dying man purportedly filled out the form. Did he react in any way when he came upon the critical question; was there any visible emotional change in his demeanor; did he, in fact, comprehend the full import of the question or the task which the police had asked him to undertake?

Presumably, if Root had visibly or verbally reacted to this incredible way of telling him he was about to die, it would have been noted in the police report. A written statement furnished to the police by Root's doctor and contained in the file did not resolve any of the questions. In that statement the doctor wrote that, after reviewing the form the detectives wished to present to Root, "I told [the detective] that I felt all the questions in this form were perfectly within reason for the patient to sign except that Mr. Root did not at that time know that he was about to die, and I felt that psychologically this [one] was a poor question for the patient at this time. [The detective] kindly agreed with me and proceeded to fill in remaining questions with the patient."

This statement contradicted the police report on three counts: first, that the doctor had ever consented to Root being informed, either conversationally or in writing, that he was about to die; second, that Root filled out the form by himself and responded to the crucial question; and finally and most importantly, that Root was advised that he was about to die when he repeated his version of the stabbing. These contradictions and the failure to turn up the original or facsimile of the dying declaration form in the police file, court file or upon request of the prosecutor's office, prompted the attorney who was studying the case to contact the physician.

Reacting with great consternation to the claims made in the police report that Root had knowingly made a dying declaration, the doctor insisted that he was present throughout the final interview between the police and Root, and at no time before death was Root told or, in the doctor's judgment, aware that he was about to die. The doctor stressed that he was sympathetic to the plight of the police officers, but that his obligation was to his patient who could not have coped with the information necessary to perfect the dying declaration. The doctor further asserted that he would not have consented to the officers' visiting the dying patient unless they agreed to his conditions and abandoned their intention to advise the man that he was dying. The rejection of Root's statement at Johnson's trial tends to substantiate the doctor's version of the facts.

The case against Ralph Johnson virtually died with his roommate. Johnson was acquitted by a jury that was never informed of the deceased's statements implicating the defendant. Although Johnson was not totally unpunished—he spent ten and a half months in custody prior to his trial and had been brutally assaulted by his fellow prisoners during this period—many would suggest that the length of incarceration and physical brutality endured by Johnson was hardly sufficient punishment for the crime he undoubtedly committed.

The cases of David Berkowitz and Ralph Johnson raise compelling questions concerning the administration of criminal justice. What both these cases prove is that criminal justice can work against all generally accepted standards of right and wrong. Berkowitz, whether intentionally or not, made the courts appear foolish. After stating, in front of the victims' families, "I'm a good shot," "I'd do it again," and that "____________ [one of his victims] was a whore,"[15] Berkowitz was still able to prolong his day in court. And the court was unable to sentence Berkowitz in a swift and sure manner that would alleviate the tension and bitterness this case aroused. Instead, the ordeal had to be drawn out to insure fairness on all counts. The situation seemed forced; the defendant indicated no remorse, and his capacity for viciousness cancelled the public's concern for his capacity to suffer. At the same time, the suffering of the victims' families was severe, and the entire nation sympathized with their painful position.

The irony in the Johnson case exemplifies other reasons for public concern with criminal justice. This case typified a general confusion of motives in the administration of justice. *Before* Johnson's innocence or guilt was established, he was kept in jail in the interests of mass production justice. His pretrial experience resulted from a mechanical and impersonal processing of his case. *After* Johnson's guilt seemed certain, evidentiary rules allowed him to go free in the interests of criminal justice.

Regardless of Johnson's guilt or innocence, his pretrial treatment was unfair: the police were too quick to charge; the attorneys' commitment to Johnson was ambiguous; the judge's bail determination was excessive; and the jail experience was harrowing. Johnson presented himself as an innocent man who had been indirectly punished (via convicted criminals) and who had therefore suffered grievously due to the ineptitude of the police, courts, and correctional personnel. The public, on the other hand, has certainly suffered from the final injustice of the system's inability to convict a guilty man.

Discussion Questions

1. "THE DEATH PENALTY!" is becoming a popular response to cases dealing with capital offenders like David Berkowitz. Do you feel that once a defendant's guilt is established beyond a reasonable doubt, as it was for David Berkowitz, that the death penalty is a realistic and effective conclusion to the crime and the criminal process? Or do you feel that the death penalty is an "easy way out" and reflects little more than the courts' willingness to pacify the emotional interests of the public?

2. Assuming the truth of the doctor's version of what took place in Cal Root's hospital room the last time he met with the police, numerous questions arise about the police and prosecutor's handling of the subsequent criminal case. How could the police report so incorrectly relate what took place? Unless one is willing to attribute those report errors to incompetency, which is hardly likely because they are errors in reporting, not judgment, what policy reasons could account for the fanciful version of events?

3. On the basis of the police report, Johnson was charged with murder and consigned to the county jail to await trial. Granting that the police and prosecutor believed with a moral certainty in the guilt of the defendant, did the police and prosecutor behave properly in going forward with this criminal case after Root died, after the chance of conviction was reduced to virtually nothing?

4. Johnson was punished by being in jail for ten months for a crime he very likely committed but for which he could not be convicted. Regardless of whether or not he killed Root, his pretrial detention was punishment without a conviction. Throughout the pretrial period, the prosecutor's office dawdled over defense discovery motions resulting in trial delays and the lengthening of Johnson's time in jail. Also, consider the fact that persons in jail are more likely to plead guilty, which Johnson nearly did. If one believes that Johnson killed Cal Root, can the conduct of the police and prosecution be justified? Explain and support your answer.

5. Consider the conduct of the appointed defense attorneys who never sought an earlier trial date even though their client was sitting in a county jail and who failed to pursue the prosecutors vigorously when their legitimate requests for information were virtually ignored. Most importantly, consider counsel's role in almost persuading Johnson to plead guilty in spite of his protestations of innocence. What is defense counsel's proper role when a client is trying to decide whether to plead guilty to a prosecutor's offer of a lesser offense or to "hang tough" and go to trial? Should counsel be aggressive and persuasive when dealing with his client if the attorney believes that the state has a good chance of convicting the defendant of the greater, more serious offense if the case is tried?

Notes

1. *New York Times,* August 12, 1977, p. 10.
2. Justice Felix Frankfurter, Malinsky v. New York, 324 U.S. 401, at 414 (1945).
3. In 1971 eleven inmates of the Cuyahoga County Jail filed suit charging that the facility "subjected the human beings there to a systematic brutalization and dehumanization which shocks the conscience of all but the most hardened observers." The complaint went on to state that the facility which was originally designed to house 300 prisoners, male and female combined, instead accommodated about 550-600 persons. A large percentage of them were confined for periods of three to twelve months. Further charges cited unsanitary living conditions, inadequate plumbing, poor ventilation, lack of beds, and insufficient provisions for food. The facility lacked a permanent medical staff, and prisoners were often assaulted by other prisoners for sexual reasons. To be sure, such conditions delayed and inhibited an inmate's ability to prepare for trial, or if he persisted in a plea of not guilty, of getting himself released if he was unable to meet the bond requirements.
4. Ohio Rev. Code §2901.23 (Page 1954): No person shall maliciously shoot, stab, or cut, or shoot at another person with intent to kill, wound, or maim such person: The penalty for violation of this statute is imprisonment from one to twenty years. This section of the Code was repealed January 1, 1974, and replaced by Ohio Rev. Code §2903.11 (Page 1975).
5. Ohio Rev. Code §2945.72 (Page 1954): A person shall not be held by recognizance without trial for a period of more than (3) terms to answer an indictment or information, not including a term at which a recognizance was first taken thereon, if taken in term time. He shall be discharged unless a continuance is had on his motion, or the delay is caused by his act, or there is not time to try him at such third term, in which case he shall be brought to trial at the next term to be discharged. This section of the Code was repealed January 1, 1974, and replaced by Ohio Rev. Code §2945.72 A-H (Page 1975).
6. Ohio Rev. Code §2901.01 (Page 1954): No person shall purposely, and either of deliberate and premeditated malice, or by means of poison, or in perpetrating or attempting to perpetrate a rape, arson, robbery, or burglary, kill another. The penalty for violation of this statute is death, unless the jury recommends mercy, in which case the punishment is life imprisonment. This section of the Code was repealed January 1, 1974, and replaced by Ohio Rev. Code §2903.02 (Page 1975).
7. Ohio Const., art. 1, §9.
8. Ohio Rev. Code §2937.12(1) (Page 1975).
9. Ohio Rev. Code §2901.01 (Page 1954) supra; Ohio Rev. Code §2939.22 (Page 1975).
10. Ohio Rev. Code §2943.02 (Page 1975).
11. Ohio Rev. Code §2901.05 (Page 1975): No person shall purposely and maliciously kill another. Whoever is found guilty of this section shall be imprisoned for life. This section of the Code was repealed January 1, 1974, and replaced by Ohio Rev. Code §2903.02 (Page 1975).
12. Donald J. Newman, *Conviction: The Determination of Guilt or Innocence Without Trial* (Boston: Little, Brown and Company, 1966), pp. 76-77: "Certainly the negotiated plea is only one of a series of discretionary decisions that characterize the administration of justice. From the initial decision of whether to investigate a crime to the final decision of whether to revoke a parole, the entire administrative process rests upon discretionary choices, formally recognized or

not, of men who must fit law to cases.... The same process, somewhat more visible, occurs at the conviction stage when a defendant is allowed to plead guilty to a lesser offense than the one of which he is actually guilty, or where, in exchange for his plea, he is promised a less serious sentence than would otherwise be imposed."

13. Ohio Rev. Code §2901.06 (Page 1954): No person shall unlawfully kill another. Whoever violates this section, except in the manner described in sections 2901.01 to 2901.05 inclusive, of the Revised Code, is guilty of manslaughter in the first degree, and shall be imprisoned from one to twenty years. This section of the Code was repealed January 1, 1974, and replaced by Ohio Rev. Code §2903.03 (Page 1975).
14. *McCormack on Evidence,* 2d. ed. (St. Paul, Minn.: West, 1972), p. 584.
15. *New York Times,* May 23, 1978, p. 1.

COURT

N.J.

COUNTY OF

COURT CODE NUMBER

COURT DOCKET NUMBER(S)

C–

PRIOR CASE DOCKET NUMBER

C–

COMPLAINT RESULT OF CASE RETURNED BY PROSECUTOR

Th[illegible]

Defendant:

Address:

City, State:

COMPLAINT

Complainant: ______ (NAME OF COMPLAINANT) ______ of ______

Residing at ______ (ADDRESS OF PRIVATE CITIZEN COMPLAINANT) ______

______ day of ______, 19___, in the ______ of ______

did;

Charge Number 1 N.J.S.	Charge Number 2 N.J.S.

Subscribed and sworn to before me this ______ day of ______

Signed ______ (NAME AND TITLE OF PERSON ADMINISTERING OATH)

Sig

To any peace officer or other authorized person: Pursuant to this warrant, you are [illegible] (her) forthwith before this court to answer the foregoing complaint.

WARR

Bail has been fixed by ______ in the amount of $ ______

Date Warrant Issued ______ Time ______ (AM) (P

Court Appearance Date ______

(Cases wherein judgm

Part II
Preserving Order

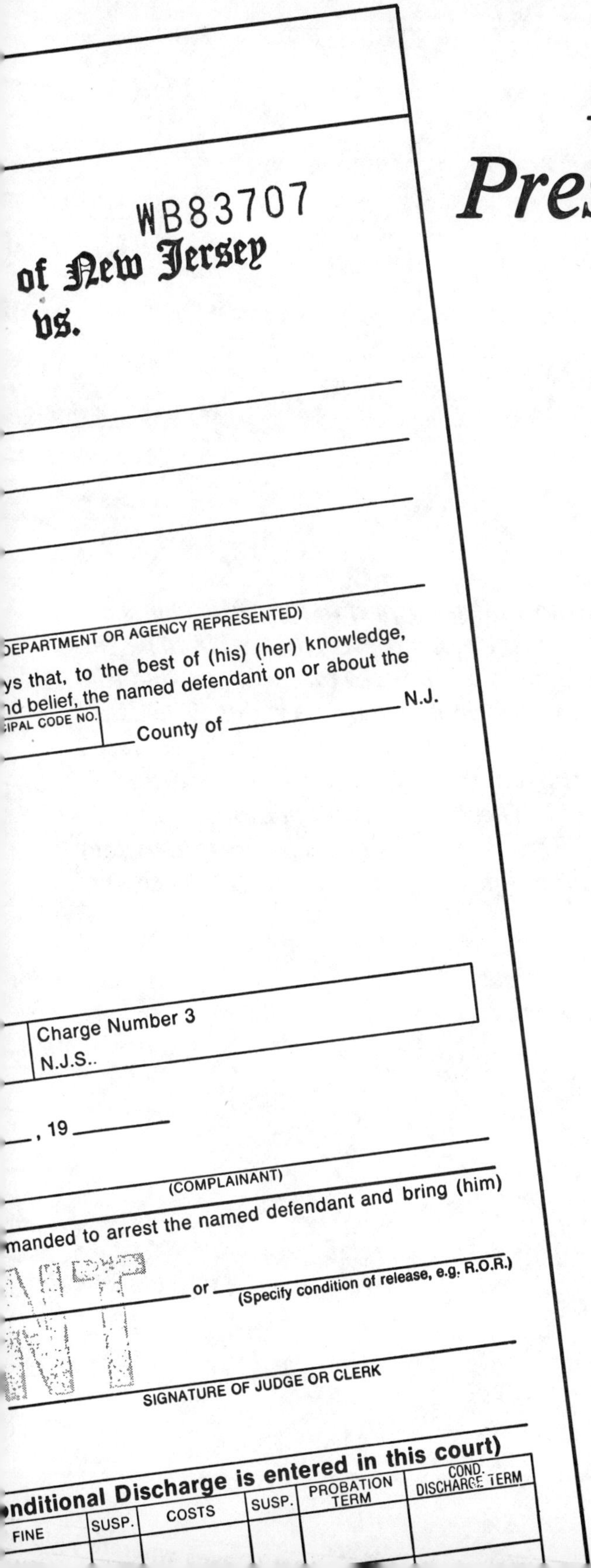

WB83707

of New Jersey

vs.

(DEPARTMENT OR AGENCY REPRESENTED)

ys that, to the best of (his) (her) knowledge,
nd belief, the named defendant on or about the
IPAL CODE NO. County of N.J.

Charge Number 3
N.J.S..

, 19

(COMPLAINANT)

manded to arrest the named defendant and bring (him)

or (Specify condition of release, e.g. R.O.R.)

SIGNATURE OF JUDGE OR CLERK

nditional Discharge is entered in this court)

FINE	SUSP.	COSTS	SUSP.	PROBATION TERM	COND. DISCHARGE TERM

3.

He told me I was the most likely suspect in the case. That's all. He proceeded to fingerprint me and everything. After he fingerprinted me he took me to a little card on the board and told me to read it which was informing me of my rights. The detective then read the card to me. I asked for an attorney because I knew one I could call, but they didn't give me an attorney. There was nothing said. There was a continuation of processing. Everything they were doing was in such a rush that they practically paid no attention to the things that I was saying. And that was it.

Policing

The suburban police officers who responded to Ralph Johnson's call for assistance, investigated the stabbing of his roommate, and built the prosecution case against him are the successors to three and a half centuries of history and tradition of American police. And although police departments are far more professional now than they have ever been in the past, Johnson's experience demonstrates an urgent need to advance police education and training further so that suspect's rights do not continue to be abused due to police haste and cases do not continue to be lost because of police inefficiency.

The traditional notion of the cop as an underpaid and either belligerent or saintly embodiment of official power has faded; today, the police view themselves and are more realistically viewed by the public as professional agents of law enforcement. As professionals, police are no longer grossly underpaid; they no longer carry the Keystone Cops stereotype of bumbling inefficiency; and as professionals and not superhumans, the police no longer enjoy the public's obsequious trust.

Policing has never been a popular profession. Even before the dawn of this age of cynicism when the public accepted police orders and directions without question, the blue uniform aroused contradictory and ambivalent emotions. That ambivalence may be attributed to the very nature and diversity of the policing task because by keeping the peace, the police alienate themselves from, as much as endear themselves to, the public.[1]

"Hue and Cry"

American police departments were formed as a result of the industrialization and concomitant increase in lawlessness during the early nineteenth century. For the previous two hundred years of European colonization of America, the cities and countryside were policed respectively by the traditional English system of constable and sheriffs who owed their great landholdings and slavish loyalty to the colonial governors.

Population growth in the states, mirrored by the accumulation of great wealth, led to the development of an impoverished class, social problems, and general unrest. And as lawlessness increased, the need for strengthening law enforcement grew. The first step taken by many towns and cities was to augment the constable's vigilance with night watches. Night watches consisted of citizen volunteers appointed to patrol the town during the night to discourage crime and other chicanery. Originating in Boston and co-opted by the Dutch in New Amsterdam, the night watchers were issued rattles which they shook as they walked through the streets of the town to reassure law-abiding citizens and to discourage potential law breakers.[2]

The Dutch in New Amsterdam were the first to create something close to a professional police department. In 1658 eight paid watchmen were appointed and sworn in to replace the volunteer rattlewatchers. When the British took the colony and renamed it New York, they retained the "professional" force but placed it under the command of a constable.[3]

Night watchers became the common response to night crime and were organized in virtually every city and town. Some cities depended upon the local militia to staff this detail, while others used civilians who either volunteered or were paid fifty cents for a night's work. In Cincinnati, Ohio, the system of conscription was used, and every male citizen over the age of twenty-one served in rotation in the twelve man force, patroling the streets with a rattle and a lantern. As the night watchers were slowly turned into the nucleus of future police departments, cities such as New York and Boston in the earliest years of the eighteenth century pioneered in the development of neighborhood precinct stations.[4]

Professional police departments were created in many European continental cities by the beginning of the seventeenth century, but the English rejected this approach fearing the type of oppression these militaristic police departments were imposing on many European cities. Consequently, the English at home and in the colonies relied upon citizen involvement—already an inbred English tradition—to aid the very few constables and watchers afoot in the towns. A citizen who was the victim or observer of a crime would raise a "hue and cry," with everyone in the vicinity adding their voices. Involvement then meant making a din and alerting everyone else who would also join in and take off after the scofflaw. The "hue and cry" was one of those early American traditions that remained with us for centuries. Persons committing crimes in the towns and cities of America could, if observed, expect to be chased and subdued by an angry crowd of irate citizens. The "hue and cry" approach was one of the principal means by which crime on the streets was controlled up to the middle of the twentieth century. It died in the 1950s with the development of the American cult of non-involvement.

On the frontier, growing lawlessness confounded the duly elected and appointed sheriffs. Naturally the wide-open countryside did not lend itself to the type of auxiliary protection that the cities found in night watches. Instead, these Westerners formed posses. Posses, however, were far from being rational or just methods of crime control. In fact, the conduct of one volunteer, John Lynch, was so notorious that his name became synonymous with his conduct, giving rise to the terms "lynch law" and "lynching."[5]

In the half century after independence was secured, the major towns of the east mushroomed into major cities and with the rapid industrialization came large-scale lawlessness. New York City was reputed to be the most crime-ridden city in the world, but the reputations of Philadelphia, Baltimore, and Cincinnati did not lag far behind. Young rowdies roamed the streets, now during the day as well as at night, assaulting and robbing people. Officials responded to this lawlessness by increasing the size of the night watch and then by adding a day watch. Crime and the problems of the cities had become so great, however, that the solution was no longer to be found in pre-independence institutions such as the watches. More comprehensive attacks upon these problems were required.[6]

The Throes of Police Professionalism

Development of the modern American police department, fashioned after the English Metropolitan Police, was not accomplished until the 1870s. Before this time, in city after city, attempts at reform, such as unification of the day and night watches, had some early successes; yet reforms were often abandoned because of the fierce rivalries that existed between competing police groups or political factions. However, the gravity of the crime problem was such that police reform became a permanent issue.

Philadelphia, Boston, and New York took the lead, followed closely by Cincinnati and Detroit, in the development of permanent professional police departments along the lines we know today. Setbacks occurred in all cities, but these were temporary and most abandoned departments were reconstituted. Because of the expanding crime rate, the necessity for departmental organization, along with permanent, professional, and responsive police, could not be denied.[7]

The first police departments were primitive; the rush with which the departments were formed resulted in a haphazard recruitment of individuals with little concern for standards and ability. Moreover, the ethnic concentration of various police departments caused resentment by various factions of the community. In general, the police at this point in their historical development were the objects of scorn and resentment, and it was not infrequent that citizens would band together to attack officers.

Few men other than new immigrants were willing to take police jobs because of the unpopularity of the profession and because salaries were low. Regardless of the importance of their task—that of preserving peace and order—the police profession lacked dignity; it is little wonder, then, that the first true police officers had little respect for the law themselves and frequently engaged in drunkenness on duty, extortion, and brutality. Instances of police heroism were rare. In fact, lacking professional support and public respect, police were as apt to openly flee from a scene of violence as they were to attempt to control it.[8]

The political authorities that controlled the police were also corrupt, and the hegemony of the police officer and the politician existed side-by-side at the expense of the common citizen. The ineptitude and corruption of city police were so great that across the country states were seizing control of city departments. This was not a satisfactory or long-range solution to the problem, however, because home rule for cities was already an American institution and, besides, more often than not, state seizures of control did not represent efforts at reform. Such usurpations were usually regarded not as efforts at real reform but as political moves by another faction trying to extend its control.

Some professionalism and stability came to the American police department towards the end of the nineteenth century. One of the first steps toward establishing policing as a true profession was the introduction of uniforms for city police. Americans had become so suspicious of a professional military and uniformed authority (largely stemming from immigrants' experiences with a repressive military in Europe) that the successful adoption of police uniforms was a major accomplishment. But the greatest move toward professionalism was the institution of civil service status for police. The patronage system was removed and administrative boards were established to replace politicians as the governing bodies of municipal police departments.[9]

The Police "Problem"

The advent of some indicia of professionalism did not eliminate the problem of police corruption and inefficacy. Police, caught up in the violence of unionization efforts of American workers in the early days of this century, were often brutal in dispersing strikers, a tendency that hardly endeared the police officer to blue-collar America. Police, themselves, sought unionization, and the resulting strikes and job actions tended to alienate still other groups within the population.[10] And that grand attempt to purify America, prohibition, accomplished little more than to cast the police into greater disrepute because of the wholesale corruption that erupted with the attempt to ban the consumption of alcohol.[11]

There were more than one hundred studies and investigations of the police problem during the 1920s. And later, a national commission reporting during the Depression called for an upgrading of qualifications and training for individual police officers and advocated the development of new management techniques and crime-fighting capabilities for police departments. The Wickersham Commission (1931), echoing earlier local reports, found the incidence of physical abuse by American law enforcement officers to be shocking:

> After reviewing the evidence obtainable the authors of the report reach the conclusion that the third degree—that is, the use of physical brutality, or other forms of cruelty, to obtain involuntary confessions or admissions—is widespread.... Brutality and violence in making an arrest also are employed at times, before the prisoner reaches the jail, in order to put him in a frame of mind which makes him more amenable to questioning afterwards....
>
> While the third degree is used mainly against arrested persons suspected of having committed a crime, it also sometimes is employed against other persons for the purpose of getting information about an offense from persons not suspected of having committed it, but only of knowing about it....[12]

Police brutality was still a significant problem, according to national commissions, in 1947 and up to 1961.[13] By 1967, the President's Commission on Law Enforcement and the Administration of Justice found that excessive force and police brutality had abated, but that verbal abuse and harassment on the part of our police was increasing:

> The Commission believes that physical abuse is not as serious a problem as it was in the past. The few statistics which do exist suggest small numbers of cases involving excessive use of force. Although the relatively small number of reported complaints cannot be considered an accurate measure of the total problem, most persons, including civil rights leaders, believe that verbal abuse and harassment, not excessive use of force, is the major police-community relations problem today.[14]

Beginning in the 1950s and extending to the present, American police departments have faced new challenges and have been criticized for different shortcomings. For instance, during the height of the civil rights movement, the police were severely criticized for their inordinate use of force against the marchers and demonstrators.[15] Similar complaints were made during the era of anti-Vietnam protests. Out of these encounters came a new surge of criticism directed toward the police: it was maintained that because the police were seemingly unsympathetic to these popular causes, they tended to be violent toward the demonstrators.

While the police have always had difficulties with certain groups within the community, they have been traditionally accepted and favored by the middle- and upper-class American. Benefiting from the favorable publicity cultivated by J. Edgar Hoover and accorded to the F.B.I., these classes of people believed that not only federal agents, but all police officers were the first line of defense for all that was good about America. If police officers harassed kids on the street or minorities in a neighborhood where they were not normally found, many Americans thought such conduct was not only excusable but desirable.

Such staunch attitudes began to erode, however, when children from middle- and upper-class families began to experiment with drugs or engage in anti-war or other protest activities that frequently resulted in police action. As a result of their own children's involvement with the law, many Americans of a comfortable economic class began for the first time to question the propriety of various police actions. To dispel middle-class support or respect even further were the revelations of F.B.I. misconduct and of Hoover's corrupt practices.

The 60s created a true dilemma for the police. Official exercises of power were suspect, from the federal government's activities to the individual actions of police officers. At the same time, not only was official authority disrespected, but the laws the police were obligated to enforce were unpopular. The enforcement of unpopular laws was resented on all fronts. For instance, police responses to sit-ins and other demonstrations were commonly regarded as unnecessary intrusions into the meaningful activities of concerned citizens.

Another serious criticism of the police that arose during the turbulence of the 60s was that the police were prejudiced, and that few departments were representative of the communities they served. In short, when increased attention was focused on the police as a result of their actions toward demonstrators, the public realized that most of the forces consisted of white males. Very few minority and women officers, in other words, were seen in the highly publicized confrontations between police and the public which took place in this decade.[16]

Through voluntary compliance, but just as often because of court-imposed plans, the hiring policies of police departments across the country have begun to change. Albeit reluctantly, police departments have begun to actively recruit black and other minority candidates, as well as women, in order to meet court-imposed quotas and goals.[17]

The lack of responsiveness of police departments to community demands and concerns has also given rise to new programs in police-community relations. Coupled with these programs have been enormous expenditures to boost police salaries and improve police training and education. And today, policing is now regarded as a serious career objective. Colleges and universities throughout the country have recognized the need and demand for programs and are offering degree programs in police science and law enforcement administration. A majority of American police officers are currently taking education continuation courses conducted by departmental academies or by colleges and universities.[18] Raising the educational levels of police officers and improving criminal justice programs will not solve the problems of crime control in America, but such efforts will enable the police to make more educated responses to the complexities of their job.

The upgrading of police, generally, and the infusion into police ranks of minorities and women have contributed to a more positive police image in the 1970s. Other events in this decade have also helped to soften the extreme views of the police held by Americans on all sides of the political spectrum. The end of America's involvement in Vietnam and with it the ebbing of constant confrontations between police and protest groups have helped to ease public criticism of the police. In addition, because of the liberalization of America's attitudes toward soft drugs, the police have been removed from the front line of the drug issue. In general, then, the 70s have had a positive effect on the police image: the day when the police officer was regarded as a symbol of righteous authority is gone. Today, the police are more realistically and sympathetically viewed as human beings with the awesome responsibility of maintaining peace and order in an unpredictable society.

The Officer on the Beat

The police officer is an important symbol of government authority and capability. Because the police represent the social order and the authority of the government, their professional conduct affects the public's confidence in its government. And that conduct is carefully monitored by the public because the police, by necessity, are invested with tremendous power. Responsible police behavior cultivates public confidence in the government; the arbitrary exercise of plenary power creates a sense of fear and resentment toward official exercises of power in general.

We have the police on the street primarily to curb incubating crime. The would-be mugger is likely to move on rather than strike if he sees a policeman nearby. Moreover, law-abiding citizens, especially in low-income areas, are apt to feel more comfortable as they go about their business if they are aware of the police presence. But police visibility also provokes hostility in a community. For instance, James Baldwin described a police officer who patrolled his native Harlem as an "occupying soldier in a bitterly hostile country."[19] Patrolling in such a hostile atmosphere is an uneasy experience and the discomfort a patrolman feels is usually reflected in his interaction with the community.

While the potential of danger is not great in every encounter, the officer is always aware that his profession entails personal risk. The patrol officer must be prepared at all times for danger. For instance, police are often wounded, even killed, in their attempts to break up what appeared to be a minor street brawl. An example of the unexpected fate hundreds of police officers have met is found in the murder of a patrolman in New York City in 1978. In that case, the patrolman began his day by warning an habitual vagrant at the Port Authority to stop harassing commuters. The vagrant's response, unlike his behavior of the past, was extreme; he grabbed the police officer's gun as the officer turned away and shot the officer to death with his own weapon. What began as a typical day on the beat concluded with the unexpected, tragic death of a police officer.[20]

Police are always in the public eye; police are always resented by some element of the society; and police are always aware that they are balancing their safety against the safety of the public at large. These points reflect the more "glamorous" side of policing. What most people are unaware of is that the police task also entails many low-visibility, low-risk, and pedestrian responsibilities. These responsibilities are commonly referred to as *service functions.* Services that the police render to the community are routine, and they are certainly less exciting than engaging in a spectacular car chase or making a dramatic arrest. Nevertheless, these services, from escorting a funeral procession to calming an hysterical accident victim, constitute a major part of the police profession.

Keeping the Peace and Community Relations

Police services include traffic control, emergency medical assistance, and "keeping the peace." "Keeping the peace" refers to the beat officer's duty, when called upon, to settle domestic disputes, neighborhood arguments, and merchant/customer altercations.

Most service functions involve keeping the peace by resolving conflicts between individuals and groups. Often, minor confrontations that may require police intervention do not necessitate arrest or prosecution. Ideally, after the police officer administers either a sage bit of advice or a light warning, the heated argument between the parties involved is cooled and the problem resolved. In reality, however, policemen often fail to adequately handle conflict-resolution crises. For instance, if an argument between a husband and a wife is interrupted by a police officer but the hostility is not properly assuaged, an assault or even a murder may occur when the officer walks out the door. One of the policeman's almost impossible responsibilities, then, is to be able to judge the effect of his personal reasoning on the emotions of others.

The difficulty of dealing with the volatile, emotional crises of individuals is exacerbated by inadequate police training in human relations.[21] The President's Commission in its report, *The Challenge of Crime in a Free Society,* pointed out that police manuals rarely discuss the hard choices the patrol officer must make in his daily contact with citizens.[22] Because education has been lacking in community relations, the police officer often bases his actions on an intuitive understanding of the problem at hand. He must decide for himself, for example, whether a group of teenagers milling about on a street corner constitutes a dangerous situation. The patrolman must also be able to assess whether a family argument merits serious intervention or if the disagreement is merely a routine squabble. The decisions a policeman makes under such circumstances involve personal evaluations that can lead to either order or serious, if not criminal, complications.

Although the policeman's training in community relations is limited, the public expects its policemen to be at once understanding *and* effective. What the public is only beginning to understand is that in the absence of comprehensive police education programs, an officer's response to community disruption is likely to be colored by his character, his background, and his biases.

Even though the decisions made in conflict-resolution crises are so critical, both to the individuals involved and to the peace of the community, these decisions are rarely reviewed—a fact that makes the public even more uncomfortable with the idea of police authority. Unlike the practice in many other countries, police in the United States are not required to report on their daily encounters with citizens.[23] Consequently, unless the problem develops into a crime or unless a citizen files a complaint, the decisions that are reached in peace-keeping endeavors remain a personal matter between the officer and the citizens involved.

Improvements in education programs along with the appearance of more policewomen and minority officers in the last decade are helping to strengthen and improve the quality and appropriateness of the police response to non-criminal situations. Resolving street incidents is at the core of the patrol officer's duty, but he is incapable of performing this duty well if he is hostile to the community and feels that he is deeply resented, even hated, there. Thus, the introduction of minority officers has helped to de-escalate the seriousness of many such police encounters. By placing black officers in black neighborhoods, police departments can be more assured that community relations, including street contact, will be less abrasive. For instance, a white officer because of racial tension, may be apt in a black neighborhood to overreact to a street argument and attempt to resolve the conflict by unnecessarily arresting one of the participants. A black officer, on the other hand, is more likely to resolve the argument in a more passive and reasonable manner. In other words, officers that understand the community's special problems are more capable of being effective mediators in delicate and emotionally charged street conflicts.[24]

The introduction of women into basic police patrols has also had a positive impact on community relations. Women officers, for example, have proven to be more effective than male officers in dealing with female victims of sexual assault. No matter how inoffensively the male officer may conduct the questioning, he is often unable to reassure a rape victim because of what she may perceive as a lack of understanding and empathy. Also, it has been reported that women police officers are as capable of dealing with angry citizens and that angry citizens are less likely to become violent toward a female officer.[25]

In the past decade, the introduction of minority and women officers has helped to change the blue-coated, white-faced, macho image the police have labored under for over one hundred years. As a consequence of improved community relations, the tension of attempting to keep the peace within a hostile setting has, to some extent, been alleviated. And improved community relations can only have a positive impact on citizen cooperation in the more arduous police tasks of detecting, investigating, and arresting for crimes.

The Investigative Function and Process

The rate of arrest in the United States will never equal the crime rate. Today, the ratio of the number of arrests made to the number of reported crimes committed is approximately twenty per cent.[26] On paper, the gap this percentage represents is disconcerting. Yet, in reality, given demographic factors, the vast range of crimes committed, the characteristics of individual police departments, and the fact that our society, as a whole, is not riddled with crime, the discrepancy between the arrest and crime rates is tolerable. The public, as well as the criminal justice system, has never expected arrests to keep pace with crimes. But when arrests in an area are noticeably low in the face of continuing crime, citizens do become concerned with and critical of their police force.

Arrest rates are predicated on sound and thorough investigation techniques. Except for those criminals who are caught "red-handed," the identification of the criminal and the accumulation and development of evidence that will justify an arrest and prosecution must be accomplished through the employment of sound investigation techniques. The principal goals of investigation are the identification, apprehension, and conviction of the criminal. Close in importance is the discovery of contraband that will end any illegal scheme and, in cases of theft, recovery of stolen property.

Responsibility for the initial investigation usually falls upon the shoulders of the uniformed officer who comes upon the crime scene inadvertently or who is the first to answer a call for assistance. Often the success or failure of any subsequent investigation depends upon the quick wits and thoroughness of the officer who is the first on the scene. That officer may have the best, and sometimes the only, chance to apprehend the offender. If the criminal is still on the scene, the officer may have to give chase, and the failure to make the arrest at that time may result in the criminal slipping away, leaving little evidence to track him down. The officer's initial observations of the scene will prove very important because he is likely to be the first witness at any trial, and he will be questioned closely as to the details of the crime scene. That officer must also act promptly to identify persons near the scene, who may have been witnesses to the crime, before they slip away. Finally, the officer must expeditiously make efforts to seal the crime scene so that nothing is lost or tampered with and so that subsequent investigation is not hampered.

Whether the officer who first appears on the scene maintains responsibility for the subsequent investigation depends upon the seriousness of the crime and the way the particular department is organized. The officer will retain authority in virtually all non-serious offenses. If there was an immediate arrest or summons issued, the officer's only likely follow-up function is to prepare a police report that will serve as the basis for a prosecution or a civil suit between the participants of the accident or crime. The importance of accurate, thorough, and well-written police reports cannot be stressed enough. Reading the police report is often the only preparation for court appearances that time allows to a busy prosecutor. If the incident involves an automobile accident, the police report may be the key evidence in determining the rights and liabilities of the participants. Even if the crime is a major offense that requires substantial investigative follow-up, each individual police report provides a piece of the jigsaw puzzle that may help to solve the crime.[27]

If the patrol officer discovers or responds to a report of a major crime, he is likely to cede his authority to departmental investigators and detectives. Often these specialized units are so preoccupied with multiple reports of serious crimes that the patrol officers, except in homicide cases, will have total responsibility for the initial investigation of the crime scene. The investigators come into the picture only when the patrol officers' reports are received and digested and a decision is made as to which crimes merit full investigation.

The modern police investigator is a highly trained professional. He has a full array of laboratory expertise and technical specialists to render assistance. The investigator must put bits and pieces, often disjointed and contradictory, together like a jigsaw puzzle in an effort to understand the crime and identify the offender. Each piece of evidence must be carefully identified and preserved, which is a herculean task because at the outset the investigator does not know what will actually be evidence and what will be a wrong lead. Everything must be carefully marked, analyzed, and the chain of custody established and protected in the event the items are to be used at a trial.

Marked advances in technology have naturally aided police investigation. Sophisticated crime labs today provide specialists who are competent in identification (including finger, foot, palm, voice, and other impressions), firearms, documents, metallurgy, photography, microanalysis, toxicology, chemistry, and physics. Crime labs are able to trace evidence and extract more information from evidence than was once imagined possible. In addition, crime labs offer field services and are able to assist in the processing of crime scenes insuring the recognition, recovery, and preservation of evidence.[28] The advent of the computer age has aided markedly in the performance of these tasks. The computer's ability to store information with its corresponding ability to retrieve it immediately can produce a list of suspects with a modus operandi (method of operation) matching that of the crime, or information about paint samples, which will enable police to identify the color and make of an automobile involved in a hit and run accident, or identify the source and manufacturer of a tool.

While a crime lab may be able to focus an investigation in a direction that would not normally have been taken without its assistance, police investigation is still centered around the hunting down of leads, making countless contacts (most of whom have little or no valuable information to offer), and sorting out information while searching for a lead that will break the case wide open. Despite the increased chance of a successful investigation stemming from the contribution of modern technology, criminal investigation remains in large part drudgery akin to searching for a needle in a haystack. Most of the work is routine and unexciting. The real contribution of the scientific experts is often limited to linking the suspect to the crime after he is traced and arrested by the investigators.

The success rate for criminal investigations in this country is not great. Investigators, like all the other personnel in the criminal justice system, carry heavy caseloads and are unable to devote enough time and resources to each crime as it might merit. Usually, an investigator is handling many cases at the same time and it is only the extremely notorious or bizarre crime that receives full attention. Investigative work involves incredible patience as the tiny parts of the jigsaw puzzle are pieced together. Questioning witnesses and others who might have some information, scouring crime scenes, and tailing suspects is far more complicated than it once was.

The Right of Privacy*

While all citizens have a duty to assist law enforcement officers in their search to solve crimes, the manner in which the police go about that quest must comport with the individual citizen's right to privacy. Essentially, the right of privacy, guaranteed by the Fourth Amendment to the Constitution, is the right to be left alone. One has the right to be peaceably on the street or in one's home without government, including police, interference. Naturally, that right is not absolute and must be balanced against society's interest in maintaining order. For instance, everyone has the obligation to assist the police in maintaining the peace of the community. We each have a duty to provide police officers with information about crimes that we have observed, and that duty is statutorily imposed in most states.[29]

The failure to assist and provide information may, itself, be a crime and an individual who fails to cooperate may be fined or prosecuted.[30] But our duty does not extend so far as providing police officers with information that may incriminate ourselves and lead to our arrest or prosecution because again, the Constitution, in the Fifth Amendment privilege against self-incrimination, protects us from having to do so.

When police investigations exceed casual encounters, the police are obligated to abide by the guidelines set forth in the law to protect individuals' constitutional rights. As the interference with individual rights

*For a complete discussion of the Exclusionary Rule relating to arrest and search and seizure principles, see Chapter 4.

resulting from an intrusion becomes greater, as in an arrest, the standards become stricter, and the police officer must have greater justification for the intrusion based upon the existing, known facts.

Stop and Frisk

Recognizing that casual public encounters can easily escalate into a full search or arrest, the Supreme Court attempted in 1968 to create standards for anything greater than the slighest street contact between a police officer and a citizen. In *Terry v. Ohio,*[31] a landmark case, the Court realized that many police stops are pretexts to conduct a full search of the individual in order to secure evidence that will then justify an arrest and the taking of the suspect into custody. The Supreme Court wanted to prevent such "free-for-all" searches without compromising the legitimate need for police officers to interfere with suspicious behavior. The *Terry* court formally recognized the authority of the police to interfere with suspicious street behavior that was insufficient to justify an arrest. It also recognized that because, under certain circumstances, an individual's right of privacy may be compromised, any limited intrusion of the police must conform to that finely honed constitutional test of "reasonableness."

The authority to stop a person arises when a police officer has a "reasonable" suspicion that the individual has just committed or is about to commit a crime. The reviewing court, in considering the propriety of the officer's conduct when the state seeks to use the evidence the officer secured from the suspect, must consider the facts that were known to the officer at the time he made the stop. The facts will determine whether the officer's suspicion that justified the stopping was reasonable. Thus, the critical issue is the conduct of the suspect just prior to the stopping, and not his appearance, nor the business which the officer believes the suspect engages in, nor even a past criminal record. What is important is what the suspect did to arouse the officer's suspicion at that time.

In *Terry,* the Supreme Court said that "the police officer must be able to point to specific and articulable facts which, taken together with rational inferences from those facts, reasonably warrant that intrusion." The reviewing court was instructed to apply an objective test to the evidence to determine whether the facts available to the officer at the time the stopping was made would "warrant a man of reasonable caution in the belief that the action taken was appropriate." The purpose of the test is to avoid police hunches that are based so often upon the police officer's prejudices rather than the facts. However, the inferences drawn by the police officer based upon his experience as an observer of street conduct are also to be taken into consideration.[32]

The police officer in *Terry* suspected that the individuals he observed were waiting for a timely opportunity to rob a jewelry store. The Supreme Court's analysis of what the officer observed is helpful in understanding when this type of intrusion is permissible:

> There is nothing unusual in two men standing together on a street corner, perhaps waiting for someone. Nor is there anything suspicious about people in such circumstances strolling up and down the street, singly or in pairs. Store windows, moreover, are made to be looked in. But the story is quite different where, as here, two men hover about a street corner for an extended period of time, at the end of which it becomes apparent that they are not waiting for anyone or anything; where these men pace alternately along an identical route, pausing to stare in the same store window roughly 24 times; where each completion of this route is followed immediately by a conference between the two men on the corner; where they are joined in one of these conferences by a third man who leaves swiftly; and where the two men finally follow the third and rejoin him a couple of blocks away. It would have been poor police work indeed for an officer of 30 years' experience in the detection of thievery from stores in this same neighborhood to have failed to investigate this behavior further.[33]

Thus the officer's observations of the suspects' conduct and the inferences which he was able to draw from that conduct based upon his thirty years' experience on the police force outweighed the right of the suspects to be left alone and justified the officer's intrusion. Later, Supreme Court and other court decisions extended the officer's basis for suspicion beyond his own observations to tips from known and anonymous informers.[34]

The purpose of a stopping is to investigate suspicious behavior. The suspect may be asked to identify himself and, if he refuses to do so, the officer may temporarily detain the individual on the street until an identification can be made. The individual need not incriminate himself, but his failure to identify himself or explain his conduct may make a further intrusion, even an eventual arrest, reasonable. Thus, for example, police officers are justified in stopping an individual who is carrying a television set down the street in the middle of the night. Even though there might not have been a report of a burglary, this is suspicious conduct. If the suspect evades the officers' questions as to why he is in the street with a television set at an irregular hour, it would be reasonable to detain the suspect for a few minutes while the officers check with headquarters to determine whether a burglary or theft of a television set has just been reported.[35] Furthermore, if the suspect fails to heed the officers' request to stop, the odd circumstances which justified their original suspicion coupled with the suspect's attempt to flee are usually sufficient ground to justify an arrest.[36]

Justification for a stop does not automatically confer authority on the police officer to conduct a search of the suspect. The right to conduct a search, and it must be a limited search, requires its own determination of reasonableness. That limited right only arises for purposes of protecting the safety of the police officer. Again, the inquiry must be based upon the facts and circumstances known to the police officer at the time he made the stop and which would justify a reasonably prudent man's "belief that his safety or that of others was in danger."[37] Courts are loathe to second guess police officers' claims of threats to their safety. Consequently, if the officer is able to articulate almost any circumstance, rather than facts that indicate that he was looking for evidence, which led him to believe that his protection required such a search, the search is likely to be upheld.

The permissible search is a limited one: a frisk for weapons. Such a frisk is conducted by patting down the outer clothing of the suspect. If the pat-down discloses an object hidden beneath that might be a weapon, the officer may go beyond the outer clothing and into the inner pockets of the suspect to retrieve the item that felt like a weapon. Because the courts are legitimately concerned with a police officer's ability to protect himself from potential danger, they bend over backwards to find justification for a limited search. In this context, it is usual for courts to admit into evidence crumpled packs of cigarettes containing marijuana or other drugs or glassine envelopes containing heroin which a police officer claimed felt like a weapon when he made the initial pat-down.[38]

Stop and frisk, now an established part of American law enforcement, is an invasion of individual privacy. The stop and frisk concept is thought to be reasonable, however, because it allows for intrusions that are relatively minor when balanced against society's need to intercept crime or to protect the lives of police officers.

Responsible police departments have recognized the need for safeguards against the abuse of stop and frisk practices. When the New York statute was enacted in 1964,[39] several years before the procedure passed constitutional muster in the Supreme Court, the New York City Police Department issued Circular No. 25 to all members of the department setting forth strict standards for the making of these stops and subsequent searches. Internal policy guidelines, such as contained in Circular No. 25, are extremely useful in shaping policy and in training patrol officers in the proper way of handling certain situations. As a result, policy guidelines such as Circular 25 have helped to exert some control over the police officer on the street:

Circular No. 25

A. GENERAL PRINCIPLES

1. The new law does not permit an officer to stop just any passer-by and search him, nor does it allow the search of any person merely because he has a criminal record.
2. The new law does not permit the stopping and searching of any person found in the vicinity of a crime scene, merely because he happens to be there.
3. The new law does not dispense with the need for adequate observation and investigation, depending upon all the circumstances, before a stop is made.
4. No officer should stop anyone, under the new law, unless he is prepared to explain, with particularity, his reasons for stopping such person.

5. No officer should stop anyone, under the new law, unless the crime he reasonably suspects is a felony or one of those misdemeanors listed in § 552 of the Code of Criminal Procedure.
6. When a person is stopped under the new law, the officer—if not in uniform—must properly and promptly identify himself to the person stopped.
7. Not everyone stopped may be searched; searches are only permitted when the officer reasonably suspects that he is in danger.
8. The right to stop provided in the new law in no way changes the previously existing authority of an officer to make an arrest without an arrest warrant, as provided by § 177 of the Code of Criminal Procedure. The new rights to stop and to search, as defined in the new statute, are separate and distinct from the established right to arrest, as provided by existing law, and to make a complete search incident to such arrest.
9. Whether or not an arrest follows a stopping under the new law, whenever any force is used in stopping the suspect, or whenever any frisk or search is made, a written report shall be made to the officer's superior officer. Form for such reports, together with instructions for their use, will be distributed with separate orders.

B. THE RIGHT TO "STOP"

1. "stop":
   The new statute gives the officer the right to stop a person under the indicated circumstances. If the suspect refuses to stop, the officer may use reasonable force, but only by use of his body, arms and legs. He may not make use of a weapon or nightstick in any fashion. (Of course, if there is an assault on the officer or other circumstances sufficient to justify an arrest, the officer may use necessary force to effect that arrest.)
2. "abroad in a public place":
   a. For the purposes of practical enforcement procedures, this phrase is viewed as being restricted to public highways and streets, beaches and parks (to include outdoor facilities open to the public even though privately owned), depots, stations, and public transportation facilities.
   b. For the purpose of practical enforcement procedures, this phrase is viewed as not including the public portions of private buildings such as hotel lobbies, moving picture theatres, licensed premises, etc.
   c. Definitions of the words "public place" as found in other laws, such as those dealing with disorderly conduct, are not to be substituted for the strict definition of "abroad in a public place" as outlined above.
3. "whom he reasonably suspects":
   a. The words "reasonably suspects" are not to be lightly regarded; they are not just an incidental phrase; they have real meaning.

"Reasonable suspicion" is clearly more than "mere suspicion." At the same time it is something less than "reasonable ground for believing" that a crime is being committed, as is necessary for an arrest.

b. No precise definition of "reasonably suspects" can be provided, other than that it is such a combination of factors as would merit the sound and objective suspicions of a properly alert law enforcement officer, performing his sworn duties. Among the factors to be considered in determining whether or not there is "reasonable suspicion" are:
   i. The demeanor of the suspect.
   ii. The gait and manner of the suspect.
   iii. Any knowledge the officer may have of the suspect's background or character.
   iv. Whether the suspect is carrying anything, and what he is carrying.
   v. The manner in which the suspect is dressed, including bulges in clothing—when considered in light of all of the other factors.
   vi. The time of the day or night the suspect is observed.
   vii. Any overheard conversation of the suspect.
   viii. The particular streets and areas involved.
   ix. Any information received from third persons, whether they are known or unknown.
   x. Whether the suspect is consorting with others whose conduct is "reasonably suspect."
   xi. The suspect's proximity to known criminal conduct.
   (This listing is not meant to be all-inclusive.)

c. "Reasonable suspicion" of any crime at all does not afford a basis for stopping under the new law; there must be reasonable suspicion that the suspect is committing, has committed, or is about to commit either any felony or one of those misdemeanors enumerated in § 552 of the Code of Criminal Procedure. (These misdemeanors are weapons crimes, burglar's tools, receiving stolen property, unlawful entry, escape, impairing, carnal abuse, indecent exposure, obscenity and other indecency provisions, sodomy, rape, narcotics, amphetamines and hypodermic needles.) Suspicion of disorderly conduct, an offense, is not for the purpose of practical enforcement procedures a basis for stopping.

C. THE RIGHT TO "QUESTION"

1. No questions are to be asked until the officer has, either by being in uniform or by showing his shield and stating he is a police officer, identified himself.
2. Promptly thereafter, the suspect should be questioned (and frisked, when appropriate) in the immediate area in which he was stopped.
3. Should the suspect refuse to answer the officer's questions, the of-

ficer cannot compel an answer and should not attempt to do so. The suspect's refusal to answer shall not be considered as an element by the officer in determining whether or not there is a basis for an arrest.

4. In ascertaining "his name" from the suspect, the officer may request to see verification of his identity, but a person shall not be compelled to produce such verification.
5. If the suspect does answer, and his answers appear to be false or unsatisfactory, the officer may question further. Answers of this nature may serve as an element in determining whether a basis for arrest exists. (But if an officer determines that an answer is "unsatisfactory" and relies upon this in part to sustain his arrest, he should be able to explain with particularity the manner in which it is "unsatisfactory.")
6. If, after he has stopped and the officer has identified himself, the suspect attempts to flee from the officer, this fact may be an element in determining whether a basis for arrest exists. However, the officer should not resort to the use of a weapon or other extraordinary means to stop the flight unless he has information which now leads him to reasonably believe that the suspect has committed a felony.

D. THE RIGHT TO "SEARCH"

1. Clearly no right to search exists unless there is a right to stop.
2. Nor is a search lawful in every case in which a right to stop exists. A search is only justified under the new law when the officer reasonably suspects that he is in danger. This claim is not to be used as a pretext for obtaining evidence. In instances in which evidence is produced as a result of a search, the superior officers, the prosecutors, and—it is anticipated—the courts, will scrutinize particularly closely all the circumstances relied upon for justifying the stopping and searching.
3. No search is appropriate unless the officer "reasonably suspects that he is in danger." Among the factors that may be considered in determining whether to search are:
   a. Nature of the suspected crime, and whether it involved the use of a weapon or violence.
   b. The presence or absence of assistance to the officer, and the number of suspects being stopped.
   c. The time of the day or night.
   d. Prior knowledge of the suspects' record and reputation.
   e. The sex of the suspect.
   f. The demeanor and seeming agility of the suspect, and whether the clothes so bulge as to be indicative of concealed weapons. (This listing is not meant to be all inclusive.)
4. Initially, once the determination has been made that the officer may be in danger, all that is necessary is a frisk—an external feeling of

clothing—such as would reveal a weapon of immediate danger to the officer.

5. **A search of the suspect's clothing and pockets should not be made unless something is felt by this frisk—such as a hard object that feels as if it may be a weapon. In such event, the officer may search that portion of the suspect's clothing to uncover the article that was felt.**
6. **If the suspect is carrying an object such as a handbag, suitcase, sack, etc. which may conceal a weapon, the officer should not open that item, but should see that it is placed out of reach of the suspect so that its presence will not represent any immediate danger to the officer.**

Stop and frisk is the least intrusive formal invasion of individual privacy recognized by American law, but even here the police officer's conduct must meet constitutional standards of reasonableness. As the intrusion intensifies, as in an arrest, the reasonableness test becomes stricter.

Arrest

The difficult decision to arrest or not to arrest is usually made by the officer on the beat. The legal definition of arrest is the deprivation of an individual's liberty and freedom of action.[40] Any seizure of the person was thought at one time by many courts to constitute an arrest, but after the development of the stop and frisk doctrine, it must be understood that the term does not include the momentary, on-the-street stopping for investigative purposes. If a stopping does become more than a very brief restriction of an individual, however, it may then be characterized as an arrest.

Theoretically, police are bound by law to arrest for every violation of the law, and the offenses committed in the officer's presence are subject to his immediate action. Under most circumstances, unless a crime is committed in the officer's presence, a *warrant* is required. A warrant is a document issued by a judge authorizing an officer to make an arrest, seize property, make a search, or execute a judgment. If a felony is committed, the police officer may arrest without a warrant and without having witnessed the violation if he has reasonable cause to believe that a crime has been committed and that the suspect is the guilty party.

A felony is generally a serious crime. At common law, any criminal act that was punishable by imprisonment in a penitentiary rather than in a local jail was regarded as a felony. While some states retain the common law definition, most states define a felony as any offense where the individual upon conviction is subject to imprisonment for more than a year.[41] The reasons for allowing warrantless arrests of suspected felons goes to the seriousness of the crime and the possibility that the individual may have done violence and may do so again. An arrest without a warrant in the case of a felony is also allowed because the seriousness of the prospective penalty may cause the individual to attempt to flee the jurisdiction to avoid arrest and prosecution.

The laws governing arrests for *misdemeanors* are significantly different from felony laws. A misdemeanor was defined at common law as an offense not punishable in a penitentiary. Today, misdemeanors are generally defined as offenses punishable by less than a year's incarceration.[42] A police officer need not have a warrant to arrest for a misdemeanor committed in his presence. Unlike felonies, however, if the misdemeanor is committed out of the officer's presence, he may not arrest without a warrant. If the officer does not personally witness the commission of the misdemeanor, judicial authorization for the arrest is required. The different rules governing arrests for felonies and misdemeanors can be understood by the different nature of the two classes of offenses. By definition, felonies are serious offenses, frequently involving violence, and the potential long prison sentence may spur the felon to take flight to avoid prosecution. On the other hand, misdemeanors are not serious crimes, usually constituting

FELONY—MISDEMEANOR DISTINCTION
Selected States & Offenses—Maximum Penalties

	RAPE		PROSTITUTION		BURGLARY		VEHICULAR HOMICIDE	
	Felony	Misdemeanor	Felony	Misdemeanor	Felony	Misdemeanor	Felony	Misdemeanor
CAL.	5 yrs.	—	—	45 days	4 yrs.	—	5 yrs.	—
FLA.	30 yrs.	—	—	60 days	5 yrs.	—	5 yrs.	—
ILL.	Life	—	—	1 yr.	20 yrs.	—	3 yrs.	—
MICH.	Life	—	—	90 days	15 yrs.	—	—	2 yrs.
N.Y.	25 yrs.	—	—	90 days	25 yrs.	—	4 yrs.	—
OHIO	25 yrs.	—	—	60 days	15 yrs.	—	—	6 mos.
PENN.	20 yrs.	—	—	lyr.	10 yrs.	—	—	5 yrs.
TEX.	20 yrs.	—	—	$200 fine	20 yrs.	—	—	1 yr.

minor breaches of the peace, and misdemeanants are less likely to flee from prosecution.

Many states have extended the authority of police officers to make warrantless arrests on reasonable cause to some misdemeanors not committed in the officer's presence. If the offense involves a breach of the peace or an assault, some states permit warrantless arrests for these misdemeanors to de-escalate a potentially violent situation.[43] Others, like the Nebraska statute here, set forth conditions for warrantless arrests not committed in the officer's presence:

1. that the offender will not be apprehended unless immediately arrested
2. that the offender may cause injury to himself or others or damage to property if not immediately arrested
3. that the offender may conceal or destroy evidence of the crime if not immediately arrested[44]

Even though an officer has the authority and intends to arrest and prosecute a misdemeanor, the person arrested will not necessarily be taken into custody. Many states allow the officer to issue a *summons* to the suspect in lieu of taking him into custody for a misdemeanor.[46] A summons is the

FORNICATION		CARRYING A CONCEALED WEAPON		ASSAULT		DRIVING WHILE INTOXICATED		POSSESSION OF MARIJUANA (Small Quantity)	
Felony	Misdemeanor	Felony	Misdemeanor	Felony	Misdemeanor	Felony	Misdemeanor	Felony	Misdemeanor
No Crime		—	6 mos.	—	6 mos.	—	6 mos.	—	$100 fine
—	60 days	5 yrs.	—	—	60 days	—	6 mos.	—	1 year[45]
—	6 mos.	—	1 yr.	—	30 days	—	1 yr.	—	30 days
No Crime		5 yrs.	—	—	1 yr.	—	90 days	—	90 days
No Crime		—	1 yr.	—	1 yr.	—	1 yr.	—	Fine
No Crime		—	6 mos.	—	6 mos.	—	6 mos.	—	$100 fine
No Crime		—	5 yrs.	—	2 yrs.	—	1 yr.	—	30 days
No Crime		—	1 yr.	—	1 yr.	—	2 yrs.	—	6 mos.

same as a traffic citation. A summons notifies the accused of the charge and informs him when to appear in court. Although many states still prefer arrests in some misdemeanor cases, the reasoning behind using a summons in lieu of an arrest is sound because a misdemeanor is not a serious offense and the likelihood of an individual receiving a jail sentence upon conviction is not great. If the suspect is a local resident and has ties to the community, facts that can be verified by the arresting officer, there is also little likelihood that he will attempt to flee the jurisdiction. Why subject the suspect to a night of humiliation and potential danger in a jail for a misdemeanor, unless the reason is to punish? And punishment is not the function of an arrest and is improper prior to conviction in all cases, serious and nonserious alike. Perhaps the most compelling reason a summons may be more practical and reasonable under certain circumstances is that an arrest takes one or two officers off the streets for at least several hours while the suspect is being booked and reports are filled out. This reduction in police visibility can hardly be justified if the arrest is not necessary either to prevent violence or to assure the suspect's presence in court. (Naturally, a summons would not be used if the individual is transient, unable to care for himself, or represents a threat of additional crimes or danger to anyone.)

Probable Cause

Naturally, an arrest is a greater intrusion on a person's privacy and liberty than that involved in the investigatory stop and frisk situation. The facts that justify the arrest, therefore, must be very solid to satisfy the constitutional test of reasonableness. The standard of reasonableness for an arrest is probable cause. Probable cause means, most simply, that it is more likely than not that a crime has been committed and it is more likely than not that the person arrested committed the crime.[47] Probable cause is necessary if there is to be a warrant issued by a judge ordering the arrest of an individual or if an arrest is to be made by a police officer without a warrant. The probable cause standard must be determined from those facts and circumstances known to the judge when he issues the warrant or to the patrol officer when making the warrantless arrest.[48] Probable cause must exist prior to the arrest.[49] Probable cause provides the justification for an arrest and cannot be established by a subsequent investigation after an arrest has been made. When a police officer makes an arrest without a warrant, the arrest will subsequently be reviewed by a court on the basis of what the officer knew before or at the time he acted.

The facts and circumstances that establish probable cause are not technical. They are the factual and practical considerations of everyday life on which reasonable and prudent men, not legal technicians, base the important decisions of their daily existence.[50] It is important to stress that at the arrest stage in the criminal process certainty is not demanded, but only that the judge issuing the warrant or the police officer making a warrantless arrest have sufficient information to justify a belief that the person arrested probably committed the crime.[51]

Information from victims or civilian witnesses is essential to many arrests, but in establishing probable cause it must be ascertained how the person providing information knows that a crime has been committed. For instance, a mere statement from an informant that a suspect has in his possession a certain quantity of heroin would not justify an arrest. If, however, the informant specifically relates how he knows that the suspect has the heroin, then there will be a probable cause justification for the arrest. Probable cause would exist if the informant's story stemmed from an overheard offer to sell, or a purchase by the informant, or the suspect's having shown the informant the heroin. Even the conclusion by a police officer that a suspect has heroin is not sufficient to justify the issuance of a warrant, unless the officer advises the judge of meaningful underlying circumstances for his conclusion.[52]

In an effort to control crime, police departments are often in the awkward position of having to secure information from people who, themselves, are on the fringes of the law and who sell information to the police. To protect informers, it is sometimes necessary to protect their identities. An informant does not have to be named if the police can present sufficient information guaranteeing his credibility, such as instances of accurate and reliable information that has been supplied by the informant in the past.[53] In the case of victims, witnesses, and other non-professional informants, their credibility, in terms of establishing probable cause, need not be proven.[54]

Because an arrest is such a severe infringement on individual liberty, prior judicial authorization of all arrests through the issuance of a warrant has traditionally been preferred.[55] Yet, while a warrant is preferable, no felony arrest has ever been declared illegal simply because of the absence of a warrant, even if the police had more than enough time to secure one. Because of the reasons cited earlier in this chapter, exceptions to the warrant requirement were initially developed at common law and have been carried over into the statutes of all American state and federal jurisdictions and have passed the constitutional test of reasonableness.

Reasonable Force

A police officer may use *reasonable force* to effect an arrest and to protect himself or others. If the arrest is for a felony, the law has traditionally permitted the use of deadly force if it becomes reasonably necessary under the circumstances to complete the arrest and prevent the suspect from fleeing.[56]

Officers who attempt to make warrantless arrests are operating without judicial predetermination of probable cause. In making a warrantless arrest, then, officers must judge first whether probable cause exists and second, whether force will be needed to make the arrest. This broad authorization to use force, deadly force if necessary, has been the subject of reconsideration in recent years.[57] The reason the use of deadly force has become a controversial subject is because police, in many instances, have resorted to deadly force in effecting arrests for non-violent crimes. For instance, police officers have often shot at suspects fleeing from crimes that did not bear any hint of personal violence. The authority to use deadly force, then, is often abused when officers cannot resist the temptation to apprehend, through any means, suspects fleeing from a crime scene, regardless of whether or not the crime itself was violent.

No one seriously questions the use of deadly force if it is reasonably necessary to prevent the completion of a dangerous felony, such as rape, arson, or armed robbery, or if it is reasonably necessary to protect the life of the arresting officer or anyone else. The propriety of its use arises only when it is utilized to prevent the flight of a person who has committed a non-dangerous felony. The Model Penal Code, which is a law of no jurisdiction but serves as a model to states reconsidering their own penal codes, proposes to limit the use of deadly force to effect an arrest to those situations where the suspected felon, himself, used or threatened to use deadly force or where there is a substantial risk that the person to be arrested will cause death or serious bodily harm if his apprehension is delayed.[58]

After Arrest. . .

Immediately after the arrest is made, the suspect is usually searched thoroughly by the arresting officers. Searches are an invasion of the Fourth Amendment right and are governed by the constitutional standard of reasonableness and the warrant requirement. Yet the warrant requirement for post-arrest searches is riddled with exceptions. Generally, a warrantless search may be reasonable if there are exigent circumstances that justify dispensing with the warrant. There are three reasons for permitting warrantless searches incident to a lawful arrest: (1) to remove weapons from the suspect in order to protect the safety of the police officer; (2) to remove evidence of the crime from the control of the suspect so that he cannot destroy that evidence; and (3) to remove anything from the suspect that will assist him in escaping from the police officers.[59]

Because the authority to conduct a search without a warrant is based upon exigent circumstances, the scope of the search is limited to those areas within the suspect's immediate reach.[60] Thus the arrest of a suspect in a room does not justify a search of the entire room, let alone the full apartment or house, but just those areas within the reach of the suspect. Obviously the suspect's body is not in issue in that context, and the Supreme Court has held that an arresting officer may make a full search of the person irrespective of the nature or seriousness of the offense for which the suspect has been arrested.[61] Several states, imposing higher standards of due process than that required by the Supreme Court under the federal Constitution, have limited such intrusions to searches for weapons unless there is reasonable cause to believe that evidence of the crime would be found on the suspect.[62] This approach prohibits full body searches, for instance, of persons arrested for traffic offenses.

Searches of automobiles immediately after the arrest of the driver or occupants presents a thornier issue. While the Supreme Court has virtually dispensed with the warrant requirement for automobiles,[63] the arrest of an individual while driving a car does not automatically justify a search of the car as incidental to the arrest. Presumably, at the time of arrest the suspect is out of the car and therefore is unable to reach a weapon or destroy evidence which may be in the car. The arresting officer is not permitted to search the car unless he has reasonable cause to believe that evidence of a crime will be found in the automobile.[64] The purpose of this limitation is to deter pretext stoppings and arrests that are made solely for the purpose of searching the car. If the car is to be impounded (taken into custody) because it was used during the commission of the crime and is subject to forfeiture to the state, or if the car is to be lawfully removed, either to satisfy a legitimate state need because it is blocking traffic or to protect the suspect's property, it is subject to a warrantless inventory search.[65] Whether an arrest automatically triggers a right to search a vehicle has been a bone of contention, but the law is clear that no such authority automatically arises.

After the search, the suspect is transported, generally by the arresting officers, to either a district police headquarters or a centralized location for processing. Once at the police station, the suspect is booked, which includes the registration of an initial charge for which the suspect was arrested, and the photographing and fingerprinting of the suspect. If the police have reasonable cause to believe that physical tests of the suspect's clothing may turn up evidence of a crime, the clothing may be taken from the suspect without prior approval by a court.[66] Physical tests may also be performed upon the accused, such as blood tests or the taking of a hair follicle, without his consent and without judicial authorization if the police have reasonable cause to believe that the tests will provide evidence of the crime.[67] The intrusion of the person without judicial authorization, however, is limited to minor intrusions. Any major bodily intrusions require court approval. For example, surgery to remove a bullet which will be evidence must be preceded by approval from a court because of the potential risk to the accused.[68] Internal examinations to search for evidence are generally permissible if they are conducted in a reasonable manner, such as having a female officer conduct the internal search of a woman suspect. Internal examinations, however, are major intrusions and may not constitutionally be performed indiscriminately or without a valid purpose. The indiscriminate internal examinations of female suspects and non-suspects by the Chicago police, discovered in 1979, obviously were not constitutionally justifiable.

The decision by patrol officers to take a suspect into custody does not automatically mean that the police will present the case to the prosecutor for formal charging. While in many cities, the patrol officer still takes the case to the prosecutor, especially where the arrest is for a misdemeanor, most large city police departments have initiated systems for internal review of the patrol officer's decision to initiate the criminal process, especially in cases involving serious felonies. The patrol officer is not apt to be aware of factors that indicate whether a case merits prosecution, such as the importance of the crime or the likelihood of securing a conviction in the particular case. Review by policy-making senior officers at this juncture of a criminal case, especially when the policies have been arrived at after consultation with the prosecutor, help to prevent the courts from being overwhelmed with cases of little merit.

In most cities, the arresting officers take a back seat immediately before or after the suspect has been booked, at least in major felony cases, and the responsibility for further investigation and the decision whether or not to pass the case on to the prosecutor is vested in specialized units, such as homicide, robbery, narcotics, or detective units. New York City detectives, for instance, used to assume responsibility for any serious felony that occurred during their shifts. In 1976, a program was initiated in that city to reorganize the detectives into specialized bureaus in the hope that more crimes would actually be solved if the detectives developed expertise in handling one category of crime.[69]

Once the detective takes over, it is his case. A complete briefing will be sought from the arresting officer, perhaps even his recommendation, but the decision whether to release the accused or recommend the case for prosecution is within the discretion of the detective. One of the detective's first efforts will be to try to get a statement from the accused. The accused does not have to make a statement. If a confession or statement obtained from a suspect is to be used at his trial, it is necessary that the arresting officer, detective, or both, advise the suspect of his rights.[70] This may be done by the arresting officers immediately after the arrest, but it should be done again to insure the accused's understanding that those rights are still operative, or to remind the accused if he has forgotten them in the hectic activities which immediately followed his physical arrest. That advice must include:

1. that the accused has the right to remain silent
2. that if the accused chooses to speak, anything he says can and will be used against him
3. that the accused has the right to consult an attorney before making the decision whether or not to speak, and that he has the right to have the attorney present while talking with the police
4. that if the accused cannot pay for an attorney, one will be provided for him[71]

The accused must be given these warnings in a manner which indicates that the police are prepared to accept his decision, even if the decision is not to cooperate.

After the detective completes the initial investigatory work, if the decision is to recommend prosecution, the authority over the case is handed over to the prosecutor. Although the detective will work in concert with the prosecutor who reviews the case and who will ultimately try the case, and while the police may be able to influence the prosecutor when it comes to plea bargaining, the power to determine whether to prosecute and whether to treat the offense as a felony is within the discretion of the prosecutor. In many towns and cities, because misdemeanors are considered less important and because it is often advantageous to conserve the limited resources of detective units and prosecuting agencies, the arresting officer often retains total power over a case until the day the case goes to trial.

The Decision to Arrest: A Practice in Discretion

While the decision to arrest will ultimately be reviewed, the decision not to arrest, because the officer chooses to ignore violations of certain offenses or to simply ignore violations committed by certain offenders, will not be reviewed by a judge nor even by the officer's commanders within the police department. It is the exercise of this enormous discretion that cloaks the officer with the mantle of legislator, prosecutor, judge, and jury. For, in effect, when making such a decision the police officer is deciding that either the law that has been broken should not exist or that the individual who broke the law should not be punished. And although the officer is but one component of the charging process, he has the power to short-circuit it. Since the immediate decision to arrest can only be made on the spot by the officer, society can only hope that his discretion will be guided by its rules, regulations, and policies.

On-the-street confrontations between the police and citizens are at best touchy situations and at worst the precursors of disorder and violence. Some of the worst urban conflagrations of the 1960s were touched off by police mishandling of street confrontations or public misconceptions regarding the overall police response. Even though the community denounces police when they react imprudently, the police often act according to the same prejudices and fears harbored by a majority of the public. Overzealous enforcement of the law often reflects these prejudices. Arrests sometimes reflect more the race, age, or appearance of the offender than the seriousness of the illegal act, which might have been overlooked by the police officer if committed by a member of another group. For instance, petty gambling operations that police wink at in affluent sections of a city may result in arrests and prosecutions in the inner-city.[72]

The same discretionary power is also used in reverse to deny full police protection in the inner-city areas. Conduct that would warrant police action elsewhere may be ignored or dismissed by the police officer in ghetto areas. For example, an assault between ghetto residents, even where there is a knifing without serious injury, may be dismissed by the patrol officer as a normal part of the subculture of the ghetto if the officer is able to restore order without making arrests. An example of police apathy in high-crime areas is also illustrated by the not uncommon opinion that "there is no such thing as rape in the ghetto."[73] Such notions offer little comfort to the victims of assault or rape. Such police reactions seem incredible, but they are reinforced by the conduct of other participants in the criminal justice process. Consider, for instance, the unspoken "40 stitch" rule that is used in Brooklyn, New York, to help expedite cases. That unofficial guide provides that two combatants arrested and brought before a court need not face felony charges unless the combined injury to one exceeds forty stitches.[74]

Situations occur daily where police officers are compelled to decide whether an arrest is of value to the criminal justice system and to the society as a whole. One of the most difficult of these situations occurs when police respond to a call for help arising out of family disputes. As stated previously in this chapter, the officers on the scene must determine what is necessary to restore order.[75] Since these disputes occur at all hours of the night and day, a social agency is not always immediately available to intervene or assist the officers in determining what type of intervention is necessary. The officer responding to the call bears the burden of making the decision. If he arrests the belligerent member of the family, the officer knows that almost invariably the next day cooler heads will prevail and the family will elect not to pursue the matter. The wheels of the justice system will have been set in motion, but they will then be halted by the victim who no longer wishes the problem to be subject to criminal jurisdiction. (With the growing attention given to the national problem of wife-beating, perhaps victims will be less reluctant to push prosecution in the future, but that is certainly not yet the case.)

Merely restoring calm in the household may not be sufficient. If the officer makes the decision not to separate the parties by arresting one, later that same night he may find that he has made the wrong decision, that the family dispute has escalated and resulted in a homicide. Consequently, if he elects not to arrest, he must assure himself that neither participant is armed (but many kitchen utensils can become deadly weapons) and that the parties are unlikely to resume their internecine warfare. In his role as peace keeper and marriage counselor, the officer must constantly keep in mind that many homicides are committed by family members and by people who have known each other. The figures of one major American city revealed that of 286 homicides in the city in one year, 133 were committed by a friend or relative.[76] Again, the police are hardly trained or equipped to be able to foresee or judge the consequences of their decisions when dealing with emotionally wrought people. At the same time, the officer does not have the time to thoroughly analyze a family uprising: the time that officers spend in dealing with such disputes removes them from the street and their duty to prevent and deter serious crimes.

The responsibility that police bear in their attempts to restore peace in a discordant household is harrowing. They are pressured by time, by the emotional and highly personal grievances of family or community members, and by the fear that their decision may be the catalyst for serious violence. Yet, even though his responsibility is so great, the police officer is accountable only to himself. His decisions are personal; unless a serious crime develops and his decision is uncovered as a major contribution to the final surge of family violence, what he says or does under the duress will never be reviewed.

Police discretion may also be exercised for purely personal reasons. In 1976 the New York City Police came under attack for exercising discretion both ways, for arresting and for not arresting. In one month it was noted that arrests were down more than 15%, though there were no changes in departmental regulations nor in complaints or calls for assistance that would explain the decrease. It was, however, a time of police protests over cutbacks and a new labor contract. One assistant district attorney explained the decrease in arrests with his theory that the police "were too preoccupied with getting off work and picketing rather than hanging around the courts. The cops have no time now for the junk cases."[77] That same year in another month, great numbers of arrests were being made by the city's uniform patrol. City police were then receiving overtime pay for court appearances following such arrests. Judges and court officers were reported at the time to have heard police officers openly boast around the courthouse that they were making all of these arrests to get overtime pay.[78] Whether or not those charges were correct, the city devised a new plan that drastically reduced the need to have the arresting officer present at the preliminary stages of criminal cases.[79]

There are countless other situations where the officer is called upon to exercise discretion in determining whether or not to make an arrest and countless rationales for those decisions. The police officer may choose not to make an arrest because of institutional concerns. He may feel that rather than using up the remainder of his shift taking in and processing a person arrested for a minor infraction, or at least one the officer considers to be only marginally important, his time can be better spend on the lookout for serious crimes. Or the officer may choose not to make an arrest because he knows the frustrating backlog of court cases and is too well aware of how many times he will have to appear in court before the case is resolved. The officer may also know that judges are typically lenient toward the particular offense at hand and may decide not to waste his time with an arrest.[80]

The decision to relieve court congestion by not making arrests for certain offenses should be the responsibility of police leadership in conjunction with the prosecutor and the courts. The officer on the street, however, by virtue of his discretionary freedom, is in the position to decide from his own narrow perspective what laws to enforce and what laws to ignore. By deciding not to enforce certain laws, the officer thwarts the will of the legislature, which is chosen by the people to enact the laws. Moreover, society runs the risk that the officer, in choosing not to enforce a particular law, may decide to administer a dose of summary justice on the street. Although a tongue lashing administered on the street by a police officer may be as effective or even more effective in correcting the ways of a minor offender than a lecture from a judge, there are potential dangers for the community from such action. In addition to the officer's becoming prosecutor, judge, and jury, the threat exists that the officer may some day be tempted to administer more than just verbal punishment. Even though most officers refrain from violence, on-the-street brands of summary justice often provoke community problems. No matter how flagrant the illegality of the wrongdoer, a confrontation between a member of the community and a police officer is often misunderstood by passers-by and leads to violence.

Overcriminalization and Police Discretion

One problem that confronts the police officer and confounds the entire society is *overcriminalization.* There are thousands of criminal offenses on the statute books of every state in this country. Many of these laws represent the actual needs of society to maintain peace and order. But just as many were enacted as a result of pressures exerted by small groups or as legislative responses to a problem of a given day. Many of these laws represent mores that no longer exist, but the laws remain on the books and are still subject to enforcement today.[81]

Overcriminalization has had a two-pronged effect on the quality of discretionary decision making on the part of the police. The problem of overcriminalization and the problem of congested court dockets has found some relief in the exercise of responsible police discretion. Responsible, effective, and realistic discretionary decisions can work to the advantage of the public and they can help to refine the criminal process. By deciding not to enforce an archaic law or by deciding not to arrest a person who may be technically but not morally guilty of a minor infraction, the police officer helps to humanize the justice machinery. The police officer who decides not to invoke an outmoded law is saving a citizen the effort of having to appear in court only to be dismissed. He is also helping to unburden the courts of cases that have little merit. Finally, it has also been suggested that the exercise of discretion in deciding not to enforce meaningless laws has helped to remove from the books statutes that are no longer relevant or necessary.[82]

Overcriminalization has also caused the police to abuse their discretionary authority. Although prosecution of a dated law may be thrown out of court, the existence of such laws provides many opportunities for abuse and corruption.[83] For example, the compromises that are made between the citizen and the arresting officer can be tainted by such illegal behavior as the policeman accepting a bribe. Also, a police officer who wishes to harass an individual can draw upon the countless outmoded laws as a basic for such harassment. Few would doubt the value of police discretion when it serves to unburden the courts of their unmanageable caseloads if we could be assured that discretion is applied evenly and did, in fact, reflect the wisdom of a community concensus. This is rarely the case, however. And the exercise of official discretion, either by a judge, prosecutor, or police officer, will always carry with it the potential for abuse.

Full enforcement of the law is not possible in our society. But the problem of police discretion and abuse should be met head-on by reviewing our tendencies toward overcriminalization, by reconsidering, in other words, all those acts our society considers criminal.[84] Until our society comes to grips with the problem overcriminalization creates for law enforcement, we will have to accept individual police officer's notions, albeit in good faith, of what is good for the community and who are the community's good and bad guys.

"Quality Control"

Arrest/Conviction Rates

One way to measure the quality of the exercise of the discretion to arrest is to determine how many arrests lead to conviction. These figures, themselves, have to be closely analyzed because taken alone they represent an unfair indictment of how the police are performing their tasks. Several surveys of major cities indicate that 60% of persons arrested on felony charges were not convicted, and a study in the District of Columbia illustrates that for that city the percentage rose to 70%.[85] In many of these cases the reasons for non-conviction are justifiable or at least cannot be laid to police failure. The non-cooperation of witnesses, for instance, or evidentiary failures that appear later in the process may account for many non-convictions; there are also other valid explanations such as the decision to forego prosecution against an offender in return for information.

Nevertheless, to a certain extent, non-conviction rates can be attributed to poor arrests,[86] many involving poor exercises of discretion and efforts to harass people. It is not uncommon for patently bad cases, where the facts are simply inadequate to justify the original charges, to be brought to court by the police. The District of Columbia project, for example, found that some police officers were far more adept at making arrests that led to convictions than others. Over half of the arrests that led to convictions in that department in 1974 were made by only 15% of the officers in that department. Most significantly, another 25% of those officers making arrests within the department made 12½ percent of all arrests, *but not one resulted in a felony conviction.*[87] It is important not to blow the significance of these figures out of proportion, but they should make us wary of passive acceptance of unchecked, on-the-street, discretion.[88]

Departmental Policies

What effect do policy decisions, whether from elected government officials or even the police hierarchy, have on an individual police officer's decision to make an arrest or permit the individual to go free? The major impact that a police department has on the quality of discretionary police decisions is in its personnel selection and training policies. Standard intelligence tests have been upgraded. But, these tests do not really examine how well an individual can respond to the police task. Today, the tests have been augmented by psychiatric evaluations and diverse, multiple interviews by panels of citizens. Through these evaluations and interviews, departments are attempting to weed-out those who seek to enter police work because of the wrong motivation. These tests help to screen the recruits and to uncover those who have inordinate drives for personal power over fellow citizens, or those who have deep-rooted prejudices or suffer from severe emotional or psychological problems.[89]

Second only to the selection of new personnel for developing a strong, professional police force is the quality of training new cadets receive after being hired. Continuous in-service training that all departmental personnel are constantly being exposed to has helped substantially to improve police performance. Also, huge amounts of federal, as well as local, money have been spent in the past fifteen years to upgrade existing training programs and to develop programs of continuing education for police personnel.[90] The repugnance of many police for community-relations training is well documented, but even that resistance is beginning to give way as police increasingly realize that their success as professionals depends on community trust and acceptance.

Once a department puts a man or woman on the street, its ability to control his or her actions is, at best, limited; but the question of who the officer comes into contact with is significantly influenced and affected by departmental policies concerning deployment of personnel. Beset by the factors of high crime rates and limitations of personnel, which are further complicated by the dollar crunch affecting more and more cities, departments must make hard decisions about the best ways to use limited personnel and still maintain an acceptable level of order within a community.[91] These decisions, in large part, set the stage for the types of persons to be arrested and the types of crimes to be prosecuted.

Cities often make a conscious choice to commit a high percentage of officers to those areas where the greatest number of crimes are reported. By saturating an area with patrol officers, it is hoped that the display of force and the extensive visibility of the police will deter persons from committing crimes. But at the same time that more violators in the high-crime areas may be apprehended, a certain amount of crime in other parts of the city goes undetected and the safety of the citizens in other parts of the city is often compromised. It must be stressed that deployment policies geared to crime rates have to be carefully monitored and constantly kept up to date. If not, a department will find that its criminals have moved to other areas in the city that have been left virtually unprotected. For instance, around Christmas when cities are attempting to protect their downtown shopping areas, great publicity is attached to the deployment of extra personnel to protect the merchants and the customers flocking to the stores. At the same time, protection in other parts of the city has to be lessened in order to free the officers deployed downtown. Even though this assignment of personnel may be logical and necessary, it also means that perpetrators of identical crimes committed in different parts of the city are less likely to be apprehended.[92]

Different police-deployment and patrol strategies were tested in Kansas City, Missouri, designed by internal task forces to guide the dispatch and deployment of patrol personnel.[93] The purpose of these tests was to enhance the crime prevention capabilities of the department by introducing modern management techniques into deployment policies. By measuring the effectiveness of patrol strategies through the systematic alteration of coverage in given areas of a city, departments can develop and evaluate strategies for best meeting the challenge of urban crime with resources which are by necessity limited by financial constraints.

The policy with respect to responding to citizen calls for assistance will similarly shape the number of crimes that are detected and the criminals who are prosecuted. Motivated by a belief that answering calls promotes citizen participation in law enforcement, Milwaukee police policy dictates that all citizen complaints and calls for assistance be answered. The response is the dispatch of a squad car to investigate the complaint. Naturally, some of the calls are without merit and divert the police officers from other more essential tasks. However, the Milwaukee policy does create a feeling of security that the police are always available if needed. This sense of security, it has been maintained, has created a greater willingness on the part of the citizens to cooperate with the police and assist in law enforcement.[94]

Milwaukee's ability to respond to all citizen complaints is based, at least to some degree, upon the luxury of not being constantly confronted with serious, violent crimes. Detroit police, on the other hand, who face urban problems of greater intensity than those in Milwaukee, cannot respond to all citizen calls. In Detroit, the police dispatcher, after receiving information from a caller, will order a squad car to investigate a complaint only if the dispatcher believes that an emergency situation exists. If the dispatcher does not believe that the caller requires immediate police intervention, he will instruct the caller to come to the police station and fill out a complaint.[95] Consequently, there is no immediate police response if the information provided by the caller is insufficient to determine whether a serious crime has been or is about to be committed. Similarly, where it is apparent that the caller as well as the person he is complaining about are in the wrong, and there is no report of violence or threat of violence, the police will decline to respond. Approaches such as the one in Detroit become necessary when there are far more calls than police are able to respond to. Citizens need immediate help when there is a prowler or burglar, or when there is a threat of violence, or when a serious crime has been or is being committed. Response time, the measure of how long it takes the police to respond to cries for help, is an issue of great concern in many cities. Many have instituted emergency phone number systems, 911, which are supposed to be limited to summons for police assistance in matters requiring immediate attention. These systems have only worked where citizens do not clog the lines with non-emergency calls. In those communities where the residents use 911 every time they have to call the police for any reason, the emergency factor is reduced and the ability of the police to respond quickly is hindered.[96]

As violent crimes that require an immediate police response increase, departments throughout the country are developing policies that free them from matters which are ancillary to their main purpose of preserving peace while preventing and detecting crime.[97] Consequently, more and more callers are being directed to appropriate social agencies in lieu of police intervention. Formerly, for instance, it was not unusual for the police to receive and respond to calls concerning stray animals. Today, in many cities, the caller is advised to notify the animal protective agency. Also, investigation of all traffic accidents, no matter how minor, remains a traditional police task throughout the country. Police in Minneapolis, however, respond only if there is a report that someone has been injured or that traffic is being blocked, because police time can be used more valuably in responding to calls about crimes and for emergency assistance. Participants in minor traffic accidents are directed to police headquarters to fill out a report about the accident.[98] Another approach to free uniformed police officers from their more mundane responsibilities is the national movement to assign many office duties to civilian personnel, thereby putting more officers on the street, in squad cars, or otherwise available to respond to calls for emergency help.

External Review of Police Decisions and Policies

Surprisingly, little mechanism exists in this democratic society for external review of an individual police officer's exercises of discretion or, for that matter, departmental policies. Both are theoretically subject to the supervision of local elected officials, who are charged with the responsibility for overseeing matters of public safety. Yet unless the police and policing become issues in political campaigns, elected officials lack both the expertise and information to exercise a meaningful role.[99] Other review mechanisms also tend to be ineffectual. Civilian review boards acting on citizen complaints, perhaps a noble product of the 1960s, met the unyielding resistance of almost all police personnel. Even when civilian review boards clearly demonstrated an absence of anti-police bias, police hostility did not abate and in most cities the review boards were short-lived.[100] Today most review is internal, with severe disciplinary action possibly subject to appeal for reconsideration and reversal to an administrative or civil service board, and, ultimately, to a court.[101]

At present, the only meaningful external review of an individual officer's decisions exists in suppression hearings held in criminal trials. That review, however, is limited only to determining the constitutionality of the police officer's conduct in certain dealings with citizens and is in the context of whether evidence secured by the officer may be used at trial against the defendant. It does not provide a full-scale review mechanism of all aspects of an individual officer's or department's conduct or policies.

Discussion Questions

1. In an article entitled, "The Police Personality: Fact or Fiction" (J. of C.L., Crim., and P.S., 63:1, 1972), Robert Balch states:

> . . . policemen are being watched and studied as never before. Liberals, minorities, and intellectuals are clamoring for greater civilian control over the police. The public has been sensitized to police brutality and prejudice, and police administrators are desperately trying to upgrade the quality of men in their departments.

In the 60s police brutality and prejudice caused extreme public animosity and distrust. These negative attitudes are now changing. What are three reasons, as discussed in this chapter, for improved relations between the public and the police?

2. Why are "service functions" one of the most difficult and demanding aspects of police work?

3. What are the principal goals of police investigation?

4. Discuss the significance of the *Terry* decision to the investigative function of the police.

5. The standard of reasonableness for an arrest is probable cause. What facts determine probable cause and therefore provide the justification for an arrest?

6. A police officer may use reasonable force to effect an arrest and to protect himself or others. What is meant by "reasonable force"?

7. After an arrest, the suspect must be advised of his rights. What are the warnings all suspects in police custody are entitled to?

8. A police officer's decisions are often personal and are rarely reviewed. They are low-visibility decisions that frequently reflect an officer's personal attitudes as opposed to his professional reasoning. Why is police discretion such an explosive issue? Discuss your answer in terms of the five ways police can use and abuse their discretionary power.

9. What three checks exist to improve and control police discretion?

Notes

1. *National Advisory Commission on Criminal Justice Standards and Goals: The Police,* (Washington, 1973), p. 39.
2. *Two Hundred Years of American Criminal Justice: An LEAA Bicentennial Study* (Washington: U.S. Department of Justice, 1976), p. 15; Harry W. More, Jr., *The American Police* (St. Paul, Minn.: West, 1976), p. 6.
3. *LEAA Study,* p. 15.

4. William J. Bopp, and Donald O. Schultz, *A Short History of American Law Enforcement* (Springfield: Charles Thomas, 1972), p. 17.
5. *LEAA Study,* p. 15; Bopp and Schultz, *A Short History,* pp. 21-22.
6. More, *The American Police,* pp. 8-9.
7. *LEAA Study,* p. 17; More, *The American Police,* p. 7; Bopp and Schultz, *A Short History,* p. 35.
8. *LEAA Study,* p. 18.
9. Ibid., p. 21.
10. Ibid.:

"The Boston Social Club, the patrolmen's fraternal organization, petitioned the American Federation of Labor for a union charter in 1919. Ired by the police commissioner's order forbidding union membership, 19 patrolmen refused to disband and were brought up on departmental charges, tried, and convicted. Sentencing was postponed as the union patrolmen demanded leniency. Ultimately, they were suspended, and this precipitated a strike. The strikers were subsequently fired, and a new police force was hired....

"Also in 1915, two Pittsburgh patrolmen founded the Fraternal Order of Police, which became a national organization concentrated in the industrial cities of the Northeast. Unlike Labor unions, it prohibited striking, but its membership included everyone from patrolmen to chiefs."

11. Ibid., p. 22:

"The biggest problem of the post-World War I era was Prohibition. Policemen either tried to enforce what quickly came to be an unenforceable law or looked the other way as America engaged in socially acceptable conduct; also see, Bopp and Schultz, *A Short History,* p. 101: "The police establishment was stung by the barrage of criticism which had been leveled at it from the survey commissions. Some police officials tried to defend themselves and their departments against charges of corruption and inefficiency, but most commissions had done their work well and indictments were painstakingly documented. While the criticism did not motivate a revolution in law enforcement, certain substantial reforms and modifications were undertaken by police agencies desirous of upgrading themselves."

12. *National Commission on Law Observance and Enforcement: The Wickersham Commission,* "Lawlessness in Law Enforcement," vol. 5, (1931), pp. 4-5.
13. *The President's Commission on Law Enforcement and Administration of Justice, Task Force Report: The Police* (Washington, 1967), p. 181.
14. Ibid., pp. 181-82.
15. *Report of The National Advisory Commission on Civil Disorders,* 1968, "Police and the Community," pp. 158-59; Bopp and Schultz, *A Short History,* p. 142.
16. Ibid., *Table A (Non-White Personnel in Selected Police Departments),* p. 169.
17. *National Advisory Commission on Criminal Justice Standards and Goals: The Police,* (Washington, 1973), pp. 329-330, where the Report states that:

"Increasing emphasis must be placed on recruiting qualified Blacks as police officers in communities with Black residents ... whenever there is a substantial ethnic minority population in any jurisdiction, the police service can be improved by employing qualified members of that group"; also see, Carter v. Gallagher, 452 F.2d 315 (8th Cir. 1971), where the Court held in part that the fire department must hire one minority group member for every three whites until 20 minority group members are hired; also see, Allen v. Mobile, 331 F.Supp. 1134 (1971), where the Court ordered the city "to consult with Black leaders in developing recruitment programs, and to direct advertising and pro motion toward the Black community."

18. *National Advisory Commission on Criminal Justice Standards and Goals: The Police,* (Washington, 1973), pp. 372-73:

"A 1969 survey by Thompson S. Crockett and John Moses, *Incentive Plans For Law Enforcement Education,* revealed that 58% of the responding 467 agencies provided some form of educational incentive for their officers."

19. James Baldwin, *Nobody Knows My Name* (New York: Dell, 1962), p. 66.
20. *New York Times,* August 1978.
21. Bopp and Schultz, *A Short History,* pp. 150-51.
22. *A Report by the President's Commission on Law Enforcement and Administration of Justice: The Challenge of Crime in a Free Society* (Washington, 1967), p. 92.
23. In Toronto, constables report all encounters with citizens as they occur. They are then joined at the scene by supervisors in mobile units who observe and direct the constable through the completion of the encounter.
24. *Standards and Goals,* pp. 329-331.
25. *National Evaluation Program: Traditional Prevention Patrol, Phase I Report* (National Institute of Law Enforcement and Criminal Justice, 1976), p. 56.
26. *Uniform Crime Reports* (issued by Clarence M. Kelly, Former Director, Federal Bureau of Investigation, 1977, *Table 20,* pp. 162-63.
27. Soderman and O'Connell, *Modern Criminal Investigation* (New York: Funk and Wagnalls, 1962); International Association of Chiefs of Police, *Criminal Investigation: Basic Procedures* (Gaithersburg, Md.: IACP, 1975); International Association of Chiefs of Police, *Criminal Investigation: Specific Offenses* (Gaithersburg, Md.: IACP, 1975).
28. Wisconsin Department of Justice Crime Laboratory Bureau, *Criminal Investigation and Physical Handbook* (Madison, Wisconsin, 1973), pp. 13-14.
29. *Ohio Revised Code* §2921.22 (Baldwin 1974); *Ill Ann Stat,* Ch 38, § 31-4 (Smith Hurd 1978).
30. *Ohio Revised Code* §2921.22(E) (Baldwin 1974).
31. Terry v. Ohio, 392 U.S. 1 (1968).
32. Terry v. Ohio, supra, at 27.
33. Terry v. Ohio, supra, at 22-23.
34. Adams v. Williams, 407 U.S. 143 (1972).
35. c.f. United States v. Mitchell, 179 F.Supp. 636 (D.D.C. 1959). This pre-Terry decision held that the officers could not detain a suspect and then check whether or not a crime had been committed.
36. See Edwards v. United States, 364 A.2d 1209 (1976), where a division of the D.C. Court of Appeals held that a police officer with an articulable suspicion that two men walking through a residential area during the early hours of the morning were carrying stolen goods had a right to chase the men into an apartment building when they fled after questioning.
37. Terry v. Ohio, supra, at 27.
38. See c.f. State v. Gannaway, 191 N.W.2d 555 (1971), where the Court suppressed the seizure of a corncob pipe from defendant's outer coat pocket by police officers during process of "frisking" defendant for weapons. The Court noted further that "it is the police officers conduct . . . which is the focus of the constitutional issue. With most commendable candor, Pelton (the officer) admits that at the point of taking defendant's pipe he had no reason to believe that Gannaway had narcotics in his possession.
39. *N.Y. Code Crim. Proc.* § 140.50 (McKinney 1971).

§ 140.50 Temporary Questioning of Persons in Public Places; Search for Weapons

1. In addition to the authority provided by this article for making an arrest without a warrant, a police officer may stop a person in a public place located within the geographical area of such officer's employment when he reasonably suspects that such person is committing, has committed or is about to commit either (a) a felony or (b) a class A misdemeanor defined in the penal law, and may demand of him his name, address and an explanation of his conduct.

2. When upon stopping a person under circumstances prescribed in subdivision one, a police officer reasonably suspects that he is in danger of physical injury, he may search such person for a deadly weapon or any instrument, article or substance readily capable of causing serious physical injury and of a sort not ordinarily carried in public places by law-abiding persons. If he finds such a weapon or instrument, or any other property possession of which he reasonably believes may constitute the commission of a crime, he may take it and keep it until the completion of the questioning, at which time he shall either return it, if lawfully possessed, or arrest such person. L. 1970, c. 996, §1, eff. Sept. 1, 1971.

40. *Black's Law Dictionary,* 4th ed. (St. Paul, Minn.: West, 1972); see also, Miranda v. Arizona, 384 U.S. 436, 444 (1965), where the Supreme Court defined arrest as a person being taken into custody or otherwise deprived of his or her freedom of action in any significant way.

41. *Crim. Code of Georgia* §26-401 (Harrison 1978); *Illinois Crim. Law and Proc.* 38 §2-7 (Smith Hurd 1978); *Indiana Crim. Code* 9-101 [2027] (Burns 1972); *Texas Code of Crim. Proc.* § 12.31-34 (Vernon 1974).

42. *Crim. Code of Georgia* §27-2506 (Harrison 1978); *Illinois Crim. Code and Proc.* 38 §2-11 (Smith Hurd 1978); *Indiana Crim. Code 9-101 [2027] (Burns 1972).*

43. *Consol. Laws of New York* § 140.15, § 140.20 (McKinney 1971); *Crim. Code of Georgia* §27-207 (Harrison 1978).

44. *Rev. Statutes of Nebraska* §29-404.02 (1974 Cum. Supp.).

45. cf. State v. Leigh, 1/18/78 (Fla. Cir. Ct., 11th Cir. (Dade County) Docket #77-267), where a trial court in Dade County, Florida granted defendant's motion to dismiss prosecution under the statute on the grounds that it was a violation of privacy. Also that the possession of small quantities of marijuana for personal use is protected by the Constitution; see also Ravin v. State, 537 P.2d 494 (Alaska 1975), where the court held that no adequate justification exists for State's intrusion into citizen's right of privacy by its prohibition of possession of marijuana by an adult for personal consumption in home, and thus possession of marijuana by adults at home for personal use is constitutionally protected.

46. *Ill. Crim. Code and Proc.* §107-11 (Smith Hurd 1978); *N.Y. Crim. Code* §140.20(2)(a) (McKinney 1971).

47. See Jerold Israel and Wayne LaFave, *Criminal Procedure in a Nutshell* (St. Paul, Minn.: West, 1975), p. 97; see also, Browne v. State, 24 Wis.2d 491, 129 N.W.2d 175 (1964), where they defined probable cause as "that quantum of evidence which would lead a police officer acting as a reasonable man, to believe that the defendant probably committed a crime; also Brooks v. United States, 159 A.2d 876 (D.C. Mun. App., 1960), where upon stopping a man carrying a player console with the price tags still on it, the police detained him to ask him some questions. When the officer pointed out the tags the suspect changed his story and was consequently placed under arrest. The Court noted that "probabilities must be measured by the standards of the reasonable, cautious and prudent peace officer as he sees them, and not those of a casual passerby." The Court therefore held that the officer acted upon probable cause.

48. Spinelli v. United States, 394 U.S. 410 (1969); See LaFave, "Improving Police

Performance Through the Exclusionary Rule—Part II: Defining the Norms and Training the Police," 30 *Mo. L. Rev.* 566, 582 (1965).

49. Israel and LaFave, *Criminal Procedure,* p. 98. Of course, when the police act without a warrant, that determination is subject to an after-the-fact review by a judicial officer upon a motion to suppress evidence found because of the arrest or search.
50. Beck v. Ohio, 379 U.S. 89 (1964).
51. Frazier v. Roberts, 441 F.2d 1224 (8th Cir. 1971).
52. Aguilar v. Texas, 378 U.S. 108 (1964).
53. Spinelli v. United States, 394 U.S. 410 (1969); also see McCray v. Illinois, 386 U.S. 300 (1967), where the Court held that probable cause was established and that the withholding of the informant's identity was valid because he had supplied reliable information in about twenty previous cases.
54. People v. Johnson, 15 Cal. App. 3d 939, 93 Cal. Rptr. 534 (1971); State v. Paszek, 50 Wis. 2d 619, 184 N.W.2d 836 (1971).
55. Beck v. Ohio, supra; United States v. Ventresca, 380 U.S. 102 (1965).
56. LaFave and Scott, *Criminal Law Hornbook* (St. Paul, Minn.: West, 1972), p. 404.
57. Edward C. Fisher, *Laws of Arrest* (Evanston, Illinois: North Western University, 1967), p. 134; Wayne R. LaFave, *Arrest: The Decision to Take a Suspect Into Custody* (Little, Brown and Company, 1965), p. 212.
58. *Model Penal Code* §3.07(2)(b)(iii).
59. United States v. Rabinowitz, 339 U.S. 58 (1950).
60. Chimel v. California, 395 U.S. 752 (1969).
61. Robinson v. United States, 414 U.S. 218 (1973); Gustafson v. Florida, 414 U.S. 260 (1973).
62. Wilkes, *"The New Federalism in Criminal Procedure: State Court Evasion of the Burger Court,"* 62 Ky. L. J. 421, 423 (1974); Howard, *"State Courts and Constitutional Rights in the Day of the Burger Court,"* 62 *Va. L. Rev.* 873, 891-907 (1976); People v. Jackson, 391 Mich. 323, 217 N.W.2d 22 (1974), which entitled a Michigan defendant to the assistance of counsel at any pre-trial line-up or photographic display; People v. Brisendine, 13 Cal. Rptr. 528, 531 P.2d 1099 (1975).
63. Texas v. White, 423 U.S. 67 (1975).
64. Chambers v. Maroney, 399 U.S. 42 (1970); c.f. People v. Cannon, 310 N.E.2d 673 (Ill. App. Ct. 1974).
65. South Dakota v. Opperman, 428 U.S. 364 (1976), where the Court reasoned that:

    "In the interests of public safety and as part of what the Court has called 'community caretaking functions,' automobiles are frequently taken into police custody. Vehicle accidents present one such occasion. To permit the uninterrupted flow of traffic and in some circumstances to preserve evidence, disabled or damaged vehicles will often be removed from the highways or streets at the behest of police engaged solely in caretaking and traffic-control activities. Police will also frequently remove and impound automobiles which violate parking ordinances and which thereby jeopardize both the public safety and the efficient movement of vehicular traffic. The authority of police to seize and remove from the streets vehicles impeding traffic or threatening public safety and convenience is beyond challenge.

    When vehicles are impounded, local police departments generally follow a routine practice of securing and inventorying the automobiles' contents. These procedures developed in response to three distinct needs: the protection of the owner's property while it remains in police custody; the protection of the police against claims or disputes over lost or stolen property; and the protection of the police from potential danger. The practice has been viewed as essential to respond to incidents of theft or vandalism. In addition, police frequently attempt to determine whether a vehicle has been stolen and thereafter abandoned."

66. United States v. Edwards, 415 U.S. 800 (1974).
67. See Blackford v. United States, 247 F.2d 745 (9th Cir. 1957), where the Court upheld the forcible removal of heroin from the suspect's anus when the examining officers noticed a greasy substance there. Later, while characterizing a rectal probe as a "disgusting sequence," courts have no great difficulty, apparently, attributing the necessity for it to the defendant's choice of an equally disgusting repository in the first place; also see State v. Riley, 303 Minn. Rept. 251, 226 N.W.2d 907 (1975), where the Minnesota Supreme Court held that a police officer following upon an observant rape sodomy victim's description of peculiar markings on her attacker's penis acted lawfully in taking the in-custody defendant to an interrogation room and having him drop his pants for inspection of the "alleged instrumentality of the offense."; c.f. Bouse v. Bussey, 573 F.2d 548 (9th Cir. 1977), where the Court held cognizable under 42 U.S.C. §1983 a civil suit for damages against a police officer for his actions in forcibly pulling hairs from the pubic area of the plaintiff after the plaintiff had repeatedly refused to give the officer the sample. While taking samples of physical characteristics that are constantly exposed to the public is such a minor intrusion that it does not constitute a search under the Fourth Amendment, but when the intrusion is a "painful and humiliating invasion upon the most intimate parts of the body, a search has been conducted requiring adherence to Fourth Amendment requirements."
68. Creamer v State, 229 Ga. 511, 192 S.E.2d 350 (1972); Adams v. State, 299 N.E.2d 834 (Ind. 1973).
69. O.W. Wilson, Roy C. McLaren, *Police Administration* (New York: McGraw-Hill, 1972), p. 371:

    "In most departments the detective function is organized according to the kind of offenses to be investigated. In the past, the organization of a detective bureau in many departments has been extremely detailed, with separate squads or details for each of the various crime categories and activities, such as homicide, burglary, robbery, bunco, fugitive, and so on. In recent years, however, there has been a tendency toward grouping the functional specialists—partly on the grounds that criminals tend to be less specialized themselves."
70. Miranda v. Arizona, 384 U.S. 436 (1965).
71. Miranda v. Arizona, supra, at 444-45.
72. See Comment, "Prosecutorial Discretion in the Initiation of Criminal Complaints," 42 *So. Cal. L. Rev.* 519, 528 (1969).
73. Ibid.
74. *New York Times,* September 27, 1976, p. 37.
75. Livermore, "Policing," 55 *Minn. L. Rev.* 649, 687-693 (1971).
76. *Cleveland Plain Dealer,* June 6, 1974, §A, at 12, col. 3.
77. *New York Times,* October 6, 1976, §A, p. 46.
78. *New York Times,* supra.
79. *New York Times,* July 29, 1976, §A, p. 1 and 40; *N.Y. Times,* September 19, 1976, §A, p. 25.
80. Kenneth Culp Davis, *Police Discretion* (St. Paul, Minn.: West, 1975), p. 14.
81. For instance, the *Illinois Crim. Code* 38 §11-8 declares that any person who

cohabits or has sexual intercourse with another not his spouse commits fornication, which is punishable by a fine not to exceed $200 or imprisonment not to exceed 6 months. Florida has a similar statute (see *Fla. Crim. Code* §794.05, also §798.01). Illinois also holds the breathing in of Isopropanol to create an intoxicated condition is also illegal, *Ill. Crim. Code* 38 §81-1 or see 38 §50-1, which requires in a public performance safety nets for trapeze, tightrope, rings, ropes or poles. A Georgia statute §26-9908, holds that "any person who shall pursue his business or the work of his ordinary calling on the Lord's day, shall be guilty of a misdemeanor."

82. Davis, *Police Discretion,* pp. 92-94.
83. Jerome Skolnick, *Coercion to Virtue* (submitted to the *President's Commission on Law Enforcement and Administration of Justice,* 1967).
84. Davis, *Police Discretion,* p. 54.
85. Frost, Lucianovic, and Cox, *What Happens After Arrest* (Washington, D.C.: Institute for Law and Social Research, 1977), p. 1.
86. Ibid., p. 23.
87. Ibid., p. 49.
88. There are legitimate reasons, as well, why an arrest may not blossom into a formal criminal charge; e.g., where a complaining witness has a change of heart and chooses not to press charges, or where the evidence is sufficient to satisfy the probable cause standard to justify an arrest but is insufficient to satisfy the standard for guilt at trial.
89. More, *The American Police,* p. 127.
90. *Task Force Report: The Police,* p. 127.
91. Kadish, "Legal Norm and Discretion on the Police and Sentencing Process," 75 *Harv. L. Rev.* 904, 908 (1962); *New York Times,* March 8, 1971, at 1, col. 3.
92. Kadish, "Legal Norm and Discretion," pp. 913-14.
93. Thomas J. Sweeney and William Ellingsworth, *Issues in Police Patrol* (Kansas City, Missouri: Kansas City Missouri Police Department, 1973).
94. *American Bar Foundation, The Administration of Criminal Justice in the United States, Pilot Project Report: Vol. 5, Milwaukee County, Wisconsin, 1-11.*
95. *American Bar Foundation, The Administration of Criminal Justice in the United States, Pilot Project Report,* vol. 2, Detroit, Michigan, 50.
96. *New York Times,* September 19, 1976, §1, p. 25.
97. Livermore, "Policing," pp. 649, 683-710.
98. Ibid., p. 170.
99. *Task Force Report: The Police,* p. 156; *Standards and Goals,* p. 472.
100. Ibid.:

    "Such boards may include a civilian police commission, the chief administrator of the jurisdiction, or the legislative body. Most of these boards were a product of the 1960s and for the most part have failed to achieve their purposes. One reason for this failure is that the police chief executive cannot give away his authority and accountability, and without that authority and accountability, a review board cannot perform adequately the function it is assigned because it cannot demand change."

101. Ibid., pp. 490-91.

4.

". . . because the constable has blundered"

— Judge Cardozo

Policing the Police

No criminal justice issue so vexes the public or divides the legal community than the exclusionary rule. Within this rule lies a panolpy of issues that this society must decide in determining its future directions in criminal justice: its aspirations of protecting individual liberty, its need to deter police illegality, and its need to deal effectively with crime and criminals.

The exclusionary rule requires that the police while enforcing the law must obey the law and respect a suspect's constitutional rights. The exclusionary rule polices the police. Here is how the rule works: when the police fail to accord a citizen his individual rights as contained in the Fourth Amendment (arrest, search, and seizure),[1] Fifth Amendment (privilege against self-discrimination),[2] and Sixth Amendment (right to counsel),[3] then the evidence that is secured, the fruits of police illegality, cannot be used by the state to convict that citizen.

It is impossible to overstate the impact of the exclusionary rule on the administration of criminal justice. Its application represents an incredible commitment to individual rights, a commitment unknown in its breadth in the criminal justice systems of all other countries,[4] and a willingness to submerge the truth-determining function of a criminal trial to a secondary position in favor of promoting and safeguarding individual rights.

The exclusionary rule was judicially created and designed in the nineteenth century[5] and given widespread application in this century to enhance and protect the rights guaranteed to all citizens through the Fourth, Fifth, and Sixth Amendments.

In 1914 the Supreme Court applied the exclusionary rule to letters and documents seized by federal officials from the home of a defendant in a criminal case. The language in that opinion is instructive in helping us to understand the purpose of the rule and its applicability to violations of the Fourth Amendment's prohibition of unreasonable searches and seizures:

> This protection reaches all alike, whether accused of crime or not, and the duty of giving to it force and effect is obligatory upon all intrusted under our Federal system with the enforcement of the laws. The tendency of those who execute the criminal laws of the country to obtain conviction by means of unlawful seizures and enforced confessions, the latter often obtained after subjecting accused persons to unwarranted practices destructive of rights secured by the Federal Constitution, should find no sanction in the judgments of the courts which are charged at all times with the support of the Constitution, and to which people of all conditions have a right to appeal for the maintenance of such fundamental rights.[6]

The Court in *Weeks v. United States* went on to say that if the government were permitted to use evidence secured illegally, the intentions of the framers of the Bill of Rights pledging that "every man's house is his castle" would be frustrated, and the provision of the Fourth Amendment might as well be stricken from the Constitution. The *Weeks* opinion also stressed that courts destroy their own integrity when they permit the government to use and profit from evidence that has been secured illegally.

Weeks, however, was applicable only to prosecutions in federal courts because at the time the specific guarantees of the Bill of Rights had not yet been applied to the states through the due process clause of the Fourteenth Amendment. When in 1948 the Court was asked to bind state courts with the same rule, the justices refused. While holding that the right of privacy inherent in the Fourth Amendment's prohibition against unreasonable searches and seizures was applicable to the states as "basic to a free society" and "inherent in ordered liberty," the Court nonetheless refused to apply the exclusionary rule. At the time, a majority of states had rejected the exclusionary rule, and the Supreme Court said that since the rule was not explicitly mentioned in the Constitution and was purely a matter of judicial implication, the states were free to devise their own methods for protecting individual privacy.[7]

Thirteen years later, in the landmark decision of *Mapp v. Ohio,* a different majority prevailed in the Supreme Court and the exclusionary rule was applied to the states. The Supreme Court said that this change was due to the fact that the other remedies for illegal searches and seizures had completely failed to secure compliance with the constitutional provisions. Now the majority established the exclusionary rule as a necessary safeguard against unreasonable searches and seizures, one of the fundamental rights guaranteed by the federal Constitution.[8]

From this lineage, standards have been developed delineating and giving substance to these constitutional principles. At the same time, these standards have provided guidelines for police intrusions into these constitutionally protected areas. For example, the Fourth Amendment's language guaranteeing individual privacy from unreasonable searches and seizures is hardly self-explanatory. Judicial interpretation was required to ascertain the limits of *reasonable versus unreasonable* intrusions. It was only in this fashion that an evolving society could learn which arrests and searches were permissible and which ones were not. Similarly, it became necessary for the courts to devise a set of guidelines for the conditions surrounding the interrogation of a suspect. The Fifth Amendment proclaims that no person shall be compelled to be a witness against himself. Certainly compulsion is not limited to the rack and thumbscrew. But to make the standard relevant to our society in this century, judicial decisions were required to re-define compulsion, and define those circumstances that rendered a statement "compelled" and in violation of the constitutional guarantee.

Operation of the Exclusionary Rule

Louisiana police had a bench warrant for the arrest of Donald Vale for failing to appear in court. The officers staking out Vale's house observed a man drive up and sound his car horn twice. Vale came out of the house, spoke to the man in the car, looked up and down the street twice, and returned inside. Vale reappeared shortly, scanned the street again, and then walked over to the car and leaned inside. The police, convinced that they had just witnessed a narcotics sale, converged on the two men. The man in the car placed something in his mouth when he saw the police approach. When both men were apprehended, the police entered Vale's house and after two searches found a large quantity of hard drugs in a bedroom.

Robert Williams, an escapee from a mental institution, was apprehended for the rape-murder of a ten-year-old girl abducted from the YMCA where Williams was living. A fourteen-year-old boy had seen Williams place a bundle wrapped in a blanket in the trunk of a car. The boy saw two legs sticking out of the bundle. Upon the advice of counsel, Williams surrendered to Davenport, Iowa, police. He was driven to Des Moines, the scene of the abduction, by police who would not let one of his attorneys accompany him in the police car, although the police did promise the attorney that they would not interrogate or mistreat Williams during the ride. Prior to the ride, Williams was advised of his rights and counselled by the attorney not to make any statements to the police. During the trip between Davenport and Des Moines, one of the detectives accompanying Williams addressed him as follows:

> "I want to give you something to think about while we're traveling down the road. Number one, I want you to observe the

weather conditions, it's raining, it's sleeting, it's freezing, driving is very treacherous, visibility is poor, it's going to be dark early this evening. They are predicting several inches of snow for tonight, and I feel that you yourself are the only person that knows where this little girl's body is, that you yourself have only been there once, and if you get a snow on top of it you yourself may be unable to find it. And, since we will be going right past the area on the way into Des Moines, I feel that we could stop and locate the body, that the parents of this little girl should be entitled to a Christian burial for the little girl who was snatched away from them on Christmas Eve and murdered. And I feel we should stop and locate it on the way in rather than waiting until morning and trying to come back out after a snow storm and possibly not being able to find it at all."

After a little more conversation, Williams directed the two officers to the place where he had hidden the body.

Vale v. Louisiana[9] and *Williams v. Brewer*[10] have several points in common: both defendants were convicted when trial judges denied motions to suppress critical evidence; the narcotics found in Vale's bedroom and the Williams' statement. Both convictions were reversed because the Supreme Court found the police practices in each case to be in violation of the defendant's constitutional rights. Each defendant could be retried following the reversal but without the tainted evidence that was ordered excluded.[11] Finally, it is likely that both convictions would have been upheld in any other country and the excluded evidence would have been admissible.

These cases illustrate the exclusionary rule in action. The exclusionary rule in both these cases precluded use of the evidence and therefore resulted in reversals of convictions of persons guilty of crimes. Although each defendant was guilty, there was an official violation of fundamental rights that resulted in the activation of the exclusionary rule at trial and the resulting suppression of evidence.[12]

Application of the Rule

To Searches

Once *Mapp* incorporated the exclusionary rule into the Fourteenth Amendment and made it a part of the due process protection of privacy applicable to the states, the extent of the federal constitutional protection against illegal arrests, searches, and seizures became the same for state illegal intrusions as it was for violations by federal law enforcement officers.[13]

How much information a police officer has prior to an intrusion—in order to justify that intrusion—determines whether or not his interference with a person's privacy is "reasonable" in the eyes of the law. If an officer notices that a person is acting suspiciously, that the person has been standing, for example, in front of a jewelry shop for two hours and that he has signalled to a car that has also been in the vicinity for the same amount of time, the officer's decision to stop and question the suspicious character would be regarded as sound and his actions reasonable beyond a doubt. An initial stopping for questioning requires that an officer act on more than a hunch, that there are some fairly strong articulatable indications that a crime is in the making.[14] On the other hand, an arrest requires that an officer act on a probable cause determination; in other words, because an arrest constitutes a tremendous intrusion into another's privacy, an officer must act according to his *conclusion* (not *suspicion*) that a crime has been committed and that the person to be arrested did commit the crime.[15]

So far, the exclusionary rule plays no role. If the suspect is unreasonably, and hence, illegally, stopped and questioned or arrested, there is nothing to suppress. An illegal arrest does not rob the court of its jurisdiction;[16] the exclusionary rule will be activated and the evidence suppressed only if the arrest leads to a search that turns up evidence. If a police officer makes an illegal arrest and then searches the suspect but finds nothing, there is likewise nothing to exclude from evidence.

On the other hand, many illegal arrests turn up incriminating evidence during the search of the suspect that automatically follows the arrest. The heroin found in a suspect's pocket may be the only evidence on which to base a prosecution. Whether or not the heroin may be used as evidence against the suspect at trial, however, depends on the legality of the arrest that led to the search. What the court will have to determine is whether the facts and circumstances known to the police officer immediately prior to the arrest provided probable cause to justify the arrest.[17] If the court finds that the officer had probable cause, then the arrest is considered legal and the subsequent search permissible, and the evidence will not be excluded at trial. If the officer was operating on a hunch or otherwise lacked probable cause, then the arrest is considered illegal, the search not legal, and the evidence must be excluded.

The very language of the Fourth Amendment providing that no warrant shall issue but upon probable cause was, itself, a reaction of the founders of this country to the General Warrants and Writs of Assistance used by the

English colonial authorities to enforce the crown's customs and tax laws against the colonists. Writs of Assistance were granted to customs officers authorizing them to enter homes and places of business at random and search for evidence of violations of the law. Once issued, the holder of a Writ did not have to seek court permission to make such searches, nor did he later have to explain his reasons for the invasion.[18] This massive repudiation of the English concept of individual privacy that a man's home was his castle and, as such, sanctuary from government intrusion was, in fact, one of the precipitous causes of the Revolutionary War. It is easily understandable that the drafters of the Bill of Rights would seek forever to keep their new government from exercising like powers. Thus it would not be likely that the relaxation of the warrant requirement for arrests would be extended to searches. Yet the history of the Fourth Amendment has not run true to that expectation.

The requirement that a warrant, supported by probable cause, is necessary before a search may be conducted of a person, or his home or effects is riddled with exceptions. Far more warrantless searches—most of them permissible under the exceptions—take place than searches with warrants. Most exceptions to the search warrant requirement originated (as did exceptions to arrest warrants) with the notion that certain conditions create emergency situations that justify immediate action rather than having the police apply to a court for a search warrant and then await its issuance. The exceptions have gone far beyond emergency situations.

Incident to a Lawful Arrest

Any time a police officer makes a lawful arrest, the arrested person and the area within his immediate reach are subject to a full search for weapons and evidence of the crime.[19] The full search of the person is applicable to traffic and minor offenses as well as serious crimes.[20]

With Consent

No warrant or probable cause is required when searches are done with the consent of the person searched. What is required is a valid consent, a free relinquishment of the constitutional right to privacy and a waiver of the requirement that the police officer secure a warrant. In order for the consent to be valid it must be freely given and represent a voluntary choice made by the person consenting. Any coercion or misinformation by the police officer invalidates the approval and any evidence found during such a search pursuant to an invalid consent will be excluded from trial. The Burger Court has defined consent as a decision which is voluntarily made and is not the product of duress. In arriving at this definition, this Court specifically rejected the idea that a police officer need advise a person of his right not to consent.[21]

Automobiles

The present Supreme Court has virtually written the warrant clause out of the Constitution when it comes to automobiles. Because of their mobility, automobiles have long been treated separately.[22] But what started as a recognition of an exception to the warrant requirement when emergency conditions justified foregoing a warrant has blossomed today into a general exception permitting warrantless searches of automobiles as long as the police officer has independent probable cause prior to the search to justify the intrusion.[23]

Other General Exceptions

When there is an emergency, it would not be good police practice nor in the interests of the community to require a police officer to secure a warrant prior to attending to the emergency situation. Consequently, when an officer is in *hot pursuit*[24] of a fleeing felon or where there is reason to believe that evidence will be destroyed if time is taken to secure a warrant, the warrant requirement will be abandoned. Similarly, search warrants are not required if the items seen and seized are in *plain view,* are in *open fields* rather than in the immediate area surrounding a house, or are *abandoned property.*[25]

To Eavesdropping

The adoption of privacy as the core protection of the Fourth Amendment automatically expanded the scope of that constitutional right to the act of eavesdropping.[26] Prior to privacy, the Amendment's protections were linked to property rights. When property was the basis of the right, it limited the scope of the Amendment's protection in the area of eavesdropping, the most insidious type of intrusion because, unlike the arrest or search of a person, eavesdropping can take place without the subject ever knowing about it. While property was the object of protection by the Fourth Amendment, only eavesdropping that involved a violation of the individual's property rights, such as an illegal entry to set a listening device in place, was covered by the constitutional tests of reasonableness and probable cause. Technology far outstripped the constitutional protection when seeing and listening devices were developed that did not require an illegal entry or even attachment of a physical object to the house.

The acceptance of the privacy notion brought with it an examination of the reasonableness of the government's intrusion, the warrant requirement, and the standard of probable cause. Without these standards, law enforcement officers could eavesdrop indiscriminately and continuously, becoming privy not only to evidence of crime but to the most personal types of communication as well. Broadening the scope of the Fourth Amendment protection to include eavesdropping certainly has not eliminated all such illegal activity by law enforcement officers. Because if the government is fiercely intent on invading and destroying individual privacy, it will always have the means. But if it does so to gather evidence of a crime for purposes of prosecution, the government must subject itself to judicial scrutiny through the warrant procedure prior to the intrusion and accept judicially imposed limitations on the intrusion, or face the suppression of any evidence so secured.

Federal legislation now authorizes limited wiretapping. The standard of reasonableness applicable to wiretapping and other forms of eavesdropping is fairly clear, the prerequisite being that a warrant must be obtained from a judge who finds that probable cause exists to believe: a crime has been or is about to be committed; that evidence concerning that crime will be obtained through this manner; and that normal investigative procedures are unlikely or too dangerous to produce that evidence. In short, wiretapping and eavesdropping are extraordinary law enforcement tools, only to be used in extraordinary circumstances and not to be nonchalantly substituted for other law enforcement techniques.[27]

All of these requirements apply when only one person to the conversation has not condoned the interception. If a person consents to a tap of his telephone, the Fourth Amendment protections are not applicable. Here again the limitation on the expectation of privacy comes into play. When one exchanges information or a confidence with another person, one always runs the risk that the person told will inform the authorities. Therefore, it is reasoned, one has a limited expectation of privacy when communicating, and Fourth Amendment standards are not applicable when one party consents to the intrusion.[28]

To Confessions

Development of the exclusionary rule with respect to confessions followed a different course than that applicable to searches and arrests. Evidence suppressed because of an illegal search may be reliable evidence of guilt but is barred from being used in a criminal trial in order to protect the Fourth Amendment rights of American citizens and to deter illegal practices. The first confessions that were barred from use in criminal trials were secured through police torture and use of third-degree methods and were considered highly unreliable because individuals could be expected to confess to anything simply to secure a cessation of the torture. A guilty verdict rendered on the basis of a forced confession could only be regarded as highly unreliable.[29]

As this area of law developed the Supreme Court continued to devise tests to determine the admissibility of confessions based upon voluntariness and illegal police practices.[30] The exclusionary rule concerning confessions reached full maturity when the Supreme Court applied the Fifth Amendment privilege against self-incrimination to state criminal proceedings through the due process clause of the Fourteenth Amendment,[31] and two years later (in 1966) rendered its landmark decision, *Miranda v. Arizona.*[32]

After *Miranda,* confessions are to be excluded unless law enforcement officials adhere to an imposed code of procedures designed to insure that confessions or other statements made by defendants in custody are not coerced. The Court reasoned that the only way to prevent coercion was to be certain that coercive elements of the police interrogation process were ameliorated by advising an accused of his right to remain silent and not make a statement or answer any questions, and by introducing a lawyer into the setting if the accused desired counsel. Thus the exclusionary rule for confessions had taken some major turns. Reliability of the confession was no longer the primary concern. Like its Fourth Amendment counterpart, the exclusion of confessions became a vehicle for promoting individual dignity and freedom by safeguarding the Fifth Amendment privilege against self-incrimination and by deterring official violations of that constitutional right.

Miranda probably provoked the most widespread and hostile criticism of any of the Supreme Court's decisions in the criminal area.[33] The Court was accused of robbing police of interrogation as an effective law enforcement technique by requiring that an accused be advised of his right to remain silent and to consult counsel before any interrogation.

The Burger Court has been offered opportunities to abandon the *Miranda* rules, but even though it has diluted the requirements and the decision's impact,[34] the Court has refused to reverse. *Williams v. Brewer,* described at the beginning of this chapter, was thought to be a vehicle through which the Burger majority might totally abandon *Miranda.* The facts in *Brewer* were compelling: (1) a brutal murder of a child; (2) a defendant having been previously advised of his rights; and (3) the interrogating officer's statement to Williams that he did not want him to answer his questions or respond to the police officer's comments about the anguish of the child's family. By the narrowest of margins, five to four, the Supreme Court refrained from reversing *Miranda* when the majority ignored the Fifth Amendment and treated it as a Sixth Amendment right to counsel case. The majority concentrated on the fact that the interrogation that took place in the police car occurred after Williams' attorney was refused permission to accompany him on the ride and was promised by the police officers that no interrogation would take place during the trip. In the face of angry dissents,[35] the majority found that Williams' response to the officer's "Christian burial" speech was not the proper kind of waiver of his right to counsel, and that courts must presume that the right is not waived unless it is specifically done.

To Derivative Evidence

Violations of fundamental constitutional rights have been likened to a growing tree. When the evidence branching from that initial violation is excluded from the trial, any subsequent derivative evidence to which the police are directed by the original inadmissible evidence is considered to be the "fruit of the poisonous tree."[36]

Examples of derivative evidence may help to clarify the analogy. If a defendant is arrested illegally and then taken to the police station where he is interrogated after having been scrupulously advised of his constitutional right to remain silent, any confession which he makes is derivative evidence of the illegal arrest. Even though the suspect was advised of his *Miranda* rights (and the confession would be admissible at trial on that score) it would still be inadmissible because it is a by-product, a "fruit," of the original illegal arrest. Similarly, if a suspect were lawfully taken into custody but then interrogated without the *Miranda* warnings, clearly any statement or confession would be inadmissible. But what if the defendant's inadmissible confession discloses where he has hidden a gun used during the commission of a crime? Should that gun, too, be suppressed and not admitted at trial? It is certainly derivative of the original constitutional violation. The branches can be extended even further. What if, when looking for the gun in the location where the suspect in his inadmissible confession indicated it would be found, police encounter a passer-by who tells them that he observed someone hiding something in that area, and later identifies the suspect as the person seen hiding an item where the weapon was found? Should the passer-by's testimony be excluded? It, too, is derivative of the original inadmissible confession.

The inquiry becomes whether or not a definitive line should be drawn between the evidence produced by the initial constitutional violation and all evidence ultimately derived from that initial violation. Largely, where an individual judge or scholar would limit the derivative evidence rule often depends upon his views concerning the validity, soundness, and desirability of the exclusionary rule.

It is plain that a confession gained through an illegal arrest would not have been forthcoming, except under the most unusual of coincidences, had the suspect escaped detection. Nevertheless, many courts are loosening up on derivative evidence principles; and by accepting certain types of evidence obtained through illegal police practices, these courts are cutting down on the scope of the exclusionary rule.

Although there are no hard and fast rules in the area, two tests have emerged to aid courts in determining whether or not certain evidence derived from an illegal police practice is too tainted to be admitted into the court. The first test permits the courts to decide whether or not the constitutional violation was still operating at the time the police acquired the derivative evidence. What the court must decide is whether the derivative evidence was the direct product of the illegal arrest or whether the illegal arrest was too remote a factor in the overall scheme of events to be regarded as a primary determinant of the confession. For example, in one case a defendant who was illegally arrested was freed on bail. Obviously suffering from a guilty conscience, the suspect returned to the police station and confessed. The Supreme Court held that the confession was the product of the defendant's free will rather than a direct consequence of the original illegal arrest. Even though the defendant may never have confessed if he had not been arrested, the amount of elapsed time between the arrest and his admission of guilt took precedence over the initial issue—the illegality of the arrest. His confession was realistically regarded by the Court as bearing little relation to the illegal arrest: the fact that the suspect was compelled to confess even after the initial effects of the illegal arrest had worn off convinced the Court that the arrest had a relatively insignificant role in this case.[37]

Regardless of a suspect's willingness to confess or to offer information, there are some cases where a court could never accept a guilt admission or other proffered evidence by the suspect. These cases are generally based on confessions or offered bits of evidential information made by a suspect under the immediate influence of an illegal arrest. For instance, in one case a suspect who was arrested and given the *Miranda* warning confessed to her crime within two hours. Although the suspect volunteered to confess, the arrest was considered the proximate cause of the confession, and therefore it could not be admitted.[38] No court could ever accept such a confession because its relation to the illegal arrest renders it far too impure to pass constitutional muster.

Derivative evidence may also be admissible, notwithstanding the constitutional violation, if the prosecution can establish an independent source for that evidence and demonstrate that the evidence would have been inevitably discovered in the course of a lawful investigation even if it had not been secured as a result of the original police misconduct.[39] Thus a gun found at the scene of the crime as a result of a statement given by the suspect while being interrogated without having been advised of his *Miranda* warnings may still be admissible as evidence at trial. That gun would not be barred as inadmissible evidence if the prosecution can establish that the crime area would have been thoroughly searched, and the weapon would have been discovered in the course of normal police investigation.[40] Often, however, trial courts appear to deviate from this rule; instead of determining whether the item *would* have been discovered, courts have accepted questionable evidence after a showing by the prosecution that it *could* have been discovered. This tendency is wrong, however, because a showing that evidence *could* have been discovered does not at all demonstrate that it *would* have been found other than through exploitation of the constitutional violation.

"Because the Constable Has Blundered..."

The exclusionary rule has been a controversial subject since its inception. Even when it was used in the confession area solely to exclude statements from defendants secured through the use of third-degree methods, its adoption was attacked and law enforcement officers devised methods to avoid its application. In brutality cases, the rule has been used to exclude inherently unreliable evidence that could lead to the conviction of innocent persons. When the rule is used to exclude evidence found by the police during an illegal search and seizure, however, it is being used to exclude reliable evidence of guilt because of the manner in which the evidence was secured. Yet, by excluding reliable evidence, the accuracy and reliability of the truth-determining process is affected. Because of the operation of the rule, many guilty persons have gone free. Obviously, the adoption of a rule that detracts from the system's ability to convict guilty defendants must be based upon very strong policy reasons and premises.

Proponents and detractors of the exclusionary rule differ violently on the validity and soundness of those policy reasons. Those who favor its retention and maintenance at full strength consider the exclusionary rule to be the greatest evidence of this society's commitment to individual freedom and the protection of the rights and dignity of each citizen. They maintain that by excluding evidence secured in violation of these fundamental rights enumerated in the Amendments to the federal Constitution, this society reaffirms its commitment to the rule of law and the supremacy of the individual over government expediency by demonstrating that it holds those constitutional rights to be more important than its interest in convicting criminals. They point to the period of history prior to the widespread application of the exclusionary rule as testimony that other available legal remedies are inept at preventing illegal police practices that violate individual constitutional rights. They argue that even if the exclusionary rule has not satisfactorily deterred illegal police practices, its abandonment now would make these practices rampant and significantly increase the incidence of police-state tactics.

Those who would significantly curtail the operation of the exclusionary rule argue with equal vehemence that the device is nothing more than a windfall for the criminal and not protective of the constitutional rights of the community as a whole. Their principal argument is that the cost of the exclusionary rule to the society is too high, and that the return on the investment is not guaranteed. Obviously, the community as a whole suffers when reliable evidence is excluded and guilty defendants go free because of constitutional violations committed by law enforcement officers. The rule's opponents contend that this remedy hardly enhances the fundamental rights enumerated in the Bill of Rights and results in the community's loss of confidence in the criminal justice system. This position was first and most eloquently voiced by then New York Court of Appeals Judge Cardozo, later a United States Supreme Court Justice, when he questioned the propriety and wisdom of a rule that permits "[t]he criminal. . . to go free because the constable has blundered."[41] The trump card offered by opponents of the rule is that empirical studies tend to show that the exclusionary rule has little effect upon the day-to-day conduct of police officers,[42] and that if an officer wishes to harass a citizen or run roughshod over that citizen's constitutional rights, the possible application of the exclusionary rule will not prevent it. Finally, they argue that alternative remedies offer more appropriate means of enforcing constitutional rights.

No constitutional right limiting the powers of government is self-enforcing. In any society rights are vindicated only if a competent and alert judiciary is able and willing to enforce those rights by telling other branches of government that they have exceeded their powers and must back off. The guarantees enumerated in the Bill of Rights are no different. The Fourth Amendment's guarantee of privacy, the right to be left alone, is a meaningless collection of words unless the government is willing or is forced to abide by them.

The exclusionary rule, itself, does not stop illegal arrests or searches, nor does it prevent coercive interrogation. Nor can the exclusionary rule independently prevent recurrences of these constitutional violations. Its success in doing so must be predicated upon a grass-roots reaction to the loss of convictions resulting from constitutional violations. If the general community were to assert itself and put heat on its elected representatives, who in turn would bear down on the police hierarchy, police commanders would be compelled to make their subordinates cognizant of the fact that the loss of convictions resulting from the exclusion of evidence because of constitutional violations is totally unacceptable. Internal police disciplinary action would be geared to insure that the lesson is learned. Training programs for field officers would stress police procedures consistent with the constitutional limitations so that individual officers would be schooled in how they may react and how far they may go. In other words, for the exclusionary rule to deter illegal police practices, the in-court rejection of evidence is not enough. Prosecutors, sworn to uphold the Constitution as part of their oath of office, are obligated to express their chagrin at the loss of criminal cases resulting from constitutional violations and should exercise their ability to pressure the police to conform to the constitutional mandates.

Since the rule's adoption, the ensuing reaction has not been directed towards the constable whose intentional misconduct or blunder caused the loss of the case, but instead consternation was heaped upon the constitutional rule and the courts that have applied it. Police, prosecutors, and politicians have fueled this reaction rather than recognizing their responsibilities in the area.

Persons are stopped and searched on streets without concern for reasonableness, let alone probable cause, as demanded by the Constitution. Telephones are tapped indiscriminately without securing a warrant. Judges issue warrants authorizing searches and taps without consideration for whether the law enforcement officers have shown a reasonable basis to justify the intrusion. Defendants are arrested and then questioned without being advised of their rights because the police officers want a statement and do not care about the constitutional niceties designed to protect the accused.

Some violations committed by the police are not so blatant and intentional. Some violations involve good faith errors of judgment or the failure to adhere to technical requirements, such as proper signatures on the warrant, and perhaps should be treated differently.[43] The differences in the nature of the violations create some of the controversy and raise questions as to whether the results of all violations should be treated alike, but the vast majority are neither technical, products of errors of judgment, or unintentional. Usually, the violations occur because law enforcement officers want to conduct a search or interrogation and ignore the constitutional standards because they believe that if they adhere to the law, desirable evidence will be lost.

Discussion Questions

1. What is the purpose of the exclusionary rule? How does it work?

2. What is meant by the following statement:
"The community suffers because the constable has blundered."

3. Opponents of the exclusionary rule frequently charge that it "handcuffs the police" and that the only way to effectively deal with crime and criminals is to abolish the exclusionary rule. Discuss the meaning of this statement. Are these opponents of the exclusionary rule limiting their criticism to the rule or does their criticism go beyond the rule to the Fourth Amendment protection?

4. Why should evidence which is derivative of an illegal search or improperly secured confession be also barred from use at trial under the exclusionary rule? Is that extension of the rule necessary or would the purposes of the exclusionary rule be sufficiently satisfied if derivative evidence could be used by the prosecution?

5. What principles of criminal justice are operating in the confession area that make it desirable to have police advise a suspect of his rights prior to their interrogation of him?

Notes

1. Weeks v. United States, 232 U.S. 383 (1914); Mapp v. Ohio, 367 U.S. 643 (1961).
2. Miranda v. Arizona, 384 U.S. 436 (1966).
3. Brewer v. Williams, 430 U.S. 387 (1977).
4. In Canada, for example, all evidence secured through illegal arrests or searches is admissible; "involuntary" confessions are excluded.
5. Boyd v. United States, 116 U.S. 616 (1886).
6. Weeks v. United States, 232 U.S. 383, at 392 (1914).
7. Wolf v. Colorado, 338 U.S. 25 (1949).
8. Mapp v. Ohio, 367 U.S. 643 (1961).
9. Vale v. Louisiana, 399 U.S. 30 (1970).
10. Williams v. Brewer, 430 U.S. 387 (1977).
11. After Williams' conviction was reversed in the Supreme Court, he was retried and convicted again in Iowa.
12. It is important to note that a defendant is not immune from conviction as long as there is sufficient, untainted evidence on which to convict. For example, the landmark Miranda case dealing with confession was in reality a consolidation of

four confession cases from Arizona, New York, California, and a federal court. All four convictions were reversed because of the manner in which the confessions were secured, but all four defendants were retried and convicted without those confessions.

It does not always work that way, however, and often without the tainted evidence there is no evidence on which to base a second trial and conviction. A good example is Escobedo v. Illinois, a case that set the groundwork for the Miranda decision decided two years later. Escobedo was convicted of the murder of his brother-in-law. He made a statement to Chicago police after they had denied his request to see his lawyer who was in the anteroom. The Supreme Court reversed Escobedo's conviction and he was not retried because the state did not have enough other evidence to warrant the expenditure of resources on a retrial. Escobedo was subsequently convicted and imprisoned for later offenses, but the original case is noteworthy because the operation of the exclusionary rule foreclosed use of the confession and conviction for the earlier offense.

13. Ker v. California, 374 U.S. 23 (1963); Aguilar v. Texas, 378 U.S. 108 (1964).
14. Terry v. Ohio, 392 U.S. 1 (1968).
15. See Kamisar, LaFave, and Israel, *Modern Criminal Procedure,* 4th ed. (St. Paul, Minn.: West, 1974), pp. 254-55.
16. Frisbie v. Collins, 342 U.S. 519 (1952); cf. United States v. Toscanino, 500 F.2d 267 (2d Cir. 1974), where the accused claimed that he was kidnapped, tortured, and returned to this country to stand trial.
17. Beck v. Ohio, 379 U.S. 89 (1964).
18. While England has abolished the Writ of Assistance, it is still used in Canada to search for narcotics.
19. Chimel v. California, 395 U.S. 752 (1969).
20. United States v. Robinson, 414 U.S. 218; Gustafson v. Florida, 414 U.S. 260 (1973).
21. Schneckloth v. Bustamente, 412 U.S. 218 (1978).
22. Carroll v. United States, 267 U.S. 132 (1925).
23. Chambers v. Maroney, 399 U.S. 42 (1970); Texas v. White, 423 U.S. 67 (1975). Police may also make inventory searches of automobiles that they tow away or otherwise lawfully seize, all done without a search warrant. See South Dakota v. Opperman, 428 U.S. 364 (1976).
24. Warden v. Hayden, 387 U.S. 294 (1967).
25. See Israel and LaFave, *Criminal Procedure in a Nutshell* (St. Paul, Minn.: West, 1975), pp. 89-94.
26. Katz v. United States, 389 U.S. 347 (1967).
27. *Title III, Omnibus Crime Control and Safe Streets Act of 1968,* 18 U.S.C. 2510 et seq.
28. Rathbun v. United States, 355 U.S. 107 (1957).
29. Brown v. Mississippi, 297 U.S. 278 (1936).
30. See e.g., Ashcraft v. Tenn., 322 U.S. 143 (1944); Spano v. New York, 360 U.S. 315 (1959); Crooker v. California, 357 U.S. 433 (1958).
31. Malloy v. Hogan, 378 U.S. 1 (1964).
32. Miranda v. Arizona, 384 U.S. 436 (1966).
33. For example, see F. Inbau and J. Reid, *Criminal Interrogation and Confessions,* 2nd ed. (Baltimore, Md.: Williams and Wilkins, 1967), where on page 1, the authors wrote, "The unfortunate consequences [of the Miranda decision] will not rest upon ... [the police officers who will be denied confessions] but rather upon the shoulders of the makers [The Supreme Court] of the rules."

34. See e.g., Michigan v. Mosley, 423 U.S. 96 (1975); Harris v. New York, 401 U.S. 222 (1971).

35. Chief Justice Burger wrote the angriest dissent characterizing the result as "intolerable in any society which purports to call itself an organized society."

36. Nardone v. United States, 308 U.S. 338 (1939).

37. Wong Sun v. United States, 371 U.S. 471 (1963).

38. Brown v. Illinois, 422 U.S. 590 (1975).

39. Nardone v. United States, 308 U.S. 338 (1939).

40. People v. Fitzpatrick, 32 N.Y.2d 499, 300 N.E.2d 139, cert. denied, 414 U.S. 1050 (1973); LaCount and Girese, "The 'Inevitable Discovery'Rule: An Evolving Exception to the Constitutional Exclusionary Rule," 40 *Albany L. Rev.,* 483 (1976).

41. People v. Defore, 242 N.Y. 13, 150 N.E. 585 (1926).

42. Oaks, "Studying the Exclusionary Rule in Search and Seizure," 37 *U. of Chicago L. Rev.* 665 (1970); see also, summary of studies testing efficacy of Miranda in American Law Institute, *Model Code of Pre-Arraignment Procedures* (Study Draft #1, 1968), pp. 101-149.

43. Supreme Court Justice Byron White in Stone v. Powell, 428 U.S. 465, at 536 (1976), advocated modification of the exclusionary rule "so as to prevent its application in those many circumstances where the evidence at issue was seized by an officer acting in the good-faith belief that his conduct comported with existing law and having reasonable grounds for this belief." In Stone, Chief Justice Burger advocated total abandonment of the exclusionary rule. Id. at 496.

No. 41-M-Commitment for Grand Jury

Municipal Court of the

______, County of ______

______ of ______

State of New Jersey

State of New Jersey,

vs.

Defendant.

CO
GRA

STATE OF NEW JERSEY, } ss
COUNTY OF

To the Sheriff, Jailor or any Constable, Marshal or any Officer
Police, or any Police Officer or Special Officer of said county:

WHEREAS, County of
of
before this Court on the complaint of of
of the
in the State aforesaid, charging the said defendant with a

Part III
Pursuing Fairness

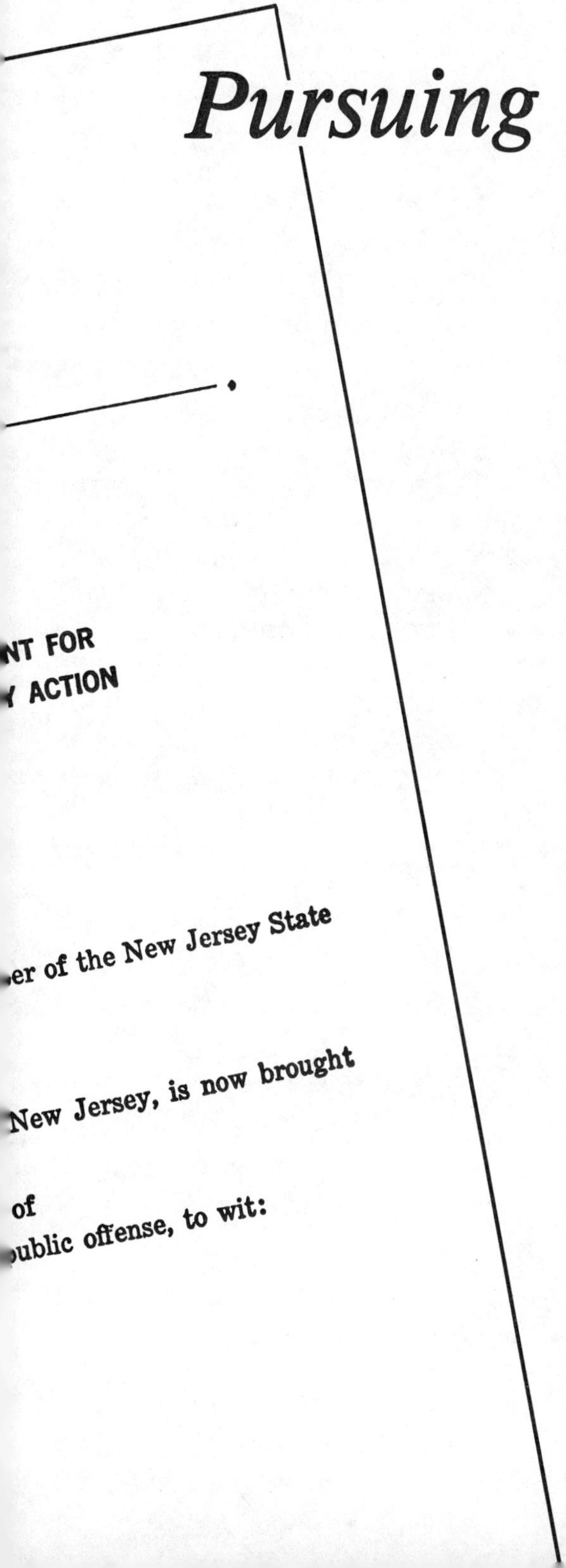

5.

They took me to court the next day. I don't recall whether the judge informed me of my rights. I was wearing handcuffs until the time when the bailiff or whoever it was called my name. There was a gentleman there who was prosecuting and he charged me at that point with stabbing with intent. They went through the process. I wasn't paying too much attention because, to tell the truth, I was afraid and I didn't know what they were doing and what was going on all the time.

The Prosecuting Power

Once the suburban police officers arrested Ralph Johnson for the knifing of his roommate, the decision whether Johnson would ever appear in court and, if so, the level of the charge to be filed against him, rested with the prosecuting attorney. The prosecuting attorney has tremendous importance in this and every society because of the enormous powers and responsibilities vested in the office. Unlike the defense attorney whose responsibilities are limited to providing effective assistance for his client, the prosecutor has a dual function. In addition to representing the state in criminal cases, the prosecutor has the obligation to see that justice is done, not simply that defendants are convicted.

The Prosecutorial Role

In most counties in the United States the prosecutor is assigned the responsibility for handling all litigation involving the governmental unit. The prosecutor represents all county offices in civil litigation, but the major responsibility and power vested in the office lie in its authority in the criminal area.

Within the context of the criminal justice process, the prosecutor is the single most important power center. As the representative of the state and the community interests, the prosecuting attorney has a tremendous amount of power; he has the responsibility to determine which offenses will be fully prosecuted, which offenses will not be prosecuted at all, and most importantly which offenders will be fully prosecuted. The enormity of this power is accentuated by the lack of accountability that is built into the system. Not only does the prosecutor make the initial policies upon which decisions to charge are based, at every stage of a criminal case he has virtually unlimited power to dismiss or pursue a prosecution.

As the agency responsible for the orderly flow of cases through the process, prosecutorial polices on screening, charging, and plea negotiations will largely determine how well the criminal justice system is capable of handling the case flow. The absence of concrete policies at this level will result in an unmanaged case flow guaranteed to result in backlogged cases, long delays, and an inability to deal with serious threats to community safety. While courts no longer permit the prosecutor to make docketing decisions and now correctly handle the management of their own calendars and the court's time, effective court management still requires the input and cooperation of the prosecuting attorney.

Another reason for the prosecutor's office being a power center is that it is the only agency that continuously works with every other component of the criminal justice system. Prosecutors must work closely with the police in the development of charging policies and the preparation of each case.[1] Prosecutors must also work closely with the defense bar to insure an orderly transfer of information and maintain a climate that is ripe for plea negotiations. While the defense attorney and the prosecutor are adversaries, the prosecutor is obligated not to over-emphasize the adversary nature of the relationship and concentrate upon winning at all costs. In his dealings with the defense attorney, the prosecutor must not lose sight of his singular and unique responsibility, to see that justice is done.

Prosecutorial Policies

There are more than 3400 county prosecutors or district attorneys in the United States.[2] Most are elected, although some states provide for appointment either by the local court or by the attorney general. Most prosecutors preside in small offices with one or two assistants. Because of the dearth of criminal work in some jurisdictions, many prosecutors are permitted to maintain a private practice, so long as it does not interfere with their official duties.[3]

While the details of prosecuting are essentially the same, how a particular prosecutor's office functions is basically determined by the size of the community. The complexity of the job increases with the size of the office which is, in turn, dependent upon the population of the community. Representing the state in a given criminal case is the same in Los Angeles, California as it is in tiny Nashville, Indiana, but the decisions as to which cases are tried and at what charge are very different. A prosecutor in a small community is usually not overwhelmed by criminal cases. The decision to prosecute, therefore, is often based on who the accused is rather than on the necessity to weed out cases from amongst hundreds—the task of the prosecutor in highly populated areas. And finally, when making decisions based upon who a potential defendant is and his place in the community, the prosecutor in a small community is more subject to the disapproval of the populace than he would be in a larger city where his actions are more likely to go unnoticed by the general citizenry.

In larger, more urban areas where there is more than one prosecutor, the decision-making process is far more complex. Offices that are comprised of two or more prosecutors must operate according to certain policies that will insure uniform decisions. The integrity of large prosecutorial offices is undermined when the decisions that are made by the individual prosecutors and their assistants represent little more than personal whims.

The policies that determine which cases will be selected for prosecution and which cases will not differ from county to county within one state. Even though each county prosecutor within one state functions under the same law, each office is autonomous. For example, there are 317 different prosecution jurisdictions in Texas,[4] which means that within that one state the application of the law from one community to another may be significantly different, depending on each prosecutor's individual policies. For instance, a surreptitious entry of a business establishment may be charged as a burglary, which is a serious felony, in one community while a prosecutor in another jurisdiction within the same state may, for the identical crime, enter a charge of breaking and entering, which is a less serious felony and, in some states, a misdemeanor.[5] The differences in policies are clearly reflected in the varying approaches to crimes that are not considered serious felonies. Several years ago, for example, the State's Attorney in Montgomery County, Maryland, adjacent to the District of Columbia, directed his assistants not to file charges against persons caught with small amounts of marijuana if the facts indicated that the drug was for the individual's personal use and not for sale or distribution.[6] Because that policy did not exist in adjoining counties, enforcement policies regarding the law against marijuana usage were significantly different within the same state.

Consider the existence of selective prosecution policies in New York City. Each of the five boroughs that comprise the city are distinct counties with separately elected district attorneys. If any one of those prosecutors adopts a policy which is significantly different from the policy in the other four boroughs, the impact and force of the law would differ within parts of one city. Theoretically, the election of prosecutors on a county level insures that the chief law enforcement officer of the county is answerable to an electorate in the immediate area and, hopefully, responsive to its needs and legitimate desires in the area of law enforcement. Nonetheless, this vesting of power at the local level does allow for radically uneven justice across a state.

One could even see the possibility for institutional unevenness within a county. Not all county prosecutors or district attorneys have total control or responsibility for the prosecution of a criminal case from the time formal charges are filed. It is not uncommon in this country for the prosecuting authority to be divided between county prosecutors and a municipal prosecutor (or city attorney) who has the responsibility for all misdemeanor cases and the earliest formal stages of felony prosecutions. Where that division of authority exists, it is the municipal prosecutors who determine which defendants will be charged with a felony and which defendants will be charged with misdemeanors. The county prosecutor's authority is limited in such situations. Therefore, if the city prosecutor decides to dispose of a case as a less serious offense, a misdemeanor, the county district attorney may be constitutionally unable to try the defendant for the greater offense.[7]

Policy decisions depend upon who the prosecutor is, who he must answer to, and how seriously he regards his responsibility to the community he serves. Unfortunately, few attorneys regard the prosecutorial office as a permanent career. Therefore, politics, inadequate salaries, and poor training, and not so much a sense of professional commitment, often determine prosecutorial policies.

Even if assistants to the prosecutor wish to pursue the office as a career, their fate is often determined by the electorate. For example, if an incumbent is ousted through an election, his assistants are very likely to be removed along with their boss. Regardless, then, of the prosecutor's or his assistants' feelings of social responsibility or commitment, politics must be a very real consideration in the development of prosecutorial policies.

The desire to be re-elected causes many prosecutors to be politically sensitive to what is popular in the community, rather than to what is necessarily right.[8] For instance, prosecution of prostitutes and pornography merchants generates media attention and public approval but at what cost? Often these campaigns are undertaken to divert public attention from prosecutorial activities or low-visibility policies that may detract from the prosecutor's positive image.

The second factor that has discouraged attorneys to make a career out of prosecuting is salary advancement. Although the starting salaries for prosecutorial assistants are comparable to the starting salaries in small- and medium-sized law firms, salary increments are usually not sufficient to encourage assistants to regard prosecuting as a permanent career.[9]

The third factor that has had a negative impact on prosecutorial professionalism is the lack of training. The President's Commission on Law Enforcement (1967) stated that the absence of training programs for future prosecutors is deplorable:

> It is clear that existing programs do not meet the need for prosecutor training. There has been deplorable inattention to the development of curricula and training techniques in the investigative, administrative, and broader law enforcement policy roles played by the prosecutor. These matters have not been seen

> as suitable subjects for the attention of law schools and the legal scholarly community. Clinical programs offering law students an opportunity to participate in the criminal process, especially as prosecutors, are helpful, but the major burden will fall on the prosecutors' offices and outside organizations. The problems posed are challenging, and their resolution should be the object of Federal, local, and professional projects.[10]

Other than a law degree and admission to the bar of the jurisdiction, there are still no special training requirements for prosecutors. Most persons elected to the office have not had extensive criminal trial work and most assistants have had very little or no legal experience. Once elected or appointed, most prosecutors and their assistants learn while on the job by making decisions and trying cases. Some large offices do have in-house training programs but most do not. To fill the need for training programs, the National District Attorney's Association, the National College of District Attorneys, and several other institutions now offer short courses for prosecutors.[11] Because of the nature of the office, however, it seems that few attorneys are interested in special training programs. Nevertheless, the National Advisory Commission on Criminal Justice Standards and Goals stressed the need to broaden training opportunities and recommended that at least all newly elected or appointed chief prosecutors be required to take one of these courses prior to taking office.[12]

Prosecutorial Discretion

Just as the police officer may decide not to arrest, the prosecutor may not file criminal charges in every case that comes into the office. The formal criminal justice process could not possibly accommodate every case. There are limited resources available and how wisely these resources are allocated largely determines the effectiveness of the criminal justice system. Effectiveness, though, should not be measured solely on case dispositions. The ability of the courts to handle and dispose of its cases is but one factor. Additional consideration must be given to whether those limited resources are used to handle matters that seriously affect the well-being and security of the community. And finally the test for effectiveness is the degree of uniformity that exists within the charging process. (Uniformity is the key to evenly-dispensed justice at this stage of a criminal case: whether two persons committing criminal acts that are substantially the same and committed under similar circumstances are both charged at the same level or not charged at all.)

The prosecutor is uniquely situated to decide which cases to prosecute. He bears the burden of deciding which cases are of sufficient critical importance to warrant introduction into the judicial maelstrom.[13] The prosecutor must also recognize that by filing charges in one case another case may have to be ignored, or that the time devoted to a more serious charge may have to be lessened in order to handle an additional case.

In making these decisions, the prosecutor is going to be beset and buffeted by diverse interests, but as the chief law enforcement officer in the jurisdiction, he is in the position to bridge those interests. The police often complicate the prosecutor's duty to screen cases by pressuring for a filing against every person they have arrested, pressure that is reinforced by the public expectation that persons committing crimes will be prosecuted. Yet, because of daily contact with the police, the prosecutor is usually aware of law enforcement needs and the pressures on the street, and knows which crimes require visible and immediate judicial action. At the same time, invested with the responsibility of representing the state in all criminal actions, the prosecutor is also painfully aware of the dilemma—overcrowded dockets—facing the courts. Balancing these critical interests, the prosecutor becomes the fulcrum in the screening process, one of the most critical stages of a criminal case.

The prosecutor has the power to not only decide which offenders to prosecute, but he is also in the position to decide which laws to enforce and which to "repeal." The vast power involved in making these decisions makes not only the police but the public uncomfortable. Their common discomfort is increased by the fact that the prosecutor's decisions are generally made quietly, unacknowledged, and with little or no opportunity available for review by the aggrieved parties. Nearly fifty years ago, one commentator wrote that to the average citizen the investiture of such vast power in the prosecutor and the manner in which it is exercised must border on anarchy.[14]

Professor Kenneth Culp Davis who has written on discretionary justice takes issue with the lack of review of prosecutorial decisions. Professor Davis' main contention is that it is unreasonable to permit the prosecutor to exercise such a vast amount of power without having to present a rational and legal basis for the choice in an open forum:

> We should reexamine the assumptions. . .that a prosecutor should have uncontrolled discretion to choose one out of six cases to prosecute, without any requirement that the one most deserving of prosecution be chosen, or to trade a lesser charge for a plea of guilty in one case but not in another, with no guiding rules or standards, without disclosing findings or reasons, without any requirement of consistency, without supervision or check, and without judicial review.[15]

Another commentator has suggested that the prosecutor's discretion *is* limited, at least when contrasted to the police decision to arrest, because the prosecutor's decision is more public, at least after an arrest has been made.[16] But this limit on discretion only exists by contrast to the almost total absence of any limits on police discretion. The degree of publicity a decision actually evokes depends on how tenacious the news media may be, and that is clearly a factor of the newsworthy value of a particular crime. Most of these decisions generate no attention whatsoever. There are certain limitations built into the legal system to review prosecutorial decisions, both to prosecute and not to prosecute, but they are generally weak, not available in most cases, and clearly not as comprehensive as Professor Davis' proposal that would require the prosecutor to file with the court his reasons for not filing a complaint when the decision is to forego prosecution.[17]

Case Screening

We have already discussed the police-arrest process, where before the case is referred to the prosecutor an officer has made an arrest and, at least in serious cases, an internal police department decision has ratified the propriety of the officer's actions by referring the case for prosecution. Most prosecutions for serious crimes arise in this manner. There are, however, two other ways that cases are cycled to the prosecutor.

Major investigations leading to prosecution may also be initiated from within the prosecutor's office without prior police action, although the very information that leads to the investigation may have originated with the police. These investigations generally involve inquiries into organized crime operations, major white-collar crimes (involving business misconduct), and official corruption. These investigations may be undertaken by the prosecutor's own investigators, or the police may be enlisted in the investigation, or the matter may be submitted to the grand jury to utilize its broad investigatory powers.

The other source of cases is through private citizen complaints. Most of the complaints originating with citizens involve less serious matters from the community's viewpoint. They often involve neighborhood or domestic disputes, nonsupport, bad check offenses, and other borderline criminal matters. Often the citizen is advised to file the complaint by the police dispatcher who considers the matter too minor to send a police officer to investigate, or by a patrol officer who intercedes on the street but is not authorized to make an arrest for the offense. In many cities, the complaint is referred to the police department for investigation.

No matter the source of the case, whether it comes from the police or a private citizen, the prosecutor must assess the value of that case from the particular perspective of the prosecuting agency. This assessment is called *screening.*[18] With the opportunity to limit the flow of cases into the criminal courts, effective screening at this stage can be a vital link in the determination of which cases merit full prosecution and which ones can be handled through alternative means.[19] Whether screening is an effective tool to limit court congestion depends upon how it is approached in each jurisdiction and how willing the prosecutor is to commit his limited manpower to the task. If it is not approached with the determination to save the court's time by totally sifting out some cases and by reducing some felonies to misdemeanors, the prosecutor's exercise of the screening power is meaningless, little more than a show of official beneficence.

Like plea bargaining, case screening and selective prosecution have been major closet issues of criminal justice. Prosecutors and others throughout the system have been hesitant to admit that not all crimes are prosecuted to the fullest extent. Perhaps the reluctance stems from their fear of the popular disillusionment that might follow. Perhaps the explanation is that by not acknowledging the practice of selective prosecution, prosecutors are able to veil the exercise of an extraordinary power that is not subject to viable review. Whatever the reason, the failure to open up about screening and selective prosecuting has stunted analysis of the practice. Only in the past decade has any such analysis been attempted and the beginnings of a methodology developed.[20]

Criteria and Methodologies

Most citizen complaints filed with the prosecutor's office involve marginal violations. Frequently these complaints arise from personal disputes that may be marginally criminal but are only of minimal importance to the community. In most situations the prosecutor will call the parties in and try to conciliate the matter rather than file criminal charges. Many of these disputes arise between members of the same household or neighbors. The crux of the dispute is rarely resolved through criminal prosecution. In Columbus, Ohio, a federally funded program was developed to provide an out-of-court method for resolving neighborhood and family disputes through mediation and counselling. The emphasis is on a lasting solution to an interpersonal problem rather than a judgment of right and wrong.[21] The Columbus concept is being recreated throughout the country. Sometimes, of course, the matter presented by a private citizen does involve serious problems or dangerous behavior that merits prosecution. In those cases the prosecutor's office will order an investigation and then review the case in the same manner that it would one referred by the police department.

Similarly, cases referred by the police to the prosecutor's office do not automatically result in the formal filing of criminal charges. The police tend to think that they should be filed, and prosecutors sometimes blindly follow these recommendations just to mollify the police, but again this involves a waste of limited resources. Mollifying the police is not one of the principal responsibilities of a prosecuting attorney; a prosecutor who automatically files on a police recommendation is not fulfilling his obligations. By not screening at this level, a prosecutor introduces into the formal process cases that do not merit full prosecution.[22]

There are distinct, identifiable issues to be considered by a prosecuting attorney when screening a case. Obviously, the seriousness of the offense is the first consideration. How effectively will the public interest be served by prosecuting this offense, either to the full extent or, possibly, as a reduced charge? If the crime is one that seriously unsettles the peace of the community, then of course the interest of the community will be served by prosecuting the offender.

Relevant characteristics of the defendant should be considered when making this determination. If the accused has a past record or if there is any other reason to believe that the accused represents a threat to the safety and well-being of members of the community, then full prosecution is warranted. If, however, the accused is a first offender, prosecution under a felony charge, even if the facts would justify it, or even for a misdemeanor, may not be necessary if other means available to the prosecutor and the criminal justice system will serve to correct the individual's behavior, dissuade him from further crime, and restore or correct the damage that was done.[23]

Another factor to be weighed by the prosecutor is whether prosecution under a particular statute is desirable and, if so, in the public interest. While it may be ethically questionable for a prosecutor to decide that a law enacted by the elected representatives of the people should be ignored, he often balances ethics against reality.[24] He asks how important is it to a community to prosecute for prostitution, gambling, obscenity, or marijuana possession if the courts are unable to fully hear cases involving serious crimes such as rape, robbery, and burglary. In the end, the prosecutor is answerable to the electorate or another appointing authority. But the absence of accountability on each of these decisions opens the door to abuse of power. Confidence in the criminal justice system is enhanced by the community's belief that the decision to charge is made uniformly without regard to factors such as race, wealth, and position in the community.

Convictability, of course, should be a prime consideration in screening a case. Even if the facts were more than sufficient to meet a probable cause test and justify police arrest, those same facts (even when coupled with whatever additional information was secured through the police investigation) may be just too weak to satisfy the standard of guilt that would be necessary to secure a conviction. For example, evidence of a narcotics buy provided by a police informant whose testimony would be rejected out-of-hand by a jury because of his own ties to the underworld and his long criminal record is likely to be rejected by a prosecutor as a useless expenditure of scarce court time and limited prosecutorial resources. It is a waste of time for the court, prosecutor, police, and witnesses to involve themselves in a case where the legally admissible evidence will not support a conviction of the charge.[25]

Notwithstanding the small percentage of felony cases that go to trial, prosecutorial decisions when screening a case must be based on the convictability of the defendant in the event of trial. Although the police consider this criterion when they arrest, the prosecutor's office has the knowledge of the law and court experience to make a more educated decision.[26] Sometimes, even where the evidence does not guarantee a conviction, a prosecutor will file because the case is so important or has raised such public interest. In the prosecution of former Secretary of the Treasury John Connally, the prosecutor was convinced of the accused's guilt despite the weakness of the government's evidence and decided to take the case to trial and let the jury decide (the jury acquitted Connally).

Beyond the strength of the case, the admissibility of the evidence should be considered. If the arrest was unreasonable and the only evidence against the defendant was secured in a search incident to that arrest, the evidence is inadmissible at trial and it would be foolish to prosecute (although the possibility exists that the accused may decide to plead guilty and not challenge the legality of the search). Finally, a prosecutor may be willing to forego prosecuting one defendant in return for information about other criminality or for testimony against other defendants.[27]

A 1970's analysis of case screening by Joan Jacoby and her associates at the Bureau of Social Science Research in Washington delved into the methodologies utilized in eighteen cities.[28] The researchers culled four prevalent policies from which the different prosecuting agencies choose to determine their own office's screening strategy. The *"legally sufficient policy"* indicates that if the elements of a crime were present, the prosecutor automatically filed the charge. Implementing this policy at the screening level only requires a cursory examination of the facts for legal defects. It was characterized as a routine and quick examination with little concern for whether the facts would justify a conviction or whether there was sufficient admissible evidence to warrant trying the case. The *"system efficiency policy"* aims for the speedy and early disposition of cases by any means possible. Thus the case is scrutinized for defects and a recommendation for an early disposition, e.g., plea of guilty to a misdemeanor, would be recommended. Particular emphasis is placed on disposal of a case at an early stage in the process. The *"defendant rehabilitation policy"* depends primarily on the circumstances, past record, and potential threat of the defendant. Prosecution on the police charge is not a goal, unless the defendant's history includes prior convictions with no evidence of rehabilitation. This policy relies heavily upon the social service resources of the community as well as the criminal justice system. The *"trial sufficiency policy"* is based upon the principle that charges will be filed only if the prosecutor is willing to have the case judged on its merits at trial and expects a conviction.

Irrespective of the policy at work in a particular jurisdiction, the Jacoby group recognized that effective screening depends upon several factors:

1. the chief prosecutor's recognition that his or her office has an independent role to play at this stage of a criminal case

2. that policy or policies are clearly formulated and articulated within the office and communicated to all personnel preferably through a permanent-type manual of operations
3. that there is a written statement for the screening decision and a review of the decisions made by assistants to insure uniformity, and that there is coordination within the office to effectuate the policy or policies throughout the life of the case[29]

The National Advisory Commission on Criminal Justice Standards and Goals, while calling for the acknowledgment of screening as a valid prosecution tool, stressed the need for such guidelines.[30] An excellent manual was developed in the Tazewell County, Illinois, prosecutor's office.[31] The prosecutor emphasized two objectives: (1) to stop proceedings against persons when further action would be fruitless ultimately because of insufficient evidence to obtain or sustain a conviction (recognizing the need for effective allocation of resources), and (2) to eliminate those cases, even where there is evidence to convict, if pursuit of formal proceedings would not be fair to the defendant or serve to reduce criminal activity in the community. The criteria and procedures for screening contained in the manual are set forth here because they help in understanding the nature of the process:

CRITERIA FOR SCREENING

A. An accused should be screened out of the criminal justice system if there is not a reasonable likelihood that the evidence admissible against him would be sufficient to obtain a conviction and sustain it on appeal. In screening on this basis, the prosecutor shall consider the value of a conviction in reducing future offenses, as well as the probability of conviction and affirmance of that conviction on appeal.

B. An accused may be screened out of the criminal justice system when the benefit to be derived from prosecution or diversion would be outweighed by the cost of such action. Among the factors to be considered in making this determination are the following:

1. The impact of discontinuing prosecution on jeopardizing the public interest in obtaining a disposition that furnishes the public adequate protection and does not depreciate the seriousness of the offense or promote disrespect for the law.
2. The value of further proceedings in fostering the community's sense of security and confidence in the criminal justice system.
3. Prolonged non-enforcement of the statute on which the charge is based.
4. The value of further proceedings in preventing future offenses by the offender, in light of the offender's commitment to criminal activity as a way of life; the seriousness of his past criminal activity, which he might reasonably be expected to continue; the possibility that further proceedings might have a

tendency to create or reinforce commitment on the part of the accused to criminal activity as a way of life; and the likelihood that programs available such as diversion or sentencing alternatives may reduce the likelihood of future criminal activity.

5. The value of further proceedings in preventing future offenses by other persons, considering the extent to which subjecting the accused to further proceedings could be expected to have an impact upon others who might commit such offenses, as well as the seriousness of those offenses.

6. The likelihood of prosecution and conviction of the offender by another jurisdiction or the fact of conviction and sentence of the offender by another jurisdiction.

7. The direct cost of prosecution, in terms of prosecutorial time, court time, and similar factors.

8. Any assistance rendered by the accused in apprehension or conviction of other offenders, in the prevention of offenses by others, in the reduction of the impact of offenses committed by himself or others upon the victims, and any other socially beneficial activity engaged in by the accused that might be encouraged in others by not prosecuting the offender. It is possible that the value of encouraging assistance to law enforcement or similar activity will outweigh the benefit to society from continuation of criminal or diversionary proceedings. In such cases, screening is appropriate. It should be recognized, however, that screening in such situations should be infrequent.

9. The impact of further proceedings upon the accused and those close to him, especially the likelihood and seriousness of financial hardship and family life disruption.

10. Any doubt as to the accused's guilt.

11. Any improper motives of the complainant.

(When formal proceedings are justified by the community's need for protection, the improper motivation of the complainant should not be a significant consideration.)

12. Attitude and feelings of those persons most directly affected by the criminal conduct of the accused, their relationship to the accused, and extent of injury, financial or personal, sustained by such persons.

PROCEDURE FOR SCREENING

It is recognized that the decision to take a person into custody should be a police decision. It is suggested that police agencies within Tazewell County should establish general guidelines for making this decision and they are encouraged to seek the advice and help of the State's Attorney's Office in creating these guidelines. It is anticipated, especially where relatively serious offenses are involved, that screening by the police through a decision not to take a suspect into custody will be less vigorous than screening by the State's Attorney's Office.

The decision to charge, to divert, to screen, or not to charge, will be made by the State's Attorney or a member of his staff. Although a police officer has the authority to arrest and book a person suspected, of a serious offense without prior prosecutorial approval, the process shall go no further than that without formal involvement of the State's Attorney's Office.

1. No complaint shall be filed or arrest warrant issued without the formal approval of the State's Attorney or a member of his staff. The initial decision to charge should involve consideration of the alternative not to charge and, where possible, the decision to screen should be made at this time.
2. Once a decision has been made to pursue formal proceedings, further consideration should be given to screening an accused as further information concerning the accused and the case becomes available. A review of the initial decision should always be made prior to Grand Jury Indictment. The prosecutor in charge of the case has a continuing duty to reevaluate a decision to charge—and not to screen—as the case progresses and further information is obtained. Information concerning the inadmissibility of some evidence or tending to suggest that formal proceedings would be inappropriate, may not be available until after an indictment has been returned.
3. The responsibility for making a screening decision is specifically placed upon the chief of the felony division on felony charges and the chief of the misdemeanor division for misdemeanor charges, subject to review by the State's Attorney upon the request of a defendant, the police or a private complainant.
4. The decision to screen should follow the criteria for screening set forth in these standards and as hereafter amended or expanded by the State's Attorney.
5. In all cases where a defendant is screened after being taken into custody on a Class A misdemeanor or felony charge, a written statement of the prosecutor's reasons shall be prepared and kept on file in the State's Attorney's Office.
6. When a case is screened out on the basis of an evidence insufficiency, the Police Agency submitting the case shall be advised so that further investigation can be conducted if warranted.
7. When a case is screened out on some other basis than evidence insufficiency, it shall be the duty of the screening prosecutor to explain the basis for the decision to the victim, police agency, or other interested party upon request.[32]

An LEAA-funded study on pretrial procedures (1971) concluded that opportunities for effective screening are critically hampered when the prosecutor's office that initiates the original charge does not have continued responsibility for the entire case.[33] The bifurcated prosecution structure exists in Cleveland, Ohio, where the city prosecutor has full responsibility for all misdemeanor cases but authority only to initiate felony cases. The ultimate responsibility for felony cases rests with the county prosecutor. Screening may be done in misdemeanor cases but the city prosecutor, subject to being second-guessed by the county prosecutor, generally avoids screening felony cases. The city prosecutor rather than pruning out cases tends to file felony complaints on the recommendation of the police, thereby introducing all cases into the felony process. Meaningful screening of felonies is, at best, deferred, and this prime opportunity to avoid unmerited felony prosecutions and attendant court congestion is lost.[34]

In Detroit, on the other hand, there is provision for a more thorough review after arrest and prior to the initiation of formal charges. Each police referral is assigned to an assistant district attorney who ultimately determines whether to institute charges. The assignment of the case not only vests the responsibility for the decision but also prevents the police from carrying a case from one assistant to another until they find one willing to prosecute.[35] The assistant district attorney reviews the police report, questions the officer or detective about the case, and requests any additional investigation that is needed. For some felonies, often in rape cases, the assistant prosecutor interviews witnesses and victims. If the suspect is already represented by counsel, the assigned prosecutor will discuss the case at the defense attorney's request prior to filing a formal complaint. Only after this brief review is completed will the assistant district attorney decide how to proceed. Reports indicate that thirty percent of felony cases in Detroit are screened out of the process at this point; the felony docket, as a consequence, is less crowded, more manageable.[36]

There is virtually no prosecutorial screening prior to the introduction of formal proceedings in New York City. Detectives from all of the borough precincts flood the complaint room of the Manhattan branch of that city's Criminal Court to file charges. The one or two assistant district attorneys stationed in the room are incapable of reviewing the cases; they are present to assist the detectives who have technical difficulties with the charging papers.[37] Thus there is no screening, other than that done by the police, until a case is presented in court. The extensive burden on prosecutors and judges caused by the incredible number of cases filed in that court casts suspicion, as well, upon the effectiveness of the in-court screening. The type of in-court screening that is done does not allow for the prosecutor to review the case and discuss it with the participants—the police, who made the arrest and conducted the investigation, and the witnesses. Consequently, this type of screening leads to case dispositions without considerations of merit.[38]

Early and careful screening is the rule of the prosecutor's office in Los Angeles County, California, the largest county in the country with over seven million inhabitants and a correspondingly large crime rate. To prosecute all or nearly all of the more than 75,000 annual felony arrests would cripple the courts. The prosecutor's office operates from the assumption that the courts cannot handle all anti-social behavior but must be reserved for the serious offenses. Consequently, the office eliminates as many cases as possible prior to filing formal charges and handles these less serious problems by other means. The use of policy directives from the main office to its seven branches located in various courthouses insures that the decision not to prosecute is uniformly made throughout the county.[39]

Unlike the situation in most cities, the Los Angeles detective who has prepared the case will not get a complaint from the prosecutor as a matter of routine. The assistant prosecutor will review the police report, the accused's prior criminal record, and the statements given to the police by the witnesses. It is not unusual for the assistant prosecutor to turn the matter back to the police for further investigation or to call in the district attorney's own investigators to secure more information. The Los Angeles screening process strives to reduce as many cases as possible to misdemeanors or to refer the suspects to social agencies. Crimes arising out of marital situations, except for the most serious felonies, are directed to the court's domestic relations commissioner to determine whether the case can be resolved without criminal sanctions. If the suspect has a lawyer, the complaint will be held in abeyance until the lawyer has an opportunity to consult with the assistant prosecutor. As a result of this extensive effort, more than sixty percent of the felony arrests are resolved by misdemeanor prosecutions, dismissals, or referral to non-judicial proceedings or social agencies.[40] Further, when an assistant prosecutor declines to charge a person arrested by the police, a written statement of the reasons for this decision is prepared and referred to the police so that the two agencies can work together more effectively.

Options

There are many options available to the prosecutor when screening a case. These options are available not only for felony cases but also for misdemeanors. However, screening and its attendant options are rarely utilized in misdemeanor cases. This is a paradox because misdemeanor defendants are often far more worthy of a non-judicial settlement than a person charged with a felony.

The major reason misdemeanor cases are usually not screened is because all misdemeanor arrests tend to result in criminal charges directly through the arresting officer and without input from the prosecutor. In addition, most persons charged with misdemeanors tend to plead guilty immediately upon their first court appearance in order to get the matter over with as soon as possible and because of the unlikelihood of a jail sentence in most of these cases. Consequently, most prosecutors are unwilling to commit any resources to these cases until the defendant appears in court. Then, if the defendant does not enter a quick plea of guilty, there may be some in-court screening rather than taking the case to trial.

With those cases that do come to the prosecutor, the prosecutor's first and most obvious option is to accept the police recommendation and file the charge. By accepting the original charge, the prosecutor is able to avoid strained relations with the police. Yet if the facts do not warrant the charge or a conviction is unlikely on the evidence, the courts will be burdened unnecessarily if the prosecutor does not use his discretion wisely.

Because the prosecutor has total control over a felony case, he may accept the police recommendation or choose to increase the degree of seriousness of the crime or expand the charge to include more than one felony count.[41] *"Bedsheeting"* is the term for the prosecutorial practice of charging a defendant with every possible crime that is applicable within the original charge. For example, a person who is apprehended by the police as he comes out of a robbery victim's home is subject to being charged with—in addition to robbery—burglary, larceny, and, if he is armed, carrying a concealed weapon.

Filing a charge that is greater than the evidence will bear is called *overcharging*. Overcharging is often done, especially where the court must rely on pleas of guilty to dispose of cases, to enable the prosecutor to make concessions during later plea bargaining. The effect upon the system, though, can be disastrous because overcharging can result in no one in the system really knowing which cases should be tried as charged and which ones have been artificially inflated and should be disposed of on a reduced charge. It would seem that in the larger courts the problem becomes insurmountable and some cases where the charges should have been reduced go to trial fruitlessly and other cases where the charge should stick are reduced and pleaded out.[42]

Conversely, the prosecutor may disagree with the police assessment of the case and the accused's conduct and refuse to file charges, thus resulting in the defendant's release from custody, or the prosecutor may institute a misdemeanor charge against the accused.[43] A misdemeanor charge at this stage of the criminal process is the easiest way to dispose of a case while still letting the offender know that the law has taken note of his conduct. Compared to a felony proceeding, a misdemeanor generally involves little court or prosecutor time. The advantage of referring the defendant's case for prosecution as a misdemeanor is that it relieves the felony process and permits more serious offenses to receive greater attention.

Most misdemeanors, at least outside New York City,[44] are handled with great dispatch. Because most persons charged with misdemeanors plead guilty at a first court appearance, the case can be disposed of where and when the defendant initially appears. A defendant who is fully aware that sufficient evidence exists to charge him with a felony is quite likely to accept the expedited procedure to free himself of any charges hanging over his head. For the defendant held by the police on a felony charge, resolution of that charge within the misdemeanor process enables him to resume his life with minimal disruption.[45] The prosecutor's reasons for washing out a case or reducing a charge at this stage are many, not the least being that the facts may make a felony conviction unlikely or questionable. Moreover, numerous cases originally prosecuted as felonies are eventually settled as misdemeanors. An early settlement in this manner relieves the pressure on the entire system.

Informal prosecutorial probation is an example of another option available to the prosecutor. This option allows the prosecutor to agree to defer charging the accused if the accused stays out of trouble. At the end of the designated period, generally six months or a year, the prosecutor will close the file if the accused has not been arrested again during that period. Prosecutorial probation is not the most desirable non-judicial settlement, however, because it does not offer the prospect of treatment or supervision for the accused.[46]

More effective non-judicial dispositions exist in the form of court diversion programs. The likelihood of this option being utilized depends upon the existence of formal programs offered in a given city and the quality and availability of social service agencies. The simplest approach is to refer the case to a welfare agency for the placement of the accused in a psychiatric, counselling, or other health-care situation. If the prosecutor determines that the defendant's criminal behavior is a result of being unemployed, the accused may be referred to a work-training program. The most effective programs are those that train the accused in a specific trade and then place him in a job after he has satisfactorily completed the training program. Naturally, a defendant need not accept placement in a diversion program, but the alternative is prosecution. If the defendant agrees, then the prosecutor will defer charging the individual. If the accused successfully completes the program, the prosecutor agrees never to institute the charge, provided that the accused is not arrested again for a specifically designated period of time.

In Philadelphia approximately sixty cases per week are handled through court diversion-probation programs. A program is available to a first offender, generally one charged with a relatively minor felony. However, if the accused is arrested again, he will be charged with the original offense as well as the one that resulted in the subsequent arrest.[47] Among the programs existing in New York City is one that in lieu of prosecution offers treatment and counselling to drug addicts accused of crimes.[48]

The advantages of such programs to both the accused and the criminal justice system are manifold. The accused is given his freedom. He is exposed to programs that provide employment training, job placement, and the opportunity for medical treatment. Above all, he comes out of the program without a criminal record and its accompanying social stigma. The benefits to society are equally significant. Without exposing the case to the overcrowded courts, the accused has been placed under supervision in a program that probably offers greater opportunity for rehabilitation than jail or prison confinement. Moreover, there is a chance that the justice system will be able to contribute a reformed, useful individual to the community, without the expense to the community of imprisonment.

The Charging Decision

The Decision Not to Charge

While many jurisdictions have placed some limits on a prosecutor's authority to terminate a prosecution once formal charges have been filed,[49] very little judicial authority exists to compel prosecution. Shortly after the Attica prison uprising, several inmates brought suit seeking the court to compel state and federal officials to investigate and prosecute those state and prison officials who had allegedly violated state and federal criminal statutes in their handling and treatment of prisoners during and immediately after the uprising. The inmates raised serious issues concerning violations of civil rights and the protection of their physical security and claimed that federal and state prosecutors had abused their discretion in not investigating and pursuing these violations. The United States Court of Appeals for the Second Circuit, in rejecting the plaintiffs' contentions, described how much mischief could be caused if courts regularly undertook to review these decisions and the difficulties that would beset a court attempting to do so. Most importantly, however, the court refused to countenance an inquiry into whether the decisions were an abuse of discretion and refused to undertake the task.[50] Obviously the courts are not prepared to impose standards on prosecutorial discretion, so an aggrieved citizen who seeks to file charges and is turned down by the prosecutor need not apply to the courts for help.

The remedies that are available to the citizen vary across the country, but none are truly effective. The most powerful remedy that has been suggested would permit private citizens to prosecute when the prosecutor fails to.[51] This approach would allow a private citizen to file formal criminal charges and hire an attorney to prosecute the case on the citizen's behalf. One proposal along these lines would compensate the private citizen for the cost of the prosecution from public funds unless it was determined that the prosecution was groundless, in which case the private citizen would be compelled to reimburse the aggrieved defendant's costs accrued in the defense of a baseless case.[52] While private prosecution affords the most meaningful remedy, it is also recognized as a "Pandora's box" solution. The courts could easily become clogged with groundless actions emanating from personal vendettas. In addition, of course, innocent defendants could be forced to bear the humiliation, anxiety, and, at least the initial costs of defending against such prosecutions.[53] Most proponents for private prosecutions admit the inherent dangers and propose an opportunity for the prosecutor to appear and present evidence as to why he dismissed a case. One American court whose rules permit private prosecution held that it would not be allowed over the objection of the prosecutor.[54]

Most jurisdictions provide alternative routes to prosecution. Either the attorney general may initiate criminal cases in any county of the state, or the attorney general or governor may appoint special prosecutors to investigate and file charges where the appointing authority believes that the local prosecutor has either abused his discretion or otherwise has been derelict in pursuing his official duties (the prosecutor can be removed from office, either through impeachment by the voters or through action by the state legislature or by court action).[55] Appointment of a special prosecutor or removal of the elected or appointed regular prosecutor does happen when there is a major breach of duty in a *cause celebre,* but those alternatives are hardly tangible for the average citizen who cannot understand why the prosecutor fails to file charges in the single case that affects him. In any event, special appointments and removals are not going to be made on behalf of the individual or group whose interests or cause is not popular or relevant to anyone else.

Finally, in states that have retained the grand jury as a means of initiating prosecutions, the possibility exists that the grand jury may undertake an investigation and present charges even if the prosecutor has refused to do so. The grand jury is empowered to investigate without the approval of the prosecutor, and a private citizen could request such an inquiry by letter. As we will later explore in greater detail, this remedy is more theoretical than real. Grand juries, while not legally under the control of the prosecuting attorney, are controlled in fact by the prosecutor and unerringly fail to deviate from the course he has set out for them.

The Decision to Charge

More common than complaints about prosecutors not filing criminal charges is the "why me?" cry of the defendant who has been snared and formally charged. If crime is as rampant as we believe and if we know that police and prosecutors choose to ignore certain crimes and certain offenders, we must listen with some understanding to the plaintive cry of the accused who must stand trial and possibly be punished for his misdeed. That is not to suggest that we excuse this person for his misconduct but only realize that what he is asking is why *he* has been singled out. When a defendant complains that he is being discriminated against in this manner, he is asserting that the state has violated his right to the equal protection of the laws guaranteed by the Fourteenth Amendment to the Constitution. However, it is not a claim that is going to be looked on with much favor because it is not accompanied by a claim of innocence.

The fact of selectivity, itself, will not carry the day for the defendant asserting his claim. The Supreme Court of the United States has made it clear that some selectivity in the enforcement of the law is not a constitutional violation.[56] What must be established is that selection was deliberately based upon an unjustifiable standard such as race, religion, or another arbitrary classification. At least one court relying on earlier Supreme Court decisions has held that in order for the defendant to prevail, the defense must not only establish that the discrimination was based upon impermissible factors (such as race, religion, or other unconstitutional classifications), but that it must also be established that the discrimination was a result of a deliberate policy, not inadvertence, negligence, or sheer ineptitude.[57] As the burden of proving the discrimination rests on the defense, the question arises as to how it can be established. It is almost an impossible burden to meet especially since all of the records and documents that may help the defense are in the possession of the prosecutor and the police. It is intended to be that way so that prosecuting attorneys will not have to justify why, other than for reasons of guilt, a particular defendant is on trial.[58]

Except in California, courts have generally held that a statistical showing that arrests for a particular crime are confined to one racial group or one neighborhood in a city is not sufficient to establish the defense of discriminatory enforcement of the law.[59] The strongest position taken in favor of this line of defense, however, was set forth in a 1973 prosecution for failure to carry a draft card. In *United States v. Falk* the defendant countered the charge by alleging that of the more than 25,000 registrants who refused to carry draft cards, he was the only one prosecuted solely because of his anti-war activism. A United States Court of Appeals held that when evidence as compelling as that presented by Falk comes before a court the presumption of the prosecutor's good faith is defeated and the defendant is entitled to a hearing to question the purpose of the prosecution.[60] It must be borne in mind that even if *Falk* were followed throughout the country its applicability will be confined to minor offenses and to those very few cases where the statistical evidence demonstrates clear discrimination.

What about the defendant charged with a serious offense who claims that, notwithstanding the heinousness of his crime, he is being prosecuted because of bad faith and antagonism towards him by the prosecuting attorney? This has not been recognized as a defense even when a disproportionate amount of government resources was used to investigate the individual in order to bring prosecution. Generally, this type of government activity meets with public approval because it involves official monitoring and close scrutiny of one who is believed to be engaged in massive illegality. Yet it does frame questions about the sheer power accorded to prosecuting agencies and the possibility of misuse. To find examples of this kind of prosecution, we need only to glance at recent history when during the Nixon era government agencies were marshalled to scrutinize the lives of persons who were on the "enemies list" and to the earlier prosecutions of Teamster Union leader James Hoffa. Some political pundits suggested that Hoffa was a marked man after he allegedly accused Robert Kennedy of being nothing but a rich man's kid who never had to earn a nickel in his life. Professor Monroe Freedman recites data that during the period Robert Kennedy was Attorney General of the United States there were more prosecutions brought against Hoffa than there were civil rights cases filed by the government in Mississippi and that there were more prosecutions against Teamster officials than there were civil rights prosecutions in the entire country.[61] Another commentator replied to Professor Freedman that it is no more a misuse of power for a prosecutor to consider the personal characteristics and dangerousness of an offender when he sets his investigative sites than when he decides to accept a plea of guilty to a lesser offense.[62] Certainly, Al Capone, the underworld figure of the prohibition era, was guilty of many crimes more serious than tax evasion, for which he was ultimately convicted and confined. Few would question here the propriety of the government's probing until an offense was found that could be proven beyond a reasonable doubt. Nonetheless, the issues raised by Professor Freedman are sound and members of a free society should be concerned when government powers and tools are susceptible for use in personal machinations.

The Formal Charge

Once the decision to prosecute is finalized, the actual preparation and filing of the *complaint* is an uncomplicated process. The *complaint* is the initial charging form in a felony case; it will ultimately be supplanted by an *indictment* or *information* at the conclusion of all the preliminary procedures. For misdemeanors, the complaint is the only charging form.

The purpose of the complaint is to notify the defendant of the nature of the charge. Therefore, it will include the name of the charge (e.g., murder, arson, robbery, rape) and the section number of the state code that defines the offense. A short statement of the major allegations required by the statute will follow, including the date of the alleged offense, the location, and the name of the victim, if any. In addition, many jurisdictions require a statement of the manner in which the offense was committed. All of this is stated in very general terms. Some states permit the charge to be simply stated in the language of the statute without any additional particulars. Additional information that the defendant is entitled to will be provided later through other means. The complaint also includes the name of the defendant and the name of the court where the charge is to be filed, and then the signature of the prosecutor, or in misdemeanor cases, often, the signature of the arresting officer.

SAMPLE COMPLAINT

State of ____________________ Case Number ____________________

vs.

____________________ In the Court of ____________________

(Name and Address of Defendant)

Complainant being duly sworn before me on ___(date)___ states that ___(Name and Address of Defendant)___, on or about ___(date)___, did commit ___(title or description of crime)___, in violation of (either "the laws of this jurisdiction" or the numerical citation of the statute involved).

Complainant by affidavit further states that (here the essential facts which support a probable cause determination are presented).

____

Complainant's Signature and Position

Sworn to and subscribed before me by ___(Name of Complainant)___ on ___(Date)___

____

Authorized Signature and Title

After the complaint is prepared and signed, it is taken to the clerk's office of the appropriate court, assigned a case number, and formally filed. If the defendant is already in custody, the case will be placed on the court's docket for the next day that court is in session. The defendant will be served with a copy of the complaint. The entire procedure, encompassing the arrest, review of the charges, and the preparation and filing of the complaint, should take less than twenty-four hours. If the defendant was arrested prior to the filing of the complaint, the state should be prepared to produce the accused and present the complaint at the next regular session of the court with initial jurisdiction over the case.

If the defendant was not arrested prior to the filing of the complaint, an arrest warrant or summons will be issued and will be served on the defendant along with a copy of the complaint. If the defendant is to be arrested, he will be taken into custody immediately upon service of the complaint and warrant, taken to the police station where he will be booked, and then probably detained, especially if the charge is a felony, until the case appears on the docket which, again, is presumably the next court day. If a summons was served instead of an arrest warrant along with the complaint, the accused will not be taken into custody but will be instructed instead on when and where to appear in court.

"Unbridled Power"

An article published in the California Law Review states:

> It is important to recognize at the outset that neither courts or commentators have creatively applied due process and equal protection values to the preaccusation stage of the criminal process. Unlike adjudicatory phases of the criminal system, which are characterized by a plethora of safeguards (e.g., public hearing, confrontation of accusor, power to subpoena, legal representation), the accusatorial stage is characterized by relatively unbridled official discretion. The preaccusation stage of the criminal system also demands development of safeguards, some of which may be constitutionally dictated.[63]

Although this observation is true, especially in regard to the prosecutorial decision-making process, some critics feel that due process and equal protection values are, to a large extent, protected by the network of relationships that exist between the prosecutor on the one hand and the police, courts, defense attorneys, and community influentials on the other. What this means is that the prosecutorial decision to charge or not to charge is affected by the interests and expectations of the other participants in the criminal process. Although these influences may be subtle and extra-legal, they exert enough pressure to confine most prosecutors to making decisions that are in the interests of the public and criminal justice system alike.

On the other hand, many critics denounce the staggering amount of power a prosecutor has as undemocratic; they claim that no prosecutor is necessarily qualified by his legal expertise to determine the "perfect" or most just decision in any given criminal case. And because such "unbridled power" can lead to serious abuses of the prosecutorial authority, these critics call for increased accountability measures. Such measures (as those proposed by Kenneth Culp Davis)[64] would help to refine the overall system by enhancing the integrity and reliability of the accusatorial stage in the criminal process.

Discussion Questions

1. What are the three ways that cases are cycled to the prosecutor?

2. Effective screening depends on what three major factors?

3. What are the five options available to the prosecutor when screening a case?

4. Why is prosecutorial screening one of the most important phases in the criminalization process? At the same time, why is case screening also one of the major closet issues of criminal justice?

5. Identify three criteria that influence the prosecutorial decision to charge.

6. Identify and explain the four prosecutorial policies uncovered by the Jacoby study of pre-trial screening.

7. An article published by the Southern California Law Review (S. Ca. L. Rev., Vol. 42, 1969) analyzes prosecutorial discretion as follows:

> [T]he prosecutor traditionally has virtually unlimited discretion of two distinct types: (1) the power to abstain from prosecution and (2) the power to selectively prosecute. It is necessary, for analytical purposes, to distinguish between these two types of discretion because the parties involved and the means available to limit the power differ. The discretion to abstain from prosecution is primarily the concern of the general public, as represented by the attorney general and the courts, and involves issues of neglect of duty. The discretion to selectively prosecute is the direct concern of the defendant and involves equal protection values.

How is the public affected by the prosecutor's decision not to prosecute for certain crimes? How does the public benefit from selective prosecution? What are the negative side effects that arise from selective prosecution?

8. What does the author of the article cited above mean when he states that "The decision to selectively prosecute is the direct concern of the defendant and involves equal protection values"?

9. Do you feel that the prosecutor possesses "unbridled power" in his decision making or do you agree with the position that the prosecutor's decision is limited by his professional relationships with other criminal justice functionaries?

Notes

1. The closeness of this relationship, though, may have undesirable effects upon the criminal justice system. While the coordination of police and prosecutorial activities is essential, the prosecutor must remain independent of the police. Otherwise, the prosecutor may be unable to overrule the police assessment of the merits of any given case.
2. *National Evaluation Program: Pretrial Screening Projects,* p. 2, (citing *First Annual Report of the National Center for Prosecution Management,* 1972).
3. In contrast, see *ABA Standards, The Prosecution Function,* §2.3.
4. *Task Force Report: The Courts: The President's Commission on Law Enforcement and Administration of Justice* (1967), p. 75.
5. Often the distinctions made between burglary and a misdemeanor breaking and entering charge rests on tenuous interpretations. See *Task Force Report: The Courts,* p. 97.
6. It may be that this response is actually the result of the prosecutor's perception of changing public opinion. See United States Attorney Manual, Title 2, §86.2-86.3, (Washington: U.S. Dept. of Justice), cited in Hutcherson v. United States, 120 U.S. App. D.C. 274, 345 F.2d 964 (1965).
7. See Waller v. Florida, 397 U.S. 387, 90 S.Ct. 1184, 25 L. Ed.2d 435 (1970), where the U.S. Supreme Court disallowed separate state and municipal prosecutions arising from the same act.
8. For standards of conduct of a prosecutor in political campaigns, see *ABA Standards, Prosecution Function,* §2.3.
9. A 1973 survey conducted by the Massachusetts Bar Association discovered that lawyers employed by the government (federal, state, and local) rank lowest among eleven categories of legal employment by personal net income. Reprinted in *Trial,* vol. 13, no. 3, March 1977, p. 32.
10. *Task Force Report: The Courts,* p. 75.
11. *A.B.A. Standards, Prosecution Function,* pp. 28-9.
12. *Courts: National Advisory Commission on Criminal Justice Standards and Goals* (1973), p. 239.
13. See Comment, "Prosecutorial Discretion in the Initiation of Criminal Complaints," 42 *So. Cal. L. Rev.* 519, 528 (1969).
14. Arnold, "Law Enforcement—An Attempt at Social Dissection," 42 *Yale L.J.* 1, 7 (1932).
15. Davis, *Discretionary Justice* (1969), reprinted in part in Kamisar, LaFave, and Israel, *Modern Criminal Procedure,* 4th ed. (St. Paul, Minn.: West, 1974), p. 823.
16. Skolnick, *Justice Without Trial* (1966), reprinted in part in Kamisar, LaFave, and Israel, *Modern Criminal Procedure,* 4th ed. (St. Paul, Minn.: West, 1974), p. 833.
17. In his analysis, Professor Davis contrasts the American system with the German system where discretionary power to withhold prosecution is denied.
18. See Miller, *Prosecution: The Decision to Charge a Suspect with a Crime* (Boston: Little, Brown and Company, 1969).
19. McIntyre and Lippman, "Prosecutors and Early Disposition of Felony Cases," 56 *A.B.A.J.* 1154 (1970).
20. National Center for Prosecution Management, *The Prosecutor's Screening*

Function: Case Evaluation and Control, Chicago: National District Attorneys Association (1973). Also Jacoby, "Case Evaluation: Quantifying Prosecutorial Policy," *Judicature,* May 1975.

21. This approach is not without the potential for tragic miscalculations. See *New York Times,* June 10, 1975, p. 39.
22. In Cleveland, Ohio, police often go to the prosecutor who presents cases to the grand jury in order to get an indictment even when probable cause is found not to exist at the preliminary hearing.
23. Relevant criteria and procedure used in diversion cases are discussed in *Alternatives to Conventional Criminal Adjudication: Guidebook for Planners and Practitioners,* National Institute of Law Enforcement and Criminal Justice, Law Enforcement Assistance Administration (1977).
24. The room for potential abuse here is discussed by Packer, *The Limits of the Criminal Sanction,* (1968) fn. 6, p. 91.
25. It may be that the criminal will be acquitted in cases where admissible evidence is not persuasive to the jury. For a discussion, see Knowlton, "The Trial of Offenders," 339 *Annals* 125 (1962).
26. "The ultimate resolution of a criminal case resulting from prosecutor screening is necessary for the maintenance of the criminal justice system. There are not enough prosecutors, defense attorneys, judges and jails to handle the massive felony docket." McIntyre and Lippman, "Prosecutors and Early Disposition of Felony Cases," 56 *A.B.A.J.* 1154 (1970).
27. A good discussion of this is contained in Miller, *Prosecution: The Decision To Charge A Suspect With a Crime* (Boston: Little, Brown and Company, 1969), pp. 253-59.
28. *Summary of Pre-Trial Screening Evaluation Phase I,* Bureau of Social Science Research, Washington (1975).
29. Ibid.
30. *Courts,* National Advisory Commission on Criminal Justice Standards and Goals, Washington (1973), p. 243.
31. *Local Standards for the Exercise of Prosecutorial Discretion in Tazewell County, Illinois,* Tazewell County State Attorney's Office (1973).
32. Ibid., pp. 4-8.
33. Here the screening prosecutor is simply passing the case on to someone else in the office who will have to deal with it at the trial level.
34. Katz, "Municipal Courts—Another Urban III," 20 *Case W. Res. L. Rev.* 87 (1969).
35. Defense attorneys know which prosecutors are sympathetic to defendants charged with certain crimes. Subin, *Criminal Justice In A Metropolitan Court: The Processing of Serious Criminal Cases In the District of Columbia Court of General Sessions* 43 (1966). Similarly, the prosecutor's sympathetic reaction will be known by police. As a result, police will try to steer cases to other prosecutors.
36. Interview with Assistant Prosecutor-Chief of Warrant Division in Detroit, Aug. 3, 1971.
37. Interview with an assistant district attorney in New York City, Nov. 29, 1970.
38. See *New York Times,* July 29, 1976, p. 1; Sept. 27, 1976, p. 37.
39. Interview with Long Beach District Attorney in Long Beach, California, Dec. 11, 1970.
40. Ibid.

41. For a discussion of multiple punishment and consecutive sentences, see Johnson, "Multiple Punishment and Consecutive Sentences: Reflections on the 'Neal' Doctrine," 58 *Calif. L. Rev.* 357 (1970).
42. The results of overcharging are difficult to rectify once the criminal is at trial. See Kamisar, et. al., *Modern Criminal Procedure,* pp. 825-6, for a discussion of attempts by judges and juries to reduce or dismiss overcharged cases.
43. "Prosecutorial Discretion," supra note 13, at 524-5.
44. In New York City an unofficial "40-stitch rule" exists where felony assault charges won't be sought unless the combined damage results in 40 stitches. In addition, most car thefts are prosecuted as misdemeanors. See *New York Times,* Sept. 27, 1976, p. 37.
45. Katz, "Municipal Courts—Another Urban Ill.," pp. 87-95.
46. *"Prosecutorial Discretion,"* supra note 13 at 529.
47. It involves first offenders or people with "minimal" police records ... If the prosecutor and the court agree that the defendant in such instances poses no risk to the community, they are taken out of the machinery and placed in a probationary status for six months or more ... Those who stay out of trouble during this time have the charges against them dropped. *New York Times,* Mar. 8, 1971 at 1, col. 3; at 26, col. 2.
48. New York has instituted a program designed to handle the problem of narcotics addicts. The new program offers counseling, often by former drug addicts, and the opportunity to obtain proper treatment in one of the thirteen drug treatment centers participating with the city in the program. If the suspect completes the rehabilitation program, the charges against him are dropped. Unfortunately, money is the greatest obstacle to the effectiveness of the program, and this prevents the courts from treating addicts in a meaningful way. *New York Times,* May 31, 1971 at 17, col. 5. This is especially critical in New York City, where it is estimated that 50 to 60% of the crimes there are committed by drug addicts. *New York Times,* Dec. 6, 1970 §1A, at 1, col. 1.
49. See *A.L.I. Model Code of Pre-Arraignment Procedure,* American Law Institute (1972), Section 320.7.
50. Inmates of Attica Correctional Facility v. Rockefeller, 477 F.2d 375 (2d Cir. 1973); for an examination of the conditions at Attica, see Wicker, *A Time to Die* (New York: New York Times Press, 1975).
51. See Kamisar, et. al., *Modern Criminal Procedure,* 4th ed., pp. 838-39.
52. Comment, 65 *Yale L.J.* 209, 233 (1955).
53. See Commentary, *A.B.A. Standard, The Prosecution Function* §2.1 (1971).
54. Tonkin v. Michael, 349 F. Supp. 78 (D.V.I. 1972).
55. See e.g., Ill. Rev. Stat. ch. 14, §6.
56. Oyler v. Boles, 368 U.S. 448, 82 S. Ct. 501, 7 L. Ed.2d 446 (1962).
57. People v. Gray, 254 Cal. App.2d 256, 63 Cal. Rptr. 211 (1967), citing Snowden v. Hughes, 321 U.S. 1, 64 S. Ct. 397, 88 L. Ed. 497 (1944).
58. See United States v. Ahmad, 347 F. Supp. 912 (M.D. Pa. 1972), aff'd. sub nom, United States v. Berrigan, 484 F.2d 171 (3d Cir. 1973), denying access to prosecution files and memoranda.
59. See Society of Good Neighbors v. Van Antwerp, 324 Mich. 22, 36 N.W.2d 308 (1949) and People v. Harris, 182 Cal. App.2d 837, 5 Cal. Rptr. 852 (Super. Ct. 1960).
60. United States v. Falk, 479 F.2d 616 (7th Cir. 1973).
61. "The Professional Responsibility of the Prosecuting Attorney," 55 *Geo. L. J.*

1030, 1034-35 (1967), reprinted in Kamisar, et. al., *Modern Criminal Procedure,* pp. 814-15.

62. Uviller, "The Virtuous Prosecutor In Quest of an Ethical Standard: Guidance From the A.B.A." 71 *Mich. L. Rev.* 1145, 1147-48 (1973), reprinted in Kamisar, et. al., *Modern Criminal Procedure,* pp. 815-16.
63. "Prosecutorial Discretion and the Initiation of Criminal Complaints," *So. Ca. L. Rev.,* vol. 42 (1969).
64. See "Confining, Structuring, and Checking Prosecuting Power," in Kenneth Culp Davis, *Discretionary Justice* (University of Illinois Press, 1971).

6.

I talked and the judge asked me questions. Then what got me was the detective who arrested me and was in court with me walked around to the judge and whispered something in his ear. After that the detective came around and stood with me and the judge set the bail at $5,000. The judge asked me if I could make the bond. I had some money but it was in check form at home, and nobody could go in the house and get it from what I understood. So therefore, I had to stay in jail, and the judge continued my case.

Bail or Jail?

Ideally, the judge who presides over preliminary appearances makes sure that each defendant, especially those charged with felonies, understands the procedures taking place, his rights, and what to expect next. Yet, this does not describe reality. Because most people who come before a court of law for the first time have little knowledge of the legal system, their initial pretrial appearances are often marked by confusion, if not paranoia. Even though Ralph Johnson appeared in a suburban municipal court, a court not harried by overloaded dockets, he understood very little of what was happening to him. His confusion, his weak position, is not atypical; most suspects, at this preliminary stage, are intimidated by the seemingly blind mechanics of the law.

The Preliminary Appearance

Formal proceedings start with a defendant's first court appearance, variously called a preliminary appearance, initial appearance, or preliminary arraignment. The preliminary appearance is the defendant's first step in the long and cumbersome journey towards a determination of guilt or innocence. For many defendants this court appearance is the first time since their arrests that they have seen anyone other than police officers or detectives. To those defendants this court appearance is reassurance that the police do not have unlimited authority to hold them endlessly and that the ultimate determination of their future will be made by someone other than the police. To establish that reassurance, the preliminary appearance must be soon after the arrest. A prompt appearance also minimizes incommunicado detention of an accused for purposes of investigation.[1] American law only authorizes arrests based upon probable cause for a specific offense, not arrests based upon suspicion. Consequently, the state is obligated to press formal charges or release the suspect.

The statutes and court rules in most jurisdictions do not specify how soon the preliminary appearance must take place, relying instead on terms like "without unreasonable delay." This term generally means no later than the next regular court session. If there are more than a couple of days until the next regular session, the judge is generally notified by the police so that a special session can be scheduled to assure that the defendant will not be held without a bail determination for a long period of time.

An unwritten rule is frequently claimed to exist authorizing police to hold a suspect up to three days without necessarily charging him in court. However, when a suspect is detained without a court appearance beyond the next regularly scheduled court session, a legal remedy does exist in the form of a *habeas corpus* action, a term which means "produce the body of the person in question and explain the detention."[2] In a *habeas corpus* action the court instructs the authorities holding the petitioner to either charge or release him immediately. Generally, a threat to file such a petition will prompt the authorities to file charges or release the suspect.

The *habeas* remedy, though, is only available to those persons who know a lawyer to call or whose arrests and detention are known by someone with presence of mind to contact a lawyer who will make inquiries and then file the petition if necessary. The idea that a person may be held for three days has probably been given substance because so few persons arrested have immediate access to an attorney or are aware of the obligation of the state to formally charge them in court without delay. The legal process is not self-activating, and remedies such as *habeas corpus* are not available until someone who seeks the legal remedy files the petition and sets the machinery in motion.

The municipal or police court in which virtually all cases originate is a court of limited or inferior jurisdiction. This court has final jurisdiction over misdemeanor cases but very limited authority over felony cases. A misdemeanor case may be handled to conclusion within this court from initial appearance to trial, although the trial will likely be handled in another courtroom and heard by a different judge. If the charge is a felony, however, the court's jurisdiction extends only through the initial appearance and preliminary hearing, a fact that tends to prolong and complicate some cases unnecessarily.

In most large cities this courtroom is not at all what the first-time observer expects, nor does it resemble the municipal court where Ralph Johnson was initially charged. Many such big-city courts are charged with the responsibility for all preliminary appearances, felony and misdemeanors, but in the busiest courts in the country there may be so many cases that felony appearances are assigned to one room and misdemeanor appearances to another. In either instance, the novice observer would be startled by the great numbers of people milling around—defendants, their families, police, lawyers, court functionaries, and sometimes witnesses and complainants.[3] Just the great numbers of people in attendance guarantees that maintaining order and decorum is no small task.

The caseload scheduled on the daily docket sheet for all these courts is staggering, frequently exceeding one hundred. The judge is obligated to get through all of these cases. If he fails to clear the docket on any given day, the preliminary appearance in each of the cases will be delayed, at least one day, and those cases will be added to the next day's docket, which can expect to fill up in its own right. Rather than taking the time and expending the energy that would be involved in maintaining order within the courtroom, most of these judges have developed a tolerance towards a certain level of disorder and, instead, concentrate their efforts on clearing their docket.

The emphasis in these courts is generally on numbers of cases disposed of, and the judges are pressured by their administrators, in some cases administrative judges who determine assignments. Their own realizations of what will be on the calendar the following day if they do not complete their docket compounds the pressure. Therefore, their own measure of success is determined to a large extent in terms of cases processed, rather than the quality of justice in their courtrooms. One New York City Criminal Court judge's actions were analogized in the press to a fast-food operation. This judge was disposing of felony cases by breaking them down to misdemeanors and securing guilty pleas from defendants at the incredible rate of two and a half minutes per case. The particular judge wielded thirty-one different rubber stamps to ink in the disposition of the cases and each matter was ended with the judge turning to his bailiff and saying, "Go, Mike," which meant bring on the next case.[4]

Judges in crowded urban courts generally have little time to consider the merits of the cases before them, the dangerousness of the offenders, or even whether the defendants know what they are agreeing to. Notions of justice and the quality of justice become totally submerged in the court's need to run through its docket; the common rationale is that any breakdown in the speed with which the cases are processed or disposed of will have a domino effect, eventually resulting in a total stoppage of the mechanics of the "justice machine."

Misdemeanors

The first court appearance for a defendant charged with a misdemeanor may very well be the last in that case. Most persons charged with misdemeanors acknowledge their guilt by pleading guilty at the first court appearance in order to end the matter as soon as possible. Misdemeanants are rarely sentenced to jail for their crimes, and certainly not if they are first offenders, especially if the defendant pleads guilty.[5] This may vary in small towns and suburbs where judges and all personnel involved in the system are still not inured to crime, but it is a safe rule of thumb in large cities.

Since most defendants are singularly interested in getting out of the process and staying out of jail, the attractiveness of a quick plea and then going home is great.

From a logical standpoint, courts are obligated to consider first the rights of a defendant charged with a misdemeanor and secondly the options that are available. Yet because case disposition is stressed, judges or bailiffs are likely to give a quick summary of rights at the beginning of the court session for all assembled. In most cases, only when a misdemeanor defendant fails to enter a quick plea of guilty, does a judge fully explain the rights and choices available to that defendant. In the busiest courts a defendant charged with a misdemeanor is called before the bar. He has presumably heard the general statement of rights offered when the court convened. The charge will be stated and the defendant will be asked to plead. If he pleads guilty, the judge will pronounce sentence, a fine or a suspended jail sentence which will not be served unless the accused gets in trouble again and a computer picks up the old charge and suspended sentence. The defendant will be requested to sign some papers indicating that he is aware of his rights and options and chooses to waive them.

If the defendant pleads not guilty or hesitates before making a plea, the judge will devote greater attention to him. The nature of the charge will be explained to the defendant, and he will be advised of his rights. Principally, the court will be concerned about setting bail, securing counsel for the defendant, and setting the case for trial. The court will set a trial date and direct the defendant to reappear for trial in the same courtroom or another branch of the same court. Prior to the overcrowding of these courts, when a defendant pleaded not guilty, the judge would call all witnesses in the case forward, swear them in quickly and hold a very brief trial in front of the bench. Courts are not likely to do that anymore because of the burden of their daily dockets and the extension of constitutional guarantees, such as the right to counsel, to some misdemeanors. If the defendant is unable to secure his release on bail, the court may review the bail situation to try to release the defendant during the interim, or, more generally, will schedule an earlier trial date, probably within a week or ten days of the initial appearance.

Besides pleas of guilty or not guilty, most jurisdictions afford an accused a third alternative, a plea of *"no contest,"* meaning that the accused will not contest the facts as stated in the charge but will permit the court to determine whether those facts constitute the crime. What the defendant signifies in most cases when entering such a plea is that he does not want to go to trial but would like the opportunity to explain his conduct. After hearing the explanation, the court pronounces its judgment, generally guilty.[6]

Felonies

Because the stakes are much higher for defendants charged with felonies—prison sentences are a greater possibility and the community through its legislature has determined the offense to be more serious—the preliminary appearance is more critical. By reason that the charge is a felony and the court has limited jurisdiction, the case is likely to be continued. What of the defendant, though, who feels true remorse for his acts and, unlike Ralph Johnson, wants to plead guilty right away and accept the penalty imposed by the court? Consider the following:

> Defendant John Doe, aged 28, was arrested as he exited through the broken glass door of a small, neighborhood supermarket. When he broke the glass and entered, an alarm sounded at a private security company and the police were alerted. Several police cars were on the scene as he came out of the market and Doe did not resist when arrested. He was carrying a substantial amount of cash when he was arrested, and freely told the police that the money came from three cash registers in the store. Doe, the sole support of his wife and two children, was unemployed and had no criminal record. He lost his truck driving job two months before the break-in when the small trucking company where he had worked for the past five years went bankrupt. Though he tried to find new employment, he was unsuccessful. His family's total savings were used up in the interim. Breaking and entering a retail establishment with the intent to steal is a felony in the jurisdiction and Doe could be sentenced to prison for one to ten years. He is a good candidate for probation because of his clean record but, even if he goes to prison, he would likely be paroled as soon as he is eligible in ten months. He feels deep remorse for his act and realizes that his conduct was not a good solution for his problem. He would like to plead guilty, try to explain the motivation behind his act, and accept whatever punishment the court imposes.

In most jurisdictions, when Doe attempts to enter his plea of guilty at the preliminary appearance, he will be stopped. The court will explain its limited jurisdiction and suggest that if Doe really wants to enter a plea of guilty, he should waive the preliminary hearing and grand jury indictment (if applicable in that state). The court will send the case over to the court with general jurisdiction and the authority to dispose of felony cases. Yet because the paperwork in transferring a case from one court to another in many cities is quite time-consuming, it may be several weeks before Doe appears in a court that can accept his plea.

Doe is unlikely to be represented by an attorney at his first appearance. He probably could not have afforded to hire one, but even if he could he probably would not have had the time to contact one after his arrest and before this preliminary appearance. If the city or state provides legal aid assistance at the preliminary appearance, the lawyer may suggest to the assistant prosecutor that Doe's case is an appropriate one to reduce to a misdemeanor so that his plea could be accepted immediately. Even if a legal aid lawyer is present, however, that outcome is not guaranteed. First, the legal aid lawyers are so over-extended with cases that one would probably not have had the opportunity to learn much about Doe. Second, the assistant prosecutor may not have this background information on Doe nor know of his willingness to plead guilty because police reports are not necessarily in the file in time for the first court appearance. Finally, not all prosecutors would permit their assistants to reduce a felony to a misdemeanor without first receiving authorization. Many assistant prosecutors get their first experience in courtrooms where initial appearances take place and are delegated very little authority. Thus, notwithstanding Doe's willingness to plead guilty and not prolong the ordeal, his case will probably work its way into the felony process. Even if he is not sentenced to prison, for he is a logical candidate for probation, he will have suffered additional weeks of uncertainty. By the time his case gets to the court of general jurisdiction, Doe may have been around the criminal process long enough to have figured out a quirk in the system: that there is no reason to plead guilty to a felony; if one waits long enough the state may reduce the charge to a misdemeanor in order to get a guilty plea. His chances of going to jail if he pleads to a misdemeanor are less, but even if he does go it would be for a shorter time.

Doe's case would likely be handled much more intelligently in a few cities. In Detroit, Michigan, for instance, Doe would have made his initial appearance in Recorder's Court, which possesses complete jurisdiction in all felony cases from the preliminary appearance through trial. As a result of the single court system operating in Detroit, the delay inherent in the two-tiered court structure is eliminated, and the judge presiding at any stage can dispose of the case. Doe's case would have been quickly disposed of in New York City, too, but for different reasons. His first appearance would have been in the New York City Criminal Court, a court of limited jurisdiction that could not have taken his guilty plea to the felony. However, the court system in that city is so hungry for dispositions that most felony defendants are permitted to plead guilty to misdemeanors. Over eighty percent of all felony cases in New York City are resolved by dismissals or guilty pleas to misdemeanors reduced from felonies in the Criminal Court.[7]

The bargaining that occurs in New York City, at least at the preliminary appearance, does not exist in most jurisdictions. After the accused is informed of the charge, the first order of business is a determination of bail. Contemporaneously, the court will advise the defendant of his right to be represented by counsel. While few courts provide counsel at the preliminary appearance (unless they make it a practice to dispose of a substantial number of cases at that junction in the process), it is nonetheless the appropriate time to advise an accused of his right to counsel, to make the determination of eligibility for court-provided legal assistance, and either to appoint an attorney or refer the defendant to the public defender. At the next step, the accused is advised of the right to a preliminary hearing and grand jury indictment, if applicable. At this point, the court must also determine whether the accused wishes to have a hearing and indictment, or chooses to waive them.[8]

Bail

The most important action taken at the preliminary appearance is the bail determination. *Black's Law Dictionary* defines bail as a verb:

> to procure the release of a person from legal custody, by undertaking that he shall appear at the time and place designated and submit himself to the jurisdiction and judgment of the court.

Bail is also defined as a noun:

> the surety or sureties who procure the release of a person under arrest, by becoming responsible for his appearance at the time and place designated.[9]

The term is commonly used in both contexts, but to the individual who has been arrested the primary significance is "getting out." Traditionally in America, "getting out" has been through the process of ransoming the accused. In exchange for a sum of money the accused is released upon his promise to return when needed in court. If the accused fails to keep that promise and does not show up, then the money is forfeited. The forfeiture, of course, is not in lieu of trying the accused; it is a penalty for failing to keep the promise to appear. The pending case will be continued and the accused will be tried if he is apprehended at a later time, and there may be additional charges added to the original resulting from the accused's flight.[10]

Bail is a disheartening concept to the general public. It is difficult, especially for victims and witnesses, to understand why the individual whom they personally know has committed a crime is free to come and go within the community, seemingly unaffected by the pending criminal charges. A case in point was raised by the dean of a college of nursing some years ago when one of her students had been the victim of a rape. On the night of the rape the police responded promptly and apprehended the student's assailant whom she was able to identify. The student was hospitalized for several days. When she was released and walking to her dorm from the hospital, she saw the man who had raped her walking on the other side of the street. The dean was understandably concerned about the psychological well-being of the victim and the vulnerability of other women on the campus. Bail had been set in the amount of $3,000 and a bail bond had been posted to secure the accused's release, presumably after he or a member of his family had paid a bondsman $300. The irony is extreme because the attacker was back on the street before his victim was released from the hospital.

With full acknowledgment of these irksome and troubling aspects of freeing individuals accused of dangerous crimes, legal scholars have traditionally cast a wary eye upon the inequities in the bail system that have allowed too many persons to spend too long a time in jail while awaiting trials. Moreover, the right to bail has to be one of the cornerstones of our notion of due process. If the presumption of innocence is to have any meaning, then pretrial incarceration—which is punishment without conviction—must be disfavored and avoided. At the same time, society has a legitimate interest and need in keeping certain persons off the street. The dilemma, then, becomes figuring out how to make fair determinations of which defendants to detain while, at the same time, devising ways to protect these defendants' rights. In America the problem has been that we have generally gone about making these decisions through the back door with less than satisfactory results for defendants and society.

History

The historical origins of the concept of bail are obscure. One theory offers that the concept derived from the English institution of hostageship, where the individual offering himself as a hostage was held responsible "until the promise of a certain person was fulfilled or a certain consequence achieved."[11] That promise, of course, was standing trial. If the promise was not kept, the hostage-surety who guaranteed the promise would submit himself to the disappointed party. A second theory suggests that the hostage-surety would not submit himself if the promise was not kept but would, instead, forfeit his property to the disappointed party.[12] The other frequently noted origin of the concept of bail is the ancient English law of debt. This law required that someone accused of a wrongful act assure payment to reimburse the injured party in case the alleged wrongdoer was found guilty. A third party would guarantee payment to the victim if liability was established, and if the debtor could not pay, the third party was ultimately responsible for payment.[13]

Whatever its true source, bail was a necessary response to the very real problems of feudal times. In those days, the system of law and order was administered by traveling magistrates whose visits to a particular region were infrequent and irregular. A year or more could pass between judicial visits, so there was a need to arrange some alternative to jail during the interim. Because local sheriffs bore the responsibility for prisoner custody, they were vested with great power to determine what to do with persons charged and awaiting trial. Frequently, sheriffs exercised this expansive discretionary power by placing a prisoner in the provisional custody of a surety. Should the defendant who had been released to a surety fail to show up on the date of trial, the surety might be imprisoned or might be required to pay a sum of money to the sheriff.[14]

Since there were no formal standards to be applied by the sheriffs in deciding whether to release on bail, it became a decision subject to arbitrariness and abuse. To combat this, Parliament, in 1275, enacted the Statute of Westminster I,[15] listing crimes that were and were not bailable and imposing fines upon the sheriffs if the standards were not obeyed. Later in the thirteenth century, justices of the peace replaced the sheriffs as grantors of bail.[16] Toward the end of the fifteenth century (1486), another act was passed that made it necessary for two justices to agree on bail for certain prisoners.[17]

To understand the significance of three additional statutes applicable to bail, it is necessary to consider them in the historical context of the Magna Carta. The Magna Carta, as early as 1215, provided that: "No freeman shall be taken, or imprisoned, or disseised, or outlawed or exiled, or in any way destroyed, nor will we go upon him, nor will we send upon him, except by the legal judgment of his peers or by the law of the land."[18] In the famous seventeenth-century case, *Darnel's Case,*[19] certain persons were imprisoned by order of the king on unstated grounds. The defendants brought a *habeas corpus* action, but the court agreed with the prosecution that the Magna Carta provision quoted above did not apply to pretrial incarceration. This resulted in an irreconcilable dilemma. If the grounds for imprisonment were not enumerated, the defendant, according to the result in *Darnel,* could be imprisoned without bail prior to trial because the Magna Carta was inapplicable. The Statute of Westminster I was also inapplicable since it listed bailable and nonbailable crimes and could not be invoked unless a defendant was charged with a specific offense. The Petition of Rights,[20] which required that grounds for detention be specified, was passed in 1628 to resolve this conflict. Thus more than four hundred years after the Magna Carta was forced from King John, the protection of the Magna Carta was finally extended to pretrial imprisonment.

Further meaning was imputed to the Magna Carta in 1676 because of a case in which bail had been refused to a defendant imprisoned for three months on bailable charges.[21] Protest over this treatment led to the passage of the Habeas Corpus Act,[22] which penalized judges who refused to grant bail where the offense charged was bailable. This practice, however, led to still another abuse, and more patchwork was required. As they could no longer refuse bail with impunity, some judges responded by imposing prohibitively high bail in certain felonies. This is still a common practice in modern American courts. The problem was attacked in the English Bill of Rights,[23] which was enacted by Parliament as William and Mary ascended the throne in 1689. The English Bill of Rights provided that excessive bail ought not to be required (nor excessive fines imposed, nor cruel and unusual punishment inflicted).[24] This law provided the model that the colonies were to use in drafting the Eighth Amendment to the new Constitution. Additional laws in nineteenth-century England permitted the justices to exercise discretion in admitting to bail anyone accused of a felony, while certain misdemeanors were bailable as of right.[25]

Because of the mobility of its people and its expanding frontiers, colonial America followed a different path in developing a bail practice. The English system of bail-surety emphasized the personal responsibility of the surety to produce the defendant at trial. The surety was invariably a friend or relative. The mobile colonists, on the other hand, developed comparatively few family ties or friends. Since a personal guarantee was unreliable in the new world, a purely monetary bail system was substituted for the surety approach.[26]

Congress first gave serious consideration to bail in Section thirty-three of the Judiciary Act of 1789,[27] which described bail as an absolute right in non-capital federal offenses. Two years later, the Eighth Amendment protection against excessive bail was adopted. The effect of these independent actions was to give the right to bail a statutory origin and the protection against excessive bail a constitutional basis.[28]

The Constitutional Right to Bail

The Eighth Amendment of the Bill of Rights is unclear regarding the actual protection it affords the accused. Adopted in 1791, it states: "Excessive bail shall not be required. . . ." Whether or not this language creates an affirmative right to bail has been vigorously argued over the years, and since the Constitution makes no other reference to bail and because the Supreme Court has never squarely faced the issue of a right to bail, it remains a subject of conjecture and dispute among constitutional authorities.[29]

The existence of the Judiciary Act has stunted the full development and interpretation of the Eighth Amendment provision on bail. Traditionally, the Supreme Court has resorted to the language of the Eighth Amendment to resolve controversies involving excessive bail;[30] and where a right to bail was at issue in a federal prosecution, the Court has avoided the constitutional issue by resolving the problem under the Judiciary Act.[31] This reliance on the Judiciary Act has avoided the necessity of deciding whether a right to bail is a constitutionally guaranteed right. But the Judiciary Act is only applicable to prosecutions in federal courts and has no impact or effect upon state criminal prosecutions, which constitute over ninety percent of all criminal cases in this country. Thus the extent of the protection of the Eighth Amendment, and its applicability to the states through the Fourteenth Amendment, remains a crucial question—crucial not only to ascertain the extent and breadth of the constitutional guarantee but also to determine the amount of interference and supervision of state criminal cases on this question that may be exercised by federal courts.

The closest the Supreme Court has ever come to interpreting whether the Eighth Amendment guarantees a right to bail was in *Stack v Boyle,*[32] a case arising from a federal prosecution where the Court was primarily concerned with the setting of excessive bail. There the Supreme Court ruled that "[b]ail set at a higher figure than an amount reasonably calculated to fulfill this purpose [to secure assurance that the defendant will stand trial] is excessive under the Eighth Amendment."[33] The Supreme Court was saying, in effect, that the Constitution prohibited courts from denying the right to bail by the indirect, though common, practice of requiring unreasonably inflated bail. If bail cannot be denied indirectly, then it would seem unlikely that it could be denied directly except in extraordinary cases based upon clearly defined standards. The implication of the Court's decision is that the Constitution guarantees a right to bail, but it is a right supported only by logically persuasive arguments and not by conclusive court decision.

Bail Determination

Even if a right to bail were found in the Eighth Amendment, it would not be absolute, as no constitutional rights are absolute. All are subject to curtailment when the government shows a compelling and justifiable need for infringement and limitation. Both state and federal governments deny bail to at least some defendants charged with an offense which could carry the death penalty.[34] The rationale for this denial of bail is obvious: no amount of money will ensure the defendant's appearance at trial if, upon conviction, he risks death. If Lee Harvey Oswald had lived to stand trial for the murder of President John F. Kennedy, would any amount of money, raised by his family, friends or sympathizers, likely have insured that Oswald would return to the Dallas courthouse and risk his life at trial?

There are reasons for denying the right to bail in non-capital cases. An individual who has a history of flight to avoid prosecution has already established his propensity to flee and need not be released on bail pending trial.[35] Similarly a defendant who has intimidated witnesses in an effort to discourage them from testifying against him or who attempts to secure perjured testimony on his behalf need not be released on bail or may have bail revoked and be recommitted to jail to await trial.[36] A common thread links these three traditional exceptions to the right to bail: *interference* with the criminal justice process, either through the unlikelihood of the defendant's reappearing for trial, or by thwarting the tribunal's ability to learn the truth through discouraging witnesses from testifying or procuring false testimony for the trial. The rationale for the established exceptions to the right to bail go directly to the purpose of bail, the double assurance that the accused will stand trial and that the court will be able to hear the evidence in the case. Yet today the public is equally concerned with bail as a "safety measure." That is, should the right to bail be extended to a defendant who is likely to threaten the safety of the community during his pretrial freedom?

That question challenges the fundamental American principle, the presumption of innocence. A "dangerous"person who has not been convicted is theoretically innocent until he is proven guilty. Therefore, pretrial incarceration or the denial of bail cannot be justified. If a person is held in jail prior to a determination of his innocence or guilt, his probable guilt or "dangerous" character would be at the root of his detention. His innocence is not presumed at all. Regardless of the possible threat this person may pose to society, his pretrial incarceration is contrary to the presumption of innocence. Thus, until the purposes to be served by bail are re-examined and exceptions to the right carefully carved out, the right to bail must be inextricably linked to the presumption of innocence doctrine.[37]

Most persons formally charged with a crime are ultimately convicted, whether after trial or upon a plea of guilty. Logically, then, some device is necessary to encourage a defendant to return and stand trial if he is to be released during the interim. If there were no penalty for failing to appear, we could assume that only those who are innocent and convinced that the tribunal will believe in their innocence would reappear. Bail is to serve the purpose of insuring the accused's return to the courthouse for trial and his submission to the judgment of the court. Bail is money or other property turned over to the court by the accused as a form of ransom to assure that the accused will return. If he fails to appear voluntarily, the money or property which was exchanged to secure the accused's release is forfeited.

If the presumption of innocence is to be maintained as a working and not just theoretical principle, bail must be within the reach of the accused and his family. Thus, if bail is a dollar amount, it should be an amount significant enough to dissuade the accused from fleeing the court's jurisdiction but not so high as to deny the accused the opportunity to secure freedom before trial. The bail determination, therefore, must be an individual matter, tailored for each defendant.

In setting customized bail there are established criteria that are almost universally imposed by statute and court rule. The Federal Rules of Criminal Procedure list the four to be used in setting bail in federal criminal prosecutions:

1. nature and circumstances of the offense charged
2. weight of the evidence against the defendant
3. financial ability of the defendant to give bail
4. character of the defendant[38]

The language may vary from jurisdiction to jurisdiction, but the criteria remain essentially the same. The first involves the charge against the accused. The more serious the crime, the greater the prospective penalty and the more inclined an accused might be to flee. The second criterion is the likelihood of a conviction. If the government has an airtight case and conviction is certain, which may increase the likelihood of a jail or prison sentence, a higher bail might be justified to encourage the accused to remain in the jurisdiction and face his trial. Third, the ability of the accused to raise bail money is critical if the amount set is to be a sum that is significant to the accused but within his reach. Fourth, and most important, is the character of the accused. Besides dealing with his past history of flight to avoid prosecution and intimidation of witnesses, this consideration delves into the accused's ties to the community. Are his ties sufficiently binding to keep him in town, or are they so weak that they fail to provide any reason why he should stay around for trial? Family ties and employment stability are frequently determinative.[39] If the defendant lives with and has helped to support his family, then there is greater likelihood that he will remain in the vicinity and maintain those ties. In such a situation, low bail or release without money bail is usually justifiable because the defendant is a good risk. The transient defendant or a resident without strong local ties is generally considered a bad risk for release.

Many communities try not to keep persons charged with misdemeanors in jail overnight or throughout the weekend until their first court appearance. Given the nature of misdemeanors and their penalties, the accused is not likely to be so frightened by the prospect of conviction and jail that he will flee rather than stand trial. Moreover, jails are often burgeoning with persons awaiting trial on serious offenses and, in any event, are not particularly safe, so the emphasis is on ways to get the misdemeanor defendant back on the street immediately without his having to spend that night in jail. *Jailhouse bail* has been devised for this purpose. The bail accepted in the police station or at the jail is determined according to a schedule adopted by statute or approved by the local court which sets the amount of bail solely upon the seriousness of the misdemeanor. Obviously, it is not an individualized decision, but it serves the purpose of securing the accused's release without vesting too much discretion in the police or sheriff by permitting neither to determine the amount. Some cities maintain night and weekend court sessions so that the accused upon arrest can be brought directly before a judge for purposes of setting bail. Still others permit the police to release a defendant immediately after arrest and booking simply upon his promise to reappear. If the police do not feel that is sufficient assurance for a particular misdemeanor defendant, they then utilize the money bail schedule. If the family cannot post the bail as prescribed by the schedule, a bail bondsman may be willing to post a bond to secure the accused's release upon payment of a premium, generally ten percent, by the defendant or his family. If none of these alternatives secures the release of the accused, he will remain in confinement at least until his first court appearance where a judge will reconsider the bail in his case.

Felony defendants are rarely eligible for jailhouse bail. Because a felony is a serious offense, the law generally requires that the bail determination be made by a judge at the preliminary appearance. Thus, the felony defendant will have at least a taste of jail and be confined until the first court appearance. Even these in-court bail determinations of felony defendants and misdemeanants unable to secure earlier release are hardly the individualized decisions that bail in a system governed by the presumption of innocence would require. The nature of the state courts where the preliminary appearances take place has already been described. Overburdened by too many cases, judges in these courts make bail decisions by rote, without considering the individual characteristics of the accused. Whenever a determination is made by rote it is almost always based solely upon the charge. Some jurisdictions acknowledge that bail is set in this manner and adopt schedules based only on the seriousness of the charge, as in Los Angeles where bail is set in accord with an approved bail schedule adopted by the judges.[40]

A judge will rarely inquire into the defendant's character in determining bail. Since there is no time to check family ties and employment records, the decision comes down to the objective material of the charge, which can be referred to superficially and rapidly. At this stage, the charge is most often the product of a police decision with, at best, cursory approval from a member of the prosecutor's staff. The police decision as to the charge has been made without considering the strength of the case, reliability of witnesses, constitutional questions relating to evidence, or importance to the community of prosecuting the charge to its full extent. The police opinion as to culpability is devoid of the realities of convictability, and thus the charge which they select is often an overcharge. If the defendant is to plead guilty, as most eventually will, it is likely that the plea will be to a lesser charge, yet the bail determination is made at this point on the initial, inflated charge. In some cities, the judge will also have the past conviction record of the accused to help him make the decision as to bail. Unfortunately, however, the pressures of the docket make it difficult for the judge to find out anything more about the accused. His decision concerning bail will be made, therefore, on the basis of the initial charge and the man's record, despite the fact that neither constitutes an adequate foundation on which to base a credible or valid decision as to how much money will ensure the defendant's presence at trial.

Attempting to avoid the rote setting of bail, many cities have bail agencies whose task is to interview the defendant prior to the court appearance and amass as much relevant information as possible about the accused's ties to the community.[41] While the time element remains a critical problem, these agencies attempt to verify the information provided by the accused pertaining to employment and place and length of residence. The bail agency's report is submitted to the judge when the accused is brought forth for the preliminary appearance and affords the court somewhat more information to go on in setting bail than just the charge and the accused's past record.

Bail determinations are subject to review by an appellate court.[42] It is one of the very few issues that may be appealed to a higher court while the case is in progress, rather than having to wait for the entire case to be terminated. Naturally, the reason for permitting *interlocutory appeals* on this issue during the life of the case is because the issue would be moot at the end of the case and the defendant would have no other way of protecting this essential right. Absent a review procedure, the court setting bail would have total and unlimited discretion in the matter. Even with appellate review available, the amount of bail or other conditions of release are within the discretion of the judge. The reviewing court will not overturn the decision and reduce the bail unless the accused can demonstrate that it is so excessive and without justification so as to amount to an abuse of that discretion.[43]

Money Bail

The power to determine bail is the authority to set bail at an amount of money that denies freedom to a defendant. This is not materially affected by the availability of appellate review because decisions on bail are rarely overturned. The attitude of the judge determines whether or not a defendant's bail will be set at an amount that he and his family can raise. If the judge favors pretrial release, then the bail will be reasonable; if not, the judge can set it beyond the means of the defendant. A court does not have to state its reasons for setting bail at a particular amount, and thus it is difficult for an appellate court to find clear evidence of discretionary abuse.

America has a long tradition of high bail and prolonged pretrial detention. John Peter Zenger spent ten months in jail awaiting trial for criminal libel against the English governor.[44] Consistent with English law operating in the colonies, Zenger was accorded his right to have bail set. The magistrate, who was responsible to the English governor, set bail at 400 pounds, notwithstanding Zenger's evidentiary showing that this exceeded his net worth ten times and that it was impossible for him to acquire the sum. But Zenger's incarceration served the colonial authorities well because it put him and his printing press out of circulation for the period between his arrest and ultimate acquittal at trial. The precedent established in the Zenger case carried over and became an American tradition, regardless of federal and state constitutional guarantees to the contrary.

Money bail is susceptible to being misused to insure pretrial detention. A judge dissatisfied with the lenient sentencing policies of his colleagues may set bail beyond the reach of an accused to give that person a taste of punishment. This represents a classic example of punishment without conviction and before guilt is ascertained. We are not so far removed from the day when it was common court policy to automatically increase the bail requirement for black defendants for the singular purpose of making it more difficult or impossible for a black defendant to regain his freedom before trial. During the height of the civil rights demonstrations, for example, an arrested demonstrator often was charged with the violation of several criminal statutes. To prevent the defendant's release on bail, all the judicial officer had to do was exact a separate bail for each charge, thereby insuring that the total sum was beyond the reach of most defendants.[45]

The burden of the bail system falls upon the poor. The affluent defendant can raise the cash and get it back; the middle-class citizen can probably raise the bondsman's fee and must pay the premium to obtain his freedom; and the poor remain in jail because of their inability to raise any bond money. None of these economic factors has a significant value in determining whether the defendant is a good risk for bail. Thus a set of procedures for selecting those who will be free on bail has evolved that has nothing to do with the purpose of bail.

The Bail Bondsman

Once bail is set, the defendant, his family, friends, employer, or even a stranger may come forth, deposit the stipulated amount, and secure the defendant's freedom. Yet few people have sufficient readily available cash, easily convertible securities, or mortgage-free real estate, and thus the scene is set for the person who truly determines bail or jail for most defendants: the professional bondsman.

Bondsmen in most large cities are responsible for over seventy-five percent of pretrial releases.[46] Most bondsmen are backed by insurance companies, but in rare instances, they operate on their own assets. Their fees depend upon the individual defendant and the amount of collateral pledged by the defendant and his family. In those states that regulate the bondsman, the statutory maximum for his services has normally been set at ten percent, although some states use a five percent maximum. Bondsmen themselves will often lower their fee to five percent if offered cash collateral. When cash collateral is submitted, it is usually put in a savings account. When the bond is subsequently discharged, the person who put up the collateral receives the original amount plus the interest and the bondsman keeps the premium. Where bondsmen are not subject to state regulation, the ceiling is provided by the market.

The individual who secures his own release without the help of a bondsman will have the money returned to him by the court at the time the case is concluded. On the other hand, the defendant whose freedom has been secured by a bondsman at the cost of ten percent of the face value of the bond has made an irretrievable expenditure for his freedom.

The introduction of the bail bondsman thoroughly confuses the issues inherent in money bail. Bail is to be set at an amount that is just right to accomplish the dual purposes of securing the accused's pretrial release and assuring that the accused returns for trial. Yet many defendants are only able to secure their freedom by paying a fee (usually one-tenth as much as the judge determined was necessary) to a stranger. The integrity of the bail system is undermined by the bondsman's profession. For instance, if the premium paid to the bondsman is sufficient up-front money from a defendant or his family, was the original bail setting excessive? If the defendant and his family can only raise the bondsman's premium (which they will never get back), instead of the full amount of bail which would be returned at the conclusion of the case, did the court setting the bail seriously consider the financial ability of the accused and his family? Is the money paid to the bondsman sufficient to assure that the defendant will return for trial?

Many bondsmen will simply refuse to write a bond unless the collateral offered is in excess of the face value of the release bond, or unless there is a guarantor for the bond with assets equal to or greater than the amount of bail. The bondsman operates within the framework of free enterprise. If, for any reason, he chooses not to write a bond for a particular accused, there is no recourse from his decision. The decision to "go or not to go bond" for an accused may be totally arbitrary and is final.[47]

The Effect of Pretrial Detention

Over half the inmate population of American prisons and jails are there awaiting trial. They are incarcerated without conviction and sentence, without a determination that they are more likely to flee than those who have been freed on bail, and without a determination that they are likely to commit additional crimes during the period between arrest and trial. They are there, enduring the same punishment that they might receive upon conviction, solely because they are poor. These prisoners are in jail because they and their families are unable to raise the bondsman's premium or show collateral sufficient to indemnify the bondsman for the full cost of the bond if the accused fails to show up for trial.

County and city jails, the holding institutions where pretrial detainees are confined, are among the worse penal institutions in the country. Often there is no distinction made in these jails between the accused and the convicted who have been sentenced to confinement or are there pending sentencing, an appeal, or transfer to a state penitentiary. Within the same cells or ranges within these jails are first offenders and persons charged with relatively minor offenses and those charged with or convicted of serious crimes.

Cells planned for one, two, or four prisoners are housing twice as many. Sanitary conditions are atrocious, health care is sparse and dental care, even on an emergency basis, virtually unknown.[48] A federal census of city and county jails undertaken at the beginning of the 1970s found that eighty-five percent had no educational or recreational facilities whatsoever, and about one-fourth have no facility for visitors.[49] Once interred, a prisoner may be confined to a cell block with no opportunity for exercise for many months, except for trips to courtrooms.

Often the institutions' rules and life styles are set by experienced inmates, and jailers are either blind to much that goes on or helpless to protect the others. The beatings and homosexual assaults endured by Ralph Johnson during his ten months' confinement were, sadly, not atypical. Young men and women introduced into this environment with no previous experience in fending off such attacks are immediately preyed upon.[50] For instance, consider the experience of a pre-law student detained in the overcrowded, decrepit New Orleans Parish Prison: the student was arrested for carrying a concealed weapon and was unable to post $500 bail or find a bondsman who would write a bond for him. He was placed in a dormitory-style cell with thirty other inmates who were accused of everything from minor offenses to armed robbery and murder. Having been warned by a guard to avoid fights at all costs, the student reluctantly obeyed a cellmate's order to take a shower. When he emerged, he discovered that his clothes had been taken. After he got to his cell he was administered a severe beating. During the nine days that he was confined, the student was forced to submit to multiple sexual acts every night by other inmates. At the end of nine days, the student appeared in court, pleaded guilty and was released after he paid a fine of fifty dollars. One year prior to the student's ordeal, the United States Department of Justice had inspected the overcrowded New Orleans facility and had recommended its immediate closing.[51]

Another ghastly illustration involves an eighteen-year-old defendant who was awaiting trial in the Cook County Jail in Chicago for being truant from school. He wrote his mother that he could not stand the beatings he was taking from other inmates. The night the letter was mailed, someone set fire to his mattress and locked him in his cell. The youth who did not smoke and had no matches was severely burned and died a few weeks later.[52]

Eruptions of violence among inmates are common, and violent rioting in protest of jail conditions fades in and out of our evening news reports. Suicides, too, are not an infrequent response to the dehumanizing conditions. One commission investigating the suicide of a young detainee who was incarcerated pending disposition of his case categorized his detention as having "succeeded only in deranging him."[53]

In addition to the physical and emotional penalties paid by the jailed defendant, there is reason to believe that pretrial incarceration has a substantial effect upon the outcome of a defendant's case in terms of likelihood of conviction and of going to prison. An accused in jail is of little value in the preparation of his defense. Aside from its many known tangible and intangible benefits, freedom for a defendant during the period between arrest and trial enables him to prepare for trial, whether that preparation involves helping a lawyer investigate and find witnesses, earning money to pay the attorney's fee, or setting a pattern of constructive behavior which may result in a lighter sentence.

The attorney must assume complete investigatory responsibility if his client is in jail. In many ways, the jailed defendant is an absolute liability to the defense attorney since the attorney must go to the jail every time he wants to see the client or check on a particular fact. Frequently the defendant in jail is virtually forgotten by his attorney. Rather than consult with the client every time a question arises, the attorney may defer looking into the matter until it is convenient to visit the jail. Jails are filled with defendants awaiting trial for several months who, like Ralph Johnson, complain bitterly that they have seen their attorneys only once or twice.

The jailed defendant is also subject to constant pressures to plead guilty. Unlike the defendant on bail, the accused in jail cannot afford to follow the advice of nearly all defense attorneys "to wait out the prosecutor." There is nothing to wait out; punishment is in progress. A guilty plea to a lesser offense could result in a short jail sentence or even probation. Most importantly, it moves the defendant closer to freedom. Defendants who are free on bail are under no pressure whatever to agree to a plea of guilty. That defendant is able to hold out for the most favorable deal, possibly until the prosecutor finally agrees to probation. If the defendant on bail is facing a hostile judge or prosecutor, he can attempt to delay trial in hopes that at a later time a different judge or prosecutor more influenced by the pending caseload might be willing to offer a more favorable deal. The individual who is in jail does not have the same leverage with which to manipulate the system; each day spent in jail is punishment.

In its massive work on standards for the administration of criminal justice, the American Bar Association in the material on pretrial release citing studies in Philadelphia, the District of Columbia, and New York indicated that "the conviction rate for jailed defendants materially exceeds that of bailed defendants."[54] Statistical surveys conducted in the Cleveland, Ohio courts did not discover a substantial difference in the percentage of defendants pleading guilty, based upon a bailed or jailed condition. These findings did concur with those in the other cities, however, on the issue of sentencing. The bailed defendant is far more likely to receive probation, while the defendant in jail has at least an even chance of being sentenced to the penitentiary or reformatory. The Cleveland figures showed that less than twenty-five percent of bailed defendants who were convicted received prison sentences, while sixty percent of the defendants who were unable to make bail went to prison.[55]

There is good explanation for these great discrepancies. While the bailed defendant is "waiting out the prosecutor," he is able to build a new record. If necessary, he can change his associates, develop a commendable work record, and reestablish his family ties. If the case is delayed for a year or more, by the time the defendant is sentenced, his attorney will be able to present to the court a good argument based upon the defendant's exemplary conduct while the case was pending, and explain away the criminal act by saying that there were mitigating circumstances involved in the crime and that the defendant should not now be sentenced to prison. The defendant in jail, on the other hand, has no opportunity to build a new record; thus it is less likely that his attorney will be able to present any mitigating circumstances, other than that the defendant has already spent time in jail. Some of the factors that lead to high bail, such as a long criminal record, will also contribute to sending a defendant to prison after conviction. But one study which considered all of these aspects came to the conclusion that notwithstanding these factors, a defendant who is in jail is more likely to have an unfavorable disposition of his case than his counterpart who is free on bail and who may have an identical criminal record.

Former New York Mayor John Lindsay, who also served as vice chairman of President Johnson's crime and justice commission, summed up the dilemma that pretrial detention presents to this society:

> Defendants are subjected to the Red Queen's jurisprudence: first the punishment, then the trial. They do time before they are found guilty of the crime.[56]

Bail Reform

Money bail, implemented by the arbitrary decisions and strong-arm tactics of the bail bondsmen, seems to work only because it is convenient. But the penalties of that convenience are high. They range from a denigration of the due process goal of maximizing pretrial freedom, to discrimination against a class of defendants based solely upon their poverty, to the great financial costs involved in unnecessarily detaining large numbers of persons. Because money bail based largely upon the police-determined charge discriminates against the poor, freedom is denied to countless defendants who would otherwise be good bail risks. Moreover, the traditional money bail system countenances and abets the excesses and blatant illegalities of the bondsman's trade.[57]

While money bail continues to be the prevailing system for securing pretrial release, it by no means enjoys the monopoly it once had. Within the past twenty years every state court system as well as the federal courts have adopted alternative routes to pretrial freedom. These have been devised to extend the constitutional ideal of bail to the poor, to alleviate the overcrowding in jails and other pretrial detention facilities, and, frankly, to break the tenacious hold of the professional sureties, the bondsmen. Notwithstanding these strong incentives, attitudes and practices are slow to change. The authority to use alternative methods of release rests with the judge setting bail, and his attitudes towards pretrial release and bail bonds will determine whether alternative methods are utilized.

Few jurisdictions have embraced the federal approach that provides for release on a surety's bond only if the alternative and favored conditions of release are not sufficient to assure the accused's presence at trial.[58] If the states have been slow to accept the federal explicit disapproval of bondsmen, they surely have resisted the American Bar Association's proposed standard which would prohibit compensated sureties.[59] Nonetheless there has been a noticeable change. A national bail study compared pretrial detention rates in 1962 at the very beginning of the bail reform movement with the rates one decade later in twenty major cities. The study found that the detention of felony defendants had decreased by one-third, from fifty-two percent to thirty-three percent, and that the percentage of misdemeanor defendants being detained had dropped from forty percent to twenty-eight percent.[60] The decrease in the detention rates was substantial in most of the twenty cities, Minneapolis being the greatest, going from fifty-four to thirteen percent of felony defendants being detained. Only Boston and Kansas City failed to show substantial reductions, both continuing to detain more than sixty percent of the felony defendants.[61]

The alternative methods for pretrial release attempt to measure the likelihood of a particular defendant's fleeing the court's jurisdiction by concentrating on the ties that may or may not bind a defendant to the locale. Additionally, some of the methods continue to utilize money bail or promises to pay while attempting, at the same time, to deal the professional bondsman out of the system. The judge making the bail decision has several options along with the traditional bail bond from which to choose.

Release on Recognizance

The Manhattan Bail Project, the prototype for most national projects, began in 1961 when a wealthy New York businessman toured one of the city's detention facilities and was overwhelmed by the human misery that he witnessed. He created the Vera Institute of Justice, the first project which was to make the use of release on recognizance programs (ROR) an acceptable procedure in New York City criminal courts and to create a program that had nationwide acceptability. A release on recognizance is based upon the accused's affirming his obligation to appear in court when necessary; the accused need not post any cash or a bond to secure that promise.

Eligibility for release on recognizance was ascertained in the Manhattan Bail Project by law students who interviewed detainees to determine whether they were good risks for such release. The questioning focused upon the individual's residential stability, employment history, family contacts in the area, and prior criminal record. After meeting with the accused, the interviewer verified through phone calls and record checks the information provided by the accused. A point system was utilized, with points awarded for positive information such as solid employment history or a long-time community residency. The point total was reduced when the accused was identified as a past criminal offender. If the total points scored registered above an established minimum, the project recommended to the judge release on recognizance. The early results were rewarding. With verified information, judges tended to release four times as many accused, ninety-eight percent of those released through the project returned to court for scheduled appearances.[62]

To place these figures in perspective, it must be kept in mind that this initial program of recognizance release excluded defendants charged with homicides, narcotics offenses, sex crimes, and police assaults. Persons charged with such crimes were excluded not so much from the belief that these people were not releasable, but from the belief of the program planners that a better public image would be fostered if a "hands off" approach were followed in the early stages. Since the Manhattan Bail Project, other similar programs have operated without this exclusionary policy, and project administrators have reported no adverse results in expanding release procedures to include those persons formerly considered "untouchable."[63]

The success of the initial project led to its city-wide adoption and emulation throughout the country. A pretrial services project has taken over the task performed by Vera's law students. Every defendant in the city is now interviewed. Originally excluded from their consideration were persons charged with homicides or charges involving serious bodily injury while the victim remained in critical condition. The elimination of these restrictions has led to at least one absurd result. Looking only at employment, family ties and length of residency and not permitted to consider the seriousness of the charge, the agency has frequently recommended release on recognizance for persons charged with murder. No judge is likely to accept that recommendation and, in fact, most New York judges deny bail to all persons charged with murder. However, one such recommendation did garner damaging publicity for the program. Shortly after his arrest, David Berkowitz, the "Son of Sam" killer who had terrorized New York for several months, was recommended for release without bail because he had a permanent residency and a steady job. Berkowitz was not released, but the press, politicians and the public began to reassess the recognizance program and its underlying philosophy.[64]

ROR is an accepted alternative to money bail. Even in cities without bail or pretrial services agencies, judges are releasing defendants whom they consider worthy without money bail. Defendants who do not meet the objective criteria used by the agencies may still be released on recognizance if the judge deems it advisable. This practice exists in New York where the "no show" rate amongst defendants who did not meet the objective criteria but were still released on recognizance by a judge is ten point three percent, only slightly higher than the nine point eight percent of defendants released on recognizance upon recommendation of the pretrial services agency.[65] The number of defendants who fail to appear is up all over the country, and the New York figures are fairly typical. The national bail study did find, however, no significant difference between the "no show" rate for defendants released on their own recognizance and those who posted money bail.[66] Even if the "no show" rate is maintained at a tolerable level, it does pose growing and perplexing problems. The Vera Institute estimated that over a period of ten years 177,000 unexecuted warrants had accumulated for defendants who failed to show for their court appearances.[67] It is often expressed that the only time a lost defendant is found is when he is arrested for another offense. There are, of course, others who reappear on their own accord and have explanations for their initial failure to appear.

Frequently substituted for or augmenting ROR is the personal bond. This approach enables an accused to secure his release upon execution of a personal bond in a specified amount for which no cash or collateral is required. If the accused fails to show up, the bond may be ordered forfeited and an attempt will be made to collect the amount from the accused when and if he is subsequently found.

Conditional Release

This approach to pretrial release permits the judge to set limitations upon the degree of freedom available to an accused. The accused may be released into the custody of another person or agency.[68] The person, generally a relative or agency, supervises the accused during the period between release and trial, keeps close tabs on the whereabouts of the accused, and reports to the court any failure of the accused to comply with the conditions. Frequently, release to an agency or organization is coupled with health care, education, or work-training programs conducted by the agency for the benefit of persons committed to its supervision. The purpose of conditional release is to provide freedom with varying degrees of restraint. In addition to release under supervision, the court may restrict the right of the accused to travel, or may restrict the hours that an accused may be away from home, or even where or with whom the accused makes his home. The most stringent provision allows release by day and return to a detention facility at night. This obviously is a significant restraint upon the individual, but it does permit one to maintain employment to support a family and raise legal fees.

In any determination of what release conditions to recommend or use, a variety of conflicting factors push and pull at the judge making the decision. Besides the preferred right of an individual to be free while awaiting trial, the flexibility offered by the alternative methods of release also offers an opportunity for the judge to consider the needs of the community. Conditional release need not be used alone. It can be used in combination with any other method and may be most helpful for an accused who may otherwise qualify for ROR but about whom the judge has the slightest hesitation.

Ten Percent Deposits

Besides the grip on the traditional bail system held by the bondsmen, their absolute power to refuse to write a bond is the financial inequity that falls upon the individual who must pay the ten percent premium to the bondsman. The individual who can post the full cash amount of the bail receives that sum in full when the case is terminated and the bail discharged. Naturally, the individual using a professional bondsman pays for that service, and the premium is retained in full by the surety after the bond is discharged. The system has always reeked of inequity, especially in the case of the defendant who could barely scrape together the bondsman's premium. If that defendant is subsequently acquitted, it has nonetheless cost him substantial out-of-pocket costs to remain free before trial.

The alternative ten percent deposit was pioneered in Illinois.[69] Essentially, the system requires the defendant for whom bail has been set to execute a bail bond and deposit with the clerk of the court an amount equal to ten percent of the bail. If the bail is less than $250, a $25 deposit must, nonetheless, be made. Rather than pay the ten percent to a bondsman, the defendant pays the money directly to the court. When the conditions of the bail bond are fulfilled and the bond is discharged, almost all of the deposit is returned to the defendant. Ten percent of the deposit, one percent of the face amount of the bond, is retained by the court to cover the administrative costs of the program. If the defendant is able to deposit the full amount of the bond, it will all be returned when the case is terminated. Variations on the Illinois plan exist throughout the country. Where all defendants in Illinois exercising the ten percent option receive all but one-tenth back, in Michigan and Wisconsin defendants who are acquitted or have their cases dismissed receive their full deposits back, while convicted defendants forfeit one-tenth of the deposit to defray the administrative costs of the program.[70]

Many states and the Federal Bail Reform Act incorporated Illinois' ten percent plan as one of the alternative methods of release. Unlike Illinois, which adopted the plan after enduring a major scandal involving bondsmen and a judge, most of the jurisdictions utilizing the ten percent plan have not prohibited professional surety bonds. Only Oregon and Kentucky followed

Illinois' lead and put the bondsman out of business.[71] The other jurisdictions using the alternative have given the judge the discretion of accepting a ten percent deposit or requiring a surety bond. Consequently, bondsmen continue to do quite well in most states and federal courts.

There is no question but that more defendants are being released now than before our national concern with the inequities of the bail system. Our often-stated preference for pretrial release is more a reality than it ever was in our history, and decisions are more likely to be made on the basis of an accused's ties to the community than ever before. Nonetheless, a national pretrial detention rate hovering around one-third clearly indicates that many defendants remain in jail during this period simply because they are poor. High bail continues to be set in some cases arbitrarily without reference to whether the accused is likely to appear in court as required, and not even based upon whether the accused represents a threat to the safety of the community. Whether or not a defendant is released prior to trial continues to depend to a great extent upon the attitude of the judge who sets bail. The preponderance of bail systems throughout the country that continue to vest virtually unlimited discretion in the judge by providing options that range from ROR to surety bonds insures the continuation of uneven results.

Preventive Detention

Preventive detention is the pretrial incarceration of a defendant, who would otherwise be entitled to have bail set, based upon a determination that the defendant is likely to commit additional crimes if free on bail and that he represents a serious threat to the safety and security of the community. Obviously this denial of freedom does not fit within the traditional justifications for denying an accused's right to bail.[72] It is a limitation of that right, not because the defendant is a poor risk and is unlikely to appear for trial, but because he is dangerous. Preventive detention involves a watering down of the lynchpin of our nation's due process ideal, the presumption of innocence.

The procedure allowing for preventive detention was adopted by Congress in 1971 and is applicable only in the District of Columbia.[73] It was intended to serve as a model for the states, but emulation of the federal proposal has not been forthcoming. Although the provision allowing for preventive detention was adopted in the 1970s, it is a notion that is as old as the nation and is practiced without formal sanction in every jurisdiction. It exists in the form of excessive bail, set at levels guaranteed to insure that the defendant remains in jail while awaiting trial. The real difference between preventive detention under the District of Columbia plan and that practiced in other courts is that the former requires a formal determination that the defendant presents a dangerous threat to the safety and the security of the community, a determination that must be based upon established criteria and is subject to review. Preventive detention as practiced elsewhere is camouflaged in high bail and is based upon the unarticulated standards, highly subjective and often unfounded, of the judge who is setting bail.

The straightforward approach to preventive detention, however, is not without its problems and weaknesses. First, it is a frontal assault upon the American ideal that bail may be used only to assure the defendant's presence at trial. While a frontal approach may be more intellectually honest than the prevailing practice which achieves the same result but disguises it, the constitutional issue must be met. The local District of Columbia court which upheld the constitutionality of the preventive detention provision did so by saying that the presumption of innocence is not linked to bail but, instead, is only a trial right dictating who has the burden of proving guilt.[74] This approach, however, does challenge and demean the relationship between the presumption of innocence and the due process ideal. That ideal requires the application of the presumption to every step of a criminal case.

A more straightforward approach is to recognize that constitutional rights are not absolute and that they are subject to abridgment when the government offers a clear and compelling case for the need to do so.[75] The right to bail, then, is also not absolute and may be abridged if the government can demonstrate a compelling need to restrict the right in a particular case. Thus to justify the curtailment of the right and the detention of a defendant in any given case, the prosecutor must establish that the particular defendant is almost certain, if released on bail, to return to the street and commit violent crimes. And this highlights the second problem and the principal weakness of preventive detention. Is the future behavior of any specific individual sufficiently predictable to justify denial of this constitutional right?

Government studies conducted while preventive detention was pending before Congress demonstrated that the art of predicting behavior is not so precise.[76] Those studies demonstrated that the standards and categories included within the provision were too broad, and that based upon the behavior of past defendants in those categories, at most, one out of four would be likely to be rearrested during the period that they were free on bail and that only five out of a hundred would likely be rearrested during that period for dangerous or violent crimes.[77] This is not the compelling and precise case that allows for the curtailment of constitutional rights.

Nonetheless, the Act with its overbroad categories was adopted by the Congress. It has been used very sparingly in the 1970s[78] because, except in the cases of very few defendants, the government is unable to prove that a defendant's "pattern of behavior consisting of his past and present conduct [demonstrates that]... there is no condition or combination of conditions which will reasonably assure the safety of the community" and that the defendant must be detained.[79] The Act has not served as a model for the states, and preventive detention will not affect the rate of crime in this country.

Preventive detention, however, is a valid and useful tool when dealing with a psychopathic killer such as David Berkowitz. Society must have the means to detain a killer like Berkowitz, even if there is no potential death penalty upon conviction. This does not apply to a substantial number of defendants, and predictability of future criminal behavior simply is not possible in all but a handful of cases. It can only be available in a case like Berkowitz's where the evidence of guilt is overwhelming and the likelihood that the defendant, if freed, will strike again is equally overwhelming.

Other means must be utilized to lessen the likelihood of criminal behavior by defendants during the period that they are free on bail while awaiting trial. And these alternative means must be consistent with the accused's right to bail. One approach is to lessen the interval between arrest and trial, decreasing the number of days that the defendants will be free on bail. A second approach is to empower bail agencies with supervisory power over individuals who are free on bail to determine that their behavior is consistent with the conditions of their release. Greater contact and closer supervision may decrease the opportunity and likelihood that bailed defendants will engage in criminal activity. While these alternative means are hardly foolproof devices for preventing criminal behavior by defendants free on bail, neither is preventive detention unless it becomes a draconian device used to deny pretrial freedom to large numbers of defendants without regard for the ability to predict the likelihood of each defendant committing criminal acts, and then it is operating outside of any constitutional framework.

Discussion Questions

1. What are the purposes served by the preliminary appearance?
2. Discuss the historical development of the right to bail in the United States. Why is excessive bail expressly prohibited in the Eighth Amendment?
3. What is meant by the following statement:
"the right to bail must be inextricably linked to the presumption of innocence doctrine"?
4. What are the three reasons for denying bail in non-capital cases? What is the common link between these three exceptions to the right to bail?
5. Explain the role of the bail bondsman. Do you feel, from a practical standpoint, that the bondsman's profession can be justified by the fact that over 75 percent of pretrial releases are achieved through the bondsman's service? Or do you agree with the point of view that the bondsman's profession undermines the integrity of the bail system and should be eliminated?

6. Why is pretrial detention a volatile issue? Include in your answer a discussion of the possible consequences of detaining persons not yet convicted of crimes.

7. What is meant by the following statement:
"Preventive detention involves a watering down of the lynchpin of our nation's due process ideal, the presumption of innocence"?

Notes

1. This principle was originally enunciated in McNabb v. United States, 318 U.S. 332 (1943) and reaffirmed by a unanimous Court in Mallory v. United States, 354 U.S. 449 (1957).
2. For a historical perspective, see Scott and Roe, *The Law of Habeas Corpus* (Chicago: T. H. Flood and Co., 1923).
3. The problem of chaos in the municipal court was examined as early as 1922 in the famous study edited by Roscoe Pound and Felix Frankfurter, *Criminal Justice in Cleveland: Report of The Cleveland Foundation Survey of the Administration of Justice in Cleveland, Ohio,* Cleveland Foundation (1922).
4. Mistakes made because of this "assembly-line" approach are often tragic as well as unnecessary. For a graphic account of one such mistake, see *New York Times,* September 19, 1974, p. 1.
5. *New York Times,* February 11, 1975, p. 1.
6. The plea is most useful in offenses arising out of automobile accidents, because, unlike a plea of guilty, it is not a confession and cannot be used later in a civil suit for damages against the defendant.
7. *New York Times,* February 11, 1975, p. 1.
8. The advice of counsel would be beneficial to most defendants when making those decisions, but few receive that aid unless a legal aid lawyer is present to offer general advice to every defendant called before the bench.
9. *Black's Law Dictionary,* 4th ed. (St. Paul, Minn.: West, 1968), p. 177.
10. E.g., a charge of false swearing. The federal statute citing penalties for failing to appear is in § 3150 of the Bail Reform Act of 1966 (Pub. Law 89-465).
11. Goldfarb, *Ransom: A Critique of the American Bail System* (New York: Harper and Row, 1965), p. 22.
12. F. Pollock and F. Maitland, *The History of English Law* (Boston: Little, Brown and Company, 1895), pp. 589-90.
13. Goldfarb, *Ransom,* p. 23.
14. Note, "The Bail System: Is It Acceptable?", 29 *Ohio St. L. J.* 1005, 1006-7 (1968).
15. 3 Edw. 1, c. 15 (1275).
16. Note, "Bail: An Ancient Practice Reexamined," 70 *Yale L. J.* 966, 967 (1961).
17. 3 Hen. 7, c. 3 (1486).
18. 14 Ency. Brit. 577 (1968).
19. 3 How. St. Sr. 1 (1627).
20. 3 Car. 1, c. 1 (1627).
21. Jenkes Case, 6 How. St. Sr. 1190 (1676).
22. 31 Car. 2, c. 2 (1679).
23. 1 W. and M. Sess. 2, c. 2 (1688).

24. Foote, "The Coming Constitutional Crisis in Bail: 1," 113 *U. Pa. L. Rev.* 959, 965-68 (1965).
25. L. Orfield, *Criminal Procedure from Arrest to Appeal,* note 5 (New York: N.Y.U. Press, 1947) pp. 101-4.
26. Note, "Bail in the United States: A System in Need of Reform, 20 *Hastings L.J.* 380 (1968).
27. 1 Stat. 73 (1789).
28. U.S. Const. amend. VIII.
29. For two opposing views of the right to bail question, see Mitchell, "Bail Reform and the Constitutionality of Pretrial Detention," 55 *Va. L. Rev.* 1223 (1969) and Tribe, "An Ounce of Detention: Preventive Justice in the World of John Mitchell," 56 *Va. L. Rev.* 371 (1970).
30. See Robinson v. California, 370 U.S. 660 (1962).
31. Stack v. Boyle, 342 U.S. 1, at 4 (1951).
32. Stack v. Boyle, 342 U.S. 1 (1951).
33. Ibid., at 5.
34. For Federal provisions affecting bail in capital cases, see § 3148 of the Bail Reform Act of 1966 (Pub. Law 89-465).
35. See State v. Whitty, 34 Wis. 2d 278, 149 N.W. 2d 557 (1967).
36. Traditionally, great discretion is vested with the trial judge to change, supplement, or revoke bail in these cases.
37. See Note, 26 *Hastings L.J.* 559, (1974).
38. Fed. R. Crim. P. 46, following 18 U.S.C. § 3146(b).
39. It is obvious that the ability to investigate these matters is severely limited by the resources of the court. See Goldfarb, *Ransom,* pp. 13-15.
40. Superior Court bail schedule, approved and adopted by the Superior Court Judges presiding in Criminal Departments on July 18, 1969 is an example.
41. The weaknesses of both public and private bail agencies and projects are discussed in Wice, *Bail and its Reform: A National Survey,* National Institute of Law Enforcement and Criminal Justice (1973), pp. 38-40.
42. Bandy v. United States, 81 S. Ct. 197, 5 L. Ed. 2d 218 (1960).
43. See Mastrian v. Hedman, 326 F. 2d 708 (8th Cir. 1964).
44. A. Schlesinger, *Birth of a Nation* 163 (1968).
45. Besides multiplying the number of violations, judges dealing with civil rights demonstrators were also known to exact separate bonds at each step of the proceedings, costing the defendants separate premiums for each bond.
46. Murphy, "State Control of the Operation of Professional Bail Bondsmen," 36 *U. Cin. L. R.* 375, at 401 (1967). The role of the bondsman in urban courtrooms is outlined in a study by the District of Columbia Bail Project, *Bail Reform in the Nation's Capital,* (1966), pp. 11-14.
47. Ibid., at 11, quoting from Pannell v. United States, 320 F.2d 698, 699 (D.C. Cir. 1963).
48. Challenges to inadequate facilities in jail for those awaiting trial have been upheld. See e.g., Jones v. Wittenberg, 323 F. Supp. 93, 330 F. Supp. 707 (N.D. Ohio 1971) and Hamilton v. Love, 328 F. Supp. 1182 (E.D. Ark. 1971).
49. *New York Times,* Jan. 7, 1971, at 1, col. 4; Professor Caleb Foote has remarked:

    "It has been established that pretrial imprisonment of the poor solely as a result of their poverty, under harsher conditions than those applied to convicted prisoners, so pervades our system that for a majority of defendants accused of anything more serious than petty crimes, the bail system operates effectively to deny rather than to facilitate liberty pending trial."

Foote, "The Coming Constitutional Crisis in Bail: 1," 113 *U. Pa. L. Rev.* 959, 960 and n. 3 (1965).

50. Alternatives to this arrangement have been urged by attorneys and judges alike. See *New York Times,* Feb. 24, 1976, p. 75.
51. "Prisons in Turmoil" *Newsweek,* Sept. 14, 1970, p. 42.
52. Davidson, "The Worst I've Ever Seen,"*Saturday Evening Post,* July 13, 1968, p. 17.
53. *New York Times,* Nov. 18, 1970, at 1, col. 7.
54. *A.B.A., Standards Relating to Pretrial Release* (1968), p. 11.
55. Katz, Litwin, and Bamberger, *Justice is the Crime* (Cleveland: Case Western Reserve University Press, 1972), Appendix A, Tables 28 and 32.
56. Statement by Mayor John Lindsay, Administrative Board of the Judicial Conference of the State of New York, Oct. 9, 1970.
57. Occasionally, the bondsman's efforts to deliver a defendant to the court lead to violence. A bondsman's assistant was killed with the defendant he was trying to take into custody in Cincinnati, Ohio. The defendant had been convicted of resisting arrest, disorderly conduct, and malicious destruction of property. *Cleveland Plain Dealer,* May 13, 1971, § A, at 7, col. 3.
58. Federal Rules of Crim. Proc. 48.
59. *A.B.A., Standards Relating to Pretrial Release,* § 5.4.
60. Thomas, *Bail Reform in America* (Berkley: U. of California Press, 1976), p. 65.
61. Ibid., pp. 37-8.
62. Davis, "Bail—An Examination of Release on Recognizance," 39 *Miss. L. J.* 303, 311 (1967-68).
63. Institute on the Operation of Pretrial Release Projects, *Bail and Summons: 1965* (1965), p. 74.
64. *New York Times,* August 19, 1977, p. 1.
65. Letter from Jack L. Highsmith, Branch Chief of Release on Recognizance of the Office of Probation for the Courts of New York City, Mar. 25, 1971.
66. Thomas, *Bail Reform,* pp. 87-118.
67. *New York Times,* June 19, 1970, at 1, col. 1.
68. Goldfarb, *Ransom,* pp. 153-54.
69. The Illinois bail procedure was upheld as constitutional in Schilb v. Kuebel, 404 U.S. 357 (1971).
70. Thomas, *Bail Reform,* p. 186.
71. Ibid., p. 187.
72. However, state courts differ in their interpretation of this matter. Contrast Rendel v. Mummert, 106 Ariz. 233, 474 P.2d 824 (1970), with In re Underwood, 9 Cal. 3d 345, 508 P.2d 401 (1973).
73. 84 Stat. 644-50.
74. Blunt v. United States, 322 A. 2d 579 (App. D.C. 1974).
75. Cantwell v. Connecticut, 310 U.S. 296 (1939); Feiner v. New York, 340 U.S. 315 (1951).
76. Ervin, Foreword to "Preventive Detention: A Step Backward for Criminal Justice," 6 *Harv. Civ. Rights - Civ. Lib. L. Rev.* 291, 294 (1971).
77. Ibid.
78. Bases and McDonald, *Preventive Detention in the District of Columbia: The First Ten Months* (1972), pp. 69-73, reprinted in Kamisar, et. al., *Modern Criminal Procedure,* 4th ed. (St. Paul, Minn.: West, 1974), pp. 790-92.
79. 84 Stat. 644-50, § 23-1322.

7.

I didn't know about the grand jury indictment until I received it. As far as I know, the only evidence presented was by the prosecutor, and as far as I'm concerned, it seems as if a person is being tried at that particular moment while not being there. Anyway, at my arraignment hearing, my name was called off, and the indictment was read. I was asked if I understood the indictment and I said yes, as far as reading it, but as far as anything else concerning the indictment, no.

Screening the Case

Ralph Johnson had a preliminary hearing in the suburban court where he made his initial appearance. The judge found cause to hold Johnson for the grand jury, which later indicted Johnson for murder in the first degree. After his case was finally concluded, Johnson still wondered why the attorney appointed to represent him at the preliminary hearing had said nothing on his behalf. He also wondered what the grand jury had to do with his case. Much time is consumed between the arrest and final disposition of a felony case because of the number of pretrial steps required by the American justice system.[1] In addition to the deliberations in the police decision to arrest, the judge's cursory examination for grounds to justify issuing an arrest warrant and the prosecutor's decision to charge, traditional American criminal procedure calls for two formal screenings of the charge, a preliminary hearing and a grand jury presentment.

Our justice system is predicated upon the belief that through procedural regularity innocent persons ultimately will not be convicted.[2] The procedures that define our criminal justice system exist to weed out the innocent and to insure that prosecution is proceeding on the basis of substantial evidence. The preliminary hearing and the grand jury are to stand between an accused and prosecution.[3] This intercession is to make certain that there is justification for requiring a defendant to suffer the expense, interruption of his life, and insecurity involved in being accused of a serious crime. How well the preliminary hearing and grand jury proceeding fulfill those purposes, and whether in fact both proceedings are necessary, will be explored in this chapter.

The Preliminary Hearing

History

The preliminary hearing is a formal review of the state's charge before a judge in an adversary setting where the accused is present and has the opportunity to challenge the state's case. It is a device that has its origins in European continental law and was eventually incorporated into English common law.[4] The preliminary hearing was not originally conceived as a protective device for defendants. The history of the preliminary hearing begins with Roman times where it was used as an accusatory technique. It was adopted by the Roman Catholic Church as part of the ecclesiastical procedures for considering criminal offenses and was codified in the French Ordonnance Criminelle of 1498.[5]

The Ordonnance operated in an inquisitorial manner. Upon receipt of a civilian or prosecutor's complaint of a crime, a French magistrate, who was the progenitor of the American prosecutor, initiated an investigation to assure himself that a crime had been committed. If convinced, the magistrate would conduct a secret investigation to discover the identity of the criminal. He used the written statement of witnesses and other means of investigation.[6] When a suspect had been identified, he was ordered to appear before the magistrate for questioning. The questioning was conducted in secret, and the suspect was not entitled to the assistance of counsel.[7] A command to appear before the magistrate and subsequent interrogation was the first notice to a prospective defendant that he had been accused of a crime. Witnesses were summoned to reappear, and their statements were read to the accused in the witness' presence. An accused could object to a statement as it was being read, but he was not permitted to have an attorney with him to advise or assist him in making objections. If the evidence indicated that the accused was guilty, the magistrate would enter a verdict of guilty. Only at this point, with the defendant already adjudged guilty, was the case called for trial, and then only for sentencing. The purpose of the French procedure was to construct an airtight case. Relying heavily upon the findings of the preliminary hearing, the trial court reviewed the evidence and privately reexamined the defendant, who was still without counsel.[8] Then the court pronounced sentence on the accused.

The first comparable English procedure, also inquisitorial in nature, was the coroner's inquest. Upon learning of an unnatural death, the coroner questioned representatives of the four townships nearest the place where the death occurred.[9] He could compel witnesses to testify under oath and could bind them over to trial should he decide a felony had been committed.[10] In 1324 when the office of justice of the peace was created, preliminary hearings were not required, but it is likely that the justices conducted some sort of examination akin to a preliminary hearing to determine probable cause.[11] A justice of the peace served in many capacities: detective, arresting officer and, if he decided that an accused should stand trial, principal witness at the trial.[12] Two hundred years later statutes required that a justice of the peace examine the defendant and witnesses.[13] Defendants were not permitted to confront these witnesses nor see their statements.[14] Evidence against the defendant was put in writing, and the witnesses could be required to appear for trial.[15] This was a closed and secret system, with the justice of the peace performing as prosecutor and arresting officer, as well as presiding over the preliminary hearing and appearing as the principal witness for the crown against the defendant.[16] Needless to say, the bias within the system created a distinct disadvantage for the defendant.

By the nineteenth century, with the emergence of professional police forces, it became necessary to redefine and separate the functions of a justice of the peace.[17] For the first time, the preliminary hearing became accusatorial, where evidence had to be developed against an accused rather than the accused being the principal provider of that evidence. The justice of the peace assumed the role of judge[18] and the police did the interrogating.[19]

In general, the preliminary hearing in America has always been accusatorial in nature.[20] In Connecticut, for example, by the end of the eighteenth century, magistrates could not examine the accused during the preliminary hearing, although defendants were permitted to present their own witnesses to counter adverse testimony.[21] Virginia followed a similar pattern but in felony cases added the Examining Court to the fact-finding process. A Virginia justice of the peace would examine the defendant, take his statement and the statements of witnesses, all without oath. After this initial determination, the justice of the peace would order the sheriff to convene an Examining Court of laymen. At this session, witnesses could be subpoenaed, the defendant could cross-examine them, and the defendant could be examined. The Examining Court sifted and screened cases, saving the trial court from having to consider all matters. If the case was considered triable, the justice of the peace and the Examining Court could bind over the defendant to the grand jury. If the case was of uncertain merit, or if the defendant requested, he could immediately be given his punishment, usually the whipping post, and be discharged.[22] This latter alternative was frequently used. It had the advantage to the defendant of being quick and cheap, since a prisoner had to pay his own upkeep in jail. The immediate punishment also protected the defendant from further prosecution and a possible death penalty, the usual penalty for most serious crimes.[23] Of course, the justice of the peace and the Examining Court did not have to accede to the defendant's request for summary punishment if the offense was serious and merited a full trial.[24]

How It Works

The preliminary hearing as it exists in twentieth century America is far different from its colonial form. It is not mentioned in the Constitution and therefore is not a guaranteed right.[25] It is, however, available under state and federal law and court rules to most persons arrested and charged with felonies.[26] It is a full adversary proceeding where the quality of the prosecution's case is first tested. It is a defendant's tool but rarely to the extent that it always was in television's portrayal of Perry Mason. Perry Mason won all of his triumphs at the preliminary hearing when, through skillful cross-examination, he succeeded in proving who actually committed the crime. Such total triumphs never occur at real preliminary hearings. Or for that matter, rarely at trials.

The preliminary hearing provides an independent evaluation by a judge of the police and prosecutor's decision to arrest and charge.[27] Unlike a trial jury, the judge at the preliminary hearing is not interested in whether the defendant is guilty beyond a reasonable doubt, but only whether the prosecution has enough evidence to establish probable cause—namely, the likelihood that the defendant has committed the crime and should be held for further proceedings. Thus, the judge is only ruling on the probability of the defendant's guilt. The state's burden of proof is minimal, although how minimal is an issue of dispute. In California, for example, the Supreme Court of that state has taken the position that if there is some evidence to support the charge, the judge should not inquire into its sufficiency.[28] A few states have been critical of that approach and argue that the preliminary hearing should serve as a true in-court screening of felony cases.[29] The cursory approach has been pejoratively described as the "heard enough" system. In other words, once a judge hears enough evidence to implicate the defendant at all, he has heard enough to terminate the hearing and bind the accused over to the grand jury. Rejecting the "heard enough" approach as insufficient, Massachusetts, as a contrary example, requires that the prosecution present enough evidence at the preliminary hearing to justify a trial judge submitting the case to the jury. Thus, there must be credible evidence on each aspect of the charge to warrant binding a defendant over.[30] The Massachusetts approach commends itself because it makes the preliminary hearing meaningful rather than a *pro forma* exercise. On the other hand, there are a couple of reasons why judges at preliminary hearings do not, on their own, generally adopt this standard. First, the judge's decision at the preliminary hearing that there is no probable cause is not final. A prosecutor who disagrees, or who is prodded by police officers who disagree, is empowered, notwithstanding the rejection of the charge at the preliminary hearing, to go to the grand jury and seek an indictment. Thus, this ever-existing threat of rendering the effort meaningless is sufficient to discourage most judges who might otherwise treat the preliminary hearing differently. Second, the hearing is in the municipal court with limited jurisdiction over felony cases, and the court is less concerned with seriously attending to felony cases over which its jurisdiction is transient than it is in clearing its own docket. It is easy for a judge to rationalize his summary consideration of felony cases by explaining that the grand jury will also consider the case and can dismiss it if it is weak. The lack of real responsibility at this level helps to dilute the formal screening process and also fails to acknowledge the realities of grand juries.

As a defense tool, the preliminary hearing is most valuable because it provides the defendant with a window on the state's case. By having to present some evidence to substantiate the charge, the prosecutor is forced to disclose the state's theory of the case and present some of its witnesses.[31] Through this process, the defense learns about some of the strengths and weaknesses of the state's case and its witnesses and is able to begin preparing a case for trial. The preliminary hearing also enables a defense attorney to help educate his client as to the seriousness of the matter and the fact that the state intends to pursue it.[32] In this context, it may even be a better device to enable the defense team to decide how best to plead in the case and what approach to take in plea negotiations.

Most states require that the preliminary hearing be held within a reasonable time of the arrest, some specifying as soon as seven days if the defendant is held in jail and ten days or two weeks if the accused is free on bail.[33] Holding the preliminary hearing promptly after an arrest certainly lessens the inconvenience to the defendant if the charges are found to be unwarranted. Despite statutory requirements, however, preliminary hearings are frequently delayed by the defense attorney, in the attorney's or client's interest. Not infrequently, an attorney's stalling is to enable the client's family to raise money for the attorney's fee.[34]

Delay may be utilized on a defendant's behalf at the preliminary hearing and sometimes in such a way that the case never gets beyond this stage. One Cleveland, Ohio, attorney related how he had appeared twice with his client for a scheduled preliminary hearing, and each time the prosecuting witnesses were present, and each time the defense attorney asked for and received a continuance, without challenge or explanation. On the third occasion, this defense attorney noticed that the state's witnesses were not present. When the case was called, the defense attorney replied that he was ready and demanded that the hearing proceed. The prosecutor was unable to account for his missing witnesses and the judge dismissed the charges. The county prosecutor could have taken the case to the grand jury, regardless of the dismissal in municipal court, but the case was relatively unimportant and was never revived. Wearing down prosecution witnesses until they become so fed up with having to reappear in court and miss additional days' work is not at all uncommon.[35]

The grand jury does offer an opportunity for a prosecutor to short-circuit the preliminary hearing process. Under the law of most states, an arrested defendant has a right to a preliminary hearing on a felony charge only until a grand jury returns an indictment.[36] Since they are both reviews of the charge and since a majority of states still provide for grand jury indictment, the latter takes precedence. Consequently, if a prosecutor tires of defense delay at the preliminary hearing, the case can be presented to the grand jury and the return of an indictment there removes the jurisdiction of the municipal court. The prosecutor does not have to wait for defense delay to do this. Any time the prosecutor wishes to deny the defense a preliminary hearing, all that need be done is to secure an indictment. He may do this to deny the defense discovery of the state's case or to protect a witness from defense cross-examination at the preliminary hearing. For example, Frank Hogan, a District Attorney who served Manhattan for thirty years, took all homicide cases directly to the grand jury to move the cases along and to deprive defendants of the discovery available at preliminary hearings. Many prosecutors in rape or sexual assault cases (especially where the victims are children) are likely to take their case directly to the grand jury in order to at least delay until trial the time when the victim will be subjected to the harsh cross-examination of the defense attorney.[37]

As the preliminary hearing is almost solely for the benefit of the accused, it is incumbent upon the defense attorney to attempt to preserve the right and not forfeit it because of unnecessary delay. Waiver of the preliminary hearing may be a logical defense tactic in certain specific situations, but that is far different from the careless loss of a valuable tool. If one of the leading prosecution witnesses is old and infirm and may no longer be available by the time a trial is held, it would be foolish for a defense attorney to insist upon the preliminary hearing and enable the state to take the witnesses' testimony. Similarly, if the state has a strong case and the defense is fully aware of it, there would be no reason to proceed with the hearing if all that would result from it is adverse publicity which would hurt the defendant's chances at trial. If there is a flaw in the prosecution's case, or if the defendant is terribly undercharged, a preliminary hearing that would alert the prosecutor to these facts would also be unwise. Chances are that the preliminary hearing will only help the defense to prepare for trial, but whether or not to waive the right is a tactical decision that should be based solely upon the total view of how best to prepare a defense in a criminal case.[38]

To achieve the most benefit from the preliminary hearing, a defendant is arrayed with a full panoply of rights. *The defendant has the right to be present, to cross-examine witnesses, and to present witnesses and other evidence in his own behalf.*[39] Real discovery, though, exists only in those jurisdictions that apply the rules of evidence standard to a trial at this stage, rather than permitting the prosecutor to establish probable cause through hearsay (that is, through a police officer relating what he has been told by the actual witnesses).[40]

An accused also has the right to the assistance of counsel at the preliminary hearing in order to secure its maximum benefits. This right was guaranteed in 1970 to those unable to hire an attorney when the Supreme Court in *Coleman v. Alabama* extended the obligation of the states to appoint counsel to the preliminary hearing. The Court did so because the ability to glean the maximum benefit out of the preliminary hearing was related to an accused's opportunity to secure a fair trial:

> Plainly the guiding hand of counsel at the preliminary hearing is essential to protect the indigent accused against an erroneous or improper prosecution. First, the lawyer's skilled examination and cross-examination of witnesses may expose fatal weaknesses in the State's case, that may lead the magistrate to refuse to bind the

> accused over. Second, in any event, the skilled interrogation of witnesses by an experienced lawyer can fashion a vital impeachment tool for use in cross-examination of the State's witness at trial, or preserve testimony favorable to the accused of a witness who does not appear at the trial. Third, trained counsel can more effectively discover the case the state has against his client and make possible the preparation of a proper defense to meet that case at trial. Fourth, counsel can also be influential at the preliminary hearing in making effective arguments for the accused on such matters as the necessity for an early psychiatric examination or bail.[41]

Prior to *Coleman* an indigent defendant either represented himself or, in most cases, waived the hearing. Because of the financial plight of most state and local governments, the response to the requirement imposed by the Supreme Court in many cities has been to provide legal aid attorneys to represent the indigent at the preliminary hearing and then to appoint either a private attorney or another legal aid attorney to handle the subsequent stages of the case. The lack of continuity of representation tends to diminish the quality of the earlier legal assistance and thus the value of the preliminary hearing. Counsel whose only responsibility is the preliminary hearing is not greatly concerned with the total development of the case or a defense to be used at trial. In many cities operating under this approach, the preliminary hearing is little more than a formal gesture; often there is no communication between nor assistance solicited by the attorney who has the ultimate responsibility for the case and the attorney who represented the indigent client at the hearing.[42]

At the preliminary hearing the defense attorney should be ever conscious of the need to prepare for trial and should attempt to learn as much as possible about the state's case. When listening to the direct examination of a state witness by the prosecuting attorney, the defense attorney focuses upon holes, weaknesses, and discrepancies in that person's account of what happened. Cross-examination is useful only to further open those holes so that if the witness attempts to clarify at the trial counsel can cross-examine, showing the discrepancy in the earlier testimony. This type of limited cross-examination is a fine art because the defense attorney must accomplish it without allowing the witness to flesh out and correct the deficiencies. That is in the domain of the prosecuting attorney who can ask questions of the witness on re-direct examination in order to clear up discrepancies. The defense job is not to demolish the witness at the preliminary hearing, as Perry Mason always did, but to leave doubt about the witness' credibility when he attempts to elaborate at the trial. In any event, if the defense attorney's interest in the case is limited to the preliminary hearing, it is doubtful that he is thinking ahead and planning how to use those inconsistencies at trial.

Aside from its principal purpose to provide an early review of the justification for the prosecution, the preliminary hearing has developed into an effective tool for the defense. This stage in the criminalization process provides the opportunity for discovery in the preparation for trial. A preliminary hearing also serves to screen cases within a jurisdiction to preserve trial court time for serious matters. How effective the preliminary hearing is, however, depends on the law of the jurisdiction and the attitudes of the judge and prosecuting attorney. Discovery for the defense and determination of the strength of the case for purposes of judicial screening are impossible goals if hearsay evidence is the cornerstone of probable cause at this stage:[43] the preliminary hearing is reduced to nothing more than ascertaining that there is some reason, no matter how negligible, for prosecuting in each case.

There is virtually no appellate review of the manner in which the judge conducts the hearing. If he views the assignment cavalierly and fails to screen effectively, the hearing will be conducted cursorily and probable cause found on the barest of evidence. When a judge recognizes the importance of the preliminary hearing to both the system and to the defense, he will permit full cross-examination of prosecution witnesses, and the state will be compelled to make a fairly full presentation.

Finally, the attitude of the prosecutor towards the preliminary hearing can be gauged by his reliance on the determination by the judge and the level of autonomy that he grants to the assistants assigned to this proceeding. Does the prosecutor accept the findings of the judge as to probable cause or are cases automatically sent to the grand jury even if the charges are dismissed at the preliminary hearing because of the absence of probable cause? Are the assistants authorized to reduce felony charges at this stage to misdemeanors if they believe the case does not merit full prosecution?

At the conclusion of the preliminary hearing the judge has three alternatives. If the state fails to establish probable cause at the preliminary hearing, the judge is obligated to dismiss the charges and discharge the accused. As already noted, the prosecutor is not required to accept this judgment and may refile the complaint or take the matter to the grand jury. Notions of *double jeopardy,* that an accused may not be prosecuted twice for the same crime, are not applicable to the preliminary hearing. Thus the defendant has no valid objection to the case going to the grand jury. When the state meets its obligation and establishes probable cause, the judge is required to bind the defendant over for the consideration of the grand jury or for trial if the state has eliminated the grand jury as the final charging institution. The third alternative occurs when the state has failed to establish probable cause for a felony but has presented enough evidence to show probable cause that the defendant committed a misdemeanor. Then the judge may dismiss the felony charge and order the defendant to stand trial on the misdemeanor in the municipal court. Again, the decision is not binding on the prosecutor and the case may be taken to the grand jury. If an indictment is returned before the misdemeanor charge is disposed of, the municipal court loses its jurisdiction and the case will be tried on the more serious felony charge. If the misdemeanor is disposed of through a plea of guilty or trial before grand jury action, the double jeopardy guarantee of the Constitution will likely bar further prosecution.[44] When such a situation arises it can lead to a power struggle amongst the courtroom protagonists. The court is attempting to pressure the prosecutor to file the misdemeanor complaint, while the prosecutor is attempting to delay complying with the court order until the grand jury has an opportunity to consider the matter. Meanwhile, the defense is likely urging the court to expedite matters in order to enter a plea of guilty to the misdemeanor to forestall a felony prosecution.

The Grand Jury

History

The grand jury is a lay panel that investigates crime and charges defendants.[45] Like the preliminary hearing, it can be traced to Rome,[46] but it first appears in England around the tenth century.[47] Exactly 100 years following the Norman conquest of England, King Henry II ordered that grand juries be summoned and used in all courts under his jurisdiction.[48] The decree required the royal sheriff to summon "twelve men of the neighborhood, or village, to declare the truth" and to report to the royal sheriff or justices the names of those persons who were believed to have committed crimes.[49] The twelve men, either knights or other freemen, acted not as judges but as accusers or witnesses. Usually the grand jury called no witnesses and took no testimony.[50] Indictments were returned on the basis of the common knowledge of the community or the personal knowledge of the members of the grand jury. After gathering and reviewing the facts surrounding a crime, the grand jury was justified in bringing an indictment only if there was "sufficient cause to call upon the party to answer" the charge.[51]

Since the grand jury was designed to function solely as a public prosecutor in the interest of the Crown, the original jury deliberated in public.[52] In the thirteenth and early fourteenth centuries, at least some members of the grand jury always served on the petit jury that tried the defendant.[53] An acquittal of the defendant by the same citizens who had found enough evidence to hold him for trial often brought the wrath of the judges down upon the jurors in the form of a jail sentence.[54]

When the grand and petit juries were separated, the independence of the grand jury began to be asserted. To protect the grand jurors and the persons they were considering from the threat of oppression by the Crown, the concept of secrecy was developed. In the fourteenth century, the practice developed of taking testimony, and the grand jury adopted the policy of hearing witnesses in private. The secrecy and eventual taking of testimony in private excluded representatives of the Crown; in this manner, the grand jury became an institution that was protective of the rights of the individual and immune from governmental pressures that sought an indictment against a private citizen. The independence of the grand jury became one of the most decisive factors in protecting individual liberty. Later, when fear of governmental coercion diminished, a representative of the Crown was admitted while testimony was taken so that the indictment could be framed in the proper manner.[55]

As the protector of individual freedom, the grand jury also exercised investigatory authority over public officials. Grand jury reports were used to publicize the misconduct of royal officers in England, and later, in the colonies, the grand jury report was used widely to investigate matters of public concern.[56] In order to conduct these investigations, the grand jury was empowered to compel the attendance and testimony of witnesses and was able to grant varying degrees of immunity from prosecution in return for information.[57]

Given its importance in assuring the protection of individual rights from governmental abuse, it is no surprise that the founders of the American colonies incorporated the grand jury into their justice system. In a society where communities were small enough so that everyone knew all the local residents and knew everyone else's business, and where there were no police or prosecutors charged with investigating and initiating criminal charges, the grand jury was the logical institution. It filled the needs of seventeenth- and eighteenth-century America. By the time the framers of the Bill of Rights adopted the right to a grand jury indictment as a part of the Constitution, it had already enjoyed a venerable past in the colonies. Virginia, which adopted the grand jury system as a result of royal decree, recreated the original notion of the grand jury in America. Virginia colonists were notified six months in advance that they were to be called for service on a grand jury and were charged during the ensuing six months to be on the look-out for crime. Thus, the grand jury in colonial Virginia indicted solely upon those facts within the knowledge of each individual juror.[58]

During the latter part of the eighteenth century, the grand jury came under attack, in England by Jeremy Bentham and in the colonies by his disciple, Edward Livingston.[59] By this time the grand jury had expanded to the extent that it could investigate not only private crime but also political and administrative misconduct. Those who favored retention of the grand jury wanted the investigation of all serious crimes to remain in the hands of the people. Bentham argued that the grand jury should be limited to reviewing whether a prosecutor had presented sufficient evidence and testimony to justify holding a suspect for a particular crime. This is essentially the way the grand jury functions in the United States today.

In 1846 the United States Congress, by statute, made the calling of a federal grand jury discretionary with the presiding judge, except in capital offenses.[60] Also, the Supreme Court in 1884 refused to include a grand jury as an essential part of the Fourteenth Amendment due process requirements [61] Following this ruling, several Western states restricted the number of situations in which a grand jury could be convened or wrote their constitutions to allow the legislature to "abolish, limit, change or amend" the existing grand jury system. Nebraska and Colorado did subsequently abolish the grand jury.[62] In short, the grand jury was regarded as an anachronism.

Since the Norman Conquest, the English have used, in addition to the grand jury, two other types of accusations: *accusation by a private person and accusation by information.*[63] In the former, a private individual who had been the victim of a crime could swear out a complaint charging the person responsible. The accused would be brought before the justice of the peace, who would hold a hearing to determine whether the complaint was sufficient to detain the accused for trial. At this hearing the accused was entitled, if he chose, to attempt to clear himself by calling witnesses and presenting evidence.

Identical to the practice in England, private citizens in the American colonies were authorized to appear before a magistrate and swear out a complaint against another citizen.[64] In Virginia, this procedure had considerable popularity because the private citizen was entitled to a percentage of the fine levied against a person who was convicted as a result of this charging method.[65]

Other procedures were developed in the colonies to circumvent the grand jury procedure. Connecticut authorized individual jurors to act independently of the full grand jury and to swear out a complaint charging that an individual had probably committed a crime.[66] Courts subsequently initiated the practice of commissioning private attorneys to originate criminal action, a technique untested by the English. The commissioning of a private attorney is the antecedent of today's prosecuting attorney and has its origin in the continental European inquisitorial procedure, a system that the colonies otherwise substantially rejected.

There were few lawyers on the frontier, and the need for a representative of the government to be present, a person solely charged with representing the community's interest, was highlighted by the great distances between the capitals of the colonies and their outlying settlements. Yet, as could be expected, the creation on the frontier of an office staffed by a law-trained official did produce imbalances. The familiarity of the prosecutor with the law and the niceties of juries and judges put the defendant in a criminal case at a disadvantage because few attorneys were available to represent the accused.[67]

The attorneys commissioned by the courts could bring charges in the form of an information. The specific origin of the criminal information is unclear. Evidence exists from the reign of Edward I that the king through his legal representatives, the sejeant of treason or the sejeant of felony (forerunners of the modern prosecutor), accused persons of felony or misdemeanor offenses in the Court of the Star Chamber and thus avoided the grand jury.[68] In this way the king used the information to control those who might oppose or criticize him. For instance, after grand juries twice refused to indict colonist John Peter Zenger for criminal libel, the Crown's governor charged Zenger by information.[69] Increasingly, with the diminished importance of the grand jury, the public prosecutor would use the information as a substitute for the grand jury indictment. This development was paralleled in the state constitutions, which in the nineteenth century almost exclusively required grand jury indictment but by the early twentieth century had been modified in some states to permit information in felony prosecutions.[70]

How It Works

In felony cases, a final charging instrument is prepared and presented to the trial court. That charging instrument, which is similar to the complaint filed in the municipal court at the inception of the case, is either an *indictment* or *information. An indictment contains the charge which the grand jury has reasonable cause to believe the defendant has committed.* In those states that have abolished the grand jury or have eliminated grand jury indictment for certain offenses, the charging instrument is an *information* prepared by the prosecutor. In other instances, a defendant may waive grand jury indictment, generally for non-capital offenses, and consent to proceed to the trial court on a prosecutor's information.[71] *In those instances, an information is the functional equivalent of an indictment and serves as the final charging instrument leading to trial.* A defendant who is anxious to plead guilty to a felony charge and accept his punishment would, if permitted in that state, waive grand jury action in his case and attempt to expedite matters by consenting to the filing of an information. Some states permit the prosecutor to refuse to accept the waiver and present the case to the grand jury instead.

Generally, an information is filed by the prosecuting attorney when the accused has been bound over for trial following a preliminary hearing. Jurisdictions that have abolished the grand jury have based their action on the realization that the preliminary hearing and grand jury indictment serve the same function, to determine the existence of probable cause. While most jurisdictions that have abandoned the grand jury preclude the filing of an information unless a judge has ruled that probable cause exists, some permit an information to be filed even though there is no preliminary hearing.[72] This procedure allows for no review of the charge until trial. The Supreme Court has inserted constitutional protection at this point to insure some minimal review. Without making a preliminary hearing or grand jury consideration constitutionally required, the Court in *Gerstein v. Pugh*[73] mandated that some form of review must exist if the accused is detained in jail prior to trial. An arrest warrant, even issued after the arrest, was deemed sufficient by the Court to satisfy this requirement.[74]

The grand jury has two basic functions. The first is to initiate charges that lead to trial. When it meets this purpose in the cases of defendants who have already been arrested, it is reviewing, and really just duplicating, the decisions already made by the police, prosecutor, and preliminary hearing court. However, there does not have to be a prior arrest or official action to commence a grand jury investigation. The grand jury can initiate an investigation on its own to determine whether criminal prosecution is warranted: its second role is to investigate wrongdoing and corruption. Both functions usually are initiated and conducted in the same manner, with the prosecuting attorney taking center stage.

The grand jury is selected at random by the presiding judge of the court of general jurisdiction. Its size varies across the country.[75] Once assembled, the jury is advised of its responsibilities, duties, and powers. A foreman, who will preside at all sessions and sign all indictments, is selected by the court. Most jurisdictions provide for that selection from among the jurors already chosen to serve, but different methods of selection may exist by state law. For instance, in Ohio the presiding judge may select any citizen, not necessarily one summoned to serve on the grand jury, as the foreman.[76] The foreman is the spokesman for the grand jury, supposedly capable of making the jury's wishes and demands known to the prosecutor and communicating to the court any grievances that may develop with the prosecuting attorney. After the initial meeting, the grand jury is dispatched to begin indicting or investigating as it sees fit. For those defendants already within the process through arrest, the grand jury was intended to serve as a citizen-barrier between overzealous, harassing police, prosecutors, and courts and the stress and ignominy of trial.[77] For wrongdoers who remain untouched by the process, the grand jury is the potential sword of citizen redress, ready to indict notwithstanding erroneous or corrupt decisions which may have been made by individual police officers or prosecuting attorneys. A similar threat supposedly exists for government officials engaged in corrupt practices who may have previously been protected by prosecutor inaction.[78]

This beacon of citizen action, however, soon dims in the grand jury room. Once ensconced, the jurors quickly learn how powerful the prosecutor is. Prosecutors, or their designated assistants, are permitted by law to be present with the grand jury at all times except when the jury is deliberating or voting. Without the prosecutor, few grand jurors would know which matters to consider, let alone how to consider them. Thus the prosecutor holds the reins in selecting which cases the grand jury will consider and which witnesses it will hear, and in which direction it will focus its investigative powers.[79] While the grand jury may at any time banish the prosecutors or may demand to have witnesses subpoenaed who have not been summoned by the prosecuting attorney, such defiance is virtually, if not totally, unheard of today. Technically, a grand jury embroiled in disagreement with a prosecutor could go to the presiding judge who has the power to resolve the conflict, including holding the prosecutor in contempt or appointing an attorney as special assistant to the grand jury to replace the prosecutor.

In large cities more than one grand jury may operate at the same time, and if the foreman or jurors in one present problems to the prosecutor, the problem cases can be directed to another grand jury. These conflicts, however, simply do not arise for two reasons. In the jurisdiction where the grand jury is used to indict in virtually all cases, it is simply too overwrought by the number of cases it must consider to flex its muscles and assert its independence. Where the grand jury is used solely or primarily for investigative matters, the subject of its inquiry is generally selected and laid out by the prosecuting attorney prior to the convening of the grand jury.

Where the grand jury is used to indict felony defendants, it may be required to consider fifty or more cases at every one of its sessions. As in each of the preceding steps in the criminal process, such a caseload is likely to encourage a quest for shortcuts. Since the grand jury, too, is only looking for reasonable cause to indict, the quality of case screening is again likely to be cursory and of marginal value.

In spite of its present ineffectiveness, the grand jury was included within the Fifth Amendment:

> No person shall be held to answer for a capital, or otherwise infamous crime, unless on a presentment or indictment of a Grand Jury...

The inclusion of the grand jury within the Bill of Rights indicates the framers' belief that the institution was a means of protecting the individual rights of defendants: in this country it was not originally conceived as a prosecutorial device.[80] However, during the past two hundred years, the mechanical operation of the grand jury and the sheer weight of its caseloads have rendered the jury an instrument of the prosecutor. Regardless, then, of its actual value to the justice process, prosecutors prefer to retain the grand jury proceeding. Unlike the preliminary hearing, the grand jury is a very effective prosecutorial tool.

The ability, then, of the institution to serve as a protector of individual rights is, at best, negligible. First of all, grand jury proceedings are *ex parte,* meaning "by or for one side." Where the preliminary hearing is conducted in an adversarial atmosphere, each side having the opportunity to present witnesses and cross-examine the other's witnesses, a defendant has no right even to be present when the grand jury considers his case. Not only does the defendant not have the right to be present while the testimony of witnesses against him is taken, he has no right to appear and present his own version of the incident.

An indictment does not have to receive the unanimous approval of the members of the grand jury. Also, the evidence on which the grand jury bases its decision to indict does not have to be, in most jurisdictions, the same type of evidence required at trial.[81] Hearsay evidence, which would not normally be admissible at a trial, may be all that the grand jury considers before it votes to indict.[82] Thus, witnesses do not have to appear if the prosecutor chooses not to summon them. In fact, a police officer may advise the grand jury what the witness is likely to say at trial and would say if personally appearing before the grand jury. In Fort Worth, Texas, the grand jury's workload is so great that it is reputed to read the police report, not hear any witnesses, and then vote on the recommendation of the prosecutor.

Hearsay evidence is not the only problem. The only constitutional protection afforded a defendant is an unbiased grand jury, presumably one selected without the systematic exclusion of racial groups or members of one sex.[83] The quantity and quality of the evidence received by the grand jury on which it based its decision to indict is not subject to review. The evidence may be all one-sided, there being no legal obligation on the prosecutor to present evidence of weaknesses in the state's case for the grand jury's consideration.[84]

While the defendant has no right to compel the grand jury to hear defense witnesses, the prosecutor may subpoena defense witnesses to appear and testify before the grand jury. This presents the prosecutor with an opportunity to discover the defense's case. Without the defendant or defense counsel in attendance, the prosecutor is able to learn how defense witnesses will testify at a subsequent trial. Without a representative of the defense, the prosecutor can also elicit statements that may be damaging to the defendant's case. The defendant will not know about it or have an opportunity to clarify these statements through cross-examination. Testimony secured during a grand jury proceeding may be used by the prosecutor to discredit a witness during cross-examination at trial if the witness gives contradictory or conflicting testimony. And in most jurisdictions a defendant is still barred from access to grand jury transcripts.[85]

Evidence that is beyond the grasp of the police may be available to the grand jury, a factor which enhances that body's investigative powers. For instance, if a crime is committed to which there are no witnesses but fingerprints are found, the probable cause requirement of the Fourth Amendment prohibits the police from making dragnet arrests of the locale to find the one among many whose fingerprints will correspond to those at the crime scene. However, if the police secure the names of those whom they may not arrest, a subpoena may be issued in the grand jury's name directing those "suspects" to appear for fingerprint tests. A grand jury subpoena is not even subject to any scrutiny for reasonableness, let alone the more rigorous standard of probable cause that governs police intrusions.[86]

The Defendant as a Grand Jury Witness

Rarely is a defendant's testimony needed by an indicting grand jury. A sufficient case has already been compiled by the police and prosecutor to satisfy the grand jury. When a grand jury is investigating to determine if criminality exists (as opposed to merely reviewing the prior decisions of the police, prosecutor, and preliminary hearing court), the testimony of a potential defendant may be desirable, although the propriety of calling a potential defendant for incriminating evidence is heatedly debated.[87]

A grand jury subpoena does not disclose the subject under inquiry nor the questions to be asked. The individual, moreover, has no right to compel disclosure of the subject of the inquiry, nor has he a right not to appear.[88] Even if suspecting the subject-matter, the witness may not challenge the grand jury's power to conduct the inquiry nor the location of the investigation.[89] Once sequestered behind the closed doors of the grand jury, the witness may be startled to find that he is the subject of the grand jury's investigation. At this point, the witness virtually is devoid of all but one constitutional protection: the Fifth Amendment privilege against self-incrimination.[90] Upon being asked a question, the answer to which may be incriminating, the witness may decline to answer on the ground that the answer may tend to incriminate him. The failure to respond will be reported to the presiding judge who convened the grand jury. If the court finds that the question is not incriminating, the witness will be directed to respond. Failure to respond after being directed to do so by the court places the witness in *contempt* of the court. Contempt carries swift punishment, commitment to jail. The witness will remain in jail until he purges himself of contempt by answering the question, or through the tenure of the grand jury, which in federal courts may last as long as eighteen months. Moreover, the end of the grand jury term does not necessarily signal the end of the witness' travail. The subject may be resubmitted to a newly empaneled grand jury which may subpoena the witness, ask the same question, and thus provoke the imposition of the same process, including commitment to jail again.[91]

On the other hand, if the court finds that the witness properly invoked the Fifth Amendment privilege, the ball is in the other court. The prosecutor must decide whether to accept that refusal or seek *immunity* for the witness. There are two types of immunity, *transactional immunity and use immunity. Transactional immunity secures for the witness freedom from prosecution on the subject matter under inquiry.* A witness' testimony may be so crucial in developing an investigation or building a prosecution against other offenders that the state will forego prosecuting him in return for his testimony. Use immunity is much more limited. *The state only agrees to forego the use of the witness' own testimony and any other evidence that his testimony leads to in a prosecution of the witness.* Thus the state is still empowered to prosecute the witness if it is able to build a case entirely separate from his own testimony. Naturally, transactional immunity is more desirable from the prospective defendant's perspective, but the type of immunity utilized is the state's decision. The limited value of use immunity has passed constitutional muster, and a defendant has no right to hold out for the greater protection.[92] Once offered either type of immunity, a witness must answer the questions or suffer being held in contempt.

Claiming one's privilege against self-incrimination is not altogether devoid of peril, even aside from the threat of contempt. A witness is entitled to being advised of the privilege against self-incrimination by the prosecutor, but the warnings, of course, are not nearly so broad or comprehensive as those that must be given by the police.[93] The warnings are not the same because the privilege is not the same. While a suspect does not have to say anything to interrogating police officers, a witness before the grand jury must answer questions unless the particular line of questioning would tend to incriminate him. Thus he must know when to assert the privilege, and the prosecutor who is questioning on behalf of the grand jury is not required to tell a witness that the question is incriminating or that the line of questioning may lead to incriminations. When to assert the privilege is critically important because a witness may be held to have waived the privilege if he fails to assert it early enough about a specific topic.[94] Obviously, then, a witness desperately needs the advice of counsel during grand jury proceedings.

While a grand jury witness is entitled to the advice of counsel, the nature and breadth of that right is severely limited. Counsel may not appear with the witness inside the grand jury chamber.[95] If the witness wishes the advice of counsel, he must request permission of the grand jury to leave the room and consult with the attorney who is presumably sitting just outside the door. This requirement is undoubtedly disruptful and time-consuming.

In 1977 the American Bar Association advocated a change in the law to permit an attorney to accompany a witness inside the grand jury room.[96] The reasoning of the Bar is obvious: since privilege and its assertion are highly technical, there is a substantial chance that the witness may not recognize the beginning of a line of incriminating questions and may unintentionally waive the privilege by risking answers without consulting with counsel. This change is being strenuously opposed by the United States Department of Justice and state prosecutors.[97]

Every society needs tools to investigate criminality. The investigative grand jury is the most powerful armament in our society's arsenal. Its ability to compel testimony and the production of documents and other physical evidence attests to its power. Because of its vast authority and the limitations upon the Bill of Rights in the grand jury room, it is an instrument that is subject to misuse. It may be misused by prosecuting attorneys in the states or by the United States Department of Justice at the federal level to inquire into matters that are not legitimate government concerns. The authority of any federal grand jury to make broad inquiry may be used as a weapon to disrupt the lives of target witnesses by making them appear before other grand juries in parts of the country far from their homes, associates, and businesses. Through such techniques, witnesses who have angered government officials, either legitimately or illegitimately, can be substantially harassed. So while the grand jury provides federal and state governments with needed tools, there has been a growing realization that clamps upon the potential mischief created by grand juries must be devised.[98]

Numerous proposals for providing such limitations on grand jury behavior and prosecutor misuse of the institution have been recently introduced. Congress has been considering various proposals that would limit only federal prosecutors and federal grand juries but would serve as models for similar state reform. Three main concerns deal with expansion of the right to counsel before grand juries; elimination of use immunity, thereby requiring the granting of transactional immunity or accepting the claim of privilege from a witness; and finally, barring grand juries from calling prospective defendants as witnesses.[99] The American Bar Association's project on minimum standards for criminal justice set forth basic proposals for operation of grand juries and their relationships with prosecuting attorneys. The proposed standards listed below are creating a solid foundation for grand jury reform and are likely to be adopted in most jurisdictions during this decade:

> 3.5 Relations with grand jury.
>
> (a) Where the prosecutor is authorized to act as legal adviser to the grand jury he may appropriately explain the law and express his opinion on the legal significance of the evidence, but he should give due deference to its status as an independent legal body.
>
> (b) The prosecutor should not make statements or arguments in an effort to influence grand jury action in a manner which would be impermissible at trial before a petit jury.
>
> (c) The prosecutor's communications and presentations to the grand jury should be on the record.
>
> 3.6 Quality and scope of evidence before grand jury.
>
> (a) A prosecutor should present to the grand jury only evidence which he believes would be admissible at trial. However, in appropriate cases the prosecutor may present witnesses to summarize admissible evidence available to him which he believes he will be able to present at trial.
>
> (b) The prosecutor should disclose to the grand jury any evidence which he knows will tend to negate guilt.
>
> (c) A prosecutor should recommend that the grand jury not indict if he believes the evidence presented does not warrant an indictment under governing law.
>
> (d) If the prosecutor believes that a witness is a potential defendant he should not seek to compel his testimony before the grand jury without informing him that he may be charged and that he should seek independent legal advice concerning his rights.
>
> (e) The prosecutor should not compel the appearance of a witness before the grand jury whose activities are the subject of the inquiry if the witness states in advance that if called he will exercise his constitutional privilege not to testify, unless the prosecutor intends to seek a grant of immunity according to the law.[100]

While most scholars recognize the need for retaining the investigative grand jury, they see little reason for perpetuation of the grand jury as an indicting institution. This view was adopted by the National Advisory Commission on Criminal Justice Standards and Goals in its 1973 report which recommended that grand jury indictment not be required in any criminal case.[101] The Commission stated that charging is the prerogative and responsibility of the prosecuting attorney who should be held accountable for those decisions through review at a preliminary hearing.

Some prosecutors remain, nevertheless, tenacious in their defense of the indicting grand jury. While the process enables the prosecutor who is so inclined to discover part of the defense case by subpoenaing defense witnesses to appear before the grand jury without surrendering anything in return, most prosecutors will insist that this is not their main concern. No one is better aware than a prosecuting attorney how few cases actually go to trial and how rarely they must make use of the grand jury for discovery of the defense case. Even if the indicting function of the grand jury were abolished, the prosecutor could direct the police to postpone arresting a suspect while the investigative grand jury looked into the case and subpoenaed potential defense witnesses. The real value, prosecutors claim, is that grand jury participation helps to keep citizen interest and understanding in the criminal justice process.

One can question the real value of such participation if it is reduced to rubber-stamping decisions already made by the local prosecutor. The grand jury stands as a facade to protect prosecutorial decisions, which are automatically affirmed by the grand jury, from public scrutiny and review. Especially when a prosecutor decides not to prosecute, it is terribly convenient to disclaim personal responsibility by laying the blame at the door of the grand jury. Rather than having to explain the reasons for the decision, the prosecutor is able to finesse the responsibility by disclaiming knowledge of the reasons for the grand jury's action. Yet, this is a transparent ploy since the prosecutor chose the evidence upon which the grand jury based its decision. This type of manipulation of the grand jury is most apparent in cases involving the misuse of force by police, or decisions not to prosecute white collar crimes or those committed by other government officials. In actuality, grand juries rarely, if ever, indict or no bill a charge contrary to the recommendation of the prosecutor.[102] Even the choice of what evidence to present to the grand jury, or more importantly what evidence not to present to the grand jury, represents a recommendation how the jury should vote in the particular case.

Return of an Indictment or Information

Once the grand jury votes to indict a defendant, the prosecutor is formally notified by the foreman that a *true bill,* a decision to charge, has been returned. The prosecutor's office drafts the indictment, setting forth the specific charges. In order to complete the process the foreman and prosecutor must sign the document. Even at this point, the prosecutor retains control. If the grand jury returns a true bill contrary to the advice of the prosecuting attorney, he does not have to sign the charging instrument; it is incomplete and will go no further.[103] If the grand jury *no bills* a charge, which is a vote not to indict, the case is over unless the prosecutor disagrees and submits the case to another grand jury. Where indictment is not used, the prosecutor merely drafts an information and signs it.

Once the indictment or information is perfected, it will be filed with the clerk of the court having final jurisdiction over the case. The case is docketed in that court, given a case number, and placed on the court's calendar for arraignment. If the defendant has already been arrested, he will be notified of the arraignment date and ordered to appear on that date. Along with the notification of the arraignment, the accused will be served with a copy of the indictment as formal notification of the charge.

Recall that not all criminal cases originate with police action and an arrest. The indictment may be the first stage of a criminal case initiating prosecution. When it is the first stage of a particular case, it is called an *original indictment,* meaning that the case began at this point. Upon the filing of the indictment or information, an arrest warrant will be issued, and the defendant will be arrested and served with a copy of the indictment or information at the same time. The arraignment, then, in the court of final jurisdiction becomes the first court appearance. The accused is not entitled to a preliminary hearing at this point because that is a review of the police decision to arrest and the prosecutor's original decision to charge. There will be no further review in these cases until trial or other final action is taken.

Are They Both Necessary?

The preliminary hearing has the potential to be a valuable facet of our justice system. Principally, it is an adversary proceeding, which commends itself over the secret, *ex parte* grand jury process. At the preliminary hearing the defendant has the right to be present with the assistance of counsel and has the opportunity to hear the state's witnesses and cross-examine them. By contrast, the grand jury offers no protection. It makes no sense to argue that the grand jury's purpose is to protect a defendant's rights when he is literally and totally shut out of the proceedings. The preliminary hearing could, on the other hand, be strengthened as a means of protecting defendants' rights by merely upping the standard of proof necessary to bind an accused over for trial. Requiring the state to establish a *prima facie* case of guilt, that is, proof on each element of the offense charged, through the presentation of evidence admissible at a subsequent trial, would clearly establish both probable cause and that the case is worthy of full felony treatment.[104] The preliminary hearing is preferable not only from the perspective of fairness and due process but also from the system's perspective of seeking the most effective screening device. Decisions at preliminary hearings are made by judges who are trained in the law and presumably capable of looking ahead to the trial stage and assessing the strengths and weaknesses of the state's case. Grand jurors are lay persons who are not familiar with the legal requirements for each crime or the rules of evidence and, consequently, are totally dependent upon the prosecuting attorney's assessment of a case and recommendation.

The question remains whether both screening institutions should be retained. Notwithstanding the dissimilarities in their operations, both the preliminary hearing and the grand jury perform the same function: determining whether there is probable cause to hold an accused for trial. This duplication of purpose results in an abdication of responsibility and inadequate screening. The charging process, originating with the police decision to arrest, involves input from the prosecutor, a review at the preliminary hearing, and a grand jury determination—all of which is time consuming and costly. The multiple-step process has been institutionalized to protect the rights of defendants and to screen criminal cases in the community's interest. Yet the multiplicity of steps and the duplication of functions retard real accomplishment. This is especially true for the preliminary hearing and grand jury actions, where neither the court nor the jurors assume the real and critical responsibilities they are delegated. Judges at preliminary hearings pass along marginal cases to the grand jury, claiming that at the indictment stage a more thorough review will be made. Instead of screening, the judge at a preliminary hearing abdicates responsibility and defers a realistic evaluation of a case for the next step on the ladder. On the next rung, however, the grand jury exists to blindly follow prosecutorial bidding.

It was stated in the first part of this chapter that the preliminary hearing and the grand jury are to stand between the accused and prosecution. They exist to screen a case for the sole purpose of determining whether or not the criminalization process should be invoked. These two procedures are critical phases in deciding an accused's case. But because the preliminary hearing is not as finely honed as it could be and because the grand jury exists for little more than prosecutorial manipulation, an accused cannot be assured that justice will be achieved. Finally, notwithstanding the involvement of the police, prosecutor, preliminary hearing court, and grand jury, no agency or institution is responsible for explaining to the community why some persons are charged and others are not.

Discussion Questions

1. What is the difference between a criminal justice procedure that is accusatory in nature as opposed to an inquisitorial procedure?
2. What are the purposes served by a preliminary hearing?
3. How does the preliminary hearing function as a defense tool?
4. Under what circumstances is it advisable for a defendant to waive his right to a preliminary hearing?
5. Trace the history of the grand jury. How does the grand jury today differ from its colonial counterpart?
6. Why has the grand jury been called "the most powerful armament in our society's arsenal" in the investigation of crimes?
7. Theoretically, the preliminary hearing and grand jury serve the same function, to determine whether there is probable cause to hold an accused for trial. It has been suggested, however, that while the preliminary hearing has the potential to be a valuable facet of our justice system, the grand jury procedure is subject to abuse and functions in many ways that are anathematic to our constitutional ideals. Discuss the reasons for these divergent views.

Notes

1. Richard Quinney, *Criminal Justice in America: A Critical Understanding* (Boston: Little, Brown and Company, 1973), p. 229.
2. See Palko v. Connecticut, 302 U.S. 319 (1937), where Justice Cardozo said that particular procedural safeguards included in the Bill of Rights were applicable to the States if they were "implicit in the concept of ordered liberty, ... and that a fair and enlightened system would be impossible without them."
3. See Coleman v. Alabama, 399 U.S. 1 (1970), where Justice Black in concurring said, "the purpose of the preliminary hearing ... is to determine whether an offense has been committed and, if so, whether there is probable cause for charging the defendant with that offense. In the absence of such a finding of probable cause, the defendant must be released from custody."
4. "The Preliminary Hearing: An Interest Analysis," 51 *Iowa L. Rev.* 164, 165 (1966): "The first known proceeding resembling the preliminary hearing was the English Coroner's inquest. Although the origin of this examination has not been definitely established, it probably began as an instrument of the King, designed to curb the political influence of the Sheriffs."
5. Ploscowe, "The Development of Present-Day Criminal Procedures in Europe and America," 48 *Harv. L. Rev.* 433, 447 (1935).
6. Ibid., p. 449.
7. Ibid., p. 450; R. Moley, *Our Criminal Courts* (New York: Minton, Balch and Company, 1930), note 32, p. 37. The French call this the period de l'instruction, covering the gathering of evidence and the formulation of the state's case for trial. The method of investigation varies, depending on the crime committed and the circumstances under which it is discovered.
8. Ploscowe, "The Development of Present-Day Procedures," pp. 451-52.

9. "The Preliminary Hearing: An Interest Analysis," 51 *Iowa L. Rev.* 164, 165 (1966).
10. See F. Nichols, *Britton* 7-8 (1901). The Sheriff's powers were very great in the 1100's and the King viewed the Sheriff with some suspicion. To alleviate the fears of the King, another official who could check the Sheriff's power and safeguard the royal interest was appointed. Thus, the coroner became a recognized figure by the beginning of the 12th century; 1 W.S. Holdsworth, *A History of English Law* 82, 3rd ed., (1922).
11. Moley, *Our Criminal Courts,* note 32, p. 15.
12. Ibid., pp. 15-16.
13. 1 & 2 Phil. & M., c. 13 (1554).
14. Ploscowe, "The Development of Present-Day Procedures," pp. 458-59.
15. L. Orfield, *Criminal Procedure From Arrest to Appeal,* (Berkley: U. of California Press, 1947), pp. 54-55.
16. Ibid., pp. 55-58.
17. Ibid., pp. 55-57; 62-64.
18. In 1836, the Prisoner's Counsel Act allowed defendants to see the written statements of witnesses that were being used against them at the preliminary hearing. And by 1848, the law required prosecution witnesses to testify at the preliminary hearing in the defendant's presence and allowed the defendant to make statements and to call witnesses in his own behalf. By this time, a defendant could be represented by counsel. In 1930, although it was not a common practice, a defendant who could not afford an attorney might have counsel appointed on his behalf at the preliminary hearing.
19. The use of physical brutality to obtain confessions became fairly common.
20. Moley, *Our Criminal Courts,* note 32, p. 20.
21. Z. Swift, *A System of the Laws of the State of Connecticut,* 377, 390 (1796).
22. A. Scott, *Criminal Law in Colonial Virginia* (Chicago: U. of Chicago Press, 1930), pp. 59-61.
23. This procedure may have provided the seeds for our present system of plea bargaining.
24. Scott, *Criminal Law,* pp. 61-62.
25. Anthony G. Amsterdam, Bernard L. Segal, and Martin K. Miller, *Trial Manual for the Defenses of Criminal Cases,* vol. I (Philadelphia, 1974) ¶ 130, pp. 2-92 and 2-93.
26. Amsterdam, et. al., p. 2-93: The "state law almost invariably gives a right to preliminary hearing—both arraignment and examination—and under state law, recent decisions may be found which enforce the right by strong remedy of reversing an otherwise valid conviction for no reason but that a preliminary examination was denied."; e.g., Manor v. State, 221 Ga. 866, 148 S.E. 2d 305 (1966).
27. See V. Rosenberry in Theis v. State, 178 Wis 98, 103, 189 N.W. 539, 541 (1922), where the posits that "the object or purpose of the preliminary hearing is to prevent hasty, malicious, improvident, and oppressive prosecutions, to protect the person charged from open and public accusations of crime, to avoid both for the defendant and the public the expense of a public trial, and to save the defendant from the humiliation and anxiety involved in public prosecution, and to discovery whether or not there are substantial grounds upon which a prosecution may be based."
28. Rideout v. Superior Court, 67 Cal. 2d 471, 432 P.2d 197 (1967).
29. Staff Comments, Proposed New York Criminal Procedure Law § 90.60 (1969).
30. Myers v. Commonwealth, 363 Mass. 843 (1973).

31. See United States ex rel. Wheeler v. Flood, 269 F. Supp. 194 (S.D.N.Y. 1961), where Weinstein, D. J. said, "Although the primary purpose served by the federal preliminary examination is to insure that there is 'probable cause,' ... in practice this hearing may provide the defense with the most valuable discovery technique available to him."
32. Amsterdam, et. al., *Trial Manual,* pp. 2-89.
33. Again, see United States ex rel. Wheeler v. Flood, supra, where the Court said, "upon a defendant's demand, a hearing is required within a 'reasonable time.' "; also see Kamisar, LaFave, and Israel, *Modern Criminal Procedure* (St. Paul, Minn.: West, 1974), p. 975: "Almost all of the states requiring prosecution of felonies by indictment have statutes or court rules providing for a preliminary hearing in felony cases."; cf., but state courts, like the federal courts, generally have held such provisions are rendered inapplicable by a prior indictment, State v. Boykin, 113 N.J. Super. 594, 274 A.2d 620 (1970).
34. Although few judges will acknowledge the reality of this situation, one candid municipal court judge remarked that he would not force a lawyer to proceed unless the attorney's fee was paid, because he knew "what it's like to have to make a living on these cases."
35. Letter from John T. Corrigan, Cuyahoga County Prosecutor, Cleveland, Ohio, April 12, 1971.
36. Amsterdam, op. cit., ¶ 21, p. 2-11.
37. Amsterdam, op. cit., ¶ 21, p. 2-11.
38. Amsterdam, op. cit., ¶ 126, p. 2-90.
39. Gideon v. Wainwright, 372 U.S. 335 (1963); Pointer v. Texas, 380 U.S. 400 (1965); Griffin v. Illinois, 351 U.S. 12 (1956).
40. See State v. Knudson, 57 Wis. 2d 270, 187 N.W.2d 321 (1971): "The issue as to credence or credibility is for the trial. The hearing as to probable cause is not the proper forum to debate and determine issues as to credibility and weight of evidence once essential facts as to probability have been established." See, *Ca. Evid. Code,* § 300, which states the usual rules of evidence apply to preliminary hearings, i.e., only evidence normally admissible at trial can be received by the magistrate; *Fed. Rule of Crim. Proc.* 5.1, as adopted provides that "the finding of probable cause may be based upon hearsay evidence in whole or in part."
41. Coleman v. Alabama, 339 U.S. 1, 3 (1970).
42. Katz, *Justice is the Crime* (Cleveland: Case Western University Press, 1972), pp. 46-47.
43. United States ex rel. Wheeler v. Flood, supra; op. cit., Amsterdam, ¶ 134, p. 2-95.
44. Waller v. Florida, 397 U.S. 387 (1970).
45. Marvin E. Frankel and Gary P. Naftalis, *The Grand Jury: An Institution on Trial* (New York: Hill and Wang, 1977), p. 19.
46. Whyte, "Is the Grand Jury Necessary?" 45 *Va. L. Rev.* 461, 463 (1959).
47. Coates, "The Grand Jury, The Prosecutor's Puppet: Wasteful Nonsense of Criminal Jurisprudence," 33 *Pa. B. Ass'n.* 311 (1962); Orfield, *Criminal Procedure,* pp. 137-39. The Assize of Clarendon, 1166, which established the first true Grand Jury, was based not on Anglo-Saxon law but upon Frankish inquests as adopted in Normandy.
48. Coates, *The Grand Jury,* note 5, p. 311.
49. Kuh, "The Grand Jury Presentment: Foul Blow or Fair Play?" 55 *Colum. L. Rev.* 1103, 1106 (1955).
50. Note, "The Grand Jury as an Investigatory Body," 74 *Harv. L. Rev.* 590 (1960-61).

51. Coates, *The Grand Jury,* note 5, p. 312.
52. Calkins, "Grand Jury Secrecy," 63 *Mich. L. Rev.* 455, 456 (1965).
53. Orfield, *Criminal Procedure,* note 5, pp. 138-139.
54. Ibid., p. 139.
55. Calkins, "Grand Jury Secrecy," p. 458.
56. Kuh, *The Grand Jury Presentment,* note 8, p. 1109.
57. Scigliano, "The Grand Jury, The Information, and the Judicial Inquiry," 38 *Ore. L. Rev.* 303, 304 (1958). Immunity was offered in cases involving public corruption or conspiracy.
58. Whyte, "Is the Grand Jury Necessary?" p. 471.
59. Younger, "The Grand Jury Under Attack," 46 *J. Crim. L. & P. S.* 26, 28 (1955-1956). Jeremy Bentham (1748-1832) was an English legal reformer who believed a professional prosecutor could perform grand jury functions more efficiently and less expensively. Edward Livingston (1764-1836) was an American disciple of Bentham. Livingston codified Louisiana's criminal laws. The Livingston Code limited the grand jury to receiving and ruling upon the indictments submitted to it.
60. Ibid., p. 31; 1 Stat. 119 (1970); U.S. Const. Amend. V.
61. Hurtado v. California, 110 U.S. 516 (1884).
62. Younger, "The Grand Jury Under Attack," note 21, p. 39.
63. Orfield, *Criminal Procedure,* note 5, p. 137.
64. Swift, *A System of the Laws,* p. 377.
65. Scott, *Criminal Law,* p. 52.
66. Swift, *A System of the Laws,* note 28, p. 375.
67. F. Heller, *The Sixth Amendment to the Constitution of the United States: A Study in Constitutional Development,* 21, 31 (1969).
68. F. Pollock and F. Maitland, *The History of English Law* (London: University Press, 1968), p. 662. The Star Chamber was not the only court using informations. The court of the Kings Bench also used informations but only in misdemeanor cases. Since the King used various court officers to represent him, justices, sheriffs, or attorneys could bring an information. The information procedure was eventually misused by Crown officials through malicious prosecutions. This abuse was remedied by the State of 4 Will. and Mary, c. 18 (A.D. 1692), which forced the Master of the Crown Office into a proceeding with a magistrate.
69. Alexander, *A Brief Narrative of the Case and Trial of John Peter Zenger* (Cambridge, Mass.: Belknap Press, 1963).
70. Scigliano, "The Grand Jury," note 18, p. 305.
71. *Ore. Const. Art.* VII, § 20; *Okla. Const. Art.* 2, § 17; see *Ohio Rev. Code* § 2941.02.1 (page 1970), where a prosecution may proceed by an information, if the punishment for the offense charged is other than death or life imprisonment and the accused has waived his right to prosecution by indictment; N.C. *Gen. Stat.* § 15-140.1 (Supp. 1969), where an accused may waive the indictment in any case in which he is charged with the exception of a capital felony; and see *Ill. Const. Art.* 1, § 7, where "no person shall be held to answer for a crime punishable by death or imprisonment unless the initial charge was brought by indictment of a grand jury or the accused has received a prompt preliminary hearing to determine probable cause."
72. See State v. Jefferson, 29 Wash. 2d 354, 485 P.2d 77 (1971); State ex rel. Hardy v. Blount, 261 So.2d 172 (Fla. 1972), where most states permitting felony prosecutions by information require a bindover at a preliminary hearing as a jurisdictional prerequisite to the filing of the information with the trial court.

73. Gerstein v. Pugh, 420 U.S. 103 (1975).

74. Gerstein v. Pugh, supra, at 120: "These adversary safeguards are not essential for the probable cause determination required by the 4th Amendment. This issue can be determined reliably without an adversary hearing. The standard is the same as that for arrest ... this is not to say that confrontation and cross-examination might not enhance the reliability of probable cause determinations in some cases. In most cases, however, their value would be too slight to justify holding, as a matter of constitutional principle, that these formalities and safeguards designed for trial must also be employed in making the 4th Amendment determination of probable cause."

75. See Ill. Crim. Proc. § 112-2, where grand jury consists of 23 persons, 16 of whom shall be necessary to constitute a quorum; Idaho Crim. Proc. [8] 19-1007 (Bobbs-Merrill), where the grand jury must consist of 16 with 12 concurring to issue an indictment; Ind. Crim. Code [8] 9-80[2117] (Burns), where the grand jury only consists of 6; and Ohio Rules of Crim. Proc. 6, where the grand jury consists of 9.

76. Ohio Rules Crim. Proc. Rule 6 (1978).

77. Wood v. Georgia, 370 U.S. 375, 390 (1962): "Historically, this body has been regarded as a primary security to the innocent against hasty, malicious and oppressive persecution; it serves the invaluable function in our society of standing between the accuser and the accused, whether the latter be an individual, minority group, or other, to determine whether a charge is founded upon reason or was dictated by an intermediating power or by malice and personal ill will."

78. Comment, "Federal Grand Jury Investigation of Political Dissidents," 7 *Harv. Civ. Rts. - Civ. Lib. Rev.* 432 (1972).

79. *Report on Prosecution: National Commission on Law Observance and Enforcement* (The Wickersham Report, 1931), p. 125: "The grand jury usually degenerates into a rubber stamp wielded by the prosecuting officer according to the dictates of his own sense of propriety and justice; c.f. In re Dymo Industries, 300 F. Supp. 529 (N.D. Cal. 1969).

This cynical description of the grand jury as a rubber stamp is simply not true. The grand jury process may at times give the appearance of a formality exercised without judgment. This appearance, however, is not the necessary result of undue control by the prosecuting agency. The very existence of the grand jury process serves as a deterrent against unwarranted accusations by the prosecuting agencies."

80. Leroy D. Clark, *The Grand Jury: The Use and Abuse of Political Power* (New York: The New York Times Book Co., 1975), p. 19.

81. Ibid., note 74.

82. Costello v. United States, 350 U.S. 359 (1956).

83. See Strauder v. West Virginia, 100 U.S. 303 (1880), where it was held that for a state to try a Negro defendant before a jury from which all members of his race had been excluded by statute is a denial of equal protection of the laws under the 14th Amendment.

84. Frankel, *The Grand Jury*, p. 71.

85. Ohio Crim. Rules of Proc. Rule 16(B)(3) (1978).

86. See State v. Dionisio, 410 U.S. 1 (1973), where the Supreme Court reversed a lower court ruling that the grand jury could not obtain voice exemplars of the witnesses by use of the subpoena power. The Supreme Court, per J. Stewart, said that "neither the summons to appear before the grand jury, nor its directive to make a voice recording infringed upon any interest protected by the 4th Amendment and accordingly there was no justification for requiring the grand

jury to satisfy even the minimal requirement of reasonableness."

87. See Kamisar, LaFave, and Israel, *Modern Criminal Procedure,* pp. 942-946.
88. See Blair v. United States, 250 U.S. 273 (1919), where the court said that "the duty to testify may on occasion be burdensome and even embarrassing. It may cause injury to a witness' social and economic status. Yet, the duty to testify has been regarded as 'so necessary to the administration of justice' that the witness' personal interest in privacy must yield to the public's overriding interest in full disclosure."
89. See Hale v. Henkel, 201 U.S. 43 (1906), which held that a witness could not properly refuse to answer a grand jury's questions because "there was no specific charge pending before the grand jury against any particular person."
90. See United States v. Winter, 348 F.2d 204 (2d Cir. 1965); United States v. Scully, 225 F.2d 113 (2d Cir. 1955), where the court held that "the principle which underlies the rule that the defendant in a criminal trial may refrain even from being sworn as a witness, has no application to proceedings before a grand jury."
91. Clark, *The Grand Jury,* pp. 51-53.
92. Kastigar v. United States, 406 U.S. 441 (1972).
93. Mandujano v. United States, 425 U.S. 564 (1976).
94. See Commonwealth v. McCloskey, 443 Pa. 117, 277 A.2d 764 (1971), where the court upheld the practice of not permitting witnesses to leave the grand jury room to consult with counsel. The court stated that it "believed that proper procedure is for the court supervising the investigating grand jury to instruct a witness when administering the oath that while he may consult with counsel prior to and after his appearance, he cannot consult with counsel while he is giving testimony."
95. See People v. Robinson, 66 Misc. 2d 639, 323 N.Y.S.2d 573 (Sup. Ct. 1971); In re Groban, 352 U.S. 330 (1957), where the court noted that a "witness before a grand jury cannot insist, as a matter of constitutional right, on being represented by his counsel; cf., in a few states, statutes provide that a witness may be assisted before the grand jury by counsel present during the examination. See Kan. Stat. Ann. § 22-3009; Utah Code Ann. § 77-19-3; Wash. Rev. Stat. § 10.27.080-.120.
96. *American Bar Association Journal,* June 1977, vol. 63, p. 790.
97. Ibid., p. 790.
98. Clark, *The Grand Jury,* p. 134; Frankel, *The Grand Jury,* p. 117.
99. H. R. 353, 95th Cong., 1st Sess. (1977).
100. *American Bar Association Project on Standards for Criminal Justice,* "The Prosecution Function," (1974), §§ 3.5-3.6, p. 90.
101. *National Advisory Commission on Criminal Justice Standards and Goals* (Washington, D.C., 1973).
102. See Interview with Geoffrey Gaulkin, Hudson County Prosecutor, in Jersey City, New Jersey, Nov. 30, 1970, where he pointed out "that if the prosecutor wishes to proceed with the prosecution of a particular case, the grand jury returns an indictment on his recommendation. If the prosecutor wishes to dispose of a case, on his recommendation the grand jury returns a no bill, which terminates the case."
103. See United States v. Cox, 342 F.2d 167 (5th Cir. 1965), where the court held that Federal Rule 7, requiring that an indictment contain the signature of the prosecutor, in effect gave the prosecutor broad discretion to "veto" the grand jury's decision to indict.
104. Lewis R. Katz, *Justice is the Crime,* p. 220.

8.

When I appeared for the preliminary hearing I had this attorney appointed by the court. This gentlemen was peculiar. I sat down and talked with him and when he got in court he didn't say or do anything. He just did nothing. I said my goodness I wanted to know what was going on, because when we stepped in court I never seen an attorney who was defending a person, supposed to be defending a person, go and become chummy and shake hands and everything with the prosecutor and everybody else. I mean it's all right to remain on friendly terms with them, but I think the way he was going at it they knew more than I knew and he knew something more too. It seems as if I'd been put on rails and I was getting ready to be shipped. I'm no attorney but I would have asked more questions in more depth and detail than the ones he asked.

Defending the Accused

An adversary proceeding is premised upon two opposing parties, theoretically equal, contesting an issue to uncover the truth. The notion that the adversaries in a criminal case are equal, however, is a myth. No matter how well-financed the defense or how capable the defense team, the defendant's resources could never match the vast arsenal of state agencies and services available to the prosecution. In an attempt, then, to reduce the disparity, the Constitution clothes a defendant in a criminal case with an array of rights, not the least being the right to counsel. No matter how base the defendant or hopeless his cause, he still must have access to an attorney who will vigorously defend his rights and require the state to prove its case through competent, legally admissible evidence presented in open court. For the adversary system to work properly, for there to be at least a chance that the truth will emerge, both the defense attorney and prosecutor must be competent individuals who are able to function within the rules of the law.

The Need for Counsel

Most people who have ever been involved at any level of the criminal justice system recognize the layman's need for counsel. Alone, the individual without legal training resembles a laboratory animal in a maze. The complexities of the legal system compound the defendant's natural fears regarding his position: the legalistic language is foreign and the people who confront him are or appear to be intimidating.

To whom should a defendant turn for guidance—the investigating officers, court functionaries, assistant prosecutors? In a heightened state of confusion, the defendant alone is more likely to do what seems to arouse the least disfavor of those who appear to control his destiny. Answer the police officers' questions? Waive the preliminary hearing? Plead guilty and try to explain? Trying hard to please, the defendant may, as soon as things have calmed down a little, find that he has surrendered precious constitutional rights without realizing what he was doing. He also may find himself in jail or prison. Perhaps he belongs there, but are the principles of due process and the integrity of the criminal justice system protected if the result is secured through confusion? Of greater concern to our system is: what if he did not belong in jail or prison?

Even a defendant who is prepared to plead guilty will benefit from the assistance of a lawyer. Because guilt is strictly a legal conclusion, a personal admission of guilt by the defendant is hardly conclusive of the final determination of guilt. While an individual may be able to recognize the wrongfulness of his act, without the assistance of an attorney he would not really know if his acts constituted the elements of the offense for which he was charged. For instance, most states have several classifications of burglary, descending in order of seriousness. Burglary is terribly serious when it involves breaking and entering an occupied dwelling at night. It is punished severely because of the inherent threat of danger to the human life within. On the other hand, breaking and entering into an abandoned dwelling, or a warehouse, or a closed store is treated differently and less severely because no resident's safety was at stake. Without a lawyer, an individual has little way of knowing whether he has been charged properly or whether he has pleaded guilty to a charge more serious than the one he committed. Moreover, a defendant typically does not know whether mitigating circumstances that may exist in his case can be relevant to the court's final sentencing decision.

Far more apparent is the need for legal assistance at trial. The rules of evidence, which determine what type of testimony may be elicited and how that testimony may be brought before the tribunal, both protect and limit the defendant. A lay person is likely to be confounded by the rules and unable to protect against deviations from them by the prosecutor. Rarely is the layman able to effectively present his side of the facts within these constraints. And because a legitimate defense may be barred if not properly presented, an otherwise innocent defendant may appear guilty merely because he is unable to get his side of the story to the judge or jury.

The judge may be prepared to protect the uncounseled defendant, but that protection is in reality limited to restraining an overly aggressive prosecutor. The judge may not be aware of what evidence the defendant is trying unsuccessfully to place before the court. The significance of the evidence may be totally lost because of the defendant's poor presentation. The facts on the surface may point to guilt, but without the careful and tenacious probing of an attorney, the judge or jury may assume guilt even when the facts do not fully satisfy the legal requirement for conviction under the statute. The ineptness of the lay advocate escalates at the appellate level where issues and arguments are limited to legal questions and may only peripherally involve a reconsideration of factual questions litigated at the trial. Successful attacks upon convictions have been made by defendants acting alone, but most defendants are unable to recognize the legal deficiencies of the pretrial, trial, and sentencing stages. Very few are able to define those deficiencies as understandable legal issues and marshal the support of authorities to substantiate their positions.[1]

The benefits of counsel are not limited only to the defendant in whose service the attorney labors. Our system of criminal justice is designed to separate the innocent from the guilty; many of its cumbersome qualities can be related to the insertion of numerous steps to insure that the innocent defendant escapes conviction. Our obsession with the integrity of the fact-determining and guilt-determining process is in great measure dictated by the concern for protecting the innocent. Yet our system of criminal justice can never guarantee absolute precision in separating the innocent from the guilty. But the potential for failure, for tremendous injustices to occur, is increased when the defendant's case is not championed by an advocate who knows and understands the law.

The Defense Attorney's Role

Unlike the prosecuting attorney who has the dual responsibilities of representing the state in all criminal cases and of pursuing justice (not simply convictions), the criminal defense attorney has a singular mandate: within the limitations imposed by the Canons of Ethics, the defense attorney's role is to serve as an advocate for his client. The criminal defense attorney, like all lawyers, is an officer of the court, but his duty is fulfilled by the competent and vigorous advocacy of the defendant's position.[2]

The lawyer is not concerned with the guilt or innocence of his client. Guilt as a legal conclusion can only be determined by the tribunal. Under our system of criminal justice, every defendant is constitutionally guaranteed a trial. The burden of proving guilt rests with the prosecution. Therefore the defense is entitled, and the defense attorney obligated, to question the state's case and put forth all credible defenses.

Since every defendant is entitled to legal assistance, presumably every attorney is obligated to provide that assistance, irrespective of the attorney's own feelings about the defendant's guilt or innocence.[3] This is part of a lawyer's obligations in fulfilling his duties as an officer of the court. As a result of the complexity of criminal law resulting from vast changes in the past quarter century, most lawyers no longer engage in any criminal practice, but they are bound to do so if called upon by the court to represent a defendant. In smaller communities, it is not at all unusual for the entire bar to occasionally handle criminal cases, whether on a retained basis or upon request from the court.

Historically, from John Adams' defense of British soldiers indicted for the Boston Massacre,[4] and fictionally, as in Thaddeus Finch's representation of the black defendant in *To Kill a Mockingbird,*[5] America has watched lawyers risk their position by representing an unpopular cause or hated client. Unfortunately, the country has also witnessed lawyers suffering economically and socially as a result of such undertakings, and the bar frequently turns its back on its obligations by avoiding the representation of unpopular clients.

While the lawyer's Code of Professional Responsibility does not require all attorneys to engage in criminal defense work, it does provide:

> ... The fulfillment of [making legal services fully available] requires acceptance by a lawyer of his share of tendered employment which may be unattractive both to him and the bar generally.
>
> ... Regardless of his personal feelings, a lawyer should not decline representation because a client or a cause is unpopular or community reaction is adverse.[6]

Once undertaking the defense of a person in a criminal case, the attorney is obliged to vigorously defend that client's interests and secure the defendant's acquittal within the bounds of the limitations set forth in the Code of Professional Responsibility. The defense attorney's task very simply is to challenge the state's case and insure that before the defendant is found guilty the state overcomes the presumption of innocence and proves guilt beyond a reasonable doubt.

By no means, however, is the defense attorney to become merely a "mouthpiece" for his client, manufacturing false defenses and supporting them with perjured testimony. Although the defendant's confidences are protected by the attorney-client privilege, the attorney is prohibited by the Code of Professional Responsibility from knowingly using perjured or false testimony.[7] An attorney is obligated to dissuade the client from perjuring himself. If the client accepts that advice, he will, in most cases, be benefiting himself because perjury, a separate offense itself, often looks like just what it is, a fabrication, when challenged by aggressive, skillful cross-examination. If the client persists in his intention to become a witness and perjure himself, the defense attorney's options are limited. The attorney may attempt to withdraw from the case, but only if that can be done without revealing privileged communications made in the context of the attorney-client relationship. Essentially, it is up to the individual to find his own course of action through a search of conscience and a personal decision about the role of the lawyer in the criminal justice system.[8]

The ethical problem and the lawyer's dilemma arise when a client confesses to his attorney his intent to take the witness stand and perjure himself. Otherwise, it is not the defense attorney's function to challenge a defendant's version of events. That is the prosecutor's job and will be done soon enough. Nor is it the defense attorney's prerogative or obligation to make personal determinations of the veracity of his client's account. The lawyer's obligation is fulfilled by pointing out the perils of perjury to his client and the likelihood that a fanciful account of the crime is not likely to hold up in court. The defense attorney's obligation is to use fair and honorable means in defense of a client, not to unmask the client's untruths or otherwise avoid representation of the defendant.

The Attorney-Client Relationship

The first meeting between the attorney and his client is of critical importance to the future of the case. One of the first obligations of the attorney is to advise his client not to make any statements or submit to a lineup unless he, the attorney, is present. The first meeting is also the time for the attorney to get to the heart of the case; the most effective defense investigation occurs immediately after the crime has been committed or the arrest made because critical evidence may be lost if the search is delayed. Also, the events surrounding the crime are fresh in the defendant's mind—time has not had the chance to distort or haze the facts. The attorney will also be able to obtain information that is necessary for an effective presentation before the court for low or non-money bail. Finally, the first meeting should resolve any of the defendant's fears regarding his attorney's fees.

By the time this initial interview is concluded, several things should be established: (1) the defendant believes that someone is acting on his behalf and is no longer as confused, afraid, and isolated as he was immediately after his arrest; (2) the defendant is aware of his rights and is less likely to waive them out of ignorance or panic; (3) reassured by the concern of the attorney, the defendant is likely to be candid and to provide substantial information which will be useful to the defense; and (4) the information provided by the defendant will set the stage for the development of an effective defense at any subsequent hearing or trial. Finally, if the lawyer has responded during this first meeting as both a professional and as one who regards the defendant in a humane light, the attorney-client relationship will be firmly entrenched.

The Right to Counsel

Every defendant's need for legal assistance in a criminal case is no longer contested. We now find it difficult to understand the reluctance in our country's past to extend this right, expecially to those who could not afford their own lawyers. But the fulfillment of the right to counsel has been a long and strenuous process. The forty year history of Supreme Court litigation spanning the recognition of the right to its full development presents a fascinating picture of how a specific part of the Constitution develops. This period is diffused with widespread expression of the need for legal assistance, followed by periods of retrenchment, then followed by the painfully slow step-by-step process of expansion and full maturation of the right.[9]

A Privilege or a Right?

Historically, counsel in England was available only to those accused of misdemeanors. Persons charged with felonies or treason were denied this assistance,[10] primarily because of the political climate of the feudal period and the attendant weakness of the central government. The government needed every advantage over its enemies and denial of counsel was but one way to accomplish this.[11] The political stability that resulted from the revolution of 1688 against James II was accompanied in 1695 by an act of Parliament that permitted counsel to be retained or appointed by the court in cases of high treason.[12] The courts also used their discretion to permit attorneys to argue points of law in other felony cases. By the close of the eighteenth century, counsel was permitted to conduct the entire defense, except for addressing the jury at trial's end, which was the exclusive privilege of the king's counsel.[13]

Early in the nineteenth century, English law was amended to permit all criminal defendants to retain counsel.[14] In practice, lawyers occasionally gave free legal service to indigents in felony cases.[15] But not until the Poor Prisoner's Defense Act of 1903 did impoverished felony defendants achieve the right to free legal aid.[16] And yet this right was by no means absolute, for the prisoner had to first explain his defense to the judge. The judge would then decide whether or not to appoint counsel for him.[17] Generally, except for defendants accused of murder, most requests were denied.[18] In 1930, the ineffective earlier law was replaced by the new Poor Prisoner's Defense Act, which gave an indigent accused of murder an unqualified right to counsel.[19] In other felony cases, the decision whether or not to provide counsel was entirely in the court's discretion.[20] Many of the problems inherent in this latter act were resolved in 1949 with the Legal Aid and Advice Act, which provided for the assigning of counsel to indigents in non-capital felonies.[21]

The colonies initially gave greater recognition to the defendant's right to be represented at trial by counsel. Rhode Island provided this right as early as 1660.[22] Pennsylvania's law had a three-stage development, beginning in 1701, when a defendant received the same privilege of witness and counsel as the prosecution had. In 1718, the Pennsylvania legislature extended to certain defendants charged with serious felonies the right to have counsel appointed by the court, and fifty years later authorized court-appointed counsel to all felony defendants.[23] Other statutory variations existed: in South Carolina, which in 1731 gave the defendant a right to retain counsel for murder, treason, felonies, and other capital offenses;[24] in Virginia and Delaware, which authorized counsel in all capital cases upon the defendant's request;[25] and in Connecticut, which appointed counsel without a request by the defendant, if the defendant was operating under a handicap.[26] The English rule that assistance of counsel was a matter of judicial discretion persisted in the remaining colonies.[27] As the colonies made the transformation to statehood and new states were born, the law changed and the constitutions of all states but Virginia affirmed a criminal defendant's right to be represented at trial. Even in Virginia, the due process clause of the Constitution was judicially interpreted as granting the right to counsel.[28]

But the American experience involved two avenues of development—state and federal. In the federal courts, the Sixth Amendment to the United States Constitution guaranteed the assistance of counsel to an accused in all criminal prosecutions. As a result of the Federal Crimes Act of 1790, appointment of counsel for indigent defendants in all capital cases became mandatory in federal courts.[29] State courts also faced the problem of right to counsel and their duty to appoint an attorney if a defendant could not afford one. Most state courts interpreted their constitutions as not imposing an overall duty to appoint counsel for the poor, although all states required—either by statute, constitution, or judicial interpretation—appointment of counsel in capital cases.[30]

Development of the Constitutional Right

The full recognition of the right to counsel has only occurred during the last half century, despite its inclusion in every state constitution as well as in the Bill of Rights.

The issue first gained national prominence in 1932 in the "Scottsboro Boys Case," *Powell v. Alabama.*[31] There for the first time recognition was given to the absolute need of the guiding hand of counsel. Seven black youths, ranging in age from fourteen to nineteen, were riding the rails through Alabama on the same open freight car as seven white boys and two white girls. A fight erupted between the two groups of boys and all but one of the whites and the two girls were thrown off the car. A message was sent ahead alerting the sheriff of the fight. Before the train reached Scottsboro, it was halted and a sheriff's posse took the seven blacks and the two girls into custody. By the time the posse reached Scottsboro with the seven defendants and two girls, a hostile crowd had assembled at the jail. The militia was sent in to guard the defendants and the courthouse from the day of the arrest through the trial, a period of two tense, belligerent weeks. The two girls, claiming to have been sexually assaulted six times each, identified the seven defendants as their assailants. Over the years one of the two girls repeatedly altered her version of what had happened.

The defendants were all illiterate and without funds to hire attorneys. Honoring Alabama's own requirement that counsel be appointed in cases where defendants faced the death penalty, the trial court on the day the trials began appointed counsel, in a fashion. The record discloses that the court appointed the entire bar of the county to represent the defendants. Also, an out-of-state attorney who claimed to be present as an observer offered to assist. As can be expected, it is totally unclear from the record whether any specific attorney undertook or was assigned primary responsibility, or whether they were all assigned the function and agreed to assist each other. With no opportunity, or for that matter with no request for an opportunity, to prepare a defense case for trial, the trials began on the very day counsel came into the case. Because of their number, the defendants were divided into three groups for trial. Each trial was completed in less than a day and all seven defendants were sentenced to death.

The case was appealed and eventually made it to the Supreme Court of the United States where the convictions were reversed on the grounds that the defendants were denied a fair trial because their constitutional right to counsel had been violated. The Court pointed out the disadvantages that a lay person faces when defending himself without the aid of counsel:

> Even the intelligent and educated layman has small and sometimes no skill in the science of law.... He lacks both the skill and the knowledge to adequately prepare his defense, even though he has a perfect one.... Without it, though he be not guilty, he faces the danger of conviction because he does not know how to establish his innocence.[32]

The language used by the Court left no doubt that the availability of counsel to the defendant in a criminal case goes to the very heart of the reliability and integrity of the guilt-determining process because without that assistance the innocent defendant might be convicted.

Along with the broad language indicating the imperativeness of granting counsel were statements in the decision alluding to the total inability of the Scottsboro defendants, on trial for their lives, to represent themselves. Unfortunately, the decision was unclear as to whether the Court had established a right that was universally applicable to all criminal cases, or just to all capital cases, or solely to those cases where the defendant was uneducated, illiterate and totally unable to present his own defense.

Exactly one decade later, the Supreme Court was asked to define what it had meant in the Scottsboro case. A defendant charged in a Maryland court with robbery informed the trial court that he could not afford to hire a lawyer and requested that the court appoint counsel on his behalf. The court refused because the defendant was not on trial for his life. Harold Betts pleaded not guilty, waived trial by jury, and tried his own case. Betts cross-examined the state's witnesses and called and examined his own. He was convicted and the case eventually made its way to the Supreme Court.

In *Betts v. Brady,*[33] the Court retrenched from the position it appeared to advocate in the Scottsboro case by holding that the earlier case had only required the states to provide counsel for indigent defendants accused of capital offenses. *Betts* minimally extended that rule by requiring that counsel be provided in other felony cases where the defendant, because of the complexity of the charge or defense or because of his own lack of education or experience, would be unable to represent himself. This was known as the *special circumstances* test. The Court pointed out that Betts was a mature individual with an average intelligence who was familiar with criminal courts. A closer look at the defendant, however, revealed that he was an unemployed farmhand with a fifth-grade education and that his familiarity with the criminal process was limited to one appearance before a court on a charge of petty larceny, a charge met with a plea of guilty.

Still closer analysis of the trial records reveals additional reasons why Betts was not capable of representing himself. The trial court permitted the state to violate its own evidentiary rules in several instances. Betts was convicted because he did not understand these rules and the criminal process. A non-lawyer typically does not understand that the state bears the burden of proving his guilt. Instead, the common belief is that an accused must establish his innocence. Rather than hammering away at the state's case, which the record discloses was not strong, and questioning the credibility and truth of the state's witnesses, Betts tried to prove that he was innocent. He tried to do so by establishing an alibi that he was elsewhere when the crime was committed. The alibi was a complete sham and led to his being convicted. But all the state had shown was that Betts was in the vicinity of the crime scene, not that beyond a reasonable doubt Betts had committed the robbery. Left to his own devices, Betts convicted himself by trying to talk his way out of trouble. He only succeeded in making himself look guilty.[34]

The *special circumstances*[35] test devised in *Betts* proved unworkable. Counsel was provided for all indigent defendants in capital cases but not in others. State trial judges deemed their obligations under the Constitution fulfilled when they appointed counsel for defendants on trial for their lives and denied appointed counsel to all others.[36] Very few ever took the time to consider whether the *special circumstances* test should be made applicable for the appointment of counsel in non-capital felony prosecutions as well.[37] In effect, *Betts* sanctioned an entirely different concept of the right to counsel than that promised in the Bill of Rights. What the framers of the Bill of Rights regarded as an inalienable right ("In all prosecutions the accused shall ... have the Assistance of Counsel") was interpreted as a conditional right, dependent upon the charge or the defendant's wealth.

It took another decade and *Gideon v. Wainwright*[38] for the Court to reverse itself and extend the right to counsel to all felony defendants.[39] By that time the vast majority of states had already done so as a matter of state law. During the same term that *Gideon* was decided, the Supreme Court decided another case recognizing that the denial of counsel on appeal was virtually the same as denying access to an appeal to the poor defendant. As a result of *Douglas v. California,*[40] the states were also obligated to furnish counsel for the first appeal of right. Another decade saw the Supreme Court in *Argersinger v. Hamlin*[41] extend the right to counsel to include misdemeanor defendants who face potential jail sentences.

In the immediate aftermath of *Gideon,* the right, even for felony defendants, had been limited to the trial stages of a prosecution. The Court developed a process of examining each phase of a prosecution to determine whether it was a *critical stage* requiring the assistance of counsel. A critical stage was that aspect or event in a case where through the absence of legal assistance, a defendant might (a) irrevocably waive a vital constitutional right, or (b) otherwise lose an advantage which would hinder the development of an effective defense for trial, or (c) affect the likelihood of his going to prison.[42]

Through the case-by-case process of constitutional litigation, the full development of the right to counsel unfolded and was extended to police interrogations,[43] lineups,[44] preliminary appearances and arraignments if guilty pleas that were entered and later withdrawn could be used against the defendant as evidence at his trial,[45] preliminary hearings,[46] and, finally, sentencing.[47] Whether counsel must be provided for other proceedings related to the criminal process, such as subsequent appeals, probation and parole revocation, is still decided on a case-by-case approach determined by the significance of the issues raised and the capacity of the individual defendant to protect his own interests.[48]

While the presence of a lawyer will in itself make a marked difference in the conduct of a criminal case, additional assistance may be necessary to enable the attorney to prepare an effective defense. Many defense investigations require psychiatrists, psychologists, or experts on ballistics, handwriting, or fingerprints. If the defense needs these investigative aids, they must be provided by the state. In addition, if the attorney also demonstrates a need to have a transcript of the preliminary hearing in order to prepare for trial, then the state is obligated to furnish one.[49] A transcript of the trial is essential to perfecting an appeal, so a request for this record cannot be denied simply because the defendant is unable to pay for it.[50] While the state is not obligated to equalize for the poor defendant every advantage enjoyed by a defendant with means, it must provide sufficient tools to insure each defendant with the opportunity to fully present his case.[51]

Effective Assistance of Counsel

Powell v. Alabama, the Scottsboro case, not only spoke to the right of an accused to counsel, but also made clear that the right was to the *effective assistance of counsel.* The Supreme Court said the duty of the state is not discharged by an assignment of counsel if the defendant does not receive effective aid in the preparation and trial of the case. Appointing counsel, in other words, does not exhaust the state's obligation to the defendant without means.

Courts, including the Supreme Court, have shied away from issues raised by ineffective representation. Avoidance, however, has become impossible because of the frequency with which charges of ineffective counsel are raised. Ineffective counsel can be charged by any defendant who feels his conviction resulted from his attorney's incompetence. If the defendant's contention is established, his conviction will be reversed and he will be entitled to a new trial. A reversal based on the grounds of ineffective counsel can cause an uncomfortable confrontation between the appellate court and the trial court. In effect, the appellate court has censured the trial court by saying that the trial judge was blind to an injustice committed in his presence.

One prominent federal judge, David Bazelon, has written that all too often indigent defendants are represented by " 'walking violations of the Sixth Amendment.' "[52] This observation is unfortunately true. Nevertheless, how to determine standards for effective representation and specifically how to enforce the obligation has confounded the courts.

Vigorous enforcement of effective assistance would require trial judges to intervene in the trial whenever a possible error is being committed by the defense attorney. This is not as simple as it seems. Failure of a defense attorney to make a proper objection is not necessarily a result of that attorney's ignorance of the legal point or evidentiary rules but may, in fact, represent a conscious tactical decision on the part of the lawyer. Interruptions by trial judges at such points would not only destroy the continuity of the trial, but they might destroy as well the sound tactics upon which the decision was based. There is also the fear that vigorous enforcement of the standard would make attorneys even more reluctant to engage in the criminal defense practice or to accept court appointments. Finally, it has been suggested that vigorous enforcement would further the efforts of the unethical attorney who, faced with a desperate case and sure loss, could insure his client a new trial by deliberately committing an error.[53]

Initially, the response of the courts was to avoid defining effective assistance and instead to apply a *mockery of justice* test. This test was devised to determine whether counsel was so ineffective that the trial was a farce and therefore shocking to the conscience of the reviewing court.[54] The Supreme Court avoided the issue by refusing to make an absolute rule that a lawyer was ineffective even if he came into the case on the very day trial began and had no time to personally consider the issues and prepare for trial.[55] By avoiding this issue, the Supreme Court shut its eyes to the very problem it had looked at almost a half century earlier in *Powell v. Alabama.* As Judge Bazelon has pointed out, the Supreme Court's avoidance of this issue resulted in lawyers not being held ineffective even when they appeared in court drunk or fell asleep at a trial.[56]

In the 1970s, the *mockery* test was abandoned in more than half the state and federal courts and replaced by more meaningful guidelines: these guidelines center on the following three tests: (1) was counsel's advice within the range of competence demanded of attorneys in criminal cases; (2) did counsel exercise the normal skill and knowledge which prevails within the profession at the time and place; and (3) did counsel provide a minimal standard of professional representation or reasonably effective assistance.[57]

The problem of ineffective counsel poses a dilemma for the reviewing court because its task is not to second-guess the reasonably competent attorney but to prevent injustice arising from professional ineptitude. For example, the attorney who fails to object to admission of certain testimony should not be subject to censure if the decision was consciously and conscientiously made, even though it may turn out to be wrong. But an attorney must be branded "ineffective" when he fails to object to legally inadmissible evidence because of his ignorance about the Fourth Amendment and the law concerning search and seizure.[58]

An interesting example of how a court can approach this problem arose in a rape case which was reviewed on the issue of effective assistance of counsel. The facts were in dispute and the claims of the defendant and the state's chief witness disclose the contradictions:

> *Defendant's contentions:* He was on a public street when he met the state's chief witness who was with a male companion. She offered to have sex with the defendant for two dollars. Defendant and the woman went into the alley where they began to argue concerning the time for payment. A neighbor heard the row, called the police, and the defendant was arrested.
>
> *Witness' contention:* Defendant grabbed her and dragged her into an alley where he then raped her.

The only other evidence was provided by a medical test performed upon the witness immediately after the defendant was arrested. The tests for the presence of spermatozoa seminal stains were both negative.

The defendant was represented at trial by two court-appointed attorneys. Between the time of their appointment and the beginning of trial, the two attorneys interviewed the defendant three times; once for thirty minutes, again for a lesser period, and a third time for a few minutes on the day of trial. The defendant was convicted and sentenced to twenty-five years. The court found the defendant's contention of ineffective assistance well founded and reversed the conviction. The court's opinion included the tasks that the appointed lawyers had failed to undertake:

> Counsel made no investigation of the reputation of the witness for chastity. Counsel made no attempt to determine the identity of, or to interview, the witness' male companion. Counsel made no attempt to interview the neighbor or to determine what her testimony would be. Counsel did not explain the elements of the crime of forcible rape to the defendant, including the necessity of penetration, nor did they question him in this regard. Counsel did not know that the witness had been examined medically and had no knowledge of the written, signed medical report.[59]

The issue of the ineffective assistance of counsel is by no means an attempt by courts to overprotect criminals; it is, instead, an attempt by courts to determine whether their obligations to protect an accused's Sixth Amendment right to fair trial have been satisfied.

Judge Bazelon's own court has taken the lead by adopting a set of standards for defense attorneys:

> Since "reasonably competent assistance" is only a shorthand label, and not subject to ready application, we . . . set forth some of the duties owed by counsel to a client.
>
> In General—Counsel should be guided by the American Bar Association Standards for the Defense Function. They represent the legal profession's own articulation of guidelines for the defense of criminal cases.
>
> Specifically—(1) Counsel should confer with his client without delay and as often as necessary to elicit matters of defense, or to ascertain that potential defenses were unavailable. Counsel should discuss fully potential strategies and tactical choices with his client.
>
> (2) Counsel should promptly advise his client of his rights and take all actions necessary to preserve them. Many rights can only be protected by prompt legal action. The Supreme Court has, for example, recognized the attorney's role in protecting the client's privilege against self-incrimination. . . . Counsel should also be concerned with the accused's right to be released from custody pending trial, and be prepared, where appropriate, to make motions for a pre-trial psychiatric examination or for the suppression of evidence.
>
> (3) Counsel must conduct appropriate investigations, both factual and legal, to determine what matters of defense can be developed. The Supreme Court has noted that the adversary system requires that "all available defenses are raised" so that the government is put to its proof. This means that in most cases a defense attorney, or his agent, should interview not only his own witnesses but also those that the government intends to call, when they are accessible. The investigation should always include efforts to secure information in the possession of the prosecution and law enforcement authorities. And, of course, the duty to investigate also requires adequate legal research.[60]

There has been a strong reluctance to apply the effective assistance standard to defense attorneys hired by defendants or their families.[61] One reason, of course, is that the court has not appointed the attorney as it has for the indigent defendant and thus does not share the moral and legal responsibility for the attorney's failings. Another theory for this differentiation is that the defendant made the choice of attorneys and must bear the responsibility and accept the consequences. This line of reasoning has been criticized. Initially, the state has certified the attorney as qualified to practice law and so the state's involvement does exist, though not as totally as when it appoints counsel. Second, even the defendant's ability to choose retained counsel is limited by financial realities. While it is true that the defendant made the choice, that choice was limited to those attorneys who would take the case for a fee that the defendant was able to raise. Nonetheless, it is in this limited area, assessment of the consequences of inadequate legal representation, that the indigent defendant appears to have his only edge.

Waiver of Counsel

Like any constitutional guarantee, the right to counsel may be waived by a defendant in a criminal case.[62] Most often waiver is exercised when the accused plans not to contest the charge but, instead, intends to plead guilty and seek an early termination of the case. Because legal assistance is deemed so fundamentally important to a defendant's access to a fair disposition, waiver of counsel is not treated lightly.[63] It is an issue to be considered at every critical stage of a prosecution.

The courts, recognizing the link between counsel and fairness, do not encourage waiver of the right. A defendant may waive the right if the court can be assured that the defendant "knows what he is doing and his choice is made with his eyes open."[64] The right is not dependent upon an accused's requesting counsel. The defendant must be affirmatively informed in court of the right to appointed or retained counsel, and the court record must show that the defendant, armed with this knowledge, made a conscious choice to forego exercising that right.[65] Consequently, a standard has been devised for determining the constitutional validity of a waiver of the right to counsel: it must be "knowingly and intelligently" made. The failure of the record to demonstrate a knowledgeable and intelligent waiver will result in the conclusion that it was not made.[66]

The failure to secure a valid waiver results in the automatic reversal of a conviction secured without counsel upon later challenge by the defendant. Thus it is important that the judge carefully advise a defendant of the right and closely question the defendant who asserts the desire to waive that right to protect the record of the court from subsequent attack. Former Supreme Court Justice William O. Douglas maintained that a layman should have the benefit of legal advice before his waiver is accepted. Douglas argued this premise from two angles: first that the lay defendant is not fully aware of all of the legal issues and nuances involved in a criminal prosecution and secondly, that a court has a right to insist upon conditions existing in a criminal case which are most likely to produce a fair result.[67] Some trial judges insist that an accused confer with an attorney in the courtroom and will draft a lawyer for this purpose before accepting a waiver of counsel and entry of a plea of guilty.[68]

The Right to Self-Representation

Corollary to the issue of waiver is the separate and distinct issue of whether a defendant has a right to try his own case. This issue emerged in full force in the 1960s. That decade saw the emergence of a new class of defendants, people disenchanted with the American system, who began to insist on the right to represent themselves. Other defendants belonging to this class saw trial as a political forum, as the opportunity to argue broader issues beyond guilt or innocence. Still others were simply distrustful of lawyers and believed that they had no chance for a fair trial unless they represented themselves.

Many courts rejected out of hand the proposition of self-representation and imposed counsel upon unwilling defendants.[69] These same courts typically prohibited a defendant from actively participating in his defense. A different arrangement, however, was struck in the trial of Angela Davis, a black activist college professor. Davis was granted her request by the trial court and accorded the right to participate along with counsel at her trial. This created the unique situation of a defendant's having the opportunity to argue her innocence to the jury without ever having taken the witness stand and testifying under oath and then being subjected to cross-examination.[70] In other instances where defendants have been accorded the right to self-representation, trial courts have imposed counsel upon the accused in an advisory capacity. However, whether the attorney is even consulted is strictly a matter for the defendant to decide.

In 1975 the Supreme Court spoke decisively on the issue. In *Faretta v. California*[71] the Court said that a defendant has a constitutional right to proceed without counsel when he voluntarily and intelligently elects to do so. The language of the Sixth Amendment itself was found to be the basis of the right. According to this amendment, a defendant must be informed of the charge, has the right to confront witnesses, and to have witnesses summoned in his behalf. The Court said that the right to defend is a personal and direct right of the accused, and that the assistance of counsel is an aid guaranteed to a willing defendant. In assessing whether a defendant is voluntarily and intelligently relinquishing the right to counsel, a judge may not question the defendant's technical legal knowledge because, the Court said, it is not relevant.[72] All that must be ascertained, as the Supreme Court did in *Faretta,* is that the defendant is literate and competent, and that he is voluntarily exercising his *informed* free will.

Defense Services for the Poor

There are no definitive figures on how many defendants in criminal cases are provided legal assistance without cost to themselves. Although the obligation has been imposed by the Supreme Court through its interpretation of the Constitution, fulfillment of that obligation is purely a local matter. The most commonly accepted estimate is that sixty percent of all felony defendants are represented by court-appointed counsel.[73] It is also believed that from twenty-five to fifty percent of misdemeanor defendants are unable to hire a lawyer. Not all the defendants in the latter category receive legal assistance because many plead guilty immediately and have their cases summarily terminated, as do many misdemeanor defendants who can afford to hire a lawyer.[74] Naturally, the figures for court-provided assistance vary from state to state and even between communities within the same state. The variance is dependent upon three factors: (1) the percentage of impoverished people within the community; (2) the attitude towards providing legal assistance demonstrated by the judge or judges who make the decision; and (3) the nature and quality of the representation provided by the court.

Although judges exercise a wide range of discretion in determining whether a defendant is entitled to have counsel appointed for him, most judges realize the necessity for having a defense attorney present in most criminal trials. This realization exists as a formidable control on judicial discretion: few judges are going to permit an accused who does not waive the right to plead guilty or to go to trial without an attorney, only for the reason that sentences reached under these circumstances are more vulnerable to reversal on appeal.

When a judge is required to determine the eligibility of a specific defendant for court-appointed legal counsel, he is measuring the amount of the defendant's income and resources against what the judge believes an average fee for that type of offense would be. While the flexibility is a necessity, it provides, nonetheless, for unevenness and disparity.

Although the term "indigent defendant" is commonly used to describe the individual who is entitled to legal assistance, it is not entirely precise. Indigency carries a connotation of eligibility for welfare and frequently connotes a family income of less than $2700 per annum for a single person, and less than $4500 a year for a family of four persons. But a single person with an income of $2700 or a family with earnings of $4500 is hardly likely to come up with the funds necessary to pay a lawyer. Consequently, the welfare standards are grossly inadequate in this context. The Supreme Court cases and most statutory formulas creating standards for appointment of counsel avoid the term indigency and, instead, provide that counsel shall be appointed for *any* defendant unable to retain an attorney.[75] This standard is perfect and yet imprecise. Inability to retain an attorney is not simply a reflection of family income but will vary depending upon the seriousness of the charge and the complexity of the criminal case. A defendant who is charged with drunken driving may be able to hire an attorney for approximately $350 to defend his case. The defendant who is charged with a felony, on the other hand, may not be able to muster the several thousand dollars that an attorney might ask to represent the accused in a felony case that is likely to go to trial. Attorneys, of course, are free to ask as much as they wish for their services, and their ability to get their asked-for retainer depends upon the market and their reputations.

Many of the standards that have been utilized for determining a defendant's eligibility for court-appointed counsel incorporate a provision requiring the appointment of counsel not only for those totally without funds but also for any person unable to retain an attorney "without substantial hardship to himself or his family."[76] What constitutes substantial hardship depends almost entirely upon the judge's discretion. Some judges appoint counsel simply upon the statement of the accused that he is unable to retain an attorney. Others make the appointment after minimal inquiry of the accused about his financial status. Some judges use bail as the guideline for determining eligibility for appointed counsel. If the defendant is free on bond, the court may assume that he has access to resources and refuse to make an appointment.[77] Still other judges carefully scrutinize the defendant's situation to assess whether the claim of indigency is accurate.[78]

In general, middle-class needs have not been accounted for in programs for court-appointed legal assistance. Yet a family member's expenses to defend a criminal case may be so high as to virtually destroy the family's future prospects. On a national basis, legal assistance programs have been confined to the truly indigent and little concern has been shown for those who can scrape together a fee. Virtually ignored (except in Florida) is the American Bar Associations's standard on partial eligibility, which would permit defendants in this strait to pay what the court determined they could into a general fund and receive court-appointed assistance.[79] The only prospect for middle-class relief may come in the form of prepaid legal insurance, which is comparable to medical care insurance. Most of the earliest plans, however, have excluded coverage in criminal cases.[80]

Defense services are supplied to eligible defendants[81] through the assignment of private attorneys or through the maintenance of professional public defender organizations.[82] Small communities are more apt to appoint private attorneys to represent an indigent because the cost of maintaining a permanent public defender organization would be too high. On the other hand, urban areas can rarely justify the appointment of private counsel to indigents because of the costs that would be incurred. Public defender organizations are relied on by larger communities to represent most indigent defendants.[83]

Appointments of private attorneys in felony cases generally take place after the return of an indictment or information when a case finally gets to the trial court. This court is usually the only one with statutory authority to order and approve an attorney's fee. If representation is needed at an earlier stage or in a misdemeanor case, the judge in the municipal court may seek a volunteer, may draft an attorney, or may be authorized to order payment of a nominal fee.

Most often the appointment is made by reference to a rotating list made up of members of the local bar who have indicated a desire or willingness to represent the indigent. Generally, the judge has total discretion and may entirely bypass the list. Bypasses most frequently occur in homicide cases where the judge is concerned with appointing a lawyer with extensive experience. The list may also be bypassed if the judge fears that the next attorney on that list will do nothing but plead the defendant guilty and submit a bill for services. Unfortunately, some judges ignore the list for the opposite reason and avoid appointing attorneys who will raise all possible defenses—to some judges, too many defenses. Not all communities maintain rotational lists and appointment, then, may be based upon the judge's confidence in a particular attorney's competence, friendship, political kinship, or because the judge wishes to give a young lawyer a start or realizes that a particular attorney may need the business.

Private attorneys who volunteer for assignments do so for many reasons. Many established and experienced attorneys involve themselves in indigent defense work because they believe that the attorney, like the doctor, is obligated by the nature of the profession to devote time to people who need assistance but who are unable to pay a fee. These attorneys are likely to exert the same energies for an indigent client as they do for regular clients. Because of the increased complexity of criminal law and procedure, however, fewer attorneys today feel themselves capable of providing the type of assistance that may be needed in the courtroom. Therefore, many lawyers who may feel an obligation toward indigents maintain an exclusively nontrial office practice and would be totally unfamiliar with a courtroom.

In every city there are some experienced attorneys who seek indigent assignments for the fees. Because the compensation is generally inadequate, these attorneys often move in for a quick consultation with the indigent client and then plead to the charge itself or to the best deal that can be arranged with the prosecutor. These attorneys find the accumulated "inadequate" fees lucrative and have come to depend upon them financially as they hurriedly finish one case to seek the next. A judge whose passion is for a current calendar and whose obsession is to avoid trial encourages these attorneys to mill around the courtroom during arraignments to pick up assignments.[84] The resolution of these cases is usually predicated upon the defendant's response to counsel's single question, "Did you do it?" The case is then resolved on the basis of the defendant's answer, irrespective of the defendant's motivations for admitting to the crime or of existing defenses or possible mitigating circumstances.

Indigent assignments are also made to the lawyer recently graduated from law school and admitted to practice. Though "untried," this neophyte lawyer often brings to the task a serious desire for experience and an eagerness to serve his client in the best possible way. Some communities assign the younger practitioner to assist a more experienced attorney on a number of indigent cases before accrediting the young lawyer as eligible for appointments.

In the past decade more than half the nation's accredited law schools have established clinical programs where students, generally in their last year, engage in criminal practice.[85] Generally limited by state rule to misdemeanor cases, the student has total responsibility for the case under the guidance of a law professor or staff attorney who must appear in court with the student.[86] The quality of the practice in these clinics is usually very high. Students spend an inordinate amount of time preparing each case and are closely supervised. The benefits of the programs are two-fold: clients receive high-quality, enthusiastic representation and the fledgling lawyer gains critical experience.

The Public Defender

The public defender concept arose with the belief that indigent defendants need experienced and specialized defense attorneys on a par with the talents at the disposal of the state in the prosecutor's office. The oldest public defender's office, serving Los Angeles County, was established in 1914, long before there was a federal mandate to the states to provide legal assistance. Most public defender operations are public agencies financed directly by state or local governments. Some are quasi-private agencies, generally adjunct to a Legal Aid Society, funded partially by community chest funds and public funds either from direct appropriations or fees generated by court appointments. The offices range in size from several hundred attorneys, as in Los Angeles, to one attorney serving as the public defender for two adjacent communities. During the 1970s, the public defender concept spread beyond the large cities to some smaller communities where it was decided that having one or two attorneys operating a full time defender office would be less costly than the private appointment system.[87]

Essential to the effectiveness and success of a public defender operation is the person selected to head the office. The devotion and zeal that the director brings to the task, to a large extent, will determine the caliber of representation provided by that office. If it is a small office, the director's ability as an advocate will be constantly tested. If the director is coordinating the services provided by a large staff, his management and leadership qualifications will set the tone for the operation. Consequently, the method of selection and compensation for the position are highly important.[88]

Recent law school graduates just admitted to the bar staff most defender offices. Unlike their peers in private practice, the young defenders are instantly immersed in criminal law and procedure problems, the volume of which necessitates a rapid growth of expertise in the area unattainable in all but very few private practices. Like the prosecutor's office, though, the public defender's office is not regarded favorably as a career objective. There are frequent and massive turnovers after the lawyers gain a year or two of experience.[89]

The public defender's office creates a cadre of lawyers expert in the criminal practice. The public defender operation also offers the courts readily available lawyers for all phases of a criminal case, including those where the state has not authorized payment of a fee. In the larger cities, however, this has usually resulted in one attorney handling the bail hearing, another the preliminary hearing, and still another the trial.[90]

Many communities have resisted a full defender program, choosing instead a defender office with appointments shared between the defender and the private bar.[91] Some cities assign all cases to the public defender unless that office's caseload is greater than the staff can handle or if there is more than one defendant in a criminal case and representation of all by the same attorney would create a conflict of interest.[92] The National Commission on Criminal Justice Standards and Goals recommended the creation of a public defender office and a coordinated assigned counsel system that would involve substantial participation of the private bar.[93] One of the reasons offered for the commission's proposal was the need to force members of the bar to become involved in the criminal justice system and to upgrade the bar's participation in the criminal process. Further, the commission stressed that the private bar's portion of cases should be significant.

No matter what defense service is made available, the indigent defendant is less able to develop confidence toward the person who is representing him than the defendant who has a private attorney. Missing is the intangible bond that seems to exist when a defendant chooses his own lawyer and pays the bill.[94] The indigent almost never has a voice in the selection of his attorney. Instead, the indigent defendant faces the reality that both the choice of his lawyer and the payment of that lawyer's fee come directly from the system which the defendant believes is seeking to take away his liberty. It is inherently difficult for an indigent defendant to accept that the attorney will be working for him and not acting in collusion with the rest of the system.

The indigent defendant lacks someone with whom he can candidly discuss his case. In many cases, he is also beset by doubts created by the infrequency of attorneys' visits along with the horror stories he hears from other inmates pertaining to the injustices, some real and some apocryphal, done by their attorneys.[95] A further barrier to the establishment of a trusting relationship is the unlikelihood that the indigent defendant will see an attorney before his first court appearance. Counsel is often appointed after an indictment or information is returned and the arraignment is scheduled. To compound the defendant's sense of insecurity regarding counsel is the fact that the lawyers indigents usually have at the earlier stages of the criminal prosecution are legal aid attorneys who are assigned to a single courtroom, with one assisting the accused at the preliminary appearance and then another at the preliminary hearing. This piecemeal system of representation may continue throughout the life of the case, with no attorney assigned permanent responsibility for the defense. In the worst arrangements, a defendant may be brought to court for trial only to meet, for the first time, the attorney assigned to represent him.[96] Obviously, no valued or effective attorney-client relationship can be forged under these conditions.

Every defendant must depend on his attorney to put forth his best efforts for the case. The defendant must also depend on his attorney's advice. We come full circle here because the soundness of that advice is directly related to how well informed the attorney is about the case. Much of the information upon which the attorney's assessment is based must come from the defendant. Without a relationship of trust, the defendant's disclosures to the attorney are not likely to be either truthful or complete. And yet the attorney will be called upon to advise the defendant: whether to go to trial; whether to plead guilty as charged; whether to accept the prosecutor's offer and plead guilty to a reduced charge or to hold out for a better offer. All are decisions to be made by the defendant, presumably after consultation with his lawyer. In order to make intelligent choices, the defendant must have the guidance of a counsellor he trusts.

Discussion Questions

1. Why is the defense attorney indispensable to a defendant in the pretrial stage of a criminal case?

2. What is meant by the statement: "Guilt is strictly a legal conclusion"? How does this statement relate to the defense attorney's obligations as an officer of the court? To his responsibilities as an advocate for the defendant? (Include in your answer the defense attorney's position in relation to perjured testimony, planned or executed by the defendant.)

3. Why is the first meeting between an attorney and his client critical? What purposes are achieved through this initial interview?

4. Trace the history of the constitutional right to counsel (colonial period to Betts).

5. The text states:

> In effect, Betts sanctioned an entirely different concept of the right to counsel than that promised by the Bill of Rights. What the framers of the Bill of Rights regarded as an inalienable right was interpreted as a conditional right, dependent upon the charge or the defendant's wealth.

Many critics regard Betts as taking a step backwards in the unfolding of the constitutional right to counsel. Do you agree or disagree? (Include in your answer the significance of the special circumstances test in relation to the Sixth Amendment right to counsel guarantee.)

6. Why have the state courts and Supreme Court avoided issues raised by ineffective representation?

Notes

1. See *Equal Justice for the Accused* (Association of the Bar of the City of New York and the National Legal Aid and Defender's Association, 1959); *The Problem of Assistance to the Indigent Accused* (Joint Committee on Continuing Education of the American Law Institute and the American Bar Association, 1961); Kamisar, "The Right to Counsel and the Fourteenth Amendment: A Dialogue on 'The Most Pervasive Right' of an Accused," 30 *U. Chi. L. Rev.* 1 (1962). [Hereinafter cited as *"Right to Counsel"]*.
2. *A.B.A. Code of Professional Responsibility* (1970), Dr 7-101.
3. See F.R. Marks, "A Lawyer's Duty to Take all Comers and Many Who Do Not Come," 30 *U. Miami L. Rev.* 915 (1976).
4. See Hanson, *The Boston Massacre: An Episode of Dissent and Violence* (New York: Hastings House, 1970).
5. Lee, *To Kill A Mockingbird* (Philadelphia: Lippincott, 1960).
6. *A.B.A. Code of Professional Responsibility* (1970), Ec 2-26, Ec 2-27.
7. Ibid., Ec 7-26.
8. See Heather, "Attorney-Client Confidentiality: A New Approach," 4 *Hofstra L. Rev.* 685 (1976) and Lawry, "Lying, Confidentiality, and the Adversary System of Justice," *Utah L. Rev.* 653 (1977); c.f. M. Freedman, *Lawyer's Ethics in an Adversary System* (New York: Bobbs-Merrill, 1975).
9. Powell v. Alabama, 287 U.S. 45 (1932); Betts v. Brady, 316 U.S. 455 (1942); Gideon v. Wainwright, 372 U.S. 335 (1963); Argersinger v. Hamlin, 407 U.S. 25 (1972); and see Kamisar, LaFave, and Israel, *Modern Criminal Procedure,* 4th ed. (St. Paul, Minn.: West, 1974), pp. 42-126.
10. Blackstone, *Commentaries on the Law of England* (Portland: T. B. Wait, and Co., 1807), pp. 354-355. Only where a point of law required debate was the accused permitted counsel. Id. at 355.
11. W. S. Holdsworth, *A History of English Law* (London: Methuen and Co., 1922), p. 193.
12. By singling out these defendants, some measure of protection was afforded controversial members of Parliament who were charged with high treason. 7 & 8 W. 3, c. 3, Sess. 1 (1695).
13. W. Beaney, *The Right to Counsel in American Courts* (Ann Arbor: University of Michigan Press, 1955), pp. 8-10.
14. 6 & 7 W. 4, c. 114, Sess. 1 (1836).
15. Beaney, *The Right to Counsel,* pp. 10-12.
16. 3 Edw. 7, c. 38, Sess. 1 (1903).
17. Beaney, *The Right to Counsel,* pp. 12-13.
18. L. Orfield, *Criminal Procedure from Arrest to Appeal* (New York: University Press, 1947), note 72, p. 362.
19. 20 & 21 Geo. 5, c. 32 (1930).
20. Beaney, *The Right to Counsel,* p. 13.
21. 12 & 13 Geo. 6, c. 51 (1949).
22. Beaney, *The Right to Counsel,* pp. 17-18.
23. Ibid., pp. 16-17.
24. Ibid., p. 17.
25. Ibid., pp. 16-17.
26. Ibid., p. 16. The handicap warranting automatic appointment of counsel was the inability of the defendant to understand the applicable law or to plead properly to the charge.

27. Beaney, *The Right to Counsel,* p. 18.
28. Ibid., pp. 80-89.
29. Federal Crimes Act of 1790, 1 Stat. 112 (1790), reenacted as 18 U.S.C. 563 (1940).
30. Beaney, *The Right to Counsel,* pp. 82-83, 86, 138.
31. Powell v. Alabama, 287 U.S. 45 (1932).
32. Ibid., at 69.
33. Betts v. Brady, 316 U.S. 455 (1942).
34. For a discussion of the Betts case, see Kamisar, "Right to Counsel," p. 42.
35. "Asserted denial (of due process) is to be tested by an appraisal of the totality of facts in a given case. That which may, in one setting, constitute a denial of fundamental fairness, shocking to the universal sense of justice, may, in other circumstances, and in the light of other considerations, fall short of such denial." Betts v. Brady, supra, at 462.
36. See Kamisar, "Betts v. Brady Twenty Years Later: The Right to Counsel and Due Process Values", 61 *Mich. L. Rev.* 219 (1962); Allen, "The Supreme Court, Federalism, and the State Systems of Criminal Justice," 8 *DePaul L. Rev.* 213 (1959).
37. The few cases that came before the Supreme Court were all reversed utilizing the test devised in Betts, but since so few convictions ever get to the Supreme Court, the capital/non-capital replaced the special circumstances test in all but the cases that the Supreme Court did hear.
38. Gideon v. Wainwright, 372 U.S. 335 (1963); A. Lewis, *Gideon's Trumpet,* (New York: Vintage Books, 1966).
39. The response of the trial judge to Clarence Earl Gideon's request for counsel is indicative of the short shrift lower courts gave to the special circumstances test: "The Court: Mr. Gideon, I am sorry, but I cannot appoint Counsel to represent you in this case. Under the laws of the State of Florida, the only time the Court can appoint Counsel to represent a Defendant is when that person is charged with a capital offense. I am sorry, but I will have to deny your request to appoint Counsel to defend you in this case."
40. Douglas v. California, 372 U.S. 353 (1963).
41. Argersinger v. Hamlin, 407 U.S. 25 (1972).
42. "The determination whether the hearing is a 'critical stage' requiring the provision of counsel depends, as noted, upon the analysis 'whether potential substantial prejudice to defendant's rights inheres in the ... confrontation and the ability of counsel to help avoid that prejudice.' " Coleman v. Alabama, 399 U.S. 1, at 9 (1970).
43. Escobedo v. Illinois, 378 U.S. 478 (1964); Miranda v. Arizona, 384 U.S. 436 (1966).
44. United States v. Wade, 388 U.S. 218 (1967).
45. White v. Maryland, 373 U.S. 59 (1963).
46. Coleman v. Alabama, supra.
47. Mempa v. Rhay, 389 U.S. 128 (1968).
48. Gagnon v. Scarpelli, 411 U.S. 778 (1973) (probation revocation hearing); Sanders v. United States, 373 U.S. 1 (1963) (waiver of indictment); Ross v. Moffitt, 417 U.S. 600 (1974) (appeals to Supreme Court, state and federal post-conviction remedies).
49. Roberts v. LaVallee, 389 U.S. 40 (1967). But see, Britt v. North Carolina, 404 U.S. 226 (1972), where the Court found "an informal alternative which appears to be a substantial equivalent to a transcript" (at 230), to be sufficient.

50. Griffin v. Illinois, 351 U.S. 12 (1956). A full transcript need not be provided if alternative means (such as a partial transcript) will serve the defendant's needs. See Mayer v. Chicago, 404 U.S. 189 (1971).
51. Ross v. Moffitt, 417 U.S. 600 (1974).
52. Bazelon, "The Defective Assistance of Counsel," 42 *U. Cin. L. Rev.* 1, 2 (1973). Bazelon, a Judge of the Court of Appeals for the District of Columbia since 1950, has been a leading advocate of more concrete standards for the effective assistance of counsel.
53. See generally, Finer, "Ineffective Assistance of Counsel," 58 *Cornell L. Rev.*, 1077 (1973); Waltz, "Inadequacy of Trial Defense as a Ground for Post-Conviction Relief in Criminal Cases," 59 *Nw. U. L. Rev.* 289 (1964); Grano, "The Right to Counsel: Collateral Issues Affecting Due Process," 54 *Minn. L. Rev.* 1175; "Note, Effective Assistance of Counsel for the Indigent Defendant," 78 *Harv. L. Rev.* 1434 (1965); "Note, Effective Assistance of Counsel", 49 *Va. L. Rev.* 1531 (1963).
54. Bell v. Alabama, 367 F.2d 243 (5th Cir. 1966); Williams v. Beto, 354 F.2d 698 (5th Cir. 1965); People v. Washington, 41 Ill.2d 16, 241 N.E.2d 425 (1968).
55. Chambers v. Maroney, 399 U.S. 42 (1970).
56. Bazelon, "The Realities of Gideon and Argersinger," 64 *Georgetown L. Rev.* 811, at 819 (1976). [Hereinafter cited as "Gideon and Argersinger"].
57. Moore v. United States, 432 F.2d 730, 737 (3rd Cir. 1970); United States ex rel. Green v. Rundle, 434 F.2d 1112, 1113 (3rd Cir. 1970).
58. People v. Ibarra, 60 Cal.2d 460, 386 P.2d 487 (1963).
59. Coles v. Peyton, 389 F.2d 224, 226 (4th Cir. 1968).
60. United States v. DeCoster, 487 F.2d 1197, 1203 et seq. (D.C. Cir. 1973).
61. O'Malley v. United States, 285 F.2d 733 (6th Cir. 1961); United States ex rel. Darcy v. Hardy, 203 F.2d 404 (3rd Cir. 1953); Weatherman v. Peyton, 287 F.Supp. 819 (W.D. Va. 1968).
62. Johnson v. Zerbst, 304 U.S. 458 (1938).
63. Von Moltke v. Gillies, 332 U.S. 708 (1948); Adams v. United States ex rel. McCann, 317 U.S. 269 (1942). Also see, Potts, "The Right to Counsel in Criminal Cases," 28 *Texas L. Rev.* 419, 500 (1950); and Grano, "The Right to Counsel," pp. 1190-1208.
64. Adams v. United States ex rel. McCann, supra at 279.
65. Carnley v. Cochran, 369 U.S. 506 (1962).
66. Ibid., at 516: "Presuming waiver from a silent record is impermissible."
67. Douglas, J., dissent in Adams v. United States ex rel. McCann, supra.
68. The summary fashion with which waivers of counsel and guilty pleas are routinely accepted from misdemeanor defendants in municipal courts would probably not pass constitutional muster. The practice persists because so few misdemeanor convictions are ever subsequently attacked.
69. People v. Sharp, 499 P.2d 489 (1972) (California); Louisiana v. Frizzel, 273 So.2d 831 (1973).
70. A. Davis delivered an opening statement to the jury lasting almost two hours.
71. Faretta v. California, 422 U.S. 806 (1975).
72. Whether a defendant's technical legal knowledge is relevant or not to determination of his right to try his own case, it certainly will be relevant as soon as the trial begins.
73. *The President's Commission on Law Enforcement and the Administration of Justice, Task Force Report: The Courts* (Washington, 1967), p. 56.

74. Ibid., p. 134.

75. 18 U.S.C. §3006A(a), "furnishing representation for any person financially unable to obtain adequate representation"; Mass. Ann. Laws, ch. 221, §34D (Michie/Law. Co-op), "unable to obtain counsel by reason of inability to pay"; S.C. Code §17-3-10, "financially unable to retain counsel."

76. *A.B.A. Project on Standards for Criminal Justice: Providing Defense Services* (New York, 1967; Approved 1968), Standard 6.1, p. 10.

77. There are obvious problems with this reliance on an accused's bail determination. First, a defendant may have bail posted by relatives or friends who are reasonably assured that they will get their money back, but who are unwilling to hire an attorney with money they may never see returned. Secondly, it forces some defendants to choose between constitutional rights, counsel and bail, and they are hardly interchangeable.

78. The hostility of some judges toward appointing counsel is based upon their concern for the costs to the community and a belief that some people pleading poverty are chiselers.

79. Fla. Stat. Ann. §27.56(4) (West).

80. Deitch, *Prepaid Legal Services* (Toronto: Lexington Books, 1976), p. 45. See generally, *A.B.A. Special Report to National Conference on Prepaid Legal Services* (Washington, D.C., 1972).

81. Krantz, *Right to Counsel in Criminal Cases* (Cambridge, Mass.: Ballinger, 1976), p. 233.

82. A third approach, which has been recommended by national agencies as being preferable, is a system providing representation through a mixed public defender-private appointment method.

83. Frequently, the perpetuation of the court-appointed attorney system in urban areas and the rejection of the defender concept can be attributed to the opposition of the practicing bar to the institutionalization of legal services and the resulting loss to the private bar of fees, even though rarely adequate, paid to private attorneys for indigent representation.

84. 3 L. Silverstein, *Defense of the Poor in Criminal Cases in American State Courts* (A Field Study and Report for the Am. B. Foundation, 1965) p. 589, where it is reported that in Montgomery County, Ohio (Dayton), this procedure has been observed.

85. See D. R. Vetri, "Educating the Lawyer: Clinical Experience as an Integral Part of Legal Education," 50 *Oregon L. Rev.* 57 (1970); M. J. Anderson, G. O. Kornblum, "Clinical Legal Education: A Growing Reform," 57 *A.B.A.J.* 591 (1971).

86. But cf. People v. Perez, 147 Cal. Rptr. 34 (1978), where the California Supreme Court held that representation by a law student and silent supervising attorney was not effective assistance of counsel.

87. L.A. Benner, "Tokenism and the American Indigent: Some Perspectives on Defense Services," 12 *Am. Crim. L. Bull.* 667, at 669 et seq. (1975).

88. See *National Advisory Commission on Criminal Justice Standards and Goals: The Courts* (Washington D.C., 1973), 267 et seq. [Hereinafter cited as *National Advisory Commission].*

89. Wice, Suwak, "Current Realities of Public Defender Programs: A National Survey and Analysis," 10 *Crim. L. Bull.* 161, 164 (1974).

90. Ibid., pp. 172-73; and Wice, Pilgrim, "Meeting the Gideon Mandate: A Survey of Public Defender Programs," 58 *Judicature* 400, 406-07 (1975). This does reduce the keenness of counsel that could be expected from one attorney's having responsibility for a case from beginning to end.

91. *Report to the National Defender Conference* (Sponsored by the Justice Department and the ABA, 1969), p. 96.
92. In Holloway v. Arkansas, 435 U.S. 475 (1978), the Court held that the failure to appoint separate counsel violated the 6th Amendment, warranting automatic reversal.
93. *National Advisory Commission,* p. 263, Standard 13.5.
94. See Casper, *Criminal Courts: The Defendant's Perspective* (Washington, D.C.: U.S. Government Printing Office, 1978).
95. See Casper, "Did You Have a Lawyer When You Went to Court? No. I Had the Public Defender," 1 *Yale Rev. L. & Soc. Act.* 1094 (1971); See United States v. Katz, 425 F.2d 928 (2d Cir. 1970), where defense counsel was observed to be sound asleep during the examination of prosecution witnesses. Also see generally, Bazelon, "Gideon and Argersinger."
96. See Chambers v. Maroney, supra.

9.

Throughout this period I saw my attorney quite often and many times I called he was right down. I was told both attorneys were going to file motions but I never knew exactly what those motions were because I put my complete confidence in them. I think I learned they were only trying to get me for second-degree murder at the pretrial conferences which ran into the trial. I really didn't know what was happening then because I didn't understand what they were saying as far as the legal terms they were using and all that. And no one ever told me I could get bail when the charge was changed. I sure didn't think I could get bail then. But I could have gotten somebody to bail me out, if I had been told.

Sporting Justice

The post-indictment period is the time to sharpen the issues in dispute in a criminal case. It is also the time for both sides to evaluate the strengths of their respective cases. Theoretically, this period is to be used to prepare for trial; in reality, prosecutors and defense attorneys are far more interested in spending this time devising strategies to avoid trial. True preparation, unfortunately, is reserved for only the more notorious criminal cases that will definitely culminate in trial. In general, and in almost all cases, notorious or not, the momentum towards disposition of criminal cases is lost during the period between the return of an indictment and the commencement of trial.

The Arraignment

The only formal proceeding between the return of an indictment or information and the commencement of trial in all felony cases is the *arraignment.* It is almost a replay of the preliminary appearance, which serves as the only arraignment in misdemeanor cases. For felonies, however, the arraignment differs from the preliminary appearance in that it is conducted in the court of ultimate jurisdiction, i.e. the court that has jurisdiction to try and take pleas in felony cases.

Modern arraignments have changed little from their eighteenth century English origins.[1] Traditionally, the principal function of an arraignment has been to formally notify the defendant of the charges. In most cases the defendant has been made aware of the charges at the time of arrest, at the preliminary appearance and hearing, or during the grand jury presentment, especially if he was called as a witness before the grand jury. It is only in that fraction of felony cases which originate with the grand jury, not preceded by an earlier arrest and court proceeding, that the arraignment continues to serve as a formal beginning.

Essentially, the same events take place at the arraignment that occurred at the preliminary appearance. Besides notification of the charge, the court will reset the bail in the case. Although the original bail set at the preliminary appearance is often continued, this court is in no way bound by the decisions of the earlier court. If the accused has been in jail during the interim, the court may reevaluate the conditions set by the lower court for release or may reduce the amount of money bail to facilitate the accused's release pending trial. For an accused who has been on bail throughout this period, the fact of his reappearance in court is generally sufficient evidence that he will reappear again when required and the original bail or bond will be continued.

Even though the presumption of innocence will serve as a mantle for the defendant until a verdict in the case is returned, that presumption diminishes somewhat as the defendant advances towards trial. The case has already survived several screenings and reviews, and the mere fact that the case has survived begins to make the charges look more substantial. The defendant is being looked at more carefully, more critically. Consequently, the court may indeed raise or lower the bail amount or toughen the nonmoney conditions for release.

Finally, one of the most important actions undertaken at the arraignment is the appointment of counsel for indigent defendants. In the vast majority of American communities, the first meeting between the indigent defendant and his appointed attorney takes place at the arraignment. The representation up until now, whether during police interrogation or at a preliminary hearing, will likely have been casual, performed by an agency or volunteer attorney and not by a committed defense attorney with the responsibility to see the accused through the disposition of the case.[2]

Pleas

The arraignment is the stage in which, in felony cases, the defendant will be asked to plead. The options are the same as those for misdemeanors: no contest *(nolo contendere)*, guilty, or not guilty.

No contest

No contest or *nolo contendere* pleas are essentially admissions to the facts, a statement of the accused's willingness to have the court apply the law to the facts as charged and enter a judgment of guilty or innocent.

Although a no contest plea was customarily not available to felony defendants, it is now accepted as a plea in most jurisdictions.

The no contest plea originated in misdemeanor cases to permit a defendant to avoid pleading guilty and still avoid a trial. It is an acceptance of the facts as stated in the charge but at the same time is not a confession of guilt which later might be used by the victim in a civil suit for damages. The plea is most useful in criminal cases arising out of automobile accidents which generally spawn suits for damages but its usage has spread to other offenses. Because it is not a confession, the judge may reject it in a criminal case as an insufficient act of contrition and require either a plea of guilty or that the defendant stand trial.

Guilty

A defendant who has wanted to plead guilty since his arrest will get his chance at the arraignment. Depending upon local procedures, his opportunity will come anywhere from one week to three months after the initial appearance.

Anytime either a plea of guilty or a no contest plea is entered in felony cases, the court is obligated to treat the admission very seriously, even more so if the defendant is also waiving the assistance of counsel in determining whether to plead guilty. A defendant entering a guilty plea is waiving several constitutional rights essential to the American concept of a fair trial. By pleading guilty the defendant is forfeiting the Fifth Amendment privilege against self-incrimintion. He is, in fact, proving the state's case by confessing guilt. Additionally, the accused is surrendering Sixth Amendment trial rights: the right to a jury trial, the right to confront his accusers, and the right to force the state to prove each and every element of the offense beyond a reasonable doubt. Therefore, in accepting such a plea, the trial court must assure itself that the accused understands that he is relinquishing many of his constitutional rights, that he understands the charge against him and possible penalties, and that the decision to enter the plea is an intelligent and voluntary one and not the product of unacceptable coercion. The requisite assurance must come from the judge's personally questioning the accused in open court and establishing that the defendant fully understands the consequences of his decision and that the decision is freely made.[3] The court record must show the dialogue between the judge and the defendant, and the intelligence and voluntariness of the defendant's decision must clearly emerge from that record.[4]

One state appellate court suggested a script to be followed by the trial judges in its jurisdiction when a guilty plea is to be entered:

> Before a guilty plea is accepted, good practice would dictate that the trial court should advise the defendant of his constitutional rights and privileges and obtain a response indicating his understanding of the following:
>
> 1. He is proposing to enter a plea of guilty to a felony. Inform

him of the nature of the charge and statutory penalties for the crime, both as to minimum and maximum sentence.

2. He has a right to confront and cross examine his accusers and any witness against him.

3. He does not have to testify at the trial.

4. He has a right to a trial by jury or he can waive the trial by jury and have a trial by the court.

5. He has compulsory process for obtaining witnesses in his favor.

6. If he is tried he is presumed innocent and the prosecution has the burden of proving him guilty beyond a reasonable doubt.

7. No one can make any promises on behalf of the court as to the manner and disposition of the case and in the event defendant is referred to the probation department for a presentence report this does not mean that the defendant will be placed on probation.

Further, before a guilty plea is accepted the trial court should make the following additional inquiries and obtain appropriate responses:

1. Age, education and employment of the defendant.

2. Does the defendant have confidence in his lawyer?

3. Did the defendant's lawyer explain to him his constitutional rights and the nature of the charge and the consequences of the defendant's entering a plea of guilty?

4. Were any promises, threats or inducements made to the defendant to get him to enter a plea of guilty?

5. Does the defendant or his lawyer have any evidence to present which would raise doubt of the defendant's guilt or show he is innocent of the crime to which he is entering a plea of guilty?

6. Does the defendant understand everything that has transpired? Does he have any questions about his rights and about any of the procedures that have taken place?

7. Does the defendant want to withdraw his plea of not guilty and enter a plea of guilty? If his response is in the affirmative, ask the defendant how he pleads to the charge.

8. Is he making this plea of his own free will and volition?[5]

Withdrawal of a Guilty Plea

Because an accused's relinquishment of rights is viewed as a serious matter, not even the in-court colloquy between the judge and the defendant necessarily terminates the case. Defendants are permitted to change their minds and withdraw guilty pleas, although most states limit this prerogative to the time between the entry of the plea and the judge's pronouncement of sentence, which may be several weeks later.[6] Few states follow the federal rule which permits withdrawal of pleas even after sentencing.[7] No withdrawal of plea, however, is a matter of right. It is within the discretion of the court to permit the defendant to withdraw his guilty plea. Few statutes or court rules provide standards to guide a judge in the exercise of this discretion, although in the federal courts if a defendant offers a "fair and just reason" a withdrawal is generally permitted.[8] Certainly, an accused's ability to demonstrate that he was misled into pleading guilty by an unkept promise of a specific sentence, whether by the prosecutor or his own attorney, would be sufficient reason to permit the change of plea.

Not Guilty

Most felony defendants plead not guilty at their arraignments, even though few will maintain that plea up to trial. Later, most will change the plea to guilty, as a result of plea bargaining. Therefore, even though the trial judge will set a date for trial upon entry of the not guilty plea, no one expects it to be kept. The time between the entry of the plea and the original trial date will be spent on the filing of motions and discovery of each side's case. Serious plea negotiations may not even begin until the date originally scheduled for trial to begin.

The Motions Practice

From the time of arraignment until the date scheduled for trial, the little in-court activity that does take place is confined to the motions practice. A *motion* is the mechanism by which a party to a lawsuit challenges one or all aspects of the proceeding, or requests something from the court, or requests the court to order the opposing party to take some action. Each motion, unless it is uncontested, requires an answer, and either side may request an opportunity to argue in court on the validity of the motion. Motions going to the legality of the methods used by law enforcement agencies in securing evidence require an evidentiary hearing to determine whether that evidence shall be excluded or may be used at trial. When properly used, the motions practice provides an opportunity to narrow, hone, and clarify some of the issues in the case and to determine whether a trial is necessary and justified as serving the interests of either the state or the defendant. However, motions can also be used as a device for delaying the case, tying up opposing counsel, or occupying judges.[9]

Challenges to the indictment or information are properly raised at this point. Challenges that go to the jurisdiction of the grand jury may be in the form of the charge, the improper joining of several offenses within the indictment, or the failure of the indictment to state facts which constitute the charged crime. By way of example, the last issue is raised when an indictment omits an element of the statutory offense. If robbery is a theft from a person by force or the threat of force, then the failure in the indictment to allege that the defendant used or threatened to use force precludes that defendant from being found guilty of robbery. A similar defect may appear pertaining to the date on which the crime occurred. It is common for states to require that all felonies except for homicide be charged within six years. Thus a charge not brought within the time prescribed in the *statute of limitations* would be subject to a pretrial motion to dismiss. The statutes of limitations in most states require that felonies other than murder be commenced within six or ten years of the felonious conduct.[10]

Most court rules favor, and some require, that all matters which may be resolved prior to trial be raised shortly after the arraignment or a prescribed number of days prior to the commencement of trial.[11] There are two sound reasons for this requirement: rulings on some motions make a trial unnecessary, and the resolution of others prior to trial prevents constant interruptions and the prolonging of trials.

A motion to dismiss an indictment on *double jeopardy* grounds illustrates how a favorable decision on a defense motion may make a trial unnecessary. Contained within the Fifth Amendment and applicable to the states[12] through the Fourteenth Amendment due process clause is the following protection:

> "nor shall any person be subject for the same offense to be twice put in jeopardy of life and limb[.]"

The purpose of this guarantee is to protect an accused from having to run a gauntlet of trials for the same offense until the prosecution obtains the result it seeks. Theoretically, a defendant is entitled to have a verdict from the first impaneled jury and is not supposed to be subject to the government's calling off a trial in midstream so that it can start anew and have a better crack at a conviction.[13] Like all constitutional rights, this Fifth Amendment right is not absolute and is subject to substantial limitations.[14] The clearest exception occurs when an accused or defense counsel engages in repeated acts of misconduct during a trial, creating a "manifest necessity" for a mistrial.[15] If this should happen, the defendant is subject to a new trial before a newly impaneled jury. The issue of double jeopardy is properly raised before trial when the defense can demonstrate that there was no manifest necessity for the judge to terminate the initial trial. If this assertion is deemed correct, the motion will be granted and a new trial barred.[16]

A motion to suppress evidence (whether it be evidence taken from the defendant's person, home, car, or from a confession allegedly obtained illegally by the police) illustrates reasons behind the requirement that such motions be raised prior to trial. Denial or granting of the motion may make a trial unnecessary. A granting of the motion and an order suppressing the evidence may convince the prosecutor to dismiss the charges because the state may have no other evidence to use at trial to prove guilt. Conversely, a denial of the motion may convince the defendant that the wiser course of action is now to plead guilty because of the incriminating nature of the admissible evidence. Even if the case proceeds to trial, the pretrial resolution of the issue prevents it from being raised again during the trial. If it were to be litigated during the trial, the trial would be interrupted and the jury would have to be excused during the hearing because the issue is whether the evidence may be presented and heard by the jury.

Finally, the motions practice revolves around the attempts by both the defendant and the prosecution to learn about the other side's evidence and the strengths and weaknesses of the adversary's case.

Discovery

In both civil and criminal cases, pretrial discovery of some aspects of the opponent's case is generally accepted and encouraged.[17] Expansive discovery rights are now available in civil cases. Discovery in criminal cases, on the other hand, has lagged far behind.[18]

Discovery was expanded in civil litigation to reduce the risk of surprise, limit the issues in a case, assure presentation of all relevant evidence, narrow the differences between parties, and encourage settlement. Full discovery tends to encourage settlement of disputes without trials because it enables each side to realistically evaluate the strength of its own case relative to that of the opposition's. For example, in a personal injury suit arising out of an automobile accident, disclosure of the plaintiff's medical expenses and doctor's reports will permit the defendant to assess the seriousness of the plaintiff's injuries and make a realistic settlement offer. If that settlement offer is satisfactory, the costs of litigating the matter at trial will be averted, resulting in substantial savings to both sides and the court as well.

One of the basic reasons that criminal practice does not follow the model of civil practice is that a criminal case is not, even in theory, a two-sided search for truth with each party equally bound to further that search. The burdens rest with the prosecution. No demand is made upon the adversaries to join together in a search for the truth. In a civil suit, however, despite unequal allocation of the burden of proof, there is such a demand and expectation.

As stated in Chapter 8, the defense attorney's sole duty and obligation in a criminal case is to his client. This obligation is fulfilled by obtaining a fair trial for the defendant or, if no trial is held, by securing the best deal possible through a guilty plea to a reduced charge. This distinct difference between civil and criminal litigation has prompted prosecutors to argue that they, as the representatives of the state, are the only ones committed to a search for the truth.[19] This is their primary objection to expansion of discovery in the criminal process.

The one-sidedness of this search is perhaps the most frequently heard and oldest lament about broadening criminal discovery. Judge Learned Hand, universally considered one of the few really brilliant judges in America's history, summed up this position when he said that "the accused has every advantage" and should not "in advance have the whole evidence against him to pick over at his leisure, and make his defense, fairly or foully."[20]

Explicit in Judge Hand's contention is that defendants will use "fair or foul" means, whichever proves necessary, to prevail. This is premised upon the notion that the defendant in a criminal case, having so much more at stake than his counterpart in a civil suit, will not resist the temptation to bribe or frighten witnesses prior to trial or to elicit perjured testimony. This line of reasoning reflects the dwindling of the presumption of the defendant's innocence—why would an innocent defendant have to resort to such desperate tactics? It may be, as well, a commentary upon the repute with which attorneys engaged in the criminal practice are held by members of the legal profession because a client's personal access to discovered information comes only through his lawyer.

Hand's second assumption is that all defendants in criminal cases have trials, a point no longer true. The very survival and continuing operation of the criminal justice system in most American cities depends on the overwhelming majority of defendants *not* having trials. The basic orientation for formulating criminal procedures has failed to shift to the reality that in some jurisdictions more than ninety percent of the convictions result from guilty pleas.

Even though these axioms about discovery and criminal procedure are not necessarily valid, the system is not fully ripe for an extensive expansion of discovery in criminal cases. The underlying basis for expansion of discovery in civil litigation was the mutual obligation to disclose evidence that could be fairly demanded of both plaintiff and defendant. Such a reciprocal obligation does not, and cannot, exist in a criminal case. The defendant is protected by certain rights that limit the state's ability to discover his case.[21] While the defendant obtains discovery of the state's case, he is, at the same time, not obligated to present any evidence at a criminal trial. The obligation to present evidence and prove guilt rests solely upon the prosecution. This imbalance has been properly addressed by federal courts and many jurisdictions through rules permitting the defendant in a criminal case to decide whether to seek discovery. Once the defense makes a demand for discovery under these rules, it triggers for the prosecution a comparable right to discover corresponding parts of the defendant's case.[22] Thus the objection to the lack of mutuality has been overcome. One further remaining obstacle is the Fifth Amendment privilege against self-incrimination. The defendant need not be a witness at his own case, and consequently the state has no right to discover the defendant's own personal account of what happened. Of course, the prosecution may well have discovered the defendant's own account from police interrogation immediately after arrest.

. . . for the defense

There are two types of discovery available to defendants, the information which the prosecutor is constitutionally obligated to disclose and the emerging mutual discovery available through statutes or court rules.

As previously discussed, a prosecuting attorney has two functions in a criminal case, to represent the state in all criminal prosecutions and to see that justice triumphs by preventing the conviction of innocent defendants. The accused's constitutional right to a fair trial protects defendants from ambitious prosecutors who wish only to secure convictions irrespective of their other obligation to secure justice. The due process guarantee, then, restricts the use of unethical prosecutorial tactics, including the withholding of information that will benefit the defense and point to the accused's innocence.

A prosecutor is obligated, like his defense counterpart, never to use perjured testimony and not to mislead the court and jury. A flagrant example of prosecutorial dishonesty was the basis for the Supreme Court's reversal of a conviction in *Miller v. Pate.*[23] In that case the defendant was convicted of the murder of a young girl whose death resulted during a sexual attack. A vital piece of evidence presented by the prosecutor was a pair of men's undershorts covered with reddish-brown stains which the prosecutor claimed were made by Type A positive blood, that of the victim. After the conviction, it was discovered that the prosecutor had known all along that the stains were not from the blood of the victim, but were paint stains. Nonetheless, throughout the trial the prosecuting attorney had persisted in waving the "bloody shorts" at the jury.

The Supreme Court said that the due process principle "cannot tolerate a state criminal conviction obtained by the knowing use of false evidence."[24] Beyond abstaining from personally making false claims, the prosecutor is obligated to correct the perjured testimony of state witnesses if he knows them to be perjured[25] and also to reveal witnesses' statements contrary to their trial testimony, even if the prosecutor believes that the testimony given at trial is the correct and truthful version.[26]

Additionally, a prosecuting attorney must disclose evidence favorable to the defendant which is material to either guilt or punishment.[27] This is in keeping with the prosecutor's duty to see that justice is done and reflects a recognition of the superior position the state enjoys in investigating a criminal case and accumulating evidence. But it is not known how fully this duty to disclose is followed in practice. Because the purpose of the Constitution in the criminal area is to set only the minimal standards of fairness, the Constitution cannot be expected to be the moving force behind the development of criminal discovery.

Discovery beyond that mandated by the Constitution to insure a fair trial has been the product of the last two decades. The Federal Rules of Criminal Procedure, applicable only to federal criminal cases, have set an example for the development of comparable rules in many states. Federal Rule 16 provides that the government shall disclose upon receiving a request from the defense:

A. Statements [including confessions] made by the defendant.
B. A copy of the defendant's prior criminal record.
C. Books, papers, documents, photographs, tangible objects, buildings or places, which are material to the preparation of the defense case or are intended for use by the government as evidence, or were obtained from or belong to the defendant.
D. Results or reports of physical or mental examinations, and of scientific tests or experiments, which are material to the preparation of the defense case or are intended for use by the government as evidence.

Many states have not gone as far as the provisions contained in the federal rules. Others have expanded upon those provisions and provide greater discovery. For example, the federal provision limits access to the defendant's own statement or confession, while some states also grant access to statements made by co-defendants.[28] Similarly, the federal rules do not obligate the United States Attorney to disclose the names of witnesses the government intends to call at trial and specifically precludes pretrial discovery of statements of witnesses or prospective witnesses. Some state provisions include discovery of this information as a matter of course and only bar discovery of these items upon a showing by the prosecutor of the need to maintain the witness' confidentiality until the beginning of trial.[29] Grand jury testimony is secret and generally not subject to inspection by a defendant, although the sacrosanct nature of grand jury testimony is beginning to give way. California's lead has been followed by several other states in granting a defendant an absolute right to inspect grand jury minutes prior to the commencement of trial.[30]

. . . for the prosecution

While it is the prosecution who starts with the immense advantage of having as its resource all the investigative powers and prowess of local, state, and sometimes federal law enforcement agencies, the opposition to discovery in criminal cases has been spearheaded by prosecutors. To overcome their objection to the one-sided nature of discovery, its development, as already discussed with respect to the federal rules, has been predicated upon mutuality. Thus, in order for the defense to learn of the prosecution's case, it must be willing to allow discovery by the government. In return for providing information to the defense, the government, too, is entitled to scrutinize books, papers, medical reports, and other tangible objects that the defense intends to produce at trial.[31] This equitable approach has helped to resolve the impasse in many state jurisdictions and the federal courts.

Aside from disclosure obligations imposed upon the defense through the theory of mutuality, there are two types of information which the defense is obligated to furnish without first setting off that obligation by its own demand upon the state. Many states require that neither a defense based on *insanity* or on an *alibi* may be sprung upon the prosecution at trial, but that both must be pleaded in advance so that the state has an opportunity to investigate and consider their merit and counter them.[32] The privilege against self-incrimination and the burden imposed upon the state to prove its allegations of guilt have not barred those procedural rules which require that a defendant plead these defenses prior to trial, or forfeit them.

The constitutionality of the notice-of-alibi statutes was litigated before the Supreme Court in 1970. A Florida statute was imposed that required the defense to notify the court and prosecutor of its intent to prove an alibi and to disclose the identity of the proposed alibi witnesses. This statute, which also authorized the state to take depositions of those witnesses, was held not to violate a defendant's constitutional rights.[33] The Florida statute is arguably at odds with the basic Anglo-American legal principle that the burden of proof rests exclusively with the state. According to this principle, the defendant need not produce anything unless the prosecution first demonstrates at trial that its case is sufficient to go to the jury. Statutes such as the one in Florida require that the defendant produce information without a prior test of the sufficiency of the prosecution's case. This statute represented a major breakthrough in compelling disclosure by the defense and paved the way for substantial two-way discovery. The Supreme Court later inserted a requirement on the notice-of-alibi statutes, linking its constitutionality to the state's having to provide comparable notification of the identity of its witnesses who would rebut the claim of alibi.[34]

Provided that there is sufficient mutuality of disclosure, the alibi-notice statutes could open the door to provisions requiring the defense to notify the court and prosecution in advance of trial of any defense it intended to use. Yet the decisions authorizing discovery by the prosecution do not emasculate the defendant's constitutional protections because no decision has authorized pretrial discovery of any information that the defendant was not intending to disclose at trial. All that the decisions have taken away from an accused is the right to choose when to disclose it.

Time Pressures

A major concern with the criminal justice system has been its inability to dispose of criminal cases in a timely manner.[35] We have previously explored the examples of judges who are so beset by overclogged dockets that they dispose of serious felonies at the preliminary appearance in a matter of minutes. Their concern for justice is subordinated to the need for relieving pressure. At the other end of the spectrum is the equally disconcerting aspect that felony cases which survive the preliminary stages of the process tend to remain within the system for an inordinate amount of time apparently resisting disposition. Legal literature is replete with claims that slowness reflects thoughtfulness and judiciousness and that delay within the criminal process should not provoke consternation. It is more realistic, however, to recognize that delay, especially between the arraignment and the commencement of trial or other disposition, is the result of all sides, defense and prosecution countenanced by judges, seeking to avoid trials.

Resentment burns on both sides of this issue. The public expresses outrage at the ability of defendants free on bail to avoid trial. Outrage is also felt on behalf of defendants who are lingering in jail during this period and are not brought to trial. These defendants are the victims of delay, and when occasionally the innocence of one surfaces, the plight of these defendants receives critical attention. One such case received national publicity in 1975 when a truck driver in New York was freed after fourteen months in jail awaiting trial on charges involving two deaths from a motor vehicle accident. Worse than the fourteen-month delay was the disclosure that two assistant district attorneys had known for the entire period that two eyewitnesses corroborated the defendant's claim that he was not the driver of the car.[36] The innocent defendant evokes anxiety because his imprisonment could happen to any one of us.

Delay also affects the ability of a criminal court to determine the truth of the matter in controversy. No matter how startling or horrible the event, memories fade. A witness' ability to recollect exactly what he saw or heard is not likely to be as precise months or years after the incident occurred. A judge or jury at a trial held long after the commission of the alleged crime is often confronted with witnesses who either cannot remember details or who embellish their stories to flesh out fading memories.

It is not unusual for prosecution witnesses to hear nothing about the case for many months until a subpoena is served upon them, directing them to appear at a particular courtroom for trial. These witnesses are not advised as to what to expect when they testify and thus are susceptible to making minor mistakes in their testimony. These mistakes not only make the witnesses appear foolish; a witness' errors can cause the state to lose what began as a strong case.

Under the worst conditions, a witness may receive subpoenas every time the case is scheduled for trial, with no one making the effort to nullify the order to appear even when the prosecutor and defense attorneys have already agreed to continue the case and not try it on the scheduled date. These witnesses are instructed to reappear on the next scheduled date without any reassurance that the matter will be heard on the new date. After several postponements, few witnesses are willing to continually readjust their daily schedules. Even crime victims have been known to give up and drop charges because of such unnecessary delays and inconveniences.

Such delays obviously affect the willingness of witnesses to testify. Rarely are witnesses notified of the case's progress. Perhaps a victim can keep abreast of the case by calling periodically and asking the assistant prosecutor questions. Yet all but the most persistent will generally stop calling when their inquiries are met by disinterest or evasiveness. Although a good prosecutor should keep in touch with the state's witnesses and attempt to maintain their cooperation, overworked attorneys will often rely on investigating officers to contact witnesses and get their statements. At times, prosecutors will never have talked to a witness for the state prior to trial.

At the same time, the defendant must rely on his attorney to keep in contact with defense witnesses. In many cases, unfortunately, this is not possible. Either the attorney is not really committed to the case and is lackadaisical, or the attorney is just one of a string of lawyers appointed to represent an indigent defendant at different stages of his case. Although the defense should maintain close ties with its witnesses, many defendants must rely on their own devices to insure that their witnesses remain available and ready to appear in court. This is almost an impossible task if the defendant is in jail.

When witnesses do get their "chance" to testify, their testimonies are often demolished under cross-examination. Lawyers are able to take advantage of trial delays by paying close attention to details and by spotting contradictions in the witness' trial testimony and that witness' earlier accounts of the crime. A disinterested witness who originally came forward out of a sense of duty is apt to regret his involvement when he is made out to be either a liar or a fool. Exiting along with this disillusioned witness may be the prosecutor's or defense's otherwise truthful and credible case.

Victims often find that their testimonies are fair game for defense lawyers who take advantage of delays. Minor discrepancies in the victim's original accounts and his trial statements can severely weaken the state's case by being blown out of proportion by the defense. The victim of a nighttime assault in an alley might not remember, months later, the color or texture of the jacket worn by the assailant; yet the failure to recollect that detail may well be the basis for a jury's rejection of the victim's otherwise faultless identification. Thus the passage of time is reflected in the testimony of witnesses and may affect the reliability of the jury's verdict.

Controlling Delay

There are two mechanisms available for the control of delay, (1) the constitutional guarantee of a speedy trial and (2) federal and state statutes and court rules mandating that trials commence within a certain number of days after arrest or indictment.

Right to a Speedy Trial

The effect of delay upon defendants in jail has plagued justice systems for centuries. In 1215 the nobles exacted the Magna Carta from King John.

This document contained the king's promise not to delay justice to any man.[37] The grievance against King John arose from the long delays between accusation and trial caused by the infrequent sessions of his courts.[38] Circuit riding judges, responsible for holding court in many towns and settlements covering vast geographic areas, brought the same problem with them to America.[39]

It is no surprise that the right to a speedy trial heads the list of "fair trial" rights enumerated in the Sixth Amendment to the Constitution. Similar provisions exist in every state constitution and the federal guarantee has been made applicable and binding upon the states.[40] Its preeminence is understandable, for without a trial there can be no justice.

The Constitution offers no clue to the framers' concept of a "speedy trial." Therefore the Supreme Court has attached a standard of *reasonableness* to the right which involves a balancing of interests: that is, weighing the effects of delay in a particular case against the causes and justification for the delay to determine whether the defendant's right has been violated. In setting its standard, the Supreme Court in *Barker v. Wingo,*[41] set forth four factors to be applied to decide the issue. They are: (1) length of delay; (2) the prosecution's justification for the delay; (3) whether the defendant demanded a speedy trial or attempted to benefit both from the delay and the constitutional prohibition; and (4) the prejudice caused to the defendant by the delay. Utilizing the four-pronged test, the Court in *Barker* found that a four-year delay under the circumstances of the case did not constitute a constitutional violation. This finding rested upon certain facts in the case. The prosecution's chief investigator suffered a prolonged illness. Also, the defendant seemed willing to await the outcome of his accomplice's trial. While the failure of the defense to demand a trial did not automatically decide the issue, it helped to show that the defendant did not suffer prejudice—no claim of impairment of his ability to defend against the charges, no pretrial incarceration, and no claim of anxiety resulting from the delay. Nonetheless, the failure of the Supreme Court to find this four-year delay a constitutional violation seriously impaired the value of that promise in the Bill of Rights. Moreover, since few defendants are aware of the complexities surrounding the right, few will make a personal demand for a speedy trial and depend upon their attorneys for doing so. While the Court in *Barker* insisted that a demand was not a prerequisite to application of the right, the absence of a demand certainly seemed decisive in that case.

Like all the provisions of the Bill of Rights, the guarantee of a speedy trial is a measure devised solely to protect the rights of individual defendants. It does not and was not intended to protect the state from delay caused by defendants. Presumably that protection could be afforded by a vigilent prosecutor and by the trial court's capacity to set its calendar and order the commencement of trials. Even if a judge failed to note the lapse of time, he would be called to task by whoever's interest would be served by a prompt trial, the prosecutor on behalf of the state or the defense attorney on behalf of the defendant. But prosecutors beset by too many cases often ignore the legitimate interest of their community and fail to demand speedy trials. The answer, if there is one, has to be found beyond the constitutional guarantee.

Federal and State Statutes

There is no consensus among the states as to the meaning of "speedy trial" as contained in the original state statutes and court rules. Some of the state formulations require that trial commence within a certain number of days after the defendant is arrested or indicted, but those requirements vary from sixty days to one year. There is not even agreement as to which group of defendants are protected or what remedies to apply when pretrial periods are deliberately prolonged. Some states apply the protection only to those defendants who are not free on bail.[42] The failure to commence trial within the stipulated period results in the dismissal of charges in some states and in others the release of the defendant on bail to await trial. When the remedy for delay is dismissal of the charges, some states permit the prosecutor to refile and begin the prosecution anew and others do not. Under the state formulations, legal redress is usually available only in the cases where a defense demand for speedy trial is not met. And in most states, a defendant will not be entitled to the applicable remedy if any part of the delay is attributable to him or to his attorney. Often defendants are not even aware of requests for continuances made by their attorneys, but those continuances are nonetheless chargeable to the defendant.

A new thrust, however, seeks not only to protect the rights of the defendant but also the interests of the community. The federal Speedy Trial Act of 1974[43] is an example of this approach and, although the remedies did not become effective until 1979, it created quite a stir. While only applicable to federal criminal cases, it is indicative of the type of statute being considered in many states and may serve as a model for others.

The essence of the Act is that it does not rely upon a defendant or defense attorney's demand for a speedy trial to activate the time requirements. The past twenty years has shown that few defendants actually want a trial, and delay has become a principal defense technique. And when the defense's case is weak, delay as an avoidance tactic is definitely not in the community's interests. Moreover, the Act's provisions appear to recognize that the community's interests are not adequately protected by judges and district attorneys. Judges, not just federal judges, have long set court calendars solely for the convenience of attorneys, without regard for the community's needs, witnesses' convenience, or even defendants' rights. In the past judges have granted continuances to attorneys upon request, especially when the continuance was consented to by the opposing lawyer. These failures, of course, partially result from the pressures of too many cases, a condition afflicting the judges as well as the prosecuting and defense attorneys.

Part of the failure, however, has to be attributed to the fraternity of lawyers, which brings with it certain accommodations that have little to do with justice. Thus the provisions of the Act are to operate automatically and become a speedy trial guarantee for all defendants, whether they want it or not, and for the interests of the community as well.

The Act requires that defendants be brought to trial within one hundred days of arrest. Specifically, this period is broken down into three segments: thirty days from arrest to indictment or information, ten days from indictment or information to arraignment, and sixty days from arraignment to trial. The law was enacted in 1974 but because of the opposition to it, a four year transition period with less stringent time limits was enacted to permit the courts and attorneys to adjust themselves to the new expectations. During the transitional period, even though the sanctions were not applicable during those years, most federal district courts found that they were able to comply with the time limits in the substantial majority of the cases. The ultimate remedies are dismissal of charges, although it is in the discretion of the trial judge to permit the refiling of the charges depending upon the legitimacy of the delay, and fines and suspensions for government and defense attorneys who unjustifiably engage in delaying tactics or file frivolous motions.

The imposed time limits have been criticized by judges and lawyers on both sides of a criminal case as being too rigid. Even Chief Justice Burger who has been an advocate of greater efficiency within the judicial system complained about the rigidity of even the transitional time limits. It is likely that there will be some congressional amendments relaxing the 30-10-60 standard to relieve the pressures on the courts. The Judicial Conference of the United States proposed in 1977 that Congress amend the Act to change the time limits to sixty days between arrest and indictment, twenty days between indictment and arraignment, and one hundred days between arraignment and trial.

The most innovative aspect of the Speedy Trial Act is the way continuances are treated. One purpose of the law is to end delay used as a defense technique and also to curtail delay caused for the convenience of attorneys. Congress recognized the need for certain delays within criminal cases and stipulated the types of delay excluded from the time limits. Rather than grant broad discretion to the court, the law enumerates acceptable delays—i.e., delays resulting from psychiatric examinations, unavailability of witnesses—and in some instances, where a court has a motion under consideration, the amount of time that may be excluded. As no enumeration would ever be totally adequate, the law does provide a broad catch-all and permits excludable delay "in the interest of justice." But even the broad catch-all is controlled by requiring that the judge state on the record the justification for this type of delay.

Even an amended version of the Speedy Trial Act will serve its purpose. A model for comparable state legislation, it serves notice that if the courts and lawyers ignore society's interests in favor of their own convenience, then legislatures representing the society can exert controls by limiting the discretion of the judges to order the affairs of that society's courts.

Discussion Questions

1. Why is an accused's relinquishment of his rights viewed by the courts as a serious matter?
2. What are the plea options available to a defendant at his arraignment? Trace the steps that follow each individual plea.
3. Explain the value of the motions practice during the pretrial stage of a criminal case. How can a motion serve the interests of the defense? Of the state?
4. A motion to dismiss an indictment on double jeopardy grounds illustrates a favorable decision on a defense motion. Why? What is double jeopardy?
5. Civil proceedings are enhanced by expansive discovery rights. Why? Why is it that criminal discovery has lagged far behind the civil model?
6. How does discovery "work" for the defense? (Include in your answer the two types of discovery available to defendants.)
7. What are some reasons why under certain circumstances the defense would want to delay the commencement of trial for as long as possible. Why do prosecutors typically want to avoid trials? And finally, why do many judges contenance this common desire on both sides to delay the criminal process?
8. What are the negative effects of delay in the criminal justice system? Discuss these effects in terms of the public's attitudes, the defendant's perspective, and the state's obligation to see that justice is achieved.
9. What is the significance the Supreme Court Case of Barber vs. Wings?
10. Explain the Speedy Trial Act of 1974.

Notes

1. Blackstone, *Commentaries On The Law of England* (Portland: T. B. Wait and Co., 1807), pp. 321-340.
2. In most cities the public defender officer will have represented the accused at each stage but without continuity in who represents the client.

3. McCarthy v. United States, 394 U.S. 459 (1969).
4. Boykin v. Alabama, 395 U.S. 238 (1969).
5. State v. Griffey, 29 Ohio App. 246, 252-3, 281 N.E.2d 32, 37 (1972).
6. Kamisar, LaFave, and Israel, *Modern Criminal Procedure,* 4th ed. (St. Paul, Minn.: West, 1974), pp. 1186-1188.
7. See Federal Rules of Criminal Procedure 32(d).
8. Note, 40 *N.Y.U.L. Rev.* 759 (1965).
9. Katz, Litwin, and Bamberger, *Justice Is The Crime* (Cleveland: Case Western Reserve University Press, 1972), pp. 179-181.
10. 21 Am. Jur.2d Criminal Law, §§ 154-164 (Rochester: Lawyers Co-op Pub. Co., 1965).
11. See Federal Rules of Criminal Procedure 12(b).
12. Benton v. Maryland, 395 U.S. 784 (1969).
13. Note, *Yale L. J.* 262 (1965).
14. United States v. Perez, 9 Wheat. (22 U.S.) 579 (1824); Illinois v. Summerville, 410 U.S. 458 (1973).
15. Kamisar, LaFave, and Israel, *Modern Criminal Procedure,* p. 1447.
16. Downum v. United States, 372 U.S. 734 (1963); United States v. Jorn, 400 U.S. 470 (1971).
17. Glasser, *Pretrial Discovery and the Adversary System* (New York: Russell Sage Foundation, 1968).
18. For a discussion of the pros and cons on discovery in criminal cases, see the majority and dissenting opinions in State v. Tune, 13 N.J. 203, 98 A.2d 881 (1953).
19. See Flannery, "The Prosecutor's Case Against Liberal Discovery," 33 *F.R.D.* 74 (1963).
20. United States v. Garsson, 291 Fed. 646 (S.D.N.Y. 1923); see also, Kaufman, "Discovery In Criminal Cases," 44 *F.R.D.* 481 (1968).
21. Scott v. State, 519 P.2d 774 (Alaska 1974).
22. See Federal Rules of Criminal Procedure 16.
23. Miller v. Pate, 386 U.S. 1 (1967).
24. Ibid., at 7.
25. Napue v. Illinois, 360 U.S. 264 (1959); Mooney v. Holohan, 294 U.S. 103 (1935).
26. Giles v. Maryland, 386 U.S. 66 (1967).
27. Brady v. Maryland, 373 U.S. 83 (1963).
28. See e.g., Ohio Rules of Criminal Procedure 16(B)(1).
29. Kamisar, LaFave, and Israel, *Modern Criminal Procedure,* pp. 1233-1243.
30. See Cal. Penal Code § 938. In some parts of California it is customary for the defendant to be given the full transcript of the grand jury testimony in his case at the time of arraignment.
31. See Federal Rule of Criminal Procedure 16(b)(1)(A).
32. See *A.B.A. Standards—Discovery and Procedure Before Trial,* § 3.3 and commentary (Approved Draft 1970).
33. Williams v. Florida, 399 U.S. 78 (1970).
34. Wardius v. Oregon, 412 U.S. 470 (1973).
35. See Church et al, *Pretrial Delay: A Review and Bibliography* (Williamsburg, Va.: National Center for State Courts, 1978).
36. *New York Times,* May 21, 1975, p. 1.
37. Magna Carta, c. 29, translated in Coke, *The Second Part of the Institutes of the Laws of England 45* (London: E. and R. Brooke), p. 45.

38. Ibid., p. 43.
39. The great distances separating settlements on the American frontier tended to exacerbate this problem and increase the span of time between judicial visits far beyond that experienced in England.
40. Klopfer v. North Carolina, 386 U.S. 213 (1967).
41. Barker v. Wingo, 407 U.S. 514 (1972).
42. Katz, Litwin, and Bamberger, *Justice is the Crime,* pp. 62-69.
43. 18 United States Code § 3161 et seq.

10.

I had become so disgusted. Everybody was saying that you don't have a chance, you don't have a chance and this and that and the other. I said maybe I don't have a chance after being in jail almost a year.

The Bargained Plea

Until very recently, plea bargaining was the most protected secret of our legal system. Now, however, because the practice is so pervasive, plea bargaining is widely acknowledged as one of our most volatile criminal justice issues.[1] Nevertheless, there is still an attempt to keep the public in the dark as to the realities of the practice. Prosecutors frequently deny that their offices engage in the practice and defense attorneys talk about it with their clients in a hush-hush manner.[2] It is little wonder, then, that the public regards plea bargaining as seamy and dishonest and that defendants frequently view themselves as having been "sold out" by their attorneys as a consequence of plea negotiations.

Approximately ninety percent of misdemeanor defendants plead guilty to avoid trial. Most defendants pleading guilty to misdemeanor charges do so outright at the first court appearance, usually without counsel, in response to a judge's request for a plea. Sixty to seventy-five percent of all felony defendants are likely to plead guilty as a result of plea bargaining. Some misdemeanor defendants and most felony defendants who plead guilty enter this plea after negotiations and in return for consideration.[3]

A negotiated plea is a plea of guilty entered by the defendant in return for which the state makes a promise that it is entitled and willing to make. The concession made by the prosecution may take several forms but ultimately it will affect sentencing. That concession may involve a reduction in charge, dismissal of some charges contained in a multi-count indictment, or a recommendation to the court that the defendant be placed on probation or given a light sentence. These concessions and the attendant pleas of guilty that they induce are the essence of plea bargaining.

Why the Prosecutor Bargains

Surprising as it may seem, plea bargaining neither originated in this country nor in this century. In seventeenth and eighteenth century England, plea bargaining was used as a device to mitigate the harshness of the statutorily mandated sentence imposed upon defendants convicted of felonies. In that period, English law required the death penalty upon a verdict of guilty for all felons. Public demand for lesser penalties resulted in English barristers representing the crown offering to reduce a felony charge to a misdemeanor if the accused would confess guilt and plead guilty. Upon the defendant's entering the plea of guilty, he was sentenced to prison and thus his life was saved.[4] The practice is still used to mitigate sentences imposed by the legislature. When, for instance, a statute imposes a harsh mandatory sentence upon an individual convicted of a certain offense, the prosecutor may allow an accused to escape that penalty by offering to reduce the charge in return for a plea of guilty. This decision by the prosecutor may be based upon any number of factors, but primarily it is warranted by an accused's lack of a prior criminal record. Burglary, for example, may end up as burglary of an unoccupied dwelling or any number of lesser burglary offenses, or breaking and entering, or even trespass if the defendant's criminal record is negligible. Robbery, similarly, may end up as a theft or assault offense.[5]

It would be misleading, however, to even hint that plea bargaining by the state springs from humanitarian motives. The primary reason for plea bargaining in this country is attributable, as are so many problems within the criminal justice system, to the horrendous crime rate and the inability of the system to try all persons charged with crime. Just to maintain the status quo the prosecution is compelled to "deal" the vast majority of defendants out of the system.[6] Even though few felony trials occur in most jurisdictions, any significant increase in their number would reduce the system to shambles.

The avoidance of trials through plea bargaining also helps to keep the state's costs down. Trials are expensive, while pleas of guilty are far less so. The difference in cost to the state when a defendant charged with murder pleads guilty to manslaughter rather than putting the state through a long trial may be tens of thousands of dollars. In addition, the courtroom, judge, prosecutors, and jurors are free for other cases, witnesses are not kept from their jobs, and police officers involved in the case may return to their beats.

A third justification for plea bargaining is that the process does result in convictions, which is one of the prosecutor's two responsibilities. Even if the gravity of the offense is watered down through plea bargaining, the offender is branded as a criminal at the same time that the prosecutor is achieving tremendous savings for the state. Through plea bargaining and concessions made to an accused, the state may also be able to secure the defendant's cooperation or vital information leading to the prosecution of other persons involved in criminal activity. Sometimes a favorable offer to a lower echelon member of an organized crime operation leads to the snaring of persons higher up in the operation. Under those circumstances, the crimes of the cooperative defendant are often totally forgiven and the charges dismissed.

Finally, humanitarian reasons may justify substantial concessions on the part of the state. Those humanitarian reasons, however, need not reflect sympathy for the defendant. Instead, they usually reflect solicitude for the victims of the offense who, if the case proceeds to trial, may have to relive once more, the nightmare of the crime. The tendency has been to consider concessions most strongly in rape and other sexual abuse cases, where the glare of publicity about a trial might increase the misery of the victim. We may see a change in that attitude in the next few years as rape crisis centers increase in number along with the prompting that those centers bring for full prosecution of sexual offenders. State concern for the trial hazards of victims will likely continue, however, where the principal witness is a child.

Why the Defendant Bargains

The defendant who pleads guilty because of the bargain struck between his attorney and the prosecutor is surrendering his right to force the state to prove his guilt. Naturally, he demands from the state something in return for his waiver and the substantial savings in time, money, and trouble that he is bestowing. An accused's primary concern is his sentence, and reduction in the time to be served is the tangible reward that defendants seek.[7] This expectation is met by a reduction in the charge, thereby reducing the minimum and maximum punishment that the court may impose, or by promises going directly to sentencing. Since freedom is the accused's ultimate objective, an offer of probation is the most enticing promise. But even if immediate freedom is not attainable, most defendants are sufficiently realistic to weigh the possible sentence if they are convicted as charged against the probable sentence on a plea to a reduced charge. A defendant can be quite practical if he believes that the chances of his being convicted are great. Even a defendant who is uncertain about the likelihood of conviction may be willing to accept the certainty surrounding a reduced charge rather than risk the uncertainty of going to trial and being convicted of the greater offense.

In addition to sentencing, other factors may influence a defendant's decision. Avoidance of trial benefits the defendant who is bearing the cost of his own defense. Attorneys' fees are based upon an expectation of the amount of time each case will take, and the fee for pleading a defendant guilty is substantially less than that charged for a trial that may last several days or longer. The accused, too, may want to sidestep the negative publicity which may flow from a trial or the stigma attached to conviction for a felony, especially for sexual offenses. The accused may also waive trial in order to plead guilty to an offense which disguises the real nature of his crime. Many times, defendants plead guilty to a misdemeanor to avoid being labeled a felon. The defendant, then, is not an unwilling participant in plea bargaining. He has a vital interest in learning how good a deal can be arranged in his case, and in many instances, he is the beneficiary of the process.

The Issues

Although there are some positive sides to plea bargaining, the problems this practice holds for our justice system are sizeable. So sizeable, in fact, that the Standards and Goals published by the National Advisory Commission on Criminal Justice in 1973 included this sweeping prohibition:

> As soon as possible, but in any event no later than 1978, negotiations between prosecutors and defendants—either personally or through their attorneys—concerning concessions to be made in return for guilty pleas should be prohibited....[8]

Yet while the proposed prohibition received a sympathetic reaction, the practice of plea bargaining across the country has changed little.[9]

Plea Bargaining

... *as an avenue toward repentance*

Aside from rewarding a defendant for saving a court and prosecutor the trouble and expense of a trial, the theoretical justification for leniency toward a defendant pleading guilty is that the plea is a demonstration of remorse. Remorse for past errors is a healthy step towards rehabilitation, but in the context of plea bargaining it is not a valid consideration. Defendants rarely plead guilty because of guilt feelings; they usually plead guilty to secure the concessions that the prosecutor is willing to make in return for the plea. Nonetheless, the remorse that allegedly accompanies the guilty plea is cited as a justification for plea bargaining.[10]

... *as an out*

Not to be underestimated is the possibility of innocent defendants pleading guilty to avoid the uncertainties of trial. The temptation may be greatest for the accused in jail who would otherwise face continued pretrial detention while awaiting trial.[11] Also, a defendant charged with a felony that carries a potential sentence of more than one year in prison might be sorely tempted to plead guilty to a misdemeanor charge when the prosecutor promises to recommend probation.

The American Bar Association's standards for prosecutors and defense attorneys require both to advise the court when an accused agrees to plead guilty but also continues to maintain his innocence.[12] The Supreme Court has refused to invalidate a guilty plea where the defendant pleaded guilty but at the same time disclaimed guilt. The Court has said that as long as evidence in the record substantiated the defendant's guilt, if the plea represented a voluntary and intelligent choice by one represented by competent counsel, the plea was valid.[13] Several states have refused to follow the Supreme Court's lead in this area and maintain prohibitions on accepting pleas of guilty from defendants who continue to assert their innocence, while others have reversed earlier positions and have accepted the Supreme Court standard.[14] The Maryland high court, when it reversed its earlier prohibition, offered an incredible explanation: "[T]he assertion of innocence does not necessarily negate any admission of guilt."[15]

... as a means of disguise

Few states have followed the federal rules provision requiring a judge to make a factual determination of guilt prior to accepting a guilty plea. Consequently, in many states, when a judge accepts a plea of guilty, he may be totally oblivious to the facts of the crime. Especially when the plea is entered to a substantially reduced charge, the judge is likely to base a sentence determination solely upon his notion of the reduced charge in the abstract and remain ignorant of the actual seriousness of the crime committed by the accused. Thus, the judge who accepts a rape defendant's guilty plea to indecent assault may impose sentence totally ignorant of the horror of the actual crime. The judge is relying upon the prosecutor under these circumstances to protect the community interest and will rarely inquire into the nature and facts of the crime. But the prosecutor may be reacting instead to the internal pressure caused by too many cases and may have relegated community needs to a position of minor significance.

... as a delaying tactic

Hand in hand with plea bargaining is the defense strategy to wait out the prosecution. This tactic grew from the notion that the older and staler a case, the more eager the prosecutor will be to avoid trial and hence the more attractive will be the forthcoming offer from the prosecutor to obtain disposition through a plea. This strategy, frequently communicated from defense attorneys to their clients, perpetuates the idea. Though the attorney cannot postpone judgment entirely, if the case is delayed many months the prosecutor may indeed be willing to come across with a favorable sentence or be willing to accept a plea to a lesser offense just to have the case closed. The logic is impeccable, especially for the bailed defendant who faces certain conviction and long imprisonment. While enjoying the luxury of freedom on bail and postponing imprisonment as long as possible, the defendant watches the chances grow as each month goes by that one of the state's witnesses may become unavailable or unwilling to testify, and the prosecutor will be forced to deal.[16]

Plea bargaining as a factor in delay is not limited to the defense side. A good defense case may be weakened by delay in the same manner as a good prosecution case atrophies, and state-induced delay may result in pressure on the defendant to deal and plead guilty once a good defense evaporates with time. The prosecution may also delay trial in order to pressure the defendant in jail to plea bargain and avoid the additional delay of waiting for trial. Delay may also be sought by the prosecutor to mitigate the strong desires for retribution on the part of the victims and arresting officers so that the prosecutor can bargain without the restraining pressure imposed by victims and police officers who feel that they are being sold out.[17]

... as a false concession

The expectation of plea bargaining in every case has reduced the criminal courts to an Arab bazaar, with all of the techniques utilized for marketplace haggling. From the onset of most criminal cases there is little reason to believe that any particular case will be the one out of ten that eventually goes to trial. Consequently, while ostensibly acting in anticipation of trial, each side is trying to maneuver into the most favorable bargaining position. If the prosecuting attorney knows that he is going to have to negotiate to relieve the pressure on the system and avoid trial, then the position sought at the beginning is the strongest for negotiating purposes. Consequently, prosecutors are not adverse to overcharging—indicting the defendant for a more serious offense than the evidence will bear at trial, or including every possible offense in the indictment—in order to make concessions during negotiations. This partially accounts for sloppy screening and the willingness of some prosecutors to faithfully accept the police-recommended charge, with the expectation that the charge is inflated but will be reduced in order to get a guilty plea.[18]

Defense attorneys complain about overcharging, but many boast to their clients that the ensuing reduction from the blatant overcharge was the result of herculean efforts and bargaining which the attorney exerted on the client's behalf. The defense attorney feels that he must present to the defendant some substantial concession by the state in return for the plea of guilty. Reduction of an overcharge offers that concession, and only the client is fooled.

... as a penalization

Plea bargaining penalizes the defendant who exercises his constitutional right to trial. A defendant in a criminal case has an absolute constitutional right to a trial and the right to compel the state to prove his guilt beyond a reasonable doubt. It would be an outright violation of that constitutional guarantee if a court were to impose a stiffer sentence upon a defendant who exercises that right.[19] When a court automatically rewards a defendant who waives the right and pleads guilty, does that constitute an automatic penalty upon defendants who go to trial?

Judges may be foreclosed from pressuring a defendant by threatening a more severe sentence if the accused fails to plead guilty, but even when a judge remains silent on the issue the threat hangs heavy in the air; virtually all empirical studies have proven that defendants who plead guilty get lighter sentences than those who are convicted at trial.[20] The fact that virtually all defendants who plead guilty are automatically rewarded with lighter sentences serves to discourage all from exercising their absolute right to trial and forcing the prosecution to prove their guilt. Not only the timid and guilty will shun the risk of a harsher sentence and waive their right to be proven guilty.

In many English-speaking countries, notwithstanding statutory minimum and maximum terms, there is a normative prison sentence for each crime depending upon the offender's past criminal record, say eighteen months for a defendant convicted of burglary with no past convictions. In this country, such norms are virtually non-existent.[21] While some judges on multi-judge courts may discuss sentences amongst themselves to insure some degree of uniformity, this is still highly unusual. Consequently, in each case a judge exercises enormous discretion within the broad parameters provided in statutes. Without normative sentences, there is no way for a defendant truly to weigh his options. If an accused were to know that the general practice is to reduce a three-year sentence by three months if the court is not put to the trouble of a trial, then of course that accused could weigh his options more intelligently. But there is no standard practice in this country. As it is, the defendant can only measure the promise of leniency or the offer of a particular sentence against the possibility of receiving the statutory maximum sentence. Usually the promise or offer looks far better. On the other hand, automatic reductions from normative sentences would be subject to condemnation as an overt attempt to chill the exercise of constitutional rights, and judges would have to studiously avoid that appearance, if not that stance. Thus the sentencing judge is granted tremendous latitude, and this discretion appears to exact a high cost from the defendant who exercises his constitutional right to trial.

... as a handmaiden of discretion

As in the screening process, the prosecutor has virtually unfettered power to grant any concession to a defendant. While a court is not obliged to accept an agreement recommended by the prosecutor if it is not in the public interest, it usually does. Most judges make no inquiry beyond establishing the voluntary and intelligent nature of the defendant's guilty plea and waiver of rights. In fact, the judge is likely to be as relieved as the participants that the trial has been avoided.

. . . as a constitutional issue

When one realizes that the vast majority of cases are disposed of through plea bargaining and that more criminal cases are generally dismissed than are tried, the avenues for the possibilities of corruption become readily apparent. Inquiry is so infrequently made into a prosecutor's reasons for the bargain struck in a particular case that the generalization has developed that the prosecutor's authority is total. Compounding the absence of substantial checks on discretion is the secrecy which still surrounds the process in so many courts. And the secrecy cloaks inequities, favoritism, corruption, and abuses of discretion that undermine the integrity of our criminal justice system.

The earliest judicial recognition and pronouncements on plea bargaining were negative. Eighteenth century state courts attacked plea bargaining, one labeling it a "corrupt agreement" and another, "essentially immoral."[22] Contemporary judges in many states continue to echo these earlier sentiments, and it is the emphatic recommendation of the National Commission on Standards and Goals that the practice be prohibited.[23]

Despite these misgivings, the Supreme Court avoided general statements on the process until the 1970s. In numerous cases considering the validity of bargained pleas, the Supreme Court acknowledged the possible benefits to both the prosecution and the defendant in particular cases but avoided general pronouncements on the subject.[24] Finally, in 1971 the Supreme Court placed its imprimatur on plea bargaining in *Santobello v. New York* when Chief Justice Burger wrote:

> Disposition of charges after plea discussions is not only an essential part of the process but a highly desirable part for many reasons. It leads to prompt and largely final disposition of most criminal cases; it avoids most of the corrosive impact of enforced idleness during pretrial confinement for those who are denied release pending trial; it protects the public from those accused persons who are prone to continue criminal conduct even while on pretrial release; and, by shortening the time between charge and disposition, it enhances whatever may be the rehabilitative prospects of the guilty when they are ultimately imprisoned. . . .[25]

Again in 1977 and 1978, the Supreme Court commented upon the desirability of the practice: "Whatever might be the situation in an ideal world, the fact is that the guilty plea and often concomitant plea bargain are important components of this country's criminal justice system."[26] Despite the subtle acknowledgment in this statement that plea bargaining is *practical*—an acknowledgment that differentiates this later opinion from the all-out endorsement in *Santobello*—it is clear that the Supreme Court is not ready to declare the practice unconstitutional, even though the later language seems to relegate it to a necessary evil. Instead, the Supreme Court's efforts have been directed towards making the practice somewhat less clandestine so that the quality of the defendant's choice may be tested for fairness. Over the years, the Supreme Court has insisted upon a public record indicating that the plea was knowingly and voluntarily made and that the prosecutor's promises which induced the guilty plea be kept.[27] Furthermore, the Court has stressed the importance of counsel for the accused during the process and while making the choice.[28]

The Prosecutor's Role

Obviously, the prosecutor realizes the need for the prompt disposition of criminal cases. Keenly aware of the necessity for keeping the process smooth by avoiding trials, the prosecuting attorney is in the unique position of representing the state while offering concessions to a defendant so he will agree that a trial is unnecessary. As the recipient of all police reports in any case, the prosecutor is also best suited—far better than the judge who will ultimately have to ratify a deal but will only have the information provided by the prosecution and defense when doing so—to determine what the society's interests are and how far society can safely go in making concessions to a particular defendant.[29] (The decisions made at this time are not unlike the decisions made when the accused is charged, except now the reality of a trial looms much greater if the prosecutor takes a hard line.)

Balancing the competing interests appears on the surface to be a rational approach except that plea bargaining is not always rational. The prosecutor's offer is rarely arrived at calmly by determining just how much protection society requires from a given defendant. Thoughtfulness that may enhance a rational decision is rare because of pressures that plague the prosecutor. Abstractly those pressures may be necessary because they often constitute the only checks upon the prosecutor's discretion, but the pressures are not necessarily directed at a fair resolution or a resolution that will adequately protect the community. In so many cities, uppermost in the prosecutor's mind is the clamor of the docket. Where the docket is extraordinarily crowded, the prosecutor must weigh whether it is at all feasible to take a hard line and risk a trial that simply cannot be accommodated. The inability to actually try all defendants often prevents the prosecutor from weighing the dangerousness of the accused. Instead, he must compare the dangerousness of the accused to the other defendants whose cases may be shunted aside and ignored when one case goes to trial. Often it is the judges who tip the scales. While supposedly not involved in the plea bargaining process, judges may be so obsessed with congested court calendars that they hammer away at the prosecutor until he virtually gives cases away.[30] LIFE magazine once recorded an instance in a New York City courtroom where a prosecutor was pressured by a judge into "recommending" a one-year sentence for a man charged with attempting to rape a four-year-old child. The defendant had a long record of rapes, assaults, sodomy, and armed robbery, but the judge persisted "in light of the calendar" until the assistant district attorney gave way and agreed to accept the plea to the reduced charge and minimal sentence.[31] Giveaways like this are not unusual in a court that is so swamped that it cannot focus beyond its calendar. New York City's problems are by no means unique; it is only the massive proportion of the problem there that singles out the New York courts.

Giveaways to keep dockets moving are common in many American cities. Because of crowded dockets, prosecutors are often reduced to recommending whatever the defendant is willing to take. Trials are avoided at all costs, and those costs are usually borne by the community in the form of repeated offenses by persons who are processed through and out of the criminal justice system. In New York City, this giveaway syndrome even applies to homicide cases. One study of murder and manslaughter indictments in the entire city for one year disclosed that eighty percent of 1,326 adult indictments in homicide cases were disposed of on the basis of negotiated pleas. Incredibly, twenty percent of that group were placed on probation after pleading guilty and, in all, seventy-eight percent received probation or sentences of less than ten years. The survey indicated that the harshest sentences were reserved for those defendants who were convicted after a trial rather than after a plea of guilty. Blame for this result was placed on the judges by the district attorneys, and upon the district attorneys by the judges. But both groups acknowledged, "The bigger the backlog, the lighter the sentences."[32] If homicide is treated so cavalierly, it is no wonder that robberies are reduced to assaults, burglaries to illegal entries, and sexual assaults to disorderly conduct.[33]

Because the need is to move cases, there is little evaluation of the factual basis supporting the original charge and little concern demonstrated for whether the defendant will be involved again in criminal activity. It is the same in many cities; the deal is usually made irrespective of the facts of the case or the theoretical goals of the criminal law. The highly negotiable commodity in which everyone deals is time. A reduction in the charge guarantees to the defendant a reduction in the length of both the minimum and maximum sentences that he may be forced to serve. Although the negotiations may be based upon the charge, the actual currency is always the time that will be served. Even where prosecutors disclaim plea bargaining and will not reduce charges, deals are struck concerning the type of recommendation the prosecutor will make in court as to sentencing in return for the defendant's guilty plea.[34]

The opposite pull may be imposed by the victims and police who insist that the prosecutor not make concessions in a particular case. If too susceptible to this type of influence, the prosecutor may end up giving away other cases where the victim and police interest are not as sustained and may pursue the cases on which he is pressured, all irrespective of the seriousness of the offenses and the dangerousness of the offenders involved.[35]

Except in courts like New York City where the pressure is overt, few defendants in other cities understand that the prosecuting attorney is as ready as they are to avoid trial. Defendants typically feel that the prosecutor is "out to get them" and that the judge is prepared to assist the prosecutor in achieving that goal.[36] These defendants assume that the promises or threats made by the prosecutor will be carried out automatically by the judge. Therefore, when accepting a defendant's guilty plea and determining whether that plea is intelligently and voluntarily made, the essential problem for the court is to ascertain whether the defendant understands the real value of the promises made by the prosecutor to induce the defendant's plea.[37]

Contrary to what many defendants believe, the prosecutor's promises do not bind the court.[38] Without first clearing the arrangement with the court, the prosecutor may not make a representation about what the judge will do. What the prosecutor can do, however, has a powerful effect on the defendant's decision to negotiate a plea. Without prior approval, the prosecutor can agree to reduce the charge and dismiss one or all of the original charges in the indictment or make promises as to recommendations that will be made to the court regarding probation or the sentence.[39]

Prosecutors, to avoid trial, will often make outlandish promises that they know will not be honored by the court. Yet because defendants are so intent upon receiving the most desirable sentence put before them by the prosecutor, they regard his promise or recommendation as absolute.[40] Defendants, for example, often feel that the prosecutorial bargain carries with it an assurance of a specific sentence. This, of course, is not the case. Courts do reverse convictions and permit defendants to withdraw guilty pleas when the sentencing judge failed to follow the prosecutor's recommendation after the prosecutor expressed a belief that the court would do so.[41] In most cases, however, prosecutorial recommendations are regarded by courts as recommendations only, and any lavish promises given to induce a guilty plea are considered unethical and subject the conviction to reversal. An attack upon a guilty plea and subsequent conviction and sentencing will generally center upon the factual questions of what was promised by the prosecutor.[42] Did the prosecutor promise a specific sentence which the defendant did not receive or did the prosecutor simply promise to *recommend* a specific sentence which was rejected by the court?

Defendants are entitled as a matter of law to have prosecution promises concerning charge reductions and sentence recommendations honored.[43] If the prosecutor fails to dismiss other pending criminal cases as promised, or fails to insure the type of after-conviction care as promised, or fails to recommend probation or a specific sentence as promised, then the guilty plea based upon these promises is invalid. Sometimes the broken promise does not come to light until after a conviction has been entered on the guilty plea and the defendant sentenced. This may happen because the accused was too rattled during the court hearing to raise the alarm or failed to understand what actually transpired. But the defendant's confusion does not release the prosecution from the obligations created by its promises. Even a defendant's in-court statement to the judge that the guilty plea is not the result of any promises made by the prosecutor does not dismiss the matter. The accused may later challenge the conviction on that basis and is entitled to an evidentiary hearing to determine whether his claim is true. If the promise was made, the accused is entitled to specific enforcement of that promise or, if that is not possible because the prosecution misrepresented its ability to influence the court on sentencing, then the defendant, even after conviction, is entitled to withdraw that guilty plea and go to trial or enter into a new plea agreement. In *Santobello v. New York,* which established this principle, the Surpeme Court stressed that proper safeguards of the plea bargaining process were so crucial that even in that case, where the prosecutor inavertently failed to fulfill the promise not to make any recommendation about sentence and the sentencing judge stated on the record that he was not influenced by the prosecutor's recommendation, the defendant was entitled to the remedy.[44]

Not long ago it was commonly believed that while promises were permissible to induce a guilty plea, threats were not.[45] This theory, of course, was linked to the voluntariness of the defendant's guilty plea. A guilty plea induced by a promise to do something which the prosecutor otherwise need not do demonstrated the voluntariness of the defendant's action and clearly showed that he had freedom of choice which he would have been deprived of if he were responding to the state's threat against him. Some might argue that a promise implicitly carries a threat: unless the defendant waives his assertion of innocence, the promised beneficence will be withheld. Notwithstanding the uneven bargaining positions of the parties, a promise to bestow a benefit on the defendant which the state is in no way obligated to grant cannot be viewed as carrying a countervailing threat. The threat, if anything, is to force the defendant to stand trial as charged and to face the possibility of receiving the maximum penalty allowed by statute if he is convicted. On the other hand, direct threats, even of legal action by the state, are considered to be unfair pressure, robbing both the defendant of choice and the criminal justice system of fairness.[46]

The distinction, however, between promises and threats is no longer clear as a result of a 1978 Supreme Court case. In *Bordenkircher v. Hayes,*[47] the Supreme Court let stand a conviction carrying a life sentence that was clearly the result of the defendant's failure to plead guilty. In this case, the accused was indicted for forging a check for $88.30, an offense carrying a penalty of two to ten years in prison under Kentucky law. During plea negotiations with the defendant and his attorney, the prosecutor offered to recommend a prison sentence of five years. Additionally, if Hayes refused to plead guilty, the prosecutor threatened to return to the grand jury and obtain indictment based upon Hayes' two prior convictions under Kentucky's habitual offender law which carries a mandatory life sentence. Hayes refused to plead guilty and the prosecutor made good his threat. The defendant was convicted as an habitual offender and sentenced to life imprisonment. The Supreme Court held that the prosecutor had not exceeded constitutional bounds in making the threat or subsequently making good on it. The Supreme Court reaffirmed its long-standing principle that to punish someone for doing what the law allows him to do is impermissible, but failed to see that permitting the state to charge the accused with the greater crime simply because he refused to cooperate with the prosecutor constituted a violation of the original principle. In essence, Hayes was punished for doing what the law allows any defendant to do: that is, insisting upon a trial.

The justices attempted to analyze what happened to Hayes but failed to regard his sentence as a stroke of retaliation or vindictiveness on the state's part. The Court reached the following conclusion: "But in the 'give-and-take' of plea bargaining there is no such element of retaliation so long as the accused is free to accept or reject the prosecution's offer."[48] That decision certainly strengthens the hand of prosecutors during plea negotiations and may even eventually mean that the prosecutor may promise or threaten to do anything that is not illegal. To put the decision in its proper perspective, however, it has long been the practice for prosecutors to overcharge and indict defendants for every conceivable offense and then promise to dismiss those charges in return for a plea of guilty. But there is an important distinction between overcharging and what happened to Paul Hayes. In Hayes' case the prosecutor had previously chosen not to indict under the habitual offender law and, moreover, in plea discussions had indicated his belief that a five-year sentence would satisfactorily serve the interests of the state. Otherwise, why would he have offered to recommend a five-year sentence? It is difficult to categorize the subsequent imposition of a life sentence as anything but vindictive and retaliatory for the defendant's decision to exercise his constitutional right to trial and his refusal to "save the court the inconvenience and necessity of a trial."[49]

The Defense Attorney's Role

An attorney's assistance and counsel is indispensible to the defendant during plea bargaining.[50] He helps the defendant understand the realities of the situation he faces, insures that the defendant understands that he has options, and helps the defendant weigh the value of those options. An attorney, additionally, is better able than a layman to assess the real value, if any, of the prosecutor's promises. The decision to plead guilty, however, does not belong to the attorney. That decision should be made personally by the defendant, involving as it does his waivers of the constitutional protection against self-incrimination, right to trial, and right to confront his accusers.[51]

It is frowned upon for prosecutors to engage defendants directly in the plea negotiation process, and they will not deal directly with a defendant who has an attorney.[52] The most frequent prosecutor-defendant negotiations occur at preliminary appearances or arraignments before counsel is retained or appointed. Hurried arrangements made during rushed conversations in the tumult of the arraignment room are most suspect. Without guidance of counsel, the defendant is unlikely to ever know whether the agreement was a fair one or at all in his interests. Rather than accepting pleas of this sort, some judges refuse to allow the accompanying waiver of counsel and require the defendant to consult with any attorney who happens to be in the courtroom. After a minute or two of consultation, the defendant generally returns to the bar accompanied by "his counsel" and enters the plea of guilty. This hardly constitutes effective representation of counsel because the attorney under those conditions is unlikely to have learned much about the case, let alone about possible defenses or deficiencies in the state's case. But perhaps, sadly, the attorney's input may be better than none.[53]

Sometimes the prosecutor is forced to negotiate directly with a defendant because the accused has spurned the offer of legal assistance, believing that he can negotiate a better deal for himself. That decision is probably fatal because legal assistance is as necessary in negotiating a deal as it is at trial. Few defendants are familiar enough with the criminal law to recognize all of the possible strengths and weaknesses of each side. Acceptability of the prosecutor's offer should not depend only on the extent of the concession but should be weighed by the defense along with an assessment of the strength of the prosecutor's "hand." What appears on the surface to be a moderately generous, and hence acceptable, deal may not be one at all to someone who can spot enormous deficiencies in the state's case. If, for example, a conviction rests upon the state's ability to use evidence it secured during a search or interrogation of questionable legality, an experienced criminal lawyer can use that potential defense to his client's advantage. In rejecting the original offer, the defense attorney can point out the search or confession issue and recommend a more lenient counter offer or suggest that the Fourth or Fifth Amendment issue be heard by the court and, if the state prevails, then recommend the state's offer to the defendant. Counsel is also needed because only the recidivist defendant who has appeared often in court will be fully versed in what the prevailing reductions are in each category of offense. A defendant who elects to proceed alone and negotiates a burglary charge down to felonious theft cannot complain later if he learns that other defendants' lawyers were able to get burglary reduced to breaking and entering or even the misdemeanor of illegal entry. Even when the state's case is excellent and the plea bargaining involves little more than a plea for mercy for the defendant, a lawyer arguing his client's positive qualities is more likely to achieve a reduced sentence than the felony defendant who advises the court of his own virtues.[54]

The defendant needs counsel to not only negotiate with the prosecutor, but to make an intelligent decision about how to plead: counsel's advice on whether or not to accept the negotiated plea is of critical importance to the defendant. The situation is too complex for one to simply say that the attorney presents the deal to the client and the client makes the choice. For that choice to be intelligent, the defendant must fully understand all the consequences of that choice. It must be acknowledged that even though an accused has an absolute right to go to trial, that decision may be a disastrous one for a defendant in a particular case. The attorney must assist his client in understanding the likely consequences of each course of action: what are the probabilities of conviction for the charged offense and what type of sentence is likely after such a conviction compared to the sentence that the defendant is likely to receive on the negotiated plea? What are the consequences of each sentence beyond statutory minimum and maximum terms of imprisonment, such as probation, parole, and the nature of the institution where the defendant is likely to be committed?[55]

Moreover, a plea of guilty in all but a very few states prevents the defendant from ever raising defenses that may have precluded conviction, such as an illegal search.[56] The defendant should know when he makes his decision what his attorney's expectations are if the defense would make a motion to suppress the evidence secured during the search. The defendant should be aware that the granting of such a motion may have a substantial effect on the likelihood of his being convicted. How fully the defendant is informed of all these matters bears upon how intelligently he is able to make the choice and waive his constitutional rights. It stands to reason since so great a proportion of criminal cases are disposed of by guilty pleas that more challenges to convictions from prisoners in penitentiaries are based upon the ineffective assistance of counsel during this critical period in the life of a case than are resulting from the mistakes of defense attorneys at trial.[57]

It is unconscionable for an attorney to recommend a plea of guilty to a defendant who maintains that he is innocent, and the American Bar Association standards require that the counsel advise the court when such a defendant pleads guilty.[58] It would also be unconscionable for an attorney not to advise his client of the likelihood of conviction despite his continued assertions of innocence. The ethical dilemma for a lawyer who believes in his client's claim of innocence is acute. In Albert Alschuler's study of defense attorneys and plea bargaining, this problem was presented to the defense attorneys and most responded that they would never enter a guilty plea if they believed that their client was innocent. One attorney described a case where the state's evidence in a rape prosecution was virtually air-tight, but because his client insisted that he was innocent, the lawyer turned down a prosecution offer that would have insured a sentence no greater than one year. After his conviction at trial, the defendant was sent to a penitentiary for one to ten years. Alschuler also points out how the "ethical" rule encourages defense attorneys to employ interrogation techniques with clients who assert their innocence and that such techniques are destructive of the attorney-client relationship.[59]

Defense attorneys frequently urge their clients to plead guilty and accept the negotiated package, notwithstanding that the decision is to be the personal one of the defendant. In most cases it is probably the proper and best choice for the client, but the force commonly exerted by the defense attorney clearly diminishes the defendant's ability to convince himself that it was his own decision and a wise one. Critical to this process is the thoroughness of the attorney's preparation and total knowledge of the case before he is presumptuous enough to substitute his own knowledge and feelings for those of the client. It is important to remember that while the defense attorney and the client are a team, only one half of the team will serve the sentence and pay the consequences for the "team's" decisions. On the other hand, the attorney's understanding of the case is probably much greater than the defendant's if the lawyer has done his homework. Unfortunately, some defense attorneys are only prepared to plead guilty, not to try cases. One has to question whether the negotiated plea is actually in the accused's best interests or his lawyer's. The deals that some attorneys are able to work out with their prosecution counterparts are often not the best ones that could be obtained. Just as defense lawyers can generally sense when prosecutors are bluffing and trying to claim a stronger case than the state actually has, prosecutors also know which defense attorneys will not go to trial. When all that a defense attorney is seeking is some concession from the state to take back to his client, the prosecutor does not have to offer the best deal because he knows that the attorney will recommend acceptance of any offer simply to avoid trial.[60] In persuading a client to plead guilty, these lawyers adopt hard-sell tactics. The system cannot be sanguine about the way the lawyer presents the prosecution's offer to the defendant. Contained within the attorney's presentation may be promises which the prosecutor never dreamed of considering. These misrepresentations may be the basis for a later attack upon the guilty plea process and the conviction, but they are difficult to prove.[61]

Judicial "Interests"

The person with the power to consummate the agreement between the defense and prosecuting attorneys is the judge. Through his authority he can accept the plea and then pronounce sentence upon the defendant. In the vast majority of cases, the judge will abide by the prosecutor's recommendation because he has a direct interest in shoring up the prosecutor's credibility in his negotiations with defense attorneys. The prosecutor's ability to obtain pleas and dispose of cases without going to trial is as great a benefit to the judge as it is to the prosecutor, since the judge has the responsibility to insure that the criminal justice system appears sound. The judge is satisfied that the state's interests are protected when the prosecutor is satisfied with the outcome of a particular case. The prosecutor's, and hence the state's, satisfaction may not, however, always be consistent with the community's need for protection from a particular defendant. Thus the judge's compliance in the bargain and assurance that the community's interest has been respected may not be justified.

In all fairness to judges, it must be noted that they lack independent investigative resources and therefore can do little to effectively question the correctness and fairness of the deal being offered. A judge in this situation has little recourse but to accept the representations made by the prosecutor and agreed to by defense counsel. Inaccuracies are not likely to be uncovered when a judge's inquiries face the concerted desires of both the prosecuting and defense attorneys to have their proposed agreement accepted by the court. Some appellate courts have even limited the discretion of a trial judge to reject a plea of guilty, requiring that the judge state the reasons for the rejection on the record so that they may be reviewed.[62] Under that condition a judge is even less likely to resist the united efforts of the state and defense because the plea of guilty and subsequent conviction is not likely to be subject to later attack. Consequently, only the most patently absurd agreements, if even those, are likely to be challenged by a judge. Even then a judge may hesitate and avoid an overt challenge to the two attorneys' decision. Most judges are loath to slow the process and jeopardize the state's ability to engage in free-wheeling negotiations, confident of its ability to dispose of large numbers of cases on its recommendations. The judge who pays scant attention to the facts of particular cases and instead relies upon the prosecutor's judgment undoubtedly approves some giveaways, but that judge enables the system, over which theoretically he is the master, to survive. Unfortunately, quantity, not quality, is the key to survival.

Recommendations for probation or other forms of mercy made by rote by assistant prosecuting attorneys are accepted by rote by sentencing judges. The *Yale Law Journal* sent a questionnaire to all federal judges and more than half responded indicating their accommodating reactions to defendants' guilty pleas. It should be noted that federal judges in most parts of the country do not share the same burden in terms of number of cases that their colleagues in the state courts face. Also, these judges are aided in their assessments by fairly sophisticated pre-sentence reports prepared by probation departments. Nonetheless, two-thirds of the responding judges said they consider the guilty plea to be a relevant factor in determining sentence, and four out of five of that group indicated that the defendant pleading guilty routinely received a more lenient sentence than the one who did not.[63]

Contrary to popular belief, guilty pleas rarely reflect a defendant's sense of remorse. The negotiated guilty plea typically serves as a cover for paying the defendant off for allowing the government to avoid a costly trial. The defendant may be "paid" twice for his plea: once, in the concession of a reduced charge by the prosecutor and second, in the form of a reduced sentence by the judge. And finally, the judge's acceptance of the plea serves to replenish the sentimental belief that a guilty plea reflects the defendant's repentance.

Not all judges are content with their role in the plea bargaining process. They recognize that a judge is to be neutral and detached, ready to try cases.

Few are willing to see themselves as auctioneers squeezing bids out of the opposing adversaries in desperate attempts to avoid trials. Consider an example of one judge who sits on a court where an administrative judge constantly prods him to clear cases. This administrator rewards those judges who clear the most cases with favorable assignments and punishes those judges who do not clear cases with banishment to night court. This judge described his reactions to the system and his role in it:

> I remain terribly frustrated and increasingly annoyed with this court. We are being pressured constantly to "produce," which means forcing pleas to lesser charges just to dispose of cases. I feel like a fool and a clerk in a bargain basement, and part of the terrible system, helping in the denigration of our brilliant judicial heritage. I don't know how much longer I can take this....[64]

The sense of emotional depression which he conveys has grown from his realization that resistance to the status quo is generally futile. Conscientious judicial resistance can be negated in several ways. To avoid the judge who challenges the propriety of pleas, a lawyer can get the case delayed until it is assigned to a different judge or until a different judge is assigned to that task. Meanwhile the personal cost to the independent judge may be high. He must be prepared to accept the hostility of other judges because the resistance is, in effect, a repudiation of their willingness to accept accommodations. Where the presiding or administrative judge has discretion to make individual assignments, the resisting judge can anticipate receiving the least desirable ones, such as constant assignment to night court.[65]

An attempt at controlling such abuses, followed under the federal rules and in a few state jurisdictions, is to require that the record show some evidence of a basis in fact for the guilty plea.[66] The protection was created, of course, for the innocent defendant who is pleading guilty out of fear or to avoid further inconvenience and risk. But the measure is hardly air-tight, and the evidence that supplements the plea need not be substantial and can be fabricated. It offers no protection against the give-away negotiated deal. Even where evidence of guilt is not required in addition to the guilty plea, the judge is constitutionally required to engage the defendant personally in conversation to examine the intelligence and voluntariness of his decision to plead guilty.[67] This questioning has been refined in most jurisdictions so that it becomes clear in the record that the defendant has made the choice in return for a concession from the prosecution. The defendant is also told, unless the deal has been previously cleared or the court is prepared automatically to accept the state's recommendation, that the judge is not bound by the prosecutor's suggestion. In some cities, however, the old practice still persists whereby the judge and the defendant engage in a charade with the defendant asserting that no representations have been made to him and that he simply and spontaneously has decided to plead guilty.[68]

The ceremony surrounding the entry of a guilty plea is designed to create the illusion that the parties have reconciled their differences and have brought the matter before a neutral judge who, having played no prior role in the settlement, is in a position to act out of great wisdom and either approve or disapprove the settlement. In most instances, he is prepared to accept any settlement, so long as the case can be terminated. If it is necessary to encourage a settlement, the judge will pressure one or the other attorney if he feels that the attorney is hanging back and not dealing. In some jurisdictions, the judge, rather than being detached, may play an active role, alternately cajoling and pressuring one side and then the other, until the attorneys reach agreement. When the judge pushes and pressures the participants to reach agreement and avoid trial, it can hardly be claimed that the subsequent plea bargain represents the decision of the state that the community's interests are protected and the decision of the defense that the defendant's best interests have been served. It amounts to an accommodation imposed by a court whose interest was directed at nothing but avoiding a trial.[69]

The Need for Reform

The practice of plea bargaining is in drastic need of reform. The concept of abolishing this practice is terribly attractive because just the idea that criminal cases can be resolved by accommodation is in itself fairly repugnant. Equally distasteful is the wide latitude that plea bargaining leaves for misuse and corruption. Yet the realities of the American criminal justice system do not lend themselves to an expectation that the practice will be abandoned in the near future.[70] Whenever the problems related to plea bargaining are recognized, the emphasis has been on reform rather than abolition. A suggestion that must eventually be considered is that perhaps these problems are barnacled to plea bargaining and may not be susceptible to real reform until the institution of plea bargaining is either substantially revamped or eliminated altogether.

The significant reform effort has been to lift the shroud of secrecy that surrounds the practice.[71] A greater opportunity for abuse exists where details are obscured and when the fact is hidden that the plea is a product of negotiation and compromise. Conversely, the more open the process, the more likely the result will be subject to scrutiny and greater the chance that unscrupulous deals will be discovered and ultimately prevented. One small step towards that end was taken when the Supreme Court imposed upon state courts as well as federal trial courts the obligation to directly address the defendant to find out the nature of his decision to plead guilty. However, a defendant can be coached on how to respond to the judge's questions and may not necessarily disclose the reasons why he has decided to waive his rights. The defendant who is coerced into agreeing to the compromise plea is the least likely, because of his fear, to acknowledge the basis for his decision. For that very reason, the defendant's in-court disclaimer of coercion, threats, and promises is not an absolute blockade to a later attack upon the voluntariness of his plea. The only viable way to protect defendant's rights in this context is through the effective assistance of a lawyer who recognizes that his sole obligation is to protect the legitimate interests of the client. Similarly, the community's legitimate interests can only be protected by a prosecuting attorney who places that obligation above his own convenience and that of judges.

Another step adopted in the federal rules governing the procedure in federal courts is to require that full disclosure of the agreement be made and included in the official record of the case.[72] This not only permits the judge who must review and approve the agreement to see the case in detail, but it also subjects it to public scrutiny in the event the news media suspects a "give-away."

A great hurdle to overcome is the intermeddling of the judge during the negotiation process, usually pushing either or both parties towards a settlement. Appellate case reports contain entries of convictions which have been reversed because of the pressure imposed by the trial court judge upon reluctant defendants to "voluntarily" waive their rights and plead guilty.[73] This pressure most often takes the form of oblique threats to impose maximum penalties if the accused persists in his plea of innocence and refuses to save the court the inconvenience of a trial. But these claims are difficult to prove, and judges throughout the country are overstepping their bounds every day. Moreover, there is no way to review those instances where judicial pressure is applied to the prosecuting attorney to consent to a give-away. The judge does not belong in the negotiating process. The proper role for the judiciary is to oversee the fairness of the process and the resulting agreement to insure that the defendant's rights and the community's interests are amply protected. Removal of the court from the bargaining process does not require that the negotiated plea be entered without first testing the judge's willingness to accept it. The same federal rule that requires full disclosure of all agreements protects the independence of the judiciary by reserving the right of the judge to reject the deal. If the court rejects the agreement as unacceptable, the judge advises the defendant in court of that fact and offers the accused an opportunity to withdraw the guilty plea and go to trial. The court is also obliged to inform the defendant that if he persists in maintaining the guilty plea, the disposition of the case may be less favorable to the defendant than contemplated in the plea agreement; unless, of course, the judge rejects the agreement as too harsh on the defendant, in which case the accused is likely to persist in maintaining his guilty plea.[74] By its very nature, the rule establishes an independent, supervisory role for the judge.

One of the most troubling aspects of plea bargaining that has received little attention is the unevenness of the resulting deals. Often, the outcome is dictated more by the leverage that the defense can exert by indicating the defendant's willingness to go to trial than on the seriousness of the crime allegedly committed by the accused or his past criminal record. Uneven results are frequently attributed to overcharging, which, it is contended, is necessary to permit the defendant to believe that he is receiving a tremendous concession for his guilty plea. Be that as it may, protection of the integrity of the criminal justice system requires some standardization to introduce a measure of equality in the results and prevent give-aways. Additionally, standardization may even make prosecutors more cautious in charging and eventually may end the practice of overcharging.

There have been two notable attempts to introduce standardization of the plea bargaining process into two prosecutors' offices, one relatively small (Tazewell County, Illinois) and the other one of the largest offices in our country (New York County, Manhattan). The guidelines issued by the Tazewell County State's Attorney specifically prohibit threatening a defendant if he does not plead guilty with additional charges not ordinarily included under the original charge or with a more severe sentence. Those standards also require full disclosure of all "exculpatory evidence material to guilt or punishment" *prior to* entering into negotiations. Finally, and most uniquely, the standards require that a final date be set for plea negotiations, so that any case not resolved through bargaining will be firmly assigned to the trial calendar, and only guilty pleas to the original charge will be accepted after that date. That last standard will eliminate the most frantic plea bargaining on the eve of trial when the greatest injustices are perpetrated.[75]

While the Tazewell County standards provide guidelines for the conduct of assistant prosecutors, the New York standards offer guidelines for the actual agreement, which if actually implemented would tend to standardize settlements. The standards promulgated by former District Attorney Richard Kuh in Manhattan generally limited reductions of charges by one degree and then, only after there was a pre-pleading investigation conducted by the office. Although on the basis of the pre-pleading investigation, "in the interests of justice" a prosecutor might consent, with the approval of a supervisor, to a two degree reduction or even dismissal. The internal standards also provide guidelines concerning aggravating circumstances (e.g., no reduction when the pre-pleading investigation determines that the defendant charged is engaged in the sale of hard drugs for profit and is a non-user; public officials charged with official misconduct are not to be permitted to plead to a misdemeanor even if the offense would only be a misdemeanor if committed by one who is not a public official) and mitigating circumstances (e.g., no prior criminal record; forgiveness on the part of the victim, though not solely determinative; willingness to make restitution to victims). Real keys to the New York procedure were standardized reductions based upon published criteria, review of each assistant's recommendations, and specific guidelines for sentencing recommendations.[76] There is no data indicating how well these standards were implemented during Kuh's brief tenure in office, nor how well assistant district attorneys were able to overcome the pressures exerted by judges to clear cases.

These are, for the most part, isolated, hesitant steps towards reform of the plea bargaining process. Efforts at bringing the practice under control can be expected to continue: the continuation of the effort is critical because in no other aspect is the integrity of the criminal justice system more on the line.

Discussion Questions

1. Thomas Church in his article "Plea Bargains, Concessions, and the Courts: Analysis of a Quasi-Experiment" states: "It is unclear how any fundamental shift away from bargain justice could occur without an even more fundamental change in the incentive structures of the participants." (LAW & SOCIETY REVIEW, c 1976.) Explain this statement.

2. Discuss the three primary reasons prosecutors engage in plea bargaining. Do you feel that these reasons justify the practice? Support your answer.

3. Why does a defendant consent to plea bargaining? What factors influence his final decision?

4. Explain the relationship of plea bargaining to the prosecutorial practice of overcharging. Why do prosecutors overcharge, and how does overcharging benefit the defense attorney?

5. Discuss the significance of the Supreme Court Case of Santabello v. New York. Do you agree with Justice Burger's opinion that plea bargaining is not only essential but desirable in the administration of justice?

6. Discuss judicial involvement in the plea bargaining process. How are the judge's "interests" served by the practice? What are objections that have been raised by judges who are not comfortable with feeling like "fool(s) in a bargain basement"?

7. Because of the inequities and injustices perpetrated by plea bargaining practices, it is widely recognized that the institution is in drastic need for significant reform. Discuss the four reform efforts introduced in this chapter which have as their common objective the lifting of the "shroud of secrecy" that surrounds this increasingly disreputable practice.

Notes

1. Donald Neuman, "Pleading Guilty for Considerations: A Study of Bargain Justice," and Arnold Trebach, "Cop Out." Both in George F. Cole, *Criminal Justice, Law and Politics* (Belmont, California: Duxbury Press, 1972).
2. See "Plea Bargaining—Justice off the Record," 9 *Washburn L. Jour.* 430 (1970).
3. Cf. see Neuman, "Pleading Guilty," p. 192, where he cites (56.7%) as the percentage of admitted bargaining.
4. Again, see "Plea Bargaining—Justice off the Record."
5. See People v. Fratianno, 6 Cal. App. 3rd 211, 85 Cal. Rptr. 755 (1970), where grand larceny was reduced to petty larceny; also see People v. Clairborne, 29 N.Y. 2d 950, 280 N.E. 2d 366 (1972), where murder was reduced to voluntary manslaughter.
6. Trebach, "Cop Out," p. 201.

7. James E. Bond, *Plea Bargaining and Guilty Pleas,* (New York: Clark Boardman, 1978), p. 18.
8. Standard 3.1, *National Advisory Commission on Criminal Justice Standards and Goals Courts* (1974).
9. Cf. in Alaska the Attorney General has prohibited all state prosecutors from plea bargaining, and the State Supreme Court has forbidden trial judges from engaging in the practice. State v. Buckalew, 561 P. 2d 289 (Alas. 1977); also see State v. Carlson, 555 P.2d 269, 272 (Alas. 1976), when it was said: "we are concerned that a judge's involvement as a plea negotiator would detract from the judge's neutrality."
10. Comment, "The Role of Plea Negotiation in Modern Criminal Law," 46 *Chicago-Kent L. Rev.* 121 (1969).
11. See Trebach, "Cop Out," p. 202, where the author found that "it is important to inquire into the conditions at these places of detention since a prisoner may spend months there and since harsh conditions may adversely affect an individual's determination to exercise his constitutional right to fight the case through to a trial by jury."
12. ABA Standards, "The Prosecution Function," § 4.2; also see § 4.25, where the defense counsel has a similar responsibility.
13. North Carolina v. Alford, 400 U.S. 25 (1970).
14. Stanley P. Golde and Jules F. Bonjour, Jr., *Plea Bargaining* (Berkely, California: California Continuing Education of the Bar, 1975), p. 27.
15. Williams v. State, 10 Md. App. 570, at 574, 271 A. 2d 777, at 779 (1970) in Alschuler, "The Defense Attorney's Role in Plea Bargaining," 84 *Yale L. Jour.* 1179, at 1298 (1975).
16. Mills, "I Have Nothing to do With Justice," *Life,* March 12, 1971, at 66.
17. Similarly, the prosecutor may delay in an effort to induce a guilty plea when it is unlikely that the complaining witness or other witnesses will actually be willing to testify when a trial is finally held.
18. See Johnson, "Multiple Punishment and Consecutive Sentences: Reflections on the 'Neal' Doctrine," 58 *Calif. L. Rev.* 357 (1970).
19. See Thomas v. United States, 368 F.2d 941, 946 (5th Cir. 1966), where the court concluded that the sentencing differential (which may also violate equal protection strictures) may dull the exercise of fundamental constitutional rights.
20. Newman, *Conviction: The Determination of Guilt or Innocence Without Trial,* (Boston: Little, Brown, 1966), p. 216; see Dewey v. United States, 268 F. 2d 124, 128 (8th Cir. 1959), where the court took "judicial notice of the fact that trial courts quite generally impose a lighter sentence on pleas of guilty than in cases where the accused pleaded not guilty but has been found guilty by a jury." Cf. Dr. William Rhodes, *Plea Bargaining: Who Gains? Who Loses?* (Washington, D.C.: The Institute for Social Research), where "the data show that many offenders who entered a guilty plea would have been acquitted had they stood trial; and defendants who pled guilty were not routinely rewarded with charge and sentence reduction."
21. Anthony Davis, "Sentence for Sale: A New Look at Plea Bargaining in England and America," 1971 *Crim. L. Rev.* 157: "It has been shown that in practice American courts almost invariably do reward guilty pleas with leniency, even without looking for evidence of actual remorse or any other mitigating factor."
22. Golden v. State, 49 Ind. 424 (1875); Wight v. Rindskopt, 43 Wis. 344, 355 (1877); and see Shelton v. United States, 242 F. 2d 101, 113 (5th Cir. 1957), where Judge Rivers said, "Justice and liberty are not the subjects of bargaining and barter."

23. See *Application of Buccheri,* 431 P.2d 91 (Ariz. 1967), where plea bargaining was held per se illegal; *Recommendations of the National Advisory Commission on Criminal Justice Standards and Goals,* § 3.1 (1973).
24. See Nagelberg v. United States, 377 U.S. 266 (1964), where in a per curiam opinion the Supreme Court hinted at its permissive views on plea bargaining; Brady v. United States, 397 U.S. 742 (1970); McMarin v. Richardson, 397 U.S. 759 (1970); Parker v. North Carolina, 397 U.S. 790 (1970); Bordenkircher v. Hayes, U.S. (1978).
25. Santobello v. New York, 404 U.S. 257, at 261 (1971).
26. Ibid., at 260.
27. Boykin v. Alabama, 395 U.S. 238 (1969); also see Tipton v. State, 498 P.2d 429, 432 (1972), where the court said "the test established by Boykin is whether a guilty plea was voluntarily and understandingly entered. If the record shows that the plea is so entered, then the record is not silent as to the waiver of these three express federal constitutional rights."
28. Kitchens v. Smith, 401 U.S. 847 (1971); Moore v. Michigan, 355 U.S. 155 (1957); Berry v. New York, 375 U.S. 160 (1964); Vecchiolli v. Maroney, 372 U.S. 768 (1963).
29. Davis, "Sentence for Sale," pp. 156-157, "both the D.A. and U.S. Attorney have assumed upon themselves certain discretions ... as a result ... in America the prosecutor can offer inducements, such as charge reductions, with the courts making only the most perfunctory scrutiny of his actions."
30. Note, "The Unconstitutionality of Plea Bargaining," 83 *Harv. L. Rev.* 1387 (1970).
31. Mills, "I Have Nothing to do With Justice," pp. 57, 64.
32. H. Jay Folkerg, "The Bargained for Guilty Plea—An Evaluation," 4 *Crim L. Bull.* 201 (1968).
33. See People v. Whitfield, 40 Ill. 2d 308, 239 N.E. 2d 850 (1968), where an offer to reduce a charge from murder to manslaughter with the recommendation of probation was made to defendant's counsel; see *New York Times,* Feb. 9, 1971, at 38, Col. 3 where:

    Two such giveaways resulted from the congestion in the courts of New York City. Stanley Poler, a New York resident, sounded the public alarm in one such case. Poler aided the police in the capture of two burglary suspects. Both of the suspects were recidivists and had engaged in a great many burglaries. Despite their history, both defendants were permitted to plead guilty to the charge of trespassing, a relatively minor offense. But the community's safety from the two burglars was short-lived, as one was sentenced to two months in jail and the other to nine months. Stanley Poler was justified in commenting that our prisons have revolving doors.

    Another beneficiary of a "giveaway" plea was Albert Jones. He admitted that he strangled Beverly Ribet, June 5, 1970, after forcing his way into her car. Although Jones was originally charged with murder, murder while committing a robbery, and murder while committing rape, the defendant was permitted to plead guilty to the reduced charge of manslaughter.

    In Gary, Indiana, a defendant was charged with assault and battery with intent to kill after he had shot his girlfriend in the chest and right thigh, and then shot her daughter twice in the leg. The prosecutor accepted a plea of guilty to the charge of carrying a pistol without a permit. (Cause No. 37763, Criminal Court, Lake County, Indiana.)
34. Donald J. Newman, *Conviction,* p. 79.
35. Kuh, "Plea Copping," 24 *N.Y. County Bar Bull.* 160 (1966-67).
36. Jonathan D. Casper, *Criminal Courts: The Defendants Perspective,* (U.S.

Department of Justice, Feb. 1978), p. 25, where "Prosecutors are seen as agents bent upon convicting and punishing defendants."

37. See Federal Rule of Criminal Procedure 11, which requires that the defendant know the consequences of his plea before it can be voluntary and intelligent; McCarthy v. United States, 394 U.S. 459 (1969); Boykin v. Alabama, 395 U.S. 238 (1969).
38. See People v. Dixon, 242 N.W.2d § 20 (Mich. 1976), where prior to receipt of defendant's plea, the prosecutor disclaims any knowledge of the arrangement, the state cannot be held to the terms. Cf. Santobello v. New York, 404 U.S. 257, 262 (1971), where C.J. Barger declared, "when a plea rests in any significant degree on a promise or agreement of the prosecutor, so that it can be said to be part of the inducement or consideration, such promise must be fulfilled."
39. See Santobello v. New York, supra.
40. See State v. Brown, 367 A.2d 417 (N.J. 1976), where a court vacated a plea-based conviction where there was no clear promise if a layman might have misunderstood and therefore may have been misled.
41. See People v. Eck, 197 N.W. 2d 289 (Mich. 1972), where a prosecutor promised that "statements made to police not be used against him, but they were included in the presentence report"; also see United States v. Brown, 500 F.2d 375 (4th Cir. 1974), where the court even found a "broken promise where the prosecutor failed to argue for his sentence recommendation enthusiastically."
42. See Johnson v. Beto, 466 F.2d 478 (5th Cir. 1972); Walters v. Harris, 460 F.2d 988 (4th Cir. 1972).
43. See Santobello v. New York, 404 U.S. 257, 262 (1971), where the court said that "the staff lawyers in a prosecutor's office have the burden of 'letting the left hand know what the right hand is doing or has done' "; Giglio v. United States, 405 U.S. 150 (1972).
44. Santobello v. New York, supra, at 262: "This phase of the process of criminal justice, and the adjudicative element inherent in accepting a plea of guilty, must be attended by safeguards to insure the defendant what is reasonably due in the cc's. Those cc's will vary, but a constant factor is that when a plea rests in any significant degree on a promise or agreement of the prosecutor, so that it can be said to be part of the inducement or consideration, such promise must be fulfilled."
45. People v. Bowman, 40 Ill 2d 116, 239 N.E. 2d 433 (1968).
46. See People v. Darrah, 33 Ill. 2d 175, 210 N.E. 2d 478 (1965), where the defendant pleaded guilty to burglary. During the course of the trial, the defense counsel was informed by the judge that a "considerably greater" sentence would be composed if the case went to the jury.
47. Bordenkircher v. Hayes, 434 U.S. 357 (1978).
48. Ibid., at 363.
49. See Blackledge v. Perry, 417 U.S. 21 (1974), where the court confronted the issue of a "realistic likelihood of 'vindictiveness' " on the part of the prosecution.
50. Brady v. United States, 397 U.S. 742 (1970).
51. Albert W. Alschuler, "The Defense Attorney's Role in Plea Bargaining," 84 *Yale L. Jour.* 1179, 1309 (1975).
58. *American Bar Association Project on Standards for Criminal Justice,* "The Defense Function," § 5.3, p. 128.
59. Alschuler, "The Defense Attorney's Role," p. 1282.
60. See Leano v. United States, 457 F.2d 1208 (9th Cir. 1972). Besides providing an expert evaluation of the appropriateness of defendant's plea, the lawyer can negotiate desirable concessions from the prosecution in exchange for its submis-

52. Cf. Alschuler, "The Defense Attorney's Role," p. 1272:

> At the time of my visit in 1968, the initial contact between prosecutors and unrepresented defendants usually occurred in the holdover room itself. A dozen or more defendants were assembled in this lockup, and a single prosecutor then entered the room. He spoke to each defendant individually and commonly asked, "Do you want a lawyer, or do you want to talk to me today?" In most misdemeanor cases, the prosecutor's offers seemed irresistible. He frequently explained that the defendant "could be home by Saturday night" or—even more often—that he "could go home today" if he wanted to. "Of course," the prosecutor sometimes added, "if you want a lawyer, that is your right, but we will have to reset your case. I don't know when your trial might be. You will have to take your turn."
>
> Clyde W. Woody explained, "The defendants are professionals at this sort of thing, and they are the ones who have to do the time."

The practice of bargaining with unrepresented defendants does lend itself to abuse, but the usual abuse was not the imposition of harsh sentences. The real danger is that a person is likely to plead guilty when he is innocent.

53. People v. Gonzalez, 352 N.Y.S.2d 7 (1974), where the defendant did not receive effective assistance of counsel where his Legal Aid Society attorney knew nothing about the case.; also, "Restructuring the Plea Bargain," 82 *Yale L. Jour.* 286, 295 (1972), where some critics accuse public defenders of deliberately sacrificing a particular client's interest for the collective interest of all their clients; also see Turner v. State, 303 F.2d 507 (4th Cir. 1962), where the court was skeptical of the counsel's competence when he sees his client only once, and then for only a few minutes before pleading him guilty.
54. Alschuler, "The Defense Attorney's Role," p. 1187, where Boston attorney Paul T. Smith claimed, "that a lawyer gets more by fighting."
55. Brady v. United States, supra.
56. McMann v. Richardson, 397 U.S. 759 (1970).
57. See Sullivan v. Warden, 540 P.2d 112 (Nev. 1975), which states the defendant bears the burden of proving that his counsel was inadequate; Moore v. Michigan, 355 U.S. 155 (1963); "Effective Assistance of Counsel for the Indigent Defendant," 78 *Harv. L. Rev.* 1434, 1440 (1965), where it was recognized that mistakes made at that stage are difficult and sometimes impossible to cure at a later time.

sion. In this case the court rejected an incompetence charge where the lawyer negotiated dismissal of five serious charges; see also Dixon v. State, 287 So. 2d 698 (Fla. 1973), where the court found counsel's assistance ineffective when he failed to confer with his client during the 3½ months the defendant was in jail. When counsel did confer with his client, he sought only to persuade him to plead guilty.

61. If the defense attorney misleads his client into pleading guilty on the basis of promises made or agreed to by the prosecutor, the plea of guilty is not intelligently entered.
62. United States v. Ammidown, 497 F.2d 615 (D.C. Cir. 1974).
63. Comment, "The Influence of the Defendant's Plea on Judicial Determination of Sentence," 66 *Yale L. Jour.* 203, 206 (1956).
64. Lewis Katz, *Justice is the Crime* (Cleveland, Ohio: The Press of Case Western Reserve University, 1972), pp. 218-219.
65. Bond, *Plea Bargaining,* § 4.09[3], pp. 191-192; Newman, *Conviction,* p. 212, in which he alludes to a defense attorney's ability to steer the case to the proper judge.
66. Federal Rule of Criminal Procedure 11.

67. Boykin v. Alabama, 395 U.S. 238 (1969).

68. Katz, *Justice is the Crime,* p. 210.

69. See Rogers v. State, 136 So. 2d 331 (Miss. 1962), which held that the judge's participation was by its very nature coercive. ("Because of the nature of the judicial junction and the power and prestige of a circuit judge, any acts or words of his containing promises or tending to persuade have a much greater significance than acts or words of others.")

70. Newman, *Conviction,* p. 232.

71. Katz, *Justice is the Crime,* pp. 211-215.

72. See Federal Rule of Criminal Procedure 11.

73. Again see McCarthy v. United States, 394 U.S. 459 (1969).

74. Federal Rule of Criminal Procedure 11.

75. *Local Standards for the Exercise of Prosecutorial Discretion in Tazwell County, Illinois,* Tazwell County State Attorney's Office (1973).

76. Richard H. Kuh, "Plea Bargaining: Guidelines for the Manhattan District Attorney's Office," 11 *Crim. L. Bull.* 48 (1975).

11.

Under our Constitution, the condition of being a boy does not justify a kangaroo court.

In re Gault

The Juvenile Justice System

Technically, juvenile courts are not criminal courts but they do affect the lives of the people subject to their jurisdiction as greatly as adult criminal courts. In fact, juvenile justice is almost a microcosm of criminal justice in America, plagued by many of the same volatile issues and problems confronting the criminal justice system. A study of American criminal justice would not be complete if it did not include the critical issues which this society must confront when considering the problems of juvenile crime. This chapter concentrates upon the procedures and rights applicable to a juvenile who is charged as a delinquent for acts which would be a crime if committed by an adult.

The twentieth century dawned with demands and proposals for the creation of separate juvenile courts that would be less formal than adult courts, less concerned about the criminal behavior of the juvenile, and totally committed to the welfare of the child.[1] The movement was spawned by the unseemly sight of children being tried, incarcerated, and punished in adult courts, jails, and penal institutions.[2] The century of reform was to change all this. The problems of children were to be handled by courts staffed by professionals and judges who would become specialists in the needs of the child, who would dispense with complicated legalisms, and who would be devoted, instead, to helping the child develop into a useful, functioning member of society. Associated with these goals was the vision of a fatherly judge who would informally chat with the errant child and set him straight.[3]

Several factors combined to prevent the realization of these dreams. The commitment was never total, and the separation of the juvenile process from the adult criminal process was never completed. Today, while some jurisdictions maintain separate juvenile courts, the jurisdiction over juveniles in many locales is simply a part of the workload of general jurisdiction courts, and juveniles share courthouses, courtrooms, and judges with adult criminal defendants.[4] Most frightening is that many juvenile offenders continue to be processed through adult jail facilities; one study places the number at over a half million annually.[5]

The notions of informality and the fatherly chat may have been flawed dreams from the outset. They were premised upon the court's sole concern with the welfare of the child and the necessity to rehabilitate him. Unfortunately, these altruistic commitments were not adaptable either to the realities of the system or to the problems of juvenile delinquency. History has demonstrated that juveniles are capable of committing serious crimes; that juvenile delinquents are not only vandals, joy riders, and purse snatchers, but rapists and murderers as well.[6] A "fatherly chat" between a concerned judge and a thirteen year old who has committed murder is very likely to be a meaningless and futile exchange. If the chat does affect the juvenile, what good is achieved if the judge finds no punishment option available but to send the child to a grim reformatory? And finally, today more than ever before, the hopes of rehabilitating juvenile delinquents have dwindled. Psychologists and sociologists alike have proven that an individual's values reflect one's environment—his home and his community. Can a child raised in a slum and versed in crime be taught the necessary values of human life in a reformatory? In short, although it is difficult to think of a ten year old as a hardened criminal, statistics have proven otherwise, and our juvenile courts and correctional systems can no longer afford to provide only kind counsellors and reformers.

The juvenile justice movement did achieve its desired goal of informality, which has largely been foresaken and partially reversed in the last decade. Initially, the idea of dispensing, in juvenile proceedings, with the legal mumbo-jumbo typical of adult criminal proceedings, seemed to be sound. Yet, by attempting to create an "informal" system, the juvenile courts sacrificed procedural regularity. As a result, unchecked discretion and the total absence of fairness have plagued the juvenile justice system for years. Under the guise of attending solely to the welfare of the child, coupled with the claim that the juvenile court decisions were not at all like those being made in criminal courts, children were being taken from their homes and institutionalized by proceedings that were patently unfair, resulting from an absence of standards and meaningful review of juvenile court decisions. By the 1960s it became apparent that the informality of juvenile courts had only served to rob the subjects of the court's jurisdiction of essential constitutional rights.[7] And, as Chief Justice Burger recognized in 1975, "[I]n terms of potential consequences, there is little to distinguish an adjudicatory hearing [in a juvenile case] ...from a traditional criminal prosecution."[8] The awakening to the evil attendant upon total informality has resulted in the evolution of the procedure in juvenile court trials so that it is virtually indistinguishable from the procedure in criminal courts, except for the absence of juries and public trials.

While the emphasis here has been on the failing ideal, it is important to note that the ideal itself has continuing merit and its implementation has not been all bad. It was essential to remove most juveniles from the adult criminal process and to handle their illegal conduct in a setting that protected their identities from public scrutiny and the stigma attached to criminal proceedings. In almost all jurisdictions, identities of juvenile offenders remain protected from media and public disclosure in order not to stigmatize the juvenile for life.[9] Secondly, state informal interference into the life of a juvenile may be desirable when such intervention will correct a juvenile before he matures into an adult criminal. The dilemma has been to protect the informality when it is beneficial to the child and society and to restrict and control that informality when it merely serves as a cover for discriminatory, arbitrary, and capricious judicial behavior. The goal of juvenile court reform of the 1960s and '70s was to preserve the beneficial aspects of juvenile justice while preventing excesses. Opponents of this goal contend that any interference in the juvenile process detrimentally affects the ability of juvenile courts to achieve its traditional and principal goals, the treatment and rehabilitation of the child.[10] However, the excesses have been so great and the success of treatment and rehabilitation so speculative that the arguments against procedural regularity and against introduction of constitutional rights into juvenile courts have been overcome.

Children Subject to Juvenile Court Jurisdiction

The very existence of a juvenile court is a matter for the legislature of every state. No juvenile court or separate juvenile procedures need be established. Similarly, the minimum and maximum ages for the court's special jurisdiction are established by the legislature and vary widely around the country. Most states do not set a minimum age limit for the court's jurisdiction. Naturally, where the matter involves neglect of a child the absence of a minimum age is desirable. We want our courts to have the authority to protect neglected children regardless of the child's age. It is obviously more important for a court to have that necessary authority the younger and more helpless the child. When dealing with delinquent children, however, the absence of a minimum age is somewhat of an anomaly.

Under the common law, when procedures were rough and penalties uniformly harsh and when no distinction was made about the age of the offender when it came to punishment, a minimum age did exist before a court could try a child as a criminal. Children under seven were conclusively presumed not to be responsible for their criminal acts and children between the ages of seven and fourteen were presumed not responsible, although the presumption could be rebutted.[11] A majority of American jurisdictions, however, set no minimum age for a juvenile court's jurisdiction over delinquent children. On the other hand, a majority cuts off that jurisdiction at age eighteen, with a minority varying between sixteen and nineteen.[12] Anyone accused of a criminal act who has passed the maximum age set for the jurisdiction of juvenile court will be tried as an adult in a criminal court. The statutory limits are absolutes. A youth who commits theft one week before his eighteenth birthday will likely be treated as a juvenile, but if he commits the crime eight days later he will be charged in criminal court.

Legislatures have, and some exercise, the authority to exclude certain offenses from juvenile court authority, even though the perpetrator fits within the normal age jurisdiction of the juvenile court. If a legislature chooses, a juvenile accused of murder, then, may be tried in adult criminal court subject to the penalties imposed upon adults.[13] Similarly, all states have procedures for the waiver of juvenile court jurisdiction and removal of the juvenile for trial in an adult criminal court.

Status Offenders

This substantial part of juvenile court caseloads is the most hotly debated subject concerning juvenile justice.[14] This class of children are not subject to juvenile court authority because of the neglect of others or because of their own criminal acts but because they fit a set of conditions set forth in juvenile court statutes. Status offenders find themselves in court because the legislature has extended juvenile court jurisdiction to "truants," "runaways," "disobedient," "unruly" and other such classifications.[15] In a majority of states a child may be adjudged a status offender if he or she fits into one of these categories, and most courts considering the issue have upheld the constitutionality of the classification system.[16] This system of classification provides for officials who cannot deal satisfactorily with a juvenile to seek the assistance of the court.

The procedural rules governing findings of status offenses often differ markedly from delinquency adjudications. The degree of proof may be less for a status offender, resulting in findings against status offenders upon a preponderance of the evidence, rather than requiring proof beyond a reasonable doubt as is necessary for a delinquent.[17] Similarly, the status offender may not be accorded all of the same constitutional rights that now must be provided to a juvenile who is charged with delinquency.

In a majority of states, juveniles found by a court to be status offenders are subject to the same disposition as delinquents. Little wonder, then, that authorities frequently file against juveniles as status offenders rather than as delinquents even when the filing results from commission of a criminal offense: proving the claim is easier and the disposition is likely to be the same. Prestigious groups throughout the nation have advocated abolition of status offenses, which are unconstitutional in adult criminal courts, arguing that no court should have jurisdiction over juveniles unless they commit criminal offenses.[18]

Delinquency

The great bulk of juvenile court jurisdiction involves adjudications of delinquency arising out of criminal conduct. Again, the laws vary widely across the country. The broadest delegation of authority involves statutes which vest jurisdiction over any child whose conduct would be a criminal act (a violation of a state statute or municipal violation) if committed by an adult.[19] Along the way, there are numerous variations. As mentioned, some states deprive juvenile courts of jurisdiction over children committing the most heinous crimes and vest that authority in the criminal court of general jurisdiction. Others limit juvenile court jurisdiction to criminal acts which would be a felony if committed by an adult, eliminating misdemeanors entirely.[20] Still others eliminate only traffic offenses from the juvenile court's authority.[21] Where misdemeanor or traffic cases are excluded from juvenile court authority, they are handled in the same way and in the same court as an adult's comparable offenses would be litigated. Most often, penalties for these offenses are so minor that the criminal court with authority to dispose of the matter has nowhere near the power over the individual that a juvenile court has in determining the disposition for a juvenile found to be delinquent.

Miscellaneous Jurisdiction

In many states, juvenile court authority extends beyond the child as a troublemaker or offender to the child in need. The neglected child may also come within the purview of the court's concern and that concern need not be triggered by the juvenile's criminal acts or other unruly conduct. Similarly, some juvenile courts serve as general family courts, handling all sorts of family disputes and problems. Finally, many states grant jurisdiction to their juvenile court over adults who are charged with offenses involving juveniles.[22] Thus, an adult who is charged with the criminal offense of contributing to the delinquency of a minor would be tried before a juvenile judge. In those instances, the exact procedures and constitutional rights that would apply in adult criminal courts will be observed.

Trying the Juvenile Offender as an Adult

There are three approaches commonly provided by statutes to try a juvenile in an adult criminal court, subjecting him to the same penalties that would apply to an adult offender upon conviction. Some states, however, limit the death penalty to persons over a statutorily set age.[23] The first method, already mentioned, is for the juvenile act to exclude jurisdiction over certain offenses from the juvenile court and vest them automatically in adult criminal court. These are most often the most and least heinous of offenses, murder and traffic offenses. Jurisdiction over murder may be excluded because it is felt that the treatment available through juvenile court offers insufficient protection for the community safety from repeated criminal acts by the juvenile offender. Traffic offenses are excluded because the available remedies in juvenile court may be too comprehensive and harsh compared to the penalties imposed upon adult traffic offenders.

The second approach is where concurrent jurisdiction is vested in the juvenile court and the general criminal court. Concurrent jurisdiction is generally limited to felonies or serious felonies, and the juvenile court is automatically deprived of jurisdiction when the prosecutor files charges in the adult criminal court or when the juvenile is indicted by a grand jury.[24]

The most common approach, available in all states but New York and Vermont,[25] is where the juvenile court waives the juvenile over to criminal court for trial as an adult. Because this is the most common approach and because it is fraught with the danger of arbitrariness resulting from the exercise of vast discretion, waiver of the juvenile has been treated to the most attention. Which juveniles are subject to waiver is a matter determined by statute and naturally varies from state to state, but the procedure is generally limited to older juveniles (fifteen year olds being most commonly the youngest group subject to waiver for trial as adults) who are charged with the most serious offenses.[26]

The decision to waive the juvenile for trial as an adult is made by juvenile court judges, generally at the request of the state. The criteria for waiver are again set by statute, but invariably the issue that is being determined is whether the treatment available in juvenile court is sufficiently comprehensive and of long enough duration to protect the community from the dangerous propensities and additional criminal acts of this juvenile. When determining this issue, the welfare of the juvenile is not the court's principal concern; the welfare of the community is of paramount importance. The statutes direct the court to consider the history, maturity, and prior criminal record of the child and the violence of the alleged criminal act. The ultimate question boils down to whether the services available through the juvenile courts offer the prospects for protection of the public and the likelihood of the juvenile's rehabilitation. Throughout this process the court's eye is on the length of time of the juvenile commitment. If the juvenile offender, charged with a crime of great violence, is almost eighteen and will not be under the court's supervision for long, then the court's ability to protect the public is marginal and the juvenile is likely to be waived for trial as an adult.[27]

Naturally, the decision to waive the juvenile is one of the most important that is made by the juvenile court. The result of that decision determines whether the juvenile will be treated if found delinquent or punished if convicted. Often the decision is made under great pressure, following a particularly heinous crime under the glare of news media publicity and demands by law enforcement and prosecuting authorities that the alleged offender be subjected to adult punishment. In the past, waiver decisions were made informally and haphazardly, with scant attention being paid to the statutory criteria. The Supreme Court entered into this picture in 1966 and imposed a set of standards on the waiver decision to limit arbitrariness and to insure a semblance of fairness in the decision.

In a case arising in juvenile court in the District of Columbia, *Kent v. United States,*[28] the Supreme Court held that a juvenile is entitled to a hearing before he may be waived into adult criminal court. Kent was arrested in connection with charges of housebreaking, robbery, and rape, and despite his attorney's request for a hearing and for access to the juvenile court's social service file on his client, Kent was waived to adult criminal court without rulings on his attorney's requests. The waiver order simply stated that it was done after the required "full investigation." Recognizing the critical importance of the waiver decision, the Supreme Court imposed standards to achieve procedural regularity consistent with the basic requirements of due process and fairness. Without requiring all of the procedures that would be required in a criminal case, the Court indicated that for the waiver decision to be valid there must be notice that the issue is to be determined; there must be a hearing where evidence is presented and where the case against waiver may be offered; the juvenile must be afforded effective assistance of counsel; and a statement of reasons justifying the waiver decision must appear in the record. *Kent* requires that the statement of reasons not be a general statement but one that is fairly specific, including relevant facts supporting the decision and susceptible to review.

Not all state courts have closely adhered to the *Kent* requirements. Since the case arose in the District of Columbia, some states have circumscribed the Supreme Court requirements, reasoning that the case was not premised on constitutional rights but was decided under the Supreme Court's authority as the chief court in the federal court system.[29] Later Supreme Court decisions applying various constitutional principles to the juvenile process as well as the reliance of the Supreme Court in *Kent* on fundamental requirements of due process, however, amply demonstrate the constitutional framework of the *Kent* decision and its applicability to state juvenile courts.

Constitutional Rights of Juveniles in Delinquency Proceedings

Kent v. United States was only the first step in the process of introducing procedural regularity into juvenile courts. There had been a reluctance on the part of courts to upset the informality attendant upon juvenile court proceedings. Some thought that it would be a step backward.[30] The evolution of constitutional rights that was affecting state criminal courts had sidestepped juvenile courts because delinquency proceedings are not criminal proceedings, and the outcome is not punishment but treatment. Within that framework of informality, however, resided inordinate and unchecked discretion, and there was increasing fear that the discretion was being exercised arbitrarily and frequently not in the juvenile's best interests. Finally, whether the outcome of a juvenile proceeding is called treatment or punishment, juveniles, like their adult counterparts in criminal courts, were being deprived of their freedom by being taken from the custody of their parents and placed in correctional facilities. The Supreme Court recognized that the reformatories in which juveniles are placed, regardless of the names given to such places, are institutions of confinement in which a child is incarcerated: a world with regimented routing and institutional hours, and peopled by guards, custodians, and delinquents. After reciting the similarities between juvenile institutions and jails and prisons, the Supreme Court, in a landmark decision one year after *Kent, In re Gault*[31] dealt a heavy blow to juvenile court indifference to the constitutional rights of children. Gerald Gault was picked up by police for making an obscene telephone call and was charged as a delinquent. After a proceeding in a Phoenix, Arizona, juvenile court, in which the Supreme Court indicated he had been denied the following basic rights: notice of the charges, right to counsel, right to confrontation and cross-examination, the privilege against self-incrimination, and the rights to a transcript and appellate review, fifteen-year-old Gerald Gault was adjudged a delinquent child and committed to a state institution for juveniles until released or until age twenty one. As a juvenile, Gault was sentenced for a period up to six years; had he been an adult, the maximum penalty for a comparable offense would have been a fine of five to fifty dollars or a jail sentence not exceeding two months. Limiting its decision only to those issues that had to be decided, the Supreme Court in *Gault* held: (1) that a juvenile and his parents are entitled to written notice of the specific charges to be considered; (2) that the right to counsel applies in those juvenile court cases which may result in the institutionalization of the child; (3) that the privilege against self-incrimination is to be observed in juvenile proceedings, and (4) that a juvenile has the right to confront and cross-examine witnesses against him.

The *Kent* and *Gault* decisions cut through the mythology that had surrounded juvenile courts. In both cases, the Supreme Court rejected the argument that the rehabilitative values of the juvenile process would be undercut by requiring constitutional procedures. Neither case held, and the Supreme Court has never required, that the procedures of a delinquency hearing must match identically the constitutional procedures demanded in adult criminal courts. The limitations imposed in *Kent* and *Gault*, as well as in subsequent decisions, simply mandated that juvenile court proceedings not fall below minimal levels of fairness and due process. Consistent with the Court's intent to insure minimal levels of due process while still respecting the special role and tasks of juvenile courts, later decisions have rejected the right to a jury trial[32] as inappropriate to juvenile court, while holding that the guarantee against double jeopardy[33] and the requirement that guilt be proven beyond a reasonable doubt[34] are applicable to delinquency hearings.

Juvenile Court Procedures

Except for those procedures mandated by the Constitution, the states are free to fashion their own juvenile court procedures. While this freedom leads to great diversity, there is a common pattern that is evident in the handling of juveniles.

When a juvenile is taken into custody by a police officer, all too often the initial processing is through an adult jail facility. Exposing juveniles, even for very short periods, to the atmosphere prevalent in adult jails, even if efforts are made to segregate the juveniles from adult offenders, has been severely criticized. There has been great impetus to get the child out of a jail and into a juvenile facility. Depending upon the nature of the juvenile facility, this society may well be concentrating upon nomenclature rather than upon substance, but even so the debilitating nature of jails is plainly evident to warrant the haste.

The issue whether the federal constitutional right to bail is applicable to juvenile court proceedings has not been litigated so the states have developed their own procedures.[35] Most provide for a detention hearing to be held shortly after arrest, and state statutes provide criteria for the judge to consider in determining whether to release or detain the juvenile. Naturally, the drive in most states has been to release the child into the custody of his parents as quickly as possible. However, this is not always possible. Parents may be unwilling to take a child back into their home, or they may be unable to reliably promise to insure his presence in court when needed, or the juvenile may be a danger to himself or others in the community. Before a juvenile may be detained, though, due process must be observed, requiring that the decision not be arrived at carelessly and informally. Some courts have held that a probable cause determination that the juvenile is delinquent is a constitutional prerequisite to a detention order.[36] Evolving out of the many lower court decisions is a pattern requiring that juvenile court judges explain the reasons justifying the detention order and that the reasons be based upon evidence presented at the hearing.[37] Once the decision is made to detain the juvenile, almost all states require that he be detained in a specialized facility, and some have recognized that the juvenile's right to treatment begins at the moment of detention and may not be delayed until after a finding that he is a delinquent and in need of special treatment.[38]

Intake procedures developed in juvenile courts present the most unique departure from adult criminal court proceedings. Reflecting the goal of the juvenile court movement, that its sole purpose is to help the child, case screening has been more finely developed in juvenile cases than in criminal cases. Most cases are weeded out at the police level and children are sent home in their parents' custody without ever involving the court. Just as in the handling of adults, this exercise of police discretion is fraught with the dangers attendant upon unbridled discretion. The decision of the police officer is likely his own, reflecting his subjective values, and is rarely monitored or controlled. Few cities have developed a set of standards and procedures like those existing for the Chicago Police Department, which requires that the family be referred to a community resource agency for follow-up care.[39]

Even when a case is referred to the juvenile court, less than half will get to an adjudicatory stage.[40] Here, too, most are screened out at the intake stage. Cases are disposed of at this stage for the same reasons that prosecutors screen out adult criminal cases—e.g. relative unimportance of the incident or lack of proof—but cases are also weeded out at this stage through informal adjustment, where a probation officer at the intake proceeding establishes a program of treatment and supervision for the child without involvement of the court. Informal adjustments are often beneficial because they provide treatment without the trauma associated with a court appearance and trial. There are drawbacks, however. The probation officer has great discretion in the controls and treatment that are prescribed, and the program may involve a significant curtailment of the juvenile's freedom and his parents' authority, without a judicial determination of delinquency, including a finding that the juvenile is in need of treatment.[41] In order to strike a balance between the benefits of informal adjustment and its dangers, many states have limited the scope of this informal interference in the juvenile's life to a period of three months in order to curtail the power of the probation officer.[42]

There is no one national approach to determining which cases will actually be heard in court. Some states rely upon the probation officer's determination, theoretically at least, based upon the age of the juvenile and the seriousness of the offense; others require review by a prosecutor, and still others preclude informal adjustment when the juvenile denies the allegations that have been made against him.[43]

Once a case reaches the adjudicatory stage, the proceedings will not be too dissimilar to a trial in a criminal court. Although juvenile cases are labeled as civil matters, statutes in most states provide that the rules applicable to criminal cases are to be observed in delinquency cases.[44] *Gault* set the framework to insure fairness in delinquency proceedings; the procedures are mandated but the question remains whether they are fully observed by the judges in juvenile courts who are still largely wed to the notion that the interests of the child are best served by a judge operating in an informal "fatherly" manner. Perhaps the most important safeguard is the presence of counsel who can insure that a determination of delinquency is premised upon relevant evidence presented in court and not based upon reports of social workers, which may be helpful in determining disposition and treatment but are irrelevant to the issue of guilt or innocence. A finding of delinquency is two-fold: the court must find beyond a reasonable doubt that the juvenile committed the criminal act upon which the delinquency claim is based and that the juvenile is in need of treatment.[45]

Disposition

Once there is a finding of delinquency, disposition is far more complex than the punishment decision in a criminal case. In the latter, the criminal court may choose the punishment that will best suit the needs of the community. In a juvenile case, disposition may take into account the needs of the community but the greatest concern must be for the welfare of the child, and the disposition must be suited to his need for treatment.

Disposition is preceded all over the country by a separate hearing. Although this phase of a juvenile case was not covered in *Kent* and *Gault,* it is fairly certain that the constitutional requirement of a hearing applies to this critical phase of a juvenile case which might result in the loss of freedom and the institutionalization of the child.[46] Likewise, the right to counsel is equally important at the disposition hearing. At this phase of the case, the procedures will be less formal and the court, in choosing the appropriate treatment, may have access to material, such as probation reports and the juvenile's prior record, which was not relevant, and consequently not admissible, at the adjudicatory hearing.[47] Traditionally, social reports were not made available to the juvenile, his parents, or lawyer, but while that practice prevails today, the substance of these reports is generally available for challenge.[48]

Juvenile court judges have great discretion in determining the appropriate treatment for delinquents, as well as those children found to be unruly and in need of guidance and neglected children. Probation in the custody of the juvenile's parents, coupled with supervision and community-based treatment, is the traditional and still most common disposition.[49] Yet, community-based probation programs suffer in many cities from the same ills affecting adult probation services, too heavy caseloads, and insufficiently funded health and vocational programs. But the judge has the authority to remove the juvenile from his parents' custody and place him in a foster home or other juvenile facility; some of these facilities have security measures rivaling in intensity the security facilities of adult prisons.

Traditionally, commitment of a juvenile to an institution was for an indeterminate period up to the juvenile's twenty-first birthday, accounting for results such as in *Gault* where a relatively minor offense resulted in a sentence of up to six years. But today reduction of the age of majority to eighteen has reduced juvenile court jurisdiction to that age in many states.[50] Still, under the guise that juvenile commitment is not punishment, incarceration resulting from a delinquency adjudication often exceeds by several years the maximum penalty that an adult might receive for committing the same act.

Emerging as a limitation on the discretion of juvenile court judges to dispose of cases as they see fit is the developing concept of the juvenile's right to treatment. If a finding of delinquency is dependent on a finding that the juvenile is in need of treatment and is not predicated on the state's right to punish an errant youth, then the juvenile has a right to be treated and not punished.[51] This right has been sought on behalf of incarcerated juveniles where the claim is that the institution is so anti-rehabilitative that it should be closed or when it is claimed that a particular form of "treatment" is so abusive or debilitating that it is anti-rehabilitative. One Texas court pioneering in this area found a corollary right "to the least restrictive alternative treatment that is consistent with the purpose of [the juvenile's] custody."[52] Under this principle, incarceration would be a last alternative and must be justified as consistent with the individual's need for particular treatment. This doctrine is consistent with the proclaimed aims of the juvenile court movement. After all, the only justification for juvenile courts, their special procedures, and in many instances questionable practices, is the rehabilitation of the juvenile offender so that he does not graduate to adult criminal court. Cast in that light it makes sense that each disposition be tested to determine whether it is appropriate and whether it is reasonably likely to aid in the fulfillment of that goal.

Discussion Questions

1. What danger occurs when a juvenile court judge feels a child's interests are best served when the judicial proceedings are conducted in an informal and fatherly manner?

2. Discuss the importance of In re Gault with respect to juvenile justice. What is the importance of guaranteeing juvenile offenders' due process rights? Why must these rights be safeguarded? Support your answer.

3. "The Kent and Gault decisions cut through the mythology that had surrounded juvenile courts." Explain this "mythology" and discuss its effect on juvenile justice.

4. If the juvenile court movement's sole purpose is "to help the child", how has this goal been thwarted and by whom? Support your answer.

5. Discuss the importance of discretion as it applies to juvenile offenders. How does discretion relate to the statement that "juvenile commitment is not punishment"?

Notes

1. The first juvenile court in America was formed in Cook County, Chicago, Illinois in 1899. The Illinois Law which created the court, aptly called the Juvenile Court Act, placed virtually all children involved with the courts under a single jurisdiction. Ten years after its inception, this court began to move toward a more clinically oriented approach and the major emphasis was placed upon finding out why a particular crime was committed. See Alan R. Coffey, *Juvenile Corrections* (Englewood Cliffs, N.J.: Prentice-Hall, 1975).

   The courts then developed an approach whereby their special weapon was probation. The probation officer would act as counselor to the child, thus providing constant contact between the court and youth. See Howard G. Paulsen and Charles H. Whitebread, *Juvenile Law Procedure* (Reno, Nevada: National Council of Juvenile Court Judges, 1974), p. 3.
2. In a paper read by Mary Carpenter, an English prison reformer, at the annual meeting of the National Conference of Charities in 1975, she stated: "In all cases, I object to large institutions for children, where individuality is destroyed, and where there cannot be any home influence." And still another reformer, Reverend Nichols, declared: "Remove a boy from his old haunts of vice, shut him out from the world, shut him up by himself, let him march with locked step, wheel him to the right, wheel him to the left with the most precise military discipline, yet know that when your manoeuvers are through, you are ignorant of the mind and soul of this tractable machine." Sanford J. Fox, "Juvenile Justice Reform: An Historical Perspective," 22 *Stan. L Rev.* 1187, 1969-70, pp. 1208-1209.
3. "The Juvenile Court," wrote Miriam Van Waters, a referee in a California juvenile court, "is conceived in the spirit of the clinic." Paulsen, *Juvenile Law,* p. 2; also see W. v. Family Court, 24 N.Y.2d 196, 198, 247 N.E.2d 253, 254 (1969), rev'd sub. nom; and In re Winship, 397 U.S. 358 (1970), where the Court

noted that "the proceedings were not designed to be punitive but were for the protection and training of a child found in difficulty; and would be administered by humane and parentally minded judges whose end was not to punish, but to save the child."

4. See Robert D. Vinter, "The Juvenile Court As An Institution," in *Task Force Report: Juvenile Delinquency Youth Crime* (The President's Commission on Law Enforcement and Administration of Justice, 1967). (Hereinafter referred to as *Task Force).*
5. Rosemary C. Sarri, *Under Lock Key: Juvenile Jail Detention* (Michigan: The National Assessment of Juvenile Corrections, 1974), p. 85.
6. See an address by Dorris Clarke, "The Nature of the Offenses of Delinquency and Crime, and Its Impact Upon the Community," in *Youth Crime,* edited by Frank J. Cohen (New York: International Universities Press, 1970).
7. See Justice Stewart's dissent in In re Gault, 387 U.S. 1, at 79 (1967), where he said that this was "a long step backwards into the 19th century ... a juvenile proceeding's whole purpose and mission is the very opposite of the mission and purpose of a prosecution in criminal court. The object of one is correction of a condition. The object of the other is conviction and punishment of a criminal act."
8. Breed v. Jones, 421 U.S. 519, 531 (1975).
9. Paulsen, *Juvenile Law,* pp. 21-22; Mich. Comp. Laws Ann. § *712A.23;* 11 Penn. Stat § 261, where they forbid the use of court or arrest records in later proceedings because of the similar fear that the child will suffer from the criminal stigma.
10. In re Gault, supra, at 79.
11. Sanford J. Fox, *Juvenile Courts Nutshell* (St. Paul, Minn.: West, 1977), p. 30.
12. See § 51.02(1)(B) *Texas Family Code.*
13. Ibid.
14. C.f. *Standards* (1976), Part 4 Judicial Services, which attacked the inadequacy of the approach to status offenders: "The report expresses dissatisfaction with the current approach to status offenders and with recent proposals to abolish judicial authority over these areas." For another approach, see Paul H. Hahn, *The Juvenile Offender Law* (Cincinnati: Anderson, 1978), pp. 268-69.
15. *Standards.*
16. District of Columbia v. B. J. R., 332 A.2d 58 (D.C. App. 1975); c.f. some courts have struck down some provisions which were overly broad, Gesicki v. Oswald, 336 F. Supp. 371 (S.D.N.Y. 1971), aff'd Oswald v. Gesicki, 406 U.S. 913 (1972).
17. Fox, *Juvenile Courts,* p. 41.
18. *Task Force,* p. 25, in which they state that "this situation is ripe for overreaching, for imposition of the judge's own code of youthful conduct."
19. Hahn, *Juvenile Offender,* 273-74.
20. Fox, *Juvenile Courts,* p. 109.
21. Ibid., p. 48.
22. See People v. Schoos, 15 Ill. App.3d 964, 305 N.E.2d 560, 562 (1973), in which the court declared that "the state has a compelling interest to protect children from abuse and neglect"; c.f. Roe v. Connecticut, 417 F. Supp. 76 (M.D. Ala. 1976), in which the Alabama statute against neglected children was held to infringe upon the privacy and autonomy of the family, some cases emphasize the detrimental effects upon children, In re Johnson, 188 Neb. 677, 198 N.W.2d 466 (1972), in which the mother's failure to keep the house clean and furnished was sufficient grounds for the court to act.
23. Rhodes v. S., 91 Nev. 17, 530 P.2d 1199 (1975).
24. Dorsey v. S., 31 Md. App. 324, 356 A.2d 290 (1976).
25. Paulsen, *Juvenile Law,* p. 132.

26. Ibid., p. 134. The author cites the fact that the states are evenly divided as to whether to restrict waiver of jurisdiction to those cases where the offense would be a felony if committed by an adult.
27. Ibid., p. 142.
28. Kent v. United States, 383 U.S. 541 (1966).
29. See Cradle v. Peyton, 208 Va. 243, 156 S.E.2d 874 (1967), in which the Virginia Supreme Court of Appeals held that *Kent* was not decided on constitutional grounds; also see Commonwealth v. Roberts, 362 Mass. 357, 285 N.E.2d 919 (1972).
30. See Justice Stewart's dissent in In re Gault, 387 U.S. 1, 79 (1967).
31. In re Gault, supra.
32. McKeiver v. Pennsylvania, 403 U.S. 528 (1971).
33. Breed v. Jones, 421 U.S. 519 (1975).
34. In re Winship, 397 U.S. 358 (1970).
35. Coffey, *Juvenile Corrections,* pp. 160-62.
36. See Moss v. Weaver, 525 F.2d 1258 (5th Cir. 1976), which applied Gerstein v. Pugh, 420 U.S. 103 (1975) to juvenile delinquents.
37. Doe v. State, 487 P.2d 47 (Alaska, 1971).
38. Creek v. Stone, 379 F.2d 106 (D.C. Cir. 1967); Fulwood v. Stone, 394 F.2d 939 (D.C. Cir. 1967).
39. Paulsen, *Juvenile Law,* p. 124.
40. Fox, *Juvenile Courts,* p. 133.
41. Ibid., p. 214.
42. See *Juvenile Justice Delinquency Prevention,* Standard 22.2 (National Advisory Committee on Criminal Justice Standards and Goals, Washington, 1976), where they discuss the necessity for state standards in intake and corrections. (Hereinafter referred to as *Standards and Goals).*
43. Coffey, *Juvenile Corrections,* p. 159.
44. *Standards and Goals,* p. 407.
45. This fundamental proposition was recognized in In re Patterson, 210 Kan. 245, 449 P.2d 1131 (1972).
46. *Standards and Goals,* p. 402.
47. Ibid., p. 445.
48. Paulsen, *Juvenile Law,* p. 172.
49. Hahn, *Juvenile Offender,* p. 313.
50. Ibid., p. 265.
51. For a discussion of rehabilitation and correctional efforts, see *Task Force,* pp. 422-24.
52. Fox, *Juvenile Courts,* p. 233.

No. 43M - Commitment---General

Municipal C

of

State of Ne

State of New Jersey,

vs.

Defendant.

STATE OF NEW JERSEY,

COUNTY OF } ss.

To the Sheriff or Jailer, or any Constable, Marshal, Police Of
to any officer or Trooper of the New Jersey State Police:

The above named defendant
having this day been convicted by the court of the offense of

(Describe the offense for which the defendant was convicted and cite specific sta
and having been sentenced to imprisonment for the period of

Part IV
The Resolution

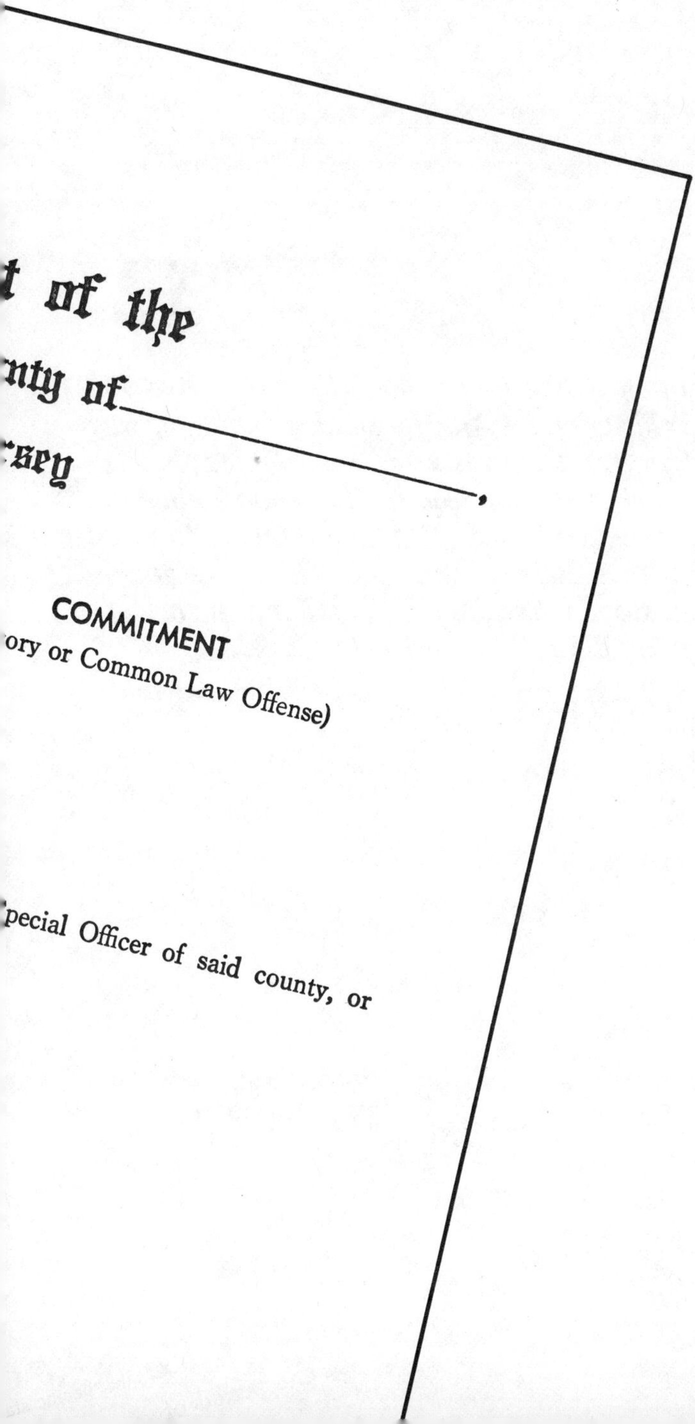

t of the

nty of________________________,

rsey

COMMITMENT

ory or Common Law Offense)

pecial Officer of said county, or

12.

The judge had gotten to the point where he said, "Are you pleading guilty to this crime?" All of a sudden it hit me, why should you plead guilty? This was what was running through my mind, now why should you plead guilty to something you didn't do? All of a sudden I said, "No, I don't want to plead guilty. Continue with these proceedings." The judge got up from his bench and stood in the door with his hands on his hips and looked at me. He didn't know what to think.

Trial and Appeal

The layman associates criminal cases with trials and courtroom drama. Yet, many citizens would be surprised at the small percentage of criminal cases that actually go to trial. While the figures vary across the country, the national average is about ten to fifteen percent of felony cases and even a smaller share of misdemeanors. More cases are dismissed outright by prosecutors than are tried. Yet almost all the pretrial procedures are designed and shaped by the needs of those few cases actually tried.

Trials vary in drama and intensity, depending upon the seriousness of the matter, the complexity of the issues, and the pretrial interest and publicity which the case has generated. A non-jury misdemeanor can be tried in less than an hour; an uncomplicated felony jury trial can be completed in a day. Some trials, however, last months, occupying and disrupting the lives of the defendants, the witnesses, and the other key participants involved in the adjudication process.

Defendant's Initial Trial Rights

A defendant's right to a trial includes his right to be present at trial.[1] Trials may not commence without the defendant's presence, although his conduct during the trial may result in a waiver of that right and its being completed in his absence.[2] As discussed in Chapter 8, the trial rights contained in the Sixth Amendment are the exclusive rights of the defendant. Thus the accused has the right to personally confront the witnesses against him and assist (and now participate) in the presentation of his defense. Even where an accused is not actively participating in the trial, his presence is essential in assisting counsel by providing details of information about state witnesses, which the defense attorney did not previously know, and to corroborate or refute for counsel's benefit statements made by witnesses.

As in other constitutional rights that we have previously discussed, the right to be present at one's own trial is not absolute. If it were, defendants would have an open license to interrupt and disrupt the proceedings. Consequently, that right to be present is conditioned upon the accused's willingness to let the trial proceed. It may be fine theatre for a defendant to shout "liar" during a prosecution witness' testimony or to rise at the conclusion, denouncing it as all lies and prejudice. But such conduct is not tolerated. If the defendant wishes to testify and be heard by the jury, his opportunity arises during the defense's presentation of evidence. At this point, the defendant, under oath, can present his side of the story. Until that point in trial, unless he is acting as counsel for himself, the defendant has no right to be heard and must refrain from denunciations of witnesses, lawyers, and judge, and not make side comments to the jury. His role at this stage is confined to providing the defense attorney with ammunition for cross-examination.

Failure on the part of an accused to abide by these rules can bring a variety of penalties. An isolated eruption by the defendant will evoke hardly more than a rebuke and admonition from the judge. Repeated disruptions, however, will elicit more severe retribution. The defendant may be held *in contempt* by the court for repeated disruptions and fined or sentenced to days in jail; a judge's pronouncement of this penalty must take place out of the hearing of the jury. More serious penalties for contempt may be forthcoming but, in that event, the defendant is entitled to a separate trial before another judge after the conclusion of the criminal case.[3] If these steps fail to deter the defendant's unruly behavior, other alternatives exist to insure that order in the court will prevail.

Judges have a wide latitude when adopting devices to achieve courtroom order. A defendant may be gagged and shackled if that is what is required for the trial to continue, or he may be entirely removed from the courtroom.[4] Both measures are reserved for extreme cases and neither helps the defendant avoid conviction. The gagging and shackling of an accused, generally accompanied by his muffled sounds and resistance to the bindings, obviously makes an accused look like a wild animal and enhances the prosecution's attempts to make him look dangerous. Removal from the courtroom denies to the defense the opportunity for the team effort that effective cross-examination of opposing witnesses requires. Consultations at the end of the court day or after the witnesses' testimony, even if daily transcripts are provided, will hardly substitute for the constant consultation that should be taking place.

An accused may waive the right to be present. If the defendant voluntarily absents himself once a trial has commenced, the trial may be continued and even a verdict may be reached.[5] Any other rule would allow a defendant to prevent the completion of his trial once it appeared that a guilty verdict would be forthcoming. Were the defendant's voluntary absence not deemed a waiver of the right, disappearances in order to cause a mistrial and prevent the return of a verdict would be common.

The defendant also has a right to a public trial.[6] This Sixth Amendment guarantee is a further attempt to check injustice. Secret trials are forbidden so that the proceedings can be publicly aired and injustices noted and corrected. Even though the Sixth Amendment solely protects defendants' rights, presumably there is no right to waive a public trial. While a secret trial may better serve the interests of the defendant by avoiding publicity and public commentary about his conduct, the right of the people to be aware of official proceedings is protected by the First Amendment's freedom of the press.[7] The right belongs to the people, and the news media have been aggressive in its pursuit. While the trial must be public, some proceedings may be properly closed to the press and public alike in order to protect the accused's subsequent right to a fair trial. Consequently, on motions to suppress evidence, courts have conducted hearings privately without access to the public or news media.[8] Since the very issue at such a hearing is whether the evidence may be used at trial, conducting the proceedings in private may be necessary to insure that evidence ruled to be inadmissible does not make its way to prospective jurors through newspapers or radio and television news reports.

The Sixth Amendment also guarantees that the public trial shall be held in the "state and district wherein the crime shall have been committed."[9] The purpose of this protection is to prevent government harassment by dragging a defendant away from home for trial. Yet sometimes the publicity surrounding a crime or local feeling generated about a particularly gruesome crime is so great that it would be virtually impossible to impanel an objective jury in the district where the crime occurred. Under these circumstances, an accused is entitled to a *change of venue,* relocation to another county or court district where a fair trial can be obtained.[10] Many jurisdictions, by statute, extend the opportunity to a change of venue to the state, as well, when the local atmosphere is riled to such heights that the prosecution could not get a fair trial.[11]

Finally, in preparation for trial, the Sixth Amendment guarantees to a defendant the state's mechanisms for "compulsory process for obtaining witnesses in his favor."[12] Thus witnesses may be compelled to appear and testify on behalf of the defense, just as they may be compelled to testify for the prosecution. Subpoenas are served according to local law in the same manner as they are to state witnesses and carry the same full backing of the court.[13] Failure to comply can lead to a finding that the witness is in contempt and the reluctant witness may be punished by the court. Without compulsory process, the backing and support of the state, a defendant might be virtually unable to convince any of his witnesses to appear and testify. Anyone, then, who is called to testify, whether he is sympathetic to the "cause" or not, must meet the defense's request.

Pretrial Publicity

An avalanche of pretrial publicity can undermine the atmosphere necessary for a fair trial.[14] Full-scale media coverage of a crime can fill the minds of potential jurors to the extent that they may be unable to separate what they hear at trial from what they have previously read and heard about the crime prior to the trial. Moreover, when a suspect is apprehended, news reports are filled with details, some true and some false, about that person's life and prior criminal record. Often the information is fed to the media by law enforcement officials and personnel in the prosecutor's office. Much of the information is not verified, often it is hearsay, and frequently it is irrelevant to the issues that will be litigated at trial (and as such are inadmissible).

To the schooled eye, both police and prosecutorial efforts frequently seem to be aimed at trying the case in the newspapers and on television before the trial ever begins. In most cities there is too much crime for the media to concentrate upon one specific incident and suspect. But invariably in every large community each year one sensational crime does occur which sorely tests the accused's constitutional right to a fair trial. In such cases, the defense is faced with potential jurors whose minds have been conditioned to believe in the suspect's guilt from "evidence" that they have been exposed to and which may or may not be corroborated at trial.

Patty Hearst's prosecution was one that involved an unprecedented amount of national publicity. Hearst was kidnapped by the Symbionese Liberation Army and made the subject of bizarre ransom demands. She apparently was converted to her captors' cause (although at her trial the claim was made, only to be rejected by the jury, that she was forced to join them) after which she participated in a string of criminal acts, primarily a bank robbery for which she was tried and convicted in federal court. As a fugitive for over a year, Hearst was "fair game" for the press and public officials and she was constantly condemned, to the extent that even the Attorney General of the United States referred to her as "a common criminal."[15] By the time she was captured, only two kinds of potential jurors could claim to have been oblivious to the extensive publicity: those who would lie simply to serve as jurors for such a sensational case and those who would claim a total ignorance of and disinterest in news events.

Courts are faced in situations like Hearst's with balancing the accused's Sixth Amendment rights to a fair trial and the public's right to know, which is protected within the First Amendment clause guaranteeing the freedom of the press. Until very recently the Supreme Court was loathe to even suggest that in these circumstances a court should restrain the right of the press to publish what it saw fit. However, in *Nebraska Press Association v. Stuart,*[16] a 1977 case involving a mass murder, a bare majority of the Supreme Court indicated that under some circumstances some restraint upon the press might be tolerated. Fittingly, the conditions imposed in that opinion are so stringent, and even then only subscribed to by a bare majority of the Court, that it is unlikely that they will serve as the basis for future restraints. Even to consider restraint upon the press, it must be clear on the record, and not simply conjecture, that "publicity, unchecked, would so distort the views of potential jurors that twelve could not be found who would, under proper instructions, fulfill their sworn duty to render a just verdict exclusively on the evidence presented in open court."[17] Before even weighing this course of action, a court must first consider alternatives to it, such as a change of venue. Then if the alternatives do not work prior to imposing a restraining order, the court must establish "the probability ... with [a] degree of certainty"[18] that a fair trial will be impossible without very limited restraints upon the press. The Court in *Nebraska Press Association* intended to make trial courts hesitate and proceed cautiously before barring the press from pretrial proceedings, at the same time that it made that option available. In 1979, however, the Court, demonstrating its recent hostility to the press, relaxed the earlier standards and indicated that the press may be barred from pretrial hearings when a trial court balances the press' First Amendment rights against a defendant's Sixth Amendment rights, and finds a closed hearing necessary to protect the defendant's interests in a fair trial.[18]

Alternatives discussed by the Court will work in most cases. Changing the location of trial to another county where the news media has not given the crime much publicity provides an effective remedy in many cases. It would not have in the Hearst prosecution because the barrage of publicity was national in scope. Postponement of trial until the attention focused on the case subsides was also suggested by the Supreme Court, but that remedy is far from perfect. Once the rescheduled date nears, extensive follow-up coverage of the case will also resume. Further there is the risk, regardless of the time that has elapsed, that information about the case will be imbedded in the subconscious minds of the jurors and weigh heavily upon an individual juror's decision in the case.

Most frequently courts have been relying upon "gag orders" not upon the press but upon public officials and the lawyers involved in a case. Public officials are subject to the court's authority, and lawyers as officers of the court must also respond to its directives.[19] Theoretically, this should work since most trial information is fed to the press by the police and lawyers. The American Bar Association standards, while calling for restraint by the news media, recognized that the main obligation to assure a fair trial rests upon lawyers. To that end, the Association advocated revision of the *Canons of Professional Ethics* to reflect that obligation:

> From the time of arrest, issuance of an arrest warrant or the filing of a complaint, information, or indictment in any criminal matter until the commencement of trial or disposition without trial, a lawyer associated with the prosecution or defense shall not release or authorize the release of any extrajudicial statement, for dissemination by any means of public communication, relating to that matter and concerning:
>
> 1. The prior criminal record (including arrests, indictments, or other charges of crime), or the character or reputation of the accused, except that the lawyer may make a factual statement of the ac-

cused's name, age, residence, occupation, and family status, and if the accused has not been apprehended, a lawyer associated with the prosecution may release any information necessary to aid in his apprehension or to warn the public of any dangers he may present.

2. The existence or contents of any confession, admission, or statement given by the accused, or the refusal or failure of the accused to make any statement.
3. The performance of any examinations or tests or the accused's refusal or failure to submit to an examination or test.
4. The identity, testimony, or credibility of prospective witnesses, except that the lawyer may announce the identity of the victim if the announcement is not otherwise prohibited by law.
5. The possibility of a plea of guilty to the offense charged or a lesser offense.
6. Any opinion as to the accused's guilt or innocence or as to the merits of the case or the evidence in the case.[20]

To be effective, these standards must be applied in all cases and made applicable by the courts to the police. This has not been the common experience in this country and, instead, "gag orders" in particular cases have been imposed. There are several problems with gag orders, however, that limit their effectiveness and make them, in some instances, unfair. The order is generally not made until the trial court has jurisdiction, which can often be a month or more after an arrest and many months after the commission of the crime. By that time, the news may well have been filled with information provided by the police and lawyers. Also a defendant may not have a lawyer at the outset of the case and a gag order imposed later may be unfair because the press has aired police and prosecutor information for months. The Hearst case is a classic example: by the time F. Lee Bailey was hired to represent Patty Hearst, she had already been the subject for over a year of extensive, negative publicity. The order restraining the participants in the case from discussing it publicly seemed even-handed but, in fact, simply prevented the defense from "catching up." Finally, one of the major problems with enforcing a gag order is that reporters are unwilling to identify the source of the "leak." Confident of this fact, lawyers and police can avoid a gag order with impunity virtually because they know that few reporters are willing to divulge valuable sources of information.

Gag orders offer limited protection then. The most that can be accomplished is the creation of a "sanitary" atmosphere in the immediate period before trial with the hope that what has come before has not unalterably sullied the system's ability to afford an accused a fair trial.

Once trial commences, the court's ability increases. Jurors are admonished not to discuss the case with anyone nor to read newspaper accounts or listen to radio or television reports about the case. Moreover, when the coverage is extensive because of widespread interest in the case, the court may order the jury sequestered, sheltered in a hotel and isolated from the rest of the community. As to pretrial publicity, when a change of venue is neither desirable nor granted, the defense attorney must rely upon his ability to pick good jurors and to utilize the opportunities afforded during the jury selection process to educate them as to their functions and obligations.

Jury Trial

The right to a jury trial perhaps is secondary only to the right to counsel as the most important right enumerated in the Sixth Amendment. Maintenance of the jury system was one of the first rights of Englishmen incorporated into the constitutions of the first American states.[21] A "jury of one's peers" has traditionally been viewed as essential to criminal defendants in order to prevent oppression, "to protect against unfounded criminal charges brought to eliminate enemies and against judges too responsive to the voice of higher authority."[22] Lay jurors also represent the voice of the "ethical morality," permitting the common concepts of "right" and "wrong" to be heard in a determination of guilt or innocence.

The federal constitutional right to a trial by jury extends to all prosecutions of serious offenses, defined as those crimes carrying a possible penalty of more than six months.[23] Independent of the federal guarantee, many state constitutions and statutes extend the right further to offenses carrying a substantial fine or any potential loss of liberty.[24]

The federal constitutional guarantee as it applies to the states, however, does not extend to a jury of twelve. The Supreme Court has upheld the right of a state to impanel juries of as few as six persons, that number deemed sufficient to promote group deliberation, to prevent outside intimidation, and to provide a fair opportunity for obtaining a cross section of the community.[25] Nonetheless, the twelve-person jury, still required in all federal prosecutions, is maintained in most states as a matter of state law.[26]

Because the defendant has the right to waive a constitutional right, he may waive his right to a jury trial and elect to be tried by a judge instead. This right to waive, however, is limited in some states where by statute the prosecution also has a right to a jury trial.[27] Waiver of the right by a defendant may be sound, depending upon the circumstances. The details of a heinous crime may, themselves, be so prejudicial that a jury would be unable to render a fair verdict based solely upon the evidence produced at trial. Similarly, a defendant's reputation in his community may be so bad that the defense fears it cannot obtain a fair verdict from a jury. Under circumstances like these, defendants are well-advised to reject the jury trial in hope that a verdict rendered by a judge would be more dispassionate and truly reflect only the proof at trial. On the other hand, a woman accused of the death of her physically abusive husband would undoubtedly want a verdict by a jury because, whether the evidence of self-defense is strong or not, she is likely to benefit from the community's sense of morality. Anytime a plausible argument for sympathy for the accused's plight can be aroused from the circumstances surrounding the crime or the defendant's life, the defense will want a lay jury's verdict rather than the dispassionate verdict of a judge based solely and totally upon the evidence and its application to the law. These considerations should not be misunderstood as improper maneuvering for they are highly proper, embodying an acceptable and traditional purpose for inclusion of the lay jury in the Anglo-American criminal justice system.

Jury Selection

The language of the Sixth Amendment grants a defendant only an impartial jury, yet the Anglo-American concept of trial by jury embraces the notion of a jury of one's peers, meaning equals of comparable rank.[28] Unfortunately, this comforting democratic notion falls short of reality. Critics of America's jury system point to several hard facts that detract from the idealistic image that is conjured by the image of "a jury of one's peers": first, since jury selection lists are compiled from registered voters, noncitizens are automatically excluded. Can it be argued that an alien is tried by a jury of his peers when all persons sharing his nationality are barred from jury service? Similarly, can a resident of an inner-city ghetto be tried by a jury of his peers when voting lists, and consequently juries, are dominated by white suburbanites? The issue has been commonly avoided by the courts since the guarantee is satisfied when the appointed jury represents a randomly selected cross section of the community, provided that there is no unconstitutional systematic exclusion of classes of persons.[29] Thus the exclusion of black persons through direct or indirect means from service on grand or *petit*(trial) juries is unconstitutional and any conviction obtained under such a system is subject to a successful post-conviction attack.[30] There have also been jury appointive systems which, without directly barring women, made their inclusion on a jury panel unlikely by methods such as providing automatic exemptions unless a women filed a written declaration of her desire to be subject to jury service. In 1975 this practice was also deemed as depriving a defendant of a jury composed of a representative segment of the community.[31] On the other hand, those other statutes have been upheld that permit exemptions for certain professions, such as lawyers, doctors, teachers, or for persons with sick persons or young children at home.[32]

During the questioning of prospective jurors, the lawyers on both sides of a case try to learn as much as possible about the candidates, their backgrounds, attitudes, and prejudices. It is the time for the lawyers to attempt to offset the negative aspects of pretrial publicity by educating the prospective jurors about their proper role and obligations. During this questioning, the lawyer attempts to secure a commitment from each prospective juror that the individual will set aside everything that he or she has heard about the case or the defendant and any other biases and make judgments based only upon the evidence presented in the case. The defense attorney is especially concerned with educating each juror as to the roles of each side in a criminal case and with establishing in the prospective juror's mind an understanding that the state has the burden of proving the defendant's guilt beyond a reasonable doubt. The defense lawyer tries to get a character reading on each prospective juror to determine which way he or she is leaning and how objective an evaluation of the evidence the person will be able to make. The accused will frequently be consulted by his attorney to get his feelings on a prospective juror, and psychiatrists and psychologists are beginning to appear at a few defense tables in courtrooms during jury selections for their assistance in sizing up potential jurors. In the end, however, the lawyers are dealing in guesswork and frequently will accept or dismiss a juror solely on the basis of a hunch formed during the brief questioning. The ability of the lawyers to engage potential jurors in direct questioning has been curtailed in recent years in many state and federal courts. To expedite jury selection, judges today are frequently asking all the questions of prospective jurors, thereby denying to the lawyers in the case the opportunity to pursue their own lines of questions or the opportunity to extract a commitment of objectivity from the juror.[34]

Members of the *venire* (prospective juror panel) will be excused by the court on the motion of either side to strike the individual from the panel on the basis of bias or just cause. In either instance, the judge must rule on the validity of the claim of bias or cause. Cause is delineated by statute and varies from state to state but generally includes a prior or continuing relationship with the defendant or others involved in the case.[35] Bias involves a predetermination of the merits of a case. That bias must be stronger than simply admitting to a prior opinion about guilt or innocence and will not be accepted as satisfactory grounds for challenge if the court is satisfied that the juror is able and willing to render an impartial verdict on the evidence.[36] Additionally, both sides in a criminal case are entitled to a number of peremptory challenges, giving each side the right to reject a prospective juror without offering a reason. Peremptory challenges, which may be used for any reason, are miserly conserved by the parties.[37] They may be used, for instance, to strike a juror when the court has rejected a challenge for cause or to satisfy a hunch about a prospective juror that one side has acquired. Depending upon statutory requirements, one or two alternate jurors will also be chosen. Alternate jurors sit with the jury throughout the trial and will step in and replace a regular juror if one becomes ill or otherwise unable to serve. Once a case is submitted to the jury for its deliberations, any remaining alternates will be excused and will not replace a member of the regular panel anytime after the jury has commenced its discussions and deliberations.

Although the selection process may appear cumbersome, in most criminal trials the jury is selected within a day. However, the selection process has been known to last for weeks; the time required depends upon the notoriety of the case and how long the case will take to be tried. When a jury is expected to be sequestered for a lengthy period of time, constant replenishment of the panel of potential jurors may be needed before the requisite number is found who cannot offer a plausible and acceptable reason why they could not order their affairs to arrange for a prolonged absence from home or employment.

Rules of Evidence

Trials are conducted under the rules of evidence which are prescribed in the statutes, court rules, and prior court decisions of all jurisdictions. Particularities vary from state to state but essentially these rules are the same, having been spawned from the English trial tradition. Although extremely technical in nature, these rules are postulated upon common sense and are designed to produce an orderly and disciplined unfolding of the facts for the jury.

All evidence including tangible objects and documentary evidence is brought before the jury through the testimony of witnesses. The only exception to this is a jury's visit to the site of the alleged crime when absolutely necessary to the facts of the case. These visits are tightly controlled and limited to observation. In most cases, a site visit will not be allowed by the court and the picture of the scene will be created through the testimony of witnesses.

Witnesses at a trial must be legally *competent* to testify. The English common law rules on competency were strict and inclusive but have been worn away with time.[38] Under those rules, for example, an insane person or a child was incompetent to testify. Today the issue of competency is handled individually, and the judge must determine whether the prospective witness has sufficient intelligence and understanding to tell the truth and sufficient capacity to recall and recount what was seen. Even if the judge finds the witness competent to testify, the opposing party will have the opportunity to impeach that testimony and attempt to persuade the jury to disregard it as incredulous.

Persons convicted of crimes and husbands or wives of defendants were disqualified at common law but these restrictions, too, have generally eroded. Through cross examination, the jury is now advised of a witness' criminal conviction or personal relationship and is thus given the opportunity to decide for itself whether or not to believe that witness' testimony.[39] The laws of most jurisdictions still restrict the calling of a spouse, but not because of the incompetency of the witness but because of the privilege accorded by the law to the marital relationship. Certainly the defendant may waive the privilege and call his wife to testify on any matter, while the state may use the defendant's wife to testify on all matters except those related specifically to the marital relationship. Certain other privileges exist to protect the confidentiality of the defendant's communications with his clergyman, doctor, and lawyer.[40]

Competent witnesses may only testify about matters which are *relevant* to the issues at trial. Relevancy is determined broadly by all of the facts that are raised in the charge and by any defense the defendant offers. Background evidence, such as to prove a motive, is highly relevant and is not excluded as immaterial to the facts in issue. A common fallacy is the assumption that only direct, not circumstantial, evidence or proof of guilt is sufficient for conviction. Direct evidence may make the fact more certain, but circumstantial evidence is the sole basis for many convictions. Circumstantial evidence requires the jury to infer an ultimate fact from what the witness observed.[41] Picture for example the following crime scene as described by a witness:

> I observed the defendant duck into a blind alley carrying a machete in one hand and then moments later saw the defendant run out of the alley. I immediately investigated the alley and found the victim lying on the ground with the machete in his back. (No one else was seen entering or leaving the alley by the witness or anyone else.)

The observation of the defendant entering the alley with a machete and leaving the alley within moments without the machete is direct proof of the defendant's presence at the scene of the crime. The entire testimony of the witness is circumstantial evidence that the defendant committed the alleged crime. It is circumstantial evidence because the witness did not observe the defendant striking the victim with the machete but, instead, requires the jury to draw a conclusion from all that the witness observed. If the witness is credible and the jury believes the testimony, it would be sufficient evidence to justify a conviction.

Tangible items and documentary evidence are also brought to the jury's attention through the testimony of witnesses. The machete found in the victim's back could not just be passed around to the jury. A proper foundation must be laid before it will be accepted as evidence. The police officer who first came on the scene would have to testify that he saw the machete in the victim's back and would also have to testify about the proper *chain of custody* between the time it was found and the day it is produced at the trial. This testimony is to insure that it is the same weapon and not a substituted one and that it has not been tampered with to conform to the description of the machete offered by the witness who saw the defendant carrying it. Documentary evidence must also be *authenticated* to establish that it is in fact the writing, official document, or business or medical record that it is claimed to be. In order to prevent fraud or error in transmittal, the document must also be the *best evidence,* the original writing or a copy acceptable under the law of the particular jurisdiction.[42]

Direct Examination

Each party to a law suit in its turn calls witnesses to present its side of the story. The witnesses describe what they observed and together their testimonies offer a composite picture of what that side is trying to prove. Assembling that picture from the bits and pieces offered by each witness is a difficult task because the picture must be both coherent and thorough.[43]

The direct examination of a witness is conducted by the party to the suit who called the witness, offering the witness' testimony as truth. There are two approaches to elicit direct testimony: through a string of successive questions or through a general question permitting the witness to offer a narrative of what he or she observed. A narrative type of testimony appears more genuine to a jury, but essential observations may be omitted by the witness. Also, the narrator is subject to constant interruption if the testimony strays beyond observation and includes opinions, immaterial items, and information about which the witness is not competent to testify.

On direct examination, the attorney may not ask the witness leading questions that suggest the answer sought by the attorney. A question is leading based upon its form or content. It would be improper for the prosecutor to ask the witness who saw the defendant carrying the machete into the alley the following question:

> Did he not have a machete in his right hand?

Opposing counsel would immediately object and the court would order the prosecutor to rephrase the question. Instead, the proper method to extract this information would be for the prosecutor to ask the witness:

> Q. Was the defendant carrying anything when you saw him?
> A. Yes.
> Q. Describe for the jury what you saw him carrying.
> A. A machete.

Even though the well-prepared attorney has previously interviewed his witnesses and knows exactly how each will testify, the purpose of a trial is to permit the jury to hear that testimony from the witness, not from the lawyer.

A witness may only testify about what he or she observed. Deviation from observation and an outpouring of opinions by the witness, unless an expert witness, is not permissible. Non-expert witnesses may offer opinions only about matters which every person is accustomed and competent to form, such as whether a defendant appeared drunk at the time he was observed by the witness. Expert witnesses, however, may offer opinions in their areas of expertise after their credentials as experts are established. Like the testimony of all witnesses, however, the opinions of the most renowned expert may be accepted or rejected by the jury.[44]

Just as the opinions of the witness are generally not admissible, neither is that witness' recitation of *hearsay*.[45] Hearsay, essentially, is second-hand information. It is barred because the person who supplied the information is not present in court, testifying under oath, subject to cross-examination, and personally observed by the jury. Recall how critical the ban on hearsay was to Ralph Johnson. If all those who heard Johnson's roommate describe Johnson as his assailant had been permitted to relate those accusations in court, the jury would undoubtedly have returned a verdict of guilty. Sometimes the conditions under which the out-of-court statement are made are deemed sufficiently reliable to insure that the person who made the statement was telling the truth. When this happens, hearsay statements will be admitted as evidence. If Johnson's roommate had been advised that he was about to die, his hearsay statement would have been admissible under the dying declaration exception at Johnson's trial. Besides dying declarations, other general exceptions[46] to the ban on hearsay evidence are:

Testimony taken at a prior hearing or trial
Admissions and confessions
Declarations against interest
Spontaneous declaration
Records of past recollection
Regularly kept records
Official written statements and certificates

One distinction should be kept in mind. It is not hearsay for a witness to testify that another person made an out-of-court statement, if that testimony is offered merely to prove that such a statement was indeed made. The ban on hearsay applies when the testimony is offered to prove the truth of the content of that statement.

Cross-Examination

When the direct examination of a witness is completed, the opposing attorney has an opportunity to cross-examine. Here is the essence of our adversary system: the truth is most likely to emerge at trial through testimony elicited from one party to a law suit and questioned and challenged by the other party. To assure that truth emerges, great leeway is permitted on cross-examination and, at times, it is not only rigorous but may be harsh and brutal. In cross-examination, the attorney is out to challenge every unfavorable assertion made by the witness.[47]

The cross-examiner probes to raise questions in the minds of the jury about the accuracy of the witness' recitation of what he or she observed and about the credibility of that witness. These ends may be accomplished by showing contradictions in the witness' recitation or inconsistencies between the witness' testimony at trial and prior statements. Counsel will dissect the ability of the witness to observe what he or she claimed to have seen, questioning about the angle of sight, duration of observation, the quantity of light, and any other factor that would affect the witness' ability to observe accurately. Leading, although not argumentative, questions are permissible on cross-examination, and the attorney may question the witness about his or her faculties for recognition and recollection.

Bias, parented by hostility, favor, or self-interest, may be unveiled through cross-examination. Similarly, a witness' character is subject to attack in order to challenge his credibility and make the jury question the truthfulness of his account. Bad character may be exemplified by the prior misconduct of the witness, prior criminal convictions (limited to felonies in some jurisdictions or offenses involving moral turpitude), or the general poor reputation of the witness in the community for truth and veracity. The object, of course, of all cross-examination is to apprise the jury of all relevant information so that it may properly decide whether or not to accept and believe a witness' testimony.[48]

Expert witnesses are also subject to intensive cross-examination involving their credentials, their level of actual expertise, bias, and the correctness of their opinions. An expert will be asked on cross-examination about differing opinions by other experts, a technique which serves the dual purpose of questioning the quality of the expert witness' conclusion and reminding the jury that there are other, opposite expert views about the same subject.[49]

Cross-examination can be great fun, but an attorney must know when to stop. The persistent cross-examiner who zeroes in on a target and then with relish proceeds to devastate the witness runs the risk that his humiliation of the witness will backfire. Instead of rejecting the witness' testimony, the jury may feel such sympathy for the person under attack that it strains to accept and believe his account of the facts.

Once the opposing attorney completes cross-examination, the party originally calling the witness will have an opportunity to clarify matters confused during cross-examination or to attempt to rehabilitate the credibility of the witness. Upon completion, the opposing attorney will also have another crack at the witness. Judges, too, may ask questions to bring out more information and to clarify points raised by the witness.

Defendant's Right to Confront His Accusers

The right to confront one's accusers is fundamental to the Anglo-American system of criminal justice. It includes the defendant's right to be present in court and to see his accusers and extends to the right of a defendant to have an opportunity to fully cross-examine those making accusations against him.[50] Like all constitutional rights, the guarantee of confrontation is limited and the exceptions to the hearsay rule have long ago passed constitutional muster.

The issue arises most frequently outside of the usual hearsay exceptions when the state seeks to use at trial the testimony from an earlier proceeding in the case of a witness who is not available to testify at trial. The first question that a court must ask deals with the unavailability of the witness. Is the witness truly unavailable or did the prosecution fail to make a good faith effort to locate the witness and secure his attendance at trial? Death, of course, provides the ultimate example of unavailability, and the testimony of a witness at the preliminary hearing may be introduced at trial even though the witness has died since the preliminary examination. On the other hand, the fact that a witness is imprisoned in another state does not render him unavailable, and consequently that witness' prior testimony may not be used.[51] Thus "unavailability" means just that. In order to overcome the accused's right to confront his accusers, the difficulty, cost, or the inconvenience of bringing back a witness will not suffice.

The second criterion that must be met to use the prior testimony of an unavailable witness is that the original testimony must have been made under oath and that the defense must have had a full opportunity to cross-examine the witness when the testimony was given. Obviously this requires that the defendant be represented by an attorney, or affirmatively have waived that right, at the earlier hearing, and that the judge not restrict the right of the defense to thoroughly cross-examine the witness. These exceptions pose a dilemma for a defense attorney. Frequently, cross-examination at a preliminary hearing is cursory and the defense elects to reserve its weaponry for trial. Full cross-examination at a preliminary hearing may alert the witness to holes in his testimony that may be conveniently filled by the time of trial. But if the defense attorney refrains from extensive cross-examining and the witness subsequently becomes unavailable, the defense may be faced with the prior testimony being accepted at trial without the defense having an opportunity to ever demonstrate the lack of accuracy of the testimony and the witness' lack of credibility.[52]

Defendant's Privilege Against Self-Incrimination

The Constitution guarantees a defendant, through the Fifth Amendment, the absolute right to remain silent at trial. Whether or not a defendant takes the witness stand is entirely up to the defendant and his attorney. The prosecutor may not comment upon a defendant's failure to take the witness stand.[53] Moreover, the defense is entitled to an instruction to the jurors informing them about the defendant's privilege and admonishing the jury not to draw inferences of guilt from the defendant's reticence. Deciding whether or not the jury should be instructed poses a difficult choice. The instruction itself may raise the issue in the minds of the jury and despite the court's admonition the jury may infer guilt. On the other hand, the defense runs the risk that one or more jurors may already be thinking about the fact that the defendant was not a witness and may need a reminder that such a fact should not weigh in their deliberations.

There are many reasons why an innocent defendant may not take the witness stand. Once sworn in as a witness, the defendant is subject to the same cross-examination as any other witness. Prior criminal convictions and relevant misconduct that will undoubtedly be exposed to the jury during cross-examination may cause the jury to reject the defendant's otherwise truthful account of the facts in the case. Some people simply make terrible witnesses because of incoherence or other personal traits and may appear to be liars when, in fact, they are not. Many defendants cannot take the witness stand, of course, because if they did they would have to fully admit to the crime or lie. In the end, the defendant and his attorney have to decide whether their case would be hurt or helped by the defendant's testifying in his own behalf, ever mindful of the fact, however, that jurors have been proven to be favorably impressed by the defendant, with no prior criminal record, who testifies at his own trial.[54]

The Trial Process

Whether a case is tried by a judge or jury, the order in which the evidence is presented is essentially the same as it has developed in Anglo-American systems over the last three hundred years. The major distinction between a case tried by a jury and one tried before a judge without a jury is that the latter is less likely to be as formal. Without a jury in attendance, a judge attempts to expedite matters and will not countenance as many objections to the manner in which evidence is presented.

Opening Statements

Each side has a first crack at the jury before any evidence is presented, with the prosecution always going first. Although some lawyers choose to waive opening statements, it is not a wise course of action. Soon evidence will be presented to a jury in bits and pieces by the witnesses. The unfolding of evidence is similar to constructing a jigsaw puzzle, and the opening statement offers counsel an opportunity to display the cover picture to the jury so that they will know what each side's puzzle should look like when all the pieces of the evidence presented are fit together. Without opening statements, the jury will not know what to expect and may well miss critical parts of the puzzle when presented.

The opening statement serves several purposes: (1) it familiarizes the jury with one's position; (2) it gives the jury an idea as to how that position will be established; and (3) it reveals the theory upon which the evidence will rest. Opening statements by each side also help to foster and maintain the jury's sense of objectivity. It is important that the defense refute, as soon as possible, any observations made during the prosecutor's opening statements that may damage its position in the eyes of the jury. Even though some courts permit defense attorneys to reserve their opening statements until after the presentation of the state's case and just before the defense begins offering its own evidence, the choice to delay is rarely advantageous. In most instances, the defense's acceptance of the option to delay its opening remarks is, at best, risky. An unrefuted opening statement by a prosecutor may create such a strong belief of the defendant's guilt in the minds of the jury, which will then be reinforced by the state's evidence, that it cannot be overcome later.[55]

During opening statements, upon the motion of either side, witnesses who will testify at the trial are ordered from the courtroom by the judge. There is wisdom in this approach because a witness cannot hear what he is expected to offer as information from the attorney and pattern the testimony after that expectation. The witnesses will be excluded until each in turn is called to testify, again so that they do not hear each other's testimony and fashion their own to conform to what a prior witness has said.

Presentation of the State's Case

As the party that has the burden of proof in a criminal case, the prosecution must produce evidence on each and every element of the crime charged. The evidence must be relevant to the issues of the case and must be offered by competent witnesses.

Motion for Acquittal

At the conclusion of the state's case and before the defense offers any evidence, a motion for acquittal—or for dismissal of the charges—will be made by the defense attorney. The purpose of this motion is to test the sufficiency of the prosecution's case against the defendant. Both attorneys will argue on the motion out of the hearing of the jury. The motion is granted if the state has failed to make a *prima facie* case of guilt by failing to produce evidence on each and every element of the offense. A motion for acquittal is also granted if the evidence that is presented on each and every element is so weak that a jury could not convict on that evidence even if it totally disregarded any later refutation offered by the defense.

Presentation of the Defense

Even if the motion for acquittal is denied, the defense need not present any evidence. It is unusual but perfectly proper for the defense to rest its case immediately after being called upon for its evidence. Defense strategy in that event is to indicate that the state's case is too weak and full of holes for a jury to believe in it beyond a reasonable doubt. Usually, however, the defense will offer evidence to rebut the state's case or present evidence of an *affirmative defense,* such as alibi, self-defense, or necessity.

Rebuttal and Surrebuttal Evidence

At the conclusion of the defense presentation, the state will be given another opportunity to offer evidence. It is improper to use the second opportunity to rehash evidence originally presented. This stage is reserved to rebut defenses and new points made during the defense case. If the state offers rebuttal evidence, a similar opportunity will be afforded with the same limitations to the defense for a surrebuttal.

Motion for a Directed Verdict of Acquittal

When all of the evidence has been presented and both sides have finally rested, the defense attorney will be permitted to make a motion for a directed verdict of acquittal. In essence the defense is claiming that the prosecution has hopelessly failed to meet its burden of proof and that there is no issue to present to the jury. The motion allows the court to test the sufficiency of the state's case one final time before submitting it to the jury for a verdict. A directed verdict of acquittal will be ordered by the court after reviewing all of the evidence presented at trial and resolving all issues of credibility of witnesses in favor of the state if the court finds as a *matter of law* that reasonable persons could not find the defendant guilty beyond a reasonable doubt as charged or of any lesser offense.[56] If there is any possibility that reasonable individuals considering all of the evidence could entertain the possibility of the defendant being guilty, the court, regardless of a weak prosecutorial presentation, will deny the motion. Naturally, a motion for a directed verdict of guilty made by the prosecutor is not permitted in a criminal case because that would deny the defendant his constitutional guarantee to a trial (and verdict) by a jury.

Summations

Each side has a chance to argue one final time to the jury, although in most jurisdictions the prosecutor has the first opportunity and again the final word after the defense argument. Final arguments, critical to each side, provide an opportunity for the lawyers to put all of the evidence in perspective. First, the attorney will remind the jurors of their earlier commitment to withhold judgment and remain objective until all of the evidence and arguments have been heard. Secondly, the lawyers in turn will discuss with the jury the applicable statutes upon which the charges were brought, and other legal principles, such as the state's duty to prove guilt beyond a reasonable doubt. Naturally, the lawyers will see the law quite differently and are permitted generous margins in their arguments within the parameters prescribed beforehand and enforced during the summation by the court. A prosecutor, for example, will stress the limitations upon the reasonable doubt standard as not requiring elimination of every conceivable possibility which the prosecutor will likely stress would be impossible unless each juror personally witnessed all the events. Obviously the defense attorney will view the standard as a protection against conviction of the innocent, and emphasize the obligation it imposes upon the state. Then each attorney will review the evidence of the case, stressing the strengths of his witnesses and other evidence and the weaknesses of the other side's, with particular attention paid to any information that might have discredited the opponent's witnesses. Finally, the prosecutor will summarize the misconduct of the defendant and remind the jury of the tolls that conduct had upon its victims, while the defense attorney extols the good qualities of the defendant and concludes by trying to denigrate the state's case to secure a finding of not guilty. The final word, though, belongs to the prosecutor.

Charge to the Jury

Final pronouncements to the jury before it retires to consider its verdict are made by the judge in the form of instructions covering each issue of the case. The judge is required to explain all of the law to the jury, and where there is uncertainty on the law, to rule on that matter and provide a framework in which the jury may make its findings of fact. In so doing, the judge is advising the jury of the role it will play in determining the defendant's guilt or innocence.

Legal questions are the province of the court and the jury is to make its factual determinations within the boundaries of the law as defined by the judge. In a murder prosecution, if the defense has relied upon self-defense as justification for the homicide, the judge will instruct the jury on the legal definition and requirements for self-defense and how to find whether the defendant's conduct met those legal requirements. The judge's instructions will also cover all theories offered by the prosecution and all defenses reasonably raised by the evidence. The jury will also be advised how it is to treat the testimony of witnesses for both sides. As the finders of fact, the jurors have complete discretion to believe or disbelieve the testimony of any witness, and some states require the court to instruct the jury to treat a police officer's testimony like that of any other. In a small number of states, the defendant is entitled to have the jury instructed that it is the final arbiter of the law and the facts in the case. This is a throwback to John Peter Zenger's criminal libel prosecution in colonial New York where, although the Crown had proven Zenger's guilt under the statute, the jury returned a verdict of not guilty because it rejected the statute. This is called *jury nullification* and although the instruction is given in only a handful of states, juries everywhere retain the power to do as they see fit in the sanctity of the deliberation room.[57]

The court will also remind the jury of the presumption of innocence and explain the burdens placed upon the state to overcome that presumption. In that context, the court will define the meaning of proof beyond a reasonable doubt and attempt to help the jury reach some understanding of how much doubt is "reasonable" doubt. It is the practice in a minority of state jurisdictions and in the federal courts for the judge also to summarize and comment upon the weight of the evidence.[58] This is often attacked as an invasion of the jury's province because of the great deference that will probably be given to the judge's remarks by the jurors, and even where this practice is recognized it is subject to attack on appeal after conviction if the judge's comments are not measured and restrained.

Finally, the court after advising on how to proceed to a verdict will provide the jury with all of the various acceptable verdicts from which it may choose. Besides guilty and not guilty to the principal charge, the court will submit to the jury all of the lesser included offenses which it may consider. In a first-degree murder case (traditionally requiring proof of an intentional killing with malice aforethought, premeditation, and deliberation), the court will also instruct the jury on second-degree murder (an intentional killing with malice aforethought, but without premeditation and deliberation), voluntary manslaughter (intentional killing without malice), involuntary manslaughter (unintentional killing committed recklessly or during the commission of an unlawful act) and, if the evidence permits, on and on to assault and battery (an unlawful touching). Not only will the court advise the jury about lesser included offenses, it must also advise about the legal requirements for finding the accused guilty under each.

The charge to the jury is rarely succinct, often tedious and boring, but nonetheless crucial. More than one prosecutor and defense attorney have watched a hoped-for verdict go up in smoke because the jurors, distracted by boredom, mentally wandered just as the judge reached an important instruction upon which their theory of the case rested. One source claims that more convictions are reversed because of errors in jury instructions than from all other components in criminal cases.[59] The instructions that are given to the jury are the responsibility of the trial judge, but he has had the input of the prosecuting and defense attorneys. After the defense has finally rested, each side will submit to the court and opposing counsel a set of proposed instructions on the law. Whether the court accepts or rejects some or all of these instructions is its prerogative, but an objection will be noted in the record by the defense attorney and may be the basis for a subsequent appeal if the defendant is convicted.

Jury Deliberation and Verdict

After the case is given to the jury for deliberation and the jury retires, the foreman is elected. Once this is accomplished, how deliberations proceed is entirely up to the jury members. One condition is certain, however: for the duration of its deliberation, the jurors will have access to the outside world only through the court. It is also not given access to law books, copies of the instructions, or documentary evidence or a record of the testimony of witnesses. And, because jurors generally are not permitted to make notes during trial because of the possibilities of error, questions that arise during deliberation must be answered by the court in the presence of the defendant and both lawyers. In addition, the jury may request a rereading of certain instructions, additional instructions, or a reading of the trial transcript of all or portions of a witness' testimony. The judge may or may not accommodate those requests.

Jury deliberations may be swift and a verdict returned immediately with no time taken for anything other than the election of a foreman and a vote on guilt or innocence. On the other hand, jury deliberations may drag on while the jurors painstakingly review all of the evidence and then try to persuade each other as to the wisest decision regarding the defendant's fate. A verdict in almost every state and in federal courts must be the unanimous decision of the jury, although the Supreme Court has upheld the constitutional validity of non-capital convictions under an Oregon statute which permits verdicts of ten to two and a Louisiana statute which permits verdicts of nine to three.[60] According to the Supreme Court, the constitutional standard requiring proof beyond a reasonable doubt goes only to the thought processes of the individual jurors and not to the number of jurors voting for conviction or acquittal, as long as the conviction is the vote of a substantial majority of the jury.

When a jury reports to the court that it is unable to arrive at a verdict and is deadlocked, the court may accept that as the result of the trial or, if the deliberations have not gone on for too many days, send the jury back to its deliberation room to try again. Returning the jury for further deliberations after it has asked to be discharged does create the possibility that a single holdout may give in, not because he or she is convinced of the correctness of the majority's position, but simply from fatigue or an unwillingness to accept responsibility for keeping the others from their homes and families. The Supreme Court has approved the use of an additional instruction to a jury unable to reach a verdict, which has been characterized as a "dynamite charge." It nudges the minority to reconsider its position by reminding them that:

> [I]n a large proportion of cases absolute certainty could not be expected; that, although the verdict must be the verdict of each individual juror, and not a mere acquiescence in the conclusion of his fellows, yet they should examine the question submitted with candor, and with a proper regard and deference to the opinions of each other; that it was their duty to decide the case if they could conscientiously do so; that they should listen, with a disposition to be convinced, to each other's arguments; that, if the larger number were for conviction, a dissenting juror should consider whether his doubt was a reasonable one which made no impression upon the minds of so many men, equally honest, equally intelligent with himself. If, upon the other hand, the majority were for acquittal, the minority ought to ask themselves whether they might not reasonably doubt the correctness of a judgment which was not concurred in by the majority.[61]

Although attacked over the years as likely to produce compromise verdicts, that charge is used in federal and numerous state courts.

Once a verdict or hopeless deadlock is reached, the jury notifies the judge and the result is returned in open court in the defendant's presence. After a reading of the verdict, upon the request of either side, the individual jurors may be polled to assure that they concur in the verdict. If the verdict is not guilty, the defendant is discharged by the court and is free to resume his life.

Following a deadlocked or hung jury, the defendant will be remanded to custody or permitted to remain free on bail while the prosecution decides whether to retry the defendant. Retrial is not barred under the concept of double jeopardy when the first or even second trial ends in a deadlock. A date for sentencing will be set if the verdict is guilty and the defendant will be ordered to jail or permitted to remain on bail while the court considers the proper sentence.

Appeals

Direct Appeals

Nowhere does the Constitution mention a defendant's right in a criminal case to appeal after conviction. Moreover, the Supreme Court stated in the nineteenth century that a state need not maintain an appellate process and it still maintains that position today.[62] Yet every state maintains an appellate procedure providing appeal from a conviction in a criminal case, and there is a comparable federal process for defendants convicted in federal courts. Most states make the right to at least a first appeal absolute.

Most states, like the federal government, maintain a two-tiered appellate process with an intermediary appellate court, generally called a *Court of Appeals,* and a high court, generally a *Supreme Court.* (Demonstrating that titles are sometimes meaningless, in New York State the intermediary appellate court is the Supreme Court and the high court is the Court of Appeals.) The first appeal of right goes to the intermediary court of appeals. There the legal issues raised by the defendant (now appellant) are thrashed out. Legal briefs are submitted by both sides, containing a statement of the essential facts of the case, the legal issues raised on appeal, and the argument supported by judicial precedents why the appeal should be granted or denied. Oral argument is generally permitted, with the appellate judges frequently and briskly interrupting the attorneys with questions and comments. At the conclusion of the arguments, the judges adjourn to discuss and vote on the case amongst themselves. After the vote, one member of the majority will be assigned to write the opinion of the court, and the other judges may write concurring opinions agreeing with the majority or dissenting opinions pointing out the fallacies of the majority's position. Appellate court decisions are kept secret until the court is ready to release its opinion. A great tradition of secrecy envelopes the United States Supreme Court's judicial conferences and decision-making process. It is probably the only branch of the national government where information usually does not seep out prior to official announcement.

Appellate review of convictions is not a retrial nor a rehash of the factual determinations leading to the result at trial. An appellate court will not consider claims that a jury made a mistake or that the jury accepted the testimony of a witness who was not credible. Appeals, which are on issues of law, review the correctness of the pretrial procedures and decisions made by the court at trial and sentencing. Were a defendant's constitutional rights properly protected? Did the trial court err in admitting certain evidence? Should the trial judge have ruled as a matter of law that the state had failed to prove its case and have entered a verdict of acquittal instead of submitting the case to the jury for its decision? Did the trial court improperly limit the defense attorney's opportunity to cross-examine prosecution witnesses? Did the trial judge fail to explain properly the law in his instructions to the jury? In other words, the purpose of an appeal is to test the soundness of the legal framework in which the jury made its decision. It is not to second-guess the jury.[63]

Few trials are error free. Momentary lapses by a judge may result in the failure to sustain objections to improperly phrased questions. Some may not be momentary lapses; there are judges who are not properly schooled in the rules of evidence and may not recognize or understand properly made objections. However, the existence of error does not automatically guarantee success on appeal. If the error is substantial and may have had an influence on the outcome of the case, then it is prejudicial and the conviction may not stand.[64]

Even constitutional errors committed at the trial and during pretrial procedures may be ruled harmless and the conviction affirmed. Courts, however, are required to treat constitutional errors differently from procedural errors not involving constitutional rights. The burden is on the appellant seeking to reverse the result at trial to show the prejudicial nature of nonconstitutional errors. When the error involves constitutional rights, the burden shifts to the appellee, the state seeking to preserve the conviction, to demonstrate that the error was harmless, for a presumption exists that a constitutional error is prejudicial. The burden on the state is to prove beyond a reasonable doubt that the constitutional error did not contribute to the verdict at trial.[65] A rule of *automatic reversal* applies to some constitutional errors believed to be so inherently prejudicial that they can never be considered harmless. A defendant's coerced confession improperly admitted into evidence calls for automatic reversal because a confession is the strongest piece of evidence that the state can produce and is assumed to have influenced the jury. The categories of constitutional errors requiring automatic reversal have been whittled down by the Burger Court and they are, today, very few in number.[66]

Once reversible error is established, in almost all cases the appellate court may only reverse the conviction and remand it to the trial court for a new trial in conformity with the appellate court's decision on the law. In a rare instance, if the trial court's error was failing to recognize the deficiencies of the state's case by dismissing the charges or entering a directed verdict of acquittal because of those deficiencies instead of giving the case to the jury, then the appellate court can reverse the conviction without remand. This is because the prosecution, as a matter of law, failed to meet its burden and therefore a second trial would be improper. Similarly, a minority of states permit the appellate court to review the correctness of the trial judge's sentence, and when error is found the appellate court may revise the sentence without remanding the case.[67]

Defendant's Right to Appeal

As already indicated, almost every state provides one appeal from conviction as a matter of right. The fact of a defendant's indigency may not be used to prohibit his access to the appellate process. Thus the state is obligated to provide counsel to the indigent defendant for the first appeal of right and also to furnish the defendant with a transcript of the trial proceedings which is necessary to perfect an appeal.[68]

A defendant may not be penalized for appealing a conviction. The purpose of this rule is to protect a defendant's right to appeal and also to protect society's interest in correcting erroneous convictions and injustices. A defendant who is charged with murder in the first degree and convicted of murder in the second degree may be retried only for murder in the second degree after a successful appeal. The first jury's failure to return a guilty verdict on the murder one charge is a silent acquittal and the double jeopardy guarantee protects against reinstatement of the more serious charge. To permit the state to retry the defendant on the more serious charge would have a chilling effect upon the defendant's right to appeal and would force a defendant to choose between the result of an error-laden trial or the risk of conviction of the more serious offense.[69] Similarly, a judge may not automatically impose a more stringent sentence upon a defendant who is convicted a second time following a successful appeal. Harsher sentences are not barred *per se,* but if a more severe sentence is imposed following a successful appeal, a statement explaining the justification for the additional harshness must appear in the record of the case to insure that the additional penalty is warranted by the facts that came out at the second trial and is not imposed because of the appeal.[70]

At the appellate stage, the presumption of innocence has evaporated with the finding of guilt, and the burden now rests on the defendant to show why the conviction should be overturned. Thus if there is no basis for a claim of substantial error the appeal is frivolous and should not be taken. However, a blanket endorsement to disregard the qualified right to appeal might result in the rights of indigent defendants being given short-shrift by attorneys who do not wish to exert themselves further for their non-paying clients. To prevent that from happening and also to forestall frivolous appeals being made by rote, the Supreme Court has set down a procedure for an attorney representing an indigent defendant to end the appellate process with built-in safeguards for the indigent. When appointed counsel finds that there is no basis to the defendant's appeal, the attorney should advise the appellate court and request permission to withdraw. Along with that request, however, the lawyer must furnish a brief referring to anything in the record that might arguably support the appeal. After the defendant has an opportunity to read the brief and supplement it, the appellate court decides whether the appeal is unworthy and whether the attorney should be relieved of the assignment. A minority of the Supreme Court labeled this process as quixotic, chiding the majority on its assumption that a letter written by an appointed attorney stating that an appeal is frivolous can not be trusted.[71]

Once the first appeal of right is concluded, the direct appeal process is terminated. Access to the second appeal level, the state's highest court, is generally within the discretion of that court. Through a *Writ of Certiorari* the highest court of the state may accept an appeal from the intermediary appellate court if it believes that the appeal raises issues of importance for the state. Where the issues on appeal raise federal constitutional questions, an appellant can also seek a *Writ of Certiorari* to the United States Supreme Court to litigate the constitutional issue after exhaustion of the state appellate process. Whether or not the Supreme Court grants the writ is solely within its discretion and is largely dependent upon the national significance of the constitutional issue raised. The concurrence of four of the nine justices of the Supreme Court is required for issuance of the writ before the case will be heard in Washington. The great bulk of the Supreme Court's work centers around its consideration and rejection of petitions for the writ.[72] Thus, we have three channels of potential review for state defendants: the state intermediary appellate court, the state high court, and where federal constitutional rights are at stake the United States Supreme Court. Criminal defendants in federal prosecutions, of course, have only two steps for an appeal from a conviction, a United States Court of Appeals, and a petition for a *Writ of Certiorari* to the Supreme Court.

Prosecution's Right to Appeal

Naturally, the state or federal governments may not appeal an acquittal or a conviction by claiming that the accused should have been convicted of a greater offense. That is, if a defendant is charged with murder in the first degree but found guilty only of murder in the second degree or manslaughter, the state cannot appeal on the ground that the defendant should have been convicted as charged. The double jeopardy clause of the Fifth Amendment has always barred the federal government from such appeals, and the last decision of the Warren Court applied the ban to the states through the due process clause of the Fourteenth Amendment.[73]

When a defendant successfully appeals and a conviction is reversed on a matter of law, however, the prosecution may contest the correctness of that legal ruling by seeking appeal to the next highest level, and by a petition for a *Writ of Certiorari* to the Supreme Court. Aside from pursuing appeals initiated by the defendant, a few states permit the prosecution to initiate appeals from acquittals and convictions solely for the purpose of correcting legal errors committed at trial. The appellate court's pronouncements in such cases are strictly advisary and can have no affect upon the defendant.

Habeas Corpus—Appeal of Custody

Even the conclusion of the appellate process does not necessarily bring a criminal case to a final conclusion. While our society has an interest in finalizing court cases, our law reflects an overriding interest in protecting against injustices. Therefore, the prisoner has access to a civil proceeding that will allow him to challenge the legality of his detention.[74] A petitioner who seeks a post-conviction appeal is claiming that errors committed during the criminal process or at trial were so fundamental that the proceeding was grossly unfair; consequently, the sentencing court lost its jurisdiction and hence its right to punish the accused. The prisoner's objective in seeking an appeal of custody is to attack the legality of his detention. If the petitioner is successful, the court will grant the prisoner a writ of *habeas corpus.* What this means is that the court will issue a formal order that the person ("corpus") detained be brought before the court to investigate the legality of the restraint of his liberty. Habeas corpus exists as a tool to protect against the possibility of illegal imprisonment.[75]

When an appeal of custody is from a state prisoner to the federal court, the prisoner must claim that the state authorities deprived him of federal constitutional rights, resulting in the illegality of the subsequent conviction and punishment. When a federal writ is granted, the state official having custody or supervision over the prisoner is required to appear before the federal court and justify the legality of that detention. During the Warren Court's expansion of individual rights and constitutional protections, habeas corpus was extended to all constitutional defects in state criminal convictions.[76] There has been a cutback of the fullness of that protection by the Burger Court. Fourth Amendment issues, challenging the admission at trial of evidence secured as a result of an illegal search and seizure, may no longer be the basis for habeas relief in federal courts if the accused had an opportunity for a full hearing on the issue in the state system.[77] Even if state trial and appellate courts wrongly decide a search and seizure issue, it will not provide the basis for a petition for habeas corpus in federal court. Four members of the present Supreme Court would cut further into habeas jurisdiction and limit it to claims of constitutional error which affect the reliability of the guilt-determining process at trial, creating the possibility that an innocent defendant was convicted. The exclusion of Fourth Amendment claims from habeas consideration could be the harbinger of further limitations excluding other constitutional claims as the basis for habeas relief. The present Supreme Court also has consistently denied habeas relief in cases where the defendant and defense counsel fail to raise the defect in the state proceeding,[78] cutting back on another Warren Court landmark decision which held that procedural forfeitures at the state level were not barriers to federal habeas corpus unless that forfeiture was a deliberate, tactical bypass of the state system.[79] Unquestionably concerned about the number of habeas petitions being filed in federal courts challenging state convictions, the Burger Court already has cut back on the scope of the writ and can be expected to further limit its availability in the future.

Although the current trend is to restrict federal habeas relief, there is no possibility that this remedy will be whittled away to nothing. Regardless of the Burger Court's approach, habeas corpus is so important and intrinsic to this country's adherence to due process that the Constitution forbids its suspension except during rebellion or invasion "when the public safety may require it," and when the courts are unable to function. So, although we can expect limitations on its use and availability, the habeas relief will continue to exist to protect against the unjust restraint of a person's liberty.

Discussion Questions

1. What are three remedies for counteracting adverse publicity regarding a criminal case that will go to trial?

2. In regard to pretrial publicity, what is the defense attorney's obligation in protecting his client's right to a fair trial? What information, according to the lawyer's Canons of Professional Ethics, should not be divulged by the prosecutor or the defense attorney?

3. Why would a defendant choose to waive his constitutional right to a jury trial?

4. It was stated that several hard facts concerning America's jury selection practices detract from the democratic notion that juries are composed of "one's peers." List and explain three examples of the inequities inherent in jury selection procedures.

5. Describe the six major steps of the trial process.

6. Why are judicial instructions to the jury following summations by both sides considered so crucial to the final verdict? What are the positive and negative aspects of judicial counseling to the jury?

7. What is the purpose of an appellate court? And why are appeals based on issues of law only and why is the purpose of the appellate process not to second guess the jury?

8. What is the present position of the U.S. Supreme Court regarding appeals of custody? Why is the habeas corpus remedy so intrinsic to this country's adherence to the due process ideal?

Notes

1. Snyder v. Massachusetts, 291 U.S. 97 (1934).
2. Illinois v. Allen, 397 U.S. 337 (1970).
3. Bloom v. Illinois, 391 U.S. 194 (1968). The Court found that the right to trial by jury for criminal contempt charges arises when possible penalties exceed six months imprisonment.
4. Illinois v. Allen, supra.
5. Taylor v. United States, 414 U.S. 17 (1973).
6. In re Oliver, 330 U.S. 257 (1942).
7. Nebraska Press Association v. Stuart, 427 U.S. 539 (1976).
8. See e.g., State v. Meek, 9 Ariz. App. 149, 450 P.2d 115, 31 ALR3d 808 (1968).
9. For a discussion by the Supreme Court on this provision, see Travis v. United States, 364 U.S. 631 (1961).
10. Fed. R. Crim. P. 21.
11. N. M. Stat. Ann. § 21-5-3.
12. Washington v. Texas, 388 U.S. 14 (1967).
13. State v. Dehler, 257 Minn. 549, 102 N.W.2d 696, 89 ALR2d 496 (interpreting Minn. Const.) (1960).
14. Irvin v. Dowd, 366 U.S. 717 (1961).

15. Saxbe called Hearst a "fugitive" and stated he believed she was "not a reluctant participant." He also stated that the S.L.A. was a bunch of "common criminals" and that Hearst was one of them. *New York Times,* April 18, 1974, p. 1.
16. Supra, note 7.
17. Ibid., p. 569.
18. Gannett Co., Inc. v. DePasquale, 443 U.S., 387 (1979).
19. Sheppard v. Maxwell, 384 U.S. 333 (1966), at 361: "[T]he trial court might well have prescribed extra-judicial statements by any lawyer, party, witness, or court official which divulged prejudicial matters..."
20. *A.B.A. Code of Professional Responsibility* Dr7-107(B), (C).
21. Moore, *The Jury* (Cincinnati: Anderson, 1973); 1 Busch, *Law and Tactics in Jury Trials* (Indianapolis: Bobbs-Merrill, 1961), p. 14.
22. Duncan v. Louisiana, 391 U.S. 145 (1968) at 156.
23. Ibid.
24. Ohio Rev. Code Ann. § 2945.17 (for any imprisonment and any fine greater than $100); Oklahoma Const. Art. II, § 20; Vermont Const. Chap. I, Art. 10.
25. Williams v. Florida, 399 U.S. 78 (1970). In Apodaca v. Oregon, 406 U.S. 404 (1972), the Court held that unanimity was not required in jury decisions. In Ballew v. Georgia, 435 U.S. 223 (1978), the Court found a jury of five to be insufficient for due process guarantees.
26. State v. Cox, 8 Ark. 436 (1848); Work v. State, 2 Ohio St. 296 (1853); Collins v. State, 88 Ala. 212, 7 So. 260 (1890). For a decision subsequent to Williams v. Florida, supra, holding a twelve-man jury necessary, see *Advisory Opinion to Senate,* 278 A.2d 852, 47 ALR3d 878 (Rhode Island, 1971).
27. Some state laws requiring prosecution to approve of waiver of trial by jury are: Ark. Stat. Ann. § 43-2108; California Const. Art. I, § 7; N.D. Cent. Code § 29-16-02. At old English common law, a defendant who refused a jury trial was subjected to "peine forte et dure" and tortured until he accepted a jury or died. Pollock and Maitland, *History of English Law* (London: Cambridge Univ. Press, 1968).
28. MacPhail, "A Jury of Peers?" 42 Penn. *A.B.Q.* 412 (1971); Note: "The Representative Cross Section Standard: Another Sixth Amendment Fundamental Right," 21 *Loyola L. Rev.* 995 (1975).
29. Swain v. Alabama, 380 U.S. 202 (1965).
30. Strauder v. West Virginia, 100 U.S. 303 (1880); Neal v. Delaware, 103 U.S. 370 (1881). In Cassell v. Texas, 339 U.S. 282 (1950), this holding was extended to grand juries. In Peters v. Kiff, 407 U.S. 493 (1972), a white man successfully challenged his conviction on the grounds that Negroes had been systematically excluded from jury service. This was found to violate his federal rights.
31. Taylor v. Louisiana, 419 U.S. 522 (1975).
32. United States v. Arnett, 342 F. Supp. 1255 (D. Mass. 1970). See generally Kamisar, LaFave, Israel, *Modern Criminal Procedure,* 4th ed. (St. Paul, Minn.: West, 1974).
33. Bailey, Rothblatt, *Fundamentals of Criminal Advocacy* (Rochester: Lawyer's Cooperative, 1974), § 318 et seq.
34. Hamer v. United States, 259 F.2d 274 (9th Cir. 1958).
35. Busch, *Law and Tactics,* p. 641.
36. Ibid., p. 718.
37. Ibid., p. 797.
38. 2 Wigmore, *Evidence* (Boston: Little, Brown, 1961), §§ 483-721.

39. Ibid., §§ 519-524, 600-620. The constitutional validity of these common law restrictions is questionable after Washington v. Texas, supra, that held a restriction unconstitutional which barred the persons charged or convicted as co-participants in the same crime from testifying for each other.
40. See generally McCormick, *Evidence,* 2d ed. (St. Paul, Minn.: West, 1976), pp. 151 et seq.
41. 2 Wigmore, *Evidence,* § 25.
42. See generally McCormick, *Evidence,* pp. 524 et seq.
43. 3 Busch, *Law and Tactics,* pp. 1 et seq.
44. See Ladd, "Expert Testimony," 5 *Vand. L. Rev.* 414 (1952); Voorhis, Expert Opinion Evidence, 13 *N.Y.L.F.* 651 (1967).
45. See generally Binder, *The Hearsay Handbook* (Shepard's Citations, Colorado Springs, Colo., 1975).
46. See McCormick, *Evidence,* pp. 579 et seq.
47. Amsterdam, *Trial Manual for the Defense of Criminal Cases* (American Law Institute, 1974), at §§ 370-382, p. 115.
48. McCormick, *Evidence,* p. 49.
49. 4 Busch, *Law and Tactics,* pp. 127 et seq.
50. Pointer v. Texas, 380 U.S. 400 (1965).
51. Ibid.
52. Dissent of Judge Brennan, in California v. Green, supra.
53. Griffin v. California, 380 U.S. 609 (1965).
54. Kalven, Zeisel, *The American Jury* (Boston: Little, Brown, 1966), pp. 177-181.
55. See Amsterdam, *Trial Manual,* §§ 341-353.
56. See Winningham, "The Dilemma of the Directed Acquittal," 15 *Van. L. Rev.* 699 (1962); Cooper, "Directions for Directed Verdicts: A Compass for Federal Courts," 55 *Minn. L. Rev.* 903 (1971).
57. See Kamisar, LaFave, Israel, *Modern Criminal Procedure,* pp. 1293 et seq.
58. The right was confirmed for federal judges in Patton v. United States, 281 U.S. 276 (1930). See Wright, "The Invasion of Jury: Temperature of the War," 27 *Temple L. Q.* 137 (1958); and Holtzoff, "Modern Trends in Trial by Jury," 16 *Wash. & Lee L. Rev.* 27 (1959).
59. Bailey, Rothblatt, *Fundamentals of Criminal Advocacy,* p. 502.
60. Apodaca v. Oregon, supra; Johnson v. Louisiana, 406 U.S. 356 (1972).
61. Allen v. United States, 164 U.S. 492 (1896).
62. Griffin v. Illinois, 351 U.S. 12 (1956); McKane v. Durston, 153 U.S. 684 (1894).
63. 4 Am. Jur. 2d Appeal and Error, § 76.
64. See Saltzburg, "Another Ground for Decision—Harmless Trial Court Errors," 47 *Temple L. Q.* 193 (1974).
65. Chapman v. California, 386 U.S. 18 (1967).
66. See Field, "Assessing the Harmlessness of Federal Constitutional Error—A Process in Need of a Rationale," 125 *U. Pa. L. Rev.* 15 (1976).
67. See Mueller, "Penology on Appeal: Appellate Review of Legal but Excessive Sentences," 15 *Vand. L. Rev.* 671 (1962); Weigel, "Appellate Revision of Sentences: To Make the Punishment Fit the Crime," 20 *Stan. L. Rev.* 405 (1968).
68. Douglas v. California, 372 U.S. 353 (1963); Griffin v. Illinois, supra.
69. Green v. United States, 355 U.S. 184 (1957).
70. North Carolina v. Pearce, 395 U.S. 711 (1969).
71. Anders v. California, 386 U.S. 738 (1967).

72. Cf. Johnson and Harper, "The Supreme Court: Time Charts and Group Decision," 31 *U. Cin. L. Rev.* 241 (1962); Hart, "The Time Chart of the Justices," 73 *Harv. L. Rev.* 84 (1959).

73. Benton v. Maryland, 395 U.S. 784 (1969).

74. See Kamisar, LaFave, Israel, *Modern Criminal Procedure,* pp. 146, 1496 et seq.; Sokol, *A Handbook of Federal Habeas Corpus* (Mitchie, Charlottesville, Va., 1965); and Wright, *Law of Federal Courts,* 3d ed. (St. Paul, Minn.: West, 1976), pp. 236-248.

75. Federal habeas corpus is so important and intrinsic to this country's adherence to due process that the Constitution forbids its suspension except during rebellion or invasion "when public safety may require it." That has been limited to times when a battle is raging and the courts are unable to function. Ex Parte Milligan, 4 Wall. 2 (1866).

76. Townsend v. Sain, 372 U.S. 293 (1963); Fay v. Noia, 372 U.S. 391 (1963).

77. Stone v. Powell, 428 U.S. 465 (1976).

78. Francis v. Henderson, 425 U.S. 536 (1976) (failure to challenge Grand Jury composition); Estelle v. Williams, 425 U.S. 501 (1976), (failure to challenge defendant's being forced to wear prison clothes at trial); Henderson v. Kibbe, 431 U.S. 145 (1977), (failure to object to improper jury instruction); Wainwright v. Sykes, 433 U.S. 72 (1977), (failure to raise claim of misunderstanding Miranda rights at trial).

79. Henry v. Mississippi, 379 U.S. 443 (1965).

13.

If this is the way her majesty treats her prisoners, she doesn't deserve to have any.

Oscar Wilde

Sentencing and Punishment

Almost everyone has seen depictions of French prisoners being led to the guillotine; we have seen woodcuts of Dickensian figures huddled together in a damp English prison cell; we have all been exposed to pictures in our high school history books of unlucky colonists pinned in the stocks; and finally, who has not perused a corrections textbook that does not include the 1950ish photographic series of a man being strapped in the electric chair and electrocuted?

These standard portrayals of social punishments exemplify the violence occasioned by legally sanctioned responses to crimes. But despite this violence, our national conscience has yet to discredit "it serves him right" as a moral justification for capital punishment. Is capital punishment a valid conclusion to justice? Is the death penalty as potentially satisfying to the public as it is distasteful?

A Brief Look at the Past

As societies mature, the relationship between the crime a person commits and the punishment he receives becomes complicated. And when societies evolve, the "eye for an eye" approach is almost inevitably denounced as barbaric, and sociological theories regarding deviance and societal wrongs and obligations give rise to correctional philosophies that are reminiscent, in their simplest form, of William Penn's ideas in the seventeenth century. Yet the study of correctional theories and practices becomes interesting, in the very least, when we become witness to the cyclical nature of public sentiment and conscience in regard to the fate of criminals.

The American colonies were notorious in their attitudes towards the treatment of criminals. Modeling much of their punitive methods after England, the colonies made extensive use of the death penalty and allowed vast discretion for sentencing judges. In the first colonies, conviction of a felony was punished, as in England, by death and forfeiture of property. As in England, judges could excuse felonies committed by the well-born, educated, and the clergy. Misdemeanants were punished by public whippings, by being locked in the stocks, and by having fines imposed upon them. The Puritans, of course, were punished for acts that we would not consider crimes, and dissenters were banished and Quakers executed. Confinement in jails was limited generally to persons awaiting trial, repeated misdemeanor offenders, and violators of Sunday blue laws. Drunkenness, common among the early colonists, was severely punished—six months imprisonment for a first offense, one year for the second, and life for the third.[1]

As the colonies developed, a revulsion grew towards the extreme methods of punishment being practiced. Penal reform was introduced in this country by William Penn, the founder of Pennsylvania. In Pennsylvania, Penn retained the death penalty only for murder and treason. Corporal punishment and physical disfigurement were replaced by imprisonment in workhouses and the imposition of fines. The themes of Penn's work were deterrence, reform of the offender, and recompense for the victim. Penn's ideas, however, were ahead of his time; demands more exigent than living up to a more ethical code regarding the treatment of criminals occupied the growing colonies. Consequently, there soon was a reversion to the more practical yet cruel methods of the past. After the War for Independence, Quaker descendants in Pennsylvania attempted to revive Penn's ideas, and it is these ideas that held the key to future American penal reform.

The first modern jail in America was the Walnut Street Jail founded in the last decade of the eighteenth century, not surprisingly, in Pennsylvania. In the Walnut Street Jail, the first attempts were made to treat and reform offenders. Inmates were put to work and were paid for their labors. Hardened criminals were isolated by solitary confinement. When prisoners were released, they left the institution with money that they had earned. The Walnut Street Jail served as a model for institutions in ten other states. One final legacy of the Walnut Street Jail is our modern concept of "good time" where a prisoner is released through a reduction of sentence for good behavior in the institution and recommended to the state governor for early pardon.

By 1800, the Quakers were forced out of the supervision of the Walnut Street Jail and its reputation subsequently declined. The recommendations for early pardons were misused by being sold for profit. The jail became overcrowded and prisoner labor lost its reformatory aspect and was exploited. Even the segregation of hardened criminals was abandoned and intermittent rioting occurred in the institution between 1817 and 1821. The reformatory nature of the Walnut Street Jail failed not because of flaws in Penn's original ideas, but because of general mismanagement.[2] With the downfall of the treatment-oriented Walnut Street Jail, other similar facilities soon fell out of public favor.

The criminal justice system's response to the failure of reformatory institutions was the establishment of penitentiaries. An abrupt turnabout took place, and conditions in the successor institutions were harsh and cruel. Penitentiaries were designed so that prisoners could be penitent. Inmates were isolated; even when they worked together at hard labor, a regimen of silence was imposed. By the mid-nineteenth century, prison officials abandoned their concepts of reformation through silence and were concerned instead with exploitation of prisoners as cheap labor for hire to enterprising entrepreneurs. The atmosphere was purely punitive and did not even seek disguise as treatment.[3]

Reaction to the penitentiary system developed in 1870 when the antecedent to the present American Correctional Association was formed. The Association adopted a Declaration of Principles that echoed Penn's theories. This declaration stated that:

1. Prison discipline is for reformation of criminals, not for the infliction of vindictive suffering.
2. Prisoners should enjoy a measure of self-destiny.
3. Prison discipline must gain the will of the prisoner.
4. Prisoner self-respect should be cultivated.
5. Prison discipline should be aimed at development of upright citizens, rather than orderly and obedient prisoners.[4]

Essentially, these are the same principles espoused today by those penal reformers who are persistent in their beliefs that prisons are not to punish but to correct and reform. Out of the Association's early work came the creation of reformatories, institutions for offenders under the age of thirty, where inmates worked their way through categories towards release on parole. Inmate labor was utilized here as well as in the penitentiaries, but greater emphasis was placed upon the development of job skills for future employment. The reformatory concept also included educational advancement for inmates. It stands to reason that reformatories for youthful offenders would concentrate upon rehabilitating the individual and preparing him for a useful, productive adult life. Yet the reformatory concept did not lead to significant developments that were capable of demonstrating the value of future-oriented treatment in prisons. It has been suggested that reformatories failed because they incorporated too many features of penitentiaries: stone-walled, grim prisons with an over-emphasis on security.[5]

Twentieth century American penology is more sophisticated, but in the main has retained the framework developed in the past century. Prisoner labor is less exploited today because the profit motive has been removed by federal laws prohibiting competition with the free labor market. The movement has continued for improvement of prison conditions, and a new element has been imposed by the courts in recent years delineating minimally acceptable conditions and carving out a body of prisoner rights. Additionally, classification of prisoners has grown more sophisticated, providing for gradations of security and restriction. But in essence little has changed. American prisons have not been reformed; in fact, the charge heard most often is that our prisons have produced better criminals. For instance, recidivism rates of persons who have served time in correctional institutions indicate that those institutions have not fulfilled their obligation to prepare prisoners for lives as free and responsible citizens.

About 300,000 adult offenders are housed in American prisons.[6] Those persons, like Ralph Johnson, are subject to the constant threat of physical violence and sexual assault. Without an orderly system for their reintegration into society, those persons represent a time bomb in our midst and upon release are likely to repay society in kind for what they have endured.

Objectives and Justifications

One reason for the corrections morass in this country is that we, as a people, have never defined a philosophical objective for punishment. For two hundred years Americans have wavered between revulsion at inhumane prison conditions and impatience with overly humane treatment, the former denounced as barbaric and the latter as "coddling criminals." Consequently, there is little national structure to punishment in America and little uniformity of objectives or treatment from case to case.

Throughout the history of the justice system in this country, the fate of convicted criminals has shifted according to national values in vogue at any specific period and their applicability to both protecting society and safeguarding human rights. Essentially, there have been four objectives upon which punishment has been based: *retribution ("just desserts"), restraint, deterrence,* and *rehabilitation.* These objectives obviously overlap, for when a prisoner is behind bars, society is revenged; the prisoner is restrained from committing further criminal acts; other would-be criminals are made aware of the possible consequences of crime; and depending upon the actual policies of the individual prisons across the nation, confinement, coupled with solid educational programs, can lead to perhaps a partial reformation of the prisoner's character.

Retribution

Societal vengeance as the underlying justification for punishment is as old as the recorded history of mankind. The passage in Chapter 21 of the Book of Exodus has provided countless individuals and justice systems down through the centuries with a rationale for meeting violence with violence. This well-known passage states:

> Now these are the judgments which thou shall set before them . . .
> 23. And if any mischief follow, then thou shall give life for life,
> 24. Eye for eye, tooth for tooth, hand for hand, foot for foot,
> 25. Burning for burning, wound for wound, stripe for stripe.

Under the retribution model of punishment, society exacts revenge from the wrongdoer on the theory that one who causes harm to another deserves to suffer himself for that wrongful conduct. On the surface, many reject retribution as a proper basis for punishment in a civilized society, yet collective vengeance quite often is the principal motivation behind a specific sentence in a criminal case.

It is often difficult when society must deal with a convicted criminal to be objective, to endorse a sentence that does not have at its root true outrage. Respect for the concept of justifiable retribution rarely seems out of place in all but the most sophisticated of circles when a killer has indicated no remorse or sense of humanistic shame in regard to his heinous act. In such extreme cases, can we expect society to quelch its anger and look ahead instead to the day when a killer such as David Berkowitz is returned to society, freshly "rehabilitated?" In dealing with such hardened criminals, society's need to see justice done is immediate, and the rehabilitative value of imprisonment becomes, at best, a secondary issue.

The current social preoccupation with the need to punish criminals and not with the question as to whether the criminal is entitled to rehabilitative efforts is illustrated by the gaining popularity of the death penalty. Consider Justice Stewart's opinion in *Gregg v. Georgia:*

> In part, capital punishment is an expression of society's moral outrage at particularly offensive conduct. This function may be unappealing to many, but it is essential in an ordered society that asks its citizens to rely on legal processes rather than self-help to vindicate their wrongs. The instinct for retribution is part of the nature of man, and channeling that instinct in the administration of criminal justice serves an important purpose in promoting the stability of a society governed by law. . . . Retribution is no longer the dominant objective of the criminal law, but neither is it a forbidden objective nor one inconsistent with our respect for the dignity of men. Indeed, the decision that capital punishment may be the appropriate sanction in extreme cases is an expression of the community's belief that certain crimes are themselves so

> grievous an affront to humanity that the only adequate response may be the penalty of death.[7]

Restraint

An individual who poses a continuing threat of repeated criminal behavior must be isolated from society. Unlike societal retribution or deterrence as correctional objectives, restraint as a correctional objective is based on the *practical* needs of society. Restraint provides its own justification when it is recognized that society has the right to protect itself from criminal behavior. Past crimes can also justify the isolation of an errant individual. A clear example of restraint as a sole justification for imprisonment is seen in the fate of the *habitual offender.* In many instances, a person who persists in criminal activity may be sentenced after a statutorily determined number of convictions, and the sentence may prescribe confinement for life.[8]

Deterrence

In examining the penal provisions set forth in the *National Commission on Reform of Federal Criminal Laws, Final Report,* an article in *Law and Contemporary Problems* gives us an example of how punishment functions as a deterrent to crime for the population at large:

> It is widely believed that human activity—indeed most animal activity—is governed by a pleasure-pain calculus. On that hypothesis society bases not only its deterrent penal codes, but also its entire system of affirmative rewards: profits for entrepreneurs, salary increases for bureaucrats, Nobel prizes for scientists and artists, . . . and so on. It is just as well to believe that these contingent rewards do not influence attitudes and behavior as to reject the deterrent hypothesis in criminal law.[9]

The suffering that a criminal undergoes as a result of his commission of a crime serves as a warning to other members of the community to avoid both that crime and other criminal behavior. Regardless of how valid this idea seems, though, the deterrent value of punishment in America has been criticized in recent decades. Soaring crime rates are offered as evidence that the types of punishment used in this country do not discourage criminal activity. It is claimed that the long delay inherent in the adjudication process between arrest and sentencing weakens the exemplary value of punishment. In addition, it is maintained that the great numbers of defendants who are not confined following conviction also weaken the deterrent value of punishment in this society, for few people recognize probation and fines as punishment. Finally there are few convincing arguments to support deterrence as a valuable correctional objective simply because it is impossible to analyze how many people refrain from criminal activity out of their fear of imprisonment.

Sometimes assigned as a separate philosophical justification is the educational aspect that punishment and the criminal law have upon the society wherein the public is educated to understand the mores of the society and distinguish between acceptable behavior through the criminal law and the punishment of offenders. This process becomes ingrained in individuals at a very young age and helps to deter criminal behavior by allowing maturing members of the society to learn to distinguish between right and wrong. The educational value of criminal law is terribly diminished, however, when viewed by generations as a reflection of outdated mores and as an effort to maintain a mindless status quo. The dispute between the young and the law concerning strict enforcement of marijuana may have had that effect in the 1960s. Rather than serving as a deterrent to violations, strict enforcement of drug laws seemed only to exacerbate the problem; in fact, the educational effect may have been reversed—people started questioning and disregarding other laws as well.

Rehabilitation

Given at least lip service in this century has been our commitment to rehabilitation as this society's objective in punishing criminals. The sanction imposed by law, whether community-based supervision or incarceration, is for the purpose of reforming the defendant's character so that he may eventually return to society a "renewed" man. This ideological basis for punishment dates from the time of William Penn and the subsequent Quaker experiment at the Walnut Street Jail.

Increasingly, policy makers are questioning society's ability to rehabilitate criminals. At the same time, despite the exorbitant costs to the community, there has been little evidence at any time of a national pledge and willingness to pay the costs for effective rehabilitative programs. One reason for this unwillingness, of course, is the skepticism about the ability of correctional agencies, even when well-financed, to devise and implement effective rehabilitative programs. Also, we are currently in an age when America must come to grips for the first time in its history with the finite nature of its wealth and resources, and this too is resulting in an increased unwillingness to allot substantial amounts of that limited wealth for the benefit of those who have broken society's rules.

Rehabilitation may involve treatment during institutionalization or while the criminal is under supervision but is otherwise free within the community. The ability to engage in worthwhile corrective treatment in America's penal institutions has been seriously questioned. Even with more complex means for the classification of prisoners—separating young from old, violent from non-violent, and novices from experienced criminals—the emphasis at all levels has remained, foremost, on security and not treatment. Besides, life in a prison is artificial and can hardly be conducive to preparing one for life in society. In prison, virtually all decisions are made for the prisoners who are confined only with members of their own sex. Reentry into a free society, where a person must make his own decisions and deal with members of both sexes, is like a rebirth into an entirely different world. Thus, prisons, because of their very nature, have been characterized as anti-rehabilitative.

As the outgoing and hopeful mood of the 1960s diminished into the self-absorbed, withdrawn attitudes of the '70s, the respect afforded the rehabilitative model of corrections passed. The following excerpt defines some of the reasons for this decline:

VALIDITY OF REHABILITATIVE AIMS

> [A] major source of much of the contemporary call for reform stems from an attack on rehabilitation, the treatment mode that is such an important element in the Model Penal Code's sentencing provisions. The historical antecedents of the rise of the "rehabilitative" ideal in penology and its increasing importance as the aim of criminal punishment have been described elsewhere. Benevolent purposes, concern over prevention, increased social scientific study of the correlates of crime, and continuous invention of therapeutic techniques, all have been suggested as stimulants of the rehabilitative influence in penological thought. Its influence has been widespread; for example, in addition to the Model Penal Code, the American Bar Association, in its Standards Relating to Sentencing Alternatives and Procedures, argues that among the general principles which should guide judicial discretion in fixing sentences should be "the rehabilitative needs of the defendant." The rehabilitative purpose also figures prominently in both the National Council on Crime and Delinquency's Model Sentencing Act and the 1973 National Advisory Commission on Criminal Justice Standards and Goals Sentencing Provisions.
>
> Recently, however, many scholars have become disillusioned with rehabilitative aims in penology. Two fronts have emerged in the battle against the rehabilitative ideal in sentencing: (1) charges that rehabilitative techniques and practices lack empirically demonstrated validity (2) concern over the implications of rehabilitation as a rationale for state intervention.
>
> Clear, the demonstrated achievements of rehabilitative techniques in corrections have been modest. Reviews of the empirical literature consistently conclude that the vast majority of programs fail to demonstrate a substantial rehabilitative effect. Although the literature leaves substantial room for disagreement and there con-

> tinue to be sporadic reports of successful treatment interventions, current evidence does not support the contention that rehabilitative purposes have achieved consistent or notable successes on a widespread basis. In fact, some critics question the assumption that meaningful psychological change can ever be coerced.
>
> Opponents of the rehabilitative disposition do not rest their arguments solely upon empirical grounds. Even if treatment effects were firmly established, many would still find rehabilitation an unacceptable purpose, particularly for the initial intervention by the state. These critics question the propriety of state-induced coercive change. They argue that too often overlooked are the potential abuses of political authority—which inhere in any notion of coercive change brought about by agents of the state, regardless of their motives or intentions. Under the guise of benevolence, the essentially punitive nature of the criminal sanction can be masked, a situation which may inhibit critical analysis of the proper role of the coercive power of the state. It is argued that the rehabilitative ideal can be covertly transformed to serve an essentially incapacitative purpose, the result of which can be an otherwise unwarranted extension of state power over the lives of convicted offenders.[10]

Sentencing goals are not statutorily imposed. While the literature emphasizes correction rather than punishment *per se,* that does not necessarily reflect the mood of the American people. There are aspects of all four justifications in the punishment patterns in every state, and more than one philosophy is at work in any particular sentence imposed in any given case. But today, the trend in social and correctional thought is definitely in the direction of retribution and deterrence as primary objectives of punishment. Further, judges and legislatures are not deaf to the public demand that criminals must "pay" for their crimes; and they are not blind to the failure of the correctional effort and the anti-rehabilitative nature of American prisons.

Sentencing Models

The power to sentence a defendant convicted of a crime is conferred by the legislature. Any limitations upon the discretion which accompanies that power is also imposed by the legislature. In the United States, those powers have generally been conferred upon the sentencing judge, although with very few exceptions, the power to determine how long a defendant actually serves in prison is decided by administrative personnel, either correction officials or a parole board.

Across the United States, a hodgepodge of statutory schemes provides for sentencing of offenders. Almost uniformly, the legislatures of the various jurisdictions, reflecting the uncertainties of their constituencies, have failed to enunciate and define clear correctional goals. Absent legislatively determined goals, judges are delegated broad power to choose appropriate punishment in each case. The limitations that judges work with fall somewhere between the extremes of the *indeterminate sentence* (one year to life), which depends on the discretionary powers of parole boards, and the *determinate sentence,* which follows a fixed term for imprisonment, with no minimum or maximum spread and with no possibility for parole.

The Indeterminate Sentence

A concept whose time has passed is the strict indeterminate sentence.[11] This sentencing practice is premised upon a purely correctional model of punishment. In its truest form, a person convicted of any crime would be automatically committed to prison for treatment for one day to life. The treatment would be chosen by administrative personnel with expertise in behavior modification and would be tailored solely to the character of the offender. The nature and seriousness of the offense would have no bearing upon the length of incarceration for the offender, but probably would be considered in diagnosing the type of treatment to be prescribed. The indeterminate sentence works hand-in-hand with the rehabilitative goal of corrections. It confers broad discretion on parole authorities, who are in the position to judge whether or not a prisoner is sufficiently reformed to justify his release.

Aspects of the pure indeterminate sentence are troubling to this society and have prevented its adoption. The lack of any relationship between the punishment and the crime is bothersome. Secondly, behavior modification is a concept that we neither understand nor are prepared to accept. Finally, without maximum penalties, a person committed to an institution has no idea at all how long he may be imprisoned. There is also no effective control to prevent arbitrary decisions determining length of incarceration. For these reasons, the strictly indeterminate sentence has not been utilized.

On the other hand, modified forms of the indeterminate sentence have been widely adopted in all states but California, Indiana, and Maine.[12] In some states, judges set minimum and maximum terms of imprisonment; in other states, minimum and maximum terms are set by the legislature, and the judge is afforded the discretionary authority to fix a sentence between those ranges. Sometimes the legislature sets a maximum term and allows the judge to determine the minimum; in other instances, the legislature may impose a minimum standard but leave the maximum amount of time that should be served open for the judge to decide. These systems are modified versions of the indeterminate sentence because the judge is granted broad discretion in choosing the actual sentence imposed and because the defendant is eligible for release on parole, often after only a fraction of his sentence is served.

In all states where the modified indeterminate sentence is utilized, prisoners are generally eligible for parole, and in some jurisdictions that eligibility begins immediately after sentencing. In other jurisdictions, the prisoner must serve six months before he is eligible; and still other jurisdictions require the prisoner to serve a proportion of his sentence. In addition, every state but Pennsylvania gives credit for "good time," a designated number of days lopped off the prison term for every month a prisoner stays out of trouble, providing an incentive to prisoners to maintain order during confinement.[13] Thus, even where judges in the majority of states and federal courts believe that they are sending defendants to prison for a definite period of time, in reality indefinite elements are determining the length of the offender's stay in prison.

States that rely on modified forms of the indeterminate sentence are, in essence, also relying on the integrity of the discretionary decision-making process. But the discretion exercised at every step of the correctional process is coming under increasing scrutiny and attack. For most offenses the judge has total power to determine whether an individual will be sent to prison or placed on probation. Once the decision to commit the individual is made, the judge can determine the length of that sentence within the boundaries provided by legislatures. The discretion to deny probation is not reviewable on appeal and only three states provide for review and adjustment of the length of prison sentences.[14] Decisions pertaining to early release are administratively made and the discretion exercised in that process is virtually unassailable.

Dissatisfaction has centered upon various aspects of the sentencing and correctional processes, especially the disparity in sentences, both in the initial decision to incarcerate and length of prison terms imposed. Differences in sentences are often totally irreconcilable from any objective criteria: nature and seriousness of the offense, past criminal records of defendants, or character of defendants. Secondly, the waning respect for the rehabilitative ideal is leading to demands for more practical correctional policies. Finally, dissatisfaction exists with the manner in which correctional institutions are run, and the arbitrariness with which early release decisions are made, compounded by excessive recidivist rates of former inmates.

The Presumptive Fixed Sentence

In between the indeterminate sentence and its variations and the determinate sentence is the *presumptive fixed sentence.* This sentencing model is increasing in popularity within the states, and because it is not as loose as the indeterminate sentence yet not as stringent as the determinate sentence it is also being considered as a model for federal practices.

A prisoner who is given a presumptive fixed sentence is sentenced to a certain amount of time in prison. What this means is that the legislature sets fixed *prison terms* (not ranges) that each crime type must carry. The judge, however, is given leeway in deciding whether mitigating or aggravating circumstances exist that may call for either a slight reduction or increase (usually one year or less in either direction) in the amount of time a specific offender deserves. For example, if the statute sets seven years as the presumptive fixed sentence for manslaughter, it would also build in limited discretion for the sentencing judge, permitting a reduced sentence of six years or an increased sentence of eight years, depending upon mitigating circumstances or established criteria, such as prior record or other exemplary conduct. Optimally, such criteria would be enacted by the legislature.

Under the presumptive sentencing model, the judge is still called upon to use his discretion, but his power is drastically reduced by being kept within certain limits. Parole authorities, however, would no longer retain their responsibility in determining whether or not a prisoner is ready to be released before his sentence is served.

A less extreme example of how legislative standards can limit abuses of discretion and lend certainty to the sentencing process is the proposal that legislatures adopt standards and guidelines to be followed by sentencing judges when deciding which punishment to impose. Accordingly, the legislature would set forth mitigating and aggravating circumstances to be considered by and binding upon the sentencing judge. To further limit the arbitrary exercises of discretion, the legislature would require the sentencing judge to present in the record a statement indicating what circumstances he considered in choosing punishment in each case that comes before him. At the same time, judges would also be aware that their sentencing decisions would be reviewable upon appeal.[15]

A federal approach that was adopted in 1978 by a liberal and conservative coalition in the Senate and stalled in the House of Representatives avoids the pattern of legislative guidelines. Instead, S. 1437 would establish a National Sentencing Commission charged with the establishment of sentencing guidelines and the virtual elimination of parole. The Commission would be mandated to establish categories of offenses and defendants and to promulgate guidelines for sentencing judges in federal courts. Under this system, if a particular sentence would fall outside the sentencing guidelines, the judge would be required to file reasons for the aberration and the sentence would be appealable.[16]

The Determinate Sentence

The essence of determinate sentencing is certainty and predictability. The aim of this mode of sentencing is to remove as much of the discretion as possible from judges who have had the option to choose from a wide array of punishments ranging from probation to long prison sentences. It is also an attempt to control the discretion of prison authorities who now are able to select the type of treatment a prisoner undergoes. And its ultimate aim is to remove the unfettered control of prison authorities and parole boards in determining when a prisoner is released.

Assault upon the vast discretion exercised upon prisoners was begun by prisoners themselves. Academic and political support for the approach followed suit upon the movement begun in the California prison system.

The movement for determinate sentencing generally advocates mandatory prison sentences of a determinate length for those convicted of serious crimes. California, Indiana, and Maine have abandoned all aspects of the indeterminate sentence and have adopted fixed sentences for all criminal convictions. For California, the change was most radical because it had the broadest indeterminate sentencing pattern of any other state in the country. Now in those three states when a defendant leaves a courtroom and is sent to prison, he knows exactly when he will get out. He need not convince any board that he is rehabilitated; he must serve his time. Determinate sentencing is also being considered in fifteen other states. The fixed sentence is altered only by credit for "good time" during confinement, reducing the sentence so many days for each month that an inmate stays out of trouble. Most of the proposals, patterned after the California model, abolish the parole function of providing for early release based upon rehabilitation.[17]

Under the California statute, a judge who sends an offender to prison is given limited authority. The judge is provided with a choice of three prison terms, such as two, three, or four years for robbery or assault, or sale of marijuana. The judge is required to impose the middle sentence, three years, unless specific mitigating or aggravating circumstances are proven at a sentencing hearing.[18] A component of determinate sentencing has been a legislative reduction in the length of prison terms imposed upon those incarcerated. While the indeterminate sentence held sway, lengthy prison sentences were legislatively provided and judicially imposed but rarely served. When fixed-time sentences become the rule, the number of years in a prison term must comport with the reality that the offender will, in fact, serve the imposed sentence.

Mandatory Minimum Sentences

Perhaps the greatest disparity in punishment occurs amongst defendants convicted of the same crime where a few are imprisoned but most are placed on probation. A system that allows for an enormously wide latitude of judicial discretion must expect that persons convicted of similar crimes will not necessarily be treated alike in the determination of punishment. The problem arises, however, when the basis for deciding who shall be imprisoned and who shall not is not apparent from the classification of the offense, nature of the crime, past criminal records of the offenders, or special characteristics of the defendants. Often these decisions appear arbitrarily and discriminatorily made.[19]

Consequently, hand-in-hand with determinate sentencing is the movement to require mandatory minimum prison sentences for all defendants convicted of certain offenses. Certainly, some offenses have never been probationable; the emphasis upon mandatory minimum sentences has been the effort to expand the categories of non-probationable offenses.

Mandatory prison sentences are consistent with the "get tough on criminals" policy which is fast replacing the notion that the prisoner can and should be rehabilitated. The emphasis, then, becomes one of punishing the violator and, hopefully, deterring others from following in his footsteps. Again, the punishment is tailored to the nature and seriousness of the crime committed, and not to the character of the offender. This, of course, provides the basis for the major objection to mandatory prison sentences: if American prisons are anti-rehabilitative, then the commitment to those prisons of more offenders will neither serve to correct the antisocial instincts of the offender nor lessen the likelihood of recidivist behavior after release.

Codification

One of the primary sources of disparity in sentences is the irrational structure of the criminal codes in many states. They are simply not codes but a compilation of statutes enacted by succeeding legislatures with little regard for the law in existence at that time. Traditionally the criminal law in this country has been the dumping ground for problems that arise and cannot be politically or feasibly dealt with by the legislature in any other way. Consequently, legislatures are prone to pronounce the conduct criminal and dispose of the problem in that way; often these statutory responses are unwise and made in anger. Congress and the Johnson Administration's response to mounting Viet Nam protests was an example of this. In anger, and prodded by the White House, Congress enacted a law prohibiting the burning of draft cards. Thus laws are enacted and penalties affixed without consideration of the relative seriousness of the offense compared to other conduct that is prohibited. State legislation is replete with less notorious examples of this kind of response.

Judge Marvin Frankel pointed out two examples that illustrate the point. He found California and Colorado statutes that simply bore no relationship to the penalties affixed in related offenses. An old Colorado statute provided a maximum penalty of ten years in prison for anyone convicted of stealing a dog. While that statute remained on the books, a newer one called for a maximum penalty of six months in prison and a $500 fine for anyone convicted of killing a dog. In California, the maximum penalty for stealing a car was ten years imprisonment, but a defendant could be sentenced to fifteen years for only breaking into the car to steal from the glove compartment.[20]

Following the lead of the American Law Institute's Model Penal Code, many states since the early 1960s have attempted to truly codify their criminal laws, with Illinois taking the initial lead. Real codification is a multi-faceted process. The first step is to weed out those antiquated criminal laws that reflected the morality of their times, such as Sunday blue laws. The next step is to group offenses by substantive categories so that all homicide offenses, for example, are grouped together in the same chapter. Then each offense within a chapter must be categorized in terms of its seriousness, vis-a-vis the other offenses within the chapter and vis-a-vis the seriousness of substantive subjects contained in other chapters. For instance, all homicide offenses are likely to be considered more serious than even the most serious offense prohibiting theft. Penalties are removed from the individual statutes and contained in a separate chapter dealing with penalties. Each offense then in each chapter must be categorized as a Class A, B, C, or D fclony with a similar categorization for misdemeanors, and the applicable punishment is determined by reference to the penalty section for that class of offense.[21] It is but an initial step at the legislative level to introduce rationality into the punishment ranges and towards controlling some of the disparity in sentencing. However, it is but a first step.

Sentencing the Accused

Although the sentencing judge has unfettered discretion in choosing appropriate punishment in any case, it may be severely curtailed where a legislature deems an offense non-probationable or adopts a scheme requiring determinate or mandatory prison sentences, but very few have yet to do so. It is that vast discretion which creates sentencing disparities impairing the fairness and credibility of the system for the administration of criminal justice.

Disparity results from the absence of standards. Without standards, each judge applies his own philosophy of punishment and is prone to react subjectively to each defendant and his crime. Because they lack standards, judges sitting on the same multi-judge court in large cities are imposing radically different punishments on defendants who are virtually alike in terms of the nature of their offense, their past criminal records, and their characters. These disparities result because one judge views the seriousness of a crime differently from another, or has more sympathy for a defendant or his victim than another judge, or because of prejudice, or because of friendship or professional contact with a lawyer representing one defendant but not with the lawyer representing another defendant. Judges need not explain why one co-defendant is placed on probation, and another is given a minimal prison sentence, while the third co-defendant is sent to prison for the maximum term allowed under the statute. And few appellate courts inquire into the judges' reasoning.

Most disparity can be avoided by the adoption of mandatory determinate sentences. But are we ready to go that far? It demands an acceptance of the philosophy that the punishment must fit the crime, irrespective of the character of the offender and the circumstances that surrounded his crime. Considering the anti-rehabilitative nature of American prisons and their dismal failure evidenced by recidivist crime rates, sending all convicted persons to prison could very well exchange one problem for an even greater one. For instance, an article in the *Criminal Justice Newsletter* states:

> California's new determinate sentencing law has coincided with, if not caused, a steep increase in prison commitments.[22]

California's new law, according to this article, may have reduced sentencing disparity, but at what cost?

Less draconian, but at the same time less restrictive on the exercise of discretion, are sentencing guidelines accompanied by a requirement that substantial deviations from the guidelines be explained in the record and reviewed on appeal. The value of such a procedure is the belief that making the judge accountable for his decisions will discourage arbitrary and capricious action.

Absent mandatory guidelines, there has been some training of judges aimed at creating internalized guidelines. Judges assembled at conferences are asked to impose sentences in hypothetical situations and then discuss their differences. The aim, of course, is to make each judge aware that there are opinions different from his own and to influence the extremes closer to a centrist position.[23]

The problem we are faced with is figuring out what we want from the sentencing judge. Do we want judges who are totally neutral and who determine punishment in an emotional vacuum, or do we want judges who are representative of the community and able to incorporate the aspirations and fears of that community in their decisions? Obviously neither extreme is satisfactory. We need neutral judges who are representative of the legitimate aspirations and needs, not irrationality, prejudices, and injustices, of the community. Yet the criminal justice system cannot depend on the ability of our judges to be skillful automatons. Elected judges are cognizant of public reaction, and appointed judges are often too political. Even federal judges, who have the security of life tenure, can turn out to be political, vindictive, and prejudiced. Perhaps the continental European system of training lawyers for a career as judges, rather than appointing or electing lawyers to judgeships, holds the answer, but there the risk is great that the judges will become responsive only to the bureaucratic structure of which they are a part and not responsive to the community or the ideals of the society.

Sentencing guidelines with review of decisions appears to be the best approach to controlling ill-defined exercises of discretion. While that movement spreads, however, we rely generally on enforcing due process procedures at the sentencing hearing and attempting to make the sentencing judge as informed as possible before he pronounces sentence. To provide that information, most jurisdictions supply the judge with a *presentence report.* Some jurisdictions require it in all cases, some in all felony cases, and others in felony cases where the judge is considering probation rather than imprisonment as the appropriate punishment. On the other hand, the National Advisory Commission recommends that presentence reports be required whenever imprisonment is a potential punishment.[24]

Prepared by probation departments, presentence reports are to provide the sentencing judge with as much information as possible about the character of the accused and his environment. From this information, the judge may be able to glean why the person committed the crime and whether or not additional criminal behavior can be expected from this offender. As to the nature of the crime and the facts surrounding the defendant's involvement, the judge will already have that information from trial or from the colloquy accompanying the entry of a guilty plea.

The National Advisory Commission recommended that these reports contain full information so that the judge has a complete understanding of the background and motivation of the offender. Often, however, these reports contain nothing more than a description of the offense and the defendant's past criminal record. Limited personnel and resources in probation departments frequently preclude the possibility of more extensive reports.

Whether the defense team should have access to the presentence report has been a matter of ongoing controversy. California makes disclosure automatic, while some states totally preclude its disclosure, and a majority place the decision to disclose the contents of the report in the hands of the judge. The main argument in favor of disclosure is that the defendant should have the opportunity to refute inaccurate information. Advocates of retaining the secrecy rule insist that it is the only way to assure that sources will speak freely without fear of reprisal.[25] Federal rules provide for disclosure of the report to the defense except for sentencing recommendations made by the probation department. The federal judge, however, is given discretion to withhold parts of the report if it would interfere with a program of rehabilitation or in order to protect the source of information.[26]

At the sentencing hearing, the prosecution and defense have the opportunity to introduce evidence relevant to punishment or its mitigation, and to present arguments to the court. The defendant has the absolute right to be represented by counsel at this stage of the proceeding and for that attorney to be heard by the court. The sentencing judge may rely upon all sorts of information in determining appropriate punishment in a given case. It has long been the law that a defendant has no right to confront and cross-examine persons making damaging statements about him to the court officer preparing the presentence report.[27] That position, however, is so opposite the due process developments which have come later, that its continuing viability is subject to conjecture and doubt. At least one federal Court of Appeals has taken the position that where a presentence report contains a statement damaging to the defendant which was allegedly made by the defendant to the probation officer conducting the presentence inquiry, the defense must have the opportunity to confront and cross-examine the probation officer or the court must disregard the statement.[28] Note, however, that such protection, as minimal as it is, exists only in those jurisdictions where the defense has access to the presentence report. In a majority of states the defense still has no knowledge of the contents of the presentence report, nor any inkling about which information the judge is taking into consideration and views as significant.

At the sentencing hearing, each side has an opportunity to present evidence to the court and to argue in favor of its position. Rarely does the prosecution present any evidence at this stage. Most of the evidence which it would offer is already contained in the presentence report where generally it is not subject to impeachment through cross-examination. The prosecutor in argument may offer the state's position on punishment in the particular case to the court, including a recommendation. Subject to any agreement reached during plea bargaining, the state's recommendation may range from a suggestion that probation would be sufficient protection to the community to advocacy that the court impose the greatest sentence allowed by law. If the plea bargain dictated the state's recommendation or dictated that the prosecutor must remain silent at this point and offer no recommendation, the prosecutor will be held to that agreement.[29] Unless the court participated in the plea negotiation or indicated prior approval of a negotiated agreement, the judge is totally free to disregard the recommendation of the prosecutor as well as that of the defense attorney.

Defense attorneys present evidence at this stage only slightly more often than prosecutors do. Emphasis is placed upon defense counsel's ability to argue in mitigation of punishment. Naturally, the defendant's main concern is reducing his chances of going to prison, or if imprisonment is a foregone conclusion then his concern is with the length of sentence imposed which dictates the date of his earliest possible release. When sentencing follows a verdict of guilty at trial rather than a guilty plea, defense attorney's main task is to convince the court that his client is not as bad as he was made out to be at trial. These arguments are tailored to the judge's inclinations and past record in similar cases. If the judge is believed to consider family stability as the key to preventing recidivist behavior, then the argument will attempt to show the defendant's devotion to his family. Similarly, if the judge is concerned about treatment, defense counsel will attempt to present to the court a comprehensive program for community-based treatment demonstrating supervision and treatment of the defendant's various aberrational conditions, ranging from health to employment. Sometimes defense pleas amount to nothing more than routine exercise where imprisonment is a certainty, and the defense attorney's only hope is to reduce the length of sentence.

The defendant may participate in the sentencing hearing. He is free in most states to make a statement to the court attempting to explain his behavior, ask the court's forgiveness, or discuss anything relevant to the issues at stake. With presentence report in hand and the arguments of both counsel ringing in his ears, as well as any statement offered by the defendant, the judge pronounces sentence. Except in capital cases, the judge can be reasonably assured that as the representative of the state and the community at this point, the sentence that he pronounces will not be successfully challenged or even reviewed.

Punishment Options

Even though we hear a lot from the national media about prisons and prison failures, less than one-third of defendants convicted of crimes are imprisoned.[30] Except as circumscribed by legislation, the sentencing judge has several other options among the statutorily provided forms of punishment.

Fines

Monetary penalties for violations of criminal ordinances and statutes are the form with which we are all familiar. Most Americans have paid them several times for the commission of traffic violations. This form of penalty, however, is not confined to minor traffic offenses. Legislatures often provide stiff fines as one form of punishment for serious felonies. They may be assessed in conjunction with or in lieu of prison sentences. Often, fines alone are assessed in business-related and white collar crimes, frequently involving government corruption. There is a certain illogic to this approach because if deterrence of others plays a role in the sentencing of individual offenders, potential white-collar criminals are the only group likely to be deterred from future criminal acts by the certainty of a prison sentence. Learning of monetary penalties assessed against their peers is hardly likely to frighten these would-be offenders. To the most unscrupulous of white-collar offenders, these penalties are treated as costs of doing business and may be ultimately passed on to the consumer.[31]

The assessment of fines upon the indigent defendant has been historically one of the cardinal examples of the discrimination based upon poverty built into the system for the administration of criminal justice. Until the mid-1960s, it was not at all unusual to hear sentences pronounced: "Thirty dollars or thirty days." What that meant, of course, was that a defendant who had the money could pay it and resume his customary life, but one who did not have the money would spend the following month in jail—solely because he did not have the money, not because incarceration was an appropriate penalty. The Supreme Court examined this approach and found it to be far short of meeting due process standards. Initially, the Supreme Court said that a defendant could not be kept in jail working off a fine longer than the maximum jail sentence provided in the statute.[32] Then the Supreme Court added that if the statute did not provide a jail sentence, it would be invidious discrimination to impose one upon a defendant convicted under the statute simply because he was unable to pay the fine. The Court said that a sentencing court must provide alternatives, such as installment payments, to insure that persons could comply with the fines.[33] Trial courts, so inclined, have developed ways to avoid the restriction, clearly in violation of the higher Court's intent. The restriction can be avoided if the sentencing judge has information prior to imposing the sentence that the defendant has cash on his person at the court session. Assured that the defendant has money, the judge will impose punishment in the form of a fine. If the judge is not informed that the defendant has enough money to pay the fine, then a jail sentence is imposed as the only penalty and there is no reference in the record of the case that the accused is being ordered to jail because he does not have the funds to pay a fine. There is a good lesson here for all who wish to study the criminal justice system and the law, and to possibly be a part of those institutions as a career objective: no matter how finely the law is written, the realization of justice is dependent upon the good-faith adherence to the law by the men and women who are charged with its administration.

Community-Based Corrections Programs

Most defendants are placed on probation following conviction, though frequently probation is used in conjunction with a fine. It usually involves the imposition of a prison sentence, which is suspended pending satisfaction of certain conditions. In some jurisdictions, a defendant is referred to probation without pronouncement of a sentence of confinement, and if the offender's probation is later revoked he will be sentenced.

To the defendant probation means freedom and escape from a prison sentence. For the community, however, the heart of probation is in the *conditions imposed* and *supervision* of the offender during the probationary period. The conditions, within the discretion of the sentencing judge, seek to try to undo the damage caused by the offender's crime, if that is possible, through restitution to the victims, and to redirect the life-style of the offender. The judge may select conditions ranging far and wide involving the offender's place of residence, nature of employment, evening and weekend curfews, avoidance of certain persons and hangouts, and prescribed counselling. Violations of these conditions or proof of subsequent criminal activity during the probationary period may result in revocation of the probation and the sentencing of the defendant to prison.[34]

A critical aspect of probation is the frequency, quality, and intensity of the supervision. Probation officers are supposed to keep tabs on their assigned offenders. Supervision is for the purpose of insuring that the probationer is not violating the conditions imposed by the court. The probation officer can assist those assigned to him to secure training and employment and channel the probationer into needed health and social care services. The probation officer is also available as a counsellor and a person with whom the probationer should be able to discuss personal problems and other matters which may affect his ability to adjust to a life free of criminal activity. The success of probation as an alternative to prison depends on the ability of the probation officer to meet frequently with his charges and to develop sufficient familiarity with their lives and problems. Unfortunately, case loads in this aspect of the criminal justice system reflect the overcrowded dockets of the court and, often, close supervision is simply not possible. Contact between the case supervisor and the probationer often becomes infrequent and the necessary follow-up to determine the truth of the probationer's statements becomes impossible. It is not unusual today for the contact to be limited to a monthly or bi-monthly telephone conversation, which can hardly be the basis for formation of a constructive relationship or close supervision. In some courts an offender may be sentenced to *inactive probation,* which involves no supervision or follow-up at all and amounts only to an admonition to the offender to stay out of trouble so that the probation will not be revoked and the offender incarcerated.

Whatever the inadequacies of the probation system in any given city, there are certain positive attributes. Even the closest probation supervision is far less costly than the cost of maintaining someone in prison.[35] Recidivist rates amongst those on probation tend to be lower than those who have served prison sentences. In addition, there are those who argue that prison life is so debilitating and dehumanizing that the prison experience should be reserved only for the criminal who poses a real and present danger of harm to the community.

Probation is not the only available form of community-based correctional treatment. It may take many forms that may be supplemental or independent of probationary supervision. Judges may commit the individual to the care of a social program, instead of under the direct supervision by the probation department, which is an arm of the court. The social programs may involve health care, family counselling, job training and placement, or any other of a number of social-based treatments. A fairly novel form, at least in this century, is sentencing offenders, generally those convicted of relatively minor offenses, to community service. One such program exists in Alameda County, California, where municipal judges are sentencing offenders to work-placement at voluntary and public agencies. Depending upon the nature of the criminal violation, a defendant may consent to be ordered to perform from four to over four hundred hours of volunteer work. Most often the job assignments involve clerical or maintenance work. The program has spread to forty-five other California communities and to Portland, Oregon where twenty-four hours of volunteer work is the minimally acceptable alternative to traditional criminal penalties. The significance of the volunteer-work programs is in its recognition of the inadequacies of conventional forms of punishment and the need to experiment and develop alternative means.[36]

Imprisonment

Even when the decision is made to imprison an offender, the sentencing court has some discretion, pertaining to time and the nature of the institution where the offender will be held. One of the early aims of prison reformers was classification of prisoners and the separation of the hardened criminal from the non-violent offender. In our age, that separation aims to protect the individual prisoner and society. The non-violent offender must be kept from dangerous criminals, for his own safety and also to minimize the chances of his being influenced by the undesirable characters that would surround him.

If persons convicted of misdemeanors are incarcerated they are imprisoned for less than a year and are not shipped to general prisons. They are confined, on the whole, in jails and workhouses, which usually are only extensions of city or county jails. Depending upon funds and the community's inclination, there may be education and job-skill training in these institutions for defendants who have already been convicted and sentenced. Some even have *work-release programs,* where selected prisoners are permitted to leave during the day and work at jobs they held before conviction. They might embark on new jobs found through the institution, and then return to the jail or workhouse at night. Work-release, which makes unquestioning sense for the non-dangerous offender who will be institutionalized for only a short time, is a very fragile concept. Naturally, the easiest way to maintain an institution is to keep people locked up all day and night; prisoners checking out for work and checking in upon return create complications for a bureaucracy that has difficulty fulfilling its minimal responsibilities. Aside from bureaucratic opposition, there is a public relations problem. Many in the community fear any contact with persons convicted of crime, even non-dangerous offenders, and shrink from even the thought of contact with these people. Moreover, this type of program is often categorized as "coddling criminals" and is not likely to be politically appealing. So fragile is work-release's acceptability that any negative publicity caused by the failure of one prisoner to return as expected is likely to result in public clamor for its abandonment.[37]

Depending upon state law, some felons may also be imprisoned in these local facilities. Naturally, these persons would be those who are not dangerous and for whom it is even questionable whether a prison sentence was appropriate punishment. For example, experienced penologists have long condemned prison sentences for defendants convicted of vehicular homicide. They argue that these defendants do not belong in prisons and that they are so guilt-ridden that they are unable and disinclined to protect themselves in prison and are victimized by their fellow inmates. Nonetheless, judges sometimes feel obliged to mete out prison sentences to these offenders because of the nature of the harm that they committed or because of public demand.

Many states try to distinguish classes of felons, as well, by having separate institutions for younger offenders, generally inhabited by convicted felons between the ages of eighteen and thirty, and institutions for offenders over the age of thirty and those who have committed heinous crimes. Reformatories, housing younger prisoners, are supposed to be educationally oriented, with emphasis upon training for re-entry into society. Penitentiaries, housing older and dangerous felons, have less resources for training programs and are more obsessed with restraining the offender and preventing his commission of other crimes, at least during the period of his confinement. These distinctions break down, however. Generally, throughout the nation the concern in both types of institutions is on security, and often little else. Due to a scarcity of funds, the training available in reformatories is hardly any more extensive and comprehensive than that available in penitentiaries. Prisons are so crowded today that placement categorization standards are not always followed. Because of crowded conditions, young prisoners who otherwise qualify for placement in reformatories are being sent to penitentiaries.

Essentially, American prisons are in fact anti-rehabilitative. Conditions in all prisons, except for a few federal installations labeled as "country clubs" and even fewer state reformatories, are brutal and often inhuman. Prison life has changed very little over the past hundred years. Today's institutions are remarkably like those of Victorian England which were characterized in a 1978 Broadway play depicting Oscar Wilde's imprisonment when he laments: "If this is the way her majesty treats her prisoners, she doesn't deserve to have any."[38]

While penological philosophy has made several shifts during this century, the nature of prisons and prison-life has remained unaffected. The wretchedness of some penal institutions is such that a few courts have recognized certain conditions as partial defenses to a charge of prison escape levied against inmates who have recognized claims of violence or sexual debasement committed upon a prisoner as at least a partial justification for his attempted escape. Frequently, though, that claim is only recognized if the escapee turns himself in once he has reached sanctuary.

In the early part of the 1970s, a flurry of prisoner-oriented law suits were filed against state correctional authorities. They were premised upon the conditions existing in state penal institutions. Under the rubric provided by the Eighth Amendment's prohibition against cruel and unusual punishment and made applicable to the states through the due process clause of the Fourteenth Amendment,[39] judges were declaring that confinement in some state institutions was *per se* a violation of Eighth Amendment standards, because of the harshness of the living conditions and the intolerable state of disrepair of some of these institutions. Successful suits were launched against the Alabama, Arkansas, and Rhode Island penal systems, sometimes resulting in court orders directing the states to improve prison conditions or release the inmates.[40] Local jails were also under similar attack. Some were ordered closed by federal courts and radical alterations of conditions were ordered in others.[41] For a few years it appeared almost as though the federal judiciary was prepared to take over the management of state correctional facilities in order to insure changes in conditions which would make those institutions constitutionally tolerable. While some suits are still being filed or are pending, the federal courts, after insuring some changes in state jails and prisons, have largely backed off. State penal officials, with one eye on the federal judiciary for possible interference, seem to be fully in control of their institutions and the power to determine the conditions of those prisons.

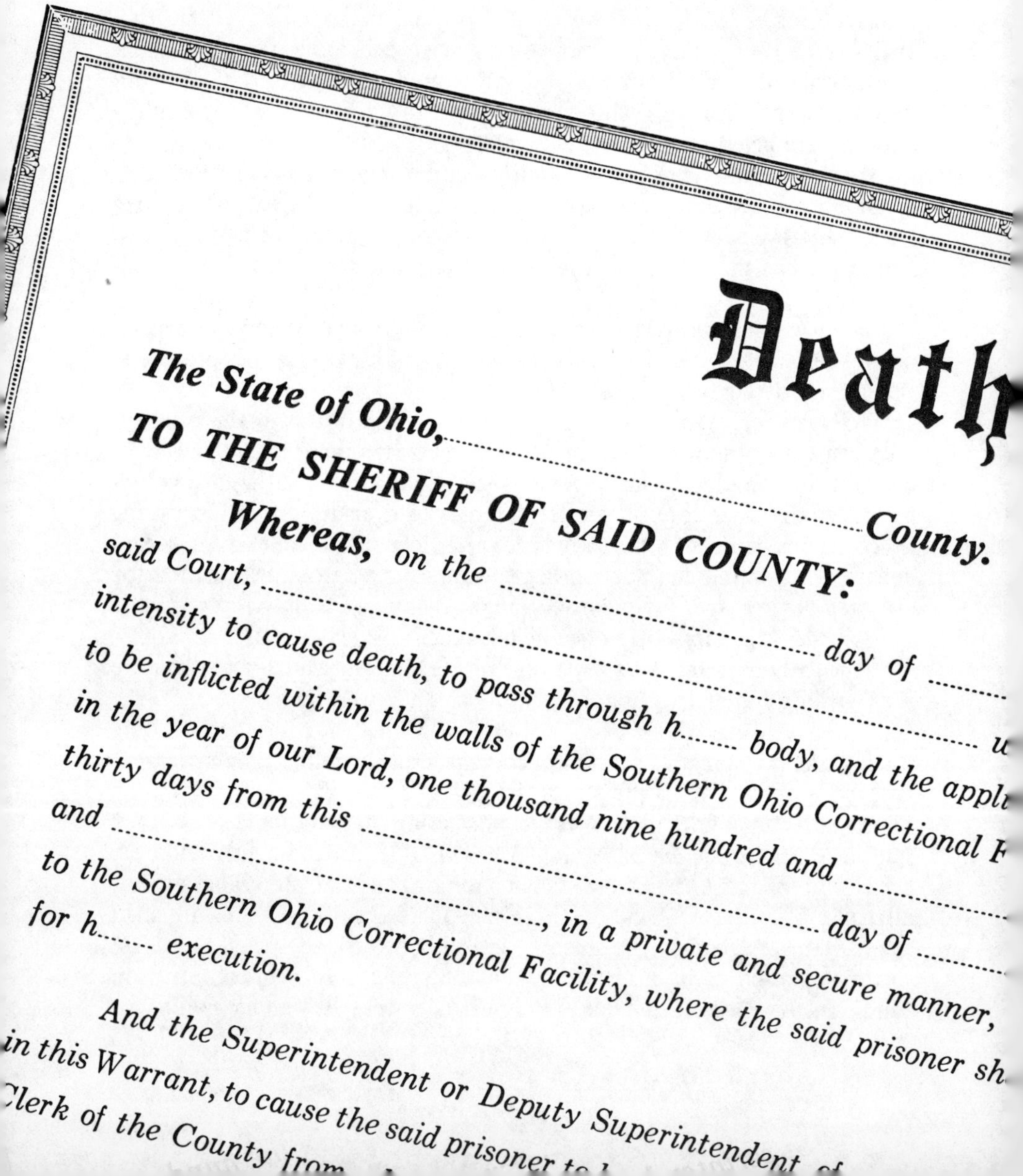
Death

The State of Ohio, ... County.

TO THE SHERIFF OF SAID COUNTY:

Whereas, on the .... day of ....

said Court, ... u

intensity to cause death, to pass through h...... body, and the appl

to be inflicted within the walls of the Southern Ohio Correctional F

in the year of our Lord, one thousand nine hundred and ....

thirty days from this .... day of ....

and ...., in a private and secure manner,

to the Southern Ohio Correctional Facility, where the said prisoner sh

for h...... execution.

And the Superintendent or Deputy Superintendent of

in this Warrant, to cause the said prisoner to

Clerk of the County from

The Death Penalty

In a landmark decision announced on the eve of the nation's 200th birthday, the U.S. Supreme Court—by a 7-2 vote—upheld the constitutionality of capital punishment.[42] The Court's action came in response to appeals by condemned men in five states who argued that the death penalty is inherently "cruel and unusual punishment" in violation of the Eighth Amendment.[43]

In affirming capital sentences from Georgia, Florida, and Texas, the majority flatly rejected this contention. "The death penalty is not," ruled the Court, "a form of punishment that may never be imposed." As long as certain procedural safeguards are observed during trial, the states are free to conduct executions at least in cases of premeditated murder.

At the same time, however, the Court overturned the statutes in North Carolina and Louisiana, which required mandatory death sentences for specified crimes. Such laws, stated the majority, are unconstitutionally cruel and unusual in that they do not allow judges and juries to consider mitigating or aggravating circumstances before imposing sentence.

. . . And Now

While the Supreme Court unequivocally answered the basic constitutional questions in issue, its ruling did not result in immediate resumption of executions. On the contrary, it neglected to address many important procedural questions, and there is as yet no certainty that the several states will ever again resume wholesale executions.

In fact, the Court itself, in the first opinion to follow its bicentennial year decision, further clouded the issues by warning that there is an as yet undefined "special responsibility" to guarantee due process in capital trials.[44] On the basis of this rather loose dicta, defense attorneys have been pressing the Court for a fuller explanation of due process standards, while prosecutors and legislators can only shudder in dismay.

"Death Wish"

Certain events that took place shortly after the 1976 decision may have contributed to the Supreme Court's recent caution and growing division over the death question. Perhaps the most dramatic—and certainly the most bizarre—development was the case of Gary Mark Gilmore.

A convicted murderer on Utah's death row, Gilmore created a sensation in late 1976 when he abruptly fired his attorneys, abandoned his appeal, and requested that his execution be carried out at the earliest possible date. Appearing personally before incredulous supreme court justices, Gilmore argued passionately that he had a "right to die." He insisted at a later news conference that successive delays would only prolong his "intolerable agony," and he advised all "do-gooders" to "butt-out" of the case.

The state court heard and rejected arguments from attorneys that Gilmore's "death wish" was "tantamount to suicide" and, therefore, clear evidence that he was insane and incapable of representing himself. As a result, all pending appeals were promptly dismissed, and the matter was referred to the state Board of Pardons. While that body examined his case, Gilmore's mother filed a petition in the U.S. Supreme Court seeking a stay of execution.[45] She argued that her son was incompetent and therefore unable to knowingly and intelligently waive his right to appeal. The high court finally rejected her petition and, in a brief written opinion, held that she had no standing, or legal position, to seek relief for her son.

By this time, the Gilmore case had taken on a tragically comic air. With his case under review by the Supreme Court, and with his execution temporarily stayed, Gilmore attempted suicide in prison by taking an overdose of sedatives. Daily news accounts of the case chronicled his pathetic love affair with a young girl who, as part of a "suicide pact," had attempted to kill herself on the same day as Gilmore. Strangely enough, an attorney was appointed by the state court to assist him in seeking an execution date. The attorney later revealed that he had a financial interest in the case, and that he had secured the exclusive right to act as Gilmore's biographer and agent.

Later, a West Coast promoter negotiated a six-figure contract giving this attorney exclusive publication and motion picture rights to Gilmore's life story. Not surprisingly, "Gary Gilmore" tee-shirts appeared, and national magazines and newspapers engaged in a bidding war to secure "exclusive" interviews and stories.

After the Supreme Court elected not to intervene, Gilmore's execution was again rescheduled—this time for January 17, 1977. Angered over this further delay and by the efforts of independent legal groups to challenge his actions through collateral law suits, Gilmore staged yet another unsuccessful attempt to suicide.

As the fateful day approached, the news media descended like locusts on the ancient state prison near Salt Lake City to begin the death watch. Consistent with contractual obligations to his agent, Gilmore refused to grant interviews with the press and spent his final hours trying to cheer his bewildered relatives. Meanwhile, a last-ditch appeal by outsiders met with momentary success when a federal judge issued a stay of execution. Within hours, however, the judge's order was vacated by a federal appellate court, and the countdown continued.

While the firing squad assembled and Gilmore was being led to the execution chamber, mobile television crews scurried around the prison grounds hoping to record the sounds of the final fusillade. Several clergymen silently picketed in front of the prison's massive gates, enduring the provocations of a "pro-death" group that threw raw eggs at them. Finally, a prison spokesman broke the news: Gary Gilmore had become the first man in ten years to be executed in an American prison.

Renewed Debate

Experts on both sides of the issue agree that the Gary Gilmore episode—for all its morbidity and sorrow—has intensified the moral debate over capital punishment. Proponents of the death penalty interpret Gilmore's cavalier stand as an example of what they have been saying all along: that a hardened criminal must be dealt with on his own terms. Gilmore's personal motives are irrelevant, they insist, and the important thing is that a convicted murderer was condemned to die and his sentence carried out. Abolitionists disagree. They view capital punishment as a brutalizing relic of the past that caused Gilmore—in anguish and horror—to view death as the only possible release.

While the debate raged on about the various implications of the Gary Gilmore story, legislators in Texas, Oklahoma, and other states wrestled with a highly controversial proposal that would replace the electric chair with lethal drug injections. The new legislation was backed by supporters of capital punishment who were genuinely horrified by the "grisly business" of electrocution. One Texas state senator who voted for the change said that in earlier hearings on animal abuse he asked a humane society representative whether or not she would approve of burning animals to death by means of electricity. "Certainly not," she replied. "We could get slapped with an injunction or prosecuted under existing state laws."

Opponents of drug injections were quick to point out several pitfalls and deficiencies in the new plan. For one thing, no licensed doctor could perform the intravenous injection because it would be a violation of his professional oath. In addition, the exact concoction of drugs to be used is not prescribed in the law, and there is no way that the precise moment of death can be determined. Several members of the opposition questioned whether the scheme would be foolproof since it is conceivable that non-lethal, coma-inducing drugs could readily be substituted. In any case, the new law will bring about a further delay while its constitutionality is tested in an appeal to the U.S. Supreme Court.

The Supreme Court and Capital Punishment

Although capital punishment is one of the country's oldest legal controversies, the U.S. Supreme Court did not become directly involved until the early 1960s. Prior to this, the death penalty debate was waged exclusively in the legislative branch, where the *wisdom* of death sentences was questioned solely on humanitarian grounds. The high court had not dealt with the problem before and consequently there was never any doubt about the essential *legality* of a death statute under the U.S. Constitution.

All this changed in 1963, however, when Justice Arthur J. Goldberg suggested that capital punishment may be a *per se* violation of the Eighth Amendment bar against "cruel and unusual punishment." Citing the alarming frequency of death sentences in rape cases, Goldberg was concerned that the practice involved "taking human life to protect a value *other* than human life." Where less severe sanctions—such as life imprisonment—are available, he said, the death penalty could amount to "unnecessary cruelty."

The First Breakthrough

Attorneys for condemned prisoners knew that Justice Goldberg was not speaking for the majority when he issued his 1963 statement; consequently, the first cases to come before the Supreme Court were argued on relatively narrow grounds to test the full court's willingness to tackle the problem. In *Witherspoon v. Illinois,* 391 U.S. 510 (1968), for example, the question was not whether capital punishment is unconstitutional, but whether or not the procedures used in capital trials are fundamentally fair. The Court ruled that the jury selection process that prevailed in most states was unconstitutional because potential jurors with religious or conscientious opposition to death sentences were systematically excluded. Such "death qualified" juries, reasoned the Court, are unconstitutional under the Sixth Amendment guarantee of an "impartial" jury. As a result, the death sentences of many inmates were reversed, and in most cases life imprisonment was substituted.

Emboldened by their success in *Witherspoon* and other cases, defense attorneys began a full-scale challenge of the death penalty under the Eighth Amendment arguments advanced by Justice Goldberg. In a series of cases, these attorneys—many of whom were associated with the NAACP Legal Defense fund—focused on the racial factors underlying jury decisions in capital cases.

It was shown by statistics that black defendants on trial in Southern states were far more likely to receive a death sentence than whites accused of the same crime. In rape cases, for example, black men who had been convicted of raping white women drew capital sentences in 98 percent of the reported cases. In contrast, no white man had ever been executed for the rape of a black woman. The probability of a white person receiving a death verdict in a murder case was three in ten; for a black person, it was nearly five in ten.

These and other statistics were combined with a mass of supporting evidence to illustrate that minorities—the black, the illiterate, and the poor—received harsher treatment than others. Thus, argued the NAACP, capital sentences are too often the product of discrimination, and it is therefore "cruel and unusual" to inflict the death penalty in such a haphazard way.

Furman v. Georgia

In 1972, a sharply divided Supreme Court finally responded and in *Furman v. Georgia,* 408 U.S. 238 (1972), it ruled that the death penalty, as then being carried out, was unconstitutional. Although the decision had great practical impact for the nation's death row inmates (most of whom later received life sentences), the difficult questions remained unanswered.

When the *Furman* decision was released, it was immediately obvious that the Supreme Court had failed to agree on the basic question of whether capital punishment is in all cases a violation of the Constitution. The Court's action was announced in a terse one-page *per curiam* order, which stated only that the cases were reversed. No two justices were able to come to complete agreement on the issues, and each wrote a separate opinion. The majority of the Court, however, objected to the fact that the decision between life imprisonment and the death penalty was "left to the uncontrolled discretion of judges and juries." The "arbitrary, wanton, and freakish" way in which some defendants were selected to die and others were allowed to live was held to be a violation of the Eighth Amendment.

The decision was greeted by a storm of protest from across the nation. With the incidence of violent crime increasing at an alarming rate, many leaders were concerned that one of the "last tools for effective law enforcement" was in serious jeopardy. What was particularly vexing was the fact that the Supreme Court offered no concrete guidelines by which the states could cure the constitutional infirmities of existing laws.

In the end, however, 35 states, as well as Congress, passed new legislation. Several jurisdictions interpreted *Furman* as a ban against jury participation in sentencing procedures; their solution was to enact statutes which provide for an automatic, or "mandatory," sentence of death if the defendant is found guilty of a specific crime. Others opted for a less rigid approach and set up detailed guidelines which limit the discretionary powers of judges and juries.

Within a short time, death houses throughout the country were once again filled with condemned prisoners, and by 1974 the Supreme Court had docketed a number of cases testing the new laws.

A Divided Court

The July, 1976, death penalty rulings were announced in five separate cases from Florida, Georgia, Louisiana, North Carolina, and Texas. The major opinion was written in the case of *Gregg v. Georgia,* 428 U.S. 153 (1976). The defendant, Troy Leon Gregg, was convicted of a particularly cold-blooded murder that occurred in November, 1973.

The Court's Holding

After several appeals in state court proved unsuccessful, Gregg's case was granted review by the U.S. Supreme Court. Initially, the majority opinion noted that while the Constitution is silent on this specific question, there are several references in the text of the Constitution which indicate that capital punishment was accepted by the Founding Fathers. For one thing, the Fifth Amendment requires a grand jury indictment in the case of a "capital or otherwise infamous crime," and prevents a person from "twice being put in jeopardy of life or limb." In addition, both the Fifth and Fourteenth Amendments speak of a person's right to *"life,* liberty, and property" in the due process clause [emphasis added]. Finally, the Court found further historical support in the fact that the first Congress—the same body that approved the Bill of Rights—also enacted the original federal criminal code, which contained death penalty provisions for certain crimes.

But simply because a particular legal sanction may have been universally accepted in 1791 is not, in the Supreme Court's view, the decisive factor. The Constitution has always been regarded as a dynamic instrument of the law, one which takes its meaning largely from contemporary values. Thus, because the Eighth Amendment only prohibits "cruel and unusual" punishment in very general terms, it is up to the courts to decide whether a certain practice is constitutional. If public floggings, facial mutilation, or other forms of corporal punishment were in issue, courts today would unquestionably rule them unconstitutional, even though such methods were widely in use at the time the Eighth Amendment was adopted.

Over the years, however, the high court focused increasingly on contemporary notions of *humane justice.*

The Court's Analysis

In its assessment of the constitutionality of capital punishment, the Supreme Court was obligated by precedent to determine whether or not contemporary American values condoned the death penalty. At the outset of his majority opinion, Justice Stewart explained that only the *objective* indications of public attitudes toward capital punishment—not the *subjective* opinions of the nine Supreme Court justices—would be considered. Accordingly, he looked to the public's response during the four years since the *Furman* case and found the following:

- The legislatures of 35 states enacted new statutes reinstituting the death penalty and provided new procedures to diminish the chances that they would be "wantonly and freakishly" imposed.
- Despite the efforts of death penalty critics, neither the federal government nor any state legislature was persuaded actually to abolish capital punishment on the strength of public opinion or the decision in *Furman.*
- In the only statewide referendum held since 1972, the voters of California overwhelmingly approved a state constitutional amendment authorizing capital punishment.
- National public opinion polls revealed that 59 percent of the population favored the restoration of capital punishment.
- Despite the claims of opponents to capital punishment, there is no conclusive proof that the death penalty fails to function as a deterrent to crime.

On the strength of this evidence the Supreme Court concluded that under the "evolving standards of decency" test, capital punishment is not a *per se* violation of the Eighth Amendment. This does not mean, however, that other constitutional limitations on the imposition of the death penalty are thereby precluded. It remains the duty of the Supreme Court to ensure that state statutes are set up so as to preserve the basic concept of "human dignity," and if in fact death is to be a penalty, defendants in capital cases may only be condemned by fair procedures.

Procedural Requirements

Having answered the threshold question of whether capital punishment is unconstitutional in all cases, the Court turned its attention to the statutory scheme under which the defendant, Troy Gregg, was sentenced to death by the trial jury. In the wake of the *Furman* decision, the Georgia legislature sought to prevent the "arbitrary and capricious" application of capital punishment by narrowing the circumstances under which the judge or jury could impose a sentence of death. If the trial is before a jury, the statute provides two separate proceedings—one to determine the issue of guilt and another to impose sentence.

Under previous statutes the jury decided both guilt and sentence at the same time. Critics of this procedure pointed out that an accused was unfairly forced to take the stand: while he may not want to open himself to damaging cross-examination, it is essential, in this life-and-death situation, that he make personal contact with the jury and thereby increase his chances for survival. Under the new Georgia statute, however, the defendant may claim the full protections of his Fifth Amendment right to remain silent during the guilt stage, and later, in the sentencing proceeding, submit evidence in mitigation and even take the stand to plead for his life.

The Georgia statute also stipulates that the death penalty may be imposed only if the jury certifies that one of ten statutorily specified "aggravating circumstances" was proved by the state. These include cases where the murder was committed for hire; where the victim was a policeman, judge, or prison guard; where the defendant was engaged in an armed robbery, burglary, or an act of arson; or where the murder was "outrageously or wantonly vile, horrible, or inhuman in that it involved torture, depravity of mind, or an aggravated (assault) to the victim."

Such standards, held the Court, satisfy the constitutional requirements of the *Furman* decision. Since the jury can only impose the death penalty on the basis of objective facts, there is little risk that passion and prejudice will play an impermissible role in the final determination. Thus, the individual circumstance of the defendant's crime—not his social or economic status—is the pivotal element.

Another requirement of the Georgia statute is that the state supreme court must review each case. The state court is to examine the trial record for any evidence of prejudice and satisfy itself that the aggravated circumstances found by the jury are supported by the evidence. Additionally, it must determine whether the sentence of death is excessive or disproportionate to the penalty imposed in similar cases. In this way, the law guards against the possibility of random and arbitrary jury action by requiring comparison with other capital cases.

No Mandatory Sentences

While the Georgia scheme was found to satisfy the constitutional requirements for jury guidance by fair and even-handed procedures, there is the additional consideration of whether the statute preserves "the respect for human dignity underlying the Eighth Amendment." Although recognizing, in classic understatement, that the death penalty is "unique in its severity and irrevocability," the majority concluded that it is only "suited to the most extreme of crimes." While the Court's opinion did not expressly address the question, it suggested that the concept of "the dignity of man" will preclude the use of capital punishment for crimes other than premeditated murder.

More importantly, however, the Court concluded that respect for human dignity requires that the jury consider all aspects of the individual's character, his past record, and the circumstances of the particular offense as part of the sentencing process in a capital trial. This "constitutionally indispensable" element was the critical factor in the two companion cases, *Woodson v. North Carolina,* 428 U.S. 280 (1976), and *Roberts v. Louisiana,* 428 U.S. 325 (1976).

Both Roberts and Woodson were condemned under mandatory death statutes. The legislatures of North Carolina and Louisiana had attempted to meet the constitutional objections of the *Furman* decision by taking all sentencing power out of the jury's hands. Consequently, if a guilty verdict is returned in a case involving certain categories of homicide, the judge is bound by law to pronounce a sentence of death.

This solution to the *Furman* case was rejected by the Supreme Court as it struck down both statutes and remanded the cases for resentencing. Invoking the "dignity of man" factor, the majority stressed the importance of taking into account the totality of circumstances in each case. The jury must be instructed to consider any mitigating factors and "focus on the circumstances of the particular offense and the character and propensities of the offender." The need for a reliable system of assuring that the death penalty is used only in appropriate cases requires that the jury look to the nature of the criminal act and the defendant's past history and character.

The Court also held that mandatory death statutes "fail to comply with *Furman's* requirement that standardless jury discretion be replaced by procedures that safeguard against the arbitrary and capricious imposition of death sentences." In support of these statutes, the states argued that *Furman* is satisfied by taking all sentencing authority away from the jury. In response, the Supreme Court pointed out that a jury's power to return a verdict for a lesser, non-capital offense gives it completely unrestrained and unreviewable discretion in determining when the death penalty is applied.

The Court's reasoning in these two cases also centered on:

> . . . the brutalizing effect of mandatory death statutes and their total disregard for sentiments of mercy and compassion. While the criminal justice system must at times be harsh and procedurally indifferent, it does not follow that all concern for individual situations is thereby forfeited.

Although the Supreme Court has decided several cases subsequent to *Gregg,* none has altered the basic fact that capital punishment is currently legal in the United States. Many of the procedures have been further defined, and several fine points resolved, but there is little chance that the Burger Court will reverse its stand on the ultimate issue.

In the meantime, it has become apparent that there is little appetite on the part of public officials to throw the switch and proceed with new executions. Yet the fact that that reluctance has already been overcome in Florida, with the execution of a convicted murderer, John E. Spenkelink on May 25, 1979, indicates that the issue of capital punishment is far from being resolved. And as the death row population swells and the capacity of prisons to house capital offenders is strained, we can only expect that this nation will have to face the ultimate test of its will to extend the legalization of capital punishment beyond the abstract and into the practical realm of everyday life.

Prisoners' Rights

In the past one hundred years there has been a drastic change in the status of American prisoners. The difference is most acutely demonstrated by the statements of two courts spanning that century. In 1871, a Virginia court commented:

> He [the convicted felon] has, as a consequence of his crime, not only forfeited his liberty, but all his personal rights except for those which the law in its humanity accords to him. He is for the time being the slave of the state.[46]

One hundred and three years later in a landmark case dealing with prisoners' rights, *Wolff v. McDonnell,* Mr. Justice White wrote:

> But though [a prisoner's] rights may be diminished by the needs and exigencies of the institutional environment, a prisoner is not wholly stripped of constitutional protections when he is imprisoned for crime. There is no iron curtain drawn between the Constitution and prisons of this country.[47]

To determine the extent of a prisoner's retained rights, a court must balance the institution's security and administrative needs against the inmate's interests in order to determine the extent to which prisoners' rights are diminished by incarceration. No one could rationally suggest that a prisoner's lot today is a satisfactory one, but the rejection of the "slave status" at least allows for the challenge of conditions and policy in a court of law and indicates that prisons are not outside the protection of the law.

The most popular forum for contesting prison conditions and asserting prisoner rights has been the federal courts. Only within the last decade, however, have prisoners had such a forum. Prior to that time, the federal courts invoked the "hands-off" doctrine and refused to review most inmate claims.[48] The doctrine was based on considerations of federalism, embodying a deference to the states, as well as a deference to the expertise of prison officials. The demise of the hands-off doctrine was a necessary corollary to the recognition that prisoners should not be stripped of certain rights. Once federal courts recognized this fact, they were obligated to see that certain inmate rights were inviolable. In the same year that the Supreme Court in *Wolff v. McDonnell* gave its imprimatur to the "retained rights" theory, it also stated in another case, "When a prison regulation or practice offends a fundamental constitutional guarantee, federal courts will discharge their duty to protect constitutional rights."[49]

State prisoner attacks are launched in federal courts through the Civil Rights Act and under habeas corpus. The principal vehicle for challenging alleged unconstitutional prison practices is through the Civil Rights Act which provides:

> Every person who, under color of any statute, ordinance, regulation, custom, or usage, of any State or Territory, subjects, or causes to be subjected, any citizen of the United States or other person within the jurisdiction thereof to the deprivation of any rights, privileges, or immunities secured by the Constitution and laws, shall be liable to the party injured in any action at law, suit in equity, or other proper proceedings for redress.[50]

Under the Civil Rights Act there is a wide range of remedies: direct orders to correctional officers to avoid certain conduct through injunctive relief to money compensation for damages suffered as a result of the violation. Individual correctional officers and their superiors as well as the governmental unit are personally liable for violations of an inmate's constitutional rights. There is, however, a defense of good faith to allegations of unconstitutional treatment. For example, if a corrections officer makes a reasonable effort to comply with prison standards issued by the state, he would probably be able to raise successfully a good faith defense and thereby avoid personal liability in a civil rights suit.

Habeas corpus, which is not as attractive as a civil rights suit because the inmate must exhaust state remedies and there can be no award of damages, must be brought when the inmate is challenging the legality of his detention.[51] If, for example, an inmate claims he was unconstitutionally deprived of good time credit as a result of a disciplinary hearing, which prolongs the duration of incarceration, he must bring suit under the habeas statute. Habeas is also available to challenge the conditions of incarceration, but again is considered less desirable by prisoners because of the limited scope of remedies available under the statute compared to the Civil Rights Act.

Access to Courts

Convicted prisoners have the same constitutional right to litigate their legitimate grievances as do persons outside of prison. Prison officials may not impede access to the courts nor can they impose restrictions on that access such as requiring prison approval before filing habeas petitions or other law suits.[52]

While the Supreme Court has never held that a convicted inmate has a right to counsel in habeas corpus proceedings, restrictions upon "jailhouse lawyers," inmates who assist others in preparing habeas petitions, have been invalidated. A state may not interfere with one inmate assisting another in the preparation of legal papers, unless the state first undertakes to provide reasonable alternative legal assistance.[53] The right extends to the assistance in the preparation of civil rights suits as well, and a prison that has not made alternative counsel arrangements also cannot bar law students from entering the prison to offer such assistance.[54] Prison officials are also bound to provide reasonable legal libraries for inmates who must prepare their own legal papers as an adjunct to protecting their right to access to the courts.[55]

Disciplinary Hearings

Often violations of prison regulations lead to disciplinary action and punishment or loss of good-time credit. The Supreme Court has extended the reach of the due process requirement of fairness to these proceedings. While an inmate has no right to either appointed or retained counsel at a disciplinary proceeding, certain procedural guarantees must be extended. An inmate is entitled to: (1) advance written notice of any alleged violation, (2) written findings including the evidence considered and the reasons for disciplinary action, and (3) the right to call witnesses and present documentary evidence, unless this would jeopardize institutional safety or correctional goals. Inmates do not, however, have the right to confront and cross-examine adverse witnesses in prison disciplinary proceedings.[56]

Freedom of Speech

Whether a prison inmate retains any vestige of the First Amendment right to freedom of speech has yet to be determined by the Supreme Court. The issue was raised in a court challenge to prison practices involving censorship of mail. The Supreme Court avoided the issue of prisoner rights but found that the regulations on mail violated the First Amendment rights of the outside correspondent. The following criteria were established for reviewing the constitutionality of prison mail regulations:

> First, the regulation or practice in question must further an important or substantial governmental interest unrelated to the sup-

pression of expression. Prison officials may not censor inmate correspondence simply to eliminate unflattering or unwelcome opinions or factually inaccurate statements. Rather, they must show that a regulation authorizing mail censorship furthers one or more of the substantial governmental interests of security, order, and rehabilitation. Second, the limitation of First Amendment freedoms must be no greater than is necessary or essential to the protection of the particular governmental interest involved. Thus a restriction on inmate correspondence that furthers an important or substantial interest of penal administration will nevertheless be invalid if its sweep is unnecessarily broad.[57]

Regulations censoring statements that "unduly complain," that express "inflammatory political, racial, religious, or other views," or that were "otherwise inappropriate" were found to be unconstitutional. Finally, the Supreme Court has held that there must be minimal procedural safeguards that accompany the decision to censor or withhold mail. The inmate must be notified of the rejection of a letter written by or addressed to him, there must be a reasonable opportunity to protest that decision, and such prisoner complaints must be referred to a prison official other than the one who rejected the correspondence for determination.[58]

The Right to Organize

Even though prison officials may permit Boy Scouts, Jaycees, and other organizations to create chapters within the walls of their prison, regulations have been upheld banning inmates from soliciting other prisoners to join a prisoner's union, barring meetings, and prohibiting the delivery of prisoner union publications for distribution among inmates. Through use of a balancing test, the Supreme Court has held that a prison's legitimate security interests outweighed whatever speech or associational rights are guaranteed to inmates.[59]

The Freedom to Worship and Proselytize

The First Amendment guarantee of religious freedom does extend to convicted inmates. There have been numerous federal court decisions, and the Supreme Court has addressed the issue once. When a Buddhist prisoner alleged that he was prohibited from using the prison chapel and from corresponding with his religious advisor, and was punished for sharing religious material with other inmates, the Supreme Court held:

> If Cruz was a Buddhist and if he was denied a reasonable opportunity of pursuing his faith comparable to the opportunity afforded fellow prisoners who adhere to conventional religious precepts, then there was a palpable discrimination by the State

against the Buddhist religion.... The First Amendment ... prohibits government from making a law prohibiting the free exercise of religion.[60]

Freedom from Racial Discrimination

Racial tensions frequently run high among prison inmates. Yet, permanent segregation is not regarded as a viable solution to racial confrontations. An Alabama statute that provided for segregated facilities was struck down as violative of the Equal Protection clause of the Fourteenth Amendment. Three members of the Supreme Court did, however, recognize the need for temporary measures in order to maintain "security, discipline, and good order in prisons and jails." Those three Justices did feel the need to caution prison officials not to misunderstand their willingness to permit temporary racial separation "as evincing any dilution of this Court's firm commitment to the Fourteenth Amendment's prohibition of racial discrimination."[61] A lower federal court commenting on the right of prison officials to temporarily segregate prisons said that the exceptional power could only be utilized after-the-fact and not before.[62]

The Right to Medical Treatment

A prisoner has the right to medical treatment and care. Deliberate indifference to serious medical needs of prisoners constitutes a violation of the Eighth Amendment as an unnecessary and wanton infliction of pain. A civil rights suit may be brought whether the deliberate indifference is manifested by prison doctors failing to respond to an inmate's needs or by prison guards who have intentionally denied or delayed access to the medical care.[63]

The Reentry into Society

There are three legal ways that a prison inmate reenters society. The most infrequent form is through presidential or gubernatorial pardon for federal and state prisoners respectively. The power to pardon is granted by statute and consists of excusing the individual for the crime. Although the pardoned prisoner retains a past criminal record, all legal disabilities are removed. An alternative means of reentry is through expiration of the prison sentence, when the statutory maximum term or lesser term imposed by a judge expires. Usually prison inmates reenter society through the parole process. Except for the couple of states (Maine and California) that have abolished parole, more than two-thirds of prison inmates are paroled prior to the completion of their sentences.[64] Eligibility for parole is determined by the statutes of each jurisdiction. As noted earlier, parole eligibility may arise immediately after incarceration or after serving six months. Most statutes, however, withhold parole eligibility until one-third, and in some states for certain offenses two-thirds, of the imposed sentence has been served.

The parole process affects the participants in the plea bargaining process, including the sentencing judge. All are aware of the parole eligibility provisions in the jurisdiction, and all are guided accordingly. In a state where a defendant is eligible for parole after having served one-third of his sentence, the judge may impose a heavier sentence than he believes is necessary or warranted to assure that one-third of that full sentence meets the judge's notions of adequacy.

Parole serves two purposes. It was devised to insure that imprisonment was tailored to the needs of the inmate. To ameliorate the harshness of long prison sentences, parole exists to hasten the prisoner's reentry into society when he is ready to function as a member of that society and no longer represents a threat to its security. Its other more subtle purpose is to assist prison authorities in maintaining order in the institutions. While the promise of parole is held out to the prisoners, the threat of its denial for misbehavior exists concurrently.

Parole decisions are generally made by administrative boards whose members often are political appointees, and not individuals well versed in the behavioral sciences. Compounding the lack of expertise of parole board members are two crippling features which permeate most aspects of the criminal justice system. Parole boards make their own decisions in each case without guidelines and standards. They are not required in most states to offer any reason for a decision to deny early release. Secondly, parole boards, like courts, are overwhelmed with heavy caseloads and are unable to give each decision due consideration. Generally, parole boards rely upon staff recommendations that are heavily influenced by the opinions of prison officials and guards. Yet they are making critically important decisions affecting the future and welfare of the inmate and society as a whole. Incursions during this decade by federal courts into the practices both of federal and state parole boards indicate that due process and basic notions of fairness can be applied to the system, but that their introduction will be slow. The Supreme Court has held that the due process clauses of the Fifth and Fourteenth Amendments apply to the parole process, and some lower federal courts have held that due process requires that reasons be given for the denial of parole.[65] On the whole, however, parole boards remain virtually unaccountable, and we are a long way from establishing standards for their actions and requiring that the boards adhere to those stands.

Once freed, the parolee is subject to the supervision of a parole officer who serves the dual functions of counselling and policing parolees. As counsellor, the officer is to ease the parolee's reentry into the society and to help him overcome hurdles created by the parolee himself and the society. The officer's ability to counsel is undoubtedly limited by his law enforcement functions. In the latter position, the parole officer is constantly on the lookout for parole violations, which will result in the parolee's return to prison; often parole officers work closely with local police in performing this function. In general, parole supervision is the closest this society has come to halfway reentry into society. Halfway houses for returning convicts exist in many cities, but they are greeted hostilely by the public, and especially the communities in which they are located. Yet these halfway houses offer refuge for inmates while they attempt to readjust to a free society. The history of halfway houses for ex-convicts as well as former residents of mental institutions is a sad one because the value of living in such a place is so frequently diluted either by poor management or by the open hostility of the neighbors.

Parole violations may result in recommitment to prison. The Supreme Court has held that due process requirements also apply at this stage of a case, but the formality of the procedures required falls somewhere between the informality of the due process requirements attaching to prison disciplinary hearings and the formalities required by the due process guarantee at a criminal trial. The parolee is entitled to written notice of the charge against him, disclosure of the evidence, an opportunity to present evidence and speak in his own behalf, a qualified right to confront and cross-examine adverse witnesses, and a hearing before a neutral and detached board that must present in writing a statement of the evidence upon which it relied and the reasons for its decision to revoke parole. There is no absolute right to counsel at a probation or parole revocation proceeding. Whether counsel should be appointed is within the discretion of hearing examiner, but the Supreme Court has indicated that counsel should be appointed when the parolee or probationer denies the charge on which the revocation is based, or if he presents substantial reasons to justify or mitigate the violation, or if the parolee or probationer is incapable of presenting his own case.[66] If ordered back to prison for parole violation, the inmate will likely serve the remainder of the full sentence, leavened only by credit for good-time while in prison.

Once discharged from prison or parole, the ex-convict faces incredible hardship. America does not heed its old shibboleth that an ex-convict "has paid his penalty" and now should be accepted back into society. Additional penalties are imposed by law. Most states continue to deprive convicted felons of their right to vote or run for election to public office. In addition, licenses for many professions, not only those involving close contact with the public or positions of trust, are statutorily barred to convicted felons. The reactions of private citizens are even more extreme, and job applications routinely request information about criminal records. Often the disabilities attached within the community far exceed the severity of the punishment imposed by a court. In the face of this disapprobation, only the heartiest and tenacious ex-convict can continue to persevere and face this fact of life. For those who cannot accept it, and those who never intended to, the cycle of crime, detection, prosecution, and punishment begins again.

Discussion Questions

1. Discuss the rationale for authorizing judges to impose sentences upon convicted criminals. What special qualifications, if any, do judges bring to this task?

2. Sentencing disparity is a valid, growing concern in this society. What are the existing means of controlling judicial discretion to limit sentencing disparities? What are the proposed measures for limiting disparities?

3. The author claims that the indeterminate sentence is an idea whose time has come and gone. What are the prime objections to indeterminate sentences? Is there any inherent contradictions between indeterminate sentencing and the due process ideal that supposedly permeates our entire system of criminal justice?

4. Determinate and presumptive fixed-time sentences are the sentencing models currently being advocated in many states. What explanations can you offer for the current popularity of these sentencing forms? What are the philosophical arguments for and against determinate sentencing?

5. Retribution as a primary justification for capital punishment has been criticized as inappropriate for a twentieth century democratic society. Recently, however, retribution has gained popularity as a viable justification for imprisonment and the death penalty. Why does this society appear ready to reject rehabilitation as the philosophical foundation for our system of punishment?

6. It has been argued that capital punishment "diminishes the society that imposes it." Explain the meaning of this charge and discuss your reasons for agreeing or disagreeing with the claim. On a practical level, discuss the arguments against capital punishment.

7. Assuming for the moment that Gary Gilmore was not irrational in requesting that he be executed, do his actions lend support to the no-capital punishment position or the advocacy position?

Notes

1. Michael Serrill, "Determinate Sentencing: History, Theory, Debate," *Corrections Magazine,* September 1977, p. 4.
2. "Three Models of Criminal Sentencing," *Fair and Certain Punishment: Report of the Twentieth Century Fund Task Force on Criminal Sentencing* (New York: McGraw-Hill, 1976), p. 87.
3. Ibid.
4. Serrill, "Determinate Sentencing," p. 6.
5. *Fair and Certain Punishment,* pp. 89-91.
6. Rob Wilson, "U.S. Prison Population Sets Another Record," *Corrections Magazine,* March 1977, p. 3.
7. Gregg v. Georgia, 428 U.S. 153 (1976).
8. Robert O. Dawson, *Sentencing: The Decision as to Type, Length, and Condition of Sentence* (Boston: Little, Brown, 1969), p. 203.
9. *Law and Contemporary Problems,* 41:1 (Winter 1977), p. 12.
10. Vincent O'Leary, Michael Gottfredson, and Arthur Gelman, "Contemporary Sentencing Proposals," *Criminal Law Bulletin,* 11:5 (1975).
11. Serrill, "Determinate Sentencing," p. 14.
12. Ibid.
13. Ibid.
14. The states that regularly review and adjust sentences are Georgia, New Hampshire, and North Carolina.
15. *Standards Relating to Appellate Review of Sentences,* American Bar Association (1968), pp. 2-5, 54-55.
16. See *Federal Criminal Code Reform,* from the National Commission to S. 1437, (a BNA Special Analysis on Criminal Code Reform in 22 *Criminal Law Reporter,* March 15, 1978).
17. Sheldon L. Messinger and Phillip E. Johnson, "California's Determinate Sentencing Statute: History and Issues," in Special Conference: Determinate Sentencing, Reform or Regression (National Institute of Law Enforcement and Criminal Justice, 1978), p. 13.
18. Ibid.
19. Dawson, *Sentencing,* p. 201.
20. Marvin E. Frankel, *Criminal Sentences: Law Without Order* (New York: Hill and Wang, 1973), pp. 8-9, cited in Kranz, *Corrections and Prisoners' Rights in a Nutshell* (St. Paul, Minn.: West, 1976), p. 7.
21. See Serrill, "Determinate Sentencing," pp. 14-15, where the range of indeterminancy is discussed.
22. *Criminal Justice Newsletter,* March 12, 1977.
23. One limitation on the discretion of the sentencing judge, however, increases the disparity in sentencing. Plea bargains resulting in a reduced charge agreed to by prosecution limits the power of the judge to impose the maximum sentence authorized for conviction of the more serious offense and creates the potential for disparity between the offender pleading guilty to the reduced charge and another offender, possibly a co-defendant, being sentenced under the original, more serious charge.
24. See *National Advisory Commission on Criminal Justice Standards and Goals: Corrections* (1973), p. 189.
25. Ibid., p. 325.
26. Ibid., pp. 188-89.
27. Ibid.
28. State v. Kunz, 55 N.J. 128, 259 A2d 895 (1969).
29. Santobello v. New York, 404 U.S. 257 (1971).
30. *National Advisory Commission: Corrections,* p. 74.

31. Ibid., pp. 162-63.
32. Williams v. Illinois, 399 U.S. 235 (1970).
33. Tate v. Short, 401 U.S. 395 (1971).
34. Dawson, *Sentencing,* pp. 151-52.
35. Ibid., p. 159.
36. "Offenders Avoid Imprisonment by Volunteer Work," *LEAA Newsletter,* June-July 1978, pp. 1 and 9.
37. James Beba, Kenneth Carlson, and Robert Rosenblum, *Sentencing to Community Service* (National Institute of Law Enforcement and Criminal Justice, October 1977), pp. 51-52.
38. This quote is from John Gay's play, "Wilde About Oscar," and may be found in the review of that play in *Newsweek,* April 24, 1978.
39. Robinson v. California, 370 U.S. 660 (1962).
40. Pugh v. Locke, 406 F.Supp. 318 (M.D. Ala. 1976), aff'd sub. nom.; Neuman v. Alabama, 559 F. 2d 283 (5th Cir. 1977); Holt v. Sarver, 309 F. Supp. 362 (E.D. Ark. 1970), aff'd, 442 F. 2d 304 (8th Cir. 1971).
41. *National Advisory Commission: Corrections,* pp. 308-09.
42. Gregg v. Georgia, 428 U.S. 153 (1976).
43. Ibid.; Proffitt v. Florida, 428 U.S. 242 (1976); Jurek v. Texas, 428 U.S. 262 (1976); Woodson v. North Carolina, 428 U.S. 280 (1976); Roberts v. Louisiana, 428 U.S. 633 (1976).
44. Gardner v. Florida, 430 U.S. 349 (1977).
45. Gilmore v. Utah, 429 U.S. 1012 (1976).
46. Ruffin v. Commonwealth, 62 Va. 790, 796 (1871).
47. Wolff v. McDonnell, 418 U.S. 539, 555-56 (1974).
48. See Ruffin v. Commonwealth, 62 Va. 790 (1871), which typified this outlook. The court stated there that, "He [the convicted felon] has, as a consequence of his crime, not only forfeited his liberty, but all his personal rights except those which the law in its humanity accords to him. He is for the time being, the slave of the State." Ibid., p. 796.
49. Procunier v. Martinez, 416 U.S. 396, 405-06 (1974).
50. 42 U.S.C. § 1983.
51. See 28 U.S.C. § 2254, which is available to persons "in custody in violation of the Constitution or laws or treaties of the United States; if a prisoner is challenging the fact or duration of confinement, he is required to use *habeas corpus* rather than § 1983"; Preiser v. Rodriguez, 411 U.S. 475 (1973).
52. Ex Parte Hull, 312 U.S. 546 (1941); also see, Coffin v. Reichard, 143 F. 2d 443 (6th Cir. 1944) cert. denied, 325 U.S. 887 (1945), which espoused the "retained rights" theory: "A prisoner retains all the rights of an ordinary citizen except those expressly taken from him by the law." Ibid., p. 445.
53. Johnson v. Avery, 393 U.S. 483 (1969).
54. Procunier v. Martinez, 416 U.S. 396 (1974).
55. Bounds v. Smith, 430 U.S. 817 (1977).
56. Wolff v. McDonnell, 418 U.S. 539 (1974).
57. Procunier v. Martinez, 416 U.S. 396, at 413-414 (1974).
58. Ibid., at 418-419.
59. Jones v. North Carolina Prisoner's Labor Union, 433 U.S. 119 (1977).
60. Cruz v. Beto, 405 U.S. 319, at 322 (1972).
61. Lee v. Washington, 390 U.S. 333, at 334 (1968).
62. Wilson v. Kelley, 294 F. Supp. 1005 (N.D. Ga. 1968).
63. Estelle v. Gamble, 429 U.S. 97 (1976).
64. See *Task Force Report: Corrections,* (President's Crime Commission, 1967), pp. 27-28.
65. Morrissey v. Brewer, 408 U.S. 471 (1972).
66. Gagnon v. Scarpelli, 408 U.S. 921 (1972).

GLOSSARY

ABANDONED PROPERTY: A legal term relating to the rule that items for which the property rights have been relinquished lose all Fourth Amendment protection and may be seized and introduced as evidence in a court of law without prior judicial authorization.

ACQUITTAL: The dismissal of criminal charges based upon a finding of not guilty. A directed verdict of acquittal is ordered by the court if after reviewing the trial process the court determines that a reasonable jury could not find that the defendant's guilt had been proven beyond a reasonable doubt.

ALIBI: Any defense that offers evidence that the defendant was in a different place at the time the offense was committed.

ARRAIGNMENT: The court appearance of a person who is charged with a crime. An arraignment consists of three parts: (a) calling a defendant by name; (b) reading the indictment; and (c) asking the defendant to plead.

ARREST: The deprivation of an individual's liberty and freedom of action prior to a finding of guilt or innocence.

BAIL: Property given as assurance that a person released from pretrial detention will return at an appointed time for trial.

BEDSHEETING: The term for the prosecutorial practice of charging a defendant with every possible crime that is applicable within the original charge.

BEST EVIDENCE: Documentary evidence: the original writing or copy acceptable under the law of the particular jurisdiction.

CHANGE OF VENUE: The relocation of a criminal case to another county or court district where a fair trial, a trial unmarred by pretrial publicity, can be obtained.

CIVIL RIGHTS ACT: Federal legislation making it a crime or civil violation for any person or groups of persons, under claim of authority of law, to deprive or attempt to deprive another citizen of federal constitutional rights.

COMPLAINT: The initial charging form in a felony case used to notify the defendant of the nature of the charge against him.

CONTEMPT: A willful disregard of public authority. A person found in contempt of court is subject to being jailed.

DETERMINATE SENTENCE: A criminal sentence in which the offender is committed to prison for a fixed amount of time, with no minimum or maximum range, precluding both judicial discretion in sentencing and parole decisions regarding an early release.

DETERRENCE: A correctional objective whereby the punishment of convicted criminals discourages the public at large from committing deviant acts.

DISCOVERY: A method by which the opposing parties to a lawsuit may obtain full and exact factual information concerning the entire area of their controversy, via pretrial depositions, interrogatories, requests for admissions, inspections of books and documents, physical and mental examinations, and inspection of land or other property. The purpose of discovery is to uncover the genuine points of factual dispute and to facilitate adequate preparation for trial, or encourage settlement before trial.

EAVESDROPPING: An extraordinary law enforcement tool whereby to secure evidence of a crime, a law enforcement officer listens secretly to a private conversation. For evidence secured in this manner to be accepted by the courts, officers must obtain either a warrant from the judge who has made a probable cause determination or consent from one party to the conversation.

EXCLUSIONARY RULE: This rule requires that the police while enforcing the law must obey the law by respecting suspects' constitutional rights. This rule was judicially created in the nineteenth century and given widespread application in this century to enhance and protect the rights guaranteed to all citizens through the Fourth, Fifth, and Sixth Amendments. Simply stated, the rule is: evidence secured through a violation of constitutional rights, such as an unreasonable search and seizure, will not be admissible in court.

FELONY: A serious crime, such as murder or robbery: usually various crimes in various jurisdictions for which the penalty can be death or imprisonment in a penitentiary.

FINES: Monetary penalties for violations of criminal ordinances and statutes.

GRAND JURY: A lay panel that investigates crime and indicts defendants.

HABEAS CORPUS: A Latin term that means "produce the body of the person detained and explain the detention." This action is a legal remedy to protect against illegal imprisonment, requiring a person to be brought before a judge or court for purposes of investigating a restraint of that person's liberty.

HABITUAL OFFENDER: An individual who has been convicted of several offenses and for which he will be subjected to greater penalties.

HOT PURSUIT: A legal term referring to the immediate and continuous police pursuit of a person who is attempting to avoid arrest. An officer who is in "hot pursuit" of a suspect need not secure a warrant prior to the chase or before entering private property to pursue the fleeing suspect.

INDETERMINATE SENTENCE: A criminal sentence in which the offender is committed to imprisonment for a period ranging from one day to life.

INDICTMENT: A formal accusation presented by the grand jury and usually required for the prosecution of felonies and other serious crimes.

INDIGENT: The state of lacking the necessities of life because of poverty. In criminal cases, the term refers to one who is financially unable to retain an attorney.

INFORMATION: A formal accusation or complaint filed by the prosecutor, without the interposition of the grand jury, charging the accused with a crime.

INTERLOCUTORY APPEALS: Determinations that are appealed to a higher court while the defendant's case is in progress.

JAILHOUSE BAIL: Bail determined in the police station or jail according to a schedule adopted by statute or approved by the local court that sets the amount of bail according to the seriousness of the offense committed.

MOCKERY OF JUSTICE TEST: A test devised by the courts to determine whether counsel in a given trial was so ineffective as to render the trial proceedings a farce.

MODEL PENAL CODE: Adopted by the American Law Institute in 1962, in which a sentencing model and suggested revision of the substantive criminal law is set forth.

MAXIMUM SENTENCE: A sentence stipulating the maximum amount of time a prisoner can be incarcerated.

MINIMUM SENTENCE: A sentence stipulating the minimum amount of time a prisoner must spend in jail before he can be eligible for release.

MISDEMEANOR: A crime less serious than a felony, usually stipulating no more than one year of incarceration to be served in a county jail or workhouse, rather than a penitentiary.

MOTION: The mechanism by which a party to a lawsuit challenges one or all aspects of the proceeding, or requests something from the court, or requests the court to order the opposing party to take some action.

NO BILL: A grand jury vote not to charge.

NO CONTEST (NOLO CONTENDERE): A plea available to a defendant whereby the defendant chooses not to contest the facts as stated in the charge against him, but will permit the court to determine whether those facts constitute the crime. A plea in criminal cases whereby the defendant tacitly admits his guilt by throwing himself on the mercy of the court.

NOTICE-OF-ALIBI STATUTES: State statutes that require any defense based on an alibi be pleaded in advance of trail so that the state has an opportunity to investigate those claims.

OPEN FIELDS: A legal term relating to the rule that items which are situated in an area fifty to one hundred yards from a defendant's residence are not protected by the Fourth Amendment right of people to be secure in their persons, houses, papers, and effects and may be seized and introduced as evidence in a court of law without a search warrant.

ORIGINAL INDICTMENT: A criminal charge that originates with a grand jury indictment.

OVERCHARGING: The prosecutorial practice of filing a charge that is greater than the evidence will bear.

OVERCRIMINALIZATION: The maintenance in state statute books of criminal offenses that are outdated yet still subject to enforcement.

PAROLE: The conditional release of an individual from prison prior to the end of the maximum sentence imposed by the sentencing judge.

PENITENTIARIES: Places of imprisonment housing predominately mature and dangerous felons.

PLAIN VIEW: A legal term relating to the rule that items which are in plain view of an officer who is lawfully present on the premises may be seized and introduced as evidence in a court of law without a search warrant.

PRELIMINARY APPEARANCE: The defendant's first court appearance whereby he is informed of the charge against him and is subject to a bail determination.

PRELIMINARY HEARING: The first formal review after arrest of the state's charge before a judge in an adversary setting where the accused is present, represented by counsel, and has the opportunity to challenge the sufficiency of the state's case.

PRESENTENCE REPORT: Reports prepared by probation departments to provide the sentencing judge with information about the accused's character, environment, and crime.

PRESUMPTION OF INNOCENCE DOCTRINE: The constitutional principle that a person who is accused of a crime is innocent until he is proven guilty.

PREVENTIVE DETENTION: The pretrial detention of a defendant, who would otherwise be entitled to have bail set, based upon a determination that the defendant is likely to commit additional crimes if free on bail.

PROBATION: A community-based corrections program that allows offenders to go at large under supervision in accordance with certain conditions and restrictions.

PROBATION, INACTIVE: A probation program that involves no imposed conditions or supervision but serves as an admonition to an offender to stay out of trouble or his probation will be revoked.

PUBLIC DEFENDER: Public officer representing indigent defendants who are unable to retain private counsel.

RECIDIVISM: Repeated or habitual relapse into criminal activity by individuals who have previously been convicted of crimes.

REFORMATORIES: Penal institutions originally designed to reform young criminal offenders.

REHABILITATION: A correctional objective whereby convicted criminals are involved in treatment programs designed to improve or correct their characters and to prepare them for useful lives within society.

RELEASE ON RECOGNIZANCE (ROR): An alternative to money bail whereby the defendant is granted pretrial release based upon his affirmation that he will appear at the appointed time in court.

SCREENING: Prosecutorial assessment of the value of a case from the perspective of the prosecuting agency, including prosecutorial analysis of the seriousness of the crime and the possibility of achieving conviction.

SERVICE FUNCTIONS: Routine responsibilities rendered by the police in the form of such community services as traffic control, emergency medical assistance, and minor domestic or neighborhood dispute settlements.

SPECIAL CIRCUMSTANCES TEST: The Supreme Court requirement stipulating that counsel be provided in any capital felony case where the defendant, because of the complexity of the charge or defense or because of his own lack of education or experience, would be unable to represent himself.

STATUTE OF LIMITATIONS: State and federal statutes that fix various periods of time within which a lawsuit must be commenced and after the expiration of which the claimant will be forever barred from the right to bring the action.

SUMMONS: A court order or writ commanding the sheriff to notify a party named therein to appear in court on or before a specified date and to answer the charges contained in the complaint.

TEN PERCENT DEPOSITS: An alternative to money bail whereby the defendant is required to execute a bail bond and deposit with the clerk of the court an amount equal to ten percent of the bail. This ten percent deposit is, in part, returned to the defendant when the conditions of the bail bond are fulfilled.

TRANSACTIONAL IMMUNITY: A legal remedy for a reluctant witness who refuses to answer questions and chooses to invoke the Fifth Amendment privilege against self-incrimination. The prosecutor, to obtain the witness' testimony, secures for that witness freedom from prosecution on the subject matter under inquiry.

TRUE BILL: A formal charge handed down by a grand jury.

USE IMMUNITY: A legal remedy for a reluctant witness who refuses to answer questions and chooses to invoke the Fifth Amendment privilege against self-incrimination. The state agrees to forego the use of the witness' testimony and any other evidence that his testimony leads to in a prosecution of the witness, and in return the witness is required to answer otherwise possibly incriminating questions before a grand jury. (Use immunity is narrower than transactional immunity.)

VENIRE: Prospective juror panel.

WARRANT: A document issued by a judge authorizing an officer to make an arrest, seize property, make a search, or execute a judgment.

WIRETAPPING: An extraordinary law enforcement technique of tapping telephone or telegraph wires for evidence or other information. For evidence secured by this method, a warrant must be obtained from a judge who has made a probable cause determination.

WORK-RELEASE PROGRAMS: Community-based corrections programs in which selected prisoners are permitted to leave during the day to work at the jobs they held before conviction.

WRIT OF CERTIORARI: An original writ whereby a case is removed from an inferior court to a superior court for review.

APPENDIX

Supreme Court Litigation* and the Development of Selected Constitutional Rights

Section 1 Scope of Due Process
- *Palko* v. *Connecticut*
- *Duncan* v. *Louisiana*
- *Griswold* v. *Connecticut*

Section 2 Arrest, Search and Seizure
- A. The Exclusionary Rule
  - *Mapp* v. *Ohio*
  - *Stone* v. *Powell*
- B. The Right of Privacy
  - *Katz* v. *United States*
- C. Reasonableness and Probable Cause
  - *Brinegar* v. *United States*
  - *Aguilar* v. *Texas*
- D. Warrantless Intrusions
  - *United States* v. *Watson*
  - *United States* v. *Robinson*
  - *Chimel* v. *California*
- E. Consent Searches
  - *Schneckloth* v. *Bustamonte*
- F. Stop and Frisk
  - *Terry* v. *Ohio*

Section 3 Police Interrogation and Confessions
- *Miranda* v. *Arizona*
- *Harris* v. *New York*
- *Michigan* v. *Mosley*
- *Brewer, Warden* v. *Williams*

* The cases contained in this appendix are heavily edited; they are intended to provide the student with the essence of the Court's thinking on each issue. These cases are presented as examples of the development of constitutional rights and illustrate the fleshing-out and narrowing process that occurs in constitutional litigation in the Supreme Court of the United States.

SECTION 1
THE SCOPE OF DUE PROCESS

Palko was indicted for murder in the first degree. A jury found him guilty of murder in the second degree and he was sentenced to life imprisonment. The State appealed and the conviction was reversed. At the second trial, Palko claimed that he was being placed in jeopardy twice for the same offense in violation of the Fourteenth Amendment of the Constitution. His claim was overruled, a new jury selected, a verdict of guilty of murder in the first degree returned, and Palko was sentenced to death. The Supreme Court's initial interpretation of the scope of the protection offered by the due process clause of the Fourteenth Amendment is contained in this opinion.

Palko v. *Connecticut,* 302 U.S. 319 (1937)

Cardozo, J.

The argument for appellant is that whatever is forbidden by the Fifth Amendment is forbidden by the Fourteenth also. The Fifth Amendment, which is not directed to the States, but solely to the federal government, creates immunity from double jeopardy. No person shall be "subject for the same offense to be twice put in jeopardy of life or limb." The Fourteenth Amendment ordains, "nor shall any State deprive any person of life, liberty, or property, without due process of law." To retry a defendant, though under one indictment and only one, subjects him, it is said, to double jeopardy in violation of the Fifth Amendment, if the prosecution is one on behalf of the United States. From this the consequence is said to follow that there is a denial of life or liberty without due process of law, if the prosecution is one on behalf of the people of a state.

. . .

We have said that in appellant's view the Fourteenth Amendment is to be taken as embodying the prohibitions of the Fifth. His thesis is even broader. Whatever would be a violation of the original bill of rights (Amendments 1 to 8) if done by the federal government is now equally unlawful by force of the Fourteenth Amendment if done by a state. There is no such general rule.

The Fifth Amendment provides, among other things, that no person shall be held to answer for a capital or otherwise infamous crime unless on presentment or indictment of a grand jury. This court has held that, in prosecutions by a state, presentment or indictment by a grand jury may give way to informations at the instance of a public officer. . . . The Fifth Amendment provides also that no person shall be compelled in any criminal case to be a witness against himself. This court has said that, in prosecutions by a state, the exemption will fail if the state elects to end it. . . . The Sixth Amendment calls for a jury trial in criminal cases and the Seventh for a jury trial in civil cases at common law where the value in controversy shall exceed $20. This court has ruled that consistently with those amendments trial by jury may be modified by a state or abolished altogether. . . .

On the other hand, the due process clause of the Fourteenth Amendment may make it unlawful for a state to abridge by its statutes the freedom of speech which the First Amendment safeguards against encroachment by the Congress . . ., or the like freedom of the press . . ., or the free exercise of religion . . ., or the right of peaceable assembly, without which speech would be unduly trammeled . . ., or the right of one accused of crime to the benefit of counsel . . . . In these and other situations immunities that are valid as against the federal government by force of the specific pledges of particular amendments have been found to be implicit in the concept of ordered liberty, and thus, through the Fourteenth Amendment, become valid as against the states.

The line of division may seem to be wavering and broken if there is a hasty catalogue of the cases on the one side and the other. Reflection and analysis will induce a different view. There emerges the perception of a rationalizing principle which gives to discrete instances a proper order and coherence. The right to trial by jury and the immunity from prosecution except as the result of an indictment may have value and importance. Even so, they are not of the very essence of a scheme of ordered liberty. To abolish them is not to violate a "principle of justice so rooted in the traditions and conscience of our people as to be ranked as fundamental." . . . Few would be so narrow or provincial as to maintain that a fair and enlightened system of justice would be impossible without them. What is true of jury trials and indictments is true also, as the cases show, of the immunity from compulsory self-incrimination. . . . This too might be lost, and justice still be done. Indeed, today as in the past there are students of our penal system who look upon the immunity as a mischief rather than a benefit, and who would limit its scope, or destroy it altogether. No doubt there would remain the need to give protection against torture, physical or mental. . . . Justice, however, would not perish if the accused were subject to a duty to respond to orderly inquiry. The exclusion of these immunities and privileges from the privileges and immunities protected against the action of the States has not been arbitrary or casual. It has been dictated by a study and appreciation of the meaning, the essential implications, of liberty itself.

We reach a different plane of social and moral values when we pass to the privileges and immunities that have been taken over from the earlier articles of the Federal Bill of Rights and brought within the Fourteenth Amendment by a process of absorption. These in their origin were effective against the federal government alone. If the Fourteenth Amendment has absorbed them, the process of absorption has had its source in the belief that neither liberty nor justice would exist if they were sacrificed. . . . This is true, for illustration, of freedom of thought and speech. Of that freedom one may say that it is the matrix, the indispensable condition, of nearly every other form of freedom. With rare aberrations a pervasive recognition of that truth can be traced in our history, political and legal. . . . Fundamental too in the concept of due process, and so in that of liberty, is the thought that condemnation shall be rendered only after trial. . . . The hearing, moreover, must be a real one, not a sham or a pretense. . . . For that reason, ignorant defendants in a capital case were held to have been condemned unlawfully when in truth, though not in form, they were refused the aid of counsel. . . . The decision did not turn upon the fact that the benefit of counsel would have been guaranteed to the defendants by the provisions of the Sixth Amendment if they had been prosecuted in a federal court. The decision turned upon the fact that in the particular situation laid before us in the evidence the benefit of counsel was essential to the substance of a hearing.

Our survey of the cases serves, we think, to justify the statement that the dividing line between them, if not unfaltering throughout its course, has been true for the most part to a unifying principle. On which side of the line the case made out by the appellant has appropriate location must be the next inquiry and the final one. Is that kind of double jeopardy to which the statute has subjected him a hardship so acute and shocking that our polity will not endure it? Does it violate those "fundamental principles of liberty and justice which lie at the base of all our civil and political institutions"? . . . The answer surely must be "no." . . . The state is not attempting to wear the accused out by a multitude of cases with accumulated trials. It asks no more than this, that the case against him shall go on until there shall be a trial free from the corrosion of substantial legal error. . . . This is not cruelty at all, nor even vexation in any immoderate degree. If the trial had been infected with error adverse to the accused, there might have been review at his instance, and as often as necessary to purge the vicious taint. A reciprocal privilege, subject at all times to the discretion of the presiding judge . . ., has now been granted to the state. There is here no seismic innovation. The edifice of justice stands, its symmetry, to many, greater than before.

The judgment is affirmed.

In the thirty years between Palko and Duncan more had changed than the members of the Supreme Court. Due process had become a much more expansive protection, and the due process clause of the Fourteenth Amendment, through the process of incorporation, now contained most of the guarantees contained in the first through eight Amendments. In Duncan, the Court enunciates the present standard for determining whether a right contained in the Bill of Rights is applicable to the states through the Fourteenth Amendment. The right involved in Duncan is jury trial, one which Mr. Justice Cardozo in Palko said was not fundamental to ordered liberty and therefore was not a part of the Fourteenth Amendment.

Duncan v. *Louisiana,* 391 U.S. 145 (1969)

White, J.

Appellant, Gary Duncan, was convicted of simple battery in the Twenty-fifth Judicial District Court of Louisiana. Under Louisiana law simple battery is a misdemeanor, punishable by a maximum of two years' imprisonment and a $300 fine. Appellant sought trial by jury, but because the Louisiana Constitution grants jury trials only in cases in which capital punishment or imprisonment at hard labor may be imposed, the trial judge denied the request. Appellant was convicted and sentenced to serve 60 days in the parish prison and pay a fine of $150. Appellant sought review in the Supreme Court of Louisiana, asserting that the denial of jury trial violated rights guaranteed to him by the United States Constitution. The Supreme Court, finding "[n]o error of law in the ruling complained of," denied appellant a writ of certiorari. . . .

[A]ppellant sought review in this Court, alleging that the Sixth and Fourteenth Amendments to the United States Constitution secure the right to jury trial in state criminal prosecutions where a sentence as long as two years may be imposed.

I.

The Fourteenth Amendment denies the States the power to "deprive any person of life, liberty, or property, without due process of law." In resolving conflicting claims concerning the meaning of this spacious language, the Court has looked increasingly to the Bill of Rights for guidance; many of the rights guaranteed by the first eight Amendments to the Constitution have been held to be protected against state action by the Due Process Clause of the Fourteenth Amendment. That clause now protects the right to compensation for property taken by the State; the rights of speech, press, and religion covered by the First Amendment; the Fourth Amendment rights to be free from unreasonable searches and seizures and to have excluded from criminal trials any evidence illegally seized; the right guaranteed by the Fifth Amendment to be free of compelled self-incrimination; and the Sixth Amendment rights to counsel, to a speedy and public trial, to confrontation of opposing witnesses, and to compulsory process for obtaining witnesses.

The test for determining whether a right extended by the Fifth and Sixth Amendments with respect to federal criminal proceedings is also protected against state action by the Fourteenth Amendment has been phrased in a variety of ways in the opinions of this Court. The question has been asked whether a right is among those " 'fundamental principles of liberty and justice which lie at the base of all our civil and political institutions' " . . .; whether it is "basic in our system of jurisprudence" . . .; and whether it is "a fundamental right, essential to a fair trial" . . . . The claim before us is that the right to trial by jury guaranteed by the Sixth Amendment meets these tests. The position of Louisiana, on the other hand, is that the Constitution imposes upon the States no duty to give a jury trial in any criminal case, regardless of the seriousness of the crime or the size of the punishment which may be imposed. Because we believe that trial by jury in criminal cases is fundamental to the American scheme of justice, we hold that the Fourteenth Amendment guarantees a right of jury trial in all criminal cases which—were they to be tried in a federal court—would come within the Sixth Amendment's guarantee. Since we consider the appeal before us to be such a case, we hold that the Constitution was violated when appellant's demand for jury trial was refused.

. . .

[B]y the time our Constitution was written, jury trial in criminal cases had been in existence in England for several centuries and carried impressive credentials traced by many to Magna Carta.

. . .

Jury trial came to America with English colonists, and received strong support from them.

. . .

Objections to the Constitution because of the absence of a bill of rights were met by the immediate submission and adoption of the Bill of Rights. Included was the Sixth Amendment which, among other things, provided:

> "In all criminal prosecutions, the accused shall enjoy the right to a speedy and public trial, by an impartial jury of the State and district wherein the crime shall have been committed."

The constitutions adopted by the original States guaranteed jury trial. Also, the constitution of every State entering the Union thereafter in one form or another protected the right to jury trial in criminal cases.

Even such skeletal history is impressive support for considering the right to jury trial in criminal cases to be fundamental to our system of justice, an importance frequently recognized in the opinions of this Court.

. . .

The guarantees of jury trial in the Federal and State Constitutions reflect a profound judgment about the way in which law should be enforced and justice administered. A right to jury trial is granted to criminal defendants in order to prevent oppression by the Government. Those who wrote our constitutions knew from history and experience that it was necessary to protect against unfounded criminal charges brought to eliminate enemies and against judges too responsive to the voice of higher authority. The framers of the constitutions strove to create an independent judiciary but insisted upon further protection against arbitrary action. Providing an accused with the right to be tried by a jury of his peers gave him an inestimable safeguard against the corrupt or overzealous prosecutor and against the compliant, biased, or eccentric judge. If the defendant preferred the common-sense judgment of a jury to the more tutored but perhaps less sympathetic reaction of the single judge, he was to have it. Beyond this, the jury trial provisions in the Federal and State Constitutions reflect a fundamental decision about the exercise of official power—a reluctance to entrust plenary powers over the life and liberty of the citizen to one judge or to a group of judges. Fear of unchecked power, so typical of our State and Federal Governments in other respects, found expression in the criminal law in this insistence upon community participation in the determination of guilt or innocence. The deep commitment of the Nation to the right of jury trial in serious criminal cases as a defense against arbitrary law enforcement qualifies for protection under the Due Process Clause of the Fourteenth Amendment, and must therefore be respected by the States.

. . .

Our conclusion is that in the American States, as in the federal judicial system, a general grant of jury trial for serious offenses is a fundamental right, essential for preventing miscarriages of justice and for assuring that fair trials are provided for all defendants.

II.

. . .

Louisiana's final contention is that even if it must grant jury trials in serious criminal cases, the conviction before us is valid and constitutional because here the petitioner was tried for simple battery and was sentenced to only 60 days in the parish prison. We are not persuaded. It is doubtless true that there is a category of petty crimes or offenses which is not subject to the Sixth Amendment jury trial provision and should not be subject to the Fourteenth Amendment jury trial requirement here applied to the States. Crimes carrying possible penalties up to six months do not require a jury trial if they otherwise qualify as petty offenses, . . . But the penalty authorized for a particular crime is of major relevance in determining whether it is serious or not and may in itself, if severe enough, subject the trial to the mandates of the Sixth Amendment. . . .

. . . It is sufficient for our purposes to hold that a crime punishable by two years in prison is, based on past and contemporary standards in this country, a serious crime and not a petty offense. Consequently, appellant was entitled to a jury trial and it was error to deny it.

The judgment below is reversed and the case is remanded for proceedings not inconsistent with this opinion.

Is the American notion of due process limited to the specific rights enumerated in the Bill of Rights? The answer was provided in this case where a 7-2 majority of the Supreme Court struck down a Connecticut statute which made it a crime for married persons as well as single persons to use contraceptives and also prohibited the dissemination of medical advice on how to prevent conception.

Griswold v. *Connecticut,* 381 U.S. 479 (1965) Douglas, J.

. . .

[S]pecific guarantees in the Bill of Rights have penumbras formed by emanations from those guarantees that help give them life and substance. Various guarantees create zones of privacy. The right of association contained in the penumbra of the First Amendment is one, as we have seen. The Third Amendment in its prohibition against the quartering of soldiers "in any house" in time of peace without the consent of the owner is another facet of that privacy. The Fourth Amendment explicitly affirms the "right of the people to be secure in their persons, houses, papers, and effects, against unreasonable searches and seizures." The Fifth Amendment in its Self-Incrimination Clause enables the citizen to create a zone of privacy which government may not force him to surrender to his detriment. The Ninth Amendment provides: "The enumeration in the Constitution, of certain rights, shall not be construed to deny or disparage others retained by the people."

. . .

The present case, then, concerns a relationship lying within the zone of privacy created by several fundamental constitutional guarantees. And it concerns a law which, in forbidding the *use* of contraceptives rather than regulating their manufacture or sale, seeks to achieve its goals by means having a maximum destructive impact upon that relationship. Such a law cannot stand in light of the familiar principle, so often applied by this Court, that a "governmental purpose to control or prevent activities constitutionally subject to state regulation may not be achieved by means which sweep unnecessarily broadly and thereby invade the area of protected freedoms." *NAACP* v. *Alabama,* 377 U.S. 288, 307. Would we allow the police to search the sacred precincts of marital bedrooms for telltale signs of the use of contraceptives? The very idea is repulsive to the notions of privacy surrounding the marriage relationship.

We deal with a right of privacy older than the Bill of Rights—older than our political parties, older than our school system. Marriage is a coming together for better or for worse, hopefully enduring, and intimate to the degree of being sacred. It is an association that promotes a way of life, not causes; a harmony in living, not political faiths; a bilateral loyalty, not commercial or social projects. Yet it is an association for as noble a purpose as any involved in our prior decisions.

SECTION 2
ARREST, SEARCH AND SEIZURE

A. THE EXCLUSIONARY RULE

Mapp v. *Ohio ranks as one of the most controversial Supreme Court decisions in American history. And today there are still efforts to reverse the decision and return to the law that existed prior to 1961. It is also one of the most significant decisions in American history because of its effect upon criminal justice in the states.*

Mapp v. *Ohio,* 367 U.S. 643 (1961)

Clark, J.

Appellant stands convicted of knowingly having had in her possession and under her control certain lewd and lascivious books, pictures, and photographs. . . . As officially stated in the syllabus to its opinion, the Supreme Court of Ohio found that her conviction was valid though "based primarily upon the introduction in evidence of lewd and lascivious books and pictures unlawfully seized during an unlawful search of defendant's home. . . ."

. . .

On May 23, 1957, three Cleveland police officers arrived at appellant's residence in that city pursuant to information that "a person [was] hiding out in the home, who was wanted for questioning in connection with a recent bombing, and that there was a large amount of policy paraphernalia being hidden in the home." Miss Mapp and her daughter by a former marriage lived on the top floor of the two-family dwelling. Upon their arrival at that house, the officers knocked on the door and demanded entrance but appellant, after telephoning her attorney, refused to admit them without a search warrant. They advised their headquarters of the situation and undertook a surveillance of the house.

The officers again sought entrance some three hours later when four or more additional officers arrived on the scene. When Miss Mapp did not come to the door immediately, at least one of the several doors to the house was forcibly opened and the policemen gained admittance. Meanwhile Miss Mapp's attorney arrived, but the officers, having secured their own entry, and continuing in their defiance of the law, would permit him neither to see Miss Mapp nor to enter the house. It appears that Miss Mapp was halfway down the stairs from the upper floor to the front door when the officers, in this highhanded manner, broke into the hall. She demanded to see the search warrant. A paper, claimed to be a warrant, was held up by one of the officers. She grabbed the "warrant" and placed it in her bosom. A struggle ensued in which the officers recovered the piece of paper and as a result of which they handcuffed appellant because she had been "belligerent" in resisting their official rescue of the "warrant" from her person. Running roughshod over appellant, a policeman "grabbed" her, "twisted [her] hand," and she "yelled [and] pleaded with him" because "it was hurting." Appellant, in handcuffs, was then forcibly taken upstairs to her bedroom where the officers searched a dresser, a chest of drawers, a closet and some suitcases. They also looked into a photo album and through personal papers belonging to the appellant. The search spread to the rest of the second floor including the child's bedroom, the living room, the kitchen and a dinette. The basement of the building and a trunk found therein were also searched. The obscene materials for possession of which she was ultimately convicted were discovered in the course of that widespread search.

At the trial no search warrant was produced by the prosecution, nor was the failure to produce one explained or accounted for. At best, "There is, in the record, considerable doubt as to whether there ever was any warrant for the search of defendant's home." . . .

The State says that even if the search were made without authority, or otherwise unreasonably, it is not prevented from using the unconstitutionally seized evidence at trial, citing *Wolf* v. *Colorado,* 338 U.S. 25 (1949), in which this Court did indeed hold "that in a prosecution in a State court for a State crime the Fourteenth Amendment does not forbid the admission of evidence obtained by an unreasonable search and seizure." . . . On this appeal, . . . it is urged once again that we review that holding.

I.

. . .

[I]n the year 1914, . . . this Court "for the first time" held that "in a federal prosecution the Fourth Amendment barred the use of evidence secured through an illegal search and seizure." . . . This Court has ever since required of federal law officers a strict adherence to that command which this Court had held to be a clear, specific, and constitutionally required—even if judicially implied—deterrent safeguard without insistence upon which the Fourth Amendment would have been reduced to "a form of words." . . . It meant, quite simply, that "conviction by means of unlawful seizures and enforced confessions . . . should find no sanction in the judgments of the courts . . .," . . . and that such evidence "shall not be used at all."

. . .

. . . The Court, in *Olmstead* v. *United States,* 277 U.S. 438 (1928), in unmistakable language restated the . . . rule:

> "The striking outcome of the [case developing the exclusionary rule] and those which followed it was the sweeping declaration that the Fourth Amendment, although not referring to or limiting the use of evidence in court, really forbade its introduction if obtained by government officers through a violation of the Amendment."

II.

In 1949, 35 years after [the rule] was announced, this Court in *Wolf v. Colorado, supra,* again for the first time, discussed the effect of the Fourth

Amendment upon the states through the operation of the Due Process Clause of the Fourteenth Amendment. It said:

> "[W]e have no hesitation in saying that were a State affirmatively to sanction such police incursion into privacy it would run counter to the guaranty of the Fourteenth Amendment." . . .

Nevertheless, after declaring that the "security of one's privacy against arbitrary intrusion by the police" is "implicit in 'the concept of ordered liberty' and as such enforceable against the States through the Due Process Clause," . . . and announcing that it "stoutly adhere[d]" to the [decision in which the rule was set forth], the Court decided that the . . . exclusionary rule would not then be imposed upon the States as "an essential ingredient of the right." . . .

[W]e note that the second basis elaborated in *Wolf* in support of its failure to enforce the exclusionary rule against the States was that "other means of protection" have been afforded "the right of privacy." . . . The experience of California that such other remedies have been worthless and futile is buttressed by the experience of other States. The obvious futility of relegating the Fourth Amendment to the protection of other remedies has, moreover, been recognized by this Court since *Wolf*. . . .

III.

[T]oday we once again examine *Wolf's* constitutional documentation of the right to privacy free from unreasonable state intrusion, and, after its dozen years on our books, are led by it to close the only courtroom door remaining open to evidence secured by official lawlessness in flagrant abuse of that basic right, reserved to all persons as a specific guarantee against that very same unlawful conduct. We hold that all evidence obtained by searches and seizures in violation of the Constitution is, by that same authority, inadmissible in a state court.

IV.

Since the Fourth Amendment's right of privacy has been declared enforceable against the States through the Due Process Clause of the Fourteenth, it is enforceable against them by the same sanction of exclusion as is used against the Federal Government. Were it otherwise, . . . the assurance against unreasonable federal searches and seizures would be "a form of words," valueless and undeserving of mention in a perpetual charter of inestimable human liberties, so too, without that rule the freedom from state invasions of privacy would be so ephemeral and so neatly severed from its conceptual nexus with the freedom from all brutish means of coercing evidence as not to merit this Court's high regard as a freedom "implicit in the concept of ordered liberty." . . .

V.

Moreover, our holding that the exclusionary rule is an essential part of both the Fourth and Fourteenth Amendments is not only the logical dictate of prior cases, but it also makes very good sense. There is no war between the Constitution and common sense. . . .

There are those who say, as did Justice (then Judge) Cardozo, that under our constitutional exclusionary doctrine "[t]he criminal is to go free because the constable has blundered." . . . In some cases this will undoubtedly be the result. But, . . . "there is another consideration—the imperative of judicial integrity." . . . The criminal goes free, if he must, but it is the law that sets him free. Nothing can destroy a government more quickly than its failure to observe its own laws, or worse, its disregard of the charter of its own existence. As Mr. Justice Brandeis, dissenting, said in *Olmstead* v. *United States,* 277 U.S. 438, 485 (1928): "Our Government is the potent, the omnipresent teacher. For good or for ill, it teaches the whole people by its example. . . . If the Government becomes a lawbreaker, it breeds contempt for law; it invites every man to become a law unto himself; it invites anarchy." Nor can it lightly be assumed that, as a practical matter, adoption of the exclusionary rule fetters law enforcement. Only last year this Court expressly considered that contention and found that "pragmatic evidence of a sort" to the contrary was not wanting. . . .

The ignoble shortcut to conviction left open to the State tends to destroy the entire system of constitutional restraints on which the liberties of the people rest. Having once recognized that the right to privacy embodied in the Fourth Amendment is enforceable against the States, and that the right to be secure against rude invasions of privacy by state officers is, therefore, constitutional in origin, we can no longer permit that right to remain an empty promise. Because it is enforceable in the same manner and to like effect as other basic rights secured by the Due Process Clause, we can no longer permit it to be revocable at the whim of any police officer who, in the name of law enforcement itself, chooses to suspend its enjoyment. Our decision, founded on reason and truth, gives to the individual no more than that which the Constitution guarantees him, to the police officer no less than that to which honest law enforcement is entitled, and, to the courts, that judicial integrity so necessary in the true administration of justice.

Reversed and remanded.

Mapp by no means put an end to the debate concerning the desirability and wisdom of the exclusionary rule. In 1976, the Court in this case took the opportunity to limit federal courts' authority to enforce the rule in state criminal proceedings when it held, "Where the State . . . has provided an opportunity for full and fair litigation of a Fourth Amendment claim, a state prisoner may not be granted federal habeas relief on the ground that evidence obtained through an unconstitutional search and seizure was introduced at his trial. In this context, the contribution of the exclusionary rule, if any, to the effectuation of the Fourth Amendment is minimal as compared to the substantial societal costs of applying the rule." (See Chapters 4 and 12 for discussion of the impact of this case.) In separate opinions, Chief Justice Burger (concurring in the Court's decision) and Justice White (dissenting from the Court's decision) set forth what they would do with the exclusionary rule.

Stone v. *Powell,* 428 U.S. 465 (1976)

Burger, C.J., concurring

I concur in the Court's opinion. By way of dictum, and somewhat hesitantly, the Court notes that the holding in this case leaves undisturbed the exclusionary rule as applied to criminal trials. . . . [I]t seems clear to me that the exclusionary rule has been operative long enough to demonstrate its flaws. The time has come to modify its reach, even if it is retained for a small and limited category of cases.

Over the years, the strains imposed by reality, in terms of the costs to society and the bizarre miscarriages of justice that have been experienced because of the exclusion of reliable evidence when the "constable blunders," have led the Court to vacillate as to the rationale for deliberate exclusion of truth from the factfinding process. The rhetoric has varied with the rationale to the point where the rule has become a doctrinaire result in search of validating reasons.

In evaluating the exclusionary rule, it is important to bear in mind exactly what the rule accomplishes. Its function is simple—the exclusion of truth from the factfinding process. . . . The operation of the rule is therefore unlike that of the Fifth Amendment's protection against compelled self-incrimination. A confession produced after intimidating or coercive interrogation is inherently dubious. If a suspect's will has been overborne, a cloud hangs over his custodial admissions; the exclusion of such statements is based essentially on their lack of reliability. This is not the case as to *reliable* evidence—a pistol, a packet of heroin, counterfeit money, or the body of a murder victim—which may be judicially declared to be the result of an "unreasonable" search. The reliability of such evidence is beyond question; its probative value is certain.

. . .

[The exclusionary rule] is now used almost exclusively to exclude from evidence articles which are unlawful to be possessed or tools and instruments of crime. Unless it can be rationally thought that the Framers considered it essential to protect the liberties of the people to hold that which it is unlawful to possess, then it becomes clear that our constitutional course has taken a most bizarre tack.

. . .

The rule is based on the hope that events in the courtroom or appellate chambers, long after the crucial acts took place, will somehow modify the way in which policemen conduct themselves. A more clumsy, less direct means of imposing sanctions is difficult to imagine, particularly since the issue whether the policeman did indeed run afoul of the Fourth Amendment is often not resolved until years after the event. The "sanction" is particularly indirect when . . . the police go before a magistrate, who issues a warrant. Once the warrant issues, there is literally nothing more the policeman can do in seeking to comply with the law. Imposing an admittedly indirect "sanction" on the police officer in that instance is nothing less than sophisticated nonsense.

Despite this anomaly, the exclusionary rule now rests upon its purported tendency to deter police misconduct, . . . although, as we know, the rule has long been applied to wholly good-faith mistakes and to purely technical deficiencies in warrants. Other rhetorical generalizations, including the "imperative of judicial integrity," have not withstood analysis as more and more critical appraisals of the rule's operation have appeared. . . . Indeed, settled rules demonstrate that the "judicial integrity" rationalization is fatally flawed. First, the Court has refused to entertain claims that evidence was unlawfully seized unless the claimant could demonstrate that he had standing to press the contention. . . . If he could not, the evidence, albeit secured in violation of the Fourth Amendment, is admissible. . . . Despite its avowed deterrent objective, proof is lacking that the exclusionary rule, a purely judge-created device based on "hard cases," serves the purpose of deterrence. Notwithstanding Herculean efforts, no empirical study has been able to demonstrate that the rule does in fact have any deterrent effect. In the face of dwindling support for the rule some would go so far as to extend it to *civil* cases. . . .

In my view, it is an abdication of judicial responsibility to exact such exorbitant costs from society purely on the basis of speculative and unsubstantiated assumptions. . . .

In *Bivens* [*v. Six Unknown Named Agents,* 403 U.S. 388 (1971)], I suggested [in dissent] that, despite its grave shortcomings, the rule need not be totally abandoned until some meaningful alternative could be developed to protect innocent persons aggrieved by police misconduct. With the passage of time, it now appears that the continued existence of the rule, as presently implemented, inhibits the development of rational alternatives. The reason is quite simple: incentives for developing new procedures or remedies will remain minimal or nonexistent so long as the exclusionary rule is retained in its present form.

It can no longer be assumed that other branches of government will act while judges cling to this Draconian, discredited device in its present absolutist form. Legislatures are unlikely to create statutory alternatives, or impose direct sanctions on errant police officers or on the public treasury by way of tort actions, so long as persons who commit serious crimes continue to reap the enormous and undeserved benefits of the exclusionary rule. And of course, by definition the direct beneficiaries of this rule can be none but persons guilty of crimes. With this extraordinary "remedy" for Fourth Amendment violations, however slight, inadvertent, or technical, legislatures might assume that nothing more should be done, even though a grave defect of the exclusionary rule is that it offers no relief whatever to victims of overzealous police work who never appear in court. . . . And even if legislatures were inclined to experiment with alternative remedies, they have no assurance that the judicially created rule will be abolished or even modified in response to such legislative innovations. The unhappy result, as I see it, is that alternatives will inevitably be stymied by rigid adherence on our part to the exclusionary rule. I venture to predict that overruling this judicially contrived doctrine—or limiting its scope to egregious, bad-faith conduct—would inspire a surge of activity toward providing some kind of statutory remedy for persons injured by police mistakes or misconduct.

. . .

White, J., dissenting

. . .

I feel constrained to say, however, that I would join four or more other Justices in substantially limiting the reach of the exclusionary rule as presently administered under the Fourth Amendment in federal and state criminal trials.

Whether I would have joined the Court's opinion in *Mapp* v. *Ohio,* had I then been a Member of the Court, I do not know. But as time went on after coming to this bench, I became convinced that both *Weeks* v. *United States,* 232 U.S. 383 (1914), and *Mapp* v. *Ohio* had overshot their mark insofar as they aimed to deter lawless action by law enforcement personnel and that in many of its applications the exclusionary rule was not advancing that aim in the slightest, and that in this respect it was a senseless obstacle to arriving at the truth in many criminal trials.

The rule has been much criticized and suggestions have been made that it should be wholly abolished, but I would overrule neither *Weeks* v. *United States* nor *Mapp* v. *Ohio.* I am nevertheless of the view that the rule should be substantially modified so as to prevent its application in those many circumstances where the evidence at issue was seized by an officer acting in the good-faith belief that his conduct comported with existing law and having reasonable grounds for this belief. These are recurring situations; and recurringly evidence is excluded without any realistic expectation that its exclusion will contribute in the slightest to the purposes of the rule, even though the trial will be seriously affected or the indictment dismissed.

An officer sworn to uphold the law and to apprehend those who break it inevitably must make judgments regarding probable cause to arrest: Is there reasonable ground to believe that a crime has been committed and that a particular suspect has committed it? Sometimes the historical facts are disputed or are otherwise in doubt. In other situations the facts may be clear so far as they are known, yet the question of probable cause remains. In still others there are special worries about the reliability of secondhand information such as that coming from informants. In any of these situations, which occur repeatedly, when the officer is convinced that he has probable cause to arrest he will very likely make the arrest. Except in emergencies, it is probable that his colleagues or superiors will participate in the decision, and it may be that the officer will secure a warrant, although warrantless arrests on probable cause are not forbidden by the Constitution or by state law. Making the arrest in such circumstances is precisely what the community expects the police officer to do. Neither officers nor judges issuing arrest warrants need delay apprehension of the suspect until unquestioned proof against him has accumulated. The officer may be shirking his duty if he does so. . . .

In these situations, and perhaps many others, excluding the evidence will not further the ends of the exclusionary rule in any appreciable way; for it is painfully apparent that in each of them the officer is acting as a reasonable officer would and should act in similar circumstances. Excluding the evidence can in no way affect his future conduct unless it is to make him less willing to do his duty. It is true that in such cases the courts have ultimately determined that in their view the officer was mistaken; but it is also true that in making constitutional judgments under the general language used in some parts of our Constitution, including the Fourth Amendment, there is much room for disagreement among judges, each of whom is convinced that both he and his colleagues are reasonable men. Surely when this Court divides five to four on issues of probable cause, it is not tenable to conclude that the officer was at fault or acted unreasonably in making the arrest.

When law enforcement personnel have acted mistakenly, but in good faith and on reasonable grounds, and yet the evidence they have seized is later excluded, the exclusion can have no deterrent effect. The officers, if they do their duty, will act in similar fashion in similar circumstances in the future; and the only consequence of the rule as presently administered is that unimpeachable and probative evidence is kept from the trier of fact and the truth-finding function of proceedings is substantially impaired or a trial totally aborted.

Admitting the evidence in such circumstances does not render judges participants in Fourth Amendment violations. The violation, if there was one, has already occurred and the evidence is at hand. Furthermore, there has been only mistaken, but unintentional and faultless, conduct by enforcement officers. Exclusion of the evidence does not cure the invasion of the defendant's rights which he has already suffered. . . .

B. THE RIGHT OF PRIVACY

Katz was convicted under an indictment charging him with transmitting wagering information by telephone across state lines. FBI agents secured evidence against Katz by attaching an electronic listening and recording device to the outside of the telephone booth from which he made the calls. This evidence was admitted at Katz's trial when it was held that there was no Fourth Amendment violation since there had been no physical entrance into the area occupied by Katz. The Supreme Court reversed, abandoning the property right basis for Fourth Amendment protection and substituting instead the concept that the Fourth Amendment protects people rather than places.

Katz v. *United States,* 389 U.S. 347 (1967)

Stewart, J.

. . . [T]he Fourth Amendment protects people, not places. What a person knowingly exposes to the public, even in his own home or office, is not a subject of Fourth Amendment protection. . . . But what he seeks to preserve as private, even in an area accessible to the public, may be constitutionally protected. . . .

The Government stresses the fact that the telephone booth from which the petitioner made his calls was constructed partly of glass, so that he was as visible after he entered it as he would have been if he had remained outside. But what he sought to exclude when he entered the booth was not the intruding eye—it was the uninvited ear. He did not shed his right to do so simply because he made his calls from a place where he might be seen. No less than an individual in a business office, in a friend's apartment, or in a taxicab, a person in a telephone booth may rely upon the protection of the Fourth Amendment. One who occupies it, shuts the door behind him, and pays the toll that permits him to place a call is surely entitled to assume that the words he utters into the mouthpiece will not be broadcast to the world. To read the Constitution more narrowly is to ignore the vital role that the public telephone has come to play in private communication.

The Government contends, however, that the activities of its agents in this case should not be tested by Fourth Amendment requirements, for the surveillance technique they employed involved no physical penetration of the telephone booth from which the petitioner placed his calls. It is true that the absence of such penetration was at one time thought to foreclose further Fourth Amendment inquiry, . . . for that Amendment was thought to limit only searches and seizures of tangible property. But "[t]he premise that property interests control the right of the Government to search and seize has been discredited." . . . Thus, although . . . [the] Court [once] supposed . . . that surveillance without any trespass and without the seizure of any material object fell outside the ambit of the Constitution, we have since departed from the narrow view on which that decision rested. Indeed, we have expressly held that the Fourth Amendment governs not only the seizure of tangible items, but extends as well to the recording of oral statements, overheard without any "technical trespass under . . . local property law." . . . Once this much is acknowledged, and once it is recognized that the Fourth Amendment protects people—and not simply "areas"—against unreasonable searches and seizures, it becomes clear that the reach of that Amendment cannot turn upon the presence or absence of a physical intrusion into any given enclosure.

We conclude that the underpinnings of [our earlier decisions] . . . have been so eroded by our subsequent decisions that the "trespass" doctrine there enunciated can no longer be regarded as controlling. The Government's activities in electronically listening to and recording the petitioner's words violated the privacy upon which he justifiably relied while using the telephone booth and thus constituted a "search and seizure" within the meaning of the Fourth Amendment. The fact that the electronic device employed to achieve that end did not happen to penetrate the wall of the booth can have no constitutional significance.

Harlan, J., concurring

. . .

As the Court's opinion states, "the Fourth Amendment protects people, not places." The question, however, is what protection it affords to those people. Generally, as here, the answer to that question requires reference to a "place." My understanding of the rule that has emerged from prior decisions is that there is a twofold requirement, first that a person have exhibited an actual (subjective) expectation of privacy and, second, that the expectation be one that society is prepared to recognize as "reasonable." Thus a man's home is, for most purposes, a place where he expects privacy, but objects, activities, or statements that he exposes to the "plain view" of outsiders are not "protected" because no intention to keep them to himself has been exhibited. On the other hand, conversations in the open would not be protected against being overheard, for the expectation of privacy under the circumstances would be unreasonable.

. . .

The critical fact in this case is that "[o]ne who occupies it, [a telephone booth] shuts the door behind him, and pays the toll that permits him to place a call is surely entitled to assume" that his conversation is not being intercepted. The point is not that the booth is "accessible to the public" at other times, but that it is a temporarily private place whose momentary occupants' expectations of freedom from intrusion are recognized as reasonable.

C. REASONABLENESS AND PROBABLE CAUSE

The Fourth Amendment protects only against unreasonable intrusions and provides that no warrant shall issue but upon probable cause. The Supreme Court has applied the probable cause requirement to warrantless arrests, searches and seizures as well as to those authorized by a warrant. But what is probable cause? In Brinegar the Supreme Court attached a definition to that phrase, which it has cited approvingly during the subsequent thirty years, and in Aguilar, the Court began to set the standards to satisfy the definition.

Brinegar v. *United States,* 338 U.S. 160 at 175, 176 (1949)

Rutledge, J.

. . .

In dealing with probable cause, . . . as the very name implies, we deal with probabilities. These are not technical; they are the factual and practical considerations of everyday life on which reasonable and prudent men, not legal technicians, act. The standard of proof is accordingly correlative to what must be proved.

"The substance of all the definitions" of probable cause "is a reasonable ground for belief of guilt." And this "means less than evidence which would justify condemnation" or conviction, as Marshall, C. J., said for the Court more than a century ago in *Locke* v. *United States,* 7 Cranch 339,

348. Since Marshall's time, at any rate, it has come to mean more than bare suspicion: Probable cause exists where "the facts and circumstances within their [the officers'] knowledge and of which they had reasonably trustworthy information [are] sufficient in themselves to warrant a man of reasonable caution in the belief that" an offense has been or is being committed. *Carroll* v. *United States,* 267 U.S. 132, 162.

These long-prevailing standards seek to safeguard citizens from rash and unreasonable interferences with privacy and from unfounded charges of crime. They also seek to give fair leeway for enforcing the law in the community's protection. Because many situations which confront officers in the course of executing their duties are more or less ambiguous, room must be allowed for some mistakes on their part. But the mistakes must be those of reasonable men, acting on facts leading sensibly to their conclusions of probability. The rule of probable cause is a practical, nontechnical conception affording the best compromise that has been found for accommodating these often opposing interests. Requiring more would unduly hamper law enforcement. To allow less would be to leave law-abiding citizens at the mercy of the officers' whim or caprice.

. . .

Aguilar v. *Texas,* 378 U.S. 108 (1964)
Harlan, J.

This case presents questions concerning the constitutional requirements for obtaining a state search warrant.

Two Houston police officers applied to a local Justice of the Peace for a warrant to search for narcotics in petitioner's home. In support of their application, the officers submitted an affidavit which, in relevant part, recited that:

> "Affiants have received reliable information from a credible person and do believe that heroin, marijuana, barbiturates and other narcotics and narcotic paraphernalia are being kept at the above described premises for the purpose of sale and use contrary to the provisions of the law."

The search warrant was issued.

In executing the warrant, the local police, along with federal officers, announced at petitioner's door that they were police with a warrant. Upon hearing a commotion within the house, the officers forced their way into the house and seized petitioner in the act of attempting to dispose of a packet of narcotics.

At his trial in the state court, petitioner, through his attorney, objected to the introduction of evidence obtained as a result of the execution of the warrant. The objections were overruled and the evidence admitted. Petitioner was convicted of illegal possession of heroin and sentenced to serve 20 years in the state penitentiary.

. . .

In *Ker* v. *California,* 374 U.S. 23, we held that the "Fourth Amendment's proscriptions are enforced against the States through the Fourteenth Amendment," and that "the standard of reasonableness is the same under the Fourth and Fourteenth Amendments." Although *Ker* involved a search without a warrant, that case must certainly be read as holding that the standard for obtaining a search warrant is likewise "the same under the Fourth and Fourteenth Amendments."

An evaluation of the constitutionality of a search warrant should begin with the rule that "the informed and deliberate determinations of magistrates empowered to issue warrants ... are to be preferred over the hurried action of officers . . . who may happen to make arrests." . . . Reasons for this rule go to the foundations of the Fourth Amendment. A contrary rule "that evidence sufficient to support a magistrate's disinterested determination to issue a search warrant will justify the officers in making a search without a warrant would reduce the Amendment to a nullity and leave the people's homes secure only in the discretion of police officers." . . . Under such a rule "resort to [warrants] would ultimately be discouraged." . . . Thus, when a search is based upon a magistrate's, rather than a police officer's, determination of probable cause, the reviewing courts will accept evidence of a less "judicially competent or persuasive character than would have justified an officer in acting on his own without a warrant," . . . and will sustain the judicial determination so long as "there was substantial basis for [the magistrate] to conclude that narcotics were probably present." . . . As so well stated by Mr. Justice Jackson:

> "The point of the Fourth Amendment, which often is not grasped by zealous officer, is not that it denies law enforcement the support of the usual inferences which reasonable men draw from evidence. Its protection consists in requiring that those inferences be drawn by a neutral and detached magistrate instead of being judged by the officer engaged in the often competitive enterprise of ferreting out crime." *Johnson* v. *United States,* [333 U.S. 10, 13 (1948)]

Although the reviewing court will pay substantial deference to judicial determinations of probable cause, the court must still insist that the magistrate perform his "neutral and detached" function and not serve merely as a rubber stamp for the police.

In *Nathanson* v. *United States,* 290 U.S. 41, a warrant was issued upon the sworn allegation that the affiant "has cause to suspect and does believe" that certain merchandise was in a specified location. . . . The Court, noting that the affidavit "went upon a mere affirmation of suspicion and belief *without any statement of adequate supporting facts,"* . . . announced the following rule:

> "Under the Fourth Amendment, an officer may not properly issue a warrant to search a private dwelling unless he can find probable cause therefor from *facts or circumstances* presented to

> him under oath or affirmation. Mere affirmance of belief or suspicion is not enough."

The Court, in *Giordenello* v. *United States,* 357 U.S. 480, applied this rule to an affidavit similar to that relied upon here. Affiant in that case swore that petitioner "did receive, conceal, etc., narcotic drugs . . . with knowledge of unlawful importation. . . ."
The Court announced the guiding principles to be:

> "that the inferences from the facts which lead to the complaint '[must] be drawn by a neutral and detached magistrate instead of being judged by the officer engaged in the often competitive enterprise of ferreting out crime.' *Johnson* v. *United States,* 333 U.S. 10, 14. The purpose of the complaint, then, is to enable the appropriate magistrate . . . to determine whether the 'probable cause' required to support a warrant exists. The Commissioner must judge for himself the persuasiveness of the facts relied on by a complaining officer to show probable cause. He should not accept without question the complainant's mere conclusion. . . ." 357 U.S., at 486.

The Court, applying these principles to the complaint in that case, stated that:

> "it is clear that it does not pass muster because it does not provide any basis for the Commissioner's determination . . . that probable cause existed. The complaint contains no affirmative allegation that the affiant spoke with personal knowledge of the matters contained therein; it does not indicate any sources for the complainant's belief; and it does not set forth any other sufficient basis upon which a finding of probable cause could be made." *Ibid.*

The vice in the present affidavit is at least as great as in *Nathanson* and *Giordenello.* Here the "mere conclusion" that petitioner possessed narcotics was not even that of the affiant himself; it was that of an unidentified informant. The affidavit here not only "contains no affirmative allegation that the affiant spoke with personal knowledge of the matters contained therein," it does not even contain an "affirmative allegation" that the affiant's unidentified source "spoke with personal knowledge." For all that appears, the source here merely suspected, believed or concluded that there were narcotics in petitioner's possession. The magistrate here certainly could not "judge for himself the persuasiveness of the facts relied on . . . to show probable cause." He necessarily accepted "without question" the informant's "suspicion," "belief" or "mere conclusion."

Although an affidavit may be based on hearsay information and need not reflect the direct personal observations of the affiant, . . . the magistrate must be informed of some of the underlying circumstances from which the informant concluded that the narcotics were where he claimed they were, and some of the underlying circumstances from which the officer concluded that the informant, whose identity need not be disclosed, . . . was "credible" or his information "reliable." Otherwise, "the inferences from the facts which lead to the complaint" will be drawn not "by a neutral and detached magistrate," as the Constitution requires, but instead, by a police officer "engaged in the often competitive enterprise of ferreting out crime," . . . as in this case, by an unidentified informant.

We conclude, therefore, that the search warrant should not have been issued because the affidavit did not provide a sufficient basis for a finding of probable cause and that the evidence obtained as a result of the search warrant was inadmissible in petitioner's trial. . . .

Reversed and remanded.

D. WARRANTLESS INTRUSIONS

Although the Supreme Court has regularly stated its preference for warrants, it has never invalidated a warrantless arrest so long as there was probable cause. In this case, the Court was forced to come to grips with the issue. Here the arresting postal inspectors had more than enough time to secure an arrest warrant. No exigent circumstances demanded immediate action.

United States v. *Watson,* 423 U.S. 411 (1976)

White, J.

This case presents questions under the Fourth Amendment as to the legality of a warrantless arrest. . . .

II.

A major part of the Court of Appeals' opinion was its holding that Watson's warrantless arrest violated the Fourth Amendment. Although it did not expressly do so, it may have intended to overturn the conviction on the independent ground that the two credit cards were the inadmissible fruits of an unconstitutional arrest. . . . However that may be, the Court of Appeals treated the illegality of Watson's arrest as an important factor in determining the voluntariness of his consent to search his car. We therefore deal first with the arrest issue.

Contrary to the Court of Appeals' view, Watson's arrest was not invalid because executed without a warrant. Title 18 U.S.C. § 3061 (a)(3) expressly empowers the Board of Governors of the Postal Service to authorize Postal Service officers and employees "performing duties related to the inspection of postal matters" to

> "make arrests without warrant for felonies cognizable under the laws of the United States if they have reasonable grounds to believe that the person to be arrested has committed or is committing such a felony."

. . . Because there was probable cause in this case . . . the inspector and his subordinates, in arresting Watson, were acting strictly in accordance with the governing statute and regulations. The effect of the judgment of the Court of Appeals was to invalidate the statute as applied in this case and as applied to all the situations where a court fails to find exigent circumstances justifying a warrantless arrest. We reverse that judgment.

Under the Fourth Amendment, the people are to be "secure in their persons, houses, papers, and effects, against unreasonable searches and seizures, . . . and no Warrants shall issue, but upon probable cause. . . ." Section 3061 represents a judgment by Congress that it is not unreasonable under the Fourth Amendment for postal inspectors to arrest without a warrant provided they have probable cause to do so. This was not an isolated or quixotic judgment of the legislative branch. Other federal law enforcement officers have been expressly authorized by statute for many years to make felony arrests on probable cause but without a warrant. . . .

Because there is a "strong presumption of constitutionality due to an Act of Congress, especially when it turns on what is 'reasonable,' " "[o]bviously the Court should be reluctant to decide that a search thus authorized by Congress was unreasonable and that the Act was therefore unconstitutional." . . . Moreover, there is nothing in the Court's prior cases indicating that under the Fourth Amendment a warrant is required to make a valid arrest for a felony. Indeed, the relevant prior decisions are uniformly to the contrary.

"The usual rule is that a police officer may arrest without warrant one believed by the officer upon reasonable cause to have been guilty of a felony." . . . Just last Term, while recognizing that maximum protection of individual rights could be assured by requiring a magistrate's review of the factual justification prior to any arrest, we stated that "such a requirement would constitute an intolerable handicap for legitimate law enforcement" and noted that the Court, "has never invalidated an arrest supported by probable cause solely because the officers failed to secure a warrant."
. . .

The cases construing the Fourth Amendment thus reflect the ancient common-law rule that a peace officer was permitted to arrest without a warrant for a misdemeanor or felony committed in his presence as well as for a felony not committed in his presence if there was reasonable ground for making the arrest. . . . This has also been the prevailing rule under state constitutions and statutes. "The rule of the common law, that a peace officer or a private citizen may arrest a felon without a warrant, has been generally held by the courts of the several States to be in force in cases of felony punishable by the civil tribunals." . . .

The balance struck by the common law in generally authorizing felony arrests on probable cause, but without a warrant, has survived substantially intact. It appears in almost all of the States in the form of express statutory authorization In 1963, the American Law Institute undertook the task of formulating a model statute governing police powers and practice in criminal law enforcement and related aspects of pretrial procedure. In 1975, after years of discussion, A Model Code of Pre-arraignment Procedure was proposed. Among its provisions was § 120.1 which authorizes an officer to take a person into custody if the officer has reasonable cause to believe that the person to be arrested has committed a felony, or has committed a misdemeanor or petty misdemeanor in his presence. The commentary to this section said: "The Code thus adopts the traditional and almost universal standard for arrest without a warrant."

This is the rule Congress has long directed its principal law enforcement officers to follow. Congress has plainly decided against conditioning warrantless arrest power on proof of exigent circumstances. Law enforcement officers may find it wise to seek arrest warrants where practicable to do so, and their judgments about probable cause may be more readily accepted where backed by a warrant issued by a magistrate. . . . But we decline to transform this judicial preference into a constitutional rule when the judgment of the Nation and Congress has for so long been to authorize warrantless public arrests on probable cause rather than to encumber criminal prosecutions with endless litigation with respect to the existence of exigent circumstances, whether it was practicable to get a warrant, whether the suspect was about to flee, and the like.

Watson's arrest did not violate the Fourth Amendment, and the Court of Appeals erred in holding to the contrary.

. . .

Powell, J., concurring

. . .

Since the Fourth Amendment speaks equally to both searches and seizures, and since an arrest, the taking hold of one's person, is quintessentially a seizure, it would seem that the constitutional provision should impose the same limitations upon arrests that it does upon searches. Indeed, as an abstract matter an argument can be made that the restrictions upon arrest perhaps should be greater. A search may cause only annoyance and temporary inconvenience to the law-abiding citizen, assuming more serious dimension only when it turns up evidence of criminality. An arrest, however, is a serious personal intrusion regardless of whether the person seized is guilty or innocent. Although an arrestee cannot be held for a significant period without some neutral determination that there are grounds to do so, see *Gerstein, supra,* no decision that he should go free can come quickly enough to erase the invasion of his privacy that already will have occurred. . . . Logic therefore would seem to dictate that arrests be subject to the warrant requirement at least to the same extent as searches.

. . .

The historical momentum for acceptance of warrantless arrests, already strong at the adoption of the Fourth Amendment, has gained strength during the ensuing two centuries. Both the judiciary and the legislative bodies of this Nation repeatedly have placed their imprimaturs upon the practice and, as the Government emphasizes, law enforcement agencies have developed their investigative and arrest procedures upon an assumption that warrantless arrests were valid so long as based upon probable cause. The decision of the Court of Appeals in this case was virtually unprecedented. Of course, no practice that is inconsistent with constitutional protections can be saved merely by appeal to previous uncritical acceptance. But the warrantless felony arrest, long preferred at common law and unimpeached at the passage of the Fourth Amendment, is not such a practice. Given the revoluntionary implications of such a holding, a declaration at this late date that warrantless felony arrests are constitutionally infirm would have to rest upon reasons more substantial than a desire to harmonize the rules for arrest with those governing searches. . . .

Moreover, a constitutional rule permitting felony arrests only with a warrant or in exigent circumstances could severely hamper effective law enforcement. Good police practice often requires postponing an arrest, even after probable cause has been established, in order to place the suspect under surveillance or otherwise develop further evidence necessary to prove guilt to a jury. Under the holding of the Court of Appeals such additional investigative work could imperil the entire prosecution. Should the officers fail to obtain a warrant initially, and later be required by unforeseen circumstances to arrest immediately with no chance to procure a last-minute warrant, they would risk a court decision that the subsequent exigency did not excuse their failure to get a warrant in the interim since they first developed probable cause. If the officers attempted to meet such a contingency by procuring a warrant as soon as they had probable cause and then merely held it during their subsequent investigation, they would risk a court decision that the warrant had grown stale by the time it was use. Law enforcement personnel caught in this squeeze could ensure validity of their arrests only by obtaining a warrant and arresting as soon as probable cause existed, thereby foreclosing the possibility of gathering vital additional evidence from the suspect's continued actions.

In sum, the historical and policy reasons sketched above fully justify the Court's sustaining of a warrantless arrest upon probable cause, despite the resulting divergence between the constitutional rule governing searches and that now held applicable to seizures of the person.

. . .

Stewart, J., concurring

The arrest in this case was made upon probable cause in a public place in broad daylight. The Court holds that this arrest did not violate the Fourth Amendment, and I agree. The Court does *not* decide, nor could it decide in this case, whether or under what circumstances an officer must obtain a warrant before he may lawfully enter a private place to effect an arrest.

. . .

[In a dissent, attacking the accuracy of the majority's historical analysis, Mr. Justice Marshall advocated applying the same rule to arrests that is applied to searches: that an arrest warrant is required except in carefully limited exceptions which would allow for the immediate arrests of the most dangerous criminals.]

Unlike its approach for arrests, the Supreme Court has more steadfastly held to the warrant requirement for searches. A warrant is required before a police officer may conduct a search without consent unless there are exigent circumstances fitting the situation into one of categories of exceptions authorizing warrantless searches. One exception is a warrantless search incident to a lawful arrest. In this case and Chimel, which follows, the Supreme Court grappled with the permissible scope of such searches.

United States v. *Robinson,* 414 U.S. 218 (1973)

Rehnquist, J.

Respondent Robinson was convicted in United States District Court for the District of Columbia of the possession and facilitation of concealment of heroin. . . .

On April 23, 1968, at approximately 11 p.m., Officer Richard Jenks, a 15-year veteran of the District of Columbia Metropolitan Police Department, observed the respondent driving a 1965 Cadillac near the intersection of 8th and C Streets, N. E., in the District of Columbia. Jenks, as a result of previous investigation following a check of respondent's operator's permit four days earlier, determined there was reason to believe that respondent was operating a motor vehicle after the revocation of his operator's permit. This is an offense defined by statute in the District of Columbia which carries a mandatory minimum jail term, a mandatory minimum fine, or both.

. . .

Jenks signaled respondent to stop the automobile, which respondent did, and all three of the occupants emerged from the car. At that point Jenks informed respondent that he was under arrest for "operating after revocation and obtaining a permit by misrepresentation." It was assumed by the Court of Appeals, and is conceded by the respondent here, that Jenks had probable cause to arrest respondent, and that he effected a full-custody arrest.

. . .

[Officer Jenks patted down the outer clothing of Robinson.] . . . During this patdown, Jenks felt an object in the left breast pocket of the heavy coat respondent was wearing, but testified that he "couldn't tell what it was" and also that he "couldn't actually tell the size of it." Jenks then reached into the pocket and pulled out the object, which turned out to be a "crumpled up cigarette package." Jenks testified that at this point he still did not know what was in the package:

> "As I felt the package I could feel objects in the package but I couldn't tell what they were. . . . I knew they weren't cigarettes."

The officer then opened the cigarette pack and found 14 gelatin capsules of white powder which he thought to be, and which later analysis proved to be, heroin. Jenks then continued his search of respondent to completion, feeling around his waist and trouser legs, and examining the remaining pockets. The heroin seized from the respondent was admitted into evidence at the trial which resulted in his conviction in the District Court.

. . .

We concluded that the search conducted by Jenks in this case did not offend the limits imposed by the Fourth Amendment, and we therefore reverse the judgment of the Court of Appeals.

I

It is well settled that a search incident to a lawful arrest is a traditional exception to the warrant requirement of the Fourth Amendment. This general exception has historically been formulated into two distinct propositions. The first is that a search may be made of the *person* of the arrestee by virtue of the lawful arrest. The second is that a search may be made of the area within the control of the arrestee.

Examination of this Court's decisions shows that these two propositions have been treated quite differently. The validity of the search of a person incident to a lawful arrest has been regarded as settled from its first enunciation, and has remained virtually unchallenged until the present case. The validity of the second proposition, while likewise conceded in principle, has been subject to differing interpretations as to the extent of the area which may be searched.

. . .

Throughout the series of cases in which the Court has addressed the second proposition relating to a search incident to a lawful arrest—the permissible area beyond the person of the arrestee which such a search may cover—no doubt has been expressed as to the unqualified authority of the arresting authority to search the person of the arrestee. . . .

Thus the broadly stated rule, and the reasons for it, have been repeatedly affirmed in the decisions of this Court since *Weeks* v. *United States*, . . . nearly 60 years ago. Since the statements in the cases speak not simply in terms of an exception to the warrant requirement, but in terms of an affirmative authority to search, they clearly imply that such searches also meet the Fourth Amendment's requirement of reasonableness.

II

In its decision of this case, the Court of Appeals decided that even after a police officer lawfully places a suspect under arrest for the purpose of taking him into custody, he may not ordinarily proceed to fully search the prisoner. He must, instead, conduct a limited frisk of the outer clothing and remove such weapons that he may, as a result of that limited frisk, reasonably believe and ascertain that the suspect has in his possession. While recognizing that *Terry* v. *Ohio*, 392 U.S. 1 (1968), dealt with a permissible "frisk" incident to an investigative stop based on less than probable cause to arrest, the Court of Appeals felt that the principles of that case should be carried over to this probable-cause arrest for driving while one's license is revoked. Since there would be no further evidence of such a crime to be obtained in a search of the arrestee, the court held that only a search for weapons could be justified.

Terry v. *Ohio, supra*, did not involve an arrest for probable cause, and it made quite clear that the "protective frisk" for weapons which it approved might be conducted without probable cause. . . .

This Court's opinion explicitly recognized that there is a "distinction in purpose, character, and extent between a search incident to an arrest and a limited search for weapons."

. . .

Terry, therefore, affords no basis to carry over to a probable-cause arrest the limitations this Court placed on a stop-and-frisk search permissible without probable cause.

. . .

The Court of Appeals in effect determined that the *only* reason supporting the authority for a *full* search incident to lawful arrest was the possibility of discovery of evidence or fruits. Concluding that there could be no evidence or fruits in the case of an offense such as that with which respondent was charged, it held that any protective search would have to be limited by the conditions laid down in *Terry* for a search upon less than probable cause to arrest. Quite apart from the fact that *Terry* clearly recognized the distinction between the two types of searches, and that a different rule governed one than governed the other, we find additional reason to disagree with the Court of Appeals.

The justification or reason for the authority to search incident to a lawful arrest rests quite as much on the need to disarm the suspect in order to take him into custody as it does on the need to preserve evidence on his person for later use at trial. . . . The standards traditionally governing a search incident to lawful arrest are not, therefore, commuted to the stricter *Terry* standards by the absence of probable fruits or further evidence of the particular crime for which the arrest is made.

Nor are we inclined, on the basis of what seems to us to be a rather speculative judgment, to qualify the breadth of the general authority to search incident to a lawful custodial arrest on an assumption that persons arrested for the offense of driving while their licenses have been revoked are less likely to possess dangerous weapons than are those arrested for other crimes. It is scarcely open to doubt that the danger to an officer is far greater in the case of the extended exposure which follows the taking of a suspect into custody and transporting him to the police station than in the case of the relatively fleeting contact resulting from the typical *Terry*-type stop. This is an adequate basis for treating all custodial arrests alike for purposes of search justification.

. . .

A police officer's determination as to how and where to search the person of a suspect whom he has arrested is necessarily a quick *ad hoc* judgment which the Fourth Amendment does not require to be broken down in each instance into an analysis of each step in the search. The authority to search the person incident to a lawful custodial arrest, while based upon the need to disarm and to discover evidence, does not depend on what a court may later decide was the probability in a particular arrest situation that weapons or evidence would in fact be found upon the person of the suspect. A custodial arrest of a suspect based on probable cause is a reasonable intrusion under the Fourth Amendment; that intrusion being lawful, a search incident to the arrest requires no additional justification. It is the fact of the lawful arrest which establishes the authority to search, and we hold that in the case of a lawful custodial arrest a full search of the person is not only an exception to the warrant requirement of the Fourth Amendment, but is also a "reasonable" search under that Amendment.

IV

The search of respondent's person conducted by Officer Jenks in this case and the seizure from him of the heroin, were permissible under established Fourth Amendment law. . . . Since it is the fact of custodial arrest which gives rise to the authority to search, it is of no moment that Jenks did not indicate any subjective fear of the respondent or that he did not himself suspect that respondent was armed. Having in the course of a lawful search come upon the crumpled package of cigarettes, he was entitled to inspect it; and when his inspection revealed the heroin capsules, he was entitled to seize them as "fruits, instrumentalities, or contraband" probative of criminal conduct. . . . The judgment of the Court of Appeals holding otherwise is

Reversed.

Chimel v. *California,* 395 U.S. 752 (1969)
Stewart, J.

This case raises basic questions concerning the permissible scope under the Fourth Amendment of a search incident to a lawful arrest.

The relevant facts are essentially undisputed. Late in the afternoon of September 13, 1965, three police officers arrived at the Santa Ana, California, home of the petitioner with a warrant authorizing his arrest for the burglary of a coin shop. The officers knocked on the door, identified themselves to the petitioner's wife, and asked if they might come inside. She ushered them into the house, where they waited 10 or 15 minutes until the petitioner returned home from work. When the petitioner entered the house, one of the officers handed him the arrest warrant and asked for permission to "look around." The petitioner objected, but was advised that "on the basis of the lawful arrest," the officers would nonetheless conduct a search. No search warrant had been issued.

Accompanied by the petitioner's wife, the officers then looked through the entire three-bedroom house, including the attic, the garage, and a small workshop. In some rooms the search was relatively cursory. In the master bedroom and sewing room, however, the officers directed the petitioner's wife to open drawers and "to physically move contents of the drawers from side to side so that [they] might view any items that would have come from [the] burglary." After completing the search, they seized numerous items—primarily coins, but also several medals, tokens, and a few other objects. The entire search took between 45 minutes and an hour.

. . .

. . . This brings us directly to the question whether the warrantless search of the petitioner's entire house can be constitutionally justified as incident to that arrest. The decisions of this Court bearing upon that question have been far from consistent, as even the most cursory review makes evident.

. . .

In 1950, . . . came *United States* v. *Rabinowitz,* 339 U.S. 56, the decision upon which California primarily relies in the case now before us. In *Rabinowitz,* federal authorities had been informed that the defendant was dealing in stamps bearing forged overprints. On the basis of that information they secured a warrant for his arrest, which they executed at his one-room business office. At the time of the arrest, the officers "searched the desk, safe, and file cabinets in the office for about an hour and a half," and seized 573 stamps with forged overprints. The stamps were admitted into evidence at the defendant's trial, and this Court affirmed his conviction, rejecting the contention that the warrantless search had been unlawful. The Court held that the search in its entirety fell within the principle giving law enforcement authorities "[t]he right 'to search the place where the arrest is made in order to find and seize things connected with the crime. . . .' "

Rabinowitz has come to stand for the proposition, *inter alia,* that a warrantless search "incident to a lawful arrest" may generally extend to the area that is considered to be in the "possession" or under the "control" of the person arrested. And it was on the basis of that proposition that the California courts upheld the search of the petitioner's entire house in this case. That doctrine, however, at least in the broad sense in which it was applied by the California courts in this case, can withstand neither historical nor rational analysis.

. . .

Nor is the rationale by which the State seeks here to sustain the search of the petitioner's house supported by a reasoned view of the background and purpose of the Fourth Amendment. Mr. Justice Frankfurter wisely pointed out in his *Rabinowitz* dissent that the Amendment's proscription of "unreasonable searches and seizures" must be read in light of "the history that gave rise to the words"—a history of "abuses so deeply felt by the Colonies as to be one of the potent causes of the Revolution. . . ." 339 U.S., at 69. The Amendment was in large part a reaction to the general warrants and warrantless searches that had so alienated the colonists and had helped speed the movement for independence. In the scheme of the Amendment, therefore, the requirement that "no Warrants shall issue, but upon probable cause," plays a crucial part. As the Court put it in *McDonald* v. *United States,* 335 U.S. 451:

> "We are not dealing with formalities. The presence of a search warrant serves a high function. Absent some grave emergency, the Fourth Amendment has interposed a magistrate between the citizen and the police. This was done not to shield criminals nor to make the home a safe haven for illegal activities. It was done so that an objective mind might weigh the need to invade that privacy in order to enforce the law. The right of privacy was deemed too precious to entrust to the discretion of those whose job is the detection of crime and the arrest of criminals. . . . And so the Constitution requires a magistrate to pass on the desires of the police before they violate the privacy of the home. We cannot be true to that constitutional requirement and excuse the absence of a search warrant without a showing by those who seek exemption from the constitutional mandate that the exigencies of the situation made that course imperative."

. . . Clearly, the general requirement that a search warrant be obtained is not lightly to be dispensed with, and "the burden is on those seeking [an] exemption [from the requirement] to show the need for it. . . ."

. . .

. . . When an arrest is made, it is reasonable for the arresting officer to search the person arrested in order to remove any weapons that the latter might seek to use in order to resist arrest or effect his escape. Otherwise, the officer's safety might well be endangered, and the arrest itself frustrated. In addition, it is entirely reasonable for the arresting officer to search for and seize any evidence on the arrestee's person in order to prevent its concealment or destruction. And the area into which an arrestee might reach in order to grab a weapon or evidentiary items must, of course, be governed by a like rule. A gun on a table or in a drawer in front of one who is arrested can be as dangerous to the arresting officer as one concealed in the clothing of the person arrested. There is ample justification, therefore, for a search of the arrestee's person and the area "within his immediate control"—construing that phrase to mean the area from within which he might gain possession of a weapon or destructible evidence.

There is no comparable justification, however, for routinely searching any room other than that in which an arrest occurs—or, for that matter, for searching through all the desk drawers or other closed or concealed areas in that room itself. Such searches, in the absence of well-recognized exceptions, may be made only under the authority of a search warrant. The "adherence to judicial processes" mandated by the Fourth Amendment requires no less.

. . .

It is argued in the present case that it is "reasonable" to search a man's house when he is arrested in it. But that argument is founded on little more than a subjective view regarding the acceptability of certain sorts of police conduct, and not on considerations relevant to Fourth Amendment interests. Under such an unconfined analysis, Fourth Amendment protection in this area would approach the evaporation point. It is not easy to explain why, for instance, it is less subjectively "reasonable" to search a man's house when he is arrested on his front lawn—or just down the street—than it is when he happens to be in the house at the time of arrest. As Mr. Justice Frankfurter put it:

> "To say that the search must be reasonable is to require some criterion of reason. It is no guide at all either for a jury or for district judges or the police to say that an 'unreasonable search' if forbidden—that the search must be reasonable. What is the test of reason which makes a search reasonable? The test is the reason underlying and expressed by the Fourth Amendment: the history and the experience which it embodies and the safeguards afforded by it against the evils to which it was a response." *United States* v. *Rabinowitz,* 339 U.S., at 83 (dissenting opinion).

Thus, although "[t]he recurring questions of the reasonableness of searches" depend upon "the facts and circumstances—the total atmosphere of the case," . . . those facts and circumstances must be viewed in the light of established Fourth Amendment principles.

. . .

Application of sound Fourth Amendment principles to the facts of this case produces a clear result. The search here went far beyond the petitioner's person and the area from within which he might have obtained either a weapon or something that could have been used as evidence against him. There was no constitutional justification, in the absence of a search warrant, for extending the search beyond that area. The scope of the search was, therefore, "unreasonable" under the Fourth and Fourteenth Amendments, and the petitioner's conviction cannot stand.

Reversed.

E. CONSENT SEARCHES

Second in frequency to searches incident to an arrest are consent searches. Naturally, they are conducted without warrants; the police officer need not have probable cause to make the search. The only issue is whether the subject voluntarily permitted the officer to conduct the search. What constitutes a voluntary consent has been a thorny issue. Must the individual know of his right to refuse? Must the police officer advise the subject of his right to refuse to grant the consent?

Schneckloth v. *Bustamonte,* 412 U.S. 218 (1973)

Stewart, J.

It is well settled under the Fourth and Fourteenth Amendments that a search conducted without a warrant issued upon probable cause is "*per se* unreasonable . . . subject only to a few specifically established and well-delineated exceptions." . . . It is equally well settled that one of the specifically established exceptions to the requirements of both a warrant and probable cause is a search that is conducted pursuant to consent. . . . The constitutional question in the present case concerns the definition of "consent" in this Fourth and Fourteenth Amendment context.

I.

The respondent was brought to trial in a California court upon a charge of possessing a check with intent to defraud. He moved to suppress the introduction of certain material as evidence against him on the ground that the material had been acquired through an unconstitutional search and seizure. In response to the motion, the trial judge conducted an evidentiary hearing where it was established that the material in question had been acquired by the State under the following circumstances:

While on routine patrol in Sunnyvale, California, at approximately 2:40 in the morning, Police Officer James Rand stopped an automobile when he observed that one headlight and its license plate light were burned out. Six men were in the vehicle. Joe Alcala and the respondent, Robert Bustamonte, were in the front seat with Joe Gonzales, the driver. Three older men were seated in the rear. When, in response to the policeman's question, Gonzales could not produce a driver's license, Officer Rand asked if any of the other five had any evidence of identification. Only Alcala produced a license, and he explained that the car was his brother's. After the six occupants had stepped out of the car at the officer's request and after two additional policemen had arrived, Officer Rand asked Alcala if he could search the car. Alcala replied, "Sure, go ahead." Prior to the search no one was threatened with arrest and, according to Officer Rand's uncontradicted testimony, it "was all very congenial at this time." Gonzales testified that Alcala actually helped in the search of the car, by opening the trunk and glove compartment. In Gonzales' words: "[T]he police officer asked Joe [Alcala], he goes, 'Does the trunk open?' And Joe said, 'Yes.' He went to the car and got the keys and opened up the trunk." Wadded up under the left rear seat, the police officers found three checks that had previously been stolen from a car wash.

The trial judge denied the motion to suppress, and the checks in question were admitted in evidence at Bustamonte's trial. On the basis of this and other evidence he was convicted, and the California Court of Appeal for the First Appellate District affirmed the conviction. . . . In agreeing that the search and seizure were constitutionally valid, the appellate court applied the standard earlier formulated by the Supreme Court of California in an opinion by then Justice Traynor: "Whether in a particular case an apparent consent was in fact voluntarily given or was in submission to an express or implied assertion of authority, is a question of fact to be determined in the light of all the circumstances." . . . The appellate court found that "[i]n the instant case the prosecution met the necessary burden of showing consent . . . since there were clearly circumstances from which the trial court could ascertain that consent had been freely given without coercion or submission to authority. . . ."

Thereafter, the respondent sought a writ of habeas corpus in a federal district court. It was denied. On appeal, the Court of Appeals for the Ninth Circuit, . . . set aside the District Court's order. . . . The appellate court reasoned that a consent was a waiver of a person's Fourth and Fourteenth Amendment rights, and that the State was under an obligation to demonstrate, not only that the consent had been uncoerced, but that it had been given with an understanding that it could be freely and effectively withheld. Consent could not be found, the court held, solely from the absence of coercion and a verbal expression of assent. Since the District Court had not determined that Alcala had *known* that his consent could have been withheld and that he could have refused to have his vehicle searched, the Court of Appeals vacated the order denying the writ and remanded the case for further proceedings. . . .

II.

It is important to make it clear at the outset what is not involved in this case. The respondent concedes that a search conducted pursuant to a valid consent is constitutionally permissible. . . . And similarly the State concedes that "[w]hen a prosecutor seeks to rely upon consent to justify the lawfulness of a search, he has the burden of proving that the consent was, in fact, freely and voluntarily given." . . .

The precise question in this case, then, is what must the prosecution prove to demonstrate that a consent was "voluntarily" given. And upon that question there is a square conflict of views between the state and federal courts that have reviewed the search involved in the case before us. The Court of Appeals for the Ninth Circuit concluded that it is an essential part of the State's initial burden to prove that a person knows he has a right to refuse consent. The California courts have followed the rule that voluntariness is a question of fact to be determined from the totality of all the circumstances, and that the state of a defendant's knowledge is only one factor to be taken into account in assessing the voluntariness of a consent. . . .

B.

. . . [T]he question whether a consent to a search was in fact "voluntary" or was the product of duress or coercion, express or implied, is a question of fact to be determined from the totality of all the circumstances. While knowledge of the right to refuse consent is one factor to be taken into account, the government need not establish such knowledge as the *sine qua non* of an effective consent. As with police questioning, two competing concerns must be accommodated in determining the meaning of a "voluntary" consent—the legitimate need for such searches and the equally important requirement of assuring the absence of coercion.

In situations where the police have some evidence of illicit activity, but lack probable cause to arrest or search, a search authorized by a valid consent may be the only means of obtaining important and reliable evidence. In the present case for example, while the police had reason to stop the car for traffic violations, the State does not contend that there was probable cause to search the vehicle or that the search was incident to a valid arrest of any of the occupants. Yet, the search yielded tangible evidence that served as a basis for a prosecution, and provided some assurance that others, wholly innocent of the crime, were not mistakenly brought to trial. And in those cases where there is probable cause to arrest or search, but where the police lack a warrant, a consent search may still be valuable. If the search is conducted and proves fruitless, that in itself may convince the police that an arrest with its possible stigma and embarrassment is unnecessary, or that a far more extensive search pursuant to a warrant is not justified. In short, a search pursuant to consent may result in considerably less inconvenience for the subject of the search, and, properly conducted, is a constitutionally permissible and wholly legitimate aspect of effective police activity.

But the Fourth and Fourteenth Amendments require that a consent not be coerced, by explicit or implicit means, by implied threat or covert force. For, no matter how subtly the coercion was applied, the resulting "consent" would be no more than a pretext for the unjustified police intrusion against which the Fourth Amendment is directed. . . .

The problem of reconciling the recognized legitimacy of consent searches with the requirement that they be free from any aspect of official coercion cannot be resolved by any infallible touchstone. To approve such searches without the most careful scrutiny would sanction the possibility of official coercion; to place artificial restrictions upon such searches would jeopardize their basic validity. Just as was true with confessions, the requirement of a "voluntary" consent reflects a fair accommodation of the constitutional requirements involved. In examining all the surrounding circumstances to determine if in fact the consent to search was coerced, account must be taken of subtly coercive police questions, as well as the possibly vulnerable subjective state of the person who consents. Those searches that are the product of police coercion can thus be filtered out without undermining the continuing validity of consent searches. In sum, there is no reason for us to depart in the area of consent searches, from the traditional definition of "voluntariness."

The approach of the Court of Appeals for the Ninth Circuit finds no support in any of our decisions that have attempted to define the meaning of "voluntariness." Its ruling, that the State must affirmatively prove that the subject of the search knew that he had a right to refuse consent, would, in practice, create serious doubt whether consent searches could continue to be conducted. There might be rare cases where it could be proved from the record that a person in fact affirmatively knew of his right to refuse—such as a case where he announced to the police that if he didn't sign the consent form, "you [police] are going to get a search warrant;" or a case where by prior experience and training a person had clearly and convincingly demonstrated such knowledge. But more commonly where there was no evidence of any coercion, explicit or implicit, the prosecution would nevertheless be unable to demonstrate that the subject of the search in fact had known of his right to refuse consent.

The very object of the inquiry—the nature of a person's subjective understanding—underlines the difficulty of the prosecution's burden under the rule applied by the Court of Appeals in this case. Any defendant who was the subject of a search authorized solely by his consent could effectively frustrate the introduction into evidence of the fruits of that search by simply failing to testify that he in fact knew he could refuse to consent. And the near impossibility of meeting this prosecutorial burden suggests why this Court has never accepted any such litmus-paper test of voluntariness. . . .

One alternative that would go far toward proving that the subject of a search did know he had a right to refuse consent would be to advise him of that right before eliciting his consent. That, however, is a suggestion that has been almost universally repudiated by both federal and state courts, and, we think, rightly so. For it would be thoroughly impractical to impose on the normal consent search the detailed requirements of an effective warning. Consent searches are part of the standard investigatory techniques of law enforcement agencies. They normally occur on the highway, or in a person's home or office, and under informal and unstructured conditions. The circumstances that prompt the initial request to search may develop quickly or be a logical extension of investigative police questioning. The police may seek to investigate further suspicious circumstances or to follow up leads developed in questioning persons at the scene of a crime. . . .

Consequently, we cannot accept the position of the Court of Appeals in this case that proof of knowledge of the right to refuse consent is a necessary prerequisite to demonstrating a "voluntary" consent. Rather, it is only by analyzing all the circumstances of an individual consent that it can be ascertained whether in fact it was voluntary or coerced. It is this careful sifting of the unique facts and circumstances of each case that is evidenced in our prior decisions involving consent searches.

. . .

In short, neither this Court's prior cases, nor the traditional definition of "voluntariness" requires proof of knowledge of a right to refuse as the *sine qua non* of an effective consent to a search.

. . .

Our decision today is a narrow one. We hold only that when the subject of a search is not in custody and the State attempts to justify a search on the basis of his consent, the Fourth and Fourteenth Amendments require that it demonstrate that the consent was in fact voluntarily given, and not the result of duress or coercion, express or implied. Voluntariness is a question of fact to be determined from all the circumstances, and while the subject's knowledge of a right to refuse is a factor to be taken into account, the prosecution is not required to demonstrate such knowledge as a prerequisite to establishing a voluntary consent. Because the California court followed these principles in affirming the respondent's conviction, and because the Court of Appeals for the Ninth Circuit in remanding for an evidentiary hearing required more, its judgment must be reversed.

. . .

Brennan, J., dissenting

. . . The Court holds today that an individual can effectively waive this right even though he is totally ignorant of the fact that, in the absence of his consent, such invasions of his privacy would be constitutionally prohibited. It wholly escapes me how our citizens can meaningfully be said to have waived something as precious as a constitutional guarantee without ever being aware of its existence. In my view, the Court's conclusion is supported neither by "linguistics," nor by "epistemology," nor, indeed, by "common sense." I respectfully dissent.

F. STOP AND FRISK

Plain clothes detective McFadden on a downtown beat observed three men on a street corner acting suspiciously. He watched two of the men walk, one at a time, to a jewelry store, peer into the store window, and then return to the corner where the three conferred. They repeated this conduct twenty-four times. McFadden approached the three men, identified himself as a policeman, and asked for their identification. When the three "mumbled something," McFadden spun Terry around, patted down his outer clothing, and felt a pistol in Terry's pocket. Unable to remove the pistol, McFadden ordered the three men into the jewelry store where he removed the gun from Terry's pocket, patted down the others, and then removed a gun from one of their pockets. The two with guns were charged with carrying a concealed pistol. The issues arising in the case were: (1) whether a police officer may interfere with on-the-street behavior before he has probable cause to justify an arrest; (2) whether a police officer may conduct even a limited "frisk" (search) for weapons when he does not have probable cause to make an arrest; and (3) whether what is found during that search may be the basis for subsequent arrest and prosecution and used in evidence to convict the subject.

Terry v. *Ohio,* 392 U.S. 1 (1968)

Warren, C. J.

This case presents serious questions concerning the role of the Fourth Amendment in the confrontation on the street between the citizen and the policeman investigating suspicious circumstances.

. . .

On the motion to suppress the guns the prosecution took the position that they had been seized following a search incident to a lawful arrest. The trial court rejected this theory, stating that it "would be stretching the facts beyond reasonable comprehension" to find that Officer McFadden had had probable cause to arrest the men before he patted them down for weapons. However, the court denied the defendants' motion on the ground that Officer McFadden, on the basis of his experience, "had reasonable cause to believe . . . that the defendants were conducting themselves suspiciously, and some interrogation should be made of their action." Purely for his own protection, the court held, the officer had the right to pat down the outer clothing of these men, who he had reasonable cause to believe might be armed. The court distinguished between an investigatory "stop" and an arrest, and between a "frisk" of the outer clothing for weapons and a full-blown search for evidence of crime. The frisk, it held, was essential to the proper performance of the officer's investigatory duties, for without it "the answer to the police officer may be a bullet, and a loaded pistol discovered during the frisk is admissible."

. . . .

. . . Unquestionably petitioner was entitled to the protection of the Fourth Amendment as he walked down the street in Cleveland. . . . The question is whether in all the circumstances of this on-the-street encounter, his right to personal security was violated by an unreasonable search and seizure.

We would be less than candid if we did not acknowledge that this question thrusts to the fore difficult and troublesome issues regarding a sensitive area of police activity—issues which have never before been squarely presented to this Court. Reflective of the tensions involved are the practical and constitutional arguments pressed with great vigor on both sides of the public debate over the power of the police to "stop and frisk"—as it is sometimes euphemistically termed—suspicious persons.

On the other hand, it is frequently argued that in dealing with the rapidly unfolding and often dangerous situations on city streets the police are in need of an escalating set of flexible responses, graduated in relation to the amount of information they possess. For this purpose it is urged that distinctions should be made between a "stop" and an "arrest" (or a "seizure" of a person), and between a "frisk" and a "search." Thus, it is argued, the police should be allowed to "stop" a person and detain him briefly for questioning upon suspicion that he may be connected with criminal activity. Upon suspicion that the person may be armed, the police should have the power to "frisk" him for weapons. If the "stop" and the "frisk" give rise to probable cause to believe that the suspect has committed a crime, then the police should be empowered to make a formal "arrest," and a full incident "search" of the person. This scheme is justified in part upon the notion that a "stop" and a "frisk" amount to a mere "minor inconvenience and petty indignity," which can properly be imposed upon the citizen in the interest of effective law enforcement on the basis of a police officer's suspicion.

On the other side the argument is made that the authority of the police must be strictly circumscribed by the law of arrest and search as it has developed to date in the traditional jurisprudence of the Fourth Amendment. It is contended with some force that there is not—and cannot be—a variety of police activity which does not depend solely upon the voluntary cooperation of the citizen and yet which stops short of an arrest based upon probable cause to make such an arrest. The heart of the Fourth Amendment, the argument runs, is a severe requirement of specific justification for any intrusion upon protected personal security, coupled with a highly developed system of judicial controls to enforce upon the agents of the State the commands of the Constitution. Acquiescence by the courts in the compulsion inherent in the field interrogation practices at issue here, it is urged, would constitute an abdication of judicial control over, and indeed an encouragement of, substantial interference with liberty and personal security by police officers whose judgment is necessarily colored by their primary involvement in "the often competitive enterprise of ferreting out crime." . . . This, it is argued, can only serve to exacerbate police-community tensions in the crowded centers of our Nation's cities.

In this context we approach the issues in this case mindful of the limitations of the judicial function in controlling the myriad daily situations in which policemen and citizens confront each other on the street. The State has characterized the issue here as "the right of a police officer . . . to make an on-the-street stop, interrogate and pat down for weapons (known in street vernacular as 'stop and frisk')." But this is only partly accurate. For the issue is not the abstract propriety of the police conduct, but the admissibility against petitioner of the evidence uncovered by the search and seizure. Ever since its inception, the rule excluding evidence seized in violation of the Fourth Amendment has been recognized as a principal mode of discouraging lawless police conduct. . . . Thus its major thrust is a deterrent one, . . . and experience has taught that it is the only effective deterrent to police misconduct in the criminal context, and that without it the constitutional guarantee against unreasonable searches and seizures would be a mere "form of words." . . .

The rule also serves another vital function—"the imperative of judicial integrity." . . .

The exclusionary rule has its limitations, however, as a tool of judicial control. It cannot properly be invoked to exclude the products of legitimate police investigative techniques on the ground that much conduct which is closely similar involves unwarranted intrusions upon constitutional protections. . . . Doubtless some police "field interrogation" conduct violates the Fourth Amendment. But a stern refusal by this Court to condone such activity does not necessarily render it responsive to the exclusionary rule. Regardless of how effective the rule may be where obtaining convictions is an important objective of the police, it is powerless to deter invasions of constitutionally guaranteed rights where the police either have no interest in prosecuting or are willing to forego successful prosecution in the interest of serving some other goal.

. . .

[W]e turn our attention to the quite narrow question posed by the facts before us: whether it is always unreasonable for a policeman to seize a person and subject him to a limited search for weapons unless there is probable cause for an arrest.

. . . There is some suggestion in the use of such terms as "stop" and "frisk" that such police conduct is outside the purview of the Fourth Amendment because neither action rises to the level of a "search" or "seizure" within the meaning of the Constitution. We emphatically reject this notion. It is quite plain that the Fourth Amendment governs "seizures" of the person which do not eventuate in a trip to the station house and prosecution for crime—"arrests" in traditional terminology. It must be recognized that whenever a police officer accosts an individual and restrains his freedom to walk away, he has "seized" that person. And it is nothing less than sheer torture of the English language to suggest that a careful exploration of the outer surfaces of a person's clothing all over his or her body in an attempt to find weapons is not a "search." . . .

It is a serious intrusion upon the sanctity of the person, which may inflict great indignity and arouse strong resentment, and it is not to be undertaken lightly.

. . .

The distinctions of classical "stop-and-frisk" theory thus serve to divert attention from the central inquiry under the Fourth Amendment—the reasonableness in all the circumstances of the particular governmental invasion of a citizen's personal security. "Search" and "seizure" are not talismans. We therefore reject the notions that the Fourth Amendment does not come into play at all as a limitation upon police conduct if the officers stop short of something called a "technical arrest" or a "full-blown search."

In this case there can be no question, then, that Officer McFadden "seized" petitioner and subjected him to a "search" when he took hold of him and patted down the outer surfaces of his clothing. We must decide whether at that point it was reasonable for Officer McFadden to have interfered with petitioner's personal security as he did. And in determining whether the seizure and search were "unreasonable" our inquiry is a dual one—whether the officer's action was justified at its inception, and whether it was reasonably related in scope to the circumstances which justified the interference in the first place.

If this case involved police conduct subject to the Warrant Clause of the Fourth Amendment, we would have to ascertain whether "probable cause" existed to justify the search and seizure which took place. However, that is not the case. . . . [W]e deal here with an entire rubric of police conduct—necessarily swift action predicated upon the on-the-spot observations of the officer on the beat—which historically has not been, and as a practical matter could not be, subjected to the warrant procedure. Instead, the conduct involved in this case must be tested by the Fourth Amendment's general proscription against unreasonable searches and seizures.

. . . In order to assess the reasonableness of Officer McFadden's conduct as a general proposition, it is necessary "first to focus upon the governmental interest which allegedly justifies official intrusion upon the constitutionally protected interests of the private citizen," for there is "no ready test for determining reasonableness other than by balancing the need to search [or seize] against the invasion which the search [or seizure] entails." . . . And in justifying the particular intrusion the police officer must be able to point to specific and articulable facts which, taken together with rational inferences from those facts, reasonably warrant that intrusion. The scheme of the Fourth Amendment becomes meaningful only when it is assured that at some point the conduct of those charged with enforcing the laws can be subjected to the more detached, neutral scrutiny of a judge who must evaluate the reasonableness of a particular search or seizure in light of the particular circumstances. And in making that assessment it is imperative that the facts be judged against an objective standard: would the facts available to the officer at the moment of the seizure or the search "warrant a man of reasonable caution in the belief" that the action taken was appropriate? . . . Anything less would invite intrusions upon constitutionally guaranteed rights based on nothing more substantial than inarticulate hunches, a result this Court has consistently refused to sanction. . . . And simple " 'good faith on the part of the arresting officer is not enough.' . . . If subjective good faith alone were the test, the protections of the Fourth Amendment would evaporate, and the people would be 'secure in their persons, houses, papers, and effects,' only in the discretion of the police." . . .

. . . [H]ere, two men hover about a street corner for an extended period of time, at the end of which it becomes apparent that they are not waiting for anyone or anything; where these men pace alternately along an identical route, pausing to stare in the same store window roughly 24 times; where each completion of this route is followed immediately by a conference between the two men on the corner; where they are joined in one of these conferences by a third man who leaves swiftly; and where the two men finally follow the third and rejoin him a couple of blocks away. It would have been poor police work indeed for an officer of 30 years' experience in the detection of thievery from stores in this same neighborhood to have failed to investigate this behavior further.

The crux of this case . . . is not the propriety of Officer McFadden's taking steps to investigate petitioner's suspicious behavior, but rather, whether there was justification for McFadden's invasion of Terry's personal security by searching him for weapons in the course of that investigation. We are now concerned with more than the governmental interest in investigating crime; in addition, there is the more immediate interest of the police officer in taking steps to assure himself that the person with whom he is dealing is not armed with a weapon that could unexpectedly and fatally be used against him. Certainly it would be unreasonable to require that police officers take unnecessary risks in the performance of their duties. American criminals have a long tradition of armed violence, and every year in this country many law enforcement officers are killed in the line of duty, and thousands more are wounded. Virtually all of these deaths and a substantial portion of the injuries are inflicted with guns and knives.

In view of these facts, we cannot blind ourselves to the need for law enforcement officers to protect themselves and other prospective victims of violence in situations where they may lack probable cause for an arrest. When an officer is justified in believing that the individual whose suspicious behavior he is investigating at close range is armed and presently dangerous to the officer or to others, it would appear to be clearly unreasonable to deny the officer the power to take necessary measures to determine whether the person is in fact carrying a weapon and to neutralize the threat of physical harm.

We must still consider, however, the nature and quality of the intrusion on individual rights which must be accepted if police officers are to be conceded the right to search for weapons in situations where probable cause to arrest for crime is lacking. Even a limited search of the outer clothing for weapons constitutes a severe, though brief, intrusion upon cherished personal security, and it must surely be an annoying, frightening, and perhaps humiliating experience. . . .

. . . A search for weapons in the absence of probable cause to arrest, however, must, like any other search, be strictly circumscribed by the exigencies which justify its initiation. . . . Thus it must be limited to that which is necessary for the discovery of weapons which might be used to harm the officer or others nearby, and may realistically be characterized as something less than a "full" search, even though it remains a serious intrusion.

. . .

Our evaluation of the proper balance that has to be struck in this type of case leads us to conclude that there must be a narrowly drawn authority to permit a reasonable search for weapons for the protection of the police officer, where he has reason to believe that he is dealing with an armed and dangerous individual, regardless of whether he has probable cause to arrest the individual for a crime. The officer need not be absolutely certain that the individual is armed; the issue is whether a reasonably prudent man in the circumstances would be warranted in the belief that his safety or that of others was in danger. . . . And in determining whether the officer acted reasonably in such circumstances, due weight must be given, not to his inchoate and unparticularized suspicion or "hunch," but to the specific reasonable inferences which he is entitled to draw from the facts in light of his experience. . . .

. . .

The sole justification of the search in the present situation is the protection of the police officer and others nearby, and it must therefore be confined in scope to an intrusion reasonably designed to discover guns, knives, clubs, or other hidden instruments for the assault of the police officer.

The scope of the search in this case presents no serious problem in light of these standards. Officer McFadden patted down the outer clothing of petitioner and his two companions. He did not place his hands in their pockets or under the outer surface of their garments until he had felt weapons, and then he merely reached for and removed the guns. . . . Officer McFadden confined his search strictly to what was minimally necessary to learn whether the men were armed and to disarm them once he discovered the weapons. He did not conduct a general exploratory search for whatever evidence of criminal activity he might find.

We conclude that the revolver seized from Terry was properly admitted in evidence against him. At the time he seized petitioner and searched him for weapons, Officer McFadden had reasonable grounds to believe that petitioner was armed and dangerous, and it was necessary for the protection of himself and others to take swift measures to discover the true facts and neutralize the threat of harm if it materialized. The policeman carefully restricted his search to what was appropriate to the discovery of the particular items which he sought. Each case of this sort will, of course, have to be decided on its own facts. We merely hold today that where a police officer observes unusual conduct which leads him reasonably to conclude in light of his experience that criminal activity may be afoot and that the persons with whom he is dealing may be armed and presently dangerous, where in the course of investigating this behavior he identifies himself as a policeman and makes reasonable inquiries, and where nothing in the initial stages of the encounter serves to dispel his reasonable fear for his own or others' safety, he is entitled for the protection of himself and others in the area to conduct a carefully limited search of the outer clothing of such persons in an attempt to discover weapons which might be used to assault him. Such a search is a reasonable search under the Fourth Amendment, and any weapons seized may properly be introduced in evidence against the person from whom they were taken.

Affirmed.

SECTION 3
POLICE INTERROGATIONS AND CONFESSIONS

Four cases, arising in Arizona, New York, California, and a federal court, all involving confessions, were consolidated on appeal in the Supreme Court. For thirty years the Court had grappled with the problems attendant upon confessions and the interrogation process. During those years, the Court had struck down convictions based upon coerced confessions and had tried to introduce elementary fairness concepts in the interrogation process. Obviously disturbed by its failure to insure fairness in that process and of the difficulties that courts have in ascertaining what actually takes place in the interrogation room, the Supreme Court uncharacteristically went beyond the facts of the cases before it and set forth a code of acceptable conduct during the interrogation process. The Court was badly split on this issue, and the majority opinion reflected the positions of only five members of the Court.

Miranda v. *Arizona,* 384 U.S. 436 (1966)

Warren, C. J.

The cases before us raise questions which go to the roots of our concepts of American criminal jurisprudence: the restraints society must observe consistent with the Federal Constitution in prosecuting individuals for crime. More specifically, we deal with the admissibility of statements obtained from an individual who is subjected to custodial police interrogation and the necessity for procedures which assure that the individual is accorded his privilege under the Fifth Amendment to the Constitution not to be compelled to incriminate himself.

. . .

Our holding will be spelled out with some specificity in the pages which follow but briefly stated it is this: the prosecution may not use statements, whether exculpatory or inculpatory, stemming from custodial interrogation of the defendant unless it demonstrates the use of procedural safeguards effective to secure the privilege against self-incrimination. By custodial interrogation, we mean questioning initiated by law enforcement officers after a person has been taken into custody or otherwise deprived of his freedom of action in any significant way. As for the procedural safeguards to be employed, unless other fully effective means are devised to inform accused persons of their right of silence and to assure a continuous opportunity to exercise it, the following measures are required. Prior to any questioning, the person must be warned that he has a right to remain silent, that any statement he does make may be used as evidence against him, and that he has a right to the presence of an attorney, either retained or appointed. The defendant may waive effectuation of these rights, provided the waiver is made voluntarily, knowingly and intelligently. If, however, he indicates in any manner and at any stage of the process that he wishes to consult with an attorney before speaking there can be no questioning. Likewise, if the individual is alone and indicates in any manner that he does not wish to be interrogated, the police may not question him. The mere fact that he may have answered some questions or volunteered some statements on his own does not deprive him of the right to refrain from answering any further inquiries until he has consulted with an attorney and thereafter consents to be questioned.

. . .

At the outset, if a person in custody is to be subjected to interrogation, he must first be informed in clear and unequivocal terms that he has the right to remain silent. For those unaware of the privilege, the warning is needed simply to make them aware of it—the threshold requirement for an intelligent decision as to its exercise. More important, such a warning is an absolute prerequisite in overcoming the inherent pressures of the interrogation atmosphere. It is not just the subnormal or woefully ignorant who succumb to an interrogator's imprecations, whether implied or expressly stated, that the interrogation will continue until a confession is obtained or that silence in the face of accusation is itself damning and will bode ill when presented to a jury. Further, the warning will show the individual that his interrogators are prepared to recognize his privilege should he choose to exercise it.

. . .

The warning of the right to remain silent must be accompanied by the explanation that anything said can and will be used against the individual in court. This warning is needed in order to make him aware not only of the privilege, but also of the consequences of forgoing it. It is only through an awareness of these consequences that there can be any assurance of real understanding and intelligent exercise of the privilege. Moreover, this warning may serve to make the individual more acutely aware that he is faced with a phase of the adversary system—that he is not in the presence of persons acting solely in his interest.

The circumstances surrounding in-custody interrogation can operate very quickly to overbear the will of one merely made aware of his privilege by his interrogators. Therefore, the right to have counsel present at the interrogation is indispensable to the protection of the Fifth Amendment privilege under the system we delineate today. Our aim is to assure that the individual's right to choose between silence and speech remains unfettered throughout the interrogation process. A once-stated warning, delivered by those who will conduct the interrogation, cannot itself suffice to that end among those who most require knowledge of their rights. A mere warning given by the interrogators is not alone sufficient to accomplish that end. Prosecutors themselves claim that the admonishment of the right to remain silent without more "will benefit only the recidivist and the professional." . . . Even preliminary advice given to the accused by his own attorney can be swiftly overcome by the secret interrogation process.

. . . Thus, the need for counsel to protect the Fifth Amendment privilege comprehends not merely a right to consult with counsel prior to questioning, but also to have counsel present during any questioning if the defendant so desires.

The presence of counsel at the interrogation may serve several significant subsidiary functions as well. If the accused decides to talk to his interrogators, the assistance of counsel can mitigate the dangers of untrustworthiness. With a lawyer present the likelihood that the police will practice coercion is reduced, and if coercion is nevertheless exercised the lawyer can testify to it in court. The presence of a lawyer can also help to guarantee that the accused gives a fully accurate statement to the police and that the statement is rightly reported by the prosecution at trial. . . .

An individual need not make a pre-interrogation request for a lawyer. While such request affirmatively secures his right to have one, his failure to ask for a lawyer does not constitute a waiver. No effective waiver of the right to counsel during interrogation can be recognized unless specifically made after the warnings we here delineate have been given. The accused who does not know his rights and therefore does not make a request may be the person who most needs counsel. . . . California Supreme Court has aptly put it: . . .

Accordingly we hold that an individual held for interrogation must be clearly informed that he has the right to consult with a lawyer and to have the lawyer with him during interrogation under the system for protecting the privilege we delineate today. As with the warnings of the right to remain silent and that anything stated can be used in evidence against him, this warning is an absolute prerequisite to interrogation. . . .

If an individual indicates that he wishes the assistance of counsel before any interrogation occurs, the authorities cannot rationally ignore or deny his request on the basis that the individual does not have or cannot afford a retained attorney. The financial ability of the individual has no relationship to the scope of the rights involved here. The privilege against self-incrimination secured by the Constitution applies to all individuals. The need for counsel in order to protect the privilege exists for the indigent as well as the affluent. . . .

In order fully to apprise a person interrogated of the extent of his rights under this system then, it is necessary to warn him not only that he has the right to consult with an attorney, but also that if he is indigent a lawyer will be appointed to represent him. Without this additional warning, the admonition of the right to consult with counsel would often be understood as meaning only that he can consult with a lawyer if he has one or has the funds to obtain one. The warning of a right to counsel would be hollow if not couched in terms that would convey to the indigent—the person most often subjected to interrogation—the knowledge that he too has a right to have counsel present. As with the warnings of the right to remain silent and of the general right to counsel, only by effective and express explanation to the indigent of this right can there be assurance that he was truly in a position to exercise it.

Once warnings have been given, the subsequent procedure is clear. If the individual indicates in any manner, at any time prior to or during questioning, that he wishes to remain silent, the interrogation must cease. At this point he has shown that he intends to exercise his Fifth Amendment privilege; any statement taken after the person invokes his privilege cannot be other than the product of compulsion, subtle or otherwise. Without the right to cut off questioning, the setting of in-custody interrogation operates on the individual to overcome free choice in producing a statement after the privilege has been once invoked. If the individual states that he wants an attorney, the interrogation must cease until an attorney is present. At that time, the individual must have an opportunity to confer with the attorney and to have him present during any subsequent questioning. If the individual cannot obtain an attorney and he indicates that he wants one before speaking to police, they must respect his decision to remain silent.

This does not mean, as some have suggested, that each police station must have a "station house lawyer" present at all times to advise prisoners. It does mean, however, that if police propose to interrogate a person they must make known to him that he is entitled to a lawyer and that if he cannot afford one, a lawyer will be provided for him prior to any interrogation. If authorities conclude that they will not provide counsel during a reasonable period of time in which investigation in the field is carried out, they may refrain from doing so without violating the person's Fifth Amendment privilege so long as they do not question him during that time.

If the interrogation continues without the presence of an attorney and a statement is taken, a heavy burden rests on the government to demonstrate that the defendant knowingly and intelligently waived his privilege against self-incrimination and his right to retained or appointed counsel. . . .

Three of the dissenters in Miranda v. Arizona were soon joined by two of President Nixon's appointees to the Supreme Court, and the process of whittling away at the Miranda began. Here, the defendant made incriminating statements to the police without having been afforded the procedural safeguards required by Miranda. The prosecution could not use those statements in the presentation of its case. When the defendant took the witness stand in his own behalf, he was cross-examined by the prosecutor. During that cross-examination, Harris was questioned about the incriminating statements he had made to the police but claimed to not remember making such statements. The jury was advised that they could not consider these statements as evidence of defendant's guilt, but could consider these statements for the limited purpose of weighing the defendant's credibility and determining whether to believe the defendant's testimony.

Harris v. *New York,* 401 U.S. 222 (1971)
Burger, C. J.

. . .

At trial the prosecution made no effort in its case in chief to use the statements allegedly made by petitioner, conceding that they were inadmissible under *Miranda* v. *Arizona*. . . . The transcript of the interrogation used in the impeachment . . . shows that no warning of a right to appointed counsel was given before questions were put to petitioner when he was taken into custody. Petitioner makes no claim that the statements made to the police were coerced or involuntary.

Some comments in the *Miranda* opinion can indeed be read as indicating a bar to use of an uncounseled statement for any purpose, but discussion of that issue was not at all necessary to the Court's holding and cannot be regarded as controlling. *Miranda* barred the prosecution from making its case with statements of an accused made while in custody prior to having or effectively waiving counsel. It does not follow from *Miranda* that evidence inadmissible against an accused in the prosecution's case in chief is barred for all purposes, provided of course that the trustworthiness of the evidence satisfies legal standards.

. . .

Petitioner's testimony in his own behalf . . . contrasted sharply with what he told the police shortly after his arrest. The impeachment process here undoubtedly provided valuable aid to the jury in assessing petitioner's credibility, and the benefits of this process should not be lost, in our view, because of the speculative possibility that impermissible police conduct will be encouraged thereby. Assuming that the exclusionary rule has a deterrent effect on proscribed police conduct, sufficient deterrence flows when the evidence in question is made unavailable to the prosecution in its case in chief.

Every criminal defendant is privileged to testify in his own defense, or to refuse to do so. But that privilege cannot be construed to include the right to commit perjury. . . . Having voluntarily taken the stand, petitioner was under an obligation to speak truthfully and accurately, and the prosecution here did no more than utilize the traditional truth-testing devices of the adversary process. Had inconsistent statements been made by the accused to some third person, it could hardly be contended that the conflict could not be laid before the jury by way of cross-examination and impeachment.

The shield provided by *Miranda* cannot be perverted into a license to use perjury by way of a defense, free from the risk of confrontation with prior inconsistent utterances. We hold, therefore, that petitioner's credibility was appropriately impeached by use of his earlier conflicting statements.

Affirmed.

Brennan, J., dissenting

It is conceded that the question-and-answer statement used to impeach petitioner's direct testimony was, under *Miranda* v. *Arizona* . . . constitutionally inadmissible as part of the State's direct case against petitioner. I think that the Constitution also denied the State the use of the statement on cross-examination to impeach the credibility of petitioner's testimony given in his own defense. . . . The constitutional guarantee forbids the prosecution to use a tainted statement to impeach the accused who takes the stand: The prosecution's use of the tainted statement "cuts down on the privilege by making its assertion costly." . . . Thus, the accused is denied an "unfettered" choice when the decision whether to take the stand is burdened by the risk that an illegally obtained prior statement may be introduced to impeach his direct testimony denying complicity in the crime charged against him. We settled this proposition in *Miranda* where we said:

> "The privilege against self-incrimination protects the individual from being compelled to incriminate himself in *any* manner. . . . [S]tatements merely intended to be exculpatory by the defendant are often *used to impeach his testimony at trial. . . . These statements are incriminating in any meaningful sense of the word and may not be used without the full warnings and effective waiver required for any other statement.*" 384 U.S., at 476, 477 (emphasis added).

This language completely disposes of any distinction between statements used on direct as opposed to cross-examination. "An incriminating statement is as incriminating when used to impeach credibility as it is when used as direct proof of guilt and no constitutional distinction can legitimately be drawn."

The objective of deterring improper police conduct is only part of the larger objective of safeguarding the integrity of our adversary system. The "essential mainstay" of that system, *Miranda* v. *Arizona* . . . is the privilege, against self-incrimination, which for that reason has occupied a central place in our jurisprudence since before the Nation's birth. Moreover, "we may view the historical development of the privilege as one which groped for the proper scope of governmental power over the citizen. . . . All these policies point to one overriding thought: the constitutional foundation underlying the privilege is the respect a government . . . must accord to the dignity and integrity of its citizens." . . . These values are plainly jeopardized if an exception against admission of tainted statements is made for those used for impeachment purposes. Moreover, it is monstrous that courts should aid or abet the law-breaking police officer. It is abiding truth that "[n]othing can destroy a government more quickly than its failure to observe its own laws, or worse, its disregard of the charter of its own existence." . . . Thus, even to the extent that *Miranda* was aimed at deterring police practices in disregard of the Constitution, I fear that today's holding will seriously undermine the achievement of that objective. The Court today tells the police that they may freely interrogate an accused incommunicado and without counsel and know that although any statement they obtain in violation of *Miranda* cannot be used on the State's direct case, it may be introduced if the defendant has the temerity to testify in his own defense. This goes far toward undoing much of the progress made in conforming police methods to the Constitution. I dissent.

Next, the Supreme Court was asked to decide whether a defendant who chooses to exercise his rights and not answer questions could ever be interrogated. Mosley was arrested for two robberies. He was advised of his Miranda rights and questioned. As soon as Mosley said he did not want to answer any questions, the interrogation ceased. More than two hours later, another detective had Mosley brought from his cell and taken to an interrogation room on another floor. There, without mentioning the robbery charges, the detective repeated the Miranda warnings and questioned Mosley about an unrelated murder. Mosley made a statement implicating himself in the murder after only fifteen minutes of questioning.

Michigan v. *Mosley,* 423 U.S. 96 (1975)

Stewart, J.:

. . .

Neither party in the present case challenges the continuing validity of the *Miranda* decision, or of any of the so-called guidelines it established to protect what the Court there said was a person's constitutional privilege against compulsory self-incrimination. The issue in this case, rather, is whether the conduct of the Detroit police that led to Mosley's incriminating statement did in fact violate the *Miranda* "guidelines," so as to render the statement inadmissible in evidence against Mosley at his trial. Resolution of the question turns almost entirely on the interpretation of a single passage in the *Miranda* opinion, upon which the Michigan appellate court relied in finding a *per se* violation of *Miranda:*

> "Once warnings have been given, the subsequent procedure is clear. If the individual indicates in any manner, at any time prior to or during questioning, that he wishes to remain silent, the interrogation must cease. At this point he has shown that he intends to exercise his Fifth Amendment privilege; any statement taken after the person invokes his privilege cannot be other than the product of compulsion, subtle or otherwise. Without the right to cut off questioning, the setting of in-custody interrogation operates on the individual to overcome free choice in producing a statement after the privilege has been once invoked." . . .

This passage states that "the interrogation must cease" when the person in custody indicates that "he wishes to remain silent." It does not state under what circumstances, if any, a resumption of questioning is permissible. . . .

It is evident that . . . literal interpretations would lead to absurd and unintended results. To permit the continuation of custodial interrogation after a momentary cessation would clearly frustrate the purposes of *Miranda* by allowing repeated rounds of questioning to undermine the will of the person being questioned. At the other extreme, a blanket prohibition against the taking of voluntary statements or a permanent immunity from further interrogation, regardless of the circumstances, would transform the *Miranda* safeguards into wholly irrational obstacles to legitimate police investigative activity, and deprive suspects of an opportunity to make informed and intelligent assessments of their interests. Clearly, therefore, neither this passage nor any other passage in the *Miranda* opinion can sensibly be read to create a *per se* proscription of indefinite duration upon any further questioning by any police officer on any subject, once the person in custody has indicated a desire to remain silent.

A reasonable and faithful interpretation of the *Miranda* opinion must rest on the intention of the Court in that case to adopt "fully effective means . . . to notify the person of his right of silence and to assure that the exercise of the right will be scrupulously honored. . . ." . . . The critical safeguard identified in the passage at issue is a person's "right to cut off questioning." . . . Through the exercise of his option to terminate questioning he can control the time at which questioning occurs, the subjects discussed, and the duration of the interrogation. The requirement that law enforcement authorities must respect a person's exercise of that option counteracts the coercive pressures of the custodial setting. We therefore conclude that the admissibility of statements obtained after the person in custody has decided to remain silent depends under *Miranda* on whether his "right to cut off questioning" was "scrupulously honored."

A review of the circumstances leading to Mosley's confession reveals that his "right to cut off questioning" was fully respected in this case. Before his initial interrogation, Mosley was carefully advised that he was under no obligation to answer any questions and could remain silent if he wished. He orally acknowledged that he understood the *Miranda* warnings and then signed a printed notification-of-rights form. When Mosley stated that he did not want to discuss the robberies, [the arresting officer] immediately ceased the interrogation and did not try either to resume the questioning or in any way to persuade Mosley to reconsider his position. After an interval of more than two hours, Mosley was questioned by another police officer at another location about an unrelated holdup murder. He was given full and complete *Miranda* warnings at the outset of the second interrogation. He was thus reminded again that he could remain silent and could consult with a lawyer, and was carefully given a full and fair opportunity to exercise these options. The subsequent questioning did not undercut Mosley's previous decision not to answer [the arresting officer's] inquiries. Detective Hill did not resume the interrogation about the White Tower Restaurant robbery or inquire about the Blue Goose Bar robbery, but instead focused exclusively on the Leroy Williams homicide, a crime different in nature and in time and place of occurrence from the robberies for which Mosley had been arrested. . . .

This is not a case, therefore, where the police failed to honor a decision of a person in custody to cut off questioning, either by refusing to discontinue the interrogation upon request or by persisting in repeated efforts to wear down his resistance and make him change his mind. In contrast to such practices, the police here immediately ceased the interrogation, resumed questioning only after the passage of a significant period of time and the provision of a fresh set of warnings, and restricted the second interrogation to a crime that had not been a subject of the earlier interrogation.

For these reasons, we conclude that the admission in evidence of Mosley's incriminating statement did not violate the principles of *Miranda* v. *Arizona*. . . .

Some commentators suggested that the Supreme Court was just looking for the right case to completely overrule Miranda. Brewer v. Williams seemed to present that opportunity. Robert Williams, an escapee from a mental hospital, was charged and arrested for the abduction and slaying of a ten year old girl. On the advice of a lawyer, Williams surrendered to police, and was arraigned and committed to custody in Davenport, Iowa. He was given his Miranda warnings. His lawyer, who was in Des Moines, advised Williams over the phone that Des Moines police officers would transport him from Davenport. The lawyer assured Williams that the police officers would not interrogate or mistreat him, and that Williams should not discuss Pamela Powers, the victim, with the police officers. The police officers promised the Des Moines attorney that they would not interrogate Williams or discuss the case with him during the trip. When the officers arrived in Davenport, they met with Williams and a local attorney who was advising him. Again, Williams was fully advised of his Miranda rights. The Davenport attorney was refused permission to ride along with Williams to Des Moines, but firmly stated that the officers were not to interrogate Williams.

During the 160 mile ride, one of the detectives engaged Williams in a long discussion about religion. The detective made, what was described at trial and during later appeals as, a "Christian Burial Speech." In that speech, the detective made an emotional appeal to Williams' conscience and, as a consequence, during the remainder of the ride, Williams made incriminating statements and directed the detectives to the place where the child's body was hidden.

Brewar, Warden v. *Williams,* 430 U.S. 387 (1977) Stewart, J.

. . . [T]here is no need to review in this case the doctrine of *Miranda* v. *Arizona,* a doctrine designed to secure the constitutional privilege against compulsory self-incrimination. . . . [W]illiams was deprived of a different constitutional right—the right to the assistance of counsel.

This right, guaranteed by the Sixth and Fourteenth Amendments, is indispensable to the fair administration of our adversary system of criminal justice. . . . The right to counsel granted by the Sixth and Fourteenth

Amendments means at least that a person is entitled to the help of a lawyer at or after the time that judicial proceedings have been initiated against him—"whether by way of formal charge, preliminary hearing, indictment, information, or arraignment." . . .

There can be no doubt in the present case that judicial proceedings had been initiated against Williams before the start of the automobile ride from Davenport to Des Moines. A warrant had been issued for his arrest, he had been arraigned on that warrant before a judge in a Davenport courtroom, and he had been committed by the court to confinement in jail. The State does not contend otherwise.

There can be no serious doubt, either, that Detective Leaming deliberately and designedly set out to elicit information from Williams just as surely as—and perhaps more effectively than—if he had formally interrogated him. Detective Leaming was fully aware before departing for Des Moines that Williams was being represented in Davenport by Kelly and in Des Moines by McKnight. Yet he purposely sought during Williams' isolation from his lawyers to obtain as much incriminating information as possible. Indeed, Detective Leaming conceded as much when he testified at Williams' trial:

> "Q. In fact, Captain, whether he was a mental patient or not, you were trying to get all the information you could before he got to his lawyer, weren't you?
>
> "A. I was sure hoping to find out where that little girl was, yes, sir.
>
> "Q. Well, I'll put it this way: You was *[sic]* hoping to get all the information you could before Williams got back to McKnight, weren't you?
>
> "A. Yes, sir."

The state courts clearly proceeded upon the hypothesis that Detective Leaming's "Christian burial speech" had been tantamount to interrogation. Both courts recognized that Williams had been entitled to the assistance of counsel at the time he made the incriminating statements. Yet no such constitutional protection would have come into play if there had been no interrogation.

. . .

The Iowa courts recognized that Williams had been denied the constitutional right to the assistance of counsel. They held, however, that he had waived that right during the course of the automobile trip from Davenport to Des Moines. . . . [I]t was incumbent upon the State to prove "an intentional relinquishment or abandonment of a known right or privilege." . . . That standard has been reiterated in many cases. We have said that the right to counsel does not depend upon a request by the defendant, . . . and that courts indulge in every reasonable presumption against waiver. . . . This strict standard applies equally to an alleged waiver of the right to counsel whether at trial or at a critical stage of pretrial proceedings. . . .

We conclude . . . that, judged by these standards, the record in this case falls far short of sustaining petitioner's burden. It is true that Williams had been informed of and appeared to understand his right to counsel. But waiver requires not merely comprehension but relinquishment, and Williams' consistent reliance upon the advice of counsel in dealing with the authorities refutes any suggestion that he waived that right. He consulted McKnight by long distance telephone before turning himself in. He spoke with McKnight by telephone again shortly after being booked. After he was arraigned, Williams sought out and obtained legal advice from Kelly. Williams again consulted with Kelly after Detective Leaming and his fellow officer arrived in Davenport. Throughout, Williams was advised not to make any statements before seeing McKnight in Des Moines, and was assured that the police had agreed not to question him. His statements while in the car that he would tell the whole story *after* seeing McKnight in Des Moines were the clearest expressions by Williams himself that he desired the presence of an attorney before any interrogation took place. But even before making these statements, Williams had effectively asserted his right to counsel by having secured attorneys at both ends of the automobile trip, both of whom, acting as his agents, had made clear to the police that no interrogation was to occur during the journey. Williams knew of that agreement and, particularly in view of his consistent reliance on counsel, there is no basis for concluding that he disavowed it.

Despite Williams' express and implicit assertions of his right to counsel, Detective Leaming proceeded to elicit incriminating statements from Williams. Leaming did not preface this effort by telling Williams that he had a right to the presence of a lawyer, and made no effort at all to ascertain whether Williams wished to relinquish that right. The circumstances of record in this case thus provide no reasonable basis for finding that Williams waived his right to the assistance of counsel. . . .

The crime of which Williams was convicted was senseless and brutal, calling for swift and energetic action by the police to apprehend the perpetrator and gather evidence with which he could be convicted. No mission of law enforcement officials is more important. Yet "[d]isinterested zeal for the public good does not assure either wisdom or right in the methods it pursues." . . . Although we do not lightly affirm the issuance of a writ of habeas corpus in this case, so clear a violation of the Sixth and Fourteenth Amendments as here occurred cannot be condoned. The pressures on state executive and judicial officers charged with the administration of the criminal law are great, especially when the crime is murder and the victim a small child. But it is precisely the predictability of those pressures that makes imperative a resolute loyalty to the guarantees that the Constitution extends to us all.

. . .

Burger, C.J., dissenting

The result in this case ought to be intolerable in any society which purports to call itself an organized society. It continues the Court by the narrowest margin—on the much-criticized course of punishing the public for the mistakes and misdeeds of law enforcement officers, instead of punishing the officer directly, if in fact he is guilty of wrongdoing. It mechanically and blindly keeps reliable evidence from juries whether the claimed constitutional violation involves gross police misconduct or honest human error.

Williams is guilty of the savage murder of a small child; no member of the Court contends he is not. While in custody, and after no fewer than *five* warnings of his rights to silence and to counsel, he led police to the concealed body of his victim. The Court concedes Williams was not threatened or coerced and that he spoke and acted voluntarily and with full awareness of his constitutional rights. In the face of all this, the Court now holds that because Williams was prompted by the detective's statement—not interrogation but a statement—the jury must not be told how the police found the body.

Today's holding fulfills Judge (later Mr. Justice) Cardozo's grim prophecy that someday some court might carry the exclusionary rule to the absurd extent that its operative effect would exclude evidence relating to the body of a murder victim because of the means by which it was found. In so ruling the Court regresses to playing a grisly game of "hide and seek," once more exalting the sporting theory of criminal justice which has been experiencing a decline in our jurisprudence. With Justices White, Blackmun, and Rehnquist, I categorically reject the remarkable notion that the police in this case were guilty of unconstitutional misconduct, or any conduct justifying the bizarre result reached by the Court. . . .

[On retrial in Iowa, Williams was convicted. Chief Justice Burger's fears that the evidence relating to the body of the murder victim would be excluded proved unfounded. The trial court held that the derivative evidence rule was not applicable to the body because it would have been found by the police even if Williams had not led them to the site.]

INDEX

A

American Correctional Association, 325
American Law Institute's Model Penal Code, 337
Appeal, right to
  defendant's, 314-315
  Douglas v. California, 205
  habeas corpus and, 140, 316-317
  prosecution's, 315
Appeals
  types of
    direct, 312-314
    interlocutory, 152-153
Argersinger v. Hamlin, 206
Arraignment, 225-226
Arrest. *See also* Police
  conviction rates and, 77
  discretionary decisions and, 73-76, 77-80
  felonies for, 65-66
  misdemeanors for, 67-69
  police, 65-69
    departmental policies for, 77-80
    external review of, 80
  privacy, right of, and, 17-18
  warrantless, 65-68

B

Bail
  alternatives to, 158-161
  bondsman, 154
  constitutional right as, 148-149
  determining, 149-153
  history of, 146-148
  juvenile courts and, 281-282
  Manhattan Bail Project, 158-160
  reforms, 157-158
  Stack v. Boyle, 148-149
  types of, 151, 153
Bedsheeting, 124
Betts v. Brady, 204-205
Bill of Rights
  incorporation process, 13-14
Bordenkircher v. Hayes, 256-257
Burger Court, 19

C

Capital punishment. *See also* Death penalty
  objectives of, 326-331
  procedural requirements for, 354-356
  Supreme Court litigation and, 350-354
Civil Rights Act, 357
Coleman v. Alabama, 174-175
Community-based corrections, 342-344
Compulsory process clause, 15
Confrontation clause, 15
Counsel
  Argersinger v. Hamlin, 206
  assistance of, 206-210
  Betts v. Brady, 204-205
  Douglas v. California, 205
  effective assistance standard, 206-210
  Faretta v. California, 205
  Gideon v. Wainwright, 205-206
  indigent defendants for, 211-214, 215-217
  need for, 197-199
  Powell v. Alabama, 203-204, 206
  public defenders as, 215-217
  right to, 201-206
  role of, 199-201
    in plea bargaining, 247-248
  self-representation and, 211
  waiver of, 210
Criminal codes, 336-337

D

Death penalty. *See also* Capital punishment
  debate, 349-350
  Furman v. Georgia, 351-355
  Gregg v. Georgia, 352-353
  punishment option as a, 347
  Roberts v. Georgia, 355
  Witherspoon v. Illinois, 350-351
  Woodson v. North Carolina, 355
Defendant rehabilitation policy, 118
Defendant. *See* Defense
Defense. *See also* Counsel
  pretrial discovery and, 231-235
  right of appeal and, 314-315
  right to, 201-206
    effective legal assistance and, 20, 206-210
  sentencing hearing and, 339-341
  special circumstances test and, 205
  state evidentiary rules and, 15

Detention
    pretrial, 155-157
    preventive, 162-164
Determinate sentence, 334-335, 338
Deterrence, 328-329
Disciplinary hearings, 358
Discovery, 231-235
    Miller v. Pate, 233
Discretion
    arrest decision and, 73-76, 80
    juvenile courts and, 284
    overcriminalization and, 76-77
    prosecutorial, 113-115
    rule of law and, 21-23
    sentencing practices and, 331-336, 337-339
Double jeopardy, 16, 230
Douglas v. California, 205
Due process
    Burger Court cutbacks on, 19
    death penalty procedures and, 348, 354-356
    disciplinary hearings in, 358
    incorporation process of, 13-14
    parole procedures in, 361-362
    state courts' interpretations of, 18-19
    Warren Court enhancement of, 13-14
Duncan v. Louisiana, 297

E

Evidence. *See also* Exclusionary Rule
    derivative, 97-99
    grand jury and, 182-183
    police investigations and, 57-65
    right of privacy and, 58-65
    sentencing hearings and, 339-341
Evidentiary rules, 15
Exclusionary Rule
    applied to
        confessions, 96-97
        derivative evidence, 97-99
        eavesdropping, 95-96
        searches, 92-95
    controversies surrounding, 99-100
    defined, 89
    Fifth Amendment and, 96-97
    Fourth Amendment and, 93-96
    history of, 89-91
    Mapp v. Ohio, 90
    Miranda v. Arizona, 97-99

Exclusionary Rule—*Concluded*
Vale v. Louisiana, 92
Weeks v. United States, 90
Williams v. Brewer, 91-92, 97

F

Faretta v. California, 211
Federal criminal laws
national commission on reform of, 328
Federal Speedy Trial Act of 1974, 239-241
Felonies, 65-67, 142-145. *See also* Police; Arrest
Felons
imprisonment of, 344-346
Fines, 341-342
Fourteenth Amendment. *See also* Due Process; Warren Court
criminal justice rights and, 9
due process model and, 13-14
equal protection and, 19-21
fair trial rights and, 12
Fifth Amendment incorporated in, 16-17
Fourth Amendment incorporated in, 17-18
Sixth Amendment incorporated in, 14-16
Furman v. Georgia, 351-352, 353, 354, 355

G

Gault, in re, 280-282
Gerstein v. Pugh, 180
Gilmore, Gary, 348-350
Grand jury, 180-183
history of, 177-180
immunity, 184
indictments, 180, 187-188
information, 180, 187-188
reform, 185-187
witnesses for, 183-185
Gregg v. Georgia, 327-328, 352-353

H-J

Habeas corpus, 140, 316-317, 357-358
Habitual offenders, 328
Immunity
transactional, 184
Imprisonment. *See* Punishment
Indeterminate sentence, 332-333
Informants, police, 69
Innocence
presumption of, 11-12, 17

Interlocutory appeals, 152-153
Judges
    juvenile justice system, 273-275, 281-283
    plea bargaining and, 260-263
    sentencing practices of
        discretionary decisions and, 331-336, 337-339, 344-346
Juvenile delinquents, 277. *See also* Juvenile justice system
Juvenile justice system
    constitutional rights of juveniles, 279-280
    court dispositions, 283-284
    court filtering process, 282-283
    court procedures, 281-283
    courts, jurisdiction of, 275-279
    evolution of, 273-275
    Gault in re, 280-282
    Kent v. United States, 279

K-O

Kent v. United States, 279
Law enforcement
    President's commission on, and the administration of justice, 51, 54
Legally sufficient policy, 118
Mandatory minimum sentences, 335-336
Manhattan Bail Project, 158-160
Mapp v. Ohio, 90
Miller v. Pate, 233
Miranda v. Arizona, 97-99
Misdemeanors, 66-67, 141-142
    distinction of, from felonies by state, 66-67
Mockery of justice test, 207
Motions, 229-231
Nebraska v. Stuart, 294-295
Offenders
    habitual, 328
Overcriminalization, 76-77

P

Parole, 360-362
    determinate sentence and, 334-335
    indeterminate sentence and, 332-333
Plea bargaining, 248-252
    Bordenkircher v. Hayes, 256-257
    defendant's role in, 247-248
    defense counsel's role in, 257-260
    judges and, 260-263
    prosecutorial role in, 246-247, 253-257
    reform, 263-265

Pleas, 226-229
Police. *See also* Arrests; Exclusionary Rule
arrests
conviction rates and, 77
crime rates and, 56
defined, 65
departmental policies for, 77-80
discretion and, 73-76, 77-80
Exclusionary Rule and, 89-101
felonies for, 65-66
misdemeanors for, 67-68
reasonable force in, 69-70
warrantless, 68-69
booking procedures, 71-72
community relations, 54-56
corruption, 50-53
history, 47-49
informants, 69
investigative function of, 56-65
citizen cooperation and, 58
privacy, right of and, 58-65
technology and, 57-58
Miranda v. Arizona, 97-99
overcriminalization and, 76-77
President's Commission on Law Enforcement and the Administration of Justice, 51, 54
professionalism, 49-50, 52-53
searches, 92-94. *See also* stop and frisk *herein*
automobiles of, 71-95
consent with, 94
eavesdropping as, 95-96
lawful arrest incident to, 60-65, 94
Mapp v. Ohio, 90
post arrest, 70-71
stop and frisk, 59-61
Vale v. Louisiana, 92
warrantless, 70-71
Weeks v. United States, 90
Williams v. Brewer, 91-92, 97
service function of, 54-56
stop and frisk, 59-61
Terry v. Ohio, 59
Wickersham Commission, 51
Policy
legally sufficient, 118
Powell v. Alabama, 203-204, 206

Preliminary hearing
bail dispositions, 145-146
Coleman v. Alabama, 174-175
defense tool as a, 173-176
felonies for, 142-145
Gerstein v. Pugh, 180
history of, 170-171
misdemeanors for, 141-142
Pre-sentence reports, 339
President's Commission on Law Enforcement and the Administration of Justice, 51, 54
Presumption of innocence, 11-12, 17
Presumptive fixed sentence, 333-334
Pretrial detention, 155-157
Pretrial procedures, 235-236
arraignment, 225-226
delay and, 237-241
discovery, 231-235
motions, 229-231
pleas, 226-229
preliminary hearing, 170-171
Pretrial publicity
adverse effects of, 294-297
lawyers' professional ethics and, 295-296
Nebraska v. Stuart, 294-295
Prisoners
rights of, 356-360
Wolff v. McDonnell, 356-357
Prisons
anti-rehabilitative as, 345-346
Privacy
right of
eavesdropping and, 95-96
police arrests and, 18
police investigations and, 58-65
"reasonableness" and, 18
Probable cause, 68-69
Probation, 335-336, 339, 342-344
Procedural regularity
fair trial rights and, 11-12
presumption of innocence and, 11-12
Prosecution
non-judicial dispositions and, 124-125
pretrial discovery and, 234-235
right of appeal and, 315
sentencing hearing and, 339-341

Prosecutor
bedsheeting practices of, 124
case screening practices of
Jacoby study, 118
Tazewell County guidelines for, 119-121
charging decision and, 126-130
education of, 113
overcharging practices of, 124
responsibilities of, 109-110
role of, in plea bargaining, 246-247, 253-257
Public defender, 215-217
Punishment. *See also* Capital punishment; Death penalty
history of, 324-326
imprisonment as, 344-347
objectives of, 326-331
options, 341-347
ranges, 331-336

R-S

Reasonableness, 18
Rehabilitation, 326, 329-331, 345-346
Retribution, 327-328
Roberts v. Louisiana, 355
Searches, police. *See also* Exclusionary Rule
automobiles of, 71-95
consent with, 94
eavesdropping as, 95-96
lawful arrests incident to, 60-65, 94
Mapp v. Ohio, 90
post arrest, 70-71
stop and frisk, 59-61
Vale v. Louisiana, 92
warrantless, 70-71
Weeks v. United States, 90
Williams v. Brewer, 91-92, 97
Self-incrimination, 17
Sentencing
determinate, 334-335, 338
disparity in, 336-339
guidelines, 338
hearings, 339-341
indeterminate, 332-333
models, 331-336
Sixth Amendment
compulsory process and confrontation clauses, 15
state's evidence and, 15
trial rights, 14-16

Special circumstances test, 205
Speedy trial
  federal and state statutes concerning, 239-241
  judging criteria for, 15
  right to, 11-12, 237-238
  Speedy Trial Act of 1974, 239-241
Spenkelink, John, 356
Stack v. Boyle, 148-149
State courts
  due process model and, 18-19
Status offenders, 276-277. *See also* Juvenile justice system
Statutes of limitations, 230
System efficiency policy, 118

T-W

Terry v. Ohio, 59
Transactional immunity, 184
Trial, jury
  defendant's rights in, 12-13, 291-293, 304
  deliberations in, 310-312
  discovery procedures and, 233-234
  Duncan v. Louisiana, 297
  evidence rules of, for, 300-301
  jury selection, 297-300
  waiver of, 297-298
  witness testimony in, 302-304
Trial. *See also* Trial, jury
Trial sufficiency policy, 118
United States Constitution
  Bill of Rights and, 9-10
  criminal justice rights and, 9
  Fourteenth Amendment and, 9
Use immunity, 184
Vale v. Louisiana, 92
Victim justice, 8
Warren Court
  criticisms of, 13
  due process model and, 13-14
  state courts and, 18-19
Weeks v. United States, 90
Wickersham Commission, 51
Williams v. Brewer, 91-92, 97
Witherspoon v. Illinois, 350-351
Wolff v. McDonnell, 356-357
Woodson v. North Carolina, 355
Work-release programs, 344